Constructing Culture and Power in Latin America

THE COMPARATIVE STUDIES IN SOCIETY AND HISTORY BOOK SERIES

Raymond Grew, Series Editor

Comparing Muslim Societies:
Knowledge and the State in a World Civilization
  Juan R. I. Cole, editor

Colonialism and Culture
  Nicholas B. Dirks, editor

Constructing Culture and Power in Latin America
  Daniel H. Levine, editor

Time: Histories and Ethnologies
  Diane Owen Hughes and Thomas R. Trautmann, editors

Cultures of Scholarship
  S. C. Humphreys, editor

Comparing Jewish Societies
  Todd M. Endelman, editor

Constructing Culture and Power in Latin America

Daniel H. Levine, Editor

Ann Arbor

THE UNIVERSITY OF MICHIGAN PRESS

F1414
.C845
1993

i0472094564

2001   2000   1999   1998   6   5   4   3

A CIP catalog record for this book is available from the British Library.

Library of Congress Cataloging-in-Publication Data

Constructing culture and power in Latin America / Daniel H. Levine,
    editor.
        p.   cm. — (The Comparative studies in society and history
    book series)
    Includes bibliographical references and index.
    ISBN 0-472-09456-4 (alk. paper). — ISBN 0-472-06456-8 (pbk. :
    alk. paper)
    1. Latin America — Politics and government — 20th century.
    2. Political culture — Latin America. 3. Social change — Latin
    America. I. Levine, Daniel H. II. Series.
    F1414.C845 1993
    306.2′098—dc20   93-18122
                                                                CIP

Foreword

For more than thirty years the quarterly issues of *Comparative Studies in Society and History* have published articles about human society in any time or place written by scholars in any discipline and from any country. Those articles, inevitably reflecting the changing methods and interests within the specialized fields of research from which they grew, have presented new evidence and new techniques, challenged established assumptions, and raised fresh questions. Now this series of books extends and refocuses the comparisons begun in some of the most stimulating of those essays.

The editor of each volume identifies a field of comparative study and presents contributions that help to define it, beginning by selecting from among the articles that have appeared in *CSSH* from October, 1958, to the present and from scores of manuscripts currently being considered. Written by scholars formed in different traditions, some of whom were born before 1900 and some after 1960, the studies are chosen for their contribution to what the editor perceives as an important continuing dialogue. The volumes in this series are thus not just anthologies. Each contains especially commissioned essays never before published and designed to suggest more fully the potential range of the topic. In addition the articles taken from *CSSH* have been revised by their authors in the light of this project. Each volume is therefore a new work in the specific sense that its chapters are abreast of current scholarship but also in its broader purpose, a cooperative enterprise reconsidering (and thereby reconstructing) a common topic.

Having established the theme to be addressed and identified the scholars to do it, the editor then invited these colleagues to join in exploring the ramifications of their common interest. In most instances this included a conference in Ann Arbor, attended by contributors and by many other scholars, where issues of conceptualization, interpretation, and method could be debated. Sometimes the volume's topic was made the basis of a graduate course, with contributors giving a series of lectures in a seminar lasting a term or more and attended by a variety of interested specialists. The book, which started from an indirect dialogue in the pages of *CSSH,* thus took form through direct encounters among scholars from different disciplines and specialties. In opened-ended and lively discussion, individual manuscripts were criticized and new suggestions tried out, common concerns identified and then matched against the criteria of different disciplines and the experience of different societies. Reshaped by the community it had created, each volume becomes a statement of where scholarship currently stands and of questions that need to be pursued as a by-product of the process in which general problems were reformulated while individual chapters were reconsidered and revised.

By building from discussions conducted over the years in *CSSH,* this series extends the tradition that the journal itself represents. A scholarly quarterly is a peculiar kind of institution, its core permanently fixed in print, its rhythmic appearance in familiar covers an assurance of some central continuity, its contents influenced by its past yet pointing in new directions. *CSSH* seeks to create a community without formal boundaries, a community whose membership is only loosely determined by subject, space, or time. Just as notes and references embed each article in particular intellectual traditions while stretching beyond them, so the journal itself reaches beyond editors, contributors, and subscribers, speaking in whatever voice unknown readers respond to whenever and wherever they turn its pages. The resulting dialogues are not limited to any single forum, and the journal itself changes from within while balancing between venturesomeness and rigor as old debates are refined and new problems posed.

The books in this series further in another form aspirations acknowledged in the opening editorial to the first issue of *CSSH,* in which Sylvia Thrupp declared her belief that "there is a definite set of problems common to the humanities, to history, and to the various social sciences." Changes in the way these problems are conceived and in the vocabulary for expressing them have not lessened the determination to reject "the false dilemma" between "error through insularity and probable superficiality." Insistence upon thorough, original research has been the principal defense against superficiality, emphasis upon comparison the means for overcoming insularity. Many of the articles published in *CSSH* are systematically comparative, across time and between societies, and that is always welcome; but many are not. Each published article was independently chosen for its qualities of scholarship and imagination as well as for its broader implications. For the contributors to and readers of that journal, comparison has come to mean more a way of thinking than the merely mechanical listing of parallels among separate cases. Articles designed to speak to scholars in many disciplines and to students of different societies are recognized as intrinsically comparative by the nature of their problematic, structure, and effect.

Every piece of research deserves to be seen in many contexts: the problems and concerns of a particular society, the immediately relevant scholarly literature with its own vocabulary and evidence, the methods and goals of a given discipline, a body of theory and hypotheses, and sets of questions (established, currently in vogue, or new). Nor can any prescription delimit in advance how far subsequent comparisons of similar problems in different contexts may reach. For the past twenty years, CSSH has placed articles within rubrics that call attention to a central comparative theme among adjacent studies. In addition an editorial foreword in each issue notes other sets of connections between current articles and earlier ones, inviting additional comparisons of broad themes, specific topics, and particular problems or methods. A variety of potential discourses is thus identified, and that open-ended process has culminated in this series of books. Some of the volumes in the series are built around themes for comparative study that have always been recognized as requiring comparison, some address topics not always recognized as a field of study, creating a new perspective through a fresh set of questions. Each volume is thus an autonomous undertaking, a discussion with its own purposes and focus, the work of many authors and an editor's vision of the topic, establishing a field of knowledge, assessing its present state, and suggesting some future directions.

The goal, in the quarterly issues of CSSH and in these books, is to break out of received categories and to cross barriers of convention that, like the residual silt from streams that once flowed faster, have channeled inquiry into patterns convenient for familiar ideas, academic disciplines, and established specialties. Contemporary intellectual trends encourage, indeed demand, this rethinking and provide some powerful tools for accomplishing it. In fact such ambitious goals have become unnervingly fashionable, for it no longer requires original daring nor theoretical independence to attack the hegemony of paradigms—positivism, scientism, Orientalism, modernization, Marxism, behavioralism, etc.—that once shaped the discourse of social science. Scholars, however, must hope that the effort to think anew can also allow some cumulative element in our understanding of how human societies work; and so these books begin their projects by recognizing and building upon the lasting qualities of solid scholarship.

Combining problems freshly identified in current research with concerns traditional to a well-developed area of study, these studies of Latin America use methods and address issues now vital to (and a source of renewal in) all the social sciences and humanities. For generations the field has stimulated fruitful and systematic comparisons—of Catholic and Protestant cultures, English and Spanish colonialism, types of slavery, patterns of racial discrimination, and the nature of economic imperialism. The history of Latin America provided the fodder for dependency theory and resistant grist for theories of development. Much of this comparison, however, has worked from the outside in, applying models and assumptions based on experience elsewhere, models that then often ran aground on the shoals of empiricism.

The essays in this book work from the inside out, from concrete circumstances in nine different countries to the ways in which power and culture have been constructed out of ordinary experience and then use that analysis for comparisons with other societies and to refine more general theories. Power is recognized and probed but not simply as something imposed. Exerted by capital, markets, elites, and states, it rises as well from peasants, women, indigenous peoples, and religion. Culture is emphasized but not simply as tradition maintained or extended. Expressed in official policy, institutions, and communal life, it is constantly reconstituted out of the values, experience, and activity of all those who share it.

In making the case for this approach, Daniel H. Levine's introductory essay becomes an important methodological statement as well as an introduction to the topics and chapters that follow. Many topics long central to Latin American studies receive fresh treatment here, from the impact of the world economic system to revolution, peasant resistance, the social role of religion, the relations of state and culture, and the process of state making. As they move from the particular to the general and back again, these chapters flow into each other like a lively conversation. William W. Culver and Cornel J. Reinhart explore the rise and fall of Chile's copper industry in the context of world competition but also that of Chilean policies rooted in domestic politics and society. That emphasis upon the importance of local response is picked up in Carol A. Smith's analysis of peasant resistance and revolution in Guatemala, which determined the impact of external pressures and the nature of capitalist expansion. A. Douglas Kincaid continues the discussion of revolution and resistance, establishing the importance of the shifting identity of the communities within which Salvadorians placed themselves. Marjorie J. Becker shows how peasant resistance in Mexico, which formed its ideas from economic and religious experience, could be transformed into an official political ideology. Religion and social change is then discussed by Daniel H. Levine, who demonstrates how each necessarily recasts the other as Catholic communities in Venezuela and Colombia connect faith, popular culture, social values, and political action, inventing new forms of organization in the process. A similar intersection arises in Michael W. Foley's research on the values and experiences that shaped the organization of resistance in a Mexican town. Linda J. Seligmann expands the discussion of economic change and peasant society by focusing on the remarkable role of the market women of Peru, brokers of both commodities and cultures. Randal Johnson takes up the question of culture and the state from a different perspective, reviewing policies in Brazil that have reached a crisis after sixty years of seeking to co-opt the intelligentsia and reach the masses. Larissa Adler Lomnitz, Claudio Lomnitz Adler, and Ilya Adler reveal another expression of how the relation between state and culture emerges by combining anthropological and political analysis in their study of public ritual in Mexico elections. That raises issues about the role of elites and national myths, and José Murilo de Carvalho demonstrates their fundamental importance in the making of the Brazilian state. Politics, culture, and social structure then bring us back to revolutionary change in Susan Eckstein's even-handed assessment of Castro's Cuba and the economic and social policies that help to account for its survival in an alien world.

Notable for their stimulating surprises and significant research, these essays speak to each other because each independently integrates elements of culture and power often left apart. Each places this new research in the context of the relevant scholarly literature, and each speaks to important bodies of theory in the methods used and conclusions drawn. Contributions specialists will value, these chapters offer all readers multiple avenues of access through the general propositions they address and the comparisons they make. Together, they constitute an engaging conversation that conveys much of the fascination of Latin America.

Raymond Grew

Acknowledgments

Grateful acknowledgment is given to *Comparative Studies in Society and History* (*CSSH*) for permission to reproduce the following article in revised form:

"Capitalist Dreams: Chile's Response to Nineteenth-Century World Copper Competition" by William W. Culver and Cornel J. Reinhart first appeared in *CSSH* 31:722–44 under the same title.

The following are reproduced in unrevised form:

"Black and White and Color: *Cardenismo* and the Search for a Campesino Ideology" by Marjorie J. Becker originally appeared in *CSSH* 29:453–65.

"The Cuban Revolution in Comparative Perspective" by Susan Eckstein originally appeared in *CSSH* 28:502–34.

"Local History in Global Context: Social and Economic Transitions in Western Guatemala" by Carol A. Smith originally appeared in *CSSH* 26:193–228.

"Organizing, Ideology, and Moral Suasion: Political Discourse and Action in a Mexican Town" by Michael W. Foley originally appeared in *CSSH* 32:488–514.

"Peasants into Rebels: Community and Class in Rural El Salvador" by A. Douglas Kincaid originally appeared in *CSSH* 29:466–94.

"Political Elites and State Building: The Case of Nineteenth-Century Brazil" by José Murilo de Carvalho originally appeared in *CSSH* 24:378–99.

"Popular Groups, Popular Culture, and Popular Religion" by Daniel H. Levine originally appeared in *CSSH* 32:718–64.

"To Be in Between: The *Cholas* as Market Women" by Linda J. Seligmann originally appeared in *CSSH* 31:694–721.

Contents

Constructing Culture and Power

Daniel H. Levine

The title of this book holds much of the story. Culture and power are linked to one another in an active process—hence the gerund *constructing*. The authors whose work is collected here explore what is entailed in the construction of culture and power in Latin America, now as in the past and future. They examine constraints and circumstances under which builders of culture and power operate, consider the prospects for their success, and ask what "success" or "failure" means to those involved.

The argument and evidence collected in this volume constitute a distinct point of view about how best to understand change in Latin America and what proper understanding means for scholarly analysis more generally. As scholars, we seek a kind of inquiry that takes account of how individuals and groups define themselves and in the process refashion their encounter with enduring structures of meaning and power. We focus therefore on the phenomenology of power, power as understood by those using and used by it. This is an essential step in any effort to repeople the structures of the social sciences with recognizable human beings rather than abstractions deduced from theoretical principles. The challenge scholarship faces is not to abandon theory but, rather, to rebuild it in ways that combine inner understanding with analysis of context and verification external to the context. Such an effort has deep roots in the classic tradition of the social sciences,[1] and, if undertaken with clarity, we believe that it can advance a wide range of intellectual disciplines and creative endeavors, in Latin America and elsewhere.

Our search for answers about culture and power casts a broad empirical net: Indians and peasants in Guatemala and El Salvador; nineteenth-century elites in Chile, Brazil, and the United States; Peruvian market women; Mexican politicians and community organizers; religious groups in Colombia and Venezuela; and the shape of economy and state reform in Cuba. Looking for historical and comparative evidence on culture and power also requires searching for better questions and more effective methods of analysis. The research collected here is part of that search, and the authors separately and as a group engage central issues in social theory, issues that have also been at the heart of scholarly debates in and about Latin America. The logic of this collection is that the evolution of scholarship on Latin America has reached a particularly apt moment for reflection, with challenges posed across a range of disciplines and scholarly traditions. How these challenges are engaged and resolved will be critical to the content, focus, and likely validity of future studies.

Changes in intellectual and aesthetic discourse respond to more than the evolution of theory or the difficulties within any scholarly discipline or tradition. Empirical failure ages theories very quickly, and, in any event, the problems that present themselves as privileged subjects for study do not emerge fully formed out of thin air. They arise as the practical arts of existence press on academic discourse. The struggles and efforts of Latin Americans themselves put new issues on the scholarly table, bringing the familiar "to consciousness as something in need of being ascertained" (Habermas 1985b:400). A central goal of this volume is to find systematic ways of connecting the several "states of the art": the intellectual and aesthetic arts with the practical arts of living in Latin America. The basic assumptions, theories, and methods advanced in these essays therefore draw simultaneously on the effort to engage scholarship and push it in new directions and on the impact changing reality has had on research and reflection about it.

The objects of any study of culture and power cannot be understood as objects alone: they are created by people, active subjects with lives, interests, and dynamics of their own. The challenge for scholarship is to understand why these lives change as they do and to make sense of emerging expressions of culture and power in ways that give full credit to innovations on the ground, working "up" to explanation from the categories real people use in daily life.[2] The result will be not only a better portrait of changes in culture and power but also a richer kind of scholarship, as inquiry moves beyond a monologue with academic concerns toward a more complete understanding of life as experienced by the subjects of study.[3]

The landscape of studies on Latin America is littered with the debris of similar efforts to build a better mousetrap, so a few words are in order on the genesis and goals of this particular enterprise.[4] This book is built around nine essays recently published in *Comparative Studies in Society and History* (*CSSH*). Two new essays were also commissioned, and, where possible, authors were invited to present their work to a graduate student-faculty seminar held at the University of Michigan in Ann Arbor during the fall of 1990.[5] From its beginnings *CSSH* has staked out a distinct scholarly perspective. In theoretical terms there has been consistent effort to explore relations among society, culture, and politics in historically focused ways. Comparative study has been framed to seek the general in the particular. Working not from abstract models but, rather, from historically specific problems, research in this vein fuses analysis of big structures with the study of community, biography, and everyday life. Special stress is placed on the creation and use of institutional and cultural mediations. Using *CSSH* as the base for a volume built around a geographical area rather than a problem or issue warrants separate attention.

There can be no question that the past few decades have seen a great flowering of research, reflection, and creative effort in Latin America. A region once confidently dismissed as culturally stodgy and dependent on models copied from Europe or North America has lately been the birthplace of well-known and much imitated innovations ranging from dependency theory to liberation theology, salsa and samba to film and magical realism or testimonial forms in literature. The quality, range, and interdisciplinary character of these creative efforts has helped move work on Latin America from the periphery to the center of comparative studies. But granting all these changes and their far-reaching character, nagging doubts remain: in what sense is Latin America per se a worthwhile subject for analysis?

Latin America as a Question

Latin America is a worthwhile subject because Latin American experience presents problems for analysis in ways that challenge conventional ways of thinking about culture and power. To frame the issues, it may be helpful to begin with a brief review of the kinds of elements relied upon over the years to justify talking about Latin America as a coherent entity. Is there any reality to Latin America? Is the expression anything more than a convenient but misleading shorthand? The mixed cultural and geographical sense of the name Latin America (as opposed, for example, to Anglo-America)[6] rests on a common history with roots in the conquest and its heritage. Elements of language, economic and social structure, institutional formation, and overlapping networks (ecclesiastical, educational, literary, diplomatic, military, and migratory) make one section of the area or fragment of its history recognizable in another.

This conventional familiarity notwithstanding, it has never been easy to capture Latin America's identifying traits in any neat or simple formula. To Alexis de Tocqueville the region's identity and apparent difficulties constituted a difficult and demanding puzzle. The physical circumstances and conditions of Latin America were broadly equal to those of the North, but even by the 1840s the region already appeared mired in stagnation and oppression. Tocqueville found the decisive difference not in static conditions but, rather, in culture and mores, the practical ethos of peoples and leaders that made them engage the world in characteristic ways. The practical ethos of Anglo-Americans reflected and reinforced prevailing social equality, making them self-reliant and capable of sustained collective action. The practical ethos of Latin Americans exaggerated authority and dependence on it and made sustained collective action all but impossible. Tocqueville's view has been shared by generations of Latin America's Liberal elite, who believed that Spain cursed the region at birth with a heritage of religious and political absolutism.[7] The key to progress lay in discarding and or at least marginalizing that heritage. Prescriptions intended to emulate North America and Western Europe followed: reshaping legislatures, forming constitutions, setting economic policy, and, tempered by the racism of the times, importing white settlers to "improve" the race.

This image of a Latin America crippled by inherited culture and institutions persists in varied forms to the present day. Even such otherwise different schools of thought as "Ibero-American cultural fragments" and modernization/development share this basic assumption.[8] According to the first, Latin America is best understood as a fragment of Iberian culture implanted in the New World. Enduring themes in Iberian culture, crystallized in the Americas through institutions of religion and law and manifest in basic cultural norms about hierarchy, authority, and the use of power are what make the region distinctive. The modernization/development school explains the particularities of Latin America in terms of lag, with cultural forms lagging (and also dragging) needed economic and institutional change. Only "development" could change things, by approximating regional patterns more closely to those of the already developed world. Each school depicts culture as something inherited from the past, controlled by elites who socialize new generations and emergent groups into its principles and practices. Latin Americans thus appear as captive of their culture. The kind of stability and progressive change envisioned and desired comes either by recognizing and adapting to the demands of the existing culture or as the aftereffect of deliberate promotion of value change through "modernization." In each case, the literature points ultimately to culture as the key to understanding Latin America, with cultural transformation depicted as necessary but exceptionally difficult.

In addition to viewing culture primarily as an inheritance from the past, both schools of thought privilege ties between culture and order, leaving little theoretical room for the analysis of culture and change. This is not the place for a detailed account of these positions or of the debate over alternatives.[9] Suffice it to say that both came under growing attack in the late 1960s, with the result that culture was replaced at the heart of scholarly concern about Latin America with arguments about structures, manifest above all in resurgent concern for classical issues of political economy. The emergence of dependency theory did much to spur creative rethinking of state, class, and power in Latin America. Now the region's distinctiveness was seen to rest not on inherited traditions or lagged development in general but, rather, on specific relations with global systems of economic, political, and cultural power, which decisively shaped opportunities. Class formation, political coalitions, and the overall structure of power were cast in a new light.[10] In brief, Latin America was the way it was because of ties with already developed nations. It was therefore misleading to expect development on the North Atlantic model: Latin American possibilities were decisively constrained by the prior existence of that model and the ubiquitous presence of economic and political forces it unleashed and controlled.

Long-standing conventions about what to study and where to look in Latin America ("Brazilian literature," "Venezuelan politics," "Argentine military elites," "Andean communities," "religion among the Tzotzil," and so forth) began to lose their sharpness and force of conviction. Efforts were made to cut across these lines, for example, in work on local manifestations of world system phenomena: media networks, investment and trade patterns, flows of migration and employment opportunities.[11] Economic factors were privileged over culture, politics, law, and institutions. De Gregori, Blondet, and Lynch comment on the changing role of anthropology in Peru in terms that are relevant here. By the early 1960s identification with the Indian (*indigenismo*) and concentration on community studies began to lose their force of conviction as society urbanized and few unstudied communities remained.

But just when a search for new directions and a turn to the city became urgent, a "cold wave" of marxism engulfed us all. Structures now took precedence over actors, and attention went to the economic base, not the cultural superstructure.... The rich accumulation of anthropological monographs became little more than raw material, with concern for usages, customs or values painted as superfluous, even frivolous, in light of the urgent need to grasp the scientific (read, economic) laws, essential for the advent and ultimate success of a revolution thought to be imminent.... Suffice it to say that life showed us that social actors don't let themselves be confined by laws that reduce them to epiphenomena of structures. Culture elbowed its way in, forcing us in many tangible ways to recognize how far it was from being merely a reflection, a superstructural frill. (1986:14–15)

As these authors suggest, categories derived from Marxist and dependency scholarship quickly ran into problems of their own. The subordination of change in Latin America to the impact of global economic formations obscured critical differences and made it hard to see changes arising from other sources. In particular, the widespread return to civilian politics combined with a surge of cultural innovation and new social movements throughout the 1980s to underscore the weaknesses of economic determinism (Levine 1988b; Remmer 1991; P. Smith 1991).

One of the central lines of scholarly response to these difficulties has been an effort (visible in many disciplines) to find units of analysis capable of linking global systems with nations, regions, communities, and ordinary routine. There is also concern to study how new ideals and organizational forms are created in encounters between institutions and their potential clients. Interest then turned to detailing the character of these linkages as lived experiences, through research on the construction of social roles and connecting structures.[12] Analysis turns from abstractions like tradition, modernity, development, modernization, class, or even "culture" to a multifaceted portrait of encounters: urban migrants with city and with the state, peasants with new economic formations or with church or party organizers, encounters of men and women with family structures and gender roles in new circumstances, encounters with the new meaning of politics and with the openings literacy provides to the rest of the world. The "rest of the world" emerges more clearly then as a world constructed by people within parameters of power that they do not create but also do not accept passively.[13]

In these ways the evolution of scholarship has directed attention to units of analysis that make it possible for observers to hear the voices emerging from everyday life and to specify the midlevel organizations being created on the ground throughout the region.[14] There has been renewed concern to craft a phenomenological perspective, pointing research to work with cultural and organizational categories that make sense within a society. Doing so properly requires seeing these categories precisely as creations, making a space for change and for those who push it along. Phenomenological efforts at imaginative reconstruction therefore involve more than recreating the pattern of ideas: attention to the origins and history of these ideas, and to what makes them change, is also required.[15] The issue is important if only because groups and individuals may follow rules that vary in systematic ways from what scholars expect. Class, for example, may be mediated by culture, both by gender or race, and so forth. In broad theoretical terms, working with a phenomenological approach substantially enriches understanding of why people act as they do.

The issue takes on added significance in scholarship on Latin America given the ambiguous relation of class to organization and identity. It is a sociological truism that class position does not translate in any direct way into collective action or shared identity. This general point is reinforced in Latin America by the emergence of a kind of self-image and identity that has drawn growing attention in the social sciences as it has in art, music, religion, and literature. At issue is the creation of an identity as members of "popular sectors." Popular music, art, religion, or literature were once widely viewed as products of ignorant and uninstructed individuals. But over the last few decades these cultural products spread into media and arenas once reserved to elites. In addition, they have increasingly been seen not as distortions requiring correction (for example, through education or evangelization) but, rather, as the expression of new and valid identities being created in these societies.

The emergence of "popular" as a widespread kind of identity affects how we understand the origins of social movements and grasp their likely impact on politics. To begin with, the pace and scale of social change has made the potential base of any movement much more heterogeneous, while the near-universal experience of personal and group transformation has spurred a powerful sense of equality of condition.[16] Emergent popular identities thus combine a rough and ready egalitarianism with a claim to group autonomy and a disposition to assert rights that is new in the culture.[17] This growing capacity for collective action often comes without stable ties to larger structures of power like political parties or the state.

The lack of sustained connections can fragment political action: groups end up confined to local issues, easily manipulated, prone to splits and co-optation, and weak, with a barely defined "vocation for power" (Eckstein 1989; Portes 1989; Caldeira 1984; and De Gregori, Blondet, and Lynch 1986). But at the same time the whole effort is more widespread and flexible because it rests less on formally organized groups than on general wider currents of egalitarian belief and social capacity. The phenomenology of power and action visible here is not well understood in all-or-nothing terms. Instead, we find a repertoire of actions and understandings whose range underscores how much the effort to play the game can itself provide a means for creating and reinforcing new identities and confidence in oneself and one's community.

The preceding sketch differs from many overviews by its deliberate focus on problems rather than disciplines. There has, of course, been a regular flow of assessments of the state of the various disciplines working on Latin America. Work in this genre has oscillated between bouts of enthusiasm for new topics, and for the prospects of applying innovative theory, method, and collaborative, interdisciplinary strategies with laments about the continued marginalization of work on Latin America in the world scholarly community.[18] An important recent effort came in the mid-1980s, with essays commissioned by the Latin American Studies Association on the state of research in history, political science, economics, sociology, anthropology, and literary studies (Mitchell 1988). The results are instructive.

Overall, the essays reveal that concern about the status of Latin America as a subject (i.e., does it mean anything? Is it as good as work on Europe?) has yielded to a focus on core scholarly problems such as culture, power, identity, ideology, change, and conflict. These are framed around a desire to see how Latin Americans interpret and grapple with their own situation. Expanded scholarly interaction between Latin and North Americans has reinforced this concern, and spurred the growth of a scholarship that is problem focused and self-critical.[19] In economics, for example, "competing economic ideologies have [thus] been a central part of the modern Latin American development experience. That debate currently continues under the impulse of the most severe downturn in economic activity since the Great Depression" (Fishlow 1988:110). In sociology and anthropology there has been a double effort to redefine the proper unit of inquiry: first, away from community (anthropology) or nation (sociology) to the world system; and then to interest in how the world system is manifested in and connected with ordinary life. One notable result, according to Alejandro Portes (1988), is that there is now less concern with creating a general "sociology of development" than with using sociological theory to inform comparative and historical study of specific problems.[20]

Some of the biggest swings and sharpest changes are visible in the study of politics. From beginnings in the study of law and institutions, political analysis moved quickly through fascination with modernization and its associated tool kit of concepts and methods to an equally intense affair with the analytical categories of dependency and the explanation of authoritarianism. Attention has lately returned to political institutions, which are now understood in a more dynamic and comparative way. Efforts have also been made to confront the challenge of how best to construct and maintain viable democracies (Remmer 1991; Valenzuela 1988; Levine 1988b; P. Smith 1991). History has also returned to the center of political analysis, for example, in work on state and labor, critical junctures, and the production and reproduction of historical legacies (Collier and Collier 1991).

The evolution of scholarship on Latin America has been marked by a seemingly endless search for paradigms and saviors: theories, methods, and critical social groups, which, it is hoped, will together provide a key to analysis and action. At present, there appears to be no consensus but, rather, analytical drift and eclecticism (Remmer 1991; P. Smith 1991). The solution is not to abandon theory or to give up the search for generalization and still less to opt for some "compromise" that includes elements from all schools.[21] Rather than produce yet another review of changes in the disciplines, or even a collection of classic pieces on a given problem, the intention here is to reinforce the interchange already underway between central issues of intellectual work and the problematic that Latin America presents. It will be more fruitful to return to classic problems in social theory, using the literature to escape its bounds, while working on the enduring challenges it poses.

Central Challenges

The central challenges arising from the literature on Latin America come in the effort to understand culture and power in ways that do justice to the values and efforts of those involved without getting lost in the minutiae of individual lives and small-scale settings. The response to this challenge constitutes a thread unifying the contributions to this volume, whatever their empirical focus. It is now appropriate, therefore, to alter voice and perspective, moving away from general discussions of scholarship on Latin America to close accounts of five sets of issues that inform the research collected in this volume. These are the meaning of human agency, the impact of capitalism, the nature of resistance, the capacity to form and maintain organizations, and, in methodological terms, concern with linkages and mediations.[22]

As used here, *agency* refers to the conscious efforts of social actors to understand and work on their situations. Human beings appear as active subjects, not as objects: acting on, if not always prevailing in, the situations in which they find themselves. Addressing ourselves to agency means acknowledging that the elements that move men and women to action, and the grounds on which they judge events, may vary systematically from the notions that external observers come to verify. Marjorie Becker's discussion of peasant ideology in the Mexican revolution, in this volume, shows that the difficulty is not limited to scholars. Ignoring peasant views, the ideologues of the revolution constructed a reductionist image of peasant society and a crude explanation of ideology that derived belief exclusively from class interest narrowly defined. Peasants had a different vision, the expression of which empowered mobilization and resistance to official programs ostensibly designed in their own interest. Becker reminds us that this opposition cannot be dismissed as arising from false consciousness; peasant consciousness is different, not distorted.

Along with others in this collection, Becker's work sheds light on how expressions of popular culture emerge in negotiated relations with institutions of power and meaning. Popular culture is no pristine product, springing full blown from preexisting cultural formations. At issue is not the rejection but more commonly the reworking of these relationships. Attention to agency reflects an understanding that beliefs are rooted in but not determined by social context. The autonomy of popular cultural expression is negotiated over time with institutions such as schools, churches, media, or the state. As used in this volume, *negotiation* refers to the way programs are projected and accepted, or not, to how groups evolve criteria for selecting one theme or another, to the character of day-to-day contact between groups, members, mediators, and to the institutions that project power and meaning through the society. Attention is directed then to discourse and to its relation with organized and sustained collective action.

Incorporating agency makes social change a meaningful and reflexive process. Human beings see themselves acting and adjust both action and perception to changing circumstances they themselves create. To this rational calculus, we add moral discourse and the creation of meaningful identities. Working with moral discourse runs against the grain of much recent social science work, whose characteristic outlook on the world remains steeped in liberal and Marxist assumptions that subordinate values and belief to interest narrowly defined. It also fits badly with desires to find general laws, basic units that cumulate, and with the growing predilection for abstract modeling throughout the social sciences.[23] Despite otherwise noteworthy differences among themselves, these scholarly conventions all marginalize the analysis of moral discourse. The general position seems to be that moral claims need to be validated in history; their origin and development requires no systematic attention. But as Habermas reminds us, "we must finally relearn what we forgot during the fascist period . . . that humanitarian and moral arguments are not merely deceitful ideology. Rather, they can and must become central social forces" (1985a:76).

Meaning and moral discourse are underscored here because they are often central to how agents define themselves and make choices about what is possible, necessary, right, or wrong. Moral discourse ties motive to action, providing, in Michael Foley's words, "the context, the reasons, and the rationalizations that select among and organize motives, arranging priorities, masking certain interests and reshaping still others."[24] My study of popular groups and popular religion, in this volume, demonstrates how important it is for groups to build a coherent moral vocabulary, one that makes sense of change while providing a foundation of trust that can hold the group together through hard times.

Complete understanding of agency and discourse requires scholars to look beyond the content of ideas and to examine critical roles such as that of local organizer or broker. Systematic attention is also needed to how identities are built. Linda Seligmann's research on Peru's *cholas* illustrates the possibilities very well. Standing between peasant producers and buyers in urban or regional markets, *cholas* in effect mediate relations among ethnic groups, communities, state institutions, and levels of the economic system. Their growing economic and commercial presence undergirds the *cholas'* growing sense of themselves as independent actors with rights that can be validated through organization and sustained conflict. New identities and commitments thus arise within existing roles, expanding the boundaries of what is seen to be possible and legitimate action. Seligmann also shows how the social construction of power mixes with a social construction of physical space. The *cholas* challenge their traditionally restricted presence in public spaces by moving from commerce to political action, thereby undercutting established definitions of gender roles.[25] The *cholas* are part of a general pattern of change, visible all across the region, as peasants and migrants to cities create organizations that occupy land, hold meetings, and fill public squares with new faces. In all cases moral discourse and the consolidation of identity rework the materials of social and economic context in ways that energize the effort at collective mobilization.

Much contemporary work on agency and identity in Latin America is directed at the study of popular self-image and the promotion of popular groups. This reflects a desire to bring popular experiences and understandings to light and to make them as central to research and reflection as those of the elites on whose written record analysis has tended to rely.[26] Incorporating other methods and source (interviews, the creative use of court transcripts, documents, or sermons) has made it possible to redress the balance, giving voice to hitherto hidden transcripts of the powerless. To be sure, the study of agency cannot properly be limited to reconstructing the world of the poor. Elites and the culture of the powerful also require systematic attention. Like the poor, elites also change, innovating and reaching out continuously to contacts and tools of control. The point is taken up in this volume by Larissa Adler Lomnitz, Claudio Lomnitz Adler, and Ilya Adler, whose research sheds light on precisely how Mexican elites (in this case, leaders of the dominant party, the PRI) imagine and maintain an ideology. Their analysis of the 1988 presidential campaign shows how these elites manage to arrange institutions and order public spaces and events to ensure that such imagining is hegemonic. My study of religious groups shows the profound difference alternative elite strategies can make to popular consciousness: shaping prevailing images of church and religion and controlling the form and content of group agendas. Leaders in the Colombian Catholic church have successfully domesticated popular groups, affirmed hierarchy, and contained democratizing tendencies. In contrast, Jesuits in

Venezuela, along with small groups of priests and sisters in both countries, have made strenuous long-term efforts to promote groups in which religious revitalization goes hand in hand with activism and internal democracy.

A second general challenge arising out of scholarship on Latin America is to grasp the impact of capitalism, especially of its expansion and incomplete development. Earlier generations of Latin American Liberals argued fervently that the region was feudal in institutions and practices. In this view progress and development would only be possible with full incorporation into the capitalist market. This position has lately been refreshed by neoconservatives such as Michael Novak (1990) who hold that Latin American countries have never experienced genuine capitalism: once they do, he argues, stable democracy and steady economic growth will follow.[27] A contrary view insists that Latin America has always been an integral (but peripheral) part of the capitalist world. Writers otherwise as different as Andre Gunder Frank, Keith Griffin, Fernando Henrique Cardoso, and Eric Wolf agree that Latin America has been part of the global economic system from the beginning. In their view it is precisely this incorporation as a peripheral and dependent element in global relations that explains the region's characteristic mix of wealth, inequality, and long-term stagnation. The problem is not to create capitalism but to change the terms under which any economic system is organized in Latin America.

Each of these positions suffers from excessive generality. More effort goes to deriving outcomes from structural considerations about the world system than to reconstructing the relationship as experienced. Excessive reliance on abstract models of capitalism leave the system on automatic pilot: sometimes there seem to be no people there! Dissatisfaction with abstract and deductive work of this kind has lately spurred research designed to fill the empty spaces and document the role of local events and actors in shaping capitalism as experienced "on the ground." Studies in this volume by William Culver and Cornel Reinhart and by Carol Smith do this, moving the debate away from aggregate data and deductive formulas to detailed analysis of local variations and relationships.

Culver and Reinhart examine the failed efforts of Chilean entrepreneurs to compete in the world copper market. Their work adds to the study of capitalism in Latin America by looking at political choices made domestically rather than asserting that external factors alone determine the course of events. They show how early success turned to marginality and attribute the industry's failure not to the defects of a supposedly "precapitalist mentality" but, rather, to the weight of competing co-alitions and interests. At the other end of the social and power spectrum, Smith's study of western Guatemala uncovers a hidden history of resistance and adaptation to global economic and political forces dating from the conquest itself. Colonial rule tried to compress Indian society into an undifferentiated peasantry, but Indians sustained independent identities and created forms of resistance that changed the overall character of capitalism in Guatemala, with long-term consequences for the nature of authority and the potential for resistance. Smith's research shows that the expansion of capitalism needs to be seen not only in economic terms but also as a social and cultural phenomenon, marked by struggle and creative human agency at every point.

Note how much the state and other institutions of power and meaning are present in the daily experience of all these cases. The role of institutions is often painted in mostly negative terms, with attention to repression, exile, purges, and censorship. These are important but by themselves fail to capture the full range and dynamic of culture and power. There is much positive action as well, as formal programs and their agents reach out to arrange local agendas, compress options, and shape the culture of the future. In his contribution to this volume Randal Johnson helps rethink the scope of state power by showing that its projection is as much cultural as economic or coercive. He examines the explicit cultural policies followed by the Brazilian state, which in this century have included promoting writers and magazines, filmmaking and cinema distribution, building schools, and shaping curricula and popular festivals. Sustained efforts have also been made to infuse popular culture with suitable content, for example, by sponsoring mass sports such as soccer, "correct" samba lyrics for carnival, or the design of "proletarian" furniture. There have also been many initiatives (popular libraries, parks and recreation) intended to soak up the leisure time of urban masses and create the kind of citizen that new industrial elites wanted.[28]

Solving the challenge posed by agency and capitalism can do much to improve our understanding of resistance. The development of capitalism creates clear conditions for resistance as well as domination, not least by making it possible for human agents to fill empty social spaces with new content. The issues that energize and legitimate resistance and the way resistance crystallizes personal and collective identity varies, of course, with the particulars of the case. But whatever the specifics, in all cases the impact of economic structures and emerging class formations is mediated by other elements. My essay on popular religious groups in Venezuela and Colombia underscores the key mediating role played by links with the institutional church in shaping not only religious belief but also the nature and direction of community identity and collective action. In the same vein, Douglas Kincaid's contribution on peasant rebellion in El Salvador demonstrates that, by itself, social class cannot account for the rise of sustained peasant resistance in El Salvador: solidarities of community and religion play a key mediating role. Such solidarities are not simply "out there" waiting only to be tapped; they are created fresh in each generation. In his words, "The contemporary strength of community solidarity was [therefore], in a recreated form, the product of popular religious organizing efforts around residual community bonds . . . these ties and externally promoted organizational forms appeared mutually indispensable elements in the formation of a contestatory peasant movement."[29]

Scholarly work on resistance has been energized through the 1980s by a profuse creation of associations all across the region: independent trade unions, human rights groups, mothers' clubs, neighborhood associations, peasant organizations, and religious communities (Eckstein 1989; Mainwaring and Viola 1984; Foweraker and Craig 1990). These have pushed their way onto the public scene, exploiting and expanding spaces opened by the sharp decline of both revolution and extremes of domination. The profusion of groups opened spaces for new kinds of practice, demystifying authority by making the tools of association available to everyone. These innovations elbowed their way into theory as well, impelling observers to abandon concepts of resistance as primarily a *defense* of "tradition" or an effort to recapture some lost utopia. There is little good evidence for utopian dreams in that sense, and in any event the resistance that forces itself on our attention today is anything but a defense of tradition. It draws on the dominant culture, using its tools and pressing claims to share in its core processes and in the goods it provides.[30]

Practice and theory have combined to expand the working concept of resistance so that it now includes a range of everyday activities once dismissed as inconsequential. Study circles, day care centers, communal kitchens, neighborhood associations, religious groups, and other contemporary or historical phenomena are now regularly considered alongside conventional indicators such as strikes, votes, and violence. The result is a *repertoire* of resistance, in which these varied expressions fit as aspects of a broad acceptance or rejection of authority and of its prevailing legitimations.[31] Much of the research collected in this volume fits nicely with this broader notion of resistance: Seligmann on brokerage by Peru's *cholas,* Becker on the ideology of Mexican peasants, and Kincaid on peasant rebellions in El Salvador all come to mind, to name only a few. As noted earlier for the case of agency, analysis of repertoires is not properly restricted to popular groups. Domination has repertoires of its own; institutions and their leaders and agents work regularly to project images of right and wrong, legitimacy, and power that are essential to their own survival. For the case of Mexico, Lomnitz, Lomnitz Adler, and Adler suggest that the PRI's success in domination rests not so much on overcoming resistance with brute force as on elites' capacity to absorb it in ways that keep resistance from ever coming to the surface in organized ways.[32] Elites can also mount successful resistance to state power, for example, through social movements, economic associations (e.g., of producers, commerce, or capital), control of media, or capital flight.

That resistance often arises within existing identities and relationships and then pushes their limits outward has importance not only for analysis but also for political action. If the direction and character of action cannot be derived in any simple way either from state action or from descriptions of the socioeconomic or demographic traits of leaders or foot soldiers, where then should analysis direct attention? Who precisely are the agents likely to carry resistance forward? Where should we look? One member of the seminar commented:

> Industrial workers were considered for "the Classics" as being the "revolutionary subject." Since they did not exist, or they were just an irrelevant minority in Latin American countries, someone realized that it should be changed, and he/she discovered that peasants could also play this role. Since their rebellions have not had in general a strong effectiveness or durability, people are looking for a new idea. Some look at the elites, others to middle classes, others to social movements, etc. Even if it is not a revolutionary one, would anyone mind leading a progressive change in Latin America please?[33]

The scholarship collected and commented on in this volume affirms that neither culture nor power can be considered as exclusive attributes of any group in particular. Innovative forms of action and new values and meanings are created throughout the social order.[34] What this means for organization, action, and the nature of authority in general can be illustrated with brief comments on recent work in two key areas: religion and the churches; and state formation and political institutions.[35]

Until recently, students of Latin America shared widespread assumptions in the social sciences, making religion epiphenomenal, destined to privatization, decline, and disappearance. Secularization was viewed as inevitable and desirable: essential to the construction of "modernity." Events in Latin America and elsewhere have exploded this comfortable paradigm and affirmed the autonomy of religion and its continued ability to move elites, masses, and institutions in unexpected directions.[36] Latin America has witnessed remarkable religious innovation, and a rich vein of scholarship has dedicated itself to exploring transformations in religious ideas, organizations, and practices and the development of religious competition where Catholicism once exercised an unquestioned monopoly (Levine 1993, 1992; Martin 1990; Stoll 1990). One thread of explanation has attributed religious innovation to the effects of crisis, as those caught up in confusing and disorienting changes of all kinds turn to religion in search of solace and escape. In a crude way one might even say that innovation has been most intense where crisis has been sharpest: Central America, Chile, Brazil, or Peru, for example. But Latin American experience presents several twists that cast doubt on this "crisis-solace" model of religious change.

The model is too static. It assumes that both churches and their clienteles remain unchanged except for the external pressure of crisis. But these are active subjects, and the historical record shows that crisis leads to opportunity, not just escape. By pulling and driving experience into new channels, crisis (in the Weberian sense of expanded trade, broadened scales of action, and challenges to legitimacy) spurs cultural innovation and gives it greater resonance. That religion should be the vehicle for such innovation makes good historical and comparative sense. Cases otherwise as distinct as the Puritan revolution, the civil rights movement in the United States, the emergence of Shi'a activism and Islamic fundamentalism, and Latin America itself all attest to the power of religious metaphors and images and the wide availability of religious structures in situations of rapid change. In Latin America itself religion has, of course, been so closely intertwined for so long with structures of domination that crisis makes churches and religious practice an especially apt focal point for action.[37]

If religion is to change culture and power, religion itself has to change. Scholarship must find ways to grasp the autonomous dynamic of such inner changes (as theologies emerge and practices evolve within an active religious tradition) without losing sight of their links to the surrounding society. To this end research has lately moved away from gross characterizations of religion in general to nuanced studies of change, variation, and resistance.[38] The greatest advance has come through efforts that reach beyond formalities of institution or doctrine to address change among believers—not isolated from institutions but as integral parts of them.[39] Researchers need to follow the lead of most groups and their members, who redefine *church* and *religion* in ways that make a place for themselves. In this way analysis can get past simplistic views that make political position or world system ties primary (parallels to the Iranian revolution, links to the Vatican or to North American Protestants) to one that finds political meaning in the ways religious culture is formed every day. New religious ideas and forms of action do not emerge out of thin air. They appear on doorsteps throughout the region, carried there by agents, diffused in pamphlets, and discussed in endless meetings. That is how the institutional and the popular are put together. That is where new images of the good citizen, or right and proper behavior, and of what faith requires of power are evolved and solidified.

The crisis-solace model also suffers from an unfortunately patronizing tone. The underlying argument is that, because they lack "scientific" or "rational" (read, Marxist or Liberal) insight into the causes of their problems, men and women caught up in change escape to religion. The implication is that change is the same as disorganization and religion is a dead end, a false solution to real problems. This position is shot through with difficulties. Equating change with disorganization and religion with escape ignores the fact that those joining new religious groups are, for the most part, aspirant and mobile individuals. Religious change provides the basis for constructing new forms of control, order, and coherence—not a world of illusion. In theoretical terms the crisis-solace-escape view rests on an impoverished notion of interest, which reduces culture and values to superstructure, mere epiphenomena of presumably more basic movements of economic or political forces or interests. But the interests that individuals and groups pursue do not flow only from their position in the social structure. They are suffused with cultural significance, are value laden from the outset, and hence are as much affected by the dynamics of cultural as by economic or political change.[40]

The consolidation of power and legitimacy in state structures offers another good example of how cultural norms are constructed, given wide and authoritative social presence, and made to endure. By the 1920s state power became concentrated in a defined and increasingly professional state elite all over Latin America. Sometimes the process has deeper historical roots, as in Brazil, where José Murilo de Carvalho shows that colonial policies created a unified and relatively homogeneous state elite. He shows how the common background and training of state elites helped to undergird a style of governing and a pattern of policy that has yet to be broken, combining centralized state structures with continuing kin and regional networks.[41] The persistent power and presence of these elite formations raises serious questions about the quality and survivability of the "new" democratic political order instituted in 1985 (Hagopian 1991). The evolution of power and its cultural projection in Mexico put the issue in a slightly different light. After the upheaval of the revolution Mexicans developed a remarkably flexible and enduring political order, whose core institutions have managed to capture and domesticate social forces.[42] Lomnitz, Lomnitz Adler, and Adler show that they have done so not only by delivering material goods to the regime's clients but also, and more important, by their successful projection of cultural norms, including metaphors of identity and PRI-sanctioned practices that affirm belonging.

Nothing lasts forever, and even revolutions once apparently successful on this score can falter under the pressure of economic decay and the corrosive effect of political constraints, which create a daily experience of domination that belies rhetorical assertions of equality. Illustrative cases include the failure of Peru's military revolutionaries, the Sandinistas' recent fall from power in Nicaragua, and the current troubles of the Cuban regime. As the first and so far the only enduring Marxist political order in the hemisphere, the Cuban revolution has drawn a steady stream of scholarly interest.[43] Susan Eckstein's chapter examines the issues from a fresh point of view, with a detailed comparative account of what the Cuban revolution has and has not accomplished. She explores how the international environment impinges on the state in Cuba but emphasizes the difference that local political choices and policies can make. Her work establishes the importance of national leadership in creating opportunities for change while pointing to likely future sources of weakness and points of conflict.

To this point we have considered the challenges posed by agency, capitalism, and resistance. A common focus on these challenges connects theory and practice in new ways. Consider, for example, their complex impact on understanding associational life. The matter is partly technical: communications, roads, literacy, and access to media all make it possible to join hitherto isolated orders of domination. Action in one place can then spill over to and influence action in another. In his classic work on social structure and power in Peru, Julio Cotler (1968) coined the metaphor of a triangle with no base. Power and domination in Peru, he concluded, rested on a parallel series of networks reaching down from the elite into a divided mass. The dominated were isolated from one another, with few opportunities for contact, little sense of common interest, and no organization of shared identity. The surge of associational life noted earlier in this essay represents a self-moved effort to fill in the base of that triangle, subverting hierarchical arrangements of control on which elites have long depended.

The emergence of sustained dispositions to create and use associations in Latin America sheds light on a number of key issues. It suggests, for example, that cultures change neither by abandoning the past nor by affirming a false image of it in search of traditions to venerate. Change is rarely total; continuity makes new experiences understandable and provides connections of value and identity. Far from making for a "homeless mind," afloat in contexts where "all that is solid melts into air," the new experience of collective life suggests that cultures change and interests are plastic, not solid.[44] If they are too solid, interest and identities get brittle and break. The more common case is negotiated change, with borrowing and contradictions running across social and cultural lines.

Reflecting on American experience, Tocqueville wrote that "in democratic countries the science of association is the mother of all science: the progress of all the rest depends on the progress it has made." The experience of common effort in one area then diffused throughout the society, and people come "ultimately [to] look on public association as the universal, or in a manner, the sole means which men can employ to accomplish the different purposes they may have in view. Every new want constantly revives the notion" (1969:138, 140). He attributed North Americans' devotion to associational life to the effects of a preexisting equality of condition that isolated them, spurring a desire to congregate in groups. Latin American experience suggests a slightly different dynamic, with organization itself spurring equality of condition, furthering changes in self-image and culture that have begun to emerge in response to variations in class and circumstances already underway.

Eric Wolf addresses the problematic of culture and power in the modern world in work that takes quite a different tack. He insists on historical specification, which in his terms means subordinating the explanation of particular configurations of culture and power to "larger" and "more basic" (economic) forces operating on a world scale. Although he acknowledges that groups use cultural forms to express their interests, Wolf insists nonetheless that such expressions are neither independent nor autonomous:

> We can no longer think of societies as isolated and self-maintaining systems. Nor can we imagine cultures as integrated totalities in which each part contributes to the maintenance of an organized, autonomous whole. There are only cultural sets of priorities and ideas, put into play by determinate historical actors under determinate historical circumstances. In the course of action, these cultural sets are forever assembled, dismantled, and reassembled, conveying in varying accents the divergent paths of groups and classes. These paths do not find their explanation in the self-interested decisions of interacting individuals. They grow out of the deployment of social labor, mobilized to engage the world of nature. (1982:387, 390–91)

Wolf roots culture in power and power in economic changes that have made the modern world what it is. His argument would be more convincing if greater room were left for cultural innovations and greater attention given to their consequences for power and institutions. The authors collected here agree with Wolf on the basic point that culture cannot be detached from power or from the kinds of ordinary routine energized by economic transformations. They also concur on the need to avoid freezing culture or power in any particular form: these are historical creations, subject to continuous change. But the call for specificity and the demand that analysis deal with determinate human actors is not satisfied with reference to economic factors alone: interest cannot be so narrowly defined.[45] We differ in the greater play given to creativity and autonomous, self-moved change within a given system. Our working concept of culture and cultural change provides for a richer range of encounters and connections among levels of action: rituals and markets, rallies and routine meetings, parades and political parties, states, churches, and armies. Greater weight is given to possibilities of enduring change arising precisely out of the kinds of interaction that take place in these interstitial spaces.

This comment brings us face to face with methodological questions, in particular with how to create methods of research capable of identifying and working effectively within these encounters and interstitial spaces. At issue are linkages, regular connections that join individuals to organized groups and institutions. Focusing on linkages, as Charles Tilly points out,

> we make the necessary link between personal experience and the flow of history. The structures at issue are now relationships among persons and groups, the processes are transformations of the human interactions constituting these relationships. . . . The necessary comparisons among relationships and their transformations are no longer huge, but they gain coherence with attachment to relatively big structures and large processes. (1984:64)

A few methodological pointers follow from this injunction to seek connections.[46] One is to locate critical social spaces, venues for repeated encounters of individuals with other structures. Such spaces provide arenas in which important events are remembered and, in some form, reproduced: parades, meetings, commemorations.[47] This is where abstractions of "human agency" take on concrete form in the work by men and women who, by their actions, make and remake culture: real people, not "the people." The meaning given to these spaces and, for example, their gradual transformation as gender roles shift (with the private sphere of women pushing itself into the public terrain) must also be explored. Like any space socially and culturally defined as public, the very availability of and access to space is a matter of power and cannot be detached from what power means in any given context.[48]

Scholarship that connects the analysis of structural forms with understanding how universes of meaning and moral discourse are constructed requires a method that respects the autonomy of culture and structure while seeking connections between them. Respecting the autonomy of culture and structure means finally abandoning notions of base and superstructure and efforts to derive either one from the other.

I use *autonomy* here not to suggest isolation or to attribute ultimate causality but, rather, to insist that each sphere has a recognizable dynamic and specific configurations of its own. To be sure, this does not relieve scholars from the necessity of explaining why a particular configuration came to be the way it is. But if culture really is suffused with power and power really is laden with cultural values, then the point of analysis is surely not to separate one from another but, rather, to grasp how they shape each other: Who does the shaping, and why in these specific ways? The active and creative dimensions of the process must remain at the center of scholarship.

How best to accomplish these tasks? Choosing methods clearly entails more than simply opting for one or another technique. The methods we choose reflect the theory we work with: they are theory laden from the outset. The theory that underlies the methodological position taken here rests on a view of social change that privileges human creativity and moral discourse as critical elements in the construction of culture and power. In this light, power and culture appear not as abstract capabilities diffused throughout the social order but, rather, as creations whose very process of formation and particular content is part of their general meaning. To say that culture is wrapped up with power and to insist on the role of human agency in the "social" (or gender or cultural or class) construction of reality means to take account of how human beings make it so. They may not do so entirely as they please. Marx was, of course, correct to see how the past weighed on and limited the present. But this does not mean that there is no room for change, no chance to alter present and future dynamics. Culture is neither frozen once and forever nor simply available "in the air." Cultural analysis often has the defect of restricting the field of study to values and meaning alone. But this leaves meaning and material structures reified and separate and cannot explain why they combine in regular and predictable ways. Culture as norm and symbol must be married with the material structures that make it possible for ideas to diffuse over time and space. To put it crudely, without carriers and an audience there is no culture, and no sustained power, at least not for very long.[49]

Conclusion

Croce remarked that "each true history is contemporary history."[50] By this he implied not only the need for history to work through an imaginative reconstruction of the past as then experienced but also the notion that each generation reads its own concerns into the past. The point is apt and the injunction relevant to our purposes in this volume. Making a true account of Latin America requires not only a projection of the concerns that move scholars but also a conscious effort to engage the historical imagination of Latin Americans. That historical imagination cannot be reified or frozen in one form as if it were forever the same. It is refreshed by each new generation, whose efforts do not erase what went before but, rather, build on it, adding new voices and opening new connections. It is also remade as the defining characteristics of any generation are themselves expanded with the assertion of claims to equal voice by those long silent or, in any event, unheard.

The recent experience of change in Latin America has been particularly rich in challenges to the prevailing order of business in politics, culture, and social life. These challenges may not overturn what Emmanuel Mounier once referred to as "the established disorder," but they have done much to alter the landscape and change the terms by which it can be understood. More is at issue than simply "rereading history from below," although that is a concern that knits action and reflection together in a number of fields. More is at issue than rereading history from below, because it is precisely in the fusion of history as seen and experienced from below with power and culture as projected by elites and the institutions and agents they direct that keys to the future can be found.[51]

Methodological innovation is critical, but not because new techniques will save us. They will not, and in any case, as we have seen, much of the most fruitful recent work has less to do with new techniques than with efforts to use existing tools to answer new kinds of questions. Methodological innovation of the kind advocated here refreshes theory by opening up new angles on the questions that theory asks. Success in the effort requires us to reconceive the issues of culture and power in ways that connect hitherto isolated spaces and empower voices long silent.

The book that follows is organized so as to move the central themes of discussion from the general to the specific and back again. Moving from the general to the specific and back again makes for a richer and more compelling scholarship, one that underscores the relations among levels of action and grounds theoretical generalizations in historically specific and meaningful experiences. The arrangement of chapters pursues these goals in a way that illustrates the many levels at which "Latin America" has presented itself as a problem for analysis. Although, to be sure, all the authors engage general issues in particular circumstances, individual contributions vary notably in the level at which what we conventionally refer to as Latin America enters the argument. We begin with two chapters (Culver and Reinhart; and Smith) that reread the meaning of Latin America's overall engagement with global systems of wealth and power. These are followed by five chapters (Kincaid, Becker, Levine, Foley, and Seligmann) that direct attention to the evolution of new forms of culture and power, through detailed studies of agency, resistance, and organization. The last four chapters (Johnson; Lomnitz, Lomnitz Adler, and Adler; Murilo de Carvalho; and Eckstein) return to issues of culture and power but now with a primary focus not on resistance but rather on domination.

The first two chapters reread the impact of global forces in ways that rescue the autonomy of local actors. Culver and Reinhart reconstruct the world copper market as it appeared in the nineteenth century and show that what now appears inevitable was then a matter of intense struggle. As they rescue elite history, Smith rescues the history of Indians and their ties to the world system. She explodes the myth of Indian culture as a static and unchanging source of all else, showing how cultural forms emerged out of a long-term encounter with economic and political structures. Both studies mirror and reinforce important trends in scholarship that reread the historical record to show how and why familiar forms of culture and power came to be the way they are.[52]

The five chapters that follow begin with Kincaid's analysis of peasant resistance in El Salvador. Kincaid shows how class is mediated by ties of community and religion and demonstrates that the very effectiveness of earlier repression made the rise to revolution in the 1970s less a matter of defending tradition than of creating new identities, new cultural norms, and a new capacity for sustained collective action. Becker paints resistance in a different light, showing how failure to acknowledge the validity of a separate popular vision left revolutionary elites out of touch with those they claimed to represent.

The discussion of cultural innovation, organization, and resistance is carried forward in my chapter on popular religious groups and in Foley's analysis of moral discourse and collective action. I take the evolution of CEBs (communidades eclesiales de base, or base communities) as a window on the creation of new identities and new forms of participation, associational life, and community solidarity through religion. Democratization within groups undergirds changes in popular culture that make for greater personal confidence and sustained capacity for collective action.

Foley's discussion of moral discourse and collective action in a Mexican village illuminates common dilemmas in this effort to create a new culture. In particular, he shows that stress on combatting egoism and avoiding corruption of the "good" community by the bad influences of politics and politicians weakens local efforts by making the necessary ties with larger institutions hard to justify and harder still to operate. The middle group of chapters closes with Seligmann's work on the *cholas,* which enriches the understanding of change by showing how people in mediating roles can create new perspectives and forms of collective action. Her focus on brokerage roles clarifies the constraints and opportunities open to those who try to manipulate the system, creating a new place for themselves.

The final group of four chapters opens with Johnson's study of efforts by the Brazilian state to shape the meaning of *Brazil* and *Brazilian.* Of course, all modern nations make an effort to shape culture: that is what school systems, national anthems, and subsidies of the arts are all about. But in this case there is an unusually direct and explicit link between the elaboration of cultural policies and the self-justification of authoritarian rule. Lomnitz, Lomnitz Adler, and Adler address the issues from a slightly different angle in their chapter on the 1988 presidential campaign in Mexico. Overwhelming domination by one party long ago convinced observers that Mexican elections were of greater interest as a symbolic exercise than as a contest for power. The authors make this insight the basis for exploring how the structure, spatial organization, and sequencing of the campaign reinforces norms about the proper relation of state to individual and the nature of leadership, power, and identity. Their richly textured study offers keys for grasping the future of power in Mexico and understanding how it is built and maintained.

We close with two chapters that together shed light on how the consolidation of elites and state power can shape the character and direction of politics. Murilo de Carvalho shows how the common education and orientation of Brazil's state elite was the deliberate product of official policies aimed at preparing a core of bureaucratic and legal officials. The resulting homogeneous and unified state elite in Brazil undergirded arrangements that maintained control, order, and the centrality of plantation agriculture. Eckstein's research on the Cuban revolution, in contrast, affirms the capacity of a determined elite to change the pattern of power and privilege. Cuban revolutionaries concentrated power and implemented massive redistributions of wealth and access of goods and services. The dilemmas they now face stem from changes in the world economic and political system compounded by a general neglect of political change. This suggests major structural weaknesses. The regime is ossified and remains so tied to the original elite that legitimacy has few bases apart from the redistributive claim and the repressive apparatus.

We cast a broad net in this volume. Individual chapters work with data about individuals, communities, groups, nations, world systems, and the connections between them. We examine economic indicators, moral discourse, official programs, public and private spaces, and the effort to build and maintain identities. We strive to explain resistance, the growth of associational life, cultural and political innovation, and state formation. It is a complex program, difficult to encompass in any single work or even in a volume that collects several. But the effort points us in the right direction. In George Eliot's words: "We need not shrink from this comparison of small things with great, for does not science tell us that its highest striving is after a unity which shall bind the smallest things with the greatest? In natural science, I have understood, there is nothing petty to the mind that has a large vision of relations, and to which every single object suggests a vast sum of conditions. It is surely the same with the observation of human life" (1981:287).

NOTES

I am grateful for comments and critical suggestions on earlier drafts of this essay by Lessie Jo Frazier, Joan Font, Raymond Grew, John Guidry, Donna Harris, Douglas Kincaid, Phyllis Levine, Scott Mainwaring, Margaret Martin, and Cornel Reinhart.

1. For a classic statement of this program, see Weber 1978a.

2. Cf. Gustavo Gutierrez, the Peruvian theologian, who remarked somewhere that the challenge is to rise to the base (*subir a la base*).

3. I am indebted to John Guidry, who forced me to make this point more explicit and whose language I borrow from here.

4. Any list of reviews of the states of the art must include Diegues and Wood 1967; Wagley 1964; and Mitchell 1988; see also Morse 1989. Reviews that address specific problems or disciplines include Levine 1988a and b; and Martz 1990.

5. Original contributions were commissioned from Randal Johnson and from Larissa Lomnitz and her collaborators, Claudio Lomnitz Adler and Ilya Adler. Presentations were made to the seminar by William Culver and Cornel Reinhart, Linda Seligmann, Roberto Da Matta, Randal Johnson, Daniel H. Levine, Susan Eckstein, and Larissa Lomnitz. Papers already published in *Comparative Studies*

in Society and History by Culver and Reinhart, Eckstein and Seligmann were extensively revised for this volume. Members of the seminar (in alphabetical order) were John Cahill, Barbara Duffield, Lessie Jo Frazier, Joan Font, Scott Greenwood, John Guidry, Sarah Hernandez, Jeffrey Hinte, Mark Jones, Margaret Martin, and Steve Striffler.

6. This old dichotomy has recently been revived in interesting ways by Martin 1990.

7. This is the "black legend" that was an article of faith to Latin America's nineteenth-century Liberals.

8. Important early statements include Johnson 1958; Kling 1964; and Almond and Verba 1963. See also Binder et al. 1971. Two useful compilations and updates are Wiener and Huntington 1987; and Klaren and Bossert 1986. The lasting power of the Ibero-American heritage has been developed by Morse 1964; Dealy 1968; Wiarda 1973; and Veliz 1980. Morse (1989) provides a comprehensive and typically iconoclastic restatement of this position.

9. Debates have been more extensive than fruitful. Useful summaries and collections include Collier 1979; Klaren and Bossert 1986; O'Donnell (1973, 1978, 1982); Remmer and Merkx 1982. See also Collier and Collier 1991; and, for a particularly insightful review of changing theoretical currents, see Tilly 1984 (chap. 1).

10. See especially Cardoso 1972; Cardoso and Faletto 1979; Hamilton 1982; Kahl 1976; O'Donnell 1973 and 1978; and Wolf 1982.

11. Studies of migration or community formation, for example, now stressed inequality not marginality, struggle rather than integration. For a review, see Perlman 1976; and also the insights on theory and method that Eckstein (1978) provides in her work on the urban poor in Mexico City.

12. In their effort to rescue culture, for example, De Gregori, Blondet, and Lynch (1986) studied migrants and neighborhoods in Lima, Peru, with a variety of techniques that together capture the richness and creative variety of human experience: fieldwork, case studies, and biographies.

13. As Sosnowski indicates, questions like these reach beyond the social sciences: "the incorporation of the literary into the spaces of everyday life . . . opts for the study of intellectual history and changes in the formation of intellectual relations, rather than limit itself to the specificity of the literary text" (1988:179).

14. It is here that what Havel, following Masaryk, calls the "small-scale work" of making democracy takes place every day: "honest and responsible work in widely differing areas of life, but within the existing social order, work that would stimulate national creativity and national self-confidence" (1985:61). The focus on small-scale work that Havel suggests is an intellectual program as well as a charter for viable democratic politics.

15. Further, as Scott insists, more is involved than mere representation of the thoughts of others: interpretation is essential. "The approach taken here certainly relies heavily on what is known as phenomenology or ethnomethodology. But it is not confined to that approach, for it is only slightly more true that people speak for themselves than that behavior speaks for itself. Pure phenomenology has its own pitfalls. A good deal of behavior, including speech, is automatic and

unreflective, based on understandings that are seldom if ever raised to the level of consciousness. A careful observer must provide an interpretation of such behavior that is more than just a repetition of the commonsense knowledge of participants" (1985:46).

16. Portes states that "popular" makes sense as an identity given the weak opportunities for class-based organization that economic change and the pattern of urban settlement provide in modern Latin America (1985, 1989).

17. The resulting identity is "not classist, but popular: the self-definition is 'of the people.' In this way, issues and groups slowly gain consistency around a new popular identity, but even though these groups challenge traditional forms of state domination, they rarely crystallize into enduring collective action" (De Gregori, Blondet, and Lynch 1986:26).

18. Morse notes the "fresh topics" commended to future researchers by one widely used text on Latin American history: "regionalism, religion, bureaucracy, entrepreneurship, ideology, urbanization, mortality control, militarism, race, climatic change, epidemiology, history of science, and even those stillborn twins, dependency and underdevelopment" (1989:192). Cf. his earlier complaint that, "for a Latin Americanist who is getting on in years, the shifts of paradigm by which we construe our region of interest have accelerated to a breathless pace. Yet academic solemnity is such that mounting chaos is presented as linear advance toward more perfect knowledge" (1989:131). On the international marginalization of studies of Latin America, see Wagley's early comment that "a Ph.D. candidate could contribute to economic, sociological, or political theory more easily by a study of New Haven, Connecticut, than by a laborious study of Mendoza, Argentina" (1964:15).

19. The point is made strongly for sociology (Portes 1988:133) and anthropology (Arizpe 1988:147).

20. Cf. the recent comment by Portes and Kincaid that "the main conceptual limitation in the field has been an undue fascination with broad concepts drawn from general theory. While dramatic social problems in the advanced countries were scrutinized from every angle, earlier research on underdevelopment too often was dedicated to documenting the veracity of sweeping intuitions.... The poor record of these models in squaring with actual events should give us pause in pursuing their lead. The resilient pillars of development studies are not works of grand theory, but rather detailed studies of historical and contemporary processes" (1989:499).

21. Cf. Nader, who opens a recent work as follows:
This book has been written over many years, and for that reason has been a pleasure intellectually. I have not been in a hurry to produce a work that fits into the latest mood in anthropology. Rather, I have been able to incorporate the wealth of insight that has come from each successive contribution: the structural-functionalists, the interest in process and power, a reflective style that has forced a consideration of paradigm and the place of a critical anthropology, the world system theories, and the insight that comes from understanding cultural as well as social contraints.... In the 1990s, a composite approach, rather than attachment to any particular school of social or

cultural theory, will add to the power of anthropological analysis of the microcosm in a global system. (1990:xxiii)
For a discussion of the difficulties this all-inclusive strategy presents, see Levine 1991.

22. In identifying these issues, I was greatly aided by seminar discussions and by the written comments students provided on each of the papers.

23. See, for example, the reports recently compiled for the National Research Council: Gerstein, et al. 1988; and Luce, Smelser, and Gerstein 1989.

24. Foley (in this volume).

25. This insight has been ably developed in new work on the cultural and political dynamics of gender. See, for example, Alvarez 1990; and Drogus 1990. On shifting bases of peasant identities, see Levine 1992 (chaps. 5 and 6).

26. Cf. Levine 1986a on this trend in comparative studies of religion or, in a wholly different vein, Beverly and Zimmerman 1990 on the ties between literary form and popular struggle.

27. For example, see De Soto 1989; and Novak 1982 or 1990.

28. See also the insightful discussion in São Paulo Justice and Peace Commission 1978 (esp. chaps. 2 and 5).

29. See also Pearce 1986. Authors such as Arjomand (1986); and Calhoun (1983) have made community solidarity central to the analysis of organization and revolution. Without entering into this debate, it is still possible to acknowledge the importance of community as a source and focus of identity and collective action.

30. The same is true for past experiences of resistance being uncovered by historians. See, for example, Adorno 1988; Farris 1984; Mallon 1983; and Stern 1987.

31. In this light, invisible forms of resistance appear throughout everyday life, providing bases for enduring solidarities and future points of conflict. In Scott's words, "everyday resistance makes no headlines. Just as millions of anthozoan polyps create, willy-nilly, a coral reef, so do thousands upon thousands of individual acts of insubordination or evasion create a political or economic barrier reef of their own. There is rarely any dramatic confrontation, any moment that is particularly newsworthy. And whenever, to pursue the simile, the ship of state runs aground on such a reef, attention is typically directed to the shipwreck itself, and not to the vast aggregation of petty acts that made it possible" (1985:36). Cf. the words of one Filipino peasant organizer quoted by Ileto: "No insurrection fails. Each one is a step in the right direction" (1979:7). The judgment cannot be lightly dismissed, nor should it be incorporated into a neo-Marxist framework of inevitable revolution. To say that no insurrection fails means that each act of resistance contributes to nurturing an independent popular consciousness, thus making continued effort possible.

32. On this point, see Levine and Mainwaring 1989; and Comaroff and Comaroff 1991.

33. Joan Font, personal communication, 11 October 1990.

34. Although sharp inequalities remain the norm, the pattern of change in Latin America also bears witness to the growing assertiveness of popular culture

and efforts to give it organized form. See Matos Mar 1988 for an incisive discussion of Peru in these terms.

35. The literature is vast and ever expanding but, apart from the works already cited, see: on religion, Bruneau 1982 and 1985; Hewitt 1991; Mainwaring 1986; B. Smith 1982; and Levine 1986a and b, 1987, 1988a, 1990a and b, 1992; on state and politics, O'Donnell 1973, 1978, 1982, and 1988; Evans, Skocpol, and Rueschmayer 1985; Stepan 1985; Collier and Collier 1991; O'Donnell, Schmitter, and Whitehead 1986; and Lipset, Linz, and Diamond 1989. P. Smith (1991) and Remmer (1991) provide useful reviews of recent currents in the study of political change, with special reference to their meaning for democracy.

36. For reviews of recent work, see Levine 1986, 1987, and 1990 a and b.

37. What kinds of individuals or social groups are likely to press for new messages and be open to hearing about and taking action on them? With a historical and comparative perspective, we can see the critical role played by "masterless men": new urban migrants, displaced peasants, and, despite the gender-specific formula, women, who constitute an avid clientele for innovations in religious discourse and a prime source of new leadership. I review the issues in Levine 1986b and 1987 and undertake a detailed comparative discussion in Levine 1992 (chaps. 9 and 10).

38. Religious innovation in Latin America left most observers flat-footed. Official fears inspired belief that religion might hold unknown keys to political change; there was much fruitless searching for parallels to the Iranian revolution.

39. The pattern of religious change in Latin America is a prime example of the multiple sources of cultural transformation. Change in the churches, responding to a new sense of mission (what it means to be authentically religious), resonated strongly among new mass publics being created at the same time. The new roles created for clergy and ordinary believers sparked different kinds of social formations and led to shifts in the moral and cultural discourse of elites and mass publics. I provide a detailed discussion in Levine 1992 and 1993.

40. As Dodson and O'Shaughnessy (1990) point out, Latin American experience has much in common with Anglo-American history, including the dynamics of the English Civil War. The links between religious innovation and democratization in Latin America recalls the nineteenth-century North American experience as described, for example, by Hatch 1989. Popkin (1979, chap. 5) underscores the creative ways in which Vietnamese peasants worked with religion (among other themes) to engage and manipulate larger systems in their favor.

41. Work on colonial history in Spanish America (e.g., Burkholder 1980) confirms many of Murilo's points. For a discussion of how the Brazilian system is penetrated by continuing kin and regional networks, see Hagopian 1991; and Lewin 1979. Although the emergence of a common background and training among technical and professional elites, military officers, and politicians took longer in other cases, its effects gradually became apparent everywhere, even in the least developed states of Central America. On Central America, see Baloyra 1983; and Dunkerly 1989.

42. See P. Smith 1979; and Hansen 1971.

43. Over time there have been noteworthy variations in the enthusiasm expressed by scholars and other observers. In some ways the evolution of the

scholarly mood on Cuba foretold a similar process on Nicaragua: from a burst of enthusiasm for cultural innovation, the New Man, and the fruits of revolutionary egalitarianism to caution and disillusionment. As Weber pointed out some time ago, revolutions are as much subject to accumulations of power and inequality as any other system of rule, "for the materialist interpretation of history is also not a cab to be hailed at will, and it does not come to a halt just for revolutionaries" (1978b:222).

44. The references are to Berger, Berger, and Kellner 1973; and Berman 1979.

45. Cf. Weber's classic statement: "Not ideas but material and ideal interests directly govern men's conduct. Yet very frequently the 'world images' that have been created by ideas have, like switchmen, determined the tracks along which action has been pushed by the dynamics of interest" (1958:280).

46. No single research strategy is adequate to the task at hand. The essays collected here cast a wide methodological net: interviews and participant observation, historical reconstructions of events, analysis of documents, statistics, and the history of institutions.

47. See the instructive comparative analysis of carnivals, military parades, and processions in Da Matta 1991 (chap. 2).

48. A case in point is the evocative comment by Lomnitz, Lomnitz Adler, and Adler (in this volume) that political rallies in Mexico are more intended to demonstrate mass loyalty to the party than vice versa.

49. This is a major weakness in Beverly and Zimmerman's account (1990) of literature and politics in Central America. They move from a general account of socioeconomic and political change and an examination of literary themes and forms to an assertion of influence and audience without ever demonstrating that such an audience was there, not to mention providing evidence about what that audience may have said, thought, or did. See also Rowe and Schelling 1991. Mukerji and Schudson (1991) bring together a range of new and classic work on popular culture.

50. Cited in Hughes 1961:211.

51. Cf. Comaroff and Comaroff in which the authors note that "hegemony is invariably unstable and vulnerable. Never merely an assertion of order, it always involves an effort to redress contradictions, to limit the eruption of alternative meanings and critical awareness. From the mute experience of such tensions arise new kinds of experimental consciousness, new ideologies that point to the discrepancies between received worldviews and the worlds they claim to mirror" (1991:314).

52. See Anderson 1983 for a compelling analysis of the construction of new national identities.

REFERENCES

Adorno, Rolena. 1988. *Guaman Poma: Writing and Resistance in Colonial Peru.* Austin: University of Texas Press.

Almond, Gabriel. 1989. "The Study of Political Culture." In *A Discipline Divided: Schools and Sects in Political Science,* ed. G. Almond, 138–56. Beverly Hills, Calif.: Sage.

Almond, Gabriel, and Sidney Verba. 1963. *The Civic Culture. Political Attitudes and Democracy in Five Nations.* Boston: Little, Brown.

Alvarez, Sonia. 1990. *Engendering Democracy in Brazil: Women's Movements in Transition Politics.* Princeton: Princeton University Press.

Anderson, Benedict. 1983. *Imagined Communities: Reflections on the Origins and Spread of Nationalism.* London: Verso.

Arizpe, Lourdes. 1988. "Anthropology in Latin America: Old Boundaries, New Contexts." In *Changing Perspectives in Latin American Studies: Insights from Six Disciplines,* ed. C. Mitchell, 143–62. Stanford: Stanford University Press.

Arjomand, Said. 1986. "Iran's Islamic Revolution in Comparative Perspective." *World Politics* 38(3): 383–414.

Baloyra, Enrique. 1983. "Reactionary Despotism in Central America." *Journal of Latin American Studies* 15(2): 295–319.

Berger, Peter, Brigitte Berger, and Hansfried Kellner. 1973. *The Homeless Mind. Modernization and Consciousness.* New York: Vintage.

Berman, Marshall. 1979. *All That Is Solid Melts into Air: The Experience of Modernity.* New York: Simon and Schuster.

Bernstein, Richard, ed. 1985. *Habermas and Modernity.* Cambridge: MIT Press.

Beverly, John, and Marc Zimmerman. 1990. *Literature and Politics in the Central American Revolutions.* Austin: University of Texas Press.

Binder, Leonard, et al. 1971. *Crises and Sequences in Political Development.* Princeton: Princeton University Press.

Bruneau, Thomas. 1982. *The Church in Brazil: The Politics of Religion.* Austin: University of Texas Press.

———. 1985. "Church and Politics in Brazil: The Genesis of Change." *Journal of Latin American Studies* 17(2): 271–93.

Burdick, John. 1990. *Looking for God in Brazil: The Progressive Catholic Church in Brazil's Religious Arena.* Ph.D. diss., CUNY.

Burkholder, Mark. 1980. *The Politics of a Colonial Career.* Albuquerque: University of New Mexico Press.

Caldeira, Teresa. 1984. *A Politica dos Outros: O Cotidiano dos Moradores de Periferia e o Que Pensam do Poder e dos Poderosos.* São Paulo: Brasilense.

———. 1986–87. "Electoral Struggles in a Neighborhood of São Paulo." *Politics and Society* 15(1): 43–66.

Calhoun, Craig. 1983. "The Radicalism of Tradition: Community Strength or Venerable Disguise and Borrowed Language." *American Journal of Sociology* 88(5):886–914.

Cardoso, Fernando H. 1972. *Estado y Sociedad en America Latina.* Buenos Aires: Ediciones Nueva Vision.

Cardoso, Fernando H., and Enzo Faletto. 1979. *Dependency and Development in Latin America.* Berkeley: University of California Press.

Collier, David, ed. 1979. *The New Authoritarianism in Latin America.* Princeton: Princeton University Press.

34 / *Constructing Culture and Power in Latin America*

Collier, David, and Ruth Berins Collier. 1991. *Shaping the Political Arena: Critical Junctures, the Labor Movement, and Regime Dynamics in Latin America.* Princeton: Princeton University Press.

Comaroff, Jean, and John Comaroff. 1991. *Of Revelation and Revolution: Christianity, Colonialism and Consciousness in South Africa.* Vol. 1. Chicago: University of Chicago Press.

Cotler, Julio. 1968. *Clases, Estado, y Nacion en el Peru.* Lima: Instituto de Estudios Peruanos.

Da Matta, Roberto. 1991. *Carnivals, Rogues, and Heroes: An Interpretation of the Brazilian Dilemma.* Notre Dame: University of Notre Dame Press.

Dealy, Glen. 1968. "Prologomena on the Spanish American Political Tradition." *Hispanic American Historical Review* 48(1): 37–58.

De Gregori, Carlos Ivan, Cecilia Blondet, and Nicolas Lynch. 1986. *Conquistadores de Un Nuevo Mundo: De Invasores a Ciudadanos en San Martin de Porres.* Lima: Instituto de Estudios Peruanos.

De Soto, Hernando. 1989. *The Other Path.* New York: Harper and Row.

de Tocqueville, Alexis. 1969. *Democracy in America.* 2 vols. New York: Schocken.

Diegues, Manuel J., and Bryce Wood, eds. 1967. *Social Science in Latin America.* New York: Columbia University Press.

Dodson, Michael, and Laura O'Shaughnessy. 1990. *Nicaragua's Other Revolution: Religious Faith and Political Struggle.* Chapel Hill: University of North Carolina Press.

Drogus, Carol. 1990. "Reconstructing the Feminine: Women in São Paulo's CEBs." *Archives de Science Social des Religions* 71:63–74.

Dunkerly, James. 1989. *Power in the Isthmus: A Political History of Modern Central America.* London: Verso.

Eckstein, Susan. 1978. *The Poverty of Revolution: The State and the Urban Poor in Mexico.* Princeton: Princeton University Press.

———. 1989. *Power and Popular Protest: Latin American Social Movements.* Berkeley: University of California Press.

Eliot, George. 1981. *The Mill on the Floss.* New York: New American Library.

Evans, Peter, Theda Skocpol, and Dietrich Rueschmayer. 1985. *Bringing the State Back In.* New York: Cambridge University Press.

Farris, Nancy. 1984. *Maya Society under Colonial Rule.* Princeton: Princeton University Press.

Fishlow, Albert. 1988. "The State of Latin American Economics." In *Changing Perspectives in Latin American Studies: Insights from Six Disciplines,* ed. C. Mitchell, 87–120. Stanford: Stanford University Press.

Foweraker, Joe, and Ann Craig, eds. 1990. *Popular Movements and Political Change in Mexico.* Boulder: Lynne Rienner.

Gallegos, Romulo. N.d. *El Forastero.* Caracas: Ediciones Populares Venezolanos.

Gaventa, John. 1980. *Power and Powerlessness: Quiescence and Rebellion in an Appalachian Valley.* Urbana: University of Illinois Press.

Gerstein, Dean, et al. 1988. *The Behavioral Sciences: Achievements and Opportunities.* Washington, D.C.: National Academy Press.

Gudeman, Stephen, and Alberto Rivera. 1990. *Conversations in Colombia: The Domestic Economy in Life and Text.* Cambridge: Cambridge University Press.

Habermas, Jurgen. 1982. "A Reply to My Critics." In *Habermas: Critical Debates,* ed. John Thomas and David Held, 219–83. Cambridge: MIT Press.
———. 1984. *The Theory of Communicative Action. Vol. 1: Reason and the Rationalization of Society.* Boston: Beacon Press.
———. 1985a. "Psychic Thermidor and the Rebirth of Rebellious Subjectivity." In *Habermas and Modernity,* ed. R. Bernstein, 67–77. Cambridge: MIT Press.
———. 1985b. *The Theory of Communicative Action. Vol. 2: Lifeworld and System. A Critique of Functionalist Reason.* Boston: Beacon Press.
Hagopian, Frances. 1991. "The Compromised Consolidation: The Political Class in the Brazilian Transition." In *Issues in Democratic Consolidation: The New South American Democracies in Comparative Perspective,* ed. Scott Mainwaring, Guillermo O'Donnell, and Samuel Valenzuela. Notre Dame: University of Notre Dame Press.
Hamilton, Nora. 1982. *The Limits of State Autonomy: Post Revolutionary Mexico.* Princeton: Princeton University Press.
Hansen, Roger. 1971. *The Politics of Mexican Development.* Baltimore: Johns Hopkins Press.
Harrison, Lawrence. 1985. *Underdevelopment Is a State of Mind: The Latin American Case.* Boston: University Press of America.
Hatch, Nathan. 1989. *The Democratization of American Christianity.* New Haven, Conn.: Yale University Press.
Havel, Valcav. 1985. "The Power of the Powerless." In *The Power of the Powerless,* ed. V. Havel et al., 23–96. Armonk, N.Y.: M. E. Sharpe.
Hewitt, William E. 1991. *Base Christian Communities and Social Change in Brazil.* Lincoln: University of Nebraska Press.
Hughes, H. Stuart. 1961. *Consciousness and Society: The Reorientation of European Social Thought, 1890–1930.* New York: Vintage.
Ileto, Reynaldo. 1979. *Pasyón and Revolution: Popular Movements in the Philippines, 1840–1910.* Manila: Ateneo de Manila Press.
Johnson, John L. 1958. *Political Change in Latin America: The Emergence of the Middle Sectors.* Stanford: Stanford University Press.
Kahl, Joseph. 1976. *Modernization, Exploitation, and Dependency in Latin America: Germani, Gonzalez Casanova, and Cardoso.* New Brunswick, N.J.: Transaction Books.
Klaren, Peter, and Thomas Bossert, eds. 1986. *Promise of Development: Theories of Change in Latin America.* Boulder, Colo.: Lynne Rienner.
Kling, Merle. 1964. "The State of Research on Latin America: Political Science." In *Social Science Research on Latin America,* ed. C. Wagley, 168–213. New York: Columbia University Press.
Levine, Daniel H. 1981. *Religion and Politics in Latin America: The Catholic Church in Venezuela and Colombia.* Princeton: Princeton University Press.
———. 1986a. "Religion and Politics in Comparative and Historical Perspective." *Comparative Politics* 19(1): 95–122.
———, ed. 1986b. *Religion and Political Conflict in Latin America.* Chapel Hill: University of North Carolina Press.
———. 1987a. "If Only They Could Be More like Us!" *Caribbean Review* 25(4): 19–20.

————. 1987b. "Holiness, Faith, Power, Politics." *Journal for the Scientific Study of Religion* 26(4): 551–61.

————. 1988a. "Assessing the Impacts of Liberation Theology in Latin America." *Review of Politics* 50(2): 241–63.

————. 1988b. "Paradigm Lost: Dependence to Democracy." *World Politics* 40(3): 377–94.

————. 1990a. "Popular Groups, Popular Culture, and Popular Religion." *Comparative Studies in Society and History* 32(4): 718–64.

————. 1990b. "Considering Liberation Theology as Utopia." *Review of Politics.* 52(4): 603–22.

————. 1990c. "How Not to Understand Liberation Theology, Nicaragua, or Both." *Journal of InterAmerican Studies and World Affairs* 32(3): 229–46.

————. 1991. "Harmony, Law, and Anthropology." *Michigan Law Review* 89(6): 1766–77.

————. 1992. *Popular Voices in Latin American Catholicism.* Princeton: Princeton University Press.

————. 1993. "Protestants and Catholics in Latin America: A Family Portrait." In *Fundamentalisms Compared,* ed. Martin Marty and R. Scott Appleby, Chicago: University of Chicago Press.

Levine, Daniel H., and Scott Mainwaring. 1989. "Religion and Popular Protest in Latin America: Contrasting Experiences." In *Power and Popular Protest: Latin American Social Movements,* ed. S. Eckstein, 203–40. Berkeley: University of California Press.

Lewin, Linda. 1979. "Some Historical Implications of Kinship Organization for Family-based Politics in the Brazilian Northeast." *Comparative Studies in Society and History* 21(2): 262–92.

Lipset, Seymour, Juan Linz, and Larry Diamond, eds. 1989. *Democracy in Developing Countries, Vol. 4: Latin America.* Boulder: Lynne Rienner.

Luce, R. Duncan, Neil Smelser, and Dean Gerstein, eds. 1989. *Leading Edges in Social and Behavioral Science.* New York: Russell Sage Foundation.

Lynd, Robert. 1939. *Knowledge for What?* Princeton: Princeton University Press.

Mainwaring, Scott. 1986. *The Catholic Church and Politics in Brazil, 1916–1985.* Stanford: Stanford University Press.

Mainwaring, Scott, and Eduardo Viola. 1984. "New Social Movements, Political Culture, and Democracy: Brazil and Argentina in the 1980s." *Telos* 61: 17–52.

Mainwaring, Scott, and Alexander Wilde, eds. 1989. *The Progressive Church in Latin America.* Notre Dame: University of Notre Dame Press.

Mallon, Florencia. 1983. *The Defence of Community in Peru's Central Highlands: Peasant Struggle and Capitalist Transition.* Princeton: Princeton University Press.

Mannheim, Karl. 1936. *Ideology and Utopia.* New York: Harcourt, Brace, and World.

Martin, David. 1990. *Tongues of Fire: The Explosion of Evangelical Protestantism in Latin America.* London: Basil Blackwell.

Martz, John. 1990. "Political Science and Latin American Studies: Patterns and Asymmetries of Research and Publication." *Latin American Research Review* 25(1): 67–86.

Matos Mar, José. 1988. *Desborde Popular y Crisis del Estado*. Lima: CONCYTEC.
Mitchell, Christopher, ed. 1988. *Changing Perspectives in Latin American Studies: Insights from Six Disciplines*. Stanford: Stanford University Press.
Morse, Richard. 1964. "The Heritage of Latin America." In *The Founding of New Societies*, ed. L. Hartz, 123–77. New York: Harcourt, Brace, and World.
———. 1989. *New World Soundings: Culture and Ideology in the Americas*. Baltimore: Johns Hopkins University Press.
Mukerji, Chandra, and Michael Schudson, eds. 1991. *Rethinking Popular Culture: Contemporary Perspectives in Cultural Studies*. Berkeley: University of California Press.
Nader, Laura. 1990. *Harmony Ideology: Justice and Control in a Zapotec Mountain Village*. Stanford: Stanford University Press.
Novak, Michael. 1982. *The Spirit of Democratic Capitalism*. New York: Simon and Schuster.
———. 1990. *This Hemisphere of Liberty: A Philosophy of the Americas*. Washington: AEI Press.
O'Donnell, Guillermo. 1973. *Modernization and Bureaucratic Authoritarianism*. Berkeley: Institute of International Studies.
———. 1978. "Reflections on the Pattern of Change in the Bureaucratic Authoritarian State." *Latin American Research Review* 13(1): 3–38.
———. 1982. "Reply to Remmer and Merkx." *Latin American Research Review* 17(2): 41–50.
———. 1988. *Bureaucratic Authoritarianism: Argentina, 1966–1973, in Comparative Perspective*. Berkeley: University of California Press.
O'Donnell, Guillermo, Phillippe Schmitter, and Laurence Whitehead. 1986. *Transitions from Authoritarian Rule: Prospects for Democracy*. Baltimore: Johns Hopkins University Press.
Offe, Claus. 1985. "New Social Movements: Challenging the Boundaries of Institutional Politics." *Social Research* 52(4): 817–68.
Pearce, Jenny. 1986. *The Promised Land: Peasant Rebellion in Chalatenango, El Salvador*. London: Latin America Bureau.
Perlman, Janice. 1976. *The Myth of Marginality: Poverty and Politics in Rio de Janeiro*. Berkeley: University of California Press.
Popkin, Samuel. 1979. *The Rational Peasant: The Political Economy of Rural Society in Vietnam*. Berkeley: University of California Press.
Portes, Alejandro. 1985. "Latin American Class Structures: Their Composition and Change during the Last Decades." *Latin American Research Review* 20(3): 7–40.
———. 1988. "Latin American Sociology in the Mid-1980s: Learning from Hard Experience." In *Changing Perspectives in Latin American Studies: Insights from Six Disciplines*, ed. C. Mitchell, 121–42. Stanford: Stanford University Press.
———. 1989. "Latin American Urbanization in the Years of the Crisis." *Latin American Research Review* 24(3): 7–44.
Portes, Alejandro, and Douglas Kincaid. 1989. "Sociology and Development in the 1990s: Critical Challenges and Empirical Trends." *Sociological Forum* 4(4): 479–504.

Remmer, Karen. 1991. "New Wine or Old Bottlenecks? The Study of Latin American Democracy." *Comparative Politics* 23(4): 479–96.

Remmer, Karen, and Gil Merkx. 1982. "Bureaucratic Authoritarianism Revisited." *Latin American Research Review* 17(2): 3–40.

Rowe, William, and Vivian Schelling. 1991. *Memory and Modernity: Popular Culture in Latin America.* London: Verso.

São Paulo Justice and Peace Commission. 1978. *São Paulo Growth and Poverty.* London: Bowerdean Press.

Schoultz, Lars. 1987. *National Security and United States Policy toward Latin America.* Princeton: Princeton University Press.

Scott, James. 1976. *The Moral Economy of the Peasant.* New Haven: Yale University Press.

———. 1977. "Protest and Profanation: Agrarian Revolt and the Little Tradition." 2 pts. *Theory and Society* 4:1–38, 211–45.

———. 1985. *Weapons of the Weak: Everyday Forms of Peasant Resistance.* New Haven: Yale University Press.

———. 1990. *Rebellion and the Arts of Resistance: Hidden Transcripts.* New Haven: Yale University Press.

Silvert, K. H. 1977. "Politics, Political Science, and the Study of Latin America." In *Essays in Understanding Latin America,* ed. K. H. Silvert, 101–16. Philadelphia: ISHI.

Smith, Brian. 1982. *The Church and Politics in Chile: Challenges to Modern Catholicism.* Princeton: Princeton University Press.

———. 1990. *More than Altruism: The Politics of Private Foreign Aid.* Princeton: Princeton University Press.

Smith, Carol, ed. 1990. *Guatemalan Indians and the State, 1540–1988.* Austin: University of Texas Press.

Smith, Peter. 1979. *Labyrinths of Power: Political Recruitment in Twentieth-Century Mexico.* Princeton: Princeton University Press.

———. 1991. "Crisis and Democracy in Latin America." *World Politics* 43(4): 608–34.

Sosnowski, Saul. 1988. "Spanish-American Literary Criticism: The State of the Art." In *Changing Perspectives in Latin American Studies: Insights from Six Disciplines,* ed. C. Mitchell, 163–82. Stanford: Stanford University Press.

Stepan, Alfred. 1978. *The State and Society: Peru in Comparative Perspective.* Princeton: Princeton University Press.

———. 1985. "State Power and the Strength of Civil Society in Latin America." In *Bringing the State Back In,* ed. P. Evans, T. Skocpol, and D. Rueschmayer, 317–43. Cambridge: Cambridge University Press.

Stern, Steve, ed. 1987. *Resistance, Rebellion, and Consciousness in the Andean Peasant World: 18th to 20th Centuries.* Madison: University of Wisconsin Press.

Stoll, David. 1990. *Is Latin America Turning Protestant?* Berkeley: University of California Press.

Tarrow, Sidney. 1991. "Transitions to Democracy as Waves of Mobilization." Unpub. ms.

Thompson, E. P. 1978. "Eighteenth-Century English Society: Class Struggle without Class." *Social History* 3(2): 133-65.

Tilly, Charles. 1984. *Big Structures, Large Processes, Huge Transformations.* New York: Russell Sage Foundation.

Valenzuela, Arturo. 1988. "Political Science and the Study of Latin America." In *Changing Perspectives in Latin American Studies: Insights from Six Disciplines,* ed. C. Mitchell, 63-86. Stanford: Stanford University Press.

Veliz, Claudio. 1980. *The Centralist Tradition of Latin America.* Princeton: Princeton University Press.

Wagley, Charles, ed. 1964. *Social Science Research on Latin America.* New York: Columbia University Press.

Weber, Max. 1958. *From Max Weber: Essays in Sociology,* ed. Hans Gerth and C. Wright Mills. New York: Oxford University Press.

———. 1978a. "The Concept of Following a Rule." In *Max Weber: Selections in Translation,* ed. W. G. Runciman, 99-110. Cambridge: Cambridge University Press.

———. 1978b. "Politics as a Vocation." In *Max Weber: Selections in Translation,* ed. W. G. Runciman, 212-25. Cambridge: Cambridge University Press.

Wiarda, Howard. 1973. "Toward a Framework for the Study of Political Change in the Iberic-Latin Tradition." *World Politics* 23(2): 206-36.

Wiener, Myron, and Samuel Huntington, eds. 1987. *Understanding Political Development.* Boston: Little, Brown.

Wolf, Eric. 1982. *Europe and the People without History.* Berkeley: University of California Press.

Capitalist Dreams: Chile's Response to Nineteenth-Century World Copper Competition

William W. Culver and Cornel J. Reinhart

The rapid increase in the produce of the mines of Cuba and Chili cannot be looked upon by the British miner otherwise than as a total annihilation of the mining interests of this country. . . .
—[Editorial] "Foreign ores," *Mining Journal*
11, no. 287 (February 20, 1841): 60.

[Copper mining in Michigan] is an interest in which more than fifty million dollars of capital is engaged, an interest that is being crushed by foreign competition—the competition of convict raised ores in Chili.
—U.S. Senator Zachariah Chandler, *Congressional Globe,*
pt. 1, 40th Congress, 3d sess. (January 18, 1869): 416.

As the produce of the Chili mines now regulates the price of copper all over the world, and all speculation as to its future price must depend on the probable future yield of these mines, their condition is a subject of prime importance to all interested in the copper trade.
—James Douglas, "II. The Copper Mines of Chili,"
*Quarterly Journal of Science, and Annals of
Mining Metallurgy, Engineering, Industrial Arts,
Manufactures and Technology* 9 (1872): 159.

Chili is still, though a smaller producer than the Peninsula [Michigan], the apparent arbiter of price, and Chili Bars the standard of value.
—[Editorial] "The Movement of Copper in England
and France in 1886," *Engineering and Mining
Journal* 42, no. 4 (January 22, 1887): 56.

Hernando de Soto's recent book *The Other Path* argues that capitalism has not failed in Peru and Latin America; rather, it has not been tried.[1] Basing his case on the observation that Latin American economies are strangled by arcane policies and regulations, de Soto goes on to bolster his point by providing a fresh and powerful look at the undeniable reality of the large "informal," and thus unregulated, economic sector in Peru.[2] As with any such generalization, how strongly does its explanatory value remain when measured against specific events, over long periods of time? This article seeks just such a perspective. It examines the impact of such regulations as mining codes and mineral taxation on the efforts of Chilean copper entrepreneurs to compete worldwide in the nineteenth century. De Soto may be correct in his contention that today's highly regulated economies keep Latin Americans from being as productive as their resources justify, but to extend this view into the past ignores earlier productive accomplishments as well as significant efforts at different times and places to cast off Latin America's mercantile legacy.

Nineteenth-century copper production in Chile provides a prime case to investigate this key issue of political economy. Chilean copper was a leading world industry for several decades, gradually sliding into stagnation and eventual collapse, while major ore deposits remained untouched. Can this instance of industrial degeneration be attributed to state regulation? Perhaps, but then how can the long earlier expansion under the same regulations be explained?

Capitalism rarely exists as unregulated entrepreneurial activity. As practiced in the real world, the question that concerns us involves entrepreneurship amid governmental regulation of varying degrees and objectives, with some level of tax burden.[3] Chilean copper entrepreneurs have earned a key place in any consideration of nineteenth-century Latin American productive activity, since they had expanded their enterprise continually for sixty years under an unreformed eighteenth-century mining code. The memory of this Chilean success, however, faded following their competitive loss to their counterparts in Michigan and Montana. Why this failure occurred focuses our attention here. We contend that after the middle of the nineteenth century certain key structural innovations pursued in North America were not duplicated in Chile. In the United States following the Civil War, the state became the firm ally of entrepreneurs. In Chile it did not.[4] This made a crucial difference. While copper serves as the industrial focus of this article, political obstacles to an ever-evolving modern capitalism form its central theme.

The full significance of Chile's colonial regulatory legacy emerges only when its copper trade is placed in a broad perspective, the kind envisioned by Charles Tilly.[5] For copper this means examining the metal's mining, smelting, and sale in Great Britain, Chile, and the United States—sequentially the world's leading producers during the last century. Coupled with the extraordinary international surge in demand for copper products during the latter decades of the nineteenth century,[6] such an examination gives rise to a series of questions. Why did Chile's leading market position, founded on earlier successful competition with English copper entrepreneurs working mines in Cornwall,[7] result in the eventual denationalization of the best Andean mines? What prevented a continuing expansion of copper production, utilizing new mining methods for low-grade ore? Can we find specific evidence of strangulation by antiquated policies? What were the Chilean entrepreneurs, who built and managed the industry, doing to meet American competition? Indeed, how aware was the Chilean mining community of its competitive weakness in the 1880s and their impending collapse?[8] Was Chile's forty years as the world's leader in copper production simply an illusion?

If rigid mercantile regulations did not stop Chilean entrepreneurs from competing with, indeed closing, the copper mines in Cornwall, England, or later, smelters in Swansea, Wales, why then did Chilean mining entrepreneurs later find these same regulations hindering their competition with producers in the United States, leading to the denationalization of Chilean copper after 1900? Finally, why was the wave of state-supported mining reform that swept the world in mid-century resisted and delayed in Chile? We believe the answer to this last question provides the key to understanding Chile's loss of competitiveness. Unable to find a political consensus in a Congress dominated by agricultural interests, the copper industry remained stalemated between traditional miners, who conceived of their efforts as a speculative adventure, and modern mining engineers wanting to transform copper into a business. This split in the copper industry itself led to a political failure that echoes down through Chilean history to the present.

Chile's copper market position in the last century was based on an ability to raise increasing amounts of ore at a cost lower than all other producers from a seemingly inexhaustible supply of ore,[9] yet these immense Chilean ore reserves, centered in the northern provinces of Coquimbo and Atacama, were not sufficient to protect the Chilean industry from stagnation in the face of North American competition. The magnitude of the relative and absolute decline of nineteenth-century Chilean copper can be shown. In 1852 the United States placed far behind Chile with less than 1 percent of the world's copper production (see table 1),

TABLE 1. Production from Selected Copper Mining Countries and Percentage as a Part of World Total, 1810–1900 (in tons of 2,000 lbs.)

Year	Great Britain		Chile		United States		Spain and Portugal		World	
	Tons	Percentage	Tons	Percentage	Tons	Percentage	Tons	Percentage	Tons	Percentage
1810	6,400	35	1,653	9	0		56	.3	18,200	100
1820	8,377	44	1,653	9	0		11	.05	18,850	100
1830	12,235	45	3,004	11	0		78	.3	27,350	100
1840	12,346	34	7,114	20	0		236	.6	36,445	100
1850	13,228	27	13,607	28	728	1	431	.8	49,381	100
1860	17,967	24	37,602	51	8,064	11	2,766	3	73,907	100
1870	8,046	7	48,724	42	14,112	12	9,060	8	114,934	100
1880	3,662	3	43,628	31	30,240	21	21,940	15	142,374	100
1881	4,340	2	42,547	23	35,840	20	43,220	23	181,342	100
1882	3,880	2	48,058	24	45,323	22	43,427	21	202,036	100
1883	2,934	1	46,031	21	57,763	26	48,893	22	224,306	100
1884	3,752	2	46,646	19	72,473	30	51,984	21	245,005	100
1885	3,106	1	43,120	17	82,938	33	53,618	21	253,120	100
1886	1,648	1	39,228	16	78,882	33	55,611	23	241,089	100
1887	436	0	32,648	13	90,739	36	58,093	23	250,538	100
1888	1,680	0	34,989	12	113,180	38	67,704	23	294,803	100
1889	1,014	0	27,160	9	113,388	39	60,782	21	291,018	100
1890	1,047	0	29,254	10	129,882	43	57,680	19	305,334	100
1895	650	0	24,724	7	190,307	52	60,967	17	368,963	100
1900	870	0	28,784	5	303,059	56	59,217	11	545,439	100

Sources: C. E. Julian, *Summarized Data of Copper Production* (Washington, D.C.: Superintendent of Documents, 1928), for Great Britain, United States, and the world; Guillermo Yunge, *Estadística minera de Chile en 1906* (Santiago de Chile: Imprenta Litografía i Encuadernación Barcelona, 1909), for Chile; and the *Engineering and Mining Journal* (New York), for years 1880–90 in the United States and world.

while Chile in that same year produced more than 40 percent. By 1900 the United States had vaulted to first place, extracting 56 percent of the world's copper; Chile had fallen to fourth with only 5 percent of the world's ore coming from Chilean mines.[10] Both vein and porphyry Chilean copper ore never gave out. In fact, during the 1920s, under North American industrial control, Chile again became a leading producer.

Copper mining flourished worldwide after the 1850s, as demand for copper expanded at unprecedented rates. Entrepreneurs in Chile and the United States, simultaneously astonished and eager in the face of new levels of copper consumption created by industrial expansion (especially steam engines and electrical use), invested in numerous mining and smelting projects. These individuals risked their capital in search of substantial personal gain. At the same time they believed their efforts to be patriotic, promising new levels of material prosperity for their respective countries; yet as investment increased production, it correspondingly increased competition. Expansion of production meant lower costs, and producers unable to compete successfully were "left by the wayside." Little time or energy was wasted on regrets over failed competitors; survival went to the "strongest and fittest," failure to the "weak and defective."[11] This was believed to be as true for countries as it was for individuals.

Chilean mining entrepreneurs, more so than their counterparts in the United States, produced for world markets. Chile, of course, did not possess the domestic market potential of the United States. Interestingly, every mineral product produced in Chile for the world market, with the one exception of natural nitrate, was also produced or potentially produced after 1848 in the United States.[12] As both countries had people who were able and willing to respond to the growing industrial world economy, the two countries naturally became trade competitors. Moreover, most of their pre-1870 trade competition centered on supplying copper to the domestic market in the United States. The ultimate consequence, however, of the integration of Chile into the commercial and industrial life of the world was not the progress Chilean entrepreneurs expected.[13] By the twentieth century failed dreams were the rewards for Chile. Chile was left by the wayside.

Some observers are not surprised. For them certain nationalities of entrepreneurs were, and still remain, culturally unable to organize and adapt to meet competition.[14] Applied to Chile, this perspective minimizes the extent of national economic achievement in the nineteenth century and ignores forty years of competitive success in the world copper market.

From the vantage point of scholars in the United States, the belief that serious competition from Chilean entrepreneurs never existed is easy to hold: the footprints of Chilean efforts have been largely erased. To the extent that important nineteenth-century productive efforts in Chile are acknowledged, those efforts are typically characterized as aberrations at best or at worst incompetent efforts by culturally inferior entrepreneurs.[15] How is it known that the business decisions of these Chilean capitalists were defective? The implicit answer seems to be that the fact of failure itself proves Chilean incompetence; such explanations, however, leave much unexplained.

The scholarly origins of the belief in the Chilean inability to marshal the resources necessary for industrial projects can be traced to the historiography concerning nineteenth-century economic life in the United States. American scholars began searching for the secrets of economic growth in the period in which that country was an industrial success. N. S. B. Gras's pioneering work of the 1920s and 1930s on business history posited a stage analysis of economic evolution. For Gras the late nineteenth century could best be understood as the period of the rise of industrial capitalism in which new technology and power machinery were employed to produce low-cost products.[16]

The 1950s saw the emergence of an entrepreneurial approach to industrial development. For the group of scholars at Harvard under the Research Center in Entrepreneurial History, America's great leap forward in the 1870s, 1880s, and 1890s is best understood as a product of the entrepreneurial genius of individual business leaders.[17] Perhaps the most important scholar of the entrepreneurial school, Thomas Cochran, significantly recast the debate over industrial growth by arguing that entrepreneurs act only within a certain set of fairly well-defined economic and social values.[18] Specifically, his study of late nineteenth-century railroad industry leaders found that these men sought approval and acted within the parameters established by other East Coast business leaders.[19]

Alfred Chandler, Jr., shared this sociological perspective but emphasized bureaucratic organization.[20] For Chandler the thirty years between 1870 and 1900 saw major changes in the economic life of the United States. The creation of a national rail network and the attendant growth of urban markets created the conditions necessary for business innovation and indeed brought "Big Business" to the United States. In industry after industry the processes were the same. The dominant economic unit was one that "integrated within a single business organization the major economic processes: production or purchasing of raw materials, manufacturing, distribution, and finance."[21] Thus, for Chandler the basic economic innovation during the last half of the nineteenth century was not technological but, rather, the creation of new forms of organization and new ways of marketing. These innovations were vital for survival in the face of intense competition.

We believe one consequence of this train of thought concerning the dynamics of industrial growth was the suggestion in the North American literature treating Chilean copper that nineteenth-century Chileans did not achieve anything of industrial significance.[22] Chilean literature on the same subject and period has been silent, focusing instead on the decades when nationalization was at issue. Still, the question raised by the entrepreneurship center is important. What were Chilean copper entrepreneurs doing in the last century? This problem is best approached with a comparative examination of international competition in the copper industry over time.[23]

Nowhere was nineteenth-century international competition more intense than in the copper industry.[24] In the early decades of the century copper producers in Chile challenged and then largely eliminated their counterparts in Great Britain.[25] From the 1840s the Cornish-Welsh copper dominance had collapsed, so mining and smelting of the red metal became one of the first industries characterized by price competition for a uniform commodity with many potential producers. While production of copper took place in numerous regions of the world and trade of the metal was widespread, most of the world's copper (specifically from 1845 to 1890) came from mining regions in either the United States or Chile.[26] Copper production in both countries rose in industrial quantities to supply the unmet demands for the metal—first in Great Britain and then in the East Coast industries of the United States.[27]

The major difference between ore production in Chile and the United States was in Chile's initial lead, which was based on extensive expansion of the existing colonial mining industry by entrepreneurs. The United States had no such traditional mining. Chilean production expanded as new mines opened to ship high-grade ore and smelted metal to Swansea, Liverpool, Baltimore, and Boston. Chile from the start was export oriented. Production in the United States similarly began with an orientation toward the Swansea smelters and, as in Chile, soon developed a smelting capacity of its own.[28] By 1870, however, only small quantities of copper from the United States left the East Coast ports. In the 1880s copper producers in Michigan and the western United States once again became interested in exports and began to compete with Chileans for control of the European markets. In 1882 producers in the United States began a practice that was to last for years. They dumped surplus copper in Europe at prices well below their production costs. Table 2 illustrates the dimensions of the turnabout in the copper industry.

Contrary to the implications of the historiography of United States industrial development and of the existing literature on Chilean copper, the authors believe the failure of Chilean entrepreneurs to build the basis for their continued industrial prosperity was not in their lack of ability to bring together technology, resources, and transportation in new organizations to take advantage of market opportunities. Indeed, as long as competition hinged solely on technical, organizational, and commercial ability, strong Chilean-based competition was a reality. During the latter

TABLE 2. **New York Copper Price per Pound and Copper Production from Chile and the United States, 1810–1900**

Year	Chile		United States		Copper Price (New York)
	Tons	Percentage (world)	Tons	Percentage (world)	Cents/Pound
1810	1,653	9	0		43
1820	1,653	9	0		29
1830	3,004	11	0		22
1840	7,114	20	0		24
1850	13,607	28	728	1	22
1860	37,602	51	8,064	11	22.25
1870	48,724	42	14,112	12	22.625
1880	43,628	31	30,240	21	20.125
1881	42,547	23	35,840	20	18.125
1882	48,058	24	45,323	22	18.5
1883	46,031	21	57,763	26	15.875
1884	46,646	19	72,473	30	13.875
1885	43,120	17	82,938	33	11.125
1886	39,228	16	78,882	33	11
1887	32,648	13	90,739	36	11.25
1888	34,989	12	113,180	38	16.75
1889	27,160	9	113,388	39	13.75
1890	29,254	10	129,882	43	15.75
1895	24,724	7	190,307	52	10.875
1900	28,784	5	303,059	56	16.625

Sources: C. E. Julian, *Summarized Data of Copper Production* (Washington, D.C.: Superintendent of Documents, 1928), for Great Britain, United States, and the world; Guillermo Yunge, *Estadística minera de Chile en 1906* (Santiago de Chile: Imprenta Litografía i Encuadernación Barcelona, 1909), for Chile; and the *Engineering and Mining Journal* (New York), for years 1880–90 in the United States and world.

part of the century, however, as world competition heightened and became characterized by United States dumping of surplus production, successful United States entrepreneurs had the state at their side—developing and implementing policies favorable to extractive, commercial, and industrial projects.[29] In short, those states that collaborated with or were captured by entrepreneurial interests gave specific industries an incomparable competitive edge. Benjamín Vicuña Mackenna, largely ignored by others looking at this issue, held that the failure of progressive Chilean copper entrepreneurs was primarily political in nature.[30] Their inability to overcome the power of traditional landed interests, which were indifferent to industrial development, at a time early enough to make a difference, hampered their industry's evolution more than anything else.[31] Landed interests could not identify industrial development with their own concerns and ignored calls for policy reforms that were crucial for modernizing the copper industry.[32]

The early success of the Chilean mining community's production of copper in industrial quantities took place under an eighteenth-century mercantilist mining code. The code conceived of minerals in terms of state revenue; this conceptualization led to regulations aimed at organizing mining to provide maximum tax receipts and to prevent tax fraud by mining interests.[33] That Chilean copper thrived under a considerable tax burden is a credit to Chilean entrepreneurship. It is this restrictive mining code that ultimately distinguishes the copper industries of Chile from those of the United States. As late as the 1860s, mining in Chile was technologically the same as that in Michigan, Montana, and Arizona. During mid-century, in Chile and the United States, production was expanded extensively rather than intensively. Competition was based on exploiting resources at more points, not by increasing the sophistication of technology at given points.[34]

It was only in the 1870s, as interregional domestic competition heightened, that intensification of production appeared in the United States, and it is at this time that mining and smelting methods can be differentiated between Chile and the United States. Still, the change was a gradual one. Hand-held drills, picks, and shovels coexisted alongside newer industrial methods. Clearly, technological change, especially the application of gigantic power machinery financed by capital outside of the mining industry, set the stage for expansion and market domination by the United States, but economic expansion in copper was not a simple application of machinery, however, inventive, by "daring" entrepreneurs grappling with new organization methods to better exploit natural resources. If copper expansion required nothing more than the application of new ideas, Chile would have stayed with Michigan, Montana, and Arizona stride for stride.[35] Each region possessed extensive reserves. Entrepreneurs in each region were aware of new large-scale applications of steam and electricity.[36] They all understand the role of railroads, increased scales of production, new drills, and lighting systems. Capital was readily available for all;[37] skilled labor was at hand.[38] The crucial catalyst for the factors of production to be combined into an efficient mine operation became a national agreement on the importance of industrial progress, with debate centered on the best *means* for that progress, as opposed to debate over the *ends* of industrial growth itself. Debate regarding the means of industrial progress in the United States led to supportive public policy. In Chile such a public debate stalled, and the search for coherent modern industrial and mining policy was prolonged into the twentieth century.

Chile and the United States both had civil wars in mid-century that can be interpreted as a part of a national debate over industrial progress.[39] In the United States the Civil War helped to provide a consensus by eliminating a significant conservative perspective from the economic debate. After 1860, with elimination of social debris of the past from Congress and creation of a new national goal to include a vast internal market, a national rail network, and protective tariffs, the United States had achieved the essential institutional and political consensus needed to stimulate profound reorganization and internal growth in every phase of American economic life.[40]

In the copper industry of the United States this national direction translated into two important developments. The first was the legislating of a 1861 tariff on smelted copper, which was raised further in 1864.[41] Michigan politicians argued that higher profits and wages in the mines of the United States would ensure the development of Michigan and the West. In its hearings on the copper industry in 1865 the United States Revenue Commission heard testimony that only a tariff of six to eight cents a pound, at a time when the price for smelted copper hovered just twenty cents (see table 2), could reverse the low profits caused by stiff Chilean competition.[42] Michigan's two U.S. senators complained of low-cost Chilean copper, which was supplying upwards of one-third of the United States market and thus depressing Atlantic seaboard prices.[43] Additional arguments held that Chileans hurt the United States by their refusal to buy New England manufactures, preferring instead to spend their copper dollars in Great Britain.

The issue of national security was raised with the assertion that the United States, by importing Chilean copper concentrates and ore, had allowed itself to become dependent on a foreign supply of a vital war matériel.[44] The political campaign for ever higher copper tariffs did not peak until 1869. Pressing new moral arguments, the "Copper Senators" proclaimed, falsely, that Chilean copper should be banned via a tariff because Chilean mines relied on forced convict labor.[45] These debates over the Copper Act of 1869, which placed a five-cents-a-pound tariff on refined copper, revealed a deep hostility toward Chilean involvement in the market of the United States.[46]

While intended to protect and develop only Lake Michigan copper, the high profits generated by the tariff induced new mines to open in Montana and Arizona during the 1870s. The result of the new mines was a domestic price war.[47] The high prices that tariff protection secured for copper producers within the United States stimulated production and ultimately led entrepreneurs to engage in competition in foreign markets. In the early 1880s Western and Michigan surplus copper started arriving in Europe priced below production costs,[48] thus driving down the price of the "Chili bar."[49] This use of foreign markets was raised to the level of economic principle by Andrew Carnegie in his "Law of Surplus," which held that it was cheaper for large industrial enterprises "to run a loss for a ton or a yard than to check . . . production" during times of oversupply. "In order to keep running in hard times" and "in order to hold the market in good times," Carnegie argued, American industrialists must exploit foreign markets.[50]

The 1866 revamping of the mining code in the United States began the other major development supporting the dramatic shift in the structure of the world copper market toward control by producers in the United States. This reform allowed mineral property claims to be made and held with a minimum of bureaucracy, and it offered complete title security to the claim holder, without taxation.[51] The 1866 Mineral Lands Act constituted a formal rejection of minerals as a source of public revenue either through their sale or by taxation, and secure full possession of a mining property was made possible for individuals, corporate or corporeal, through a simple claim process.[52]

This policy approach, reaffirmed in the Mineral Development Act of 1872, was a formulation intended to meet the needs of new corporate organizations.[53] The 1872 law made investments even more secure than the 1866 law and made possible the consolidation of many small claims into one large property. Financiers believed that consolidation was obligatory to ensure large processing plants would be fed sufficient ore over a long period of time at a planned rate and at a predictable price. Only consolidated mineral properties could justify the huge investments required by new efficient plants. Planning and predictability were absolutely critical for financing to be available for ever larger installations. It was widely believed that "nothing but steady, unavoidable losses will force a mine into suspension, and therefore, the period leading to the survival of the strongest is usually much longer than is generally believed."[54] Well-financed mines, secure in their mineral property ownership, could wait out competitive losses and thus prevail in the end.

As the copper industry in the United States underwent the transformation to ever larger scale processing of ore, it required far more capital than had previously been available to the industry. Those mining and smelting capitalists able to secure stable financing outside the mining industry became the survivors. This trend was noticed in 1876 by Abram S. Hewitt, president-elect of the American Institute of Mining Engineers, who observed in an address to his fellow mining engineers that the industry had gone through many stages of leadership: from pioneer to mine engineer, from mine engineer to mechanical engineer, and lastly toward control by corporate financiers.[55] As Hewitt looked back on the previous decade, he also noted that meagerness of government supervision characterized the relationship between government and mining in the United States and that this had allowed progress to continue unimpeded. He points out that this condition was to be contrasted with the complicated mining codes of Spain, Mexico, or Chile, which may have enriched the coffers of the state but had also tied the hands of the new class of mining entrepreneurs.[56] Hewitt concluded his address by reaffirming that industrialists and financiers, freed of state control, needed to continue to forge the most important development of the century: the industrial corporation. He innocently believed that this development would be the outgrowth of a new and beneficent principle: that "the practical association of diffused capital, through the agency of corporate organization, with labor, for the promotion of economy, [worked] for the improvement of processes, and for the general welfare of mankind."[57]

The appearance of the corporation indeed constituted a momentous innovation in business organization. This new form did not just happen;

it was the conscious result of involvement of the state in the nineteenth-century social economy. The granting of the legal rights of a person to a paper entity, the corporation, and then limiting the liability of this fictitious person to the amount of capital invested must be seen as a major intervention. Limiting liability resolved the greatest fear of mining investors—that continual calls would be made for more capital, which, if not paid, would lead to forfeiture of ownership rights. Limited liability also opened the door for a major change in the United States economy: the concentration of dispersed capital into a few hands. Hewitt's hope for the general welfare, however, turned out to more closely resemble general warfare in the copper industry during the last years before the combined mining regions in the United States displaced Chile as the world's leading copper producer.

During the 1880s the mining press in the United States continually studied "how our competitors are bearing up under the strain."[58] In 1881 the San Francisco *Bulletin* carried a report on copper ore shipments from Arizona and editorialized that, with the railways now in place, Arizona could "compete successfully with Chile in supplying the English demand. . . . The future of the Arizona copper mines is bright and full of promise, and now that avenues of transportation are open by which products can reach tidewater, we ought to be able to undersell every other copper country."[59]

Warming up to the copper contest, the *Engineering and Mining Journal* took an even more dramatic line in its editorials in 1884. The editors wrote that "it seems to be a mighty struggle now between the producers in all parts of the world."[60] The same editorial went on to analyze the capacity for Chilean copper miners to continue production, noting that, as the mines remained under Chilean control, "they are probably capable and willing, with that faith which is at the same time the blessing and curse of mine ownership, to struggle at least for years to come."[61]

The North American copper mining industry felt proud and boastful, ready to take on any and all challengers. With this truculent attitude, mining capitalists in the United States were determined to force not just their counterparts in foreign copper regions but one another as well to the wall. The tactics used with foreign competitors were not more ruthless than those used with domestic ones. For Western producers, "in every case it comes to be a struggle for existence and the law of survival of the fittest applies in industry as in physical existence."[62]

As the 1880s ended New York-based copper corporations, working deposits in Montana and Arizona, along with their Boston competitors who were working the Michigan deposits, constituted a dominating influence on world copper markets. This dominance, grounded in supportive legislation at the regional and national levels,[63] had its strength in promotion of access to the financing necessary to change copper mining from a family-run, small-scale, cottage speculation to a highly developed, large-scale, mechanized business.[64] From the 1860s onward, once Southern opposition was eliminated, the United States Congress created a uniform and standardized national market. Important for the growth of the copper industry in the United States were railroad expansion, joint-stock corporations, and limited liability, but the copper tariffs and a modern mining code based on private property stand out as absolutely critical. In short, copper in the United States was able to become an aggressive, efficient, and competitive industry because the state provided the necessary legal, physical, and economic infrastructure.

The story of copper in Chile during this period contrasts sharply with what occurred in the United States. As the 1870s began, Chile outproduced all other countries in copper,[65] yet the leaders of the Chilean copper industry were concerned about the future—and rightly so. While the Chilean copper region still had the world's lowest prices and the highest output, its leaders saw the recent North American tariffs, as well as other changes in the United States, as potential threats. The progressive Chilean copper leadership began to press for legislation to rationalize Chilean mining along lines taken by the United States through its reforms of 1866 and 1872.[66]

Chilean mining reforms in 1874, however, actually made the situation worse for the copper industry. The reformed mining law strengthened surface agricultural land rights against those of entrepreneurs trying to discover, claim, and operate mines.[67] Despite the so-called reforms of 1874, Chilean mining continued to be organized under an eighteenth-century mining policy, while the competition in the United States operated under a modern capitalist code. Chile had a mining policy of state revenue; the United States had one of economic growth. There is no evidence that the world mining community of the 1870s appreciated the full implications of the difference—nor how bad the Chilean copper situation was, nor how good was that of the United States. Whatever these policy differences meant to society in general, they had critical implications for the copper regions involved in a struggle for survival.

The Chilean method of copper taxation had specific unfortunate consequences. The tax policy established in 1810 set a rate of two pesos per pound of copper when the market price was eight to ten pesos.[68] The tax basis remained the value of production, not profit. After mid-century, when copper prices began to fall, the tax became proportionally higher and harder to pay. Because the tax was on volume, not profits, it had to be paid even during periods in which the market price fell below the cost of production. Mining resentment against this difficult tax levy, combined with antagonism over the inadequate mining code, lay somewhat behind the unsuccessful Civil War of 1851 and was instrumental in the succeeding Civil War of 1859.[69]

These civil wars have traditionally been viewed in Chile as "anarchist" rebellions but were, in fact, based on policy in the North.[70] Mining operators claimed their taxes supported government projects only beneficial to urban and agricultural interests, while mining had unmet needs for roads, port facilities, and other infrastructure. In the 1859 civil war a government was formed in the North in Copiapó. One of its first acts was to suspend the copper production tax and replace it with a lower export tax.[71] The civil wars were lost by the copper interests, yet the other factors of production (principally abundant ore) were so favorable that production continued and even expanded in the 1860s despite the antagonistic policies.

The decades of the 1860s and 1870s indicate a buoyance for Chilean copper that was misleading on account of these favorable factors of production. The United States virtually dropped out of the European market after the American Civil War. Chilean mining, while strained by increasing shortages of high-grade ore, still seemed blessed. The key Chilean mining centers enjoyed all of the fruits of nineteenth-century industrial progress: electricity, gas streetlights, iron structures (Alexandre Eiffel was contracted to build a church in Coquimbo), and expansion of railroads.[72] Progress in Chile's north seemed real and irreversible but was shortly revealed to be fragile.

Michigan and Western copper producers became jubilant in 1883. They used the detailed production statistics reported in the *Engineering and Mining Journal* to proclaim the copper superiority of the United States.[73] What the Chilean mining community had seen coming for years had now happened. The United States began to sell its copper in Europe, and the relatively strong position of Chilean copper in terms of skills and abundant ore, which had postponed the crisis, was now acute. Although Chilean mines were strained to their fullest capacity to produce the copper extracted in 1883, most mines lost money. Only the hope of better prices and the fear of losing a mining property under the existing code kept more mines from suspending operation. The crisis brought renewed demands for mining reform.

About the time when Chile lost its first place for copper output, mining leaders met in Santiago to create a national mining society, the *Sociedad Nacional de Minería* (SONAMI).[74] SONAMI leadership consisted of mine owners and engineers from the north, with close connections to Liberal party members of the Chamber of Deputies and the Senate.[75] This new professional organization seems to have been a part of the worldwide rise of a middle class seeking to secure its status through organizational life.[76] SONAMI was not, however, an interest group in a pluralist sense. Born through presidential sponsorship and financed by public monies, SONAMI led the campaign for reform through intensive efforts to convince a majority of the Chamber of Deputies to legislate a mining policy more favorable to the industry. SONAMI argued that copper prosperity was directly linked to the country's underlying mining policy and that the key to future national economic prosperity was not agriculture but a strong copper industry.[77]

Boletín, the SONAMI journal, strenuously pushed for major changes in the existing mine code. Issue after issue, its pages carried the argument that the code was the principal cause of the copper industry's stagnation, which had resulted from a lack of new investment on a scale required to compete with the United States.[78] The copper mining leadership understood that its antiquated mining code sought to provide state revenue, not promote new investment. The code's logic presumed miners would not mine unless forced to do so, and it allowed anyone to claim an existing mine property, if work at that property were suspended, even for a short time.[79]

The mining conditions resulting from the old code were seen as contrary to what was necessary for the Chilean industry to compete with United States producers. The nature of United States competition called for ever larger scales of production, as did falling ore grades in Chile. Both conditions, large-scale production and low-grade ores, required consolidation of mining properties, but this was particularly difficult for Chilean producers, since their code mandated the individual working of each small claim. When consolidation was attempted, it required a team of lawyers to fend off claim challenges.[80] Such insecurity was not conducive to obtaining the capital necessary for large-scale mine development complete with steam machinery and vast smelting capacity. Thus, the existing claim system was believed to be the root cause for Chilean investment funds going elsewhere, particularly into nitrates, as well as Bolivian and Peruvian copper, which had higher ore grades and more favorable codes.[81]

SONAMI's primary goals became twofold: (1) to change the mine claim system to that of the patent system used in the United States; and (2) to abolish the copper tax in favor of an annual patent fee on each claim.[82] The mining leadership did not believe that Chilean copper could both compete worldwide and further capitalize itself if it was also expected to be the prime contributor to the state treasury.[83]

Not until 1888 did the Chilean Congress finally approve a new code.[84] This reform emerged after five years of legislative debate. Toward the end of the debate, curiously, the main opposition came from coal and nitrate mining interests as well as from agriculture. Under the colonial code in force until 1888, metal mining properties could be claimed by anyone, on any property—a right resented by landowners, who feared reform would strengthen and expand claiming rights to all minerals, not just metals. The coal and nitrate interests resisted reform for the same reason; they were unregulated by the colonial code that only conceived of metal mines.[85] So far as the old code was concerned, nitrate and coal did not exist; surface landowners could claim all subsurface coal and nitrate, free from any outsider's claims, keeping the minerals in reserve. This reserve advantage became one of the central goals of the copper reformers. In the final compromise creating the 1888 reforms, coal and nitrate were given exceptional status and continued as unregulated.[86]

With that legislative success behind it, SONAMI began to push its other proposals: northern rail consolidation, a mining college, and the holding of an international mine exposition.[87] Liberal President José Manuel Balmaceda, who provided essential support for passage of the reform in 1888, initiated efforts to rationalize the railroad situation in the copper region and thus supposedly reduce the rates for copper ore transportation. His program, which called for rail nationalization, was cut short by the Revolution of 1891. SONAMI supported Balmaceda but suspended its meetings once the revolution broke out. After Balmaceda lost power SONAMI was conciliatory toward the new agrarian-backed government.[88]

The SONAMI legislative successes of 1888 grew out of its close relations with the president and Liberals in the legislature, but the realignment of power in 1891 dissolved the willingness of both the Chamber of Deputies and the Senate to go along with further reforms. Ministerial budgets allowed for such activities as the International Mine Exposition of 1894 in Santiago, but no legislative measures in support of mining can be found until the end of parliamentary dominance in 1925.[89]

During the 1880s Chilean copper interests advocated mining code reforms that were twenty years old in the United States; they hoped to achieve what miners in Michigan and the American West had already received: legislation that bolstered capitalist practices. United States mineral policy was drafted by mining industry representatives and was aimed at rapid economic growth based on huge quick profits to individuals. One good mine fulfilled the career ambitions of a prospector, an engineer, or an investor. This was in great contrast with the Chilean copper mining industry, which had been structured under a code based on Spanish colonial goals of creating revenues for the state in the mining of precious, not industrial, metals. The Chilean reforms, both out of competitive crisis, had the intent of increasing efficiency by allowing for the large-scale, highly capitalized mining as practiced in the United States after the 1870s.

Had reform been realized earlier in Chile, there is no guarantee that Chilean copper would have prevailed in competition with the United States. Given the predatory nature of the New York–based copper mining corporations—specifically, the dumping of surplus production below cost while relying on domestic earnings created by a high tariff—it is still possible that Chilean reforms would only have delayed their submission to American industry.

The period of Congressional dominance in Chile (1891–1925), from the point of view of copper, complicated a bad economic situation. The reforms in the 1880s were too little, too late. The Revolution of 1891 simply postponed any further attempt to rationalize and modernize Chilean mining for thirty-five years. Despite the 1888 code reforms, overall mining policy during the years of congressional dominance remained indifferent to the needs of a failing copper industry. It is ironic that the reforms of 1888, while too late to revitalize Chilean copper, provided the foundation for United States capital to enter Chile. Without these reforms there would have been no large-scale foreign investment in mining.[90] Consolidation of mine holdings would have been too insecure.

During the 1890s United States copper tariffs were dropped; the Western copper industry was unquestionably preeminent worldwide. New technology had brought forth new possibilities at century's end for copper corporations in the United States. As the industry came to depend on the now workable, dispersed, low-grade copper ore (porphyry) properties, scouts from giant American copper corporations searched the planet for porphyry deposits. Since Chile had many of these deposits, mining capital from the United States moved into Chile—the same country that forty years earlier had provided the competitive excuse to build a copper tariff around the United States.

It may be that any industry structured around a given set of regulations becomes, in a sense, comfortable with those regulations. Change means uncertainty and is acceptable only in a crisis. In Chile the mid-century civil wars were based on policy in the north; their focus was limited to lowering the rate of taxation. The copper mining prosperity encountered during the 1860s and 1870s through extensive working of Chilean deposits postponed the crisis necessary to overcome entrenched antimetal mining interests. In Chile the power of agrarian and nonmetal mining interests was such that the needs of industrial copper were not taken seriously by a congressional majority until too late. Even the reforms of 1888 meant little in the face of congressional indifference to copper after the overthrow of Balmaceda in 1891, when interests hostile to metal mining settled in for years of governance.

As the nineteenth century closed, with a great American productive capacity in place and Chilean competition demoralized, United States producers began to respond to the dangers of excessive competition. An era of combinations followed, "intended to lessen the rigors of the struggle for existence by uniting the strength and interests of many individuals in a company or association or 'trust.'"[91] There was even an occasional expression of concern for the foreign competitors in the industry press: "The sooner the foreign producers appreciate the ability of our mines to supply the world with cheap copper, the sooner will they cooperate with ours in effecting some reasonable 'working basis' for marketing the large stocks, now in the country."[92] Predatory marketing, supported by tariffs favorable to mining capital, and mining codes written by mining industry representatives, combined to support a copper success in the United States only dreamed of in Chile.

Industrial mining and smelting of copper prospered in the nineteenth century not because of free enterprise but precisely its opposite, which was the extent and quality of government intervention. Had government not regulated the distribution of subsurface minerals, had mining not been freed of the obligation to contribute to general state revenues and social well-being, had transportation not been subsidized, had limited liability corporations not been legislated into existence, had tariffs not been passed, the United States copper industry would still have emerged—the ore was there—but it would have been a very different industry and perhaps not the world's aggressive dominant copper producer. Unlike the natural change of seasons, competition is not inevitable in its results. As Chilean and United States copper entrepreneurs found in their years of competition, public policy, not their individual entrepreneurial talents, was the ultimate factor in industrial success or failure and in each nation's economic development.

Issues of Politics and Development

"For our time," Charles Tilly writes,

> it is hard to imagine the construction of any valid analysis of long-term structural change that does not connect particular alterations, directly or indirectly, to the two interdependent master processes of the era: the creation of a system of nation-states and the formation of a worldwide capitalist system. We face the challenge of integrating big structures, large processes, and huge comparisons into history.[93]

The history of the competition for dominance of the nineteenth-century international copper industry of necessity responds precisely to this challenge expressed by Charles Tilly. To truly understand these complex interdependent master processes, to attempt to solve the difficult question of national economic development, we must be prepared to construct complex and often tedious historical explanations. We must be prepared to do what the late Stein Rokkan did when "confronted with a set of variations in contemporary political means and outcomes": "move back in time, looking for the crucial choices that set presumably different paths of development."[94]

Putting these ideas to work in the specific context of Chile's economic and political development requires that we look at the nineteenth-century world as it was seen by its contemporaries—a place not yet interpreted in terms of periphery and core; a place of intense competition among relative equals; a place of interconnected, international histories. Nineteenth-century Chile evolved in a context of trade and exchange with, among other countries, Great Britain, the United States, Spain, and Peru. Chile was a full partner in the movement of peoples around the globe spreading ideas and knowledge of opportunities. Chileans, or at least those with some education, were excited with illusions of their own pending national progress.

Contrary to the "obvious" inequalities today's observers see among the countries of the Western Hemisphere, in 1820 the hemisphere's emerging nation-states competed on a somewhat equal footing. We need to remember that this was a time when the people of the United States of America used the verb form *are* when referring to their country—that is, the United States of America "are"—rather than the modern post–Civil War usage, *is*. This perhaps helps to provide a useful corrective to the contemporary sense of eternal North American completeness and omnipotence. Certainly, vast and expansive possibilities existed in the United States of America, and clear natural advantages could be identified. But contemporary analysts of the enormous Spanish colonial domain emerging from its 300-year-old cocoon, or of the unexplored lands of Brazil, were no less optimistic about the coming prosperity of what is today termed Latin America.[95]

Looking back then from the vantage of our time, one can see that, out of the international trade competition of the 1800s, some countries emerged relative winners and some relative losers. Indeed, should we expect anything different from competition? No, we should not. The research for this article has led the authors to concentrate on international trade competition, tracing competitive success as a process linked to the nature of the relationship between the state and productive forces in a country.[96] Just as breakthroughs occur in technology, or business organization, they also occur in public policy's influence on things economic. As advantages through policy are pursued in one country, policy responses are logically and necessarily called for in competitor countries. This is not to suggest that policies can be merely copied to bring about automatic results; rather, trade survival requires rounds of competitive policy initiatives pursued in response to those of competitors, whether to lower costs of production, to improve product quality, or to remove some perceived bottleneck in production. Public policy innovations,

Rokkan's "crucial choices," are thus necessarily understood as one of several possible competitive steps in any world industry.

Chile and its place in the international copper industry provides a useful thread of continuity throughout the nineteenth century by which comparative analysis can be pursued. The study of this early worldwide industry involves examining the marketplace interaction of Chile with Great Britain, Australia, the United States of America, Spain, Bolivia, and Peru, in that order—the order in which each began to produce copper metal for the expanding world capitalist system. Both the United States and Great Britain have an extensive historiography illuminating public policy's impact on economic development and, indirectly, on copper.[97] But analysis of nineteenth-century Chilean economic development from the perspective of public policy influence is still emerging, despite a number of excellent studies published in recent years.[98] Taken together, these new monographs provide a corrective to the last decade's fascination with the international power and class aspects of the state. This earlier structural approach to understanding the issues of underdevelopment relegated the role of the state as a policy-making institution to the shadows. Little was written about specific policies because policy itself was perceived to be of marginal importance. The politics of public policy were seen as secondary to large structural forces about which policy could do very little.[99]

This article represents an effort by the authors to argue that politics matters, a conclusion that results from placing Chile in a comparative context of policies and trade competition. Chilean international trade in the last century, more than anything else, meant exportation of copper. Thus, this study focuses on a series of public policies that structured competition in the world copper industry during the last century. And as important as the public policies were by themselves, the specific timing of policy implementation in relation to the competitive environment is the aspect that deserves our greatest attention. The authors argue that effective policy in one decade is not necessarily effective if postponed to a later one; competitive trade environments evolve. In a sense, this study is about how politics, and thus policy, makes a difference in economic development—how mining policy made a difference in Chilean development.

The approach taken here considers the overall problem of economic development as a maze of particular practical problems facing specific industries. All too often analysts seeking to understand national economic patterns have a confused and substantially imprecise grasp of individual industrial activity. Or the reverse is true: specialists concerned with specific industries often give exclusive attention to the particular at the expense of thinking about larger development problems. What seems called for is a grasp of necessary detail set amid the overall context of development: a context of the formation of the nation-state and of expanding world capitalism.

For Chile over the long run, copper mining has constituted the prime national industry. Thus, an interest in Chilean economic development must lead to copper mining and the policies that allow copper mining to prosper. In copper mining the concerns of the mine owner, the mine engineer, and the metallurgist are to reduce the costs of extraction and mineral concentration to at least the market price, if not lower. For them national economic growth is assumed to flow from prosperous mines; larger national questions are not their day-to-day concern. Yet scholarly analysis of Chilean economic development is most often concerned precisely with the big picture and the details of mining are either glossed over or misunderstood.[100]

Perhaps the period most needing further investigation within the confines of the topics of this article, and certainly the focus of the authors' current work, is the policy-making process of Chile in the last three decades of the nineteenth century. For mining in general, and copper mining in particular, detailed work is needed on the people and activities of the Sociedad Nacional de Minería, founded in 1882. Political battles of the day involved differences in outlook between elites and the copper mine owners/managers who did not necessarily hold key positions of political influence.[101] At that time "miners" still referred to mine owners or mine engineers and not mine laborers (only during the last decade of the century did labor become a key factor in copper politics). The general approach taken by the authors, as outlined above, leads to specific efforts to understand the politics of these miners and their grasp of the domestic and international markets they faced.

The miners of the 1870s and 1880s had great industrial dreams and appear to have given considerable thought to how mineral production might best be organized and to the issue of the state's role in that process. To better understand their politics, a set of questions about copper and SONAMI need to be investigated. Whatever the answers to these questions mean to the understanding of mining, they also help us to understand the ways in which Chileans faced their *crucial choices* about national economic development. These choices are also part of the evolution of democratic institutions in Chile and set the stage for the ways these institutions confronted Chile's major twentieth-century concern:

determining the ownership of mining properties coupled with taxation of mines and distribution of tax revenues.

The political problem for miners, always in the minority and working in remote places, evolves to finding the means to influence those in power to support initiatives needed by their industry. The state has the power to influence and even create a production environment. As capitalist practices emerged and evolved little by little in nineteenth-century mining, competition began to hinge on which mining region had the most favorable production environment. In copper mining the product is an identical commodity whose competitiveness is mostly a matter of price. From a mining perspective the most favorable production environment is the one with the lowest costs.

In this context the questions to be asked about SONAMI start with the multiple reasons for its formation in the 1880s. To what extent was presidential/executive sponsorship of SONAMI essential to its creation? In what ways is it an interest group in the sense the concept is used today? Certainly Cheryl Schonhardt-Bailey's 1991 *American Political Science Review* article, cited above, is an inspiration for the kind of combined political and historical analysis of interest groups to which the authors aspire. Comparative research is needed on SONAMI and its agricultural equivalent, the Sociedad de Agricultura (SAG). Did they share membership? To what extent did their respective leadership collaborate? To what degree can SONAMI be cast in a light of middle-sector formation and the development of democratic institutions? Did SONAMI's membership reflect the younger technically oriented miners who thought of mining as investment in a business, rather than the older generation of miners who viewed their efforts as more of a speculation? And some larger questions come to mind as SONAMI is examined in the context of late nineteenth-century Chile.

How were Chileans in general doing in identifying and understanding the central problems, the crucial choices, of their era?[102] How well did Chilean institutions allow for a debate over their national future? The Civil War of 1891 is the subject of renewed interest in this centennial year, and part of the historical debate is precisely over this point. Was the ultimate collapse and denationalization of the Chilean copper industry due to political process failure or perhaps ineffectiveness in actions taken by SONAMI? Was it a failure of political leadership?

The authors' study of politics in the nineteenth century has involved a combination of efforts to study several diverse subjects: the historiographies of each country involved in the copper trade, the evolution of the science of geology and the technology of mining, the approaches to politics in each country, and the theoretical work on development. It is this combination that provides the means to deal with the sort of inquiry suggested by the work of Hernando de Soto. While his interests are contemporary, his work obliges us to go back in time. Paul Gootenberg's recent book provides insight into Peru's own nineteenth-century struggle over the issues of the Liberal state, revealing a case very different from that of Chile.[103] In Gootenberg's Peru the roots of the problems identified by de Soto are identified—a post-1852 "export liberalism" without liberalism in the establishment and running of domestic Peruvian enterprise. De Soto's, Gootenberg's, and our own work are part of an emerging generation of studies investigating the role of politics in development—indeed, the centrality of politics as people identify and debate the issues of their time.

The case of Chilean copper prior to 1880 suggests that this new direction in the study of postindependence Latin American countries is fruitful. What role did regulations and policies play in the economic development of specific industries? In Chile an entire industry collapsed and was denationalized due to some combination of policies and circumstances. Had the Chilean state prepared a mining code more supportive of capitalist copper mining, would economic circumstances still have held back the copper industry? Perhaps not.

NOTES

The authors are grateful for research support in Chile from the State University of New York, University Awards Committee, and from the National Science Foundation.

1. Hernando de Soto, *El otro sendero: La Revolución informal* (Bogotá: Editorial Oveja Negra, 1987); English ed., *The Other Path: The Invisible Revolution in the Third World* (New York: Harper and Row, 1988).

2. "Informal" refers to the unregistered, unregulated, and illegal shops, services, and production operating alongside the formal and regulated economy. De Soto estimates that 50 percent of Peru's economy falls into the informal sector.

3. Charles W. Anderson, *Politics and Economic Change in Latin America:*

The Governing of Restless Nations (Princeton, N.J.: Van Nostrand, 1967). Chapter 1, in particular, influenced the authors' thinking on this topic.

4. Ibid., 9.

5. Charles Tilly, *Big Structures, Large Processes, Huge Comparisons* (New York: Russell Sage Foundation, 1984).

6. Every issue of the *Engineering and Mining Journal* of the 1880s contained editorial commentary and news on the swelling world copper demand. *EMJ* gave copper an especially prominent role from 1882 to 1884 as overall United States production began to total more than any competitor. See Merwin L. Bohan and Morton Pomeranz, *Investment in Chile: Basic Information for United States Businessmen* (Washington, D.C.: U.S. Government Printing Office, 1960), 87, for a typical business observation about this period of increasing copper demand.

7. See R. O. Roberts, "Development and Decline of the Copper and Other Non-Ferrous Metal Industries in South Wales," *Transactions of the Honorable Society of Cymmrodorian* (South Wales: Frank Cass, 1956); and T. C. Barker and J. R. Harris, *A Merseyside Town in the Industrial Revolution: St. Helens, 1750–1900* (London: Frank Cass, 1959), 240–446, for a British interpretation of this process.

8. Clearly, twentieth-century copper politics in Chile has generated a considerable interest. An excellent and thorough analysis of the post–World War II era is found in Theodore H. Moran, *Multinational Corporations and the Politics of Dependence* (Princeton, N.J.: Princeton University Press, 1974).

9. Chile still holds approximately 40 percent of the world's copper reserves, both as vein and porphyry coppers. Reserves are estimated on the basis of ore that can be mined "economically" (where the cost of production is below a given market price). Early copper mines were based on veins (cracks in other rocks filled with concentrations of the metal); in the late nineteenth-century porphyry deposits (very low concentrations of the metal dispersed throughout a huge area) became the mainstay of the industry. See A. B. Parsons, *The Porphyry Coppers* (New York: American Institute of Mining and Metallurgical Engineers, 1933); Victor Hollister, *Geology of the Porphyry Copper Deposits of the Western Hemisphere* (New York: Society of Mining Engineers of the American Institute of Mining, Metallurgical, and Petroleum Engineers, 1978); and Alan M. Bateman, *Economic Mineral Deposits* (New York: John Wiley and Sons, 1981), 482. Given unlimited free energy, most metal reserves are limitless, as mineral distribution in very small quantities is vast, especially if ocean bottom nodules are considered. For an overview of the nodule aspect of copper, see Robert Bowen and Ananda Gunatilaka, *Copper: Its Geology and Economics* (New York: John Wiley and Sons, 1977).

10. Nicol Brown and Charles Turnbull, *A Century of Copper* (London: Effingham Wilson, 1906), 20–21.

11. This type of social Darwinist thinking and language is found in the mining journals of all countries. Mining journals were read not just by mining engineers and investors, a conservative lot to this day, but also by the investing public. For most of the last century the leading journal in the United States has been the *EMJ* and, in England, the *Mining Journal* of London. Both had an informational role like the contemporary *Wall Street Journal*. The *Mining Journal*'s original title at

its founding in 1835 was the *Mining Journal, Railway and Commercial Gazette; Forming a Complete Record of the Proceedings of All Public Companies.*

12. 1848 refers to the date after which the United States had full access to the lands of the West, lands that had earlier been a part of Mexico.

13. The best summary on the role of idea of progress in Latin America is E. Bradford Burns, *The Poverty of Progress: Latin America in the Nineteenth Century* (Berkeley: University of California Press, 1980). The authors have also been influenced by John Stanley's introduction to Georges Sorell, *The Illusions of Progress,* trans. John and Charlotte Stanley (Berkeley: University of California Press, 1969).

14. A prominent version of this argument is made by Seymour Martin Lipset: "The evidence presented thus far would seem to indicate that, regardless of the causal patterns one prefers to credit for Latin American values, they are, as described, antithetic to the basic logic of a large-scale industrial system." See his "Values, Education, and Entrepreneurship," in *Elites in Latin America,* ed. Seymour Martin Lipset and Aldo Solari (New York: Oxford University Press, 1967), 32. Lipset develops this position as an outgrowth of the ideas of Max Weber on the requisites of economic development. "Structural conditions make development possible; cultural factors determine whether the possibility becomes an actuality" (3).

An earlier holder of this view is Thomas C. Cochran, "The Legend of the Robber Barons," *Pennsylvania Magazine of History and Biography* 74 (July 1950). Cochran puts forward the position that "comparative studies need to be made of the place of entrepreneurship in varying national cultures. There seems little doubt that such studies will go further toward explaining the economic progress of different regions than will any assessment of potential natural resources. It is these cultural elements, to a very large extent, that determine who will become entrepreneurs, a culture with feudal standards of lavish living or the support of elaborate ceremonial organizations of church and state will obviously not have the capital to invest in economic development that will be available in a culture where frugal living, saving, and work are the custom" (320–21).

Another very recent expression of this view is found in Michael Novak, "Why Latin America Is Poor," *Atlantic* (March 1982). Novak extends the present into the past when he writes: "Why, then, didn't Latin America become the richer of the two continents of the New World? The answer appears to be in the nature of the Latin American political system, economic system, and moral-cultural system. The last is probably decisive" (67).

15. Most influential on this point is Clark Winton Reynolds, "Development Problems of an Export Economy: The Case of Chile and Copper," in *Essays on the Chilean Economy,* ed. Markos Mamalakis and Clark Winton Reynolds (Homewood, Ill.: Richard D. Irwin, 1965). Reynolds draws a number of observations from secondary sources about nineteenth-century Chilean copper to conclude that Chilean entrepreneurs were outdated and backward in their outlook. "There were few men in Chile at the turn of the century who had contacts with the large investment consortia and who were aware of the developments in copper technology and their potential application in Chilean mining" (212). While

these comments were directed at the years in which porphyry copper was just being developed, the statement implies, incorrectly, a chronic condition.

Less prominent but also significant in the downgrading of Chilean entrepreneurial ability is Leland Pederson's *The Mining Industry of the Norte Chico, Chile* (Evanston, Ill.: Northwestern University, 1966). A geographer, Pederson looks at silver, gold, and copper from the Conquest to the present, providing a broad historical perspective. A view similar to Reynolds is expressed: "The vast majority of Chile's mining entrepreneurs were incapable of adopting more than the simplest of the new techniques, such as oil lamps as a replacement for tallow candles" (193). Again there is a blurring of the decades. Still other studies repeat these notions: Joseph Sumwald and Philip Musgrove, *National Resources in Latin American Development* (Baltimore: Johns Hopkins Press, 1970), 167; Robert Cortes Conde, *The First Stages of Modernization in Spanish America* (New York: Harper and Row, 1974), 69–71; Lawrence MacDonnell, "The Politics of Expropriation, Chilean Style," *Quarterly of the Colorado School of Mines,* 68, no. 4 (October 1973): 195–96; and Moran, *Multinational Corporations,* 20–22.

These studies assume a lack of effective nineteenth-century entrepreneurship in Chile. They ignore the years prior to the 1880s. The studies are also strongly influenced by the bitter twentieth-century copper analyses that appeared in Santiago as Chileans debated how to respond to the dominance of United States capital in the Chilean copper industry. The classic Chilean study is Francisco A. Encina, *Nuestra inferioridad económica, sus causas y sus consequencias* (Santiago: Imprenta Universitaria, 1912); also important is Santiago Macciavello Varas, *El problema de la industria del cobre en Chile y sus proyecciones económicas y sociales* (Santiago: Universidad de Chile, 1923). Macciavello Varas is a key source for Reynolds's position on the nineteenth century. The weakness of all of these studies, from our point of view, is their lack of discrimination about the decades from the 1840s to the 1880s.

16. N. S. B. Gras, *Business and Capitalism* (New York: F. S. Crofts, 1939).

17. A useful summary of the older literature is found in Louis Galambos, "American Business History" (pamphlet, Service Center, American Historical Association, n.d.).

18. Cochran, "Legend," 320.

19. Ibid., 320–21.

20. Alfred D. Chandler, Jr., "The Beginning of Big Business in American Industry," *Business History Review* 33 (Spring 1959): 6; and argued subsequently in *The Visible Hand: The Managerial Revolution in American Business* (Cambridge, Mass.: Belknap Press, 1971).

21. Chandler, "Beginning," 9.

22. See n. 15 for a review of this literature.

23. Influential in forming this approach has been Tilly, *Big Structures.*

24. Most historical studies of the copper industry focus on just one country or mining district. There are, however, several studies that take a comparative perspective on copper from a technical point of view: Brown and Turnbull, *Century*; Parsons, *Porphyry Coppers*; Bowen and Gunatilaka, *Copper*; Hollister, *Geology of the Porphyry Copper Deposits*; and Otis Herfindal, *Copper Costs and Prices: 1870–1957* (Baltimore: Md.: Johns Hopkins Press, 1969). One popular

description of copper mines is both interesting and useful: Ira B. Joralemon, *Romantic Copper: Its Lure and Lores* (New York: D. Appleton Century, 1934).

Among the many monographs and articles on Welsh and Cornish copper, the work of R. O. Roberts stands out. Especially important is his article cited in n. 7: "Development and Decline." For the United States regions, see William B. Gates, Jr., *Michigan Copper and Boston Dollars: An Economic History of the Michigan Copper Mining Industry* (Cambridge: Harvard University Press, 1951); F. E. Richter, "The Copper Industry in the United States, 1845–1925," *Quarterly Journal of Economics* 41 (February and August 1927), 236–91 and 684–717; Angus Murdock, *Boom Copper: The Story of the First United States Mining Boom* (Calumet, Mich.: Brier and Doepel, 1964); and C. B. Glasscock, *The War of the Copper Kings* (New York: Grosset and Dunlap, 1935).

For Chile, in addition to those works previously cited, see Benjamin L. Miller and Joseph T. Singewald, *The Mineral Deposits of South America* (New York: McGraw-Hill, 1919); Markos Mamalakis, *The Growth and Structure of the Chilean Economy: From Independence to Allende* (New Haven, Conn.: Yale University Press, 1976); C. M. Sayago, *Historia de Copiapó* (Copiapó: Imprenta de "El Atacama," 1874); and James M. Little, *The Geology and Metal Deposits of Chile* (New York: Bramwell, 1926).

Two studies specifically investigate the causes for the decline of Chilean copper and the conditions that allowed for the takeover of the Chilean industry by United States capital. See Joanne Fox Przeworski, *The Decline of the Copper Industry in Chile and the Entrance of North American Capital, 1870–1916* (New York: Arno Press, 1980); and Juan Alfonso Bravo, "United States' Investment in Chile: 1904–1907" (Master's thesis, Department of History, American University, Washington, D.C., 1980).

25. The *MJ,* from 1838 through 1848 in weekly chronicles, followed the Chilean pressure on the copper mines of Cornwall. The best contemporary review of this crisis is found in *United Kingdom, House of Commons (Select Committee on Copper), British Sessional Papers,* "Copper Ore: Copies of all Memorials and Petitions Presented to the Board of Trade, and to the Chancellor of the Exchequer, Respecting the Duty on Copper Ore, and Copies of the Answers Sent to the Applications since January, 1849" (March 15, 1847).

26. Copper production statistics before 1880 are not always reliable, but they do provide a general production range useful for comparison. The mining regions listed in table 1 constitute, each in its turn, the leading pre-1900 world producers.

27. T. Egleston, "The Port Shirley Copper Works," *School of Mines Quarterly* 7, no. 4 (July 1886): 1–25; and "Commerce and Progress of Chile," *Merchants Magazine and Commercial Review* 13 (1845): 325–26.

28. Gates, *Boston Dollars,* 9–10.

29. John D. Leshy, *The Mining Law: A Study in Perpetual Motion* (Washington, D.C.: Resources for the Future, 1987). The entire book develops this theme, but chapters 1–3 are especially useful. This is the best overview of United States mining law and the law in mining history.

30. Benjamín Vicuña Mackenna, *El Libro del cobre y del carbón de piedra en Chile* (Santiago: Imprenta Cervantes, 1886). The views of Vicuña Mackenna

are further supported by correspondence from industry leaders, which arrived too late for inclusion in this classic book—correspondence stored in the Archivo Nacional de Chile, Fondo Benjamín Vicuña Mackenna. In preparation for *El Libro del cobre,* he wrote to all of the leaders in copper asking for their recollections and recommendations for the industry. Most helpful were letters from Juan Mackay, Guillermo C. Biggs, and Enrique Sewell.

31. Two sets of Chilean congressional debates chronicled the position of landed agricultural interests in the face of calls for mining code reform. In both the Chamber of Deputies and the Senate, see the *Boletín de las Sesiones Ordinarios de la Camara de Diputados* and the same for the *Senado* for 1872 to 1874; and again for 1882 through 1888.

32. The congressional debates of the 1870s and 1880s are a topic in and of themselves. Mine code reform implied restricting the rights of surface landowners. For a characteristic exchange, see *Boletín de las Sesiones Ordinarios del Senado* (July 24, 1872): 102–6.

33. Luz María Mendez Beltrán, *Instituciones y problemas de la minería en Chile, 1784–1826* (Santiago: Universidad de Chile, 1979), 16–26; and Vicuña Mackenna, *El Libro del cobre,* 495.

34. John D. Davis, *Corporations* (New York: Capricorn Books, 1961), 262. In his last chapter, focusing on the modern corporation, Davis presents an interesting discussion of the role of corporations in the shift from extensive to intensive expansion. He sees a direct correlation between corporate organization and industrial growth.

35. Eujenio Chouteau, *Informe sobre la provincia de Coquimbo* (Santiago: Imprenta Nacional, 1887). His introduction is an expression of belief in inevitable progress, cast in terms of a strong copper industry needing a new impulse of modernization.

36. For example Carlos Cousiño and Marcial Gatica were importing the latest copper smelting equipment in 1884. Minister of Hacienda Barros Luco, in *Boletín de las Sesiones Ordinarios del Senado* (October 7, 1884): 575.

37. Thomas O'Brien, in tracing the movement of Chilean capital into the Chilean nitrate mines, clearly shows that capital was available in Chile during this period, but he does not look into the copper industry's problems, in "The Antofagasta Company: A Case Study of Peripheral Capitalism," *Hispanic American Historical Review* 60, no. 1 (1980): 1–31.

38. "The native 'baretoris' or miner is a skillful workman, unsurpassed by the miner of any other country in the mere handicraft of his calling, more enduring and more expert in the handling of his tools than a Cornishman. . . . The Chilean miner . . . handles both hammer and drill, a mode of mining known as singlehand drilling, which is growing in favor in some of the mining districts of the United States." J. D., Jr., "Chili, Her Mines and Miners—II," *EMJ* 38 (July 26, 1884): 55.

39. Maxwell Whiteman, *Copper for America: The Hendricks Family and a National Industry, 1755–1939* (New Brunswick, N.J.: Rutgers University Press, 1971), 207–8. Also see Maurice Zeitlin, "Class, State, and Capitalist Development: The Civil Wars in Chile (1851 and 1859)," in *Continuities in Structural Inquiry,* ed. Peter M. Blau and Robert K. Merton (Beverly Hills, Calif.: Sage

Publications, 1981), 121–64. During the nineteenth century Chile had three separate episodes termed in the Chilean historiography as "civil wars." Two of them, in 1851 and 1859, were significant political milestones but also violent when compared with that of the United States. A third civil war occurred in 1891, and, while more important politically than militarily, it continues to be the subject of considerable historical debate. See Brian Loveman, *Chile: Legacy of Hispanic Capitalism* (Oxford: Oxford University Press, 1979).

40. Support for this interpretation of the role of the American Civil War is somewhat controversial. The authors follow the case made by Barrington Moore, Jr., *Social Origins of Dictatorship and Democracy: Lord and Peasant in the Making of the Modern World* (Boston: Beacon Press, 1966), esp. 141. The same argument is made in a novel but very useful manner by Major L. Wilson, "The Concept of Time and the Political Dialogue in the United States, 1828–1848," *American Quarterly* 19 (1907): 619–44. Wilson observes the South's insistence on clinging to the past, represented by slavery, as distorting the national debate over economic development and forcing the debate toward conflict between the parties of the "past" and the "present." Also useful is Eugene Genovese's several works on the Southern mind, especially *The Political Economy of Slavery* (New York: Pantheon Books, 1965), chap. 1. William R. Taylor makes much the same argument with different sources in his classic work, *Cavalier and Yankee: The Old South and American National Character* (Garden City, N.Y.: Doubleday, 1961).

41. U.S. Revenue Commission, *The Copper Crisis in the United States* (Washington, D.C.: 1866), 11, 13, 15, 17, and 19. See also *Congressional Globe,* 40th Cong., 3d sess. (January 18, 1969), 416.

42. U.S. Revenue Commission, *Copper Crisis,* 12.

43. During this time the American copper industry split over the struggle between smelting interests in Maryland and mines in Michigan and Tennessee. The seaboard smelters wanted low-cost, tariff-free Chilean ore. See proceedings of congressional debates on HR 1460, "To Regulate the Duties on Imported Copper and Copper Ores." The debate extended throughout the 40th Congress, 3d sess. from December 1868 to February 1869. See also the 2d sess. debates in the *Congressional Globe; EMJ* 4 (July 25, 1867): 56; and 7 (January 2, 1869): 2.

44. U.S. Revenue Commission, *Copper Crisis,* 15.

45. *Congressional Globe,* 40th Cong., 3d sess. (January 18, 1869). During the session Senator Zachariah Chandler of Michigan spoke endlessly about Chilean copper. His emotional pleas included a mixture of exaggerated and mistaken claims. "Copper is an interest that is absolutely being crushed by foreign competition—the competition of convict raised ores in Chile" (416).

46. Ibid.

47. The Montana-Michigan copper price war is thoroughly reviewed in K. Ross Toole, "A History of Anaconda Copper Mining Company: A Study in the Relationships between a State and Its People and a Corporation, 1850–1950" (Ph.D. diss., Department of History, University of California at Los Angeles, 1954).

48. A typical comment of the era is found in *EMJ* 35, no. 22 (June 2, 1883): "But yet a glance at the figures which illustrate the excessive growth of copper production will show the careful student and speculator that our American

markets can no longer stand the tension of such burdens as are heaped upon them by the ambitious operators of mines. And so we are confronted by a new question: Are we ready to try to experiment the problem of shifting the battle from home to foreign fields, where we come into competition with the pauper labor of Spanish-speaking people and the inexhaustible beds of Chile, Africa, Portugal, Spain, and Australia?" (313).

49. Since the 1840s Chilean smelted copper was exported in bars $6 \times 2 \times 2$ inches. In Europe and North America this "Chili bar" became the international standard for forward copper trading due to its consistent high quality and dominating abundance. Each bar was stamped with the name of the smelter of origin (interview with Sr. Claudio Canut de Bon Urrutia, July 17, 1980, Museo de Antropología de La Serena, Chile). Old Chili bars from several smelters are on display in the museum in La Serena.

50. Dumping of surplus production was standard procedure for North American industry during the era. See Edward D. Crapol and Howard Schonberger, "The Shift to Global Expansion, 1865–1900," in *From Colony to Empire: Essays in the History of American Foreign Relations,* ed. William Appleman Williams (New York: J. Wiley, 1972), 186.

51. The legislative fight was led by William Stewart of Nevada. See the *Congressional Globe,* 39th Cong., 1st sess., Senate bill 157, 3548.

52. Ibid.

53. William Doherty, *Minerals Conservation in the United States: A Documentary History* (New York: 1971), 542–55. See also Leshy, *Mining Law.*

54. "Foreign Copper and Lead Mines," *EMJ* 37 (1884): 456.

55. Abram S. Hewitt, "A Century of Mining and Metallurgy in the U.S.," *EMJ* 21 (1876): 609.

56. Ibid., 612.

57. Ibid., 614.

58. "Foreign Copper and Lead Mines," *EMJ* 37 (1884): 456.

59. "Copper—Arizona's Place along the Producing Regions," *San Francisco Bulletin*; reprinted in *EMJ* 32 (1881): 22.

60. "Foreign Copper," 456.

61. Ibid.

62. "The Copper Question," *EMJ* 47 (1889): 452.

63. See Toole, "History of the Anaconda," for a detailed analysis at the state level; and Frank William Tausig, *Some Aspects of the Tariff Question* (Cambridge: Howard University Press, 1915), 161–70, for an analysis of federal copper politics.

64. Walter H. Voskuil, "Copper," *Minerals in World Industry* (Port Washington, N.Y.: 1930), 226–27; and Chandler, "Beginning," 28–31.

65. Chouteau, *Informe.*

66. Vicuña Mackenna, *El Libro del cobre.* Vicuña Mackenna expressed this view clearly: "All we ask of the country, that is of government, or the legislators and of the people, is three things, simple and indispensable, urgent and lifesaving: 1. Abolition of the copper tax; 2. Reform of the mining code; and 3. A railway uniting the entire north" (604; my translation).

67. "La cuestión minera," *Boletín de la Sociedad Nacional de Minería—*

Revista Minera 1, no. 2 (January 1884): 9–10 (hereafter *Boletín*).

68. Vicuña Mackenna, *El Libro del cobre,* 513–17.

69. This is implied through numerous references in Pedro Pablo Figueróa, *Historia de la revolución constituyente, 1858–1859* (Santiago: 1889). See also an important analysis of these wars taking a somewhat different view in Zeitlin, "Class, State, and Capitalist Development."

70. Francisco Encina, *Historia de Chile desde la prehistoria hasta 1891* (Santiago: 1940), 52.

71. Figueróa, *Historia,* 31.

72. Chouteau, *Informe,* 2.

73. "Annual Review of the Metal Markets for 1882," *EMJ* 35 (January 20, 1883): 27–28.

74. *Boletín,* 1, no. 12 (April 30, 1884): 94.

75. See all issues of *Boletín* 1 (1883–84).

76. For an analysis of this process in the United States, see Robert H. Wiebe, *The Search for Order, 1887–1920* (New York: Hill and Wang, 1967).

77. *Boletín* 1 (1883–84), all issues.

78. *Boletín* 1, no. 1 (December 15, 1883): 1–2; and 1, no. 2 (January 1, 1884): 9–10.

79. Ibid.

80. Ibid.

81. Bravo, "U.S. Investment," 53.

82. Ibid.

83. *Boletín* 1, no. 12 (June 1, 1884): 101–2; and 3, no. 49 (December 15, 1885): 389.

84. *Boletín* 5, no. 4 (October 31, 1888): 15; and 6, no. 7 (January 31, 1889): 193–208.

85. There is some confusion in existing writing on various minerals and their regulations in nineteenth-century Chile. For example, in his study of the Chilean economy Markos Mamalakis touches on nineteenth-century copper at several points, making the familiar argument about the incapacity of the copper sector to modernize, but he makes an additional important reference to government policy: "If true laissez-faire ever came close to existence in Chile, it was in nitrate and copper mining" (40). While he is correct in pointing to policy as a factor to be examined, the two minerals, nitrate and copper, were produced under wholly different legal bases prior to 1888. Copper was highly regulated, nitrate not at all.

86. "Código de Minería," *Boletín* 6, no. 7 (January 31, 1889): 194.

87. *Boletín* 2, no. 9 (March 31, 1889): 237.

88. *Boletín* 2, no. 37 (July 1 and October 31, 1891): 190–92.

89. *La Riqueza Minera de Chile* 1, no. 1 (September 1921): 29.

90. Santiago Macciavello Varas, "Breve estudio," *La Riqueza Minera de Chile* 3, no. 28 (January 1925): 509.

91. "The Copper Question," *EMJ* 47 (1889): 452.

92. Ibid., 473.

93. Tilly, *Big Structures,* 147.

94. Ibid., 129–30.

95. Tom B. Jones offers a delightful review of early writings by merchants, diplomats, and travelers to South America during the period from 1820 to 1870: *South America Rediscovered* (Minneapolis: University of Minnesota Press, 1949). The chapters on Chile were very helpful in introducing the authors to this literature: 6, "The Vale of Paradise," and 7, "Innocents Abroad."

On the origins and conscious creation of the term *Latin America* in the last century, see the report: University of California SCR 43 Task Force, *The Challenge: Latinos in a Changing California* (1990), 15–21.

96. These ideas are being fully developed in our forthcoming book, *Chili Bars: Copper Trade Competition and the Politics of the Liberal State, 1800–1930.*

97. For example, the recent article in the *American Political Science Review* by Cheryl Schonhardt-Bailey, "Lessons in Lobbying for Free Trade in Nineteenth-Century Britain: To Concentrate or Not" (85, no. 1 [March 1991]: 37–58) draws on an extensive body of sources.

98. For example: Julio Pinto Vallejos y Luis Ortega Martínez, *Expansión minera y desarrollo industrial: Un Caso de Crecimiento Asociado (Chile, 1850–1914)* (Santiago: Universidad de Santiago de Chile, 1991). Pinto and Ortega provide an excellent survey of the literature, including many sources not utilized in English language investigations. However, their overall conclusion, that reluctant entrepreneurs and lack of economic transformations in the country are at the root of later economic troubles, seems incomplete. Without an examination of politics and policy debates, we may only be viewing the manifestations of something deeper when investors fail to invest.

99. These points are developed throughout his recent review of the literature by Cristobal Kay, *Latin American Theories of Development and Underdevelopment* (New York: Routledge, 1989). Chapter 7, "The Latin American Contribution in Perspective," presents Kay's arguments for a new research agenda that would take a closer look at the role of the state, especially "the relationship between state interventions and market mechanisms in development" (206–8). It is also important to recall the pioneering work of Charles Anderson, which laid out many general conceptual leads but was unfortunately ignored during the years of the dependency debates.

100. Two examples: the otherwise excellent study by Clark Reynolds of Chilean copper in this century cites works written amid 1920s policy debate as evidence of general nineteenth-century backwardness in mining; and the provocative work by Maurice Zeitlin on Chile's civil wars remarks about smelting in Chile during the 1840s, when there was none.

101. See Arturo Valenzuela's synthesis of the literature on Chilean elites in "Chile," in *Democracy in Developing Countries: Latin America,* ed. Larry Diamond, Juan J. Linz and Seymour Martin Lipset (Boulder, Colo.: Lynne Rienner, 1989).

102. This line of inquiry has been supported and clarified through reading Charles Lindblom, *Inquiry and Change: The Troubled Attempt to Understand and Shape Society* (New Haven, Conn.: Yale University Press, 1990).

103. Paul Gootenberg, *Between Silver and Guano: Commercial Policy and the State in Postindependence Peru* (Princeton: N.J.: Princeton University Press, 1989).

Local History in Global Context: Social and Economic Transitions in Western Guatemala

Carol A. Smith

It is increasingly fashionable for anthropologists to castigate themselves (or at least to castigate other anthropologists) for failing to take into account the larger or global processes that affect the small communities they study. We accuse ourselves, for example, of treating peasant communities as if they were primitive isolates and of failing to consider the external forces that created those communities and that cause them to operate the way they do. While this accusation may be warranted for the earliest work on peasant communities, I suggest that for quite some time now the anthropological perspective regarding these communities has shifted. In fact, I will argue here that many anthropologists have been all too ready to accept global views of peasant communities and social relations without proper consideration of the interplay between local and global processes.

When globalists assert, for example, that the present function of peasant communities in the world economy is to supply cheap labor to capitalist enterprises, anthropologists obligingly document how subsistence farming by peasants preserves them as a cheap labor force (cf. Clammer 1975). Or when a dependency theorist suggests that the function of Latin American civil-religious *cargo* systems (in which individuals bear the economic burden of community festivals) is to preserve relations of internal colonialism (cf. Stavenhagen 1969), anthropologists are willing to show how celebration of community festivals does little more than enrich oppressive merchants and priests engaged in selling liquor, candles, and masses (Diener 1978). Those anthropologists who doggedly cling to notions such as the "dual society," who emphasize functions of *cargo* systems that relate to local prestige, or who note the importance of ethnic over class relations (e.g., Collier 1975) are roundly criticized for their misunderstanding of the larger dynamic in the regions they study—which dynamic is capitalism (see, e.g., W. Smith 1977; and Wasserstrom 1978).[1]

While I too find fault with studies of modern peasants that ignore the interplay between international capitalism and local adaptations, I am concerned that, in their eagerness to embrace a global view, anthropologists will substitute a new kind of global functionalism for the community-integration functionalism so recently discarded. In so doing, they will fail to provide an understanding of the contradictory nature of global changes, something anthropologists are uniquely able to contribute. That is, anthropologists are usually privileged to see, and often record, how people make their own history—how people form local-level institutions that are often opposed to the interests of capitalism, how these institutions are sometimes the means by which peasants or other groups resist capitalist incorporation, and thus how they are responsible for the *particular* kind of capitalism extant in peripheral social formations. Yet anthropologists remain quite one-sided, assigning potency and causality only to the external forces. I suspect that this one-sidedness results less from conviction than from inability to conceptualize the other side of the process. How does one examine and analyze a dialectical process that involves the articulation of different layers in a multilayered system?

An obvious first step is to develop models of those structures that mediate between the local community and the world system. These structures include such things as regional class systems, state and political institutions, and specific forms of production and exchange that link the economies of small communities to the world system. Anthropologists have generally left this task to other social scientists. But since other social scientists rarely understand the dynamic existing within local communities, they describe these structures as if they came about only to meet the needs of actors operating at the higher levels of the system—regional elites, members of state bureaucracies, or international capitalists. The result is an interpretation of local history in which the masses play only a passive role. Anthropologists may not see the masses as passive, but they do see them as responding to a world made largely by others. They assume, in other words, that local communities adapt to external pressures (or die out), rarely considering the possibility that local-level processes actively shape the larger picture.[2]

Let me use as an example of this model of adaptation a well-known anthropological construct, relevant to the case I later discuss—that of the closed corporate peasant community. Eric Wolf (1957) developed this model of peasant social organization to show how peasants reacted to the exigencies of early mercantile capitalism in Latin America and Indonesia. Wolf persuaded us that the closed corporate community was no relic of past civilizations; it was, instead, an active response to ongoing economic and political processes. Through closure, leveling mechanisms, and corporate or ethnic identities, peasant communities protected themselves from the depredations of plantation (hacienda) systems, the uncertainties of a volatile market situation, and the dangers of internal polarization. In so doing, peasant communities also maintained themselves as a cheap and ready reserve of labor for the unsteady process of capitalist expansion. Wolf's model was an important first step toward understanding how global forces affected local-level systems.

Most of us, however, have neglected the other part of the argument, suggested but only weakly developed by Wolf. That argument was that the organization of peasants into closed corporate communities affected in turn how the expansion of capitalism was to proceed within the social formations producing them. It cannot be accidental that, wherever closed corporate peasant communities have formed, the social formations holding them have been plagued by the "agrarian problem"—peasantries that refuse to be easily proletarianized—as well as by countless peasant rebellions, control of the state apparatus by powerful landed oligarchies, and persistent ethnic divisions that shape the way in which regional and national political processes operate. These conditions, moreover, have produced only a weak and distorted form of capitalism, in which labor supplies must still be mobilized by force and in which the internal market is poorly developed—at least as regards the consumption of industrial goods. Yet we tend to interpret these developments as if they were the outcomes wished by capitalism all along. This could hardly be so. Some capitalists may have wanted such an outcome, but certainly not all of them did.[3]

It is much too soon to attempt a general description of how local-level processes have helped shape regional and national structures in certain types of social formation. Data are missing, especially data on the middle or regional levels of organization: how they vary and how they link to both local and higher levels. But I can attempt a first step, which is to show how various middle-level institutions, regional and national, resulted from the interplay of local and global forces in one social formation, that of Guatemala.

The sources available on Guatemala are not especially rich in the kinds of information needed to construct a history of middle-level institutions, but one is unlikely to encounter better information on any peripheral social formation.[4] One finds, on the one hand, the many standard ethnographies, contextualized as to neither time nor place, that totally ignore the impact of world capitalism on the peoples under study, and, on the other, a number of world-oriented accounts that view virtually all developments within Guatemala as nothing more than aids to world capitalist expansion. Yet, in combination, these two sources of information can be used to describe, or at least to suggest, some of the distinctive features of Guatemalan institutions, features that guided that country's particular response to global capitalism.

To orient my discussion, I have elected to use a world system history (a generalized, composite one, in order to evaluate a position rather than an individual), for two reasons. First, it is the approach dominating anthropological discourse today, and, while no more deficient than accounts that ignore global forces as regards an understanding of peripheral formations, it is equally deficient. Second, of the two approaches available, it alone pays sufficient attention to history, and one cannot understand even local processes without some knowledge about how those processes developed through time. In the following discussion I divide modern Guatemalan history into five periods: colonial (1521–1821), early independence (1821–71), early plantation (1871–1944), post–World War II (1944–78), and recent (1978–81).

What I hope to do in this brief sketch of Guatemalan history is to capture some of the tensions and dialectic of social life in a situation in which people who had noncapitalist values and institutions confronted expanding capitalism to produce a unique historical outcome. Thus, I want to show not only how capitalist expansion affected one small local system but also how local institutions interacted with externally imposed forces to create a particular dynamic that affected capitalist expansion itself. Guatemalan and other peasants of the world were changed by the new and contradictory institutions of capitalism. So too were capitalist institutions changed by the response and resistance of Guatemalan and other peasants to them. The revolutionary governments now in power in many parts of the Third World are only the most recent manifestation of the obstacles that have arisen in the path of world capitalism and to which *capitalism* has had to adapt.

The Colonial Period (1521-1821)

A typical global account of the colonial period in Guatemala would make the following points:

> The Spanish conquest forcibly integrated Guatemala into an expanding capitalist world-system, but left the area's internal structures pre-capitalist. The region developed as a classic example of a dependent socioeconomic formation in which the various systems of production present remained dominated by and subordinated to the needs of an external mode, European mercantile and industrial capitalism. As a result, the local economy suffered an unstable alternation of subsistence farming with local booms incapable of sustained growth. Those of the indigenous population who survived the shocks of the conquest took refuge in isolated highland communities structured internally by communal land tenure and the religio-political *cargo* system and externally by limited contact with the Latino world. Unlike the Spanish of Peru, the colonizers of Guatemala made only limited and localized labor demands on the Indian population.[5]

Since the colonial period in Guatemala is poorly researched, I cannot make a detailed critique of this characterization. I can, however, raise a major problem with it. Why did the dense and relatively productive population of western Guatemala remain as isolated and autonomous as it did during the colonial period? Robert Wasserstrom (1976) has shown that this was not at all the case in neighboring Chiapas, whose indigenous population was less dense and less productive. In Chiapas traditional subsistence-farming communities did not really form around cargo systems until late in the eighteenth century. During most of the colonial period, considerable labor was taken from the Chiapas Indian communities for work on lowland plantations; because of this, communal institutions barely survived. Ralph Woodward (1976) documents a similar pattern to the east of Guatemala, where slavery, mining, and indigo plantations (the latter mainly in what was to become El Salvador) either obliterated native populations or destroyed much of their preconquest heritage. Most scholars agree that the western highlands of Guatemala, in contrast, remained relatively neglected throughout the colonial period, even during the seventeenth century, when Spaniards desperately sought means of finding and holding scarce labor (MacLeod 1973:229). Most scholars also concede that the economic potential of the region was as great as that of other parts of Central America because labor was the critical scarcity throughout the colonial period. The question is: Why was western Guatemala neglected?

Certain preconquest features of Central America, ignored in the global accounts, suggest an answer. We find heavy exploitation of those Indian communities peripheral to the Quiche kingdoms but relative neglect of the Quiches and their immediate neighbors. That the Quiche peoples had achieved state-level integration before the conquest, while the more exploited groups east and west of them had not (Carmack 1981), is not likely to be an incidental fact. In other words, it seems plausible that the indigenous institutions of the Quiches made possible stronger resistance to colonial labor drafts. The Spaniards did not simply create plantation economies where and when they wanted them, but had to adapt to local conditions, which included the variable states in which native communities organized themselves after the ravages of the conquest.

Many Spaniards left Guatemalan cities in the seventeenth century to develop small indigo farming operations. But most settled in sparsely populated eastern Guatemala, where they had continuous difficulties in finding sufficient labor. Most used slave labor, raided from western Guatemala, if they had access to nonfamily labor at all (MacLeod 1973:288–309). Why did they not settle in western Guatemala, which was very densely populated? We cannot assume that the lands of eastern Guatemala were more productive, because the most successful plantation economy of Guatemala developed in western Guatemala. Nor can we assume that the colonial authorities kept them out of western Guatemala to protect the Indians there because the Spanish Crown, if it paid any attention at all, frowned on the use of Indian slaves more than on any other form of exploiting Indians. A more likely reason is that the Indians of western Guatemala were more difficult to control unless they were taken out of their home communities as slaves. Thus, the Spanish settlers in Guatemala, who used slavery more than any other form of labor control, were forced by Indian resistance to contradict what has been considered a law of global capitalist expansion: where indigenous people are abundant you use tribute extraction methods, and only where potential labor is scarce do you use slaves.[6]

In the western highlands the classic form of the closed corporate peasant community gradually emerged around the *municipio*. The *municipio* was not an indigenous institution, nor did it closely resemble any indigenous institution. It was a colonial administrative unit—the lowest level political unit and the unit subject to tribute and labor levies. The *municipio* was also the lowest level unit in which the Spanish clergy operated. As many have noted, then, this community, centered on the *municipio,* was a novel structure, meeting the needs of both the colonial administration and the peasants subject to that administration. But this is not to say that local institutions and local history did not play a role in the particular development of the closed corporate community in Guatemala. In fact, in Guatemala that community had several very distinctive features that were to make it more resilient to state control than others that developed in Latin America.

In the first place, the closed corporate community developed in western Guatemala in reaction to state taxation and authority, rather than as protection against hacienda encroachment or as resistance to other kinds of land struggle. Thus, it did not have the same functions that such communities had elsewhere. It did not, for example, develop institutions to level differences in internal wealth during the colonial period (MacLeod 1973; Carmack 1979). This made it much more difficult for the state to break the community apart later through the use of selective rewards. A peasant community could survive without leveling mechanisms in Guatemala during the colonial period because land was not a major issue then.[7] Hence there was little danger of a landless proletariat arising within the community if wealth (or poverty) were not shared equally. Because the closed corporate community in western Guatemala did not develop as an economic entity, preserving itself for continuous exploitation, but, rather, evolved as a political instrument wielded by, but also against, state authority, these Guatemalan Indians have retained greater political autonomy than native peoples in most parts of the world, even as they have been absorbed by economic systems not of their own making.

In the second place, the emergence of the *municipio* as a significant unit of peasant social organization in the colonial period did not eliminate other, more elementary, units of peasant social organization in western Guatemala. Most *municipios* were made up of several *parcialidades,* endogamous kindreds holding rights to corporate property and usually ranked in relation to each other.[8] These groups persisted as corporate units not only during the colonial period but up through the twentieth century, according to the documentation recently produced by Robert Carmack (1979) and Robert Hill (1981). Thomas Veblen (1975) showed that *parcialidades* in several Quiche-speaking *municipios* continue to hold corporate property even today; Stuart Stearns and I found that these same *parcialidades* also maintained important political, religious, and marriage-regulating functions.[9]

Most anthropologists have focused on the *municipio* as the basic unit of peasant social organization in western Guatemala, to the exclusion of other units such as the *parcialidad*.[10] Partly because of this, they have been surprised regularly by the fact that Indian ethnic identity, social traditions, and sense of community have withstood the demise of municipal institutions, such as the cargo system. We can now help account for this anomaly with the observation that what was perhaps the most important preconquest social institution for indigenous peasants, the *parcialidad,* had a more stable existence. The *parcialidad* was rarely recognized by the colonial or other Guatemalan states and thus, unlike the *municipio,* was much less subject to direct state manipulation. When the *municipio* lost its closed corporate character (because the state wished to place new demands on the peasantry), Indian communities were still able to regroup around more elementary institutions with little or no difficulty.

In summary, several institutions were important for preserving a peasant community in western Guatemala. Through the *parcialidad* Indian peasants held onto much of their land, their communal institutions, and their ethnic identity. And through municipal institutions such as the cargo system, Indian peasants developed a political strategy that allowed them to struggle with some success against the more outrageous demands of the colonial authorities. None of these developments was to turn them into an especially pliable labor force for the future. On the contrary, the preservation of the indigenous community represented the greatest barrier to capitalist development throughout Guatemalan history.

The Conservative Interlude (1821–71)

Guatemala achieved independence from Spain in 1821 and carried out the institutional reforms necessary for establishing a major export-oriented plantation economy in 1871. The period between these two years is ignored in most global accounts of Guatemalan history, which usually slide over the chaos of the early independence period as follows:

Political independence did not immediately alter established relations. Rather, it was the shift to large-scale coffee production which revolutionized Guatemala. Triumph of the Liberals in 1871 threw the full weight of the state behind the new export, and production rose dramatically, as did demand for peasant labor.

From this account, we would assume that 1871 was the period in which export production of plantation crops was first considered by Guatemalan capitalists; we would also assume that it was a fairly simple matter to develop that economy, given Guatemala's abundant supply of peasant labor. In fact, however, Guatemala was very slow to develop coffee plantations; Costa Rica had begun coffee production on an intensive scale as early as 1830 (Cardoso 1975). Why was Guatemala so slow?

In this little discussed period of Guatemalan history, peasant interests were partly in the ascendancy; their interests were represented by the Conservative regimes that held power between 1837 and 1871. The Liberals, who advocated capitalist expansion in Guatemala, were the first rulers of independent Guatemala. And they attempted to do in the 1820s and 1830s precisely what Rufino Barrios was able to do in the 1870s. Their program involved (1) the establishment of a direct head tax, reminiscent of the tribute collected by the Spaniards, which had been abolished immediately following independence, (2) heavy demands on peasant labor for the development of roads and ports, (3) the suppression of the Church tithe (some of which had aided the destitute) and the abolition of many religious holidays, and (4) a land policy that promoted private acquisition of public and communal lands as a means of increasing production (Woodward 1971). The peasant response to these programs was rebellion. A major popular uprising, described by some as a race war, began in eastern Guatemala and gathered support from peasants throughout the country.[11] The leader of this revolution was Rafael Carrera, a former peasant, who became the president-for-life of the new Guatemalan republic in 1854. Conservatives stayed in power through 1871.

Most liberal historians of Guatemala have described the Carrera regime as one wherein traditional mercantile interests won out over liberal capitalism. They make little mention of the fact that it was the peasants who were largely responsible for retaining conservative regimes in power, these peasants being considered mere tools of the conservative church. But recent historical work on this period (Woodward 1971; Miceli 1974;

Ingersoll 1972) has established that a peasant revolution put Carrera into power, that Carrera represented peasant interests more than those of any other group, and that the major consequence of Carrera's regime was the prevention for fifty years of the capitalist development of Guatemala. There was no lack of capitalist interest during Guatemala's conservative interlude, but there was considerable resistance to capitalist enterprise by peasants who presumably preferred autonomy to national integration. And for at least fifty years the interests of international capitalism were *not* served in Guatemala.

It is difficult to demonstrate that the tardiness of capitalist development in Guatemala, brought about by peasant resistance, had a major impact on the *kind* of development that was to ensue. But in the following section I will show how the system of plantation agriculture adapted to the continuing problem of insufficient labor supplies. I will also discuss the development of certain other institutions—marketing, urban, and political—which must be seen as other accommodations to local-level systems. These institutions continue to affect capitalist development in Guatemala.

The Coffee Plantation Period (1871–1944)

Ultimately, capitalist interests did triumph in Guatemala, and coffee plantations had transformed the national and local economies profoundly by the end of the nineteenth century. The Liberal regime of Rufino Barrios, which began in 1871, eventually carried out the reforms necessary for the transformation that the earlier Liberals had tried to impose. The pattern of the reforms is described in the global accounts along the following lines:

> The new government legislated and policed systems of *habilitacion* (debt servitude), *mandamiento* (forced labor), and vagrancy laws and facilitated the transfer of communal village lands into private, usually Ladino, hands. Village autonomy shattered, and the Indians were forced down into the coffee fields. Wages could be kept depressed because of the absence of a free market for labor and because wage income did not have to pay the full cost of labor maintenance/reproduction. Coffee's seasonal demand for large amounts of labor released the Indians for much of the year to support themselves as best they could on their shrinking highland plots.

What made possible in the 1870s that which was impossible in the 1830s? No anthropologist or historian has tried to answer this question because all have taken it for granted that global rather than local factors were responsible for the transformations. But I suggest that only by considering what were the internal dynamics of peasant communities during the Carrera period can we understand why Barrios's Liberal program did not evoke the widespread, violent, and effective opposition of Indian communities that had occurred earlier. While I have no direct evidence about the changes that took place in Guatemala's peasant communities in the nineteenth century, I am willing to hazard some guesses based on contemporary travelers' accounts and on what we know about peasant communities from anthropological studies undertaken in the early part of the twentieth century.[12]

Anthropologists who worked in Guatemala in the 1930s—exempli gratia, Ruth Bunzel (1952), Sol Tax (1953), and Charles Wagley (1941) as well as their associates Raymond Stadelman (1940) and Felix McBryde (1947)—describe the maintenance of certain traditional features of the closed corporate community during this period, especially of the civil-religious cargo system. But they also note the considerable involvement of the peasantry in markets and a cash economy (travelers' accounts indicate that this began in the nineteenth century), the importance of wage income for peasant subsistence, and the impact of the replacement of communal land tenure systems by holdings under private title. Two transformations of the peasant community stand out in particular: the development of significant differentiations according to wealth, wherein poorer individuals came to work for wages from richer individuals within the community, and the development of a vigorous regional marketing system manned primarily by indigenous merchants, who traded international imports as well as local commodities and who helped ease peasants out of their exclusive preoccupation with agriculture. It is not entirely clear when these changes occurred.[13] But these two developments, which shook the foundations of the closed corporate community, may well have begun before the implementation of forced labor drafts for plantation needs and have resulted instead from the increased commercial opportunities for some of the peasants in the region during the Carrera years.

At the same time, the anthropologists of the 1930s did not ignore the impact of plantation labor on peasant communities. All of them describe the abuses of the labor *enganche* system, through which poor Indians were given advance payment of wages, often during festivals and while drunk, that had to be worked off on the plantations. Most observe that, whereas poorer peasants had to seek wage labor on plantations, richer peasants were absolved from this necessity. Most also discuss chicanery on the part of plantation agents, who were often assisted by wealthy or powerful local peasants, but they describe little forcible implementation of the labor draft laws. We can take the position that these anthropologists simply refused to see the larger dynamic. Or we can use their accounts to construct a pattern whereby local changes in the native communities assisted plantation expansion, as follows.

It seems likely that the conservative Carrera regime allowed a period of economic expansion among peasants, the like of which they had never experienced before. Local production specialization and commerce were expanding during a period when tribute and labor drafts on native people were lighter than ever. Under these circumstances the peasant communities of the western highlands opened up to an unprecedented degree, and this opening was accompanied by a great deal of economic differentiation within the communities. Some peasants became much wealthier than others, and these were the people who were most likely to exercise local political power, rather than the traditional elders. Such leaders had their own instead of their community's interests in mind, and they were much less likely to be revolutionary leaders than were their more traditional predecessors.

Among other important developments during the expansive Carrera years were (1) a high rate of population increase in the native communities, brought about by improved material conditions (Veblen 1975), (2) breakup of the extended patriarchal family, brought about by, and exacerbating, economic differentiation (cf. Collier 1975), (3) decentralization of the corporate community through the movement of many peasant families to remote rural areas and to other communities (cf. Davis 1970), and (4) the loss of some urban monopolies held by Spaniards and urban Ladinos, which led to greater economic opportunities for some Indians and to greater spatial mobility for many Ladinos.[14] All of these developments undermined the corporate nature of the peasant community. The private titling of lands, a process begun with independence and reaching a fever pitch by the end of the nineteenth century, dealt only the final blow. By the first decade of the twentieth century, Indian communities had lost about half of the lands they traditionally claimed during the colonial period. But not all Indians were passive victims of this onslaught. Most Indian communities managed to survive, holding on to some land (though much less than was rightfully theirs) by obtaining both individual and group titles.[15] Thus, while the titling of land destroyed the material base of the corporate peasant community, it did not destroy a land-based peasantry.

The Barrios reforms were successful, then, because of certain changes that had already taken place within the indigenous communities. That is, Barrios was able to move this vigorously against the peasantry because, by the time he did so, these acts would have been differentially perceived within the local communities. Only the poorest members of Indian communities were forced into plantation labor, not all of them. Only Indian traditionalists lost political power, not all Indians. Only native customs that stood in the way of migratory labor movement needed to be suppressed, not all native customs. Needless to remark, the changes that ensued in native communities ultimately disadvantaged the entire community. But once opened and differentiated, the indigenous communities simply could not put up the resistance they did when closed and corporate.

There is another and equally important reason why the Barrios reforms were successful. Barrios, unlike his predecessors, used great caution in acting against the native communities and did not assault them all at once. According to David McCreery, who documents the Liberals' successes and failures of the nineteenth century:

> Barrios, who understood Indian attitudes better than many of his supporters, rejected [certain] request[s] for levies of forced labor, fearing both the disruption of the coffee labor supply and the real possibility of an Indian revolt. Quick to quash isolated opposition to his authority, he consistently avoided antagonizing the indigenous majority unnecessarily. (1976:450)

As McCreery argues the case, it was more efficient to attack communal land tenure and to assault the individual (and poorer) peasant than to impose a general head tax or massive labor conscription. Playing on the internal differentiation that had taken place within native communities was the key to Barrios's success. While the accommodation to potential peasant resistance assisted in the transformation of many indigenous institutions, it also helped maintain certain other features of native communities, and of native resistance, which were later to work against the aims of capitalist development in Guatemala. McCreery puts it this way:

The spread of coffee cultivation in Guatemala generated fundamental structural change not because it represented a transition to a new capitalist mode of production; reliance upon extra-economic coercion continues today to characterize Guatemalan owner-laborer relations. Rather, the expansion of coffee production was the first instance in Guatemala of the penetration of commercial agriculture into the fiber of indigenous society. (459)

The main failure of the Liberal program, then, was its inability to create a free wage-laboring class, the necessary ingredient for capitalist agriculture. This was not a premeditated failure, designed to keep labor cheap, for as McCreery's documentation makes clear, the Guatemalan elites wished to create a full-fledged proletariat. They even tried unsuccessfully to import such a class from Europe and the United States by offering comparatively high wages in the international labor market. Meeting little interest abroad and strong resistance at home, these nineteenth-century Liberals were unable, not unwilling, to make a successful transition to a capitalist mode of production. It remains to delineate some of the social and political consequences of this failure.

McCreery mentions one of the consequences, the development of large latifundia for export production, a system that supported a very small oligarchy. Large holdings were not the only or even the most efficient way to grow coffee for export; Costa Rican producers grew coffee for export on much smaller holdings and have always produced coffee more efficiently in terms of both land and labor. Nor were latifundia remnants of the colonial past; before coffee production few large properties existed in Guatemala. Large holdings developed in Guatemala because of the labor problem: only large producers had enough political power to obtain forced labor, which was supplied by the state, and enough economic power to afford the production inefficiencies that use of forced labor entails.

Large operations required large amounts of initial capital, a scarce resource in nineteenth-century Guatemala. Much of the capital came from the outside, mainly from German merchants, which tied Guatemalan coffee production to one particular market and which allowed the Germans to control a good deal of Guatemalan production (Jones 1940:206–8). As it turned out, the German presence was not to have long-standing repercussions because the events of World War II allowed Guatemalans to expropriate most of the German holdings. Thus, the development of large export-oriented plantations did not lead to foreign domination of production, a national problem that has a readily apparent solution. The development of large plantations, which relied on cheap forced labor and imported capital, led to certain other consequences, much more difficult to eradicate and holding much longer-term consequences for Guatemala's social and political history. The consequences were these: first, Guatemalan plantation agriculture remained undercapitalized, inefficient, and tied to relatively few crops from 1871 on; second, a small oligarchy, the latifundists, came to dominate Guatemalan politics from 1871 on; and, third, a highly centralized state apparatus developed in order to assist in the acquisition of both capital and labor, and this apparatus was to grow only stronger and more rigid after 1871.

Some of the political consequences of oligarchic control over a highly centralized state are fairly obvious. One need only point to the political histories of Guatemala and El Salvador, where this pattern emerged, as opposed to that of Costa Rica, where it did not. All three countries became dependent on export coffee production in response to global forces in the latter half of the nineteenth century. But Costa Rica became a showcase for democratic political institutions within Latin America, while Guatemala and El Salvador have had strongly centralized, repressive regimes from the beginning of the export era to the present. The oligarchies developed where peasant labor had to be coerced; the democratic regime developed where smallholders produced coffee with a free labor force.[16]

Other political consequences are less obvious, partly because they depend upon what happened to the other classes in society. In El Salvador, for example, the coffee economy gradually absorbed most of the peasantry (though not without bloodshed), because plantations could be established only where peasants already lived (Cardoso 1975). Since most peasant holdings were expropriated, proletarianization of the Salvadorean peasantry was advanced considerably over that evolving in Guatemala. From the 1930s, which saw the great *matanza,* or slaughter, of El Salvador's peasants, Salvadorean politics have reflected an ongoing struggle between a full-fledged working class (whose members retain few traces of their Mayan heritage) and a small but highly unified oligarchy.[17]

The situation was different in Guatemala. Peasants remained a distinct class in Guatemala and retained an ethnic identity separate from that of nonpeasants, at least in western Guatemala. And in the region where peasants resided, another distinctive class remained as well, an urban

Ladino class.[18] Urban Ladinos never had the political clout of the plantation oligarchy, but they did hold considerable sway over or within many Indian communities, and they helped shape the direction that economic structures took outside the plantation economy. The combination of a small, but entrenched, urban Ladino class (which controlled certain aspects of internal commerce and local-level political administration) and an even smaller and much more powerful plantation oligarchy (which directed the state apparatus) with a very large and ethnically distinct rural population (which held onto a community-centered way of life) produced in Guatemala three regional structures unique in Central America.

First, Guatemala was the only republic to develop (in the western region only) a dense, competitive, rural marketing system whose traders were almost entirely rural peasants. Elsewhere in Central America, small towns, which were also administrative centers, remained the centers for trade between rural and urban producers. The small-town pattern helped link rural producers to the national economy and to regional elites more than to each other; it also preserved a very heavy reliance on agricultural activities among the rural people. The Guatemalan pattern, however, allowed many peasants to lessen their dependence upon agriculture without requiring them to move to towns and cities, where they would have been more fully integrated into national culture. This fostered the retention of ethnic divisions in western Guatemala. The rural marketing system developed in western Guatemala at the same time the plantation system was imposed. I surmise that a rural marketing system arose because the urban commercial classes could not make their marketing practices, based on monopoly, serve the consumption needs of plantations as efficiently as could peasant traders in competition with one another. Thus, when the Liberals, who represented plantation interests, ousted the Conservatives, who represented urban Ladinos among other groups, they allowed rural marketplaces to flourish. In so doing, they divided and weakened their political opposition, for on most other issues urban Ladinos and rural peasants were united in opposition to the Liberals.

The second difference from the typical Central American pattern concerns the political position of Guatemala's urban-based regional elites. In most of Central America, regional elites had some commercial monopolies, but they also owned most of the land on which peasants worked. Through patron-client ties and direct economic coercion, regional elites were able to mobilize local support to gain national power. Thus, Central American politics usually revolved around plural interest groups, aligned in vertical segments; moreover, the potential power of regional elites always conditioned the power of the state. In Guatemala, however, regional elites had no local-level power base.[19] The enormous social and cultural gulf between Indians and Ladinos prevented patron-client ties from linking rural groups to regional interest groups, and Guatemala's regional elites rarely had the degree of economic control over peasants that was typical of the elites in the rest of Central America. On the other hand, Guatemala's regional elites were of great importance to the state in controlling the masses through political means. Nor did the state prevent these elites from intimidating, exploiting, or expropriating from peasants in any way they could—as long as they did not instigate serious rebellion or threats to state power. This treatment, of course, exacerbated the polarization between Indians (most of the rural people) and Ladinos (most of the urban people and the only people holding state offices); it also prevented the development of plural interest groups aligned in vertical segments and created instead a nationwide horizontal segmentation between the peasants and the state, and it allowed all political power to concentrate in a highly centralized state. Regional elites were merely granted state power through appointment to political office; they could not challenge state power by mobilizing local support—state-granted power was the only power they had.[20]

Because of the limited strength of regional elites, then, the plantation oligarchy in Guatemala became *the* national elite, and the power of this small group was rarely contested by any other group. El Salvador also developed a powerful plantation-based oligarchy, but its oligarchy was less removed from the masses because El Salvador's plantation system, unlike Guatemala's, encompassed the entire country. In fact, El Salvador's plantation oligarchy carried out the same political functions as Guatemala's urban Ladinos and at the same time tied the peasants to them in relations of personal dependency.

The third distinctive feature of Guatemala, which follows from the other two, was its urban system. All urban population growth and most economic infrastructure became concentrated into a single city, the national capital, while provincial towns that had previously mediated between the national and local levels, both economically and politically, languished. Only Costa Rica developed an equally top-heavy urban system. But in Costa Rica, a much smaller country, most of the rural population lived within easy reach of the capital city, even by foot. In Guatemala dense rural populations were far outside the sphere of the national capital. The direction taken by Guatemala's urban system not only fostered a greater disparity in income distribution than that of any other Central American republic but also led to increasing problems of political control.[21]

Guatemala's three distinctive sociopolitical patterns, derivative of the plantation economy established in 1871, were not fully realized until after World War II. I therefore delay elaboration on their consequences until the following section. For now I sum up the consequences of plantation agriculture apparent to the observer in the early 1940s, the end of the period under discussion here.

An accommodation had been reached between plantation development and native-community development, which must be seen as a real accommodation rather than the result of the will of capitalist expansion. Plantations obtained labor from native communities for meager wages by tapping the labor of poorer families on a seasonal basis; native communities held onto diminished community land, now mostly privately titled, and made up in wage labor, artisanry, and commerce what they had lost in agricultural self-sufficiency. The Ladino plantation-owner class gained peasant labor, but the Ladino urban merchants lost many of their commercial monopolies. Rural peasants overall lost autonomy and self-sufficiency, but some of them gained new possibilities for obtaining an income. Large-scale export agriculture was established in the lowlands, but it was not capitalist agriculture; force was still required to obtain labor. What was irretrievably lost was the old colonial system of tribute extraction, along with its complement, the closed corporate peasant community. Yet the basis for peasant resistance was not destroyed. It only changed.

The Free Wage Period (1944–78)

The global, and most widely accepted, view of Guatemala during the period following World War II is that peasants became significantly more impoverished and that the short-lived reform government that initiated the era had little impact on the continuing sway of external forces over Guatemala's internal pattern of development:

Partial integration of the indigenous population into the export economy through wage labor acted to preserve the peasant community. The community persists not because of isolation or cultural resistance, but because the contradictory effects of expanding world capitalism are such as to reproduce as well as erode precapitalist formations. Precapitalist modes of production serve capitalism in a number of ways. Indigenous peasant communities reproduce labor power cheaply and can be coerced into making it available as needed by the more advanced sectors of the economy. These communities also supply cheap goods and services through a market not dependent on industrial wages. And while the village functions to pump cheap labor into the migratory circle, the money the laborers earn there also plays an important role in sustaining and reproducing the community itself by permitting an ecological balance and population density much above that which could be sustained with available land. When Guatemala's reform government (1944–54) challenged the material base of the economy by threatening to institute land reform, it had to go.

The reform government did accomplish one thing; it abolished in 1945 all forced labor laws in Guatemala. Plantation owners shrieked that their enterprises would be jeopardized, that they would be unable to obtain necessary labor, but labor materialized on plantations without much of a hitch in response to the mere offering of a very low minimum wage. Nor did the basic pattern of seasonal labor dependence of both the peasant and plantation economies undergo any major change. If anything, plantation owners were able to utilize more seasonal labor (as opposed to permanent wage labor) than ever before—at least through the 1960s (Schmid 1967). Thus, the "free wage" era involved minimal disruption of the symbiosis existing between plantations and peasant communities. In fact, the short period of sociopolitical reform in Guatemala merely brought about a deepening of capitalist relations of production in agriculture by allowing the market rather than the government to deliver labor to plantations. It did not, however, eradicate the increasing contradiction between the peasant economy and plantation agriculture.

I shall not attempt to explain what brought on Guatemala's abortive reforms of 1944–54 because it is not necessary for my discussion and others have thoroughly covered it (see especially Jonas 1974; and Wasserstrom 1975). Suffice it to say that most analysts do not believe it represented an entirely new direction for Guatemala's economic system or its political system; it represented, instead, a power struggle within Guatemala's national bourgeoisie. The reformers, who represented the petite bourgeoisie, wanted a share of the wealth and power held by the plantation oligarchy. The established bourgeoisie, who were mainly plantation owners, did not want to share. The struggle between these two groups did allow a third power, the United States, to enter the scene more actively, and from 1954 on the United States was to play an increasingly important role in Guatemala's internal affairs. But the struggle between the principal groups did not have a significant impact on the peasantry.[22]

Anthropological opinions differ about the nature of the reform government but not about the negligible impact of the reforms it instituted on local peasant communities. Richard Adams (1957) and Robert Ebel (1957) document for several indigenous communities the process whereby Indians contested local Ladino municipal control. Most of these anthropologists conclude that the local Indian leadership squandered in factional rivalry the opportunity to take greater charge of their local affairs. Wasserstrom (1975), who has recently reviewed the materials produced by Adams (1957) and Ebel (1957), suggests otherwise. He argues that the goals of the reform government never converged with those imagined to exist in native communities, that it hoped only to develop a strong and independent form of capitalism based on peasant labor (not a new social order freeing peasants of capitalism's thrall). He also argues that the condition of the Indian communities was long past what could be seen as representing a single unified interest. Wasserstrom summarizes his thesis as follows:

> Ethnic stratification in rural Guatemala was not a particularly tenacious and long-lived form of European feudalism, as most Guatemalans believed. Having emerged during the early twentieth century as a consequence of economic development, in the highlands it had fragmented Indian society into a series of incipient social classes. One signal effect of fragmentation was apparent in the revolution: prosperous Indians made common cause with those conservative politicians in Guatemala City who shared their desire to contain, not expand, the process of agrarian reform. (1975:178)

But while anthropologists differ about the potential of the reform government for effecting reform at the local-community level, they are of one voice on the new character of the local communities. They agree that with few exceptions the last institutional remnants of the closed corporate community had now disappeared, most notably the civil-religious cargo system. They also agree that wealth and social differentiation were significant factors in local-level politics and that market dependence (whether for wages or for the sale of commodities) was well developed everywhere. As for the level of peasant welfare, anthropologists document two contradictory trends: one of increasing poverty and one of increasing wealth.

Waldemar Smith's (1977) study of three communities in the western department of San Marcos describes both patterns. Smith found that differentiation *within* communities was not nearly so marked as differentiation *among* communities: one community he describes was almost totally impoverished, sending more than 80 percent of its adult male labor force to the plantations seasonally in order to make ends meet; another community was doing very well on the whole, relatively few of its people needing to seek plantation wages in order to maintain a satisfactory level of living. What distinguished these communities was not so much the amount or quality of land retained but, rather, access to commercial and artisanal occupational alternatives.

My 1968–70 work on the regional marketing system (1976, 1978) showed this division of Indian peasant communities to be general. Those Indian communities in the western highlands that were located near major urban centers of the region (especially in the departments of Totonicapan and Quezaltenango) had more diverse occupations, more access to capital, and better standards of living than communities located in the northwestern periphery of the region (especially San Marcos, Huehuetenango, and northern Quiche). Dependence on income from seasonal labor on plantations followed the same division: communities in the northwestern periphery exported upwards of 50 percent of their adult labor force to the plantations seasonally, whereas communities in the core of the regional marketing system exported less than 10 percent. Obviously, then, it is incorrect to describe as general a pattern of increasing impoverishment of peasant communities in this period, though one could point to increasing penetration of market relations into the fiber of indigenous society.

An apparent effect of the division of the region into poorer and richer communities was the slowing down of the process of internal differentiation within the communities. Thus, John Watanabe (1981) observes that the pattern of land distribution in Santiago Chimaltenango (a peripheral community), documented earlier by Wagley, was less uneven in the 1970s than in the 1930s, even though all indications at the time of Wagley's study (1941:81–83) pointed in the opposite direction. I have found the same to be true of Totonicapan (a core community), even though the research I carried out there in 1977–78 was motivated by the hypothesis that peasant differentiation in that community would be on the increase. What accounts for this anomaly?

One of the unanticipated effects of the plantation economy for peasants is that many of the poorer peasants either became completely proletarianized and remained in the plantation area, thus relieving population pressure on the peasant community, or they returned with enough savings to begin small businesses, take up trade, or otherwise find new outlets and sources of income for themselves. (See Wagley [1941:51, 78–79] for a description of this latter phenomenon even in the earlier period, when plantation wages were much lower.) Nearly half of the present petty commodity producers I interviewed in Totonicapan in 1977–78 had obtained part or all of their initial capital from plantation work or from trade in the plantation area. And the percentage of people who took up specialized (nonagricultural) occupations in Totonicapan had more than doubled in the period between 1945 and 1978. Thus, a fairly significant number of peasants in Guatemala found in the plantation economy the means by which they could hold onto a peasant way of life. Plantation work was never a preferred occupation anywhere. But the plantation economy, both directly and indirectly, helped many peasants retain their peasant holdings and invest in measures that made their lands produce more than twice as much as they did before.[23]

So far, the argument presented here does not contradict that of the global account, which suggests that peasant communities were better maintained by dependence on plantation labor than they would have been without the economic outlet. The global account, however, suggests that economic dependence on plantation labor should be on the increase and should be associated with both increasing internal differentiation of communities and increasing poverty of Indian communities in general. And here my data contradict the global view. In my 1977–78 survey of 131 communities (rural hamlets) in the western highlands of Guatemala,[24] I found that fewer and fewer people were able to make a living from subsistence farming, as one would expect. But the slack was not taken up by increased participation in plantation labor; it was taken up by increased participation in occupations outside of agriculture altogether.

Table 1 presents data on male primary occupations (most individuals had more than a single occupation) from my survey of 1,341 males in peripheral communities, 1,556 males in core communities, and 1,263 males from communities in the intermediate zone. My survey shows that only 32.5 percent of all males reported their major occupation to be in *any* form of agriculture—whether subsistence farming (13 percent), local wage-laòor in agriculture (11.4 percent), or in plantation wage-labor (8.1 percent). (Most male respondents, however, reported a secondary or tertiary occupation in agriculture.) Nearly 10 percent reported some plantation work in association with another primary occupation, and 8 percent claimed it as their primary occupation, which yields a total of 18 percent of males ever employed on plantations. These figures were much lower than I had expected from my earlier survey (1969–70),[25] in which 30 to 40 percent of adult males worked seasonally on plantations and more than 50 percent were also employed in local peasant agriculture.

TABLE 1. Primary Occupations of Indian Males in Rural Guatemala, Percentage Distribution by Type of Community

	Core Communities (1,341 individuals)		Peripheral Communities (1,556 individuals)		All Communities (4,160 individuals)	
Agriculture		18.5		37.9		32.5
Subsistence	9.4		10.7		13.0	
Local wage	7.8		13.0		11.4	
Plantation wage	1.3		14.2		8.1	
Commerce		20.7		14.1		16.8
Manufacture		53.8		35.6		41.1
Crafts	5.4		7.9		7.0	
Artisanry	25.1		15.7		18.8	
Crafts wage	0.7		0.9		0.9	
Artisanry wage	22.6		11.1		14.4	
Construction		5.6		12.3		8.9
Building	4.1		8.8		6.1	
Building wage	1.5		3.5		2.8	
Other		1.2		0.1		0.8
Services	0.5		0.1		0.5	
Government	0.7		—		0.3	

Note: This table is based on a stratified random sample from my 1977–78 survey of rural occupations in the western highlands of Guatemala, which covered a representative 131 rural hamlets. Procedures for obtaining this information are described in note 24. I do not give a breakdown of the 1,263 individuals from intermediate communities here.

The difference between the core and peripheral zones remained marked, with only 1.3 percent of the core males dedicated primarily to plantation work (less than 5 percent working on plantations at all during the year) and only 18.5 percent primarily engaged in any form of agriculture, while 14.2 percent of peripheral males made most of their income from plantation work (24 percent working on plantations at some point in the year), and nearly 38 percent were primarily engaged in some form of agriculture.

The more recent survey year, 1977–78, can be considered a "good" year for peasants. Reconstruction after the major 1976 earthquake provided more local employment than was normally available. But the difference between a good year and a bad one would, according to local estimates, affect only about 10 percent of the population. Both individuals and communities generally reported a much lower dependence on plantation income than was formerly the case. Communities that in the 1960s had exported upwards of 60 percent of their adult male population to work on plantations were now sending as few as 10 to 15 percent.

What were the new income sources for these peasants? They were derivative of the new kind of commercial distribution system in the peasant highlands, described earlier. This system emerged during the early years of independence, it expanded alongside the plantation economy in order to keep it supplied, and it boomed throughout the period under discussion here, fueled by modern transportation, urbanization, and the increased cash incomes of peasants and workers in the region. By the beginning of the free wage era in the mid-1940s, the new commercial distribution system had eroded all the Ladino commercial monopolies to the point that rural market centers rather than Ladino-controlled urban centers accounted for most of the commerce. The initial impetus for this development came from the plantation economy, but by the end of the period under discussion a fair amount of the peasant production was intended for urban as well as rural demand. The fastest-growing cottage industry was tailoring, the market for which was not only peasant Guatemala but also the working and middle classes of Guatemala City.

Because peasants had developed a variety of ways to cope with the increasing penetration of market relations into their communities, there can be no single characterization of their stratagems. One can argue, however, that certain expectations for this period were *not* realized: there was no general trend toward increasing dependence on plantation wages, no general impoverishment, relatively little internal class polarization, and much less destruction of indigenous community organization than would be expected from the usual accounts of the period. The closed corporate community no longer existed, but in any event it had expired much earlier. Yet, contrary to anthropological expectation, social relations within indigenous communities remained coherent—organized by the traditional values of formal courtesy, reciprocity, and respect for age, hard work, and properly accumulated wealth—even without the cargo system and the other institutional devices of the closed corporate community. Indians in both poorer and richer zones maintained a steadfast stance of preserving cultural if not economic or political autonomy, and the assimilation process that had produced the Ladino culture elsewhere made little progress in the highlands.[26]

Let me turn to two other developments in the region that furthered the economic and political independence of indigenous communities, but which also hid them from view. As noted in the previous section, Guatemala's regional elites, the urban-based Ladinos, held a peculiar political and economic position. On the one hand, they were important to the state in controlling the peasant areas and held virtually all state-granted political offices. On the other hand, they had no local-level political base by which they could gain state power and through which they could influence state policy. The plantation oligarchy, domiciled in Guatemala City, was virtually the only group guiding state policy. Holding political office in a peasant area was lucrative only insofar as it could provide an official with the means to maintain commercial monopolies or otherwise obtain income from peasants. But as the Ladinos' commercial monopolies, such as control of transportation, were gradually eroded by intense competition from rural Indian *commerciantes,* and as some wealthy peasants gained the education to enter traditional Ladino occupations (law, medicine, education), the economic position of the Ladinos began to deteriorate seriously. And urban Ladinos began migrating in large numbers to Guatemala City, the only place where alternative sources of income were available.[27]

Normally, one would expect successful or wealthy peasants simply to replace the urban Ladino group as their new life-styles diverged from that of a typical peasant. But because most peasants were Indians, and because the social and political gulf separating Indians and Ladinos remained constant, relatively few Indians became Ladinos or abandoned their native communities.[28] Thus, the number of people remaining in peasant areas upon whom the state could depend to help carry out its political objectives dwindled. Nor did members of the state bureaucracy recognize the significant transformations taking place among the Indians. When Indians began successfully to operate within the Ladino world, the national census, for example, simply counted them as Ladinos (Early 1974). Thus, it appeared to the bureaucracy that the ethnic majority was shrinking rather fast. But these "new Ladinos" were hardly the trustworthy political operatives that the old Ladinos had been. And they were too new—even in Guatemala, where "passing" was widely recognized and approved by the national power-holders—to be granted much political force. Thus, the system of political control in peasant areas gradually deteriorated without anyone recognizing the extent of the problem.

Guatemala City grew between 1950 and 1973 at an unprecedented rate, accounting for almost all of the urbanization responsible for moving Guatemala's population from 30 percent to 36.4 percent urban. Most other cities grew no faster than the rural population. The people who moved into the national capital were largely Ladino, many from smaller urban centers, mostly well educated and fairly young (Roberts 1973). Guatemala City also grew in number of industrial establishments, as the plantation oligarchy diversified its investments and as foreign investors (mainly from the United States) found Guatemala City a good source of cheap labor (Adams 1970). Plantation agriculture also diversified, with cotton, sugar, and cattle becoming significant exports. Coffee production remained strong, however, for the new exports were grown in different areas of the country. Some plantations attempted to mechanize, but relatively few actually succeeded. Thus, demand for labor throughout the 1950s and 1960s remained strong (Williams 1978), and the major source of labor continued to be the peasant communities of the western highlands.

Guatemala's national economy boomed throughout the 1960s and early 1970s, both in export agriculture and in urban industrialization (CSUCA 1978a). The local economies in the Indian highlands also grew and diversified but without any greater incorporation into the national economy than had been achieved at the beginning of the era. Few Indians migrated to urban centers, ethnic artisanal production was not replaced by world system imports, and imported capital goods (fertilizer, sewing machines, and the like) only furthered the self-sufficiency of indigenous communities vis-à-vis national capitalist development. Most important, a relatively smaller amount of labor was available from the highlands for agricultural or industrial expansion than ever before.[29]

Plantations responded to dwindling labor supplies from the highlands in two ways. First, they moved against their resident work force, the *colonos*, who had in the past been retained as a labor reserve by the plantations through grants of land for use in subsistence farming. Making these partially proletarianized workers fully proletarianized by taking away their subsistence plots released more labor for expanded coffee, cotton, and cattle production throughout most of the 1970s (Winson 1978). Plantations also sought labor in urban centers, a rather new development in Guatemala (CSUCA 1978b), and in addition came to rely on labor from El Salvador, where similar movements against *colonos* had already taken place (Durham 1979). These new sources of labor, however, made for a much more volatile political situation in Guatemala, as recent developments in the region attest.

A crisis point was reached by the late 1970s, as Guatemala's industrial expansion, based on the Central American Common Market, was cut short by war and revolution in other Central American republics and as growing labor unrest on Guatemalan plantations led to work stoppages and strikes. By 1978 peasant and capitalist interests were once again in direct conflict in Guatemala, and the result of that conflict is the full-scale war now being waged against peasants by the state. Recent events show more clearly than anything else that the preservation of the indigenous community in western Guatemala was not brought about by, nor was it in the interest of, capitalist development in the region. When the free wage era ended in 1978, Guatemala's economy was still dominated by a large peasantry whose labor potential was far from being fully tapped and whose intransigence as a labor force for Guatemalan development remained a continuing problem for capital. Force was still needed as an implement to draw these peasants into capitalist relations of production.

The Prerevolutionary Crisis (1978–81)

With news that more than one hundred Guatemalan Indian peasants had been massacred at Panzos in May 1978[30] and with the documentation by Amnesty International (1981) of the following three years of murderous repression undertaken by the government of Romeo Lucas Garcia, the world has become aware that another revolution is brewing in Central America. The global explanation for the new crisis in Guatemala presents the following picture:

Changing needs of the export sector indicate a falling relative, if not absolute, demand for seasonal labor. This is forcing growing numbers of the highland population permanently out of the village community. Faced with the extinction of their communities and the loss of means to sustain themselves, increasing numbers of Guatemalan peasants have achieved some measure of revolutionary consciousness.

My recent work on local-level processes in Guatemala leads me to a very different reading of the economic processes bringing about the present revolutionary situation. I argue that in recent years increasing numbers of peasants have been able to build up their local economies to the point that fewer and fewer of them have needed to seek work on plantations. Some have achieved greater economic independence by joining colonization projects. Some have used plantation earnings to develop their own farming systems to the point that wages are no longer needed to supplement farming. More have become traders and petty commodity producers, feeding not only other specialized peasants and plantation workers but workers in the growing urban centers as well. In any event, local developments within peasant communities have created a labor shortage on the plantations, and the recent actions of the state are at least in part a response to the resulting economic crisis.

Little information exists on the current political situation in western Guatemala because of the absence of reports from sociological investigators and the virtual blockade on regular news sources. Thus, I have had to base the following analysis of this early period in the Guatemalan revolution on a systematic review of the available news accounts,[31] limited information about how locals interpreted the political situation, and virtually no knowledge of how their interpretations may have changed since 1979. Yet I think it is important to record the unfolding of the present revolution before the myths inevitably created by the victors of such struggles become the accepted view of the matter. Because I have tried to understand how Guatemalans have made their own history, even if they have made it not exactly as they have pleased, I think I can make better sense of the present situation in Guatemala than many others. It is certainly clear that events there were only influenced, but not directed, by global forces.

In 1978–79 highland Indians listened spellbound to radio reports of the Nicaraguan revolution but remained convinced until the end that the revolutionary forces would lose.[32] Not only did the Guatemalan press make it appear that the Somoza regime would ultimately prevail, but Guatemalan Indians had had enough experience with insurgent movements, local rebellions, and even peaceful reforms (1944–54) in their own country to know that such efforts rarely succeed. Even after the Sandinista victory in July of 1979, Guatemalan Indians gave little thought to revolutionary change of their own situation. The only ones interested in the possibility of a Nicaraguan-style revolution were the offspring of the most successful people in the richer communities, Indian children now attending secondary school in significant numbers for the first time in Guatemalan history.[33] Even these radical students, however, were more interested in their personal futures as teachers or other petty professionals than they were in guerrilla movements. It took a full-scale declaration of war against peasants, unions, teachers, students, journalists, and political opposition by the Lucas García regime to change Indian consciousness on armed warfare. Indian awareness of the source and nature of their oppression had always existed. But the struggles they undertook before—and these were real struggles—mostly took a nonviolent form, of the kind described above.

No one who has followed events in Guatemala since the Panzos massacre questions that the state is waging a war against its peasants and agrarian workers. There has been a clear pattern of repression directed against potential popular leadership in rural areas,[34] utilizing government forces in a countrywide reign of terror. The object has been to intimidate the entire Guatemalan population, especially the Indians, through the use of torture and brutal attacks on defenseless communities. Children, women, and elderly men have been targeted as often as potential recruits for guerrilla groups. People *are* frightened, but many have now begun to resist.

It is difficult to know exactly what the Lucas García regime had in mind—how it selected the areas in which it terrorized peasant villages, or what it hoped to gain from bloody and ruthless attacks whose effect was to mobilize peasant resistance far more successfully than could any leaflets distributed by leftists. After the state's military moves against the Indians, guerrilla groups (especially the Poor Peoples' Guerrilla Army [EGP] and the Organization of People in Arms [ORPA])[35] recruited more Indian peasants than they ever had earlier, finding support and protection in Indian areas that had formerly reported guerrilla activities to the authorities. Few Indians now volunteered for service in the Guatemalan military; in reaction, military recruitment began to concentrate on Ladino communities in the east rather than Indian communities in the west. Most Guatemalan civilians and even some members of the military forces became convinced that the repression created more resistance than it destroyed. The pattern of repression, however, suggests that the particular course chosen by Guatemalan's military regime was governed by certain considerations, as outlined below.[36]

Repressive moves against the peasants of western Guatemala began in 1975 in the northern transversal area, or "zone of the generals," so named because most of the land in the region had been recently claimed by people of high military rank—including Guatemalan presidents. Considerable development potential was thought to lie in the area, which promised both mineral and petroleum wealth. But in order for that wealth to be claimed and exploited, three changes were necessary. The land had to come under the control of people willing to promote capitalist development; the Indians, who had farmed that land for centuries, had to be removed from it; and more labor had to be released from Indian communities in order to help exploit the potential resources. In 1978 the Panzos massacre occurred as a result of these peasants' resistance to expropriation. This opened the period of outright war in the region.

When Guatemala's political leaders made their move against the peasants in the northern transversal, they must also have been aware that even more had to be done to increase the potential labor supply for capitalist development everywhere. Labor was needed on the plantations, in the cities, and in the transversal, where a major road and other infrastructure for exploiting the area had long been planned but never built because of the labor shortage.[37] Guatemala's political leaders already had a model of how to meet their various goals from what they had accomplished in eastern Guatemala in the recent past. Between 1965 and 1966 government troops had brought a similar reign of terror to eastern Guatemala, ostensibly to eliminate a few hundred guerrillas active at that time. They not only destroyed more than twenty thousand peasant lives and all active political resistance in that region but also helped eradicate the base of much peasant livelihood there.[38] Ever since the late 1960s eastern Guatemala has been an unending source of proletarianized labor—for the cities, for plantations, and for the army. Indian communities in that part of Guatemala have nearly vanished. It must have seemed plausible to Guatemala's political and military leaders in 1978 (allegedly still directed by Carlos Arana Osorio, who masterminded the CIA-assisted military campaign in eastern Guatemala) that the same methods would bring about the same effects in western Guatemala, where there was both more potential labor and more potential use for it.

Beginning with the rule of Rufino Barrios, who took office in 1871, political regimes in Guatemala have done the bidding of those wishing to promote the capitalist development of the country. The reform government of 1944–54 was no exception, different only in trying novel means to the same end. Many stratagems have been used over the years to try to incorporate peasant (especially Indian) communities within these development plans. Among the less violent were the encouragement of foreign missionary work and tourism in the Indian areas, the promotion of colonization projects that promised to make yeoman farmers out of Indians, and the various self-help and cooperative projects of aid programs directed by the United States. It must have seemed to the government in 1978 that many of these programs had backfired, locking peasant labor into community projects and encouraging peasant political ambitions at a time when peasant labor was needed for grander schemes and when peasant political leadership could only mobilize resistance. In any event, the areas where these projects had been most successful were the ones pinpointed for assault by the regime-directed death squads.

From published accounts I have tried to analyze the distribution of communities against which the government's attacks have been most persistent and brutal.[39] My survey shows that they are not located where guerrilla activities have been most successful, the southern plantation area, or guerrilla supporters most numerous, the urban centers. Instead, they have been those communities where Indian political organization has been most fully developed (Chimaltenango, Solalá); where self-help projects sponsored by missions have been most successful and peasant cooperative organizations most numerous (northern Huehuetenango, Quiche, Solalá, Chimaltenango); where colonization projects have taken root (the Ixcan, Petén, and Panzos areas); where considerable tourism-based development has taken place (Solalá, southern Quiche, and Sacatepequez); and areas of potential capitalist expansion now occupied by peasants (the transversal area of northern Quiche, northern Huehuetenango). Guerrilla groups, to be sure, now gain considerable support and some recruits from these areas, but support has come from these areas mainly as peasants have reacted to attacks on their communities, rather than because peasant revolutionary consciousness was already strong there.

This particular pattern of attack suggests to me that the Guatemalan government has been blind to the basic source of peasant resistance to the needs of Guatemalan capitalism—the internal economic growth of the peasant economy—and has assumed, like most social scientists who have worked in the region, that only where outside help and influence have been strong (through missions, tourism, cooperative projects sponsored by the Agency for International Development [AID], and the like) will peasants find the means to resist the full proletarianization always sought by Guatemalan capitalists. (Indians in the more commercialized and politically autonomous areas of Quezaltenango and Totonicapan, regions where Indian peasant resistance to the state has historically been strongest, have been relatively immune from government attack, yet these are the very areas of greatest peasant economic autonomy.) But though misguided about the underlying bases by which Guatemala's peasants have resisted the goals of Guatemala's capitalists, the military actions undertaken by the current government may nonetheless undermine these bases through its wanton destruction of peasant life. At the same time, however, the savagery of the present attack on peasants may lead to an ultimate defeat for Guatemalan capitalism. The government now encounters resistance to its program of repression and murder everywhere, and many Guatemalans, rich and poor alike, are now willing to risk everything to attempt the overthrow not only of the present regime but also of capitalism.[40]

I close this account of the latest and most savage period in Guatemalan history not knowing how it will end or who will ultimately prevail. Whatever the outcome, however, no one group will have willed it. I have emphasized the role of the Guatemalan government during the early period of violence because its leaders began and directed the concerted attack against what they perceived to be the bases of peasant resistance. I also recognize the fact that those in power have been aided and directed in their aims by global capitalist interests in Guatemalan resources. But pursuit of these interests has not produced the intended consequences. Even if the present Guatemalan government ultimately wins the present struggle, which is by no means assured, they will have produced enormous losses for international and Guatemalan capital, will have destroyed rather than released much of Guatemala's potential labor force, and will not necessarily have eliminated the basic sources of peasant resistance. Surely this was not the desired end.

At the same time, I do not think it reasonable to assert that Guatemala's peasants, if victorious, will achieve their intended objectives either. While peasant resistance to the state and to capitalism lies at the heart of the present struggle and goes much deeper than reaction to the recent political attack on them, that resistance was not initially directed toward the overthrow of the state or the elimination of capitalism in Guatemala, aims embraced by the political groups siding with the peasants. If peasants are victorious in their present struggle, they will be caught up in a new struggle that will as surely threaten their goals of cultural autonomy and economic independence as the present political economy in Guatemala. I assume, however, that a new regime will have to accommodate itself to elements of peasant resistance, as have all previous regimes.

Conclusions

In this essay I have tried to suggest ways in which the expansion of capitalism within a particular peripheral region was strongly influenced by local response and cultural resistance. Given the slow, incomplete, and peculiar development of capitalism in Guatemala, I argue that it is difficult to sustain the position that Guatemala turned out the way it did because global capitalism needed that particular pattern of development. To understand any particular local system, such as that in Guatemala, one must look instead at the interaction of global and local forces. Indeed, the dialectic of global and local forces must be considered to understand the nature and progress of world capitalism itself.

Today most anthropologists recognize that global forces help shape the environments in which local systems operate, and they actively seek information to document that process. But rarely do they look at the way in which local systems affect the regional structures, economic and political, on which global forces play, which prevents them from describing the way in which global forces have adapted to local conditions. Thus, anthropological versions of social history remain far too parochial. The work of other social scientists, who are even more likely to view local systems as the passive recipients of global process, has not been of great help in this regard. They have given us, essentially, only two models of the modern world. The older of these, whether in the guise of modernization theory or in the guise of classic Marxist thought, is that of capitalist diffusion. In this model capitalism is seen as expanding on a world scale, inexorably developing new markets, inevitably proletarianizing the masses, and constantly homogenizing culturally and making dependent economically the working classes. The process may be slow, but it is thought to be continuous. Local events are read through the lens of this model, by many anthropologists as well as others. Dependency or world system theorists, recognizing that the global expansion of capitalism has not been so constant or inexorable, have provided a revised view of the modern world, the second model.[41] This model acknowledges that there have been highly resistant pockets of noncapitalist producers, that there has been continuous segmentation of the working classes and even of the bourgeoisie, and that there have been successful, but "premature," revolutions in peasant social formations, led by neither the bourgeoisie nor the proletariat. In this model the anomalies with respect to capitalist development have been explained as being "functionally" necessary to the capitalism of the time. A preserved peasantry and segmented labor markets keep the costs of capitalist production low, premature revolutions change the status of places within the world system zones in order that accumulation can continue, and struggles among factions of national bourgeoisies allow greater penetration by world-scale capitalism. Local events are also read through this model, even by anthropologists.

The two global models are highly economistic, tending to view the international expansion of capitalism as a purely economic phenomenon. Although many anthropologists reject such economistic models, they do so not in order to reinterpret the pattern of development in the modern world; they simply eschew any attempt to deal with the relations between economy, social relations, and culture, dealing instead with culture as a process sui generis. I want to plead for a different approach. It seems to me that one way we can account for the distorted, uneven, and unanticipated events resulting from the global expansion of capitalism is to view capitalism as a social and cultural phenomenon as much as an economic one, as a process that can be and is affected by class struggle and human agency all along. And to understand the nature of social classes, not to mention the aims or objectives of social groups, we need to take social relations and cultural phenomena into account. Classes form and struggle long before the ultimate polarization takes place between wage labor and capital, and in their formations and struggle they affect whether and how capitalism is instituted in their social formations. In the approach I advocate, then, we cannot assume a universal logic to the unfolding of capitalism; instead, we must examine the social processes that produce a varied rather than a single response.

NOTES

This study was prepared for the meeting of the American Anthropological Association held in Los Angeles in December 1981. The last section, on the current revolution in Guatemala, reflects the situation at that time; no attempt has been made to bring it up to date. I would like to thank the following people for helpful comments on the first draft of this article: Richard Adams, Jeffrey Boyer, Shelton Davis, Les Field, David McCreery, Sidney Mintz, Joseph Pansini, Benjamin Paul, Edelberto Torres Rivas, Katherine Verdery, John Watanabe, Robert Williams, and Margery Wolf. I would also like to acknowledge the help I received from Ronald W. Smith and from several Guatemalan research assistants, who must remain anonymous for obvious reasons; they assisted in the fieldwork on which part of my analysis is based. Alice Saltzman, Ruth Nix, Robert Jackson, and David Jackson helped with later data analysis. The National Science Foundation supported the fieldwork through grant no. BNS 77-08179 and also provided partial support during the write-up period. The Center for Advanced Study in the Behavioral Sciences, Stanford, California, provided the facilities and additional support for the preparation of these materials.

1. Both Waldemar Smith (1977) and Robert Wasserstrom (1975, 1976, 1978) have made some useful points about the external forces affecting peasant communities in Mesoamerica. My critique is not directed at them in particular but at a whole school of thought that has been of increasing influence in anthropology.

2. I should note in this context that social historians have also faced this interpretive problem but have solved it differently. At least the "new social historians," of which the most widely known is E. P. Thompson (1966), are now trying to develop historical interpretations that credit the masses with considerable influence on the course of human events—whether or not their struggles erupt so visibly that no one could mistake them. I acknowledge the influence of these historians on my attempt to provide a social history of Guatemala.

3. It has been pointed out that I am guilty in this study of assuming a single, uncontradictory logic to capitalism. Since this is the position taken by the scholars I am trying to critique, I do not attempt to correct for this. To deal with all the contradictory elements within Guatemalan capitalism would take me far beyond the bounds of this article—indeed, it would call for several volumes. The primary task here is to introduce Guatemalan peasants as active agents of the historical development of Guatemala.

4. See, however, Adams 1970. Adams must be credited for trying to look at larger systems, regional and national, long before it became fashionable in anthropology. His analysis of Guatemalan politics has become an anthropological

classic of macro-level studies. Yet, like most social scientists who look at the larger picture, Adams tends to interpret much of Guatemalan history as if it were determined almost entirely by struggles among elites. In Adams's account the Guatemalan peasant, especially the Indian peasant, is merely a long-lived anachronism.

5. My global account can be ascribed to no particular individual, but elements of it can be found in the summaries of Guatemalan history by Adams 1970; Jonas 1974; W. Smith 1977; Stavenhagen 1969; Torres Rivas 1971; Winson 1978; and Woodward 1976.

6. This law of global development is clearly stated by Immanuel Wallerstein (1974), though many others have discussed it.

7. Land, of course, is always an issue to peasants, and considerable litigation clogged the colonial courts in Guatemala. But most of the land disputes in this period were between rival Indian *municipios* (or *parcialidades*), and those who lost these battles did not become landless but had to go much farther afield for water, firewood, or pasturage. Landlessness became a serious problem only in the latter part of the nineteenth century (see, e.g., Davis 1970). Because of the absence of mining in Guatemala, the classic land-hungry hacienda never developed there.

8. In the Quiche-Cakchiquel area of western Guatemala, the *parcialidad* was known as *chinamital,* while in the Mam area it was known as *molab*. Both groups were simultaneously neighborhoods and kinship units. Hill's work (1981) on the *chinamital* in Sacapulas shows that Spanish authorities occasionally recognized the *parcialidad* landholding tradition but preferred to impose their own categories of social organization and landholding through the municipal organization, their own creation.

9. Veblen worked primarily in Totonicapan, but he discussed *parcialidad* landholding in neighboring *municipios* as well. Stuart Stearns (personal communication) found that the *parcialidad* in Totonicapan had a variety of social functions. Stimulated by Stearns (and indirectly by Robert Carmack), I pursued this line and found that most hamlets in Totonicapan were identified with a particular *parcialidad* and that the hamlet, rather than the *municipio,* was the significant endogamous unit.

10. The smaller *municipios* in Guatemala were less likely to retain several functioning *parcialidades* in them than were the larger *municipios*. Since most anthropologists have preferred to work in the smaller *municipios,* it is understandable that the importance of the *parcialidad* might be overlooked.

11. A rash of serious peasant rebellions accompanied independence, many of them in western Guatemala (see Contreras 1951; Carmack 1979; and Falla 1971). Some rebellions were occasioned by the Bourbon reforms undertaken by the last colonial governors; others were brought on by programs attempted by the early Liberal government. The pattern of uprisings suggests that, whenever the state attempted a *general* reform program and tried to implement it through state officials, peasants were likely to rebel, regardless of the details of the particular reform. But when the state allowed municipal authorities to interpret and carry out the reform in accordance with established practice, rebellion was much less likely—even if the reform was damaging to many peasants.

12. Many nineteenth-century travelers describe aspects of Guatemalan society and most describe considerable commercial activity among Indians (see Baily 1850; Boddam Whetham 1877; Dunlop 1847; Dunn 1828; Morelet 1871; Tempsky 1858; and Thompson 1829). Unfortunately, however, none of these accounts is systematic enough to establish if or how peasant commercial activity was restricted.

13. It is clear, however, that during the colonial period marketplaces were allowed only in urban centers where they could be taxed and controlled by the colonial authorities. It is also clear that by the beginning of the twentieth century there were many rural marketplaces throughout the western highlands that were not subject to state or Ladino control. I have been unable to establish, however, whether the transformation occurred during the Conservative interlude (before the plantation economy) or with the Barrios reforms (as part of the whole effort by the Liberals to establish a freely functioning economy).

14. Population increase was pronounced throughout the nineteenth century. The other developments I mention may have taken place only with the Barrios reforms and the plantation economy. But population dispersion was well under way by 1880, when Guatemala undertook its first national census (never completed because of peasant resistance in the western highlands). Ladinos were also well established in many Indian communities by 1880. This leads me to surmise that these processes were begun much earlier than 1871.

15. Shelton Davis (1970) describes the process of land titling in northwestern Huehuetenango in the latter decades of the nineteenth century. He shows that, while most Indians gained access to some land in this period, the distribution of titled land was extremely uneven, and many people never gained clear legal title. Thus, the Barrios reforms were to have bitter, even tragic, consequences for many Indians. Yet we should not overlook the fact that most peasant victims did what they could to minimize the damage and that the lands of most peasants were not fully expropriated.

16. C. F. S. Cardoso (1975) contrasts the development of coffee export production in Guatemala, El Salvador, and Costa Rica. He shows that the three export systems differed from one another in important ways because of significant differences in the class structures of the three republics; he also shows that the consequences of coffee export production for class structures were necessarily different in each case. See also Torres Rivas 1971.

17. Alistair White (1973) observes that the ethnic traditions of El Salvador's Indians (as numerous, proportionately, as Guatemala's Indians) disappeared with their land base. Cardoso (1975) suggests that the political histories of Guatemala and El Salvador differed primarily because El Salvador successfully proletarianized its peasants, whereas Guatemala did not.

18. Joseph Pansini (1977) must be credited for making the distinction between the national Ladino class, or Guatemaltecos, who own plantations and major industrial enterprises in Guatemala City, and urban Ladinos, who live in provincial towns and hold bureaucratic offices, engage in professional occupations, or run local commercial establishments.

19. The position of regional elites in eastern Guatemala was slightly different

from the usual pattern (see Adams 1970:217–37), conforming more closely to the position of elites in the other Central American republics. But their potential power in dealings with the state was small because of their relative poverty.

20. Richard N. Adams (1970) describes the same centralization of power that I do, but he proffers a different explanation for it. Whereas I argue that regional elites in Guatemala never had a local-level power base from which they could gain access to, and influence over, national-level politics, Adams argues that local and regional elites never realized their potential power because they never exercised it collectively.

21. I have described some of the causes and consequences of the different urban patterns in Central America in greater detail elsewhere (Smith 1980). The urban systems in all five republics are immature even today, and urban primacy seems to be developing in most of them. But only in Guatemala is there such extreme disparity between the national capital and provincial towns, reflecting and exacerbating the class polarization in Guatemala.

22. Some people accord the 1944 revolution much greater significance than I do. Robert Williams (1978), for example, suggests that the struggle taking place in that period was between the old-fashioned coffee bourgeoisie and a potential industrialist class. Williams goes on to argue that the reforms enacted by the revolutionary government allowed much greater industrial development to take place than would otherwise have been the case. Adams (1970), however, shows that most supporters of the 1944 revolution were professionals, small storekeepers, or potential bureaucrats rather than potential industrialists; he also shows that considerable industrial investment was made by the traditional coffee oligarchy.

23. Watanabe (1981), for example, shows that, while individual peasant holdings in Santiago Chimaltenango have dwindled to approximately one-third of what they were in the 1920s (mainly because of population increase), these lands produce at least three times as much as they did in the 1930s because of fertilizer and alternative crop mixes.

24. Because my earlier Guatemalan fieldwork had indicated that there were twelve regional subsystems within western Guatemala, each having a distinctive pattern of occupation and market dependence (see Smith 1976), I designed the present survey so as to include three municipalities from each subsystem. The particular municipalities were selected so as to cover places in which other anthropologists had worked and so as to cover a certain amount of municipal variation (in size, language, accessibility, and so forth). For each municipality I selected randomly three or four hamlets. Within each hamlet I did a full household survey for primary occupation of household heads; from the occupational survey I then randomly selected between 20 and 35 percent of all households for further questioning. Guatemalan assistants (all Indians, most of them multilingual) carried out the household interviews; table 1 is based on information from these interviews.

25. The earlier survey was done on a municipal basis rather than a household basis. I questioned municipal authorities (almost always Indian officials) in 152 *municipios* as to the general occupations within the *municipio* and as to the number of households dependent on seasonal plantation work. This survey is likely to be much less accurate than my later one (see n. 24).

26. Most anthropologists working in Guatemala before 1970 had predicted that extreme wealth or poverty would lead individual Indians to leave their communities and to take on the cultural attributes of Ladinos. In recent years, however, it has become clear that the process of becoming a Ladino is more complex than had been thought. Most wealthy Indians stay on in their communities (as do many very poor Indians) and though they take on some "cultural" aspects of Ladinos, most of which simply reflect greater wealth, they continue to identify themselves as Indians. The people most likely to become Ladinos are young men who marry outside of their community and never return. These individuals are rather few in the western highlands. Thus, the trend toward increasing Ladinoization in Guatemala documented since the turn of the century reflects census definitions of ethnicity more than the actual rate of change in people's self-identification (see W. Smith 1977; Early 1974; Dow 1981).

27. See Adams (1970, 124–37) on the migration pattern in Guatemala during the 1960s. Adams observes that most migrants to Guatemala City are Ladinos from provincial centers, but he does not attempt to explain why this is so. My guess is that the commercial and administrative incomes of these Ladinos have been declining because of increased competition from newly prosperous and educated Indians.

28. See W. Smith (1977); Dow (1981); and Pansini (1977), on the retention by successful Indians of their ethnic identity.

29. Many Guatemalan scholars would dispute this point, given their agrarian bias in understanding peasant livelihood. Assuming that peasants farm, for someone else if not themselves, these scholars believe that dwindling peasant land (*minifundia*) translates into excess supplies of labor for plantations (*latifundia*). Since my data come from the peasant rather than the plantation side of Guatemala's economy, I cannot be sure of my interpretation. But Joseph Pansini, one of the few scholars to know something about Guatemala's plantations in recent years on a regional scale, finds evidence from the plantation side to support my interpretation (personal communication).

30. For a detailed report on the Panzos massacre that includes several perspectives on the events leading up to it, see IWGIA (1978).

31. For news on Guatemala since 1978, I have relied primarily on two periodicals, *News from Guatemala* (Toronto) and *Guatemala!* (Berkeley, Calif.). Both periodicals reprint articles from a variety of sources, including Guatemalan newspapers.

32. I was doing fieldwork in the highlands at the time, and this report is of my own observations.

33. Various scholars have remarked on the increased number of Indians attending secondary and higher-level schools, among them W. Smith (1977), William Demarest and Benjamin Paul (1981), and Leslie Dow (1981).

34. The pattern whereby rural leaders or potential leaders are selected for attack was pointed out in the Amnesty International report: "the targets for extreme governmental violence tend to be selected from grassroots organizations outside official control" (1981:6).

35. At present there are three major guerrilla organizations operating in Guatemala. The oldest of these is the Rebel Armed Forces (FAR), the organization

active in eastern Guatemala during the 1960s and composed largely of middle-class students and longtime leftists. ORPA was founded in 1975, as a FAR splinter group, and operates mainly in the western highlands among Indians. The EGP was founded in an Indian *municipio* in 1973 and includes many peasants and Indians. All of these organizations have grown considerably since 1978. A recent article in *Time* (January 15, 1982) suggests that more than three thousand people are actively engaged in guerrilla warfare against the government and another thirty thousand people are providing economic and other support to the guerrilla groups.

36. There is no documentation concerning the present goals of the military regime in Guatemala, and the following analysis is based only on my own reading of events. For a similar view, however, see the report of Frederico Gil, Enrique Baloyra, and Lars Schoultz (1981).

37. For background information on the transversal development program, see *Cultural Survival* 5, no. 3: (1981): 15–16.

38. For documentation on the government program of repression and its consequences in eastern Guatemala, see Jonas (1974) and Diener (1978).

39. The analysis is based on department figures on casualties assumed related to the present civil war, as reported in *News from Guatemala* (September 1979 through December 1981).

40. According to both *Time* (January 15, 1982) and *News from Guatemala*, the level of Indian participation in guerrilla resistance is at an all-time high.

41. This literature needs little introduction today, but, for the dependency approach, see Andre Gunder Frank (1966), and, for the world system viewpoint, see Immanuel Wallerstein (1974).

REFERENCES

Adams, Richard N. 1957. "Political Change in Guatemalan Indian Communities." In *Community, Culture, and National Change,* ed. R. N. Adams, 1–54. New Orleans: Middle American Research Institute at Tulane University, Pub. no. 24.
———. 1970. *Crucifixion by Power: Essays on Guatemalan National Social Structure, 1944–1966.* Austin: University of Texas Press.
Amnesty International. 1981. *Guatemala: A Government Program of Political Murder.* London: Amnesty International Reports.
Baily, John. 1850. *Central America: Describing Each of the States of Guatemala, Honduras, Salvador, Nicaragua, and Costa Rica....* London: Trelawney Saunders.
Boddam Whetham, J. W. 1877. *Across Central America.* London: Hurst and Blackett.
Bunzel, Ruth. 1952. *Chichicastenango: A Guatemalan Village.* Seattle: University of Washington Press.
Cardoso, C. F. S. 1975. "Historia Economica del Café en Centroamérica." *Estudios Sociales Centroamericanos* (San José, Costa Rica) 4, no. 10: 9–55.

Carmack, Robert. 1979. *Historia Social de los Quiches.* Seminario de Integración Social Guatemalteca, Pub. no. 38. Guatemala City.

———. 1981. *The Quiche Mayas of Utatlan.* Norman: University of Oklahoma Press.

Clammer, John. 1975. "Economic Anthropology and the Sociology of Development: 'Liberal' Anthropology and Its French Critics." In *Beyond the Sociology of Development,* ed. I. Oxaal, T. Barnett, and D. Booth, 208–28. London: Routledge and Paul.

Collier, George. 1975. *Fields of the Tzotzil: The Ecological Bases of Tradition in Highland Chiapas.* Austin: University of Texas Press.

Consejo Superior Universitario Centroamericano (CSUCA). 1978a. *Estructura Agraria, Dinámica de Población y Desarrollo Capitalista en Centroamerica.* San José, Costa Rica: Editorial Universitaria Centroamericana.

Contreras, J. Daniel. 1951. *Una Rebelión Indígena en el Partido de Totonicapan en 1820.* Guatemala City: Imprenta Universitaria.

———. 1978b. *Estructura Demografica y Migraciones Internas en Centroamerica.* San José, Costa Rica: Editorial Universitaria Centroamericana.

Davis, Shelton. 1970. "Lands of Our Ancestors." Ph.D. diss., Harvard University.

Demarest, William, and Benjamin D. Paul. 1981. "Mayan Migrants in Guatemala City." *Anthropology UCLA* 11:43–73.

Diener, Paul. 1978. "The Tears of St. Anthony: Ritual and Revolution in Eastern Guatemala." *Latin American Perspectives* 5, no. 2: 92–116.

Dow, Leslie. 1981. "Ethnicity and Modernity in the Central Highlands of Guatemala." Ph.D. diss., University of Michigan.

Dunlop, R. G. 1847. *Travels in Central America.* London: Longman, Brown, Green, and Longman.

Dunn, Henry. 1828. *Guatimala [sic], or the United Provinces of Central America in 1827–1828.* New York: G and C. Carvill.

Durham, William. 1979. *Scarcity and Survival in Central America.* Stanford: Stanford University Press.

Early, John D. 1974. "Revision of Ladino and Maya Census Populations of Guatemala, 1950 and 1964." *Demography* 11, no. 1: 105–17.

Ebel, Robert Ewald. 1957. "Political Modernization in Three Guatemalan Indian Communities." In *Community, Culture, and National Change,* ed. R. N. Adams, 82–152. New Orleans: Middle American Research Institute at Tulane University, pub. no. 24.

Falla, Ricardo. 1971. "Actitud de los Indígenas de Guatemala en la Epoca de la Independencia, 1800–1850." *Estudios Sociales Centroamericanos* 2, no. 4: 701–18.

Frank, Andre Gunder. 1966. *Capitalism and Underdevelopment in Latin America.* New York: Monthly Review Press.

Gil, Frederico G., Enrique A. Baloyra, and Lars Schoultz. 1981. "The Deterioration and Breakdown of Reactionary Despotism in Central America." Report prepared for the United States Department of State. MS.

Hill, Robert M. 1981. "Continuity of Highland Maya Principles of Social Organization: The *Chinamitales* of Sacapulas." MS.

Ingersoll, Hazel. 1972. "The War of the Mountain: A Study of Reactionary Peasant Insurgency in Guatemala, 1837–1873." Ph.D. diss., University of Maryland.

International Work Group for Indigenous Affairs (IWGIA). 1978. *The Massacre at Panzos.* IWGIA Doc. no. 33. Copenhagen.

Jonas, Suzanne. 1974. "Guatemala: Land of Eternal Struggle." In *Latin America: The Struggle with Dependency and Beyond.* ed. R. Chilcote and J. Edelstein. New York: John Wiley and Sons.

Jones, Chester L. 1940. *Guatemala, Past and Present.* Minneapolis: University of Minnesota Press.

McBryde, Felix W. 1947. *Cultural and Historical Geography of Southwest Guatemala.* Smithsonian Institution, Institute of Social Anthropology Pub. no. 4. Washington, D.C.

McCreery, David. 1976. "Coffee and Class: The Structure of Development in Liberal Guatemala." *Hispanic American Historical Review* 56, no. 3: 438–60.

MacLeod, Murdo J. 1973. *Spanish Central America: A Socioeconomic History, 1520–1720.* Berkeley: University of California Press.

Miceli, Keith. 1974. "Rafael Carrera: Defender and Promoter of Peasant Interests in Guatemala, 1837–1848." *The Americas* 31, no. 1: 72–95.

Morelet, Arthur. 1871. *Travels in Central America....* trans. M. F. Squier. New York: Leopold, Holt, and Williams.

Pansini, Joseph J. 1977. "'El Pilar,' a Plantation Microcosm of Guatemalan Ethnicity." Ph.D. diss., University of Rochester.

Roberts, Bryan. 1973. *Organizing Strangers: Poor Families in Guatemala City.* Austin: University of Texas Press.

Schmid, Lester. 1967. "The Role of Migratory Labor in the Economic Development of Guatemala." Ph.D. diss., University of Wisconsin.

Smith, Carol A. 1976. "Causes and Consequences of Central-place Types in Western Guatemala." In *Economic Systems,* vol. 1 of *Regional Analysis,* ed. Carol A. Smith. New York: Academic Press.

———. 1978. "Beyond Dependency Theory: National and Regional Patterns of Underdevelopment in Guatemala." *American Ethnologist* 5, no. 2: 574–617.

———. 1980. "On Urban Primacy, Export Dependency, and Class Struggle in Peripheral Regions of World Capitalism." MS.

Smith, Waldemar. 1977. *The Fiesta System and Economic Change.* New York: Columbia University Press.

Stadelman, Raymond. 1940. *Maize Cultivation in Northwestern Guatemala.* Carnegie Institution Pub. no. 523. Washington, D.C.

Stavenhagen, Rodolfo. 1969. *Social Classes in Agrarian Societies.* Garden City, N.Y.: Doubleday.

Tax, Sol. 1953. *Penny Capitalism: A Guatemalan Indian Economy.* Smithsonian Institution, Institute of Social Anthropology Pub. no. 16. Washington, D.C.

Tempsky, Gustav F. 1858. *Mitla, a Narrative of Incidents and Personal Adventure....* London: Longman, Brown, Green, and Longman.

Thompson, Edward P. 1966. *The Making of the English Working Class.* New York: Random House, Vintage Publications.

Thompson, George A. 1829. *Narrative of an Official Visit to Guatemala from Mexico*. London: John Murray.

Torres Rivas, Edelberto. 1971. *Interpretación del Desarrollo Social Centroamericano*. San José, Costa Rica: Editorial Universitaria Centroamericana.

Veblen, Thomas. 1975. The Ecological, Cultural, and Historical Bases of Forest Preservation in Totonicapan, Guatemala. Ph.D. diss., University of California, Berkeley.

Wagley, Charles. 1941. *The Economics of a Guatemalan Village*. Menasha, Wis.: American Anthropological Association.

Wallerstein, Immanuel. 1974. *The Modern World-System: Capitalist Agriculture and the Origins of the European World-Economy in the Sixteenth Century*. New York: Academic Press.

Wasserstrom, Robert. 1975. "Revolution in Guatemala: Peasants and Politics under the Arbenz Government." *Comparative Studies in Society and History* 17, no. 4: 433–78.

―――. 1976. "White Fathers, Red Souls: Ethnic Relations in Central Chiapas, 1528–1975." Ph.D. diss., Harvard University.

―――. 1978. "Population Growth and Economic Development in Chiapas, 1524–1975." *Human Ecology* 6, no. 2: 127–43.

Watanabe, John. 1981. "Cambios Economicos en Santiago Chimaltenango, Guatemala." *Mesoamerica* 2, no. 1: 20–41.

White, Alistair. 1973. *El Salvador*. New York: Praeger.

Williams, Robert. 1978. "The Central American Common Market: Unequal Benefits and Uneven Development." Ph.D. diss., Stanford University.

Winson, Anthony. 1978. "Class Structure and Agrarian Transition in Central America." *Latin American Perspectives* 5, no. 4: 27–48.

Wolf, Eric. 1957. "Closed, Corporate Peasant Communities in Mesoamerica and Central Java." *Southwestern Journal of Anthropology* 13, no. 1: 1–18.

Woodward, Ralph L. 1971. "Social Revolution in Guatemala: The Carrera Revolt." In *Applied Enlightenment: Nineteenth-Century Liberalism*. Middle America Research Pub. no. 23. New Orleans: Tulane University.

―――. 1976. *Central America: A Nation Divided*. New York: Oxford University Press.

Peasants into Rebels: Community and Class in Rural El Salvador

A. Douglas Kincaid

Peasant Communities, Rebellion, and Social Revolution

The venerable conservative credentials of "community" have been challenged vigorously and often in recent years. Perhaps nowhere has its conceptual renovation gone further than in studies of peasants and social change. Where once the solidarity of peasant communities was analyzed as an impediment to economic development and societal modernization, a growing body of work now portrays such solidarity as the basis of revolutionary upheaval from eighteenth-century France to contemporary Vietnam.

Despite differences among theorists corresponding to their disciplinary idioms and empirical referents, a general model of community-based peasant rebellion can be fairly simply stated. The traditional bonds of kinship, culture, and communal economy provide at once a shared identity and definition of outsiders. In the event of external pressure, such as attempts to expropriate peasant lands, mobilize peasant labor, or integrate the community into wider market or political systems, community solidarity can provide the organization, leadership, and objectives around which resistance will be mounted. Under certain conditions—generally involving widespread community rebellions, a weakened ruling elite and/or state apparatus, and an opportunistic social group ready to take over state control—the consequence may be a social revolution.[1]

While the term *peasant community* tends to invoke a fixed image based on well-known social scientific dichotomies,[2] it should be noted that the above argument treats community solidarity as itself a variable. Peasant communities may be more or less solidary as a result of being more or less internally stratified, cooperatively organized, or autonomous with respect to landlords and the state.[3] The argument thus is a tendency rather than an absolute: the stronger the community solidarity, the higher the potential for rebellion. At the societal level, however, peasants are not seen as capable of effecting revolutionary change by themselves, and, in the event of such change, the outcome is unlikely to restore local autonomy and privileges. In Barrington Moore's famous phrase,

> Peasants have provided the dynamite to bring down the old building. To the subsequent work of reconstruction they have brought nothing; instead they have been . . . its first victims.[4]

Nevertheless, community-solidarity theorists take a strong stand on the crucial role of the community in revolutionary social change and contrast it to other social forms offered as agents. In particular, they have singled out the urban proletariat for its comparative inefficacy. Because of their physical, economic, and cultural proximity to dominant class institutions, urban workers are regarded as likely to fall under the latter's ideological hegemony and to limit their struggles to officially sanctioned channels.[5] Alternatively, they are seen as confined to formal associational representations, which provide weaker incentives for individual participation and tend toward bureaucratized inertia.[6] Craig Calhoun sums up the case for traditional community radicalism in provocative fashion:

> Reactionary radicals have seldom, if ever, been able to gain supremacy in revolutions. But at the same time, revolutions worthy of the name have never been made without them.[7]

The community-solidarity approach confronts a variety of competing explanations, of course. Samuel Popkin's well-known formulation regards peasant movements as based on the calculated self-interest of individual peasants.[8] Other authors, while accepting the role of community solidarity in rebellions of an earlier age, argue for a more contemporary model in which urban revolutionary activists recruit individual peasant adherents through offers of tangible present or future assistance in overcoming particular economic and political problems obstructing their livelihoods.[9] Still other theorists have focused on the alternative of class solidarity. Alain De Janvry takes a classical Marxist tack, asserting that the ongoing proletarianization of peasant producers tends to create the objective basis for a revolutionary movement led by the urban proletariat with support from certain segments of the peasantry.[10] Jeffrey

Paige, on the other hand, argues that self-conscious revolutionary movements correspond to the class positions of sharecroppers and migratory laborers, in contradistinction to the more limited, isolated rebellions of autonomous peasant villages.[11]

El Salvador as a Case Study

Clearly, then, substantial debate continues around the question of community as a basis for peasant rebellion.[12] The present essay addresses this issue through a comparative historical analysis of peasant-based rebellions in El Salvador. Two related objectives will be pursued. First, the long history of agrarian unrest in that country provides a longitudinal base for evaluating the arguments of community-solidarity theorists. Hence we may seek to determine not just whether such solidarity may be assigned causal significance in one or another instance of rebellion but whether its importance has changed over time in the face of agrarian capitalist development and other significant changes in Salvadoran society.[13]

A second objective is to determine if community-solidarity theories can serve to illuminate, at least partially, the nature of conflict and change in a country that has only lately commanded international attention. A reviewer of recent works devoted to Central American crises notes that, despite the proliferation of publications, relatively little attempt has been made to interpret these crises within the framework of prevailing social-scientific theories.[14] The literature on the Salvadoran insurgency fits this description well up to a point, the principal exception being works in Spanish that interpret it within a general theory of class struggle.[15] The challenge here is to assess whether a focus on community solidarity can help to fill the theoretical gap (all the more noticeable as one moves backward in time) and modify or complement the conclusions derived by those who have emphasized class conflict.

Given the constraints of space and, above all, the availability of historical data, the comparison will be confined to the three most outstanding cases of peasant mobilization and rebellion in the country's modern history: the Nonualco rebellion of 1833, the Communist-led uprising of 1932, and the contemporary conflict beginning in the late 1960s and early 1970s. Data are drawn from secondary sources, published testimonies, and, for the contemporary period, various documents and journalistic accounts. For each case, the antecedent conditions, pattern of mobilization, basis of solidarity, and outcome (so far as it has been determined) will be reviewed.

The Nonualco Rebellion of 1833

The modern agrarian history of El Salvador is in many ways a colonial product—specifically, of the Spanish conquest and domination of the indigenous peoples dating from about 1524. Though the Indian population was devastated by wars of conquest and the spread of disease brought by the conquerors, enough of them survived to provide the Spaniards with a labor force.[16] Mineral resources were minimal, leading almost by default to the predominance of agricultural activity as a wealth-generating strategy. The Salvadoran colonial economy was centered first on cacao, from about 1540 to 1590, and then on indigo, from about 1580 on into the nineteenth century.

The Spaniards left cacao cultivation in the hands of Indian villagers, simply making its production compulsory and then appropriating the output through tribute or trade. The principal center of cultivation was around Izalco in what is now the western department of Sonsonate (see fig. 1). Dependent on substantial amounts of year-round labor, the cacao economy suffered an early demise as the Indian population dwindled during the sixteenth century.[17] It is notable, however, that the Indian producer communities retained control of their lands.[18]

By contrast, the production of indigo, which entailed both cultivation and processing activities, necessitated the direct appropriation of land by the Spaniards. Large diversified estates were carved out that relied on a small, permanent labor force of tenants and drew on nearby villages for the more extensive seasonal needs. Less ecologically confined than cacao, indigo spread rapidly across remaining lowland regions of the colonial province.[19] David Browning provides a concise summary of the social impact of this boom:

> The indigo farm became synonymous with the disruption and destruction of traditional Indian communities. Wherever established, the indigo mill drew workers from surrounding areas. Indian villages were either depopulated or absorbed as part of an estate. . . . This process of absorption and dispossession affected most parts of the colony. Where Indian villages survived, and a surprisingly large number did so especially within the central highlands, the private estate,

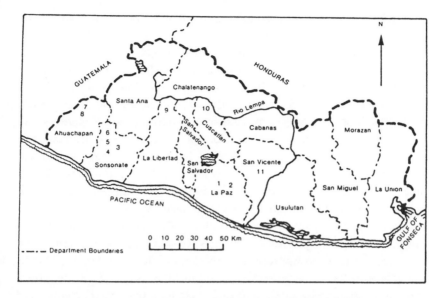

Fig. 1. El Salvador, with locations of peasant mobilization. 1833: 1. Santiago Nonualco, 2. Zacatecoluca; 1932: 3. Izalco, 4. Sonsonate, 5. Nahuizalco, 6. Juayua, 7. Ahuachapan, 8. Tacuba; 1970s: 9. Aguilares, 10. Suchitoto, 11. San Vicente.

based on indigo, cattle, resident labourers and subsistence farmers, was firmly established in close proximity to them. Away from this highland area, numerous large village communities were replaced by private estates; the pattern of settlement became characterized by dispersed populations of labourers attached to private estates or migratory subsistence cultivators seasonally dependent on them.[20]

By 1800, therefore, solidary Indian communities had largely disappeared from the colony except in certain parts of the western and central highlands. Elsewhere the processes of acculturation and miscegenation (*mestizaje*) had accompanied the creation of both internal and external peasantries dominated by an elite landowning class.[21] Prior to 1770 there was little Indian resistance to indigo expansion beyond ineffectual petitions to colonial authorities. Between 1770 and 1775 the efforts of central highland villages to block usurpation of their communal lands led to a number of small-scale uprisings. In 1789 a brief revolt erupted in the Nonualco village of Santiago over the attempt of indigo planters to convert seasonal wages from cash to kind.[22] All of these risings were easily subdued; only with a weakening of colonial power could successful protest become possible.

The collapse of Spanish royal authority after 1810 ruptured the tenuous links that had held the Central American provinces together, leading to a lengthy series of wars within and among the various provinces.[23] The conflicts were particularly intense betwen Guatemala and El Salvador, given the opposing interests of wealthy Salvadoran indigo planters and the Guatemalan merchants who had controlled Central American colonial trade. In these provinces the stakes of independence were higher for dominant groups, the wars more protracted, and the consequences more direct for peasant producers. In addition to their seasonal labor obligations on indigo plantations, Salvadoran peasant communities suffered the forcible recruitment of residents into armies opposing each other or those of Guatemala. Alongside tax and tributary obligations, they saw their communal funds appropriated to support the war efforts of bankrupt governments. Hacienda owners, meanwhile, sought to alleviate their own tax obligations by increasing their exactions from nearby villages.[24]

The economic and political disruptions accompanying the strife over independence offered a limited opening for popular protest.[25] In the wake of pro-independence revolts in Salvadoran towns during 1812–14, a new revolt broke out among the Nonualcos. Indian rebels occupied the town of Zacatecoluca, drove out Spanish officials, and called for an end to tributary obligations.[26] Though this movement was quickly defeated and its leaders arrested, the escalation of Indian demands was apparent.

In January 1833 another rebellion took place in the Nonualco region, this time of major proportions. Again originating in the village of Santiago, a movement led by Anastasio Aquino pledged to rid the Nonualcos of Hispanic control. The spark that ignited the revolt is believed to have been a confrontation between Aquino and the owner of an indigo plantation where Aquino and fellow villagers worked as day laborers. Quickly mobilizing neighboring Nonualco communities, the Indians overwhelmed local Salvadoran authorities and again occupied Zacatecoluca. Soon other towns and large estates in the area were also taken by Aquino's forces.[27]

Over the first two months of the revolt, the Nonualcos defeated several military expeditions set against them by the Salvadoran elites. Certainly this is indicative of the weakness of the Salvadoran state at the time, and contemporary observers believed that Aquino could have taken the capital city of Salvador had he chosen to do so.[28] The Nonualco leader's strategy was more limited, however, and there was no attempt to extend

Nonualco control beyond the environs of their communities. Thus allowed to regroup and reinforced by Guatemalan troops, government forces counterattacked in March, and the military tide began to turn. Aquino's capture and execution in April ended the revolt.

Little is known concerning the organization or ideology of this movement. Several accounts attest that Aquino was a community leader by neither birth nor position and came from a relatively poor family. After taking charge of the rebellion, however, he assumed the post and attire of a traditional Nonualco noble.[29] There is no indication that Nonualco community leaders opposed Aquino's movement or that support was less than unanimous within these communities. Even lower-status Ladinos residing among the Nonualcos were said to have adhered to the movement.[30] These circumstances, considered jointly with earlier manifestations of rebellion among these villages, suggest an interpretation of Aquino's movement as an attempt to forge a wider identity among solidary Nonualco communities by recreating a lapsed ethnic social and political structure. This may also help to explain the limits of the movement, however, for despite Nonualco appeals and the obvious weakness of Hispanic elites, other Indian groups failed to revolt or otherwise support the rebel movement.[31]

The limitations of Nonualco political and territorial ambitions and the failure of other Indian communities to rise to their assistance tend to confirm a prediction of the community-solidarity model of peasant rebellion and revolution. That is, with respect to the larger society, peasant rebels by themselves are unlikely to possess the vision or scale of organization necessary to effect a revolutionary transformation. Clearly, the Nonualco rebellion shook the prevailing structure of domination in El Salvador, but there were no social forces with the interests and capacity to supplant the ruling landowning elite.[32]

The Peasant Rebellion of 1932

If indigo constituted the backdrop to Aquino's rebellion, then coffee development set the stage for the events of 1932. By 1855 coffee plantations had begun to proliferate as urban and immigrant investors sought to cash in on a booming international demand. With the collapse of the international indigo market after 1860, numerous large planters joined the rush as well. The suitability of coffee to somewhat higher altitudes than indigo soon led the planters to challenge the collective holdings of peasant communities along the fertile volcanic slopes of the western and central highlands. Between 1879 and 1881 communal and municipal land-tenure forms were by law abolished in favor of private property ownership. It was generally simple work for rural and urban elites to manipulate legal and political institutions in their favor, and throughout the coffee-growing regions peasant communities were deprived of much of their holdings. By the turn of the century large coffee plantations dominated the landscape of the western highlands of Sonsonate and Ahuachapan, the central highlands to the south of the capital city, and the eastern upland zone around San Miguel.[33]

The massive expropriation of peasant lands in the context of expanding population and a nearly nonexistent agrarian frontier "freed" a large labor force for the coffee plantations. Unlike indigo, coffee required a fairly large permanent labor force as well as a major seasonal increment at harvest time. Thus, in addition to relying on migratory part-time workers, many estate owners retained, resettled, or created whole peasant villages on estate lands to provide a steady work force. At the same time, planters were reluctant to grant their workers the usual access to portions of the estate for their own cultivations, finding it more profitable to plant their entire holdings to coffee and pay higher wages to their workers.[34] In this manner a highly proletarianized and concentrated labor force took shape around the larger plantations.

The assault on peasant landholdings and subsequent rearrangement of labor patterns did not go unchallenged. Numerous violent uprisings were recorded between 1872 and 1898 among the Indian peasant communities in the western part of the country.[35] Nonetheless, these actions encountered a far different political reality from that of Aquino's rebellion a half century before. Instead of a weak and fragmented Creole elite, Indian rebels faced an ascendant, relatively homogenous dominant class in control of a much stronger state apparatus.[36] There was no longer any prospect of successful resistance on the part of isolated communities.

A different sort of political opening presented itself after about 1910. Prompted by a growing differentiation of oligarchic interests accompanying the concentration and diversification of domestic capital, elite politicians began to seek electoral support through the mobilization of urban middle-class, artisan, and peasant voters.[37] This opening was sufficient for the emergence of an urban labor movement among artisanal producers in San Salvador and other urban centers.[38]

During the 1920s the labor movement gradually acquired a more centralized and radical character. Key points in this process were the establishment of the Regional Workers Federation (FRTS) in 1924, the consolidation of communist leadership in the FRTS in 1929, and the founding of the Salvadoran Communist Party (PCS) in 1930.[39] During this decade the government alternately ignored and repressed the movement, which in any case did not represent a serious political problem. In 1929 the FRTS numbered thirty-eight affiliates, with a total membership of only one thousand five hundred.[40] The impact of the depression produced a dramatic change, however. Focusing their attention on the countryside, FRTS organizers sparked a remarkably rapid and massive mobilization of peasants, primarily coffee workers.[41]

As a result of popular discontent and a certain lapse of oligarchic control over the political arena, the 1931 election was won by Arturo Araujo, a dissident coffee planter. His platform pledged, among other measures, a redistributive agrarian reform. His inability or unwillingness to enact such a program, however, led to a wave of rural strikes, which in turn were met with violent repression by government forces. The ascending spiral of protest and repression, coupled with continuing economic decline and dissent on other fronts, led to a coup under General Maximiliano Hernández Martínez in December 1931.[42]

In the wake of the coup and a round of fraudulent local elections held in January 1932, the PCS opted to call for a revolutionary insurrection. Government forces, getting wind of the plot through informers, were waiting. By January 22, the scheduled day of revolt, most PCS leaders, including top man Farabundo Martí, had already been arrested, thus depriving the movement of its central coordination. The uprisings that did take place were mainly confined to the western coffee-growing region, where insurgent peasants occupied some important towns before succumbing to army counterattacks. The defeat of the revolt, accomplished in three days, signaled the beginning of a slaughter: in the following weeks some twenty-five thousand peasants and workers were rounded up and executed, many times the number who had actually participated in the rebellion.[43]

With respect to the issues of peasant mobilization, there are two separate, if closely related, phenomena to be accounted for in the rebellion. One is the preceding period of peasant mobilization and organization under the leadership of PCS and FRTS activists, while the other concerns the actual insurrection. With regard to the former, it is clear that most of the successful organization took place in the western departments of Sonsonate and Ahuachapan and in the central region around the capital city. Both of these were coffee-producing zones, where depression-induced wage cuts had struck hard.[44] Yet a simple reference to the economic condition of coffee workers is inadequate, since there was virtually no organization in the country's third major coffee zone to the east around San Miguel.[45]

Different mobilization processes appear to have been at work in the central and western mobilizations. In the central zone the key element was the proximity of peasant communities to the capital city. By 1910, according to PCS activist Miguel Marmol, there was substantial migration back and forth between San Salvador and the surrounding villages, and many urban artisans resided or had family ties in the villages.[46] During the 1920s Marmol and other labor activists sought to extend their organization into these communities but found their ideological exhortations ineffective against the countervailing influence of church and municipal officials. It was only after they turned to small-scale mobilizations around local problems, such as road repairs, transportation to medical facilities, and community insurance schemes, that they struck a responsive chord. Marmol recalls,

> If it had been necessary to put on a circus, we would not have hesitated to become clowns or trapeze artists, even if we would have all come unhinged as a result.[47]

From this base they were able to organize peasants over the opposition of local elites.

In the west organizing success was found precisely in the areas where Indian communities, despite being highly proletarianized, had retained a certain sociocultural autonomy. Because of their local influence, Indian caciques and *cofradía* (sodality) leaders were courted not just by radical organizers but also by oligarchic politicians and officials of the Catholic church.[48] With the advent of the depression, Indian leaders became more receptive to PCS overtures; noteworthy in this respect was the fortuitous presence of a Mexican communist organizer of Indian descent, Jorge Fernández Anaya, who toured western El Salvador in 1930 addressing Indian peasants in their own Nahuatl language.[49]

One should not overstate, however, the degree of leftist political or ideological control over Indian groups.[50] No doubt the Indian communities derived important organizational and political support, as well as a sense of belonging to a wider movement, from their association with the Left. Nevertheless, strikes and other violent incidents before the revolt represented local initiatives, while PCS leaders alternately counseled patience or sought concessions from the government in exchange for their intercession with unruly peasants.[51]

Thus, two distinct patterns of peasant mobilization emerged during the years immediately prior to the rebellion. In one, formal organizations were created by urban labor activists on the basis of community ties between peasants and artisans and around issues of mutual concern to the community. In the other, organization was superimposed over preexisting community structures through links between traditional leaders and urban activists. With these in mind, the quiescence of peasants in the eastern part of the country, both before and during the 1932 rebellion, becomes comprehensible. In that region neither the traditional ethnic community solidarity nor the peasant/artisan connection pertained.[52]

Concerning the actual insurrection, a number of interpretations have been advanced from the perspective of those directly involved on both sides. The elite version portrays massive uprisings carried out by Indians and other peasants who, imbued with quasireligious Marxist fervor, committed numerous acts of barbarism against defenseless, philanthropic landowners before flinging themselves in suicidal waves on the guns of the military.[53] On the left, two distinct versions emerged. One viewed the revolt as purposefully provoked by the government in order to justify repression of the peasants, in the face of which the PCS was obliged to take its place at the head of popular forces, albeit unsuccessfully.[54] The other emphasized the military and ideological deficiencies of the PCS in performing its vanguard role in the context of an authentic, mass revolutionary disposition.[55]

None of these versions provides a very satisfactory set of arguments. We may begin by noting that the rebellion was actually quite limited in scope, almost exclusively centered in Sonsonate and Ahuachapan, with the most significant conflicts being the attacks on the towns of Juayua, Izalco, Nahuizalco, Sonsonate, Tacuba, and Ahuachapan. The first four of these were clearly identified with Indian insurgencies directed by village leaders. Concerning the last two, there is some debate, but the evidence suggests that, even if less well articulated, ethnic community solidarity played a part there also.[56]

In explaining the absence of more widespread mobilization, some authors have focused on the predicament of the PCS at the moment of revolt, pointing to the confusion occasioned by government disinformation, the arrest of important party leaders, and internal disagreement among those remaining.[57] By this reasoning, the villages that did revolt were those that remained ignorant of this last-minute turmoil or chose to ignore it. The patterns and locations of rebellion, however, make it seem unlikely that a simple matter of broken communications determined who did or did not revolt. If it was a matter of choice, then the action must still be accounted for. The crucial factor, when preceding patterns of mobilization are taken into account, was the strength of local organization and solidarity among Indian communities in the west, which gave them the potential to act independently of the fortunes of the party's central committee.[58] This can be contrasted to the absence of action in the PCS strongholds of the central region, where the preventive government strike against party leaders left local cadres disorganized and defenseless.

On the other hand, we should not go so far as to argue that the rebellion was wholly a matter of local initiative, particularly in reaction to government provocation, and that the PCS merely responded in solidarity with the peasants. Marmol leaves no doubt that the party issued a call for revolutionary insurrection several days in advance, settling on the actual date after two postponements.[59] It is hard otherwise to account for the simultaneity of upheavals in the rebel zone. And Thomas Anderson makes the point that the government was probably not so adept as to be able to plan and execute a plot of such precise provocation.[60]

Something nearly all authors take for granted is that a revolutionary situation existed in the country in 1932, at least with regard to massive popular support for a revolutionary societal transformation. There are reasons to be cautious about this assumption, however. Araujo's reformist platform enjoyed widespread support among peasants and workers in the 1931 electoral campaign, despite the aloof attitude of the PCS.[61] Subsequent disillusionment with Araujo's administration did little to alter this orientation, and, even after Martinez's coup in December, popular enthusiasm for the January local elections was extraordinarily high. Marmol, never afraid to record observations at variance with his theories, confirms the limitations of popular will as of 1932:

> The masses fully believed that a change of authorities in the administrative apparatus would really resolve many problems. . . . To my

mind we communists did not understand that despite the ultimate weakness of that belief, it did signify the great desire of the Salvadoran workers to politicize their struggle. For it should not be forgotten that despite the violence dogging our Party and the organized labor movement, that struggle until then had been fundamentally an economic one.[62]

It seems very likely, therefore, that the failure of a massive rebellion to materialize on January 22 was not the result merely of PCS vacillation or preventive government repression but, rather, reflected also a popular unreadiness to risk all in an open insurrection.

The point here, of course, is not to blame the PCS for ill-considered or voluntaristic acts that precipitated the ultimate carnage. The government's preparations before the rebellion and, above all, its systematic, genocidal reaction afterward clearly show that the rebellion served as a pretext for the elimination of peasants and workers as a political presence.[63] In this sense the conspiratorial theory of a rebellion instigated by the government is correct in spirit, if not to the letter; had the 1932 rebellion not occurred, it would have been necessary to invent it.

Peasant Movements and Revolution in the 1970s

The interval between the 1932 rebellion and the rise of peasant movements during the 1970s witnessed major transformations in the country's economic structure. Cotton, after 1945, and sugar, after 1960, joined coffee as major export commodities. With impetus from the creation of the Central American Common Market in 1960 and the large-scale entry of foreign capital, urban industrialization began to cut into the predominance of the agrarian export sector. During the same period the urban services sector grew rapidly, and the state assumed a much greater managerial role in economic affairs.[64]

The growth and diversification of the agrarian export sector had major consequences for the peasantry but varied according to commodity. An important postwar boom in coffee production and exports was accomplished primarily through increases in productivity, as relatively little land suitable for coffee remained unplanted by that point. This development, effected through the increased use of fertilizers, pesticides, and so forth, perhaps tended to lower permanent and increase seasonal labor requirements, but overall the demand for labor in the coffee zone seems to have grown substantially during this period.[65]

The rise of cotton and sugar, however, signified the conversion of extensive cattle and grain haciendas in various lowland regions of the country and thus entailed a large-scale expulsion of peasants previously allowed to occupy estate lands. Cotton production, rapidly blanketing the Pacific coastal lowlands from La Paz to La Unión, was principally undertaken by entrepreneurs renting hacienda lands. Extensive mechanization made labor needs minimal except during the harvest season, such that little effort was made to retain peasants on or around the estates. Seasonal labor needs were drawn from migratory landless laborers, many of whom resided in dispersed groups of huts strung along the narrow strips of national lands bordering highways and rivers.[66]

Sugar cane production, along with that of other commercial crops like rice and sesame, developed primarily at the initiative of hacienda owners along the upper Lempa River valley and in the northern portions of San Vincente and Usulután departments. Though this production also utilized capital-intensive technology, enough year-round labor was required that the expulsion of peasants was less thoroughgoing. Sharecropping and tenancy rights were converted to cash rents for smaller plots, thereby necessitating a greater reliance on supplementary wage labor for affected peasants. Additional labor was drawn from the peasant population inhabiting sub-subsistence–sized plots perched on the hills above the hacienda lands.[67]

Census and survey data from the 1970s clearly reflect the pressures of postwar development on the peasantry. Between 1961 and 1971 landholdings under traditional tenancy arrangements declined by 77 percent. With rapid population growth compounding developmental effects, the proportion of farm families that were landless climbed from 12 to 41 percent between 1961 and 1975, and by the latter date an additional 34 percent possessed plots smaller than one hectare.[68] High rates of malnutrition, infant mortality, and housing inadequacy prevailed.[69] Peasant migration to cities, particularly to San Salvador, and across the border to comparatively land-rich Honduras climbed dramatically.[70] Land invasions and squatting on idle lands also reached epidemic proportions.[71]

Another effect of the crisis of peasant holdings was that by the late 1950s the production of basic grains, which was primarily carried out on small farms, could no longer meet the effective domestic demand. Faced with rising food import bills in the early 1960s, the government began efforts to shore up peasant production with a large-scale infusion of credits, technical assistance, and infrastructural support. As a result, the country was again self-sufficient in corn production by 1970, though the benefits at the production level were confined to smallholders and did nothing to either increase the availability of land (agrarian reform) or improve the situation of subfamily farms and landless peasants.[72]

The crisis in the countryside fueled three distinct peasant movements during the 1970s. The first, to be referred to as the Catholic Left, began in 1964 with the founding of the Christian Peasant Federation (FECCAS), supported by the Catholic church, the Christian Democratic party, and the Latin American Social Christian labor organization.[73] Though originally mildly reformist in orientation, FECCAS rapidly became more radicalized in its pronouncements, and by the end of the decade it was calling for revolutionary changes in the social order. By then, however, it had become weak, tiny, and ineffectual, having been cut off from its original sponsors and comprising only twenty peasant leagues numbering five hundred members between them. As a sympathetic observer noted, "It is not known to have led any strike or land invasion during the entire decade."[74] By the organization's own admission, it suffered in 1970 an internal crisis not fully resolved until 1974.[75]

Nonetheless, by 1975 FECCAS had some five thousand members, a rather remarkable growth considering the organization's internal difficulties. The key ingredient of this expansion was the convergence of FECCAS with a radicalized grass roots movement of the Catholic church. Beginning in the late 1960s religious and lay workers influenced by new, progressive church doctrines organized biblical study and self-help groups in rural and urban poor communities. The Christian Base Communities, as they were called, stressed collective over individual responses to local problems and, in some groups, sponsored the revival of communal cultivation practices.[76]

A priest's report on one such evangelical project in the parish of Aguilares during 1972–74 offers excellent insight into the process of this mobilization.[77] A Jesuit team, assigned to the parish by the archbishop and led by Rutilio Grande, toured the region (which encompassed some 18 *cantones* across 170 square kilometers) offering the pastoral mission. On the basis of requests received from the population, two-week missions were planned for various rural communities and neighborhoods within the town of Aguilares. In the act of planning and during the initial meetings and ceremonies of each mission, however, the team sought to identify and involve leadership from within the communities, provided such leaders did not appear as repressive figures among their fellows. The document bears extensive citation:

> In particular, the names were noted of those whom the dialectics of the method brought together. These came to appear as born leaders, the natural motivators with whom nightly sessions were held to evaluate the work and to correct or improve the method of dialogue, in order to animate the groups and that they themselves begin to take responsibility for the course of the mission.... The two weeks of mission activity brought out the men and women who have initiative, mobility, influence, etc., within the community.
>
> From the first day it was emphasized implicitly and explicitly that every responsibility, talent and knowledge that distinguishes an individual should be seen as "service" and not as domination. All elitism or bossism [*caciquismo*] were discouraged in order that "the rest may grow."
>
> ... On the next-to-last evening the communitarian election was held.... The community itself suggested names; the nominees were queried concerning their willingness, pros and cons, and on this basis the community approved them and voted, with a majority necessary for election. Thus were designated the Delegates of the Word of God in service to the community. In practice 1 delegate was elected for each 4 or 5 persons. The predominance of men or women as delegates has varied from one place to another....
>
> The last night of the mission they accepted publicly and individually the designation and the commitment to serve the community. From that moment they were in charge of motivating their community. They were not left alone, but rather were placed under the tutelage of another, more veteran delegation, either from outside or from another community, which could help the delegates as well as the new community to grow.
>
> The delegates were the link between the community itself and the parish, or great community.[78]

In this manner a network of base communities and elected leaders was developed simultaneously. It is worth emphasizing the combination of previous community ties and external impulse underlying the very origin of the movement; it could not be self-generated. As the same report notes:

> Tradition weighs little in Aguilares, a fact in itself ambivalent for the pastoral mission, for although change is facilitated to the extent that traditionalistic barriers do not have to be overcome, there is also lacking the scaffolding or matrix which would feed or sustain popular religiosity.[79]

The strategy was highly successful, nonetheless, as, over the nine-month period ending in June of 1973, a total of 15 missions took place in rural communities with an average participation of 150 persons. We may thus calculate totals of around 2,250 participants and 450–500 Delegates of the Word in a parish with a total population, excluding the town of Aguilares, of about 23,000. An additional 10 missions with an average of 60 participants each were carried out within the town itself, which numbered some 10,000 inhabitants.[80]

More generally, rural base communities began to address the problems of land tenure, employment, and social justice that pitted peasants against estate owners and local security forces. Community initiatives on these issues encountered brutally repressive reactions, however, and, as the level of conflict escalated, the base groups turned to more organized and coordinated activity, for which FECCAS provided a convenient and ideologically congruent outlet. This convergence caused a growing rift within the church during the mid-1970s, and religious organizers like Rutilio Grande generally sought to maintain a certain distance between church-sponsored groups and the leftist peasant organizations. Their efforts were futile in the face of mounting official and right-wing violence, however; the murder of Grande in March 1977 symbolized an irreversible process of polarization prefiguring civil war.[81]

The early strength of the Catholic Left peasant movement was concentrated around Aguilares, Suchitoto, and other points along the north-central Lempa sugar belt. In 1973 a strike was successfully carried out against an Aguilares sugar mill, and during the mid-1970s strikes and demonstrations against haciendas and mills became common. During the same period a parallel organizational development linked base communities to a formal peasant organization in the sugar region around San Vicente. Established in 1974, following an army attack on a base community group that had carried out a small land invasion, the Farm-workers' Union (UTC) had mobilized several thousand members two years later. In 1976 FECCAS and UTC formally allied themselves and in 1978 merged to form the Farmworkers' Federation (FTC), with an estimated membership of ten thousand to twelve thousand.[82]

Two other major peasant movements will be dealt with summarily as counterpoints to our focus on radical mobilization. The Salvadoran Communal Union (UCS) was set up at the initiative of organizers from the American Institute for Free Labor Development (AIFLD), as part of its program to foment noncommunist labor movements in Latin America.[83] Beginning in 1966, AIFLD sought to organize cooperatives of smallholding peasants, who were provided with leadership training, technical assistance, and credit facilitation. In 1969, when the UCS was formally constituted to represent these groups, their membership numbered around five thousand.[84]

By 1975 the UCS claimed fifty thousand members, undoubtedly a reflection of its financial good health, as it was consistently a beneficiary of United States foreign aid programs and a certain degree of political support from the state. The early locus of UCS strength was among smallholders located around and producing for major urban markets.[85] Thus, it complemented state efforts to increase food production that had been targeted on this sector. By the mid-1970s, however, the UCS had begun to advocate wage and contract improvements for peasant small-holders linked to large estates, thus bringing the organization into increasing conflict with the dominant landowning class.

The other peasant organization was also formed during the 1960s, but with a very different stamp. The National Democratic Organization (ORDEN) was established by a rightist politician and former head of the National Guard, with the active support of both large landowners and the security forces. As its acronym (*orden* is the Spanish word for order) and origins suggest, it was not intended as a vehicle for promoting change in the countryside. Rather, ORDEN's functions were to provide a rural intelligence network for detecting signs of popular unrest or mobilization and to serve as a paramilitary force for attacking and dismantling such subversive activities. Individual peasants were formed into small squads under a hierarchical chain of command, usually staffed, at the upper levels, by security officials.[86]

Despite ORDEN's subordination to ruling elite groups, it may still be considered a peasant organization in the formal sense of the term. Peasants were recruited into it (often through initial coercion) in exchange for jobs, credit, local offices, and other favors that could be dispensed by its public and private sponsors. Like a protection racket, it also guaranteed peasants some security against right-wing violence or harassment. By the late 1970s ORDEN had as many as 100,000 members, though only a small fraction were thought to be actually involved in local espionage or paramilitary activities.[87]

The oscillations between halting reforms and murderous repression with which the state and landowning elites, in varying degrees of collaboration, countered the increasingly assertive popular movements after 1975 have been extensively analyzed elsewhere and need not detain us.[88] An agrarian reform law, which if effective might yet have defused the crisis, was enacted in 1974 and initially implemented in 1976. Almost immediately, however, its provisions were legislatively gutted in the face of intense private-sector opposition, thereby exacerbating the conflict.[89] By the time a more far-reaching reform project was decreed under United States pressure, in 1979, the insurrection was under way.

Similarly, we need not dwell on the origins and intricacies of the various guerrilla organizations created by leftist activists in the 1960s and early 1970s.[90] For that period they remained small and relatively ineffectual groups drawn primarily from the ranks of urban intellectuals. As the decade progressed, however, their efforts to attract popular support for armed struggle began to be rewarded.

The Catholic Left peasant movement emerged during the mid-1970s as the core strength of pre-insurrectionary peasant mobilization. Its radicalization in this period was accompanied by an increasing scale of organization and alliance with other social sectors. In 1974 FECCAS, along with church, labor, and professional organizations, created a national popular coalition, the United Popular Action Front (FAPU), with loose links to the National Resistance guerrilla movement. In July 1975 FAPU split over political and strategic disagreements, one of which concerned the importance to be given to peasant mobilization as a revolutionary force. The pro-peasant faction created the Revolutionary Popular Bloc (BPR), to which FECCAS and UTC subsequently adhered. The BPR, in turn, was aligned with the Popular Liberation Forces (FPL), oldest and largest of the guerrilla organizations.[91]

During the 1976–79 period the BPR pursued a strategy of local organizing around limited demands, sponsoring numerous rural strikes, land invasions, and demonstrations, as well as urban protests. Nonetheless, the radical political program behind essentially economic actions was openly proclaimed. In a 1978 response to criticism from conservative sectors of the church, the leaders of FECCAS and UTC described the BPR, in terms that might have pleased Lenin, as

> a *revolutionary front of the masses* which, based on the *worker-peasant alliance with proletarian hegemony,* is the only guarantee that one day soon we will be able to rid ourselves forever of this system of exploitation and injustice.[92]

By 1980 the BPR had grown to become the largest mass organization of the Left, with about eighty thousand members. At that point, however, the escalation of conflict into open civil war had led to the submergence of BPR activity into the combined military and political tactics of the Farabundo Marti National Liberation Front (FMLN) and the Democratic Revolutionary Front (FDR).

In the pre-insurrectionary context of the late 1970s, the regional dynamic of mobilization changed considerably. In particular, the highland areas of Cabañas and especially Chalatenango, to the north of the sugar region, became the focus of revolutionary organizational efforts. In the highland region, however, despite the presence of Christian Left organizers since the early 1970s, mass mobilization can be attributed to the combined impact of generalized repressive violence on the part of the Right and the efforts of the revolutionary organizations to establish a secure base of operations beyond the effective reach of the military. While Chalatenango subsequently became the most publicized and perhaps most crucial center of rebel strength, it seems dubious that this development could have occurred without the prior sequence of mobilization and reaction to the south.[93]

On the other side of the fence, ORDEN was employed during the 1970s to attack FTC and other popular organizations in the countryside, intimidate voters during elections, and orchestrate demonstrations of support for the government. In some cases the clashes between ORDEN and the leftist groups pitted neighbor against neighbor in the same village.[94] As the level of conflict climbed, ORDEN actions became more coordinated with military and paramilitary operations. ORDEN was officially dissolved by the reformist junta in power briefly after the 1979 coup, but the organization continued to function locally as an adjunct to the security forces.[95]

The UCS was caught in the middle of the polarization of the late 1970s. Despite the hostility of the landed elite, its international ties had facilitated continual growth, which reached a peak of some 100,000 members in 1980. At that point the UCS had become an integral part of the agrarian reform program set up after the 1979 coup, with responsibility for organizing and supporting the peasant beneficiaries of planned land redistributions. For the moderate Christian Democrat and military reformists in the government and for their United States backers, the UCS represented a stabilizing rural influence and a potentially potent electoral force. The reform was sabotaged by the Right, however, which began to direct terrorist attacks on UCS members and leaders as well as on government and United States officials associated with the reform. Under this pressure, the organization split apart in late 1980, with a significant segment moving over to support the Left.[96]

In short, the objective interests of Salvadoran peasants, faced with contemporary subsistence and employment crises, found expression in profoundly different and even opposing political vehicles. One possible explanation, advanced by several authors, is that organizational differences can be linked to different class positions stemming from the internal differentiation of the peasantry in the wake of postwar development. Carlos Samaniego argues that the increasing proletarianization of peasant labor led to demands focused on wages, rents, and credit, rather than on the possession of land, and thus facilitated the alliance of rural and urban workers. The revolutionary posture of the alliance reflected the precariousness of this proletarian existence and the frustration of demands made through peaceful or legitimate channels.[97] The proletarian and radicalized basis of the Catholic Left movement can be contrasted with the smallholding constituency and limited economic demands of the UCS.[98] The membership of ORDEN is more problematic, since it reportedly mobilized peasants from a variety of class backgrounds.[99] Given the imposed and controlled nature of its program, however, this need not be taken as a setback for the hypothesis.

Nevertheless, there are two serious objections to this correspondence of political outlook with class position. The first is that proletarianization does not serve to predict very well the location of the Catholic Left peasant movement. The most thorough and disruptive process of rural proletarianization was undoubtedly that of cotton development in the Pacific lowlands. Yet the wellsprings of the movement were found almost exclusively in the areas where sugarcane and certain other commercial crops transformed the traditional haciendas. The key difference between the cotton and sugar regions only indirectly concerned the relations of production on the estates. What made the sugar belt a fertile zone for the Catholic Left was the persistence of localized peasant solidarities, around which the Christian Base Communities could be organized. The retention of a land base, however minimal, may have been crucial in this regard. In the cotton belt the dispersed and fragmented hamlets of landless laborers presented much more difficult terrain for creating local organizations.[100]

The second problem concerns the particular political character of movements associated with different objective class positions. The organization of rural labor may have challenged the interests of the dominant landowning class, but by itself that did not imply a revolutionary orientation on the part of mobilized peasants. The radicalization of the movement as a mass phenomenon appears much more the consequence of the repression unleashed against it at a time when it sought much more limited objectives.[101] Similarly, the reformism of UCS smallholders was fractured by the violent intransigence of rural elites over the agrarian reform project of 1979–80, leading many to a more radical course of action.

In arguing the importance of community solidarity to the rise of the Catholic Left peasant movement, and hence to the genesis of a popular revolutionary movement, we must be careful not to idealize or magnify its scope. Salvadoran peasant communities of the 1960s and 1970s were in no sense closed or autonomous collectives with solidary identities. Indeed, many conflicts of the period revealed the degree of internal differentiation and penetration of national political structures into village life. Rather, the contemporary strength of community solidarity was, in a recreated form, the product of popular religious organizing efforts around residual community social bonds. In this case these ties and externally promoted organizational forms appeared mutually indispensable elements in the formation of a contestatory peasant movement.

The evolution of the war after 1980 has revealed that a mass-based revolutionary movement could not by itself produce a revolutionary outcome. This tends to confirm the argument that, whatever their class basis, social revolutions are highly unlikely to succeed where dominant class unity and the coercive apparatus of the state remain largely intact.[102] In the case of El Salvador, moreover, both of these factors evidently are strongly influenced by the direction of United States foreign policy. Nevertheless, regardless of the military and political resolution of the present war, the experience of mobilization, organization, and rebellion seems destined to leave its mark on the social identity of a large segment of the Salvadoran peasantry.

Conclusion

The lessons that can be drawn concerning the significance of community solidarity in the three cases described above are tempered by the extremely long lens through which the events have been viewed. A closer look at the concrete, local-level interactions of peasants could only strengthen the analysis, and these interactions constitute a major avenue for further development of this topic.

Certain patterns and distinctions of these cases stand out strongly, nevertheless. In the first place, community solidarity has played an important role in all three instances of peasant mobilization. Mobilization leading up to rebellion has taken place at the community level. In each case the analysis has tended to confirm a fundamental hypothesis of the model: higher levels of community solidarity are associated with a greater likelihood that, given sufficient cause, particular peasant villages will be mobilized for rebellion. On this basis the geography of rebellion conforms to theoretical expectations.

Some immediate qualifications are next in order, however. The Catholic Left base communities of the 1970s have little in common with nineteenth-century Indian villages. A strong trend toward declining village autonomy is clearly observable across the three cases. Landless rebel villages in 1932 retained an important local institutional basis of solidarity and leadership, but they were far more dependent on the large coffee estates than the Nonualcos had been on the coerced-labor indigo haciendas of 1833. Peasant communities of the 1970s, in turn, were much more internally differentiated and penetrated by the administrative and coercive controls of the Salvadoran state than the villages of a half-century before.

Correspondingly, the importance of external allies increased from one case to the next. In 1833 the Nonualco rebels saw their opportunity and acted without outside support of any kind. In 1932 peasant communities were spurred to mobilization and rebellion through the efforts of urban communist organizers, though local initiatives and organization remained very important. By the 1970s, however, the role of external allies (in this case the Catholic Left) extended beyond assistance or coordination to the creation of the organizational forms around which community solidarity could be rearticulated. On this basis a radicalized movement could subsequently develop.

Finally, we may note that none of the three rebel movements offers an example of purely localized solidarities adrift in a world of larger political forces.[103] In each case, to one extent or another, efforts to foment wider solidarities have helped to determine the nature and consequences of the movement. Though detailed consideration of these solidarities would carry us into another essay, we can indicate briefly the importance of ethnicity, religion, and class as they have emerged from our analysis.

Indian ethnicity played a significant role in both the 1833 and 1932 revolts. Two forms may be usefully distinguished here, one a specific cultural identity rooted in the vestiges of pre-Columbian societies and the other a more diffuse identity as "Indians" imposed by Spanish/ Ladino elites. The first represented an important aspect of the rebellion led by Anastasio Aquino, which drew together the Nonualco communities around the recreation of a Nonualco kingdom. By 1932 this sort of collective identity no longer seems to have had any significance beyond the community level, though it undoubtedly constituted an important bond within the community. We may surmise, however, that its decline may have facilitated increased solidarity around an Indian ethnicity, considering the wider participation of western Indian communities in 1932 compared with the isolation of the Nonualco movement.

Religion seems to have played an important role only in the contemporary period.[104] The creation of the base communities in the 1970s drew strength from the traditional Catholic religiosity of Salvadoran peasants, even as it sought to redefine that outlook in a more worldly and activist manner. But the fact that this religious tradition also encompassed the Salvadoran ruling elite (whose interests the church had once faithfully served) made it difficult for church organization to be utilized directly as an instrument of intrasocietal conflict. This helps to explain both the severity of contemporary doctrinal disputes within the church and the rapprochement of the Catholic Left movement with Marxist theories and organizations.[105]

The structure of class relations around dominant export economies set the stage for all three mobilizations studied here. But while the social relations of production on indigo haciendas, coffee estates, and (less monotonically) sugar plantations provide excellent predictors of the two sides in conflict from one case to the next, the analysis of class relations with attendant objective interests proves insufficient to determine the incidence and political direction of mobilization for these cases.

In particular, the process of proletarianization was not synonymous with the rise of peasant radicalism in the contemporary period. On the one hand, it does not explain regional variations of mobilization. On the other, popular rebellion in El Salvador (as elsewhere in Central America) did not issue out of the fundamental class antagonism of capitalism. As Edelberto Torres Rivas has observed for the region as a whole:

> The force of the labor movement is present but within a popular mobilization in which are participating other social sectors, especially the various fractions of the peasantry.... A radical political antagonism has emerged which is built around diverse forms of economic demands but subsumes them, and therefore, leads not to direct confrontation with the bourgeois exploiter, but rather with the political regime and its repressive material apparatus.[106]

Might a revolutionary temperament be structurally linked to semi-proletarian, rather than proletarian, class status? Paige has argued as much for the case of revolutionary peasant mobilization in contemporary Guatemala.[107] By contrast, our analysis in this work leads to a greater emphasis on historical contingency than on structural imperatives as to the political correlates of class position. That is, the Catholic Left peasant movement would likely have taken a different course if Salvadoran elites had behaved more like their Honduran or Costa Rican counterparts.[108]

Short of revolutionary imperatives, however, might there still be a link between class status and community-based peasant mobilization? The data presented in this work are not sufficiently detailed to warrant a conclusion on their own, but recent developments in the field of urban sociology may be instructive in this regard. First, in contradiction to the classical evolutionary schema, community ties have proven a resilient organizational resource even in the cities of the developed countries.[109] Second, community-based organizations and social movements focused on issues of "collective consumption" have constituted a modal form of social action of the "urban informal" classes, in contrast to the workplace organization of the formal proletariat.[110] Finally, such activity has reflected quite variable political orientations around relatively constant material objectives.[111] The parallel of these findings with the structure of social action in the Salvadoran countryside is striking. The implication for further research in this area is that formal/informal class distinctions, with corresponding variations in patterns of mobilization, may be usefully applied in a rural setting as well.[112]

The comparative approach used here has enabled us to show that an analytical emphasis on community solidarity is consistently justified in efforts to explain revolutionary peasant mobilization in El Salvador, but not in the static version in which it is often portrayed by both critics and advocates. The model of widespread, localized peasant rebellions paving the way for the seizure of state power by some other social group is clearly of declining relevance across the cases we have examined. It fits the Nonualco rebellion rather well, despite the absence of an opportunistic revolutionary actor. The 1932 rebellion featured a transitional combination of traditional community-based and externally organized peasant groups, but the growth in the scope and complexity of state power had already rendered localized rebellion ineffective. The present-day form is indeed one in which external agency and resources are prerequisites for a large-scale peasant mobilization. At the same time, the most recent example of peasant rebellion has not come about mainly through revolutionary ideological appeals or the purchase of peasant adherence by guerrillas in individual-level exchanges. Rather, it has been mediated through prior localized mobilization and social identities. Thus updated, a theory of community solidarity retains considerable relevance for contemporary processes of social change, such as those presently gripping Central America.

NOTES

The research on which this work is based was conducted with support from the Inter-American Foundation, the Institute for the Study of World Politics, and the Central American University Confederation (CSUCA). Helpful advice or comments were offered by Marc Edelman, Alejandro Portes, Sally Ward, and reviewers; responsibility for the final product, however, rests solely with the author. An earlier version of this study was presented at the Twenty-eighth Annual Convention of the International Studies Association, Washington, D.C., March 5-9, 1985.

1. Principal works from which this summary is derived include Barrington Moore, Jr., *The Social Origins of Dictatorship and Democracy: Lord and Peasant in the Making of the Modern World* (Boston: Beacon Press, 1966); Eric Wolf, *Peasant Wars of the Twentieth Century* (New York: Harper and Row, 1969); James Scott, *The Moral Economy of the Peasant* (New Haven, Conn.: Yale

University Press, 1976); and idem, "Hegemony and the Peasantry," *Politics and Society* 7, no. 3 (1977): 267–96. A more recent statement of the radical potential of traditional communities (urban as well as rural) can be found in Craig J. Calhoun, *The Question of Class Struggle: Social Foundations of Popular Radicalism during the Industrial Revolution* (Chicago: University of Chicago Press, 1982); and idem, "The Radicalism of Tradition: Community Strength or Venerable Disguise and Borrowed Language," *American Journal of Sociology* 88, no. 5 (1983): 886–914.

2. For sociologists, the classic contrasts are those of Ferdinand Tonnies (*Gemeinschaft* and *Gesellschaft*) and Emile Durkheim ("mechanical solidarity" and "organic solidarity"). Within the discipline of anthropology, the early writings of Eric Wolf contrasted "closed, corporate communities" of peasants with "open communities" in which peasants, if present, were only one of a number of subgroups. See, for example, his "Closed Corporate Peasant Communities in Mesoamerica and Java," *Southwestern Journal of Anthropology* 13 (Spring 1957): 1–18. Further confusion may arise from the common usage of *community* to signify both a spatially bounded area of residence and the bonds of solidarity among its inhabitants. While the emphasis of the community-solidarity theories outlined above is clearly on the latter aspect, the relationship between these meanings of community may be of substantial interest for our historical analysis. Thus both are retained in the present work, though with an effort to ensure that the context of each reference to *community* makes clear which is meant.

3. Moore, *Social Origins,* 468–77; Calhoun, "Radicalism of Tradition," 897.

4. Moore, *Social Origins,* 480.

5. Scott, "Hegemony and the Peasantry," 276–77.

6. Calhoun, "Radicalism of Tradition," 908–9.

7. Ibid., 911.

8. Samuel Popkin, *The Rational Peasant: The Political Economy of Rural Society in Vietnam* (Berkeley: University of California Press, 1979).

9. See Joel Migdal, *Peasants, Politics, and Revolution: Pressures toward Political and Social Change in the Third World* (Princeton: Princeton University Press, 1974); and Theda Skocpol, "What Makes Peasants Revolutionary?" *Comparative Politics* 14, no. 3 (1982): 351–75.

10. Alain De Janvry, *The Agrarian Question and Reformism in Latin America* (Baltimore: Johns Hopkins University Press, 1981).

11. Jeffrey Paige, *Agrarian Revolution: Social Movements and Export Agriculture in the Underdeveloped World* (New York: Free Press, 1975).

12. A vast debate concerns the correct definition of *peasant* and its relationship to categories of social class. The range of definitions has encompassed a wide scope of economic, cultural, and geographic criteria deployed in varying combinations. Here we will simply take peasants to be rural cultivators from whom an economic surplus is extracted in one form or another, freely or coercively, by nonproducing classes, and will employ other terms to characterize the various class and other structural differentiations such a broad conception inevitably encloses. This usage is thus primarily descriptive rather than theoretical; it certainly does not obviate the need for clear theoretical concepts, but neither does

it forestall the contrast of theories of peasant mobilization as a matter of definition. For a recent review of alternative conceptions of peasants and peasant economy, see Klaus Heynig, "The Principal Schools of Thought on the Peasant Economy," *CEPAL Review,* no. 16 (1982): 113–39.

13. For our purpose, this method has obvious advantages over the more usual strategy of cross-national comparisons (such as those of Moore, Paige, and Skocpol, among others), which involve risky assumptions if one is attempting to evaluate the changing relevance of a particular theory over time (e.g., with respect to the evolution of capitalist development).

14. Mark Ruhl, "Understanding Central American Politics," *Latin American Research Review* 19, no. 3 (1984): 143–52.

15. Perhaps the most straightforward example is Carlos Samaniego, "Movimiento campesino o lucha del proletariado rural en El Salvador," *Estudios sociales centroamericanos,* no. 25 (1980): 125–44.

16. See Murdo MacLeod, *Spanish Central America: A Socioeconomic Survey, 1520–1720* (Berkeley: University of California Press, 1973), 38–56; and William Sherman, *Forced Native Labor in Sixteenth-Century Central America* (Lincoln: University of Nebraska Press, 1979), 20–63.

17. For a discussion of the Salvadoran cacao economy, see David Browning, *El Salvador: Landscape and Society* (Oxford: Clarendon Press, 1971), 52–65; and MacLeod, *Spanish Central America,* 80–95. Competition from other producing regions in the Spanish empire may have contributed to the decline of Salvadoran cacao as well.

18. In Guatemala and elsewhere the decline of cacao was accompanied by the displacement of Indian producer communities and the creation of large Spanish-owned cattle haciendas. See Browning, *El Salvador,* 52–65; and MacLeod, *Spanish Central America,* 80–95.

19. Mario Flores Macal, "La hacienda colonial en El Salvador: Sus orígenes," *Estudios sociales centroamericanos,* no. 25 (1980): 355–82; also Browning, *El Salvador,* 66–77.

20. Browning, *El Salvador,* 76.

21. See ibid., 111–33, for detailed discussion of the varieties of land-tenure arrangements and corresponding local social structures during the late colonial period.

22. Flores Macal, "La hacienda colonial," 365–66.

23. Concerning these conflicts, see Miles Wortman, *Government and Society in Central America, 1680–1840* (New York: Columbia University Press, 1982), 195–267; and Edelberto Torres Rivas and Julio César Pinto, *La formación del estado nacional en Centroamérica* (San José: Instituto Centroamericano de Administracíon Pública, 1983).

24. Julio Alberto Domínguez Sosa, *Ensayo histórico sobre las tribus Nonualcas y su caudillo Anastasio Aquino* (San Salvador: Ministerio de Educación, 1964), 44–47; Browning, *El Salvador,* 140–41.

25. In general, intra-elite conflicts and independence movements in Central America were tempered by elite apprehensions of the possible consequences of massive popular mobilization for their positions of dominance (Torres Rivas and Pinto, *La formación del estado,* 106–7).

26. Domínguez Sosa, *Ensayo histórico,* 44–47.

27. The description of the Nonualco rebellion presented here is drawn mainly from the text and documentary appendices of Domínguez Sosa, *Ensayo histórico,* esp. 78–95. See also Julio César Calderón, *Episodios nacionales: Anastasio Aquino y el porqué de su rebelión en 1833 en Santiago Nonualco* (San Salvador: Imprenta Moreno, 1957).

28. Domínguez Sosa, *Ensayo histórico,* 94–95.

29. Cf. the appended documents and interviews in Domínguez Sosa, *Ensayo histórico.*

30. Ibid.

31. Aquino's movement bears an instructive contrast to the Tzeltal rebellion in Chiapas (then part of Guatemala) in 1712. In that uprising Tzeltal village leaders played an instrumental role in the initial phase of mobilization against the Spaniards but were subsequently shunted aside in an effort led by a Tzeltal prophet, Sebastian Gomez, to form a pan-Indian theocratic state modeled on the Catholic church. The withdrawal of community support for Gomez's movement contributed to the later defeat of the rebellion; at the same time, Gomez found little success in efforts to recruit support among non-Tzeltal Indian villages. While the lesser initial roles of the Nonualco traditional leaders may be ascribed to the intracommunity leveling effect of closer integration into the colonial economy, via indigo, the two cases underscore the extreme difficulty faced by peasants in sustaining autonomous, supralocal organizations. On the Tzeltal rebellion, see Herbert S. Klein, "Peasant Communities in Revolt: The Tzeltal Republic of 1712," *Pacific Historical Review* 35, no. 3, (1966): 247–63; and Robert Wasserstrom, *Class and Society in Central Chiapas* (Berkeley: University of California Press, 1983).

32. Four years after the Nonualco rebellion, a series of revolts in highland Guatemalan Indian communities weakened the Liberal regime of that country and paved the way for the restoration of Conservative domination under the dictatorship of a mestizo farmer-turned-general, Rafael Carrera. While few would define the outcome as a social revolution, it did significantly retard the advance of agrarian capitalism while protecting the rights and resources of highland communities in that country. See Ralph Lee Woodward, Jr., "Social Revolution in Guatemala: The Carrera Revolt," in Mario Rodriguez et al., *Applied Enlightenment: Nineteenth-Century Liberalism* (New Orleans: Middle American Research Institute, Tulane University, 1972), 45–70; and Carol A. Smith, "Local History in Global Context: Social and Economic Transitions in Western Guatemala," *Comparative Studies in Society and History* 26, no. 2 (1984): 193–228.

33. For details of the rise of the Salvadoran coffee economy, see Browning, *El Salvador,* 155–221; Rafael Menjívar, *Acumulación originaria y desarrollo del capitalismo en El Salvador* (San José: Editorial Universitaria Centroamericana, 1980); and E. Bradford Burns, "The Modernization of Underdevelopment: El Salvador, 1858–1931," *The Journal of Developing Areas* 18, no. 3, (1984): 293–316. For a comparative perspective encompassing coffee development in the rest of Central America, see Ciro F. S. Cardoso, "Historia económica del café en

Centroamérica," *Estudios sociales centroamericanos,* no. 10 (1975): 9–55; and Ciro F. S. Cardoso and Héctor Pérez Brignoli, *Centroamérica y la economía occidental (1520–1930)* (San José: Editorial Universidad de Costa Rica, 1977), 208–74.

34. Browning, *El Salvador,* 169–71.

35. Abelardo Torres, "More from This Land," *Americas* 14, no. 8 (1962): 9.

36. The concentration of economic and political power in the hands of Salvadoran coffee planters produced the purest oligarchical structure in Central America. See Edelberto Torres Rivas, "Síntesis histórica del proceso político," in *Centroamérica hoy,* ed. E. Torres Rivas et al., 9–118. (Mexico City: Siglo XXI, 1975).

37. Rafael Guidos Vejar, *El ascenso del militarismo en El Salvador* (San José: Editorial Universitaria Centroamericana, 1982), 92–131. Nothing like a pluralistic, competitive party system was contemplated, of course; demagoguery and clientelism were the predominant styles. See also Dana G. Munro, *The Five Republics of Central America* (New York: Oxford University Press, 1918), 107.

38. Rafael Menjívar, *Formación y lucha del proletariado industrial salvadoreño* (San José: Editorial Universitaria Centroamericana, 1981), 49–102.

39. Roque Dalton, *Miguel Marmol: Los sucesos de 1932 in El Salvador* (San José: Editorial Universitaria Centroamericana, 1982), 143–57; Menjívar, *Formación y lucha,* 49–68.

40. Thomas Anderson, *Matanza: El Salvador's Communist Revolt of 1932* (Lincoln: University of Nebraska Press, 1971), 27; Menjívar, *Formación y lucha,* 66, 67.

41. Anderson states that eighty thousand agricultural workers were organized by the FRTS in the course of a few months in 1930, but this is undoubtedly too high (*Matanza,* 40). A principal PCS leader of the period, Miguel Marmol, estimates that by 1932 the combined urban and rural strength of the FRTS was seventy-five thousand (Dalton, *Miguel Marmol,* 144). While a reliable estimate may be impossible to produce at this point, suffice it to observe that by all accounts the Salvadoran oligarchy was suddenly confronted by a massive, militant popular mobilization.

42. Anderson, *Matanza,* 40–63; Guidos Vejar, *Ascenso del militarismo,* 158–83.

43. For accounts of the rebellion, see Anderson, *Matanza,* 83–146; Jorge Arias Gómez, *Farabundo Marti: Esbozo biográfico* (San José: Editorial Universitaria Centroamericana, 1972), 129–57; and Dalton, *Miguel Marmol,* 267–368.

44. Though massive unemployment is conventionally described as an effect of the depression in the coffee economy, one must be skeptical of the claim that the aggregate demand for labor declined significantly, since many estate owners sought to maintain or increase production levels after the collapse of the international market price. Only in 1932 did Salvadoran coffee output fall and then only for one year and for political, not market, reasons. See the figures provided by Guidos Vejar, *Ascenso del militarismo,* 141–43. The adjustment to low prices logically implied an attack on wage rates in order to sustain estate profits.

45. Marmol noted this omission. See Dalton, *Miguel Marmol,* 320, 330.

46. Ibid., 111–18.
47. Ibid., 123.
48. Anderson, *Matanza,* 19; Guidos Vejar, *Ascenso del militarismo,* 187.
49. Anderson, *Matanza,* 24–25, 69–71.
50. Anderson consistently errs in this regard; for example, see *Matanza,* 70.
51. See Segundo Montes, *El compadrazgo: Una estructura del poder en El Salvador* (San Salvador: Universidad Centroamericana Editores, 1979), 182; Dalton, *Miguel Marmol,* 251–53, 264–67; and Guidos Vejar, *Ascenso del militarismo,* 189. Marmol relates that on one occasion, after convincing a peasant group in Ahuachapan to desist from demonstrating outside the town's military barracks, he was sent back by the peasants with a warning to the party that if it "persisted in throwing water on the fire, the next pacifist messenger—including if it were me—would run the risk that 'the machete would strike him before falling on the class enemy.'"
52. These contrasting forms of community-based peasant organization bear striking similarity to changing forms of peasant mobilization in France during 1848–51. See Ted Margadant *French Peasants in Revolt: The Insurrection of 1851* (Princeton: Princeton University Press, 1979).
53. Despite Anderson's occasional disclaimers, this is precisely the impression conveyed by his book, which relies heavily on elite informants.
54. Abel Cuenca, *El Salvador: Una democracia cafetalera* (Mexico: Ala Revolucionaria Radical [ARR] Centro Editorial, 1962); and Alejandro D. Marroquín, "Estudio sobre la crisis de los años treinta en El Salvador," *Anuario de estudios centroamericanos* 3 (1977): 115–60.
55. Exempli gratia, Dalton, *Miguel Marmol*; Menjívar, *Formación y lucha.*
56. Anderson argues that the ethnic factor was not important in the last two cases and cites as evidence the leading role of local Ladino communists (*Matanza,* 20, 71–72). However, Tacuba residents identified their attackers as Indians (*naturales*) and offered testimony as well to the prevalence at that time of Indian dress and language among local peasants. See Montes, *El compadrazgo,* 303–23. For Ahuachapan the difficulty of the PCS in controlling peasant actions there is indicative of autonomous local solidarity. Further indirect evidence of an Indian presence in Ahuachapan can be found in the fact that the villages to the east of the town, identified by Anderson as points of departure for those attacking it, had been among those most negatively affected by the expropriation of communal lands fifty years earlier. See Browning, *El Salvador,* 206. Pedro Geoffroy Rivas suggests the same conclusion in "El problema agrario en El Salvador: Una visión histórica," *Estudios centroamericanos* 28, nos. 297–98 (1973): 435.
57. Exempli gratia, Anderson, *Matanza,* 78; Dalton, *Miguel Marmol,* 277–78.
58. Similar arguments can be found in Geoffroy Rivas, "El problema agrario," 441; and Guidos Vejar, *Ascenso del militarismo,* 189–90.
59. Dalton, *Miguel Marmol,* 267–74.
60. *Matanza,* 86.
61. Cf. Menjívar, *Formación y lucha,* 79–80.
62. Dalton, *Miguel Marmol,* 247–48.

63. Anderson, *Matanza,* 131–34; Dalton, *Miguel Marmol,* 332–42.

64. For data concerning postwar transformations of the Salvadoran economy, see Rafael Menjívar, *Crisis del desarrollismo: Caso El Salvador* (San José: Editorial Universitaria Centroamericana, 1977); and Hector Dada Hirezi, *La economía de El Salvador y la integración centroamericana, 1954–1960* (San José: Editorial Universitaria Centroamericana, 1983).

65. Dada Hirezi, *La economía,* 39; CSUCA (Confederación Universitaria Centroamericana), *Estructura agraria, dinámica de población y desarrollo capitalista en Centroamérica* (San José: Editorial Universitaria Centroamericana, 1978), 150–54. The latter study shows that coffee-growing departments became regions of attraction for internal migration during 1950–61, after having mainly experienced net out-migration between 1930 and 1950.

66. The rise and characteristics of the cotton economy are well described in Browning, *El Salvador,* 226–48. A more recent treatment can be found in Robert G. Williams, *Export Agriculture and the Crisis in Central America* (Chapel Hill: University of North Carolina Press, 1986), chaps. 2–4.

67. Perhaps because of its more recent origin (sparked by the United States embargo of Cuban sugar after 1960), the sugar export boom has been less well studied in El Salvador than the markets in cotton or coffee. The summary here is based on Napoleon Alvarado López and Jesús Octavio Cruz Olmedo, "Conciencia y cambio social en la hacienda Tres Ceibas (El Salvador): 1955–1976" (*Licenciatura* thesis, University of Costa Rica, 1978). Other relevant observations can be found in William A. Durham, *Scarcity and Survival in Central America: Ecological Origins of the Soccer War* (Stanford: Stanford University Press, 1979), 44; and Penny Lernoux, *Cry of the People* (New York: Doubleday, 1980), 69.

68. Samaniego, "Movimiento campesino," 135. See also Santiago Ruiz Granadino, "Modernización agrícola en El Salvador," *Estudios sociales centroamericanos,* no. 22 (1979): 71–100.

69. Segundo Montes, "Situación del agro salvadoreño y sus implicaciones sociales," *Estudios centroamericanos* 28, nos. 297–98 (1973): 458–75.

70. By 1969 some 300,000 Salvadorans, or about 7 percent of the Salvadoran population, resided in Honduras. The forcible return of many of these immigrants, associated with the 1969 war between the two countries, further exacerbated the demographic pressure. Concerning this and other patterns of demographic change in the Salvadoran countryside, see Durham, *Scarcity and Survival,* 54–101.

71. Browning, *El Salvador,* 256–65.

72. Samaniego, "Movimiento campesino," 132–35; Browning, *El Salvador,* 281–92. As Samaniego correctly observes, the combined effect of agrarian export development and state intervention to support food production produced an increasing differentiation of the peasantry into a mass of largely proletarianized rural workers and a smaller segment of viable small farmers.

73. On the origins of FECCAS, see Walter Guerra Calderón, "Las asociaciones comunitarias en el área rural de El Salvador en la década 1960–1970" (*Licenciatura* thesis, University of Costa Rica, 1977), 232–47; and Francisco K. Chavarría Kleinhenn and Walter Guerra Calderón, "Estructura agraria en El

Salvador: Políticas estatales y movimientos campesinos, 1880–1978" (Heredia, Costa Rica: Centro de Estudios Democráticos para la America Latina, 1978).

74. Guerra Calderón, "Las asociaciones comunitarias," 246.

75. Federación de Trabajadores del Campo (FTC), *Los trabajadores del campo y la reforma agraria en El Salvador* (El Salvador: n.p., 1982), 6.

76. Pablo Richard and Guillermo Meléndez, eds., *La iglesia de los pobres en América Central* (San José: Departamento Ecuménico de Investigaciones, 1982), 73.

77. Salvador Carranza, "Aguilares: Una experiencia de evangelización rural parroquial," *Estudios centroamericanos* 32, nos. 348–49 (1977): 838–54.

78. Ibid., 840–41.

79. Ibid., 845.

80. Ibid., 839, 844.

81. The convergence of FECCAS with the base communities occasioned major controversy within the church. On this crucial topic, see James R. Brockman, *The Word Remains: A Life of Oscar Romero* (Maryknoll, N.Y.: Orbis Books, 1982), 122–30; and Phillip Berryman, *Religious Roots of Rebellion: Christians in the Central American Revolutions* (Maryknoll, N.Y.: Orbis Books, 1984), 109–15. See also the discussions in Tommie Sue Montgomery, *Revolution in El Salvador: Origins and Evolution* (Boulder, Colo.: Westview Press, 1982), 102–7, 115–17; Higinio Alas, *El Salvador: ¿porqué la insurrección?* (San José: Permanent Secretariat of the Commission for the Defense of Human Rights in Central America, 1982), 170–84; and Robert Armstrong and Janet Shenk, *El Salvador: The Face of Revolution* (Boston: South End Press, 1982), 78–83.

82. Federación de Trabajadores del Campo, *Los trabajadores del campo,* 6, 7.

83. On the origins of AIFLD, see Serafino Romualdi, *Presidents and Peons: Recollections of a Labor Ambassador in Latin America* (New York: Funk and Wagnalls, 1967), 415–33.

84. Guerra Calderón, "Las asociaciones comunitarias," 248–55. See also Philip Wheaton, *Agrarian Reform in El Salvador: A Program of Rural Pacification* (Washington, D.C.: Ecumenical Program for Interamerican Communication and Action [EPICA] Task Force, 1980).

85. Guerra Calderón, "Las asociaciones comunitarias," 250.

86. For obvious reasons, ORDEN has not been much studied. A summary account of its creation and purposes can be found in Armstrong and Shenk, *El Salvador,* 77–78.

87. Montgomery estimates that 5 to 10 percent were participating as repressive agents (*Revolution in El Salvador,* 207).

88. See the accounts of Armstrong and Shenk, *El Salvador*; Montgomery, *Revolution in El Salvador*; Enrique Baloyra, *El Salvador in Transition* (Chapel Hill: University of North Carolina Press, 1982); and James Dunkerley, *The Long War: Dictatorship and Revolution in El Salvador* (London: Verso Editions, 1982).

89. On the origins and projected impact of the law, see the special issue, published soon after the enactment, of *Estudios centroamericanos* 31, nos. 335–36 (1976). Reflecting the rapidity of the project's demise, the following issue (no. 337) constitutes a postmortem on modifications introduced in the interim.

90. A good guide to the complex family tree of popular and revolutionary organizations can be found in Montgomery, *Revolution in El Salvador,* 119–57. For a more critical view, see Gabriel Zaid, "Enemy Colleagues," *Dissent* 29, no. 1 (1982): 13–40.

91. See the interviews with FPL and BPR leaders in Mario Menéndez Rodríguez, *El Salvador: una auténtica guerra civil* (San José: Editorial Universitaria Centroamericana, 1980); and also Federación de Trabajadores del Campo, *Los trabajadores del campo,* 7–8.

92. FECCAS-UTC, "FECCAS-UTC a los cristianos en El Salvador y Centroamérica," *Estudios centroamericanos* 33, no. 359 (1978): 777.

93. Peasant mobilization in the northern highland region has received considerable attention through the work of journalists reporting from FMLN-controlled territory in the civil war. Among the most informative recent accounts are those of Robert McCartney in the *Washington Post,* November 7, 1985, A1, A35; November 8, 1985, A1, A36; November 9, 1985, A1, A17; November 10, 1985, A1, A24; James Lemoyne in the *New York Times,* December 24, 1985, A-4; December 26, 1985, A-12; and Tim Golden in the *Miami Herald,* January 19, 1986, C-4. For a longer treatment, see Nicolas Doljanin, *Chalatenango, la guerra descalza* (Mexico City: El Dia, 1982). One must be cautious, however, in extrapolating the dynamics of sustaining peasant support for a full-blown insurgency (i.e., considerations such as logistics, security, and local administration) to account for a prior phase of mass mobilization. In our view, the latter is the more important problem for explanation. A similar view of the debate on the nature of peasant mobilization in the Vietnamese revolution is expressed in Skocpol, "What Makes Peasants Revolutionary?" 362–66.

94. Armstrong and Shenk, *El Salvador,* 100–102.

95. Baloyra, *El Salvador in Transition,* 90, 91, 109.

96. Montgomery estimates that 40 percent of UCS affiliates aligned themselves with FAPU in the wake of the split, while the remainder elected to continue their collaboration with the reform (*Revolution in El Salvador,* 123, 213). See also Wheaton, *Agrarian Reform,* 17, 18; and Baloyra, *El Salvador in Transition,* 138–39.

97. Samaniego, "Movimiento campesino," 140–41. See also Alvarado López and Cruz Olmedo, "Conciencia y cambio social," 140.

98. Guerra Calderón, "Las asociaciones comunitarias," 255.

99. Cf. Armstrong and Shenk, *El Salvador,* 100.

100. A similar interpretation of the basis of the Catholic Left's peasant strength has been argued by Andreas Scheuermeier, "Movimientos campesinos en Centroamérica" (paper presented to the Fifteenth Latin American Sociology Congress, Managua, Nicaragua, November 1983).

101. An enlightening comparison in this regard is to the Catholic Left peasant movement in neighboring Honduras; it emerged in the early 1960s under the same initiatives that gave rise to FECCAS, also benefited from the mobilization efforts of the popular church, and by the 1970s constituted the most aggressive and second largest peasant organization in the country. Nevertheless, in the context of much lower levels of violence and repression than those of El Salvador

and a genuine, though seriously flawed, agrarian reform program, the Honduran movement has consistently pursued structural change through a reformist strategy. See Robert A. White, "Structural Factors in Rural Development: The Church and the Peasant in Honduras" (Ph.D. diss., Cornell University, 1977); and J. Mark Ruhl, "The Influence of Agrarian Structure on Political Stability in Honduras," *Journal of Inter-American Studies and World Affairs* 26, no. 1 (1984): 33–68.

102. Theda Skocpol, *States and Social Revolutions: A Comparative Analysis of France, Russia, and China* (New York: Cambridge University Press, 1979); Charles Tilly, *From Mobilization to Revolution* (Reading, Mass.: Addison-Wesley, 1979).

103. Such a view is implied, for instance, in Calhoun's revision of Marx concerning French peasants in 1848: "They may have been a class *in itself* but they were only communities *for themselves.*" See "Radicalism of Tradition," 898.

104. It is quite conceivable, however, that further historical research would reveal a religious element in the local bonds and leadership of the Nonualco rebellion. Such factors played important roles in eighteenth- and nineteenth-century Indian peasant revolts in Guatemala. See Wasserstrom, *Class and Society in Central Chiapas*; and Keith Miceli, "Rafael Carrera: Defender and Promoter of Peasant Interests in Guatemala, 1837–1848," *The Americas* 31, no. 1 (1974): 72–95.

105. This issue has generated voluminous discussion in Latin America. For Central America, see Lernoux, *Cry of the People*; Brockman, *The Word Remains*; Richards and Meléndez, *La iglesia de los pobres*; and Berryman, *Religious Roots of Rebellion.*

106. Edelberto Torres Rivas, "Escenarios, sujetos, desenlaces (reflexiones sobre la crisis centroamericana)," Working Paper no. 68 (Kellogg Institute for International Studies, University of Notre Dame, 1986), 18.

107. Jeffrey Paige, "Social Theory and Peasant Revolution in Vietnam and Guatemala," *Theory and Society* 12, no. 6 (1983): 699–737.

108. A detour to the same end has been sought by the United States since 1979 through pressure on the Salvadoran state to enact basic reforms. Apart from the problem of conflicting United States strategic security policies, however, the degree of polarization induced by the war makes this at best a long-term alternative. See Enrique Baloyra, "Central America on the Reagan Watch: Rhetoric and Reality," *Journal of Interamerican Studies and World Affairs* 27, no. 1 (1985): 35–62.

109. See, for example, Avery M. Guest, "The Mediate Community: The Nature of Local and Extra-Local Ties within the Metropolis" (paper presented at the annual meeting of the American Sociological Association, Washington, D.C., August 1985).

110. Bryan Roberts, *Cities of Peasants: The Political Economy of Urbanization in the Third World* (Beverly Hills, Calif: Sage, 1979); Manuel Castells, *The City and the Grassroots: A Cross-Cultural Theory of Urban Social Movements* (Berkeley and Los Angeles: University of California Press, 1983);

Alejandro Portes, "Latin American Class Structures: Their Composition and Change during the Last Decades," *Latin American Research Review* 20, no. 3 (1985): 7–40.

111. David Collier, *Squatters and Oligarchs: Authoritarian Rule and Policy Change in Peru* (Baltimore: Johns Hopkins University Press, 1976); Alejandro Portes and John Walton, *Urban Latin America* (Austin: University of Texas Press, 1976).

112. An initial discussion of this topic can be found in Carol Smith, "What Is the Informal Sector and How Does It Affect Peripheral Capitalism?" (paper presented at conference on "New Directions in Immigration and Ethnicity Research," Duke University, May 1981).

Black and White and Color: *Cardenismo* and the Search for a Campesino Ideology

Marjorie J. Becker

It is well known that upon emerging victorious from the Mexican Revolution in 1920, the Constitutionalists confronted a dilemma. Having defeated the popular armies of Emiliano Zapata and Pancho Villa, they believed that they had won the right to construct a postrevolutionary state reflecting their interests. Yet the specters of the popular armies were to haunt them. The new revolutionary elites were forced to determine how to create a state in their own Constitutionalist image and simultaneously how to avoid provoking further popular insurrection.

Despite their passionate desire to erect a stable postrevolutionary state, the Constitutionalists' attempt to do so foundered for more than fifteen years. Their goal of pacifying the countryside proved elusive, it seems, precisely because they understood neither the motivations for popular protest nor the components of popular understandings of legitimate government. Generally not themselves campesinos, the Constitutionalist leaders seemed unable to grasp the fact that such ordinary Mexicans possessed ideological notions regarding what constituted the essence of legitimate government—the relationships between governors and governed. Instead, Constitutionalists consistently reduced campesinos to the lowest economic denominator. Believing that campesinos were motivated only by the desire for land and were susceptible only to bribery or to military power, the Constitutionalists in their search for the formula for rural pacification continually juggled the proportions of land reform and physical coercion.

The government's response to the Cristeros' 1926–29 challenge to its consolidation clearly reveals the failure of such formulas. In President Plutarco Elías Calles's version of the recipe, there was heavy reliance on the military ingredient because, for him, the civil war was basically a military problem. He saw the thousands of campesinos who fought the government as the Vatican's unpaid mercenaries, fighting because

155

they had been hypnotized by local priests. In fact, to put the argument at its most provocative, the Cristero revolt constituted an autonomous popular challenge.[1] Cristeros fought to defend their ways of life—unified realms containing songs, thoughts, and the means of production—as surely as the articles of faith. The Cristero war constituted a signal to would-be governors that their conception of government was not legitimate.

The Constitutionalists were both unable to understand that message and unsuccessful in their attempts to defeat the Cristeros militarily. Consequently, in 1929 the Constitutionalists arranged a truce with the Catholic hierarchy. Yet the pact agreed upon by secular and religious elites did not correspond to the campesinos' view of legitimacy. The area remained unpacified, the task of legitimizing the postrevolutionary state bequeathed to Calles's successor, Lázaro Cárdenas. A veteran himself of the war against the Cristeros in his native Michoacán, Cárdenas rejected a military solution to the problem. Instead, he determined to use "socialist" educators to "spiritually pacify" the region.

Though Cárdenas has been seen correctly as the architect of the modern Mexican state, in fact he, too, at first proved incapable of pacifying western Mexico. No less than Calles, Cárdenas misunderstood the nature of the problem. Incapable of viewing campesinos as equals possessing their own political visions, he attempted to institute a cultural revolution to impose a statist ideology. However, that effort provoked what Margaret Mead has called "one of those dramatic clashes which suddenly illuminate the plot of people's lives."[2] Disaffected campesinos throughout Michoacán instituted widespread continuous resistance against the centralizing state.[3] They boycotted the schools, harassed agricultural agents, and assassinated teachers.

Historians generally have minimized and misunderstood this *anticardenista* movement precisely because they have echoed the *cardenistas'* own appraisal of the campesinos as one-dimensional economic actors, devoid of ideology.[4] This essay seeks to turn that prevalent approach on its head, arguing that it was Cárdenas and the cardenistas who proved themselves to be one-dimensional in their effort to instruct the campesinos in the terms of a new social pact. This work is meant to serve as a corrective to a historiography that remains hampered by a willingness to accept Cárdenas's revolutionary claims and by a peculiar blindness both to the campesinos' ability to act autonomously and to their larger needs. It seeks to show how the cardenistas entered the routine world the campesinos considered their own in order to forge the pact: a pact based on allegiance to the state, destruction of loyalties to landowners and priests, and *ejidal* (state-directed, communal) land tenure. As they did so, the cardenistas revealed the true colors of their ideological universe. They thought in uncompromising black and white terms, and Cárdenas, at least, never forgot that his central aim was political domination.

It is ironic that, as the Michoacán cardenistas attempted to carry out their program in the realm of daily life, they provoked campesinos to uncover the usually invisible world of campesino political consciousness. This consciousness most frequently emerges from, and is concerned with, everyday issues. Though *anticardenista* sentiment was widespread in Michoacán, this article will focus only upon that expressed by a group of Tarascan Indians living on one of the Lake Pátzcuaro islands. The argument will be that the ideology revealed by those campesinos could hardly have contrasted more vividly with that of the cardenistas. Unlike rigid *cardenismo,* the Tarascan campesinos' political world was multihued—subtle, flexible, and more egalitarian than that of their would-be teachers.

While there should be little doubt that this campesino ideology was both more sophisticated and more democratic than that of the cardenistas, simply to reveal its nature and to glorify it seems both irresponsible and antiquarian. For notwithstanding the many political virtues characterizing campesino ideology, the cardenistas possessed two attributes the campesinos lacked—access to state power and the will to utilize it. These characteristics were to prove critically important in determining the configuration of rural lives. Having provoked the clash that caused the campesinos to reveal their usually hidden worlds of ideological concerns, the cardenistas, it will be argued, obtained the information that enabled them to bind the Michoacán campesinos—and campesinos all over Mexico—securely to the centralizing Mexican state. They did not hesitate to use this information to create far more subtle and permanent forms of state domination.

Cardenista Ideology in Black and White

The Michoacán cardenistas' ideology was based on three major characteristics of social reality in the state. Together these constituted the terrain most clearly identified for reconstruction under the new order.

First was the inequitable and unjust precardenista land tenure. In an overwhelmingly agricultural state, only 3 percent of the population held land. By far the vast majority of landowners owned only between one and five hectares.⁵ Second, secular political control was limited to the statehouse in Morelia. The rest of the state was composed of numerous locally controlled fiefs. Third, the vast majority of the state's population was Catholic, and many inhabitants had been willing to take up arms to defend their understandings of Catholicism. Michoacán had produced more Cristeros than any other state.

Utilizing these facts, the cardenistas constructed an ideology in schematic black-and-white terms. They blamed the prevailing social characteristics on campesino acceptance of a mentalité of deference imposed by despotic local elites. For cardenistas the foundation of this hegemony lay in the almost transcendental power of *hacendados* and priests. The hacendados, according to this myth, mesmerized campesinos to protect their fiefdoms, while the clerics proved their might by marshaling soldiers for their antigovernment crusade. In fact, however, the strength of both of these groups was waning. The Cristiada had disrupted the traditional ideological underpinnings of control. Hacendados were unwilling to fight at the side of the Cristeros during the war, while the church hierarchy had betrayed the Cristeros through both flight and, ultimately, negotiations with the state.⁶ By the time Cárdenas ascended to the presidency, the authority of local elites was seriously undermined. Armed campesinos, under the banner of the Cristiada, had already created an altered political configuration in Michoacán.

More important, the kind of deference described by the cardenistas never existed. Cardenistas consistently assumed that campesinos were intellectually imprisoned by hacendados and priests, trapped within a somber, airless world. They believed that the economic domination of the former and justification of inequity by the latter destroyed the campesinos' wills and reduced them to mere puppets. Yet, in reality, rural Mexicans were able to manipulate the strings that bound them to local elites. Campesinos drew upon traditional conceptions of paternalism and Christian notions of morality. Over the generations they had learned to use the social pact between elites and themselves for their own advantage. Despite the many political and economic constraints that they faced, campesinos knew that the old system of allegiance could also provide a certain measure of protection. Campesinos may have differed with Cárdenas over the urgency of their need to be "spiritually liberated" from the "frauds and deceivers" who "maintained them in the shadows."⁷

Yet it seems that the cardenistas were themselves captives of their view of the past. While they were intent on eradicating the old material basis for deference through their land reform and education programs, they refused to believe that campesinos could in fact shake off habits of deference to the powerful. Consequently, the cardenistas constructed an ideology calling for social control and then proceeded to imitate the old elites' techniques of control. They sought to dominate both the material basis of rural life and the arrangement of social relations. The cardenistas entered the black-and-white picture of the past that they themselves had painted and began to impersonate the elites within.

Three characteristics of the old order—as the cardenistas perceived it—particularly shaped their efforts at reconstruction: peasant Catholicism, the order of property, and *caciquismo* (political bossism). First, the idea that campesinos shaped their own understandings of peasant Catholicism was entirely foreign to the cardenistas. Rather, they believed that campesinos had been captivated by priests who utilized gimmicks to justify the old regime. Priests held campesinos in thrall through investing buildings, time periods, and specific objects with supernatural significance and through the use of rites, ceremonies, and symbolism. As school superintendent Celso Flores Zamora put it, "The Catholics, to propagate their religion, used elements of fable and symbolism of inexorable beauty . . . the birth of Jesus in the stable, the mule, the bull, the guiding star, . . . the shepherds with their little sheep adoring the child Jesus."[8] Having captured campesino loyalty, the priests orchestrated their political actions. Pátzcuaro school inspector Policarpo Sánchez complained:

This work of sabotage of the government and the authorities lies in the fanaticism and the prejudices promoted by the enemies of the proletariat: the priests and capitalism. This silent work of ambush emerges from a well organized movement perfectly directed by intellectual authors crouched in the redoubts of the sacristies.[9]

Yet, judging from the cardenistas' reactions, the priests had cast a spell on them. To explain the new social order, they mimicked the priests' methods. Expropriating churches throughout the state, they transformed them into schools,[10] often removing the icons and substituting pictures of Marx, Lenin, Venustiano Carranza, Calles, and Zapata.[11] They prohibited Sunday Mass and substituted "cultural Sunday" programs, featuring the immortal words of General Cárdenas and revolutionary songs.[12] Although not daring to justify the new social order in the name of the Trinity, they did extoll its virtues in the name of greater equality, the campesinos' own well-being, and, always, the revolution.

Thus creating a following, the cardenistas unconsciously assumed what they perceived as the traditional clerical role of directing the campesino political agenda. They claimed that their connection with higher (if political) worlds allowed them to determine what campesino demands would be tolerated by the new regime. For example, in 1934 the cardenistas organized the Congreso Femenil Socialista in Pátzcuaro. Tarascan women dressed in traditional blue shawls heard speeches extolling "schools, rather than churches; workshops, rather than seminaries; cooperatives, rather than saints and alms-boxes."[13] When the women were allowed to present their demands, it is perhaps not surprising that they echoed the cardenistas' program for rural reconstruction. As *Maestro Rural* described it, "The women asked for churches, for their cooperatives; for workshops, for schools for their children; and for arms to defend the government."[14]

The second aspect of the old social pact that imprisoned cardenista ideology and praxis was the old realm of property and its attendant deferential social relations. In the ideological sphere, cardenistas could not believe that campesinos might, at times, have masked their true opinions behind deferential behavior in order to obtain benefits. Rather, the literal-minded cardenistas seemed to confuse such masks with skin, often viewing campesinos as completely paralyzed by "fear of the owner," as one school inspector wrote.[15]

However, the cardenistas' own acts in the establishment of new forms of land tenure once again reveal the persistent power of the past. Finding it difficult to recognize that campesinos could themselves determine the details of land tenure, cardenistas—not unlike the old landowners—controlled agrarian relations. They decided who was eligible for land, what type of crops could be grown, whether or not the area would receive infrastructural aid. Often the teachers who drew up petitions for land aided in the lopsided distribution of the plots. Not unlike the hacendados, cardenistas reserved for themselves the right to banish campesinos who did not comply with the terms of the contract they had established. Francisco Frías, the school inspector of Queréndaro, informed campesinos who refused to attend cardenista schools that they would lose access to their plots of land.[16]

Nowhere is the influence of the hierarchical model the cardenistas inherited from the past more noticeable than in the third example of their ideological rigidity. In this case, the cardenistas denounced the old political domination of the landowners as unjust, stifling the political voice of the campesinos. Yet the cardenistas' behavior hardly suggests that they would have invited rural views unlike their own to coexist within the Michoacán political terrain. On the contrary, and again influenced by the hacendados' hierarchical example, the cardenistas institutionalized local petty tyrants to impose *cardenismo* on the population. Since the revolution Cárdenas had been allied with such armed strongmen, whom he utilized to control various areas of the state.

The cardenista teachers' relationship with rural *caciquismo* is particularly revealing of the ideological rigidity fostered by the cardenistas' bondage to the past. For example, educator Moisés Sáenz fully recognized the unsavory tactics that one such rural cacique employed. Ernesto Prado, a mestizo strongman, had since his 1918 alliance with Cárdenas relied on armed retainers to impose his will.[17] Sáenz described Prado's land reform, which consisted of expropriating the land of the majority and redistributing it to a tiny clique of followers:

The redistribution was neither impartial nor completely equitable. Only the heads of households from the agrarian group received plots, and not all of the confiscated farms came from outside monopolists; at times the farms had belonged to impoverished Indian families of the Cañada [the area in question].[18]

Yet notwithstanding Sáenz's disapproval of Prado's methods, an attitude that Zamora school inspector Evangelina Rodríguez Carbajal shared,[19] they both continued to sanction him, because he was "of the Revolution and of the government," as Sáenz said.[20] Clearly, the cardenistas were so bound to their ideological precepts that they refused to act on dissent, even when the dissenting opinions were their own.

Campesino Ideology in Color

The cardenistas, with their ideological color blindness, at first neither saw nor suspected the existence of campesino ideologies. To be fair to the cardenistas, such ideologies are generally difficult for outsiders to perceive, because they emerge from the varied exigencies of daily life. But for the cardenistas, bound to an intellectual credo that denied the existence of independent rural ideologies, they were at first invisible. It remains ironic, then, that the cardenistas' own involvement with Michoacán campesinos at the community level caused campesino ideologies to burst forth. In striking contrast to cardenista ideology, these ideologies were multihued, as various and flexible as campesino political behavior, which could alternately turn red when it threatened armed insurrection or tone to subtle pastel when it bargained or cajoled.

Although the variegated nature of the Michoacán economic, geographic, and cultural terrain shaped numerous rural ideologies, this study concentrates on one species of *anticardenismo* found among the farmers, fishermen, and hatmakers of the Tarascan island of Jarácuaro, on Lake Pátzcuaro. This emphasis reveals the existence of an untrammeled ideology whose analysis should clarify the specific nature of these campesinos' concepts of legitimacy.

Yet how was it possible for campesinos who described themselves as "impoverished and forsaken"[21] to create an autonomous, idiosyncratic ideology, one corresponding to the blueprints of no ideologues? How were they able to fashion a political worldview that angered both priests and cardenistas, an ideology sanctioning both communal land and ardent Catholicism? What sort of ideology would inspire a political expertise not demonstrated by local cardenistas?

It appears that part of the answer lies in the nature of precardenista politics. Before it occurred to the cardenistas that, in order to obtain legitimacy for their regime, they would be forced to go to the rural communities where the vast majority of the Mexican population lived, national elites had largely ignored community life.[22] It was consequently possible for rural communities, nestled away in niches national elites seldom disturbed, to create ideologies undetected by outsiders.

Within such a niche, the Tarascan Indians at Lake Pátzcuaro had developed a peasant Catholic ideology informed by their attempts to control their lives. The clearest testimony to the independence of the Tarascan approach can be found in the fact that both orthodox Catholic priests and cardenistas disavowed it,[23] though for different reasons. For the priests, it appears that Tarascan Catholicism was a bit too functional, that the worship and the rituals were too much directed toward the improvement of material life. The cardenistas, on the other hand, found Tarascan Catholicism too otherworldly. In fact, these objections presaged the later scholarly tendency to dissect the components of such worlds (base and superstructure). Yet from the perspective of the Tarascans themselves the worlds were integrated. Part of the material basis of their world was the reed lands that they owned communally, for they utilized profits from the reeds to support their rituals. At the same time, they believed that the performance of ritual activity determined their material well-being. As Lucio Mendieta y Nuñez has described it, "Tarascan religion is based on an interested devotion, which is granted in exchange for health, material goods, and divine protection."[24] In other words, the Tarascans had written their own ideological script.

However, when the eight Jarácuaro Tarascans affiliated with Cárdenas attempted to institute their program, the Tarascan scriptwriters learned that their relatively secluded island was no longer so isolated. In fact, these eight people taught the Tarascans a central tenet of the new social pact—that, like it or not, they were to be connected to the national center. In three ways the "Cardenista Eight" showed the other 892 Jarácuaro residents what this was to mean. First, the cardenistas expropriated the communal rush lands and redistributed them among themselves.[25] Then they closed the church, insulting and threatening the campesinos who desired that it be left open.[26] Finally, Cárdenas himself attempted to build a school on the island and to insist on the villagers' attendance.[27]

At that point, the Jarácuaro campesinos unveiled the ideology that had been bred in such a protected environment. Having seen what the cardenistas hoped to institute as legitimate government, they countered with their own vision of legitimacy. In 1937 nineteen Tarascans from Jarácuaro wrote to Cárdenas to specify that vision. Notwithstanding its homeliness and misspelling, the letter reveals an impressive degree of political self-respect. Quite simply, the campesinos told Cárdenas that, without their signatures, no social pact could be drawn up.

In fact, they reminded him, in their bargaining with him on the island they had together rewritten the contract: "You told us personally that the church would not be closed if we send our children to the school."[28] Yet, while they were fulfilling the agreement, he had reneged. They reminded him that, because such behavior on his part (or on the part of his henchmen) was not legitimate, they would not tolerate it:

Don't wait, Mr. President, for blood will run, much blood, because of bad authorities. If they continue to bother us, and if they put us in the prison because of this bargain we have made with you, you have to understand that although we are impoverished and forsaken, we will defend ourselves, so that they do not make a mockery of us.[29]

The fact that the campesinos threatened the president should not be taken to imply that they were incapable of grasping the fact that his might could affect their lives. On the contrary, it was precisely their understanding of the new source of power that prompted them to turn to him. They understood that it was he who was the ultimate arbiter and not his agents, who had stolen their land, or even the authorities, who mocked them. Indeed, they requested that he discipline his underlings. "We want you to order the governor and the rest of the authorities not to mock us, and not to mistreat us."[30]

As such petitions indicate, while the campesinos grasped Cárdenas's power, they were not paralyzed by it. Their remarks to him reflect not simply bravado, though clearly there is also a touch of that ("you have to understand that although we are impoverished and forsaken we will defend ourselves, so that they do not make a mockery of us"). Instead, they show a will to fight for their own vision of legitimate society, even when this meant working within constraints, negotiating, compromising. To do so, they identified within their possession two chips of possible utility for bargaining with Cárdenas. First, their children's attendance at the schools seemed important to him. They consequently reminded him of what satisfying their demands might mean for him. "You must keep your end of the bargain," they said, "so that our children will continue attending the school and so that they will look to you and remember you always, always, with veneration and respect you after you die."[31] Second, aware that Cárdenas was reluctant to risk greater bloodshed in the state, they threatened him. "We ask that you not be bad, and that you comply with our call of the heart, and fulfill your offer not to close the church. . . . Don't wait, Mr. President, for blood will run, much blood, because of bad authorities."

Though the Jarácuaro campesinos' style of prose might be considered inferior to that of the cardenista school inspectors' reports, it nonetheless displays a grasp of political realities (such as power relations, responsibilities of authorities and citizens, techniques to achieve desired ends) more frequently found among practitioners of politics than among those aspiring to be architects of other people's political dwellings.

These campesinos had a political strategy because, as suggested here, they also possessed a vision for their lives. To describe that vision a bit differently, its central political component was an insistence on communal control of the aspects of their lives that most deeply affected them as a community. Together the Tarascans had fashioned a seamless social fabric, stitching together both the means of production and human reflection on those means. Specifically, the Jarácuaro Tarascans' communal ownership of the rush lands allowed them to control the means of production of ritual life as a community. They believed that their rituals, in turn, controlled material life. Although private citizens owned subsistence plots, community rules governed their farming.[32] In other words, the Tarascans did not perceive private property as evil in itself. However, they sought to order the structure of private subsistence farming through community ritual means. The state's attempt at land reform, in fact, meant a privatization of communal property and short-circuited community control.

The Tarascans' world strikes the casual observer as idyllic, but their response to the local cardenistas' land "reform" demonstrates their awareness of the fact that they were being subjected to inequities of power and property. It also suggests that, far from being backward-looking romantics, they were in fact prescient regarding the new power that Cárdenas sought to impose on them. They recognized that, whereas they had previously lived within a relatively isolated niche, the new state had devised a role for the region that endangered their control.

That prescience transformed what might be referred to as a self-protective ideology informed by nascent antistatism into an idiosyncratic antistatist ideology. While viewing state incursion into their lives as illegitimate precisely because it obstructed community control, the Tarascans did not allow that perception to prevent them from pursuing their central goal: the defense of the world they had built. They consequently attempted to preserve that world through negotiation with the state's highest representative. Unlike the cardenistas, they did not allow ideological rigidity to prevent them from attempting to protect what they believed in.

Despite these virtues, it may be objected that the Tarascans' vision was too homely, too small-scale, to be classified as an ideology. While it is true that Tarascans were primarily concerned with making policy governing the details of their own lives and not with national policy, this seems to reflect their instinctive awareness that their expertise was limited to their own experiences. They did not suggest that their knowledge could be transferred to other Mexicans of unknown backgrounds and cultures, a modesty that contrasts strikingly with the cardenista tendency to posit daily rules for lives only poorly understood.

Black and White and Color

The 1937 confrontation between the cardenistas and the Jarácuaro islanders revealed the colorful tapestry of Tarascan political consciousness. Yet the purpose here has not been to revel in the mere exhibition of such tapestries, for that would seem to be a betrayal of the Tarascans' intention in affording Cárdenas a glimpse of their political vision. Recognizing that Cárdenas was for the moment willing to respond to their requests, the Tarascans determined to show him what they most valued precisely because his agents were threatening its existence.

Though Cárdenas was responsive to Michoacán campesino demands at that specific political juncture, the Tarascans had not themselves fashioned the causes for that responsiveness and therefore had little control over them. The reasons Cárdenas sought rural ratification of the social pact he hoped to institute included the fact that western Mexico had posed a military threat to national stability between 1926 and 1929. It appears that Cárdenas was anxious to avoid the economic consequences of further warfare. Also the area's economic significance as a source of foodstuffs must be stressed. The Bajio remained critical as a traditional breadbasket of Mexico. Cárdenas's goals for land reform included the creation of a rural population capable of feeding both itself and the urban population. And most important, from the perspective of the campesinos, Cárdenas hoped to create a constituency to support his economic and political programs. He consequently sought rural approbation of his program.

The need for campesinos to legitimize his government brings us full circle. That need to receive legitimation from the campesinos was so strongly felt that cardenista ideologues constructed a myth. Promulgated by the cardenista educators, the myth stressed that the revolution culminating in *cardenismo* was made by and for the campesinos. According to this myth, Cárdenas—more than any other postrevolutionary president—particularly satisfied campesino needs through his land reform and cultural program.

As this essay suggests, however, the Jarácuaro campesinos did not see it that way. Nor did the majority mestizo population of Michoacán. Although an in-depth examination of their response to *cardenismo* is beyond the scope of this essay, it should be mentioned that evidence exists which documents widespread mestizo disaffection with *cardenismo*. Despite the fact that their political cultures were distinct from those of the Tarascans, mestizos similarly displayed those cultures in expressing their *anticardenismo*. Like the Tarascans, they found schools and land reform particularly problematic, and they forcefully declared *cardenismo* illegitimate regarding precisely those points.

It is not surprising that the rest of the story that has been sketched here has not been told by cardenista ideologues. That Cárdenas was unable to create a legitimate social order until after the campesinos had first declared it illegitimate is hardly the stuff of hagiographic mythology. The fact remains that, once campesinos had shown the true colors of their ideologies to Cárdenas, he was able to institute a much more subtle and effective form of social control. Once he knew the nature of the campesino demands, he was able to fulfill them selectively, based on his state's political and economic needs for campesino support.

Although it should be suggested that the Michoacán campesinos' anticardenista challenge altered the course of Mexican history, the chief result—the creation of more stable state domination—certainly does not correspond to the campesinos' colorful ideological blueprints. Cárdenas learned from the campesinos that ideological conformity was not necessary for state control. Nor was it necessary to destroy every vestige of rural culture. Rather, a more nuanced form of domination began to emerge under Cárdenas. This national political culture sanctioned the coexistence of any train of thought that did not dispute state control and dependent capitalist economics. Today's Mexican state reflects this legacy.

NOTES

The research for this study was supported by a fellowship from the Inter-American Foundation and was partially funded also by the History Department of Yale University. The author would like to thank Steven Wilf for his careful and perceptive critique of an earlier version. She would also like to thank Jean Meyer, James C. Scott, and Emilia Viotti da Costa for their generous support of the work. Findings and views expressed in the article are, of course, solely those of the author.

1. See Jean Meyer, *La Cristiada,* Aurelio Garzón del Camino, trans., 3 vols., 7th ed. (Mexico, D.F.: Siglo veintiuno editores, 1980).

2. Margaret Mead, *Blackberry Winter* (New York: William Morrow, 1972), 247.

3. I discovered this resistance during the fifteen months of research for my dissertation, "Lázaro Cárdenas and the Mexican Counter-Revolution: The Struggle over Culture in Michoacán, 1934–1940" (Department of History, Yale University, 1988). The research was conducted from January 1984 through January 1985 and from June 1985 through September 1985.

The documentary basis for this research in Mexico included population and agrarian censuses, inspectors' evaluations of the education program implemented in Michoacán villages, cardenista plans for rural transformation, textbooks and education journals, cardenista speeches and memoirs, government documents on social banditry and reports on assassinations, transcripts of judicial proceedings, descriptions of rural political networks, campesino petitions and written complaints, campesino requests for land, and descriptions of the ensuing contests and judgments.

These documents are housed in the Archivo General de la Nación (cited herein as AGN), the Archivos Históricos de la Secretaría de Educación Pública (cited herein as AHSEP), the agrarian reform archives in Michoacán and Mexico City, the Hemeroteca of the Ciudad Universitaria, municipal and local archives in Michoacán, private archives of a Michoacán agrarian leader, the Centro de Estudios de la Revolución Mexicana Lázaro Cárdenas, A. C., and in the libraries of the Instituto Nacional de Antropologia y Historia, the Colegio de Mexico, the Colegio de Michoacán, and the Centro de Estudios Históricos del Agrarismo en Mexico. I also conducted interviews with former cardenistas, socialist teachers, and Michoacán campesinos.

4. See, for example, the work of David Raby, *Educación y revolución social en Mexico, 1921–1940* (Mexico, D.F.: Sepsetentas, 1974); and Victoria Lerner, *La educación socialista,* Vol. 6, no. 17 of *Historia de la revolución mexicana,* ed. Luis González. 23 vols. (Mexico, D.F.: El Colegio de Mexico, 1979). On the other hand, chapter 8 of James C. Scott's *Weapons of the Weak: Everyday Forms of Peasant Resistance* (New Haven: Yale University Press, 1985) constitutes a powerful and persuasive rendition of the existence of campesino ideology in the Kedah area of Malaysia. I share with Scott the intuition that campesinos with one foot in the communal past possess the expertise for constructing a more egalitarian future at least as surely as the proletarianized workers, who have never experienced such forms of communal ownership.

5. I based these calculations on information found in Estados Unidos Mexicanos, Secretaria de la Economia Nacional, Dirección General de Estadística, *Quinto censo de población 15 de mayo de 1930, estado de Michoacan,* 11; and Fernando Foglio Miramontes, *Geografía económica agrícola de estado de Michoacán,* 3 vols. (Mexico, D.F.: Imprenta de la camara de diputados, 1936).

6. Meyer, *La Cristiada.*

7. Lázaro Cárdenas, *Palabras y documentos de Lázaro Cárdenas: Mensajes, discursos, declaraciones, entrevistas, y otros documentos, 1928–1940.* 3 vols. (Mexico, D.F.: Siglo veintiuno editores, 1978), 1:169. (This and all subsequent translations are, of course, my own.) See also L. Carranco Cardosa, August 23, 1933, Departamento de enseñanza agrícola y normal rural, Instituto de acción social, La Huerta, Michoacán, Caja 259, AHSEP, Mexico, D.F.: Francisco Frías, Profesor inspector federal Michoacán, "Informe que rinde el inspector de la 17/ a zona escolar en el estado de Michoacán de la labor desarrollado en las escuelas de su dependencia durante el tercer trimestre del año escolar de 1936," Caja 412, AHSEP, Mexico, D.F.: J. Socorro Vázquez, Profesor inspector federal Michoacán, November 15, 1935, "Informe anual," Caja 412, AHSEP, Mexico, D.F.; and Teodoro Mendoza, Profesor inspector federal Michoacán, January–February 1936, Caja 412, AHSEP, Mexico, D.F.

8. Profesor Celso Flores Zamora, "Circular IV," March 7, 1936, "Colección de circulares giradas por la dirección general de enseñanza en los estados y territorios," Caja 557, AHSEP, Mexico, D.F.

9. Policarpo L. Sánchez, Profesor inspector federal Michoacán, February 12, 1936, Caja 412, AHSEP, Mexico, D.F.

10. Among the many examples, see expediente 547.4/462, ramo Lázaro Cárdenas, May 2, 1940, AGN, Mexico, D.F., on the Ario de Rayon church; expediente 547.4/220, ramo Lázaro Cárdenas, January 18, 1936, AGN, Mexico, D.F., on the Purépero church; expediente 547.3/85, ramo Lázaro Cárdenas, September 30, 1935, AGN, Mexico, D.F., on the Tarjero church; expediente 547/56, ramo Lázaro Cárdenas, February 8, 1938, AGN, Mexico, D.F., on the Cherán church; expediente 547.4/133, ramo Lázaro Cárdenas, August 18, 1939, AGN, Mexico, D.F., on a Pátzcuaro church; expediente 547.4/133, ramo Lázaro Cárdenas, AGN, Mexico, D.F., on a Uruapan region church.

11. Personal interview with Roberto Villaseñor Espinosa, March 1, 1984, Mexico, D.F.

12. Ramón Reynosa G., Profesor inspector federal Michoacán, April 29, 1936, Caja 413, AHSEP, Mexico, D.F.

13. "Las mujeres rojas de Michoacán," *El maestro rural* (Mexico, D.F.), December 15, 1934, 22.

14. Ibid.

15. Caja 259, AHSEP, Mexico, D.F.

16. Francisco Frías, Profesor inspector federal Michoacán, March 10, 1936, Caja 412, AHSEP, Mexico, D.F. See also idem. "Informe de los trabajos desarrollados durante el primer trimestre—enero, febrero, y marzo de 1936 por la inspección de la 17/a zona y escuelas dependientes de la misma en el estado de Michoacán," March 31, 1936, Caja 412, AHSEP, Mexico, D.F.

17. Moisés Sáenz, *Carapan,* 3d ed. (Morelia, Michoacán: Talleres linotipográficos del gobierno del estado, 1969), 12. My interview with Jesús Múgica Martínez on December 4, 1984, in Morelia provided additional corroborating material regarding Cárdenas's widespread utilization of rural caciques to control the population.

18. Sáenz, *Carapan,* 163.

19. Ibid., 6.
20. Ibid., 164.
21. Expediente 547.4/133, ramo Lázaro Cárdenas, AGN, Mexico, D.F.
22. Callista educators clearly intended to transform rather than ignore community life, but the Cristero civil war brought their efforts to a standstill in many parts of Michoacán.
23. Expediente 547.4/133, ramo Lázaro Cárdenas, AGN, Mexico, D.F.; and Pedro Carrasco, *Tarascan Folk Religion: An Analysis of Economic, Social, and Religious Interactions* (New Orleans: Middle American Research Institute, Tulane University of Louisiana, 1952), 11, 21.
24. Lucio Mendieta y Nuñez, ed., *Los Tarascos* (Mexico City: Universidad Nacional Autónoma de México, 1940), 161.
25. Personal interview with Jervacio López, August 31, 1985, Jarácuaro, Michoacán; personal interview with Celerino Ramírez, September 2, 1985, Jarácuaro, Michoacán; Carrasco, *Tarascan Folk Religion,* 11, 21.
26. Interview with López; personal interview with Eulario Capilla, September 2, 1985, Jarácuaro, Michoacán; expediente 547.4/133, ramo Lázaro Cárdenas, AGN, Mexico, D.F.
27. Policarpo L. Sánchez, Profesor inspector federal Michoacán, May 11, 1936, Caja 412, AHSEP, Mexico, D.F.; interviews with López, Capilla, and Ramírez.
28. Expediente 547.4/133, ramo Lázaro Cárdenas, AGN, Mexico, D.F.
29. Ibid.
30. Ibid.
31. Ibid.
32. Carrasco, *Tarascan Folk Religion,* 18.

Popular Groups, Popular Culture, and Popular Religion

Daniel H. Levine

This article examines the emergence and character of popular religious groups and considers their implications for long-term cultural change in Latin America. Particular attention is given to the link between religious change and the creation of a *popular subject,* a set of confident, articulate, and capable men and women, from hitherto silent, unorganized, and dispirited populations. I argue here that creation of such a popular subject is nurtured by transformations in key expressions of popular religion, by the way these take form in new patterns of community organization and group solidarity, and by efforts to rework the ties that bind popular groups to dominant institutions.

Popular religious groups have attracted considerable interest and have lately been the focus of much conflict in Latin America. It is worth asking why. Surely it is not for the numbers they attract; at best these groups are an active and perhaps a strategic minority. Most accounts agree that membership figures (unreliable in any case) are small and vary enormously from case to case. Supposed "politicization of religion" or accelerated social mobilization through the groups also fails to make adequate sense of the energies concentrated on them. After all, the past provides ample precedent for clashes between church and state, as for religious and political mobilization generally. Elsewhere I argue that the very definition of a "popular group" is subject to bitter dispute in churches and political groups alike (Levine 1986b, 1988; Levine and Mainwaring 1989). The matter warrants a closer look.

The meaning and value given to things "popular" in Latin America (popular groups, popular religion, popular art, and *lo popular* in general) has shifted substantially over the past few decades (Levine 1986b; Mainwaring and Wilde 1989). Not long ago, reference to *lo popular* called up images of ignorance, magic, and superstition. Popular religion was taken to mean saints, feast days, shrines, pilgrimages, or processions. Older views took popular groups as occasional agglomerations of the poor and humble, mostly logical extensions of major institutions (confraternities that "keep the saints," parish groups) or simply arms of the church like Catholic Action. From this vantage point, popular culture and action are subordinate to and ultimately derived from institutions and elites. But the same reference now commonly evokes class identity (the popular as "the people"—specifically peasants, proletarians, and so forth), comes wrapped in claims to autonomy and collective self-governance by such people and is identified in ordinary discourse with values like authenticity, sharing, solidarity, and sacrifice. When popular groups are defined in terms of class and common circumstances, then legitimate group orientations can emerge from ordinary experience and shared needs, not only from elite direction (see Davis 1974).

Reflecting the new status of popular groups (no longer just sheep to be led in a "flock"), verbs like *accompany* have entered the Catholic lexicon, replacing earlier stress on direction, instruction, and purification. These trends have been powerfully reinforced by the development of theologies (for example, liberation theology) and related institutional programs dedicated to empowering popular groups and giving them a legitimate place in religion, society, and politics (Adriance 1986; Levine 1988; Levine and Mainwaring 1989; Mainwaring and Wilde 1989). There is clearly both shadow and substance here. Much of what is presented as popular self-governance turns out on closer inspection to be little more than the old paternalism renamed. But as we shall see, given half a chance, democratization can become self-sustaining in popular groups, with important implications for reworking general cultural norms about authority, leadership, and action.

In *Democracy in America* de Tocqueville (1961) pointed out the importance of religion to the culture and practice of American democracy in terms that are relevant here. In his view, the separation of religion from state power enhanced the vitality of associational life he found to be characteristic of American life. Religion, he wrote,

> which never intervenes directly in the government of American society, should therefore be considered as the first of their political institutions, for although it did not give them the taste for liberty, it singularly facilitates their use thereof. The religious atmosphere of the country was the first thing that struck me on arrival in the United States. The longer I stayed in the country, the more conscious I became of the

important political consequences resulting from this novel situation. (1:292, 295)

Tocqueville argued that American religion fit into a broad pattern of "mores" (manners, styles of social interaction, family patterns, prevailing norms about hierarchy, equality, authority, and reinforcing links between civil and political associations) that gave American democracy its special character and strength. He gave particular stress to associations, which in his view undergirded American democracy by making habits of expression and association legitimate and possible in all walks of life. This provided citizens with everyday practice in equality and liberty, and as a result,

> in democratic countries the science of association is the mother of science; the progress of all the rest depends on the progress it has made.... When citizens can only meet in public for certain purposes, they regard such meetings as a strange proceeding of rare occurrence, and they rarely think at all about it. When they are allowed to meet freely for all purposes, they ultimately look on public association as the universal, or in a manner, the sole means which men can employ to accomplish the different purposes they may have in view. Every new want constantly revives the notion. The art of association then becomes, as I have said before, the mother of action, studied and applied by all. (1:138, 140)

Applying Tocqueville's insights to the matter of religious change, popular culture, and politics in contemporary Latin America calls for a focus on several related issues. The first involves the character and influence of new religious organizations. Are they more democratic in practice as well as in theory? Do they have discernible impact beyond the boundaries of religion, narrowly defined? The second issue concerns the origins and character of the new groups. How and why do groups get started in the first place? Do differences in origin make for variations in the nature of the group? What is their characteristic link to larger institutions (for example, church and state), and what difference do such links make to the culture and practice of groups on a day-to-day basis? The last directs our attention to changes in religion itself that may arise as part of these developments. Is involvement in different kinds of groups associated with distinct patterns of spirituality, belief, and practice? Limitations of space make complete answers impossible here.[1] The following analysis is an attempt to specify how such organizational and cultural changes get started, work, last (if they do) and to develop guidelines for understanding their possible long-term impact.

In theoretical terms, I root cultural change in evolving links among ideas, group structure and practice, class, and institutions. I give particular attention to the convergence of religious experience and associational life in the development of a new vocabulary and structural basis for independent moral judgment and group solidarity. Empirical analysis rests on field studies in peasant and urban communities and requires us to listen at length to popular voices as they reflect on and make sense of their faith, their lives, and their vision of what the future holds. These popular voices find expression in a context shaped by institutions and their agents and by the needs and understandings (derived from class, economic circumstance, gender, politics, and community tradition) popular groups bring to their encounter with institutions. As we shall see, church relations with other institutions, most notably the state, give a specific tone and character to this encounter—for example, by providing models of behavior, leadership, and organization that can encourage hierarchy or equality, activism or passivity, along with starkly contrasting notions of what religious faith requires in terms of equity, justice, and solidarity with others.

Base Communities in the Latin American Context

Recent discussion of these issues in Latin America has focused on the theory and practice of base communities, or CEBs (*communidades eclesiales de base*), popular religious groups that have garnered considerable (if uneven) attention in recent years. The churches have made CEBs a key theme in regional and national documents, in pastoral plans, and have pointed to them repeatedly as models of desired change, albeit, as we shall see, with very different goals in mind. In practical terms, CEBs have also been an effective strategy for the churches, allowing them to operate with scarce personnel in ways that appealed to an important new clientele.

Most accounts (for example, Azevedo 1987; Bruneau 1982, 1986; Hewitt 1986, 1987; Levine 1986b; Mainwaring 1986a) agree on a few points.

First, CEBs began springing up throughout Latin America in the mid-1960s, with rapid expansion starting a decade later. In all likelihood there was no *first* CEB but, rather, a process of simultaneous invention. Groups are small, gathering fifteen to twenty-five members on a regular basis (weekly or biweekly). They are also comprised mostly of poor people: peasants, rural wage workers, and urban slum and squatter settlement dwellers. The everyday life of groups turns on reading and discussion of the Bible, prayer, reflection on common needs, and some kind of cooperative action. Unlike the conventional parish, CEBs work with and reinforce existing friendship and community ties, putting religion in a familiar and accessible context. This list of traits does not exhaust the reality of CEBs. Indeed, considerable variation exists, along with sharp competition among alternatives at the institutional and grass roots levels. Before getting into the particulars of this variation, it is important to clarify how CEBs fit into the pattern of recent Latin American history. The conventional wisdom locates religious change in delayed regional reaction to the Second Vatican Council. In this view, when they met at Medellín in 1968, the region's Catholic bishops initiated broad-ranging efforts to adapt general changes in Catholicism to the particular societies in which they lived. As is well known, this effort involved both changing the churches and seeing society in new, more critical ways.

This position gets at only part of the truth; a closer inspection of the record reveals more than external stimuli at work here. Indeed, change pops up all across the region, more or less simultaneously with Vatican II and Medellín. Thus, "pastoral weeks," common in the early 1960s, were dedicated to rethinking the church's mission, devising new strategies for action, and implementing them in efforts to reach grass roots clienteles more effectively (Berryman 1984; Bruneau 1985; Carney 1987; Mainwaring 1986a, 1986b; C. Romero 1989). At first, many of these initiatives aimed simply at overcoming scarcities of clergy by creating groups that could run themselves. Emphasis was also placed on training pastoral agents (for example, catechists, community organizers, and a different style of priest or sister) to mediate between ecclesiastical structures and ordinary people. These innovations also responded to the challenge posed by a clientele on the move and no longer likely to be reached and held by traditional strategies founded on priest, parish, procession, and pilgrimage. All these strivings were clearly not created at Medellín, but, rather, brought together and given focus and continental projection. These were soon further extended by liberation theology, which emerges as such just a few years after Medellín.

CEBs can be understood as the latest in a series of organizational mediations that have become central to the discourse and practice of Latin American Catholicism. The general decline of Catholic Action and the failed promise of Christian Democracy opened the door to other visions of group structure and other norms for the proper link between popular groups and the institutions of the church. As Table 1 shows, each favored organizational form (with CEBs the latest) responds to perceived threats and issues and is shaped decisively by the images of church, society, and politics that prevail at any given moment.

The dynamic force of recent Latin American experience lies in the way changes in the church cut across other transformations. Just as the churches reach out to a new clientele, a new clientele is thrust upon them by socioeconomic change, violence, and political decay. The past few decades have brought exceptionally hard times for most Latin Americans. Despite scattered early macroeconomic growth, increasing inequality and impoverishment were the norm, and the late 1970s saw a general slide to debt and depression. A number of related structural changes also altered the meaning of poverty in ordinary life. Agrarian concentration, large-scale migration (migrant agrarian workers, along with moves to the city), improved transport, and expanded literacy and access to media combined

TABLE 1. Change and Conflict in Latin American Catholicism*

Period	Pope	Key Political Events	Key Church Events
Postwar–1958	Pius XII	Cold war	
1958–68	John XXIII	Cuban revolution	Vatican II
	Paul VI	Democratic alternatives	Medellín
1968–79	Paul VI	Rise of authoritarianism	Medellín
			Puebla
		Civil war in Central America	CELAM
1979–?	John Paul I	Central American crisis	Puebla
	John Paul II	Redemocratization	Papal visits

* Trends indicated are (1) Rise and Decline of Christian Democracy as a Model, (2) Succession of Key Issues for Church: Marxism, Politics, Violence, Human Rights, "Popular," Unity, (3) Succession of Preferred Organizational Vehicles: Catholic Action, Christian Democracy, Popular CEBs.

to undermine longstanding ties between elites and masses. Popular sectors were thus made available for new kinds of organization and experience. At the same time, escalating violence and political closure (repression, military rule) spurred group life—closing traditional national structures and driving activists to the grass roots, worsening life conditions for ordinary people and making them seek help, and giving new meaning to biblical passages about justice, suffering, and perhaps a "promised land" (Pearce 1986; Walzer 1985) to be reached after organization and struggle.

The preceding pattern is by no means universal, nor does it come about automatically. Authoritarian rule has been a growth medium for popular groups only where (as in Brazil, with Archbishop Romero of El Salvador, or with groups in Nicaragua) prior changes in ideology and leadership led churches to invest in groups and empower them in significant ways, backing leaders and giving them tools for action (Adriance 1986; Berryman 1984; Bruneau 1974; Dodson 1986; Mainwaring 1986a). Argentina is perhaps the best counter instance, with its enormous repression and a church firmly allied with the military (Mignone 1988). The rise and impact of Christian Democracy reinforces the general point. Where these parties were strong (Chile or Venezuela), activist energies remained closely tied to elites through party structures, focused on elections and partisan struggle, and kept away from diffuse grass roots work. CEBs took off in Chile only after the 1973 coup. Where they were weak

Church Ideology (Key Issue)	Ideal Church Organization	Image of the Popular	Model Latin American Case
Christendom (defense)	Catholic action Christian Democrats	Massive phenomena Ignorance (popular "piety")	Chile Brazil (Leme)
Neo-Christendom Modernization Flirtations with Marxism (reform)	Decline of Catholic action Rise of Christian Democracy	Massive phenomena Ignorance (popular "piety")	Chile Colombia
Emergence of Liberation Theology Splits (politics)	Decentralized groups CEBs	Popular as the class of poor	Brazil Colombia
Splits (popular)	CEBs	Popular as the class of poor	El Salvador Brazil Colombia

from the outset, activism moved directly to grass roots work or became instead a central point of conflict, with powerful opposition from top church leaders. Peru is a good instance of the former case, Colombia of the latter (C. Romero 1989; Levine and Wilde 1977; Levine and Mainwaring 1989).

These conjunctures provide a necessary but not a sufficient basis for understanding. As a rule, exclusive focus on conjuncture is misleading, for it suggests that the different elements in the package come together in some automatic way. This will not do; human agency needs to be built into the process in systematic ways. Transformations within religion (ideas, structures, and practice) need to be set in the context of the changes that make them resonate and ring true to ordinary people and give average men and women a chance to shape the course and content of change on their own. In this light, the central question changes from understanding the impact of conjuncture to explaining why popular groups turn to religion in the first place and what they find there (Levine 1986c). As Segundo points out:

> One of the primary ambiguities of this popular church and its base ecclesial communities is that the whole world is busy counting them, yet no one has any interest in knowing what makes them so appealing. There is an interest in taking advantage of them, no matter what the motivation or consequent praxis. (1985:140)

CEBs derive their impact from the combined appeal of religion's messages and structures. For ordinary group members the message comes mediated through the Bible and discussions of it. With rare exceptions, these members neither read theological texts nor debate general ideological concepts like class, exploitation, or power in any explicit way. The ideas are worked out indirectly, through conversation, reflection on local experience and discussion of familiar (biblical) metaphors (see Scott 1985). Such issues also reach the tiny stage most groups occupy through their effect in shifting the overall weight of church programs—for example, by spurring large numbers of clergy, sisters, and pastoral agents to "go to the people" and, in general, enhancing the dignity of ordinary people and the value of their experience (Adriance 1986; Levine 1988, 1992; Levine and Mainwaring 1989).

New messages are not enough. For enduring social and cultural change to begin and take hold, ideas need carriers and must be embedded in organizational structures and patterns of ordinary group life that make them make sense to average men and women. In this regard, variation in the character and structure of CEBs is decisive. An example may drive the point home. It is not uncommon to find leaders imposing egalitarian and democratic ideals on "their" groups in authoritarian ways: creating issues, imposing programs, making contacts all in the interests of the members, who are rarely involved in the process other than as spectators. Indeed, images of radical priests or sisters and their "flocks" are the stuff of local folklore all over Latin America (Pásara 1986, 1989). Members go along out of traditional deference to superiors or because they are simply too polite to object in public. Whatever the reason, the difficulties for long-term change are obvious. If and when the "good" father or sister leaves, the group has little to fall back on— no homegrown leaders, no experience at setting goals, no independent contacts with others.

The example is cautionary but not universal. As we shall see, new patterns of belief and practice (Bible study, prayer, understandings of sainthood and of the proper role of clergy, indeed the very meaning of "being church") gain strength and take hold within a process whereby men and women come to see themselves as equal, valued, and capable people. The more democratic, autonomous, and participatory groups work best in this regard, for they combine major religious changes with heightened opportunities for leadership and self-expression. Groups of this kind are more viable and better able to survive alone. Personal and structural aspects of change thus reflect and reinforce each other. Where they remain dependent on tightly controlled and hierarchical links to institutions, change is more constrained, and groups wither quickly. New ideas make sense in new contexts, just as altered settings may elicit opinions (including discussion of shared needs) and uncover interests and skills hitherto veiled or simply latent and never brought to the surface in ordinary discourse.

These observations suggest the outlines of a typology of CEBs that highlights the dynamic relations among church structures, institutional ties, and the beliefs, self-image, and routine practice prevailing among popular groups. Table 2 distinguishes among a radical ideal, a vision of group life centered on sociocultural transformation, and a conservative ideal. The first two share a stress on autonomy, democracy, and change but diverge with respect to the salience of class and confrontation in their discourse and the scope of commitment and action their proponents desire. The conservative ideal is little more than the old clericalism repackaged: these small groups remain utterly dependent on clergy for agendas, initiatives, and contacts with larger issues and institutions. Of course, clergy, sisters, and pastoral agents retain an important role in all three CEB types. At issue in this typology (as in reality) is less their presence and role per se than the way it is conceived and carried out and its consequent implications for the developing character of personal, group, and community life. I explore these matters further below. (See also Levine and Mainwaring 1989; Levine 1992.)

Nations, Churches, and Dioceses

It is time now to look closely at cases and to set the general patterns outlined thus far against the experience of specific nations, churches, communities, and individuals. The data that follow are drawn from research I conducted between 1981 and 1983 in Venezuela and Colombia. After preliminary work in national church organizations, I selected dioceses and communities varying widely in context and orientation: rural and urban, devotional and socially activist, autonomous and controlled, progressive and conservative. Research at the community and group level combined structured interviews with members and activists, collection of life histories, and observation of meetings. This comparative and multilevel structure allows for a more thorough exploration of the origins and pathways of change than would be possible with a focus on any

TABLE 2. A Typology of CEBs

	Radical Ideal	Sociocultural Transformation	Conservative Ideal
Origins	Early 1970s	Early–mid-1970s	Late 1970s
Exemplars	El Salvador 1970s	Peru	Colombia
	Chile 1970s	Brazil	
Prevailing ecclesiology	People of God (Liberationist)	People of God (Liberationist)	Institution Christendom
Prevailing image of "popular religion"	Religion of the oppressed	Religion, culture of the poor	Religion of the ignorant
Key values	Authenticity Solidarity	Authenticity Solidarity	Loyalty Unity
Local autonomy	Yes	Yes	No
Agenda source	Bible and "reality testing"	Bible and "reality testing"	Bible and official guides
Scope of action	Local, national	Mostly local	All local
Politics	Confrontational	Local, within group	"None"(?)
Links to church	Strong backing to popular	Coordination	Strong, vertical control

single case or dimension of the process. Figure 1 specifies the research sites and outlines the relations among levels.[2]

In earlier work (Levine 1981), I underscored the importance of national differences in setting the character of religious change in the two nations. These distinctions in economic structure, population (mobility and location), and political history for the most part remain, although attenuated to some extent by rapid urbanization and steady industrial growth over the last decade in Colombia. In Latin America as a whole, despite current waves of violence and political decay in Colombia and growing economic problems in Venezuela that pose questions about the long-term future, the two countries continue to stand out for the relative openness and democratic character of their institutions (Americas Watch 1986; Amnesty International 1988; Bagley 1989; Berry 1978; Hartlyn 1988; Lang 1988; Levine 1973, 1981, 1986a, 1992; Malavé Mata 1987; Urrutia 1985).

In religious terms, the longstanding power of the Colombian church is reinforced by tight links to other dominant institutions and by the hierarchical assumptions that unify elites across the board in fear and suspicion of popular initiatives. Elsewhere I have described Colombian Catholicism as "the leading edge of the old wave" (Levine and Mainwaring 1989). For years Colombian church leaders have provided the dominant regional voice for traditional church positions, defending hierarchical authority and institutional unity from supposed "popular" threats. This position is often associated with immobility, but nothing could be further from the truth. The Colombian church has long been a vigorous innovator: sponsoring unions, creating effective bureaucracies and social agencies, and most recently promoting actively the creation of the "right kind" of popular groups—those tightly linked to hierarchical direction and control. The overwhelming power of the institutional church in Colombia has also marginalized and radicalized independent popular groups that do get off the ground. Their typical combination of radical rhetoric and organizational weakness leaves such groups especially vulnerable to counter measures (Levine 1992). For all these reasons, analysis of Colombia provides particularly valuable insights into the way institutional constraints affect popular groups and shape their characters.

In contrast to Colombia, the Venezuelan church is weak, with no effective national or even diocesan program for group promotion. Here the convergence of institutional weakness with broad social and political

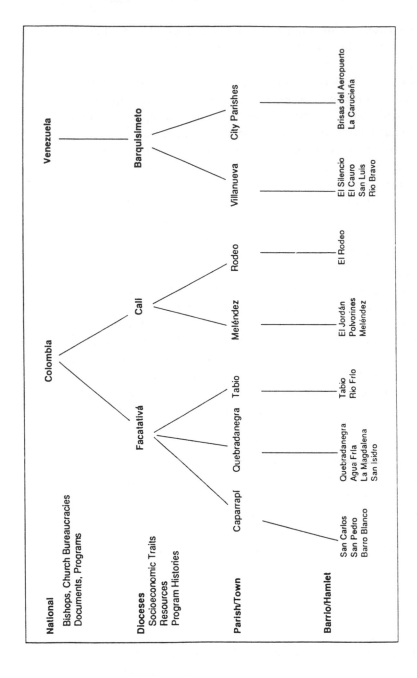

National
Bishops, Church Bureaucracies
Documents, Programs

Dioceses
Socioeconomic Traits
Resources
Program Histories

Parish/Town

Barrio/Hamlet

Venezuela

Colombia

Barquisimeto

Cali

Facatativá

Villanueva   **City Parishes**

Rodeo

Meléndez

Tabio

Quebradanegra

Caparrapí

San Carlos
San Pedro
Barro Blanco

Quebradanegra
Agua Fría
La Magdalena
San Isidro

Tabio
Río Frío

El Jordán
Polvorines
Meléndez

El Rodeo

El Silencio
El Cauro
San Luis
Río Bravo

Brisas del Aeropuerto
La Carucieña

Fig. 1. Levels of research in fieldwork

tolerance of mass mobilization has provided spaces in which autonomous popular groups could emerge along with allies and a sense of legitimacy not available to most of their Colombian counterparts. I found (and studied) striking instances of successful organizational growth and far-reaching sociocultural transformation. People in these communities are much like their Colombian counterparts in economic conditions, life experience, and religiosity, but they differ notably in the prevailing structure and image of group life and hence in its links to broader cultural transformation. As we shall see, these differences rest above all on the distinctive way popular-institutional links are organized in the two countries.

At the local level, my work in Colombia centered on peasant towns and hamlets in the diocese of Facatativá and slum neighborhoods in the archdiocese of Cali. Brief comments on these settings will help frame the discussion that follows. Within the Colombian church, Facatativá has a reputation for progressive leadership and was chosen in the late 1960s as one of several pilot dioceses for CEB development. Analysis of Facatativá thus reveals what "official" CEBs can look like in practice and shows their implications for popular culture. The diocese is almost entirely rural and lies in rough and varied topography to the west of the capital city of Bogotá. Peasant agriculture in this region is generally unproductive, marked by low technology, poor transport and communications, and harassment by armed forces and insurgents. These conditions make it hard for ordinary people to get by and limit their organizational choices severely. In practical terms, the church is often the only available forum for organized group life on the local level. High traditional religiosity and respect for clergy also give church efforts easy entry into most communities.

To reach and hold a popular clientele, the diocese has put together an elaborate program with the following characteristics: use of highly traditional groups (*cursillos de cristiandad*) as entries to CEB formation; plenty of resources (funded by a long-term contract with Catholic Relief Services [CRS]); concentration of money and personnel in pilot parishes and communities; and concern to keep local groups tied to the church. The latter is accomplished by devoting personnel (usually sisters) to promote and monitor group life and also through a complex net of "leadership schools," which meet on a monthly basis in parishes and communities. These schools provide the institutional church with the means for identifying, selecting, and training potential leaders, while keeping tabs on the groups. As we shall see, this control mutes the transformative aspects of religious change, above all by inhibiting self-expression and group independence. Only when groups fall through the cracks in some way does change and self-confidence flower.

The city of Cali is a very different environment. Cali sits at the head of the rich Valle del Cauca. Its economy, augmented lately by major industrial growth, turns on agricultural processing and transport. In the postwar period the city's population has grown explosively, fueled by migrants seeking economic opportunity, while fleeing the rural violence endemic to those years. The archdiocese has been hard pressed to keep pace. Unlike Facatativá, Cali displays no clear program other than a desperate effort to keep up, especially in the popular barrios that spread out like a fan to the south of the city's downtown. I focused on these areas, with special concern for two cases: Barrio El Rodeo, known citywide for radicalism; and Barrio Meléndez, where groups have been spurred by activist sisters as part of a general effort at changing popular culture.

All the communities I studied in Venezuela lie within the archdiocese of Barquisimeto, which has long been home to the Centro Gumilla, a Jesuit research and social action organization. Venezuela's Jesuits have made Barquisimeto one of their major national centers since the late 1960s and, like their colleagues elsewhere, have been active in organizing cooperatives, working with barrio groups, and promoting research and publication on regional and national issues. Their rural efforts center on the parish of Villanueva, and I begin here. The relevant organizational history of Villanueva starts with efforts by an Australian priest, Vincent Arthur (known widely as Padre Vicente) to establish units of the Legion of Mary. In his view, the legion was a perfect combination of intense spirituality, stress on community responsibility, and a simple structure easily run by groups on their own. He was correct: the legion spread rapidly and within a few years produced a corps of capable leaders able to command local loyalties, develop projects, and act together on a regular basis.

Most members are small-scale coffee growers, long subject to usury, abuse, and extortion by jobbers, middlemen, money lenders, and local merchants. As time passed, discussions in the legion turned to material needs, and in response Padre Vicente called on the Centro Gumilla for help. Working with existing units of the Legion of Mary, Jesuit advisers helped establish cooperatives that in short order grew from small and limited savings and local operations to include production, warehousing, marketing, and credit activities on a broad regional scale. Groups have remained closely linked—for example, by common leadership and a widely shared belief that religious values are the indispensable foundation for trust and group solidarity—to the legion from the beginning.

The city of Barquisimeto itself is much like Cali: a large, rapidly growing regional metropolis with an economy geared to commerce, transport, and agricultural processing. I studied two barrios in Barquisimeto: Brisas del Aeropuerto (an older barrio, situated as its name suggests, next to the city airport) and La Carucieña, established a few years earlier by the invasion of an unfinished public housing project. Jesuits have their residence (and educate their novices) in Brisas del Aeropuerto, where they concentrate on promoting CEBs. In La Carucieña, they work closely with two groups of nuns: four North American Medical Mission sisters, who run a mobile clinic and work with health committees throughout the city; and another group of four sisters (from the Congregation of San José de Tarbes) who had recently left their order's elite girls' school to live and work with the poor, with a stress on general education and neighborhood organization.

Tables 3–6 present a general statistical overview of the nations, churches, and dioceses. Table 7 summarizes the central traits of these cases, setting each against key questions about the origins, nature, and implications of CEBs. Subsequent sections of this paper provide the details required to give recognizable human shape and voice to these preliminary and all too general indications. I begin with a look at what they all have in common.

Common Threads

When one looks across these countries, dioceses, and communities, several striking parallels and differences come immediately to the surface. Poverty is common for all the group members, although, as we shall see, being poor can have very different meanings and needs associated with it. With rare exceptions CEB membership is not drawn from the very poorest sectors on the population. Rural groups are comprised mostly of smallholding peasant families; migrant laborers and hired hands are rare. Members may supplement their income occasionally with other work (especially so for younger men), but all have some relatively secure (if poor) base. In the cities, small-scale artisans, vendors, and

TABLE 3. Social and Economic Indicators for Venezuela and Colombia, Selected Years

	Total Population	Percentage of School Enrollment, Ages 6–11	Percentage of Labor Force in			Agriculture as Share of Total GDP	Inflation Rate
			Agriculture	Industry	Service		
Venezuela							
1950	5,034,838	—	42.9	21.4	35.8	—	—
1960	7,523,999	69	33.4	22.5	44.2	7.9	1.0 (1960–70)
1970	10,721,822	78 (1975)	26.0	24.8	49.3	7.5	8.4 (1970–80)
1980	15,024,000	83	16.1	28.4	55.6	6.5	11.0 (1980–84)
Colombia							
1950	11,548,172	—	57.2	17.9	24.9	—	—
1960	17,484,508	48	50.2	19.5	30.4	32.7	11.2 (1960–70)
1970	21,070,115	64 (1975)	39.3	23.3	37.4	28.6	21.1 (1970–80)
1980	24,933,000	70	34.3	23.5	42.3	25.8	21.9 (1980–84)

Sources: Adapted from data in the following: Inter-American Development Bank, *Economic and Social Progress in Latin America, 1986.* Special section: *Agricultural Development;* Inter-American Development Bank, *Economic and Social Progress in Latin America, 1987.* Special section: *Labor Force in Employment;* Sheahan, *Patterns of Development in Latin America;* Grindle, *State and Countryside.*

keepers of tiny shops are the norm, along with public employees like bus drivers or police officers.

Few are recent migrants; fewer still are permanently unemployed or in the so-called informal sector. The vast majority of those I interviewed came to the city (Cali or Barquisimeto) some time ago. Their barrios are already integral parts of the urban scene; recent invasion barrios are generally considered difficult to organize and work with. There is too much movement and too little permanence of housing or income for groups to get much of a foundation there.

Poverty has different meanings for men and women and presents each sex with characteristic dilemmas and lost opportunities. Women everywhere have a narrower range of occupations and more limited access to schooling than men. Those who are not full-time homemakers typically work in food service or as vendors of some kind. I also found a number of single mothers, not widows but women who had either been abandoned by their husbands or had kicked out unreliable or philandering husbands and gone on to make a life alone with their children.[3]

As these comments suggest, poverty makes for highly specific and immediate needs. Members express particular needs for education, health services, security (in housing, land, and in safety from violence), and companionship. This partial listing suggests that groups mediate access to goods and services, while at the same time providing highly prized

TABLE 4. Venezuela and Colombia, Selected Indices, into the 1980s

	Venezuela	Colombia
Surface area (kms²)	898,805	1,138,338
Population (1986)	17,914,000	29,058,000
Urban (1986)	81.3%	66.6%
Life expectancy at birth	69.0[a]	62.1[c]
Infant mortality per 1000	26.1[a]	60.9[c]
Annual population growth rate (1970–85)	2.9%	1.6%
Literacy	85.95%[b]	81%[c]
Annual growth rate GDP		
Cumulative variation (1981–85)	−9.6%	11.2%
1985 growth rate	−1.2%	2.6%
Inflation rate		
(1960–70)	1.0%	11.2%
(1970–80)	8.4%	21.1%
(1980–84)	11.4%	24.0%

Source: See sources for table 3.
[a]1985.
[b]1984.
[c]1981.

elements of friendship and mutual support. Such companionship and solidarity help members cope with the fragmentation of city life and give rural people a way to get beyond the narrow horizons of isolated hamlets or kinship groups. Indeed, such groups often provide the only available organized social life in rural areas. The peasant families I met in Facatativá knew about unions and political parties but rarely had direct experience with them.

When society is regarded "from the bottom up," major economic and cultural institutions appear as distant powers setting the conditions of local life in ways beyond the control of ordinary people: fixing the price of crops, setting the terms of credit, controlling access to schools, determining the condition of roads or other services, and so forth. Vulnerability and violence are permanent conditions, and violence is particularly associated with politics and the state. Violence has come to rural communities for the most part in connection with guerrilla activity, past and present: Villanueva was a key guerrilla zone in the 1960s; much of Facatativá still is. Peasants in Facatativá worry about the guerrillas but reserve special fear and resentment for the army, which has kept a substantial force in the area for decades. Movement is controlled, and groups are regularly harassed and intimidated. Men and women in the towns I visited (especially Caparrapí and San Pedro) commonly report abuses by both sides, display a range of nervous tics, and speak freely of their fears and nightmares.

TABLE 5. Selected Indices on the Church in Venezuela and Colombia, 1950–1980

	Dioceses	Parishes Number	Persons Per
Venezuela			
pre-1900	6	—	—
1950	13	465	10,828
1960	20	582	12,928
1970	26	1,232	13,710
1980	28	1,459	10,297
Colombia			
pre-1900	7	—	—
1950	33	1,127	10,249
1960	48	1,433	10,472
1970	56	1,850	11,389
1980	59	2,212	13,814

Source: Adapted from data in the following: Levine, *Religion and Politics in Latin America, 73;* Levine, "Continuities in Colombia," 307; *Statistical Abstract for Latin America,* vol. 23; *Catholic Almanac,* selected years; *Statistical Yearbook of the Church,* selected years.

Violence in the cities comes in the invasions that establish many barrios and also in repeated clashes between residents and police or army units over access to urban services, especially transport and water. Cali's Barrio El Rodeo was consolidated only after long and exceptionally violent confrontations involving both army and air units. Barrio Meléndez is located close to a major army barracks; this makes for added fear, tension, and clashes. As a general matter, recent years have seen a growing number of very sharp clashes in Cali's barrios among soldiers, police, residents, and guerrilla militants (Americas Watch 1986; Amnesty International 1988).

A final similarity concerns the scale and ordinary routine of groups. All the groups I studied are small (at most twenty members) and gather on a weekly or biweekly basis, depending on weather and transport. Meetings follow a common agenda: prayer, Bible reading, discussion of the text, and some effort (organized in different ways, according to the setting) to link texts to personal and community issues. Most groups also engage in some kind of community work, ranging from visits to the sick, cooperatives, charity to those poorer than themselves, building water lines, schools or bridges, and so forth.

The most critical difference among groups lies in the extent and power of links to the institutional church. These are particularly dense and strong in Facatativá. The arrangements noted earlier are reinforced in this case by a mobile team the diocese has organized (with money from

Priests		Sisters	
Number	Persons Per	Number	Persons Per
—	—	—	—
786	6,406	—	—
1,218	6,177	2,919	2,578
1,976	5,426	4,032	2,659
1,995	7,531	4,345	3,458
—	—	—	—
3,003	3,774	8,865	1,303
4,094	3,765	15,329	1,141
4,864	4,358	17,699	1,193
5,330	5,733	17,654	1,534

CRS) that brings a catechist, an accountant, a cooperative specialist, an extension agent, and a varied group of educators to bear as a group on local-level projects. These complex and overlapping linkages give the diocese a direct and permanent role in group life, manifest not only in operations but also in the very origins of groups and the reasons people join. Sometimes pastoral agents ("a flock of nuns" in one man's phrase) direct a mission to the area. Two examples follow:

> I really don't know. Some missionaries [nuns] came to the school about four years ago. Before that, we didn't know anything about it. They stayed a night and later a sister came, Sister Sara came and told us a base community was going to be set up, people were needed and who would volunteer? So she showed us how to organize the meetings and [now] we do it. (S:16)

> How? Because they told us to [*porque mandaron*]. When Sister Sara and Father Mario came and told us, at first I said no. They never asked me to a meeting, because I would not go. I don't harm anyone, I don't steal, I am not bad. But I went anyway, and I liked it. (S:61)

TABLE 6. Facatativá, Cali, and Barquisimeto, Selected Years

	Area (kms²)	Population	Parishes	Priests	Sisters	Educational Institutions
Facatativá						
1962	8,000	233,000	32	20	—	—
1970	8,000	350,000	34	65	191	17
1975	6,788	374,000	32	65	196	28
1980	6,788	483,000	32	61	230	12
1985	6,788	550,000	28	55	220	14
Cali						
1960	6,555	906,891	55	189	682	44
1970	2,712	980,000	57	190	1,000	59
1975	2,712	1,250,000	68	231	1,172	53*
1980	2,712	1,296,000	74	181	859	90
1985	2,712	1,633,699	81	185	976	113
Barquisimeto						
1960	29,906	502,820	52	82	80	21
1970	19,800	550,000	67	136	200	25
1975	19,800	733,635	72	144	227	37
1980	19,800	836,700	79	148	255	40
1985	19,800	1,115,000	88	186	232	64

Source: Annuario Pontificio, selected years.
*1976.

Groups established in this way require constant care and attention; dependence is built into the process from the beginning. Agendas come from the outside (the diocese through Sister Sara), and groups stick closely to them: there is little autonomy in selecting issues for discussion or initiatives for action. For the most part such groups are locally bounded, with all external contacts mediated through the church. Independent links to nonchurch groups are discouraged; autonomy is viewed with concern. In any event, social issues are less salient here than personal piety and individual spirituality. One young woman states that groups let people "seek a little learning, talk with God, be with God, and discuss religion with others, with songs and prayer" (S:25).

This kind of focus on conventional religiosity and things of the church is reinforced by utter dependence on clergy and pastoral agents for starting groups, finding leaders, and putting agendas together. Susan Eckstein's comments on "the irony of organization" (1979:chap. 4) are relevant here. Eckstein notes that organization can be as much a problem as a solution. When poor people are organized into groups that fit in a

TABLE 7. Field Research Sites: Selected Traits

	Colombia		Venezuela (Barquisimeto)	
	Facatativá	Cali	Rural	Urban
Main program line	Official bishops Pilot (CRS ties)[a]	Independent	Jesuit	Jesuit
Social context	Peasant, homogeneous	Urban, invasion barrios heterogeneous	Peasant, homogeneous	Urban, invasion barrios heterogeneous
Traditional religiosity	High	Low	High	Low
Key religious group	Cursillos	CEB[b]	Legion of Mary	Various
Key social group	Cooperative community stores	"Social action" sporadic organizations	Cooperative, health committees	Cooperative, health committees
Hierarchical control	Yes	No	No	No
Concentration of religious personnel	Yes	No	Yes	Yes
Pastoral agent goal	Evangelization and material aid	Cultural change	Evangelization and material aid	Material aid then evangelization
Groups explicitly Christian	Yes	Mixed	No	No
"Spillover"	Confined to locality	Limited	Yes	Limited

Source: Fieldwork in the communities.
[a]CRS is Catholic Relief Services.
[b]CEB is defined in the text as one of the religious base communities (communidades eclesiales de base).

subordinate way within a dense net of hierarchical ties, the groups become weaker and more dependent on the institution, show little capacity for action, and lack viability over the long haul. Groups with authoritarian origins (*"porque mandaron . . ."*) are likely to drop quickest of all. I found this in Caparrapí, where the diocese had put the bulk of its resources, along with its most charismatic organizer, P. Román Cortes, who died suddenly of cancer in 1981. It appears that the closer links are to the institutional church, the swifter the decline once external support or supervision is reduced.

Where links were weaker from the outset, groups appeared more capable of independent initiative and of bringing personal and community experience to the center of attention. They get used to setting their own agendas, both for specific meetings and over the long term for the group as a whole. Leadership selection becomes more open, as leaders are chosen by and from within the group, not appointed. I found this to be the case in Agua Fría, where groups were formed by local residents who returned, inspired, from motivational meetings sponsored by the churches. Groups in Cali and Venezuela are also much more independent in organization and action. This does not mean no pastoral agents are involved. As we have seen, Jesuits and independent groups of clergy and sisters play a critical role, but official links to the institutional church are much attenuated, leading to reduced emphasis on hierarchical authority and top-down directives.

The preceding comments point to a second general dimension of difference: the quality of group life. Meetings can be open or closed, freewheeling or constrained. I have attended numerous sessions in which participation was both encouraged and unhindered. Here men and women haltingly read texts and spur one another to comment and join in. But I have also sat through interminable meetings that in the last analysis are little more than charades. The priest or pastoral agent (typically sitting in front of the group) asks for comments, stating that "it is up to you, the people must decide." Silence follows: people are shy, not used to speaking in large groups, and in any event reluctant to take the first step. Experience has taught them what is about to happen. After a few moments of quiet, the priest lays out a detailed plan, which is adopted without dissent and usually without comment. In this way, shared reflection and arrangements for common action become not occasions for change but simply added practice in passivity and subordination.

Groups also vary in terms of the concentration of resources and the degree of spillover from religion to other roles and interests. One new element in church work with popular groups is the stress on team effort and coordination. The isolated priest working alone in a parish is a declining type. Groups are now the norm: three priests in a parish, four sisters in a village or neighborhood, a mix of lay activists and clerics. The fact of such concentration in an overall context of resource scarcity helps explain the scattered quality of experience; one tends to find clusters of groups rather than an even spread over a given territory. Concentration of resources also points up the role of external financing. Facatativá has relied on CRS and on the limited national help it gets as a pilot diocese. In Venezuela Jesuit connections and expertise have done the job. Individuals or independent groups of priests or sisters also typically get help from their congregations or home countries. This was the case in both of the Cali barrios I studied.

Organizational scope and spillover vary greatly from case to case. As a rule, groups in Facatativá have remained confined to local cooperatives and community stores, without regional organization or contact with organizations not affiliated to the church, such as rural unions or credit agencies. Contacts are mediated through the diocese wherever possible, thereby restricting local initiative, constraining the development of independent leadership, and reinforcing clerical control at all points. In contrast, Venezuelan experience shows what can happen when clerics deliberately work themselves out of a directive role. Of course, the Jesuits operated apart from mainline ecclesiastical structures in any case and thus felt free to start things up and then let them run. The result is great and growing independence. Leaders who cut their teeth in the Legion of Mary have moved laterally to the cooperatives, using their organizational skills to build alliances with other groups. In a short time, they overcame initial constraints of politeness and deference to clergy and moved clerical advisers out of the day-to-day management of group affairs altogether.

Now that the general contours of groups and programs are clear, it is time to consider how things appear from the bottom up. The following section presents ordinary men and women talking about their ideas and experiences. To be sure, it is always possible to find evocative quotations and use them in ways that mask or misrepresent reality, but I hope by now to have provided sufficient background and context to clarify the meaning and significance of what people say about themselves, their faith, and their church and community. Most people are sufficiently eloquent that the task is less one of search than elimination. The discussion that follows is organized under three headings: needs; religious experience and reading the Bible (both specific texts and the act of reading itself); and changes in what is conventionally termed "popular religion."

Popular Voices

Needs

Popular discussion of needs reflects less a sense of being exploited or oppressed (that is, of class opposition, discussed below) than of having been crippled from the outset in the struggle to make a good life for self and family. Such crippling is located above all in deficient health and education. Despite recent advances in the availability of formal schooling in both countries, access remains limited, especially in the countryside. Older people have bitter memories of an education truncated by closed schools, absent teachers, or the needs of the household economy. Women in particular have everywhere been deprived of schooling by cultural norms that downplay education in favor of service in the home and early marriage. Medical care is also lacking, and diets are often weak in essential protein. Medications are costly, routine preventive care (apart from antimalarial spraying) nonexistent, and access to hospitals difficult when not totally impossible. The result is endemic gastrointestinal problems, childhood diarrhea, and hepatitis; arthritis is common, and poor teeth are the norm. Many families have lost at least one child to disease.

Speaking of his town, one Venezuelan peasant stated simply: "Life is critical there. Everyone works but no one has anything. People suffer a lot in these communities" (V:104). A Colombian echoes this view, noting that obstacles had filled his life: "Not having been able to study. I would be better, more intelligent. Illness too, I have always been sick. Problems have never been lacking" (A:12). Two women describe their frustrating brush with formal schooling in the following words:

I only got through the fifth grade, because the idea then was that men should study, but women would later marry and have children, so why bother, they said. We had to respect that, and so I was left with wishes for more study. (CA:160–61)

The biggest problem here is that people don't value studies. My sister Gladys and I wanted to go on studying but they don't see it. . . . Men say why go to school if women are meant to marry and have babies, and men to handle a plow? (RF:62, 112)

The desire for education explains much of the appeal groups have to women. Meetings provide a chance to learn reading and writing (through the Bible), along with exposure to courses ranging from first aid, sewing, and cooking to theology or history. Meetings also get them out of the house and out from under the thumb of husbands, parents, and in-laws (see Drogus 1988). Many of the women I interviewed had married young in order to escape oppressive family life, only to find themselves now equally subordinate to husbands. For example, this Cali woman eloped, thinking that "in marrying I would free myself, be a different person, that marrying would be a solution. But things went bad for me, like for dogs at mass. I left that man years ago" (CR: 186).

Economic needs combine specifics like wages, credit, housing, land, or education with a general sense of powerlessness and vulnerability. A Colombian peasant put the high cost of living in context this way:

Of course it affects us because we are poor. Everything is controlled at the national level and we get screwed. Our products are worth nothing, what we purchase costs the sky. You've got to accept the price buyers impose; no bargaining is possible for what we need to buy. (A:67)

Vulnerability and powerlessness also underlie expressed needs for security. Insecurity is manifest above all in fear of police and army and general resentment of the way rich and powerful people treat the poor. One peasant man from a town under permanent military garrison (San Pedro) summed things up by telling me "from what I have seen, the rule is kick the guy who's down [al caído caerle]" (C:71).

The church was not exempt from criticisms of this kind. Questions about what it could or should do elicited a sense that even this most trusted of institutions was not living up to its stated ideals. The shepherd was not a good pastor, his flock left adrift and alone. The first speaker is a Colombian peasant; the second, a woman from Barrio Meléndez.

The priest, right? They could help us more, but they just give advice.

Actually helping a poor man—the first case hasn't been seen. A diocese or a priest, they have money, and they could say: here, I have this and I can help you build a house or buy food. Not just advice. (A:59)

For me an ideal priest would be open to dialogue, simple, easy to trust, an ordinary man, not aloof and uninterested. More conscious of his duty, of the real duty a priest has. Because you know, being a priest isn't just staying on your knees to pray. No! It is to see and know your neighbor, especially the poor, to be closer to those in need. That's what a real priest is like. (CA:256)

Being Religious, Reading the Bible, and "Becoming Church"

For many members, joining a grass roots religious group is something like a conversion experience. One repeatedly hears that "we were bad and became good, we went from darkness to light, from vice to virtue, from isolation to community. Now we know what it really means to be religious." This sense of conversion and exposure to valued new insights spurs groups in their tendency to be religious reformers. One man described how he and his companions felt:

We started thinking, we were very different. You're like two people, you go out old and return all new—new spiritually and new materially. And we began to realize the bad things we had been doing. So all this is a change in our way of living, each one in the community. (A:34)

CEBs often have a markedly Protestant-like quality, not only in the stress on Bible study and participation but also in the pervasive concern members express for religious authenticity. They regularly contrast earlier concern with processions and pilgrimages with the current focus on Bible and Eucharist. The former now appears superfluous: Why go to a shrine when God is everywhere? Why pray to a saint when Jesus is central? Why worry about one or another particular Virgin when we know that Mary is everywhere the same, just called by different names?

The frequency and regularity of meetings is much prized by ordinary people. The pattern of small-group religious meetings is new in Latin America, particularly among popular sectors. Such small and intimate settings make religious experience more accessible and familiar, thus undercutting the isolation and suspicion of rural life and helping to repair the fragmentation common to many barrios. Members also stress that, by working together in groups, each teaches the other. As a result, all learn more and more thoroughly than would otherwise be the case. This peasant man recalls that, as a youth: "You had to record questions and answers in your memory [literally: tape them]. But later I learned that Catholicism isn't learning prayers by rote, but rather that we have to incarnate prayers in ourselves and live them in our actions" (A:12). A woman from Barrio Meléndez goes further, stating that without the groups she and her neighbors would still be sunk in ignorance.

> We would just be the same. And really we even committed idolatries, kneeling before Christ and thinking he was the true God, that praying to him all our problems could be over. Now we know better, we see God in our brother, God is reflected in our brothers, in the poor. Now we understand, you see, that you've got to stand with the poor, with those who suffer because, well, doing good to your brother is doing good to God, and if you hurt your brother you hurt God too. That's what we understand. (CA:275, 76)

In many communities the mere fact of organization and regular meetings is new. Around Villanueva there was little or no regular organized activity before the Legion of Mary. The legion spread new habits and routines (e.g., punctuality, record keeping, joint effort in long-term projects) that have elicited a corps of leaders who see themselves as new men and women, spiritually regenerated and socially capable. One man comments:

> Well yes, I think that most of the people you now see working in the cooperative, before, most of them were people with no ... most of them were full of vices—lazy, drinking, no commitment whatsoever. They led bad lives. But now you see them active in the cooperative and the Legion. There has been a change in them as people. And it is precisely the area of getting together for religion [en lo católico] that has made the difference. Before, the only meeting we ever had in El Cauro was for celebrations, fiestas, Christmas, Easter, the annual mass.... Those were the only meetings. But now in the community, in every community, not a month passes without meetings, meetings

where people participate. Now people are used to getting together, and they make new opportunities to join with one another. (V:93)

The most valued experience members cite when discussing the groups is reading the Bible. The Bible is read individually (on getting up or retiring), in family groups, and in regular CEB sessions. Text and process are both important: reading the Bible is prized for the messages it brings and for the sense of personal responsibility, involvement, and self-improvement the act of reading creates. It is important to be clear about how the Bible is seen. These are not fundamentalists. In their eyes the Bible offers not an inerrant text to be followed to the letter but is, rather, a source of accessible values, ideals, and role models. The way the Bible is discussed is indicative. Passages are rarely studied in a formal, analytical way. Instead, participants jump right in to discuss how what is spoken of in a particular text is happening here and now, to people like themselves. The promised coming of the Kingdom of God is thus taken not as an injunction to prepare for personal salvation ("to get right with God" in the style of North American televangelism) but, rather, as a part of working with others now. Echoing Luke 17:20–21 ("the Kingdom of God is not coming with signs to be observed ... the Kingdom of God is in the midst of you"), members see building community and bettering social, family, and spiritual life as integral to that kingdom. This woman put the matter in terms of responsibility:

> I tell everyone that we must be real Christians walking towards our faith, walking to truth, not the kind of Christians who sit every day with rosary in hand, who wait every day for manna to fall from heaven. Because the manna is all used up, that's what I say. (CA:198)

Reading and talking about the Bible on a regular basis gives ordinary people a chance to work together as equals and reinforces confidence in each person's ability to reason, evaluate, and act. The experience can help overcome the sense of crippling and powerlessness often associated with poverty or lack of schooling. As one Venezuelan woman states: "Before we had no idea; you went to mass and that was it. But now we take ourselves into account, we have shared responsibility" (B:99). Understanding gained in this way is regarded as particularly authentic and more long-lasting than that produced by earlier rote learning. It is also independent of clergy.

Yes, yes, let's say that no priest is available for a mass. Well then we can come anyway, no? Participate, join in the church. Reading Scripture and talking about it is what's important anyway. So we go on, because religion is really for us. As they say, God is in the people. (CA:120)

The development of confidence and a capacity to judge and act independently of guidance from elites (civil or ecclesiastical) adds a new dimension to popular life. The process recalls early Puritan accounts of the Bible, which, as Zaret (1985) shows, encouraged independence and a willingness to rely on one's own unaided reason. Learning about religion through shared reflection on the Bible is very much one's own creation. As one rural leader told me, getting together regularly meant that "between us we can be a greater light, help others and see things more clearly" (S:69). When I asked one woman from Meléndez what meetings were like, she replied as follows:

Well it's like this, we develop it this way. We all work to understand better, even me, because you know there are so many things a person doesn't know. Right? The Bible. We read the Gospels and we study every little bit. And here we have people who have never known anything. They read it there [in church], the priest reads the Gospel and that's that. Because he says a world of things people pay no attention to. But here we try to explain things ourselves. We don't have them explained to us, but ourselves we draw it out, we discover what we think. . . . There's more getting together, more dialogue. Not just the priest in the pulpit telling you not to sin, not to do this or that, to repent. Because you know a person hears that stuff and then goes home and forgets it all. (CA:40, 46)

The expressed needs, focus on Bible study and authenticity, and concern for participation are common to all groups but are expressed and combined in different ways according to the degree of independence and democratization each particular group displays. For example, the more group life centers on participatory Bible reading, the more exclusive attention to personal spirituality or prayer appears as a lesser form of religion, something properly left behind. Authenticity is then found in direct links between faith and common action to help others. The Venezuelan groups clustered around Villanueva constitute perhaps the clearest example of these links. Here members combine intense piety and religious devotion with a consistent stress on solidarity and social action reaching beyond the local community. These are seen not as alternatives to religion but, rather, as essential components of it. Cases like Agua Fría or the barrios of Cali occupy a middle ground, in which growing independence and self-worth are constrained, in the first case by continued ties to the institutional church and in the second by general marginalization and scarce resources. Rural Colombian groups centered on Caparrapí, Quebradanegra, and San Isidro remain the most controlled and least changed of all. Here the ideal member continues to be deferential to superiors and focused above all on personal spirituality (*beato*, to use the local parlance). Groups in Agua Fría have been more activist but focused here on the development of what might be called miniclergy—permanent deacons or lay ministers. Groups thus remain subordinate to the institutional church's agenda; local initiatives leading to new commitments and styles of action are not legitimized in this case, as they are, for example, in Villanueva or Cali (for more details, see Levine 1992). Table 8 sums up the differences.

When changes in religious expression and organizational life do get underway, they draw strength from an emerging popular Christology that downplays Christ's mild meekness and resignation for stress on how both his life and his death point to the centrality of practical love for

TABLE 8. Key Questions on CEBs

	Facatativá		Cali	Rural Venezuela
	Agua Fría	Caparrapí Quebradanegra San Isidro	Meléndez	Villanueva
How founded	Cursillo graduates	Priests/sisters	Priests, local residents	Legion of Mary members
When founded	1970–72	1970–72	1977	1970–72 (Cooperativ later)
Meetings/size	Weekly 15–20	Weekly 12–20	Weekly 10–15	Biweekly 15–20
Agenda source	Diocese (adapted)	Diocese pastoral agents	Bible study Discussion Alternative guides	Legion guides Bible study Cooperative
Leader selection	Elected	Selected	Elected	Elected
Presence of diocese	None	Through sisters	None	None
Relation to priests and sisters	Occasional	Strong	Localized contacts with Jesuits	Through cooperative
"Spillover"	Localized	No	Localized	Strong
Ideal group	Spiritual/social	Devotional, activist	Spiritual, activist	Spiritual, activist
Ideal member	Miniclergy	"Beato"	Activist	Activist

Source: Field studies.

others. "We are like Jesus," one Venezuelan peasant commented in a meeting of the cooperative:

Jesus Christ was the first, he joined with people to see how they could get out from under. You can't separate the two things. Jesus came and celebrated; he got involved with people's problems. So with us, a day's work always ends with a celebration. The two things. So Jesus is here with us, doing the same work. (V:76)

He and his companions believe they are "like Jesus" because they too trust in God and work together to help each other and the community.[4] In a further discussion sparked by a passage (Luke 13) in which Christ compares the kingdom successively to a fig tree (that must be planted and nurtured before it bears fruit), to a grain of mustard seed (that becomes a mighty tree), and to the yeast that makes bread rise, one member said this reminded him of when the cooperative began in his town:

When we organized in El Cauro, at first there was no priest to help us. People told us no, priests don't get into that, those are not the church's things. But we know priests are involved in all the problems people have, to see how they can get out from under. They aren't just for praying. (V:75)

Choice of texts warrants separate comment. The Bible has many messages, but the interviews and observation of numbers of group meetings reveal a clear preference for some passages over others. One rarely hears discussions of Romans 13, in which subordination to authority is enjoined. Traditional injunctions to wives to be silent and obey are also for the most part absent. Instead, there is considerable stress everywhere on texts highlighting God's desire for justice and Jesus's stress on love interpreted as sharing and equality.[5] Exodus is popular, along with prophets like Amos, Jeremiah, Micah, or Isaiah, who denounce injustice in terms that are familiar to ordinary people. They talk about oppression, demand freedom for prisoners, and condemn those who, in the words of Isaiah 5:8, "add house to house and field to field until there is no more room, and you are made to dwell alone in the midst of the land." The prophets reserved particular scorn for religious hypocrites content with empty ritual, sacraments, music, and the like but who remained blind to injustice. One woman cited Isaiah as she lashed into the bishops:

> They issue statements about not getting involved in politics, but politics means that they speak about hunger and that they let the people speak about injustice, poverty and all that. They say we shouldn't slide over into other areas, but what are they really doing? They are denying the Gospels. Because if you read the Gospels—I tell you I am a Christian and I have a Bible. But I hardly know any of those Biblical citations, I only know one which is Isaiah 58, which talks about the offerings He wants, and it is to loosen the chains and break the yoke. (CR:173)

I heard a related use of the New Testament at a cooperative meeting in the crossroads community of Río Bravo, outside Villanueva. Here members had built an impressive store and warehouse serving the surrounding area and were also deeply involved in the promotion of farm gardens (to improve diets) and in natural medicine. Discussion at this meeting turned on a passage from John (15:12–13): "This is my commandment, that you love one another as I have loved you. Greater love has no man than this, that a man lay down his life for his friends." To one member this meant that "Jesus seeks us now through the family gardens, through the health committees. It is just like when God made the first man, he made a garden then." In his view texts like this affirm that their group is properly both spiritual and social. At issue was not prayer alone but, rather, "praying and lending a hand [*rezando y la mano dando*]" (V:242).

Beginning meetings with the Bible and making reference to it throughout gives activism and participation a sense of rightness it might not otherwise enjoy. One of the Jesuit organizers in Villanueva comments:

> At first we had some problems. There were a few groups who thought that all this went beyond the proper bounds of religion. Some even said it was bad, that it meant using the Legion for things for which it was not intended. I told them no, and used Gospel passages like the multiplication of loaves and fishes. I said, "Do you know why five thousand were able to eat? Because one person put his food in common. If that person had kept his bread and fish in his own pocket, Christ would not have made the miracle. Yes, and Christ is willing

to work miracles here too. But someone has to contribute his loaf, his fish, someone has to lend his hoe, lend his jeep, put something in common so that Christ can perform the miracle." And so we got started. (V:194)

A similar use of the Bible is found in Barrio Meléndez. Here groups gather every week in the evening, rotating among members' houses. Each session begins with a Bible passage, and time is explicitly set aside for related comment on personal, group, and national issues. One man comments:

People come here with such and such a problem and we start from there. This is where one can really feel the work of the group, because you know in the life of poor people there is so much pressure, so many economic problems. . . . On the one hand patience is needed to stay in the fight. On the other hand, well, you have to learn to stand up and ask for help. Not to remain closed off but to communicate, to tell your problems to your neighbors, to the group. This is the base of our activities, that all [of us] develop a critical consciousness. Because in isolation nothing gets done, nothing can be accomplished, not for oneself, not for others. (CA:106)

The concept of authentic love provides a common thread in meetings and conversations with group members. Indeed, the biblical citation repeated most often to me was 1 John 4:20–21: "If anyone says I love God and hates his brother, he is a liar, for he who does not love his brother whom he has seen cannot love God whom he has not seen. And this commandment we have from him, that he who loves God should love his brother also." Commentary on this text undergirds an evolving view of society, class relations, and what it means to "be church." The first two are portrayed in terms that downplay conflict and rancor. From this perspective the issue between the classes is less structural change or revolution than mutual understanding. Equity and justice involve greater sharing and genuine reconciliation more than sustained confrontation.[6]

Working from texts like this, "the church" no longer appears as the priest or the building down the street but is now commonly visualized as the members who work and live together: the people of God building community. The views of one Venezuelan peasant follow:

I believe we are nothing, not church, nothing if we cannot feel for our brother. How can we [then] feel for other things? Look, the church tells us that if you love the God you cannot see and you do not love the brother you do see, then you are a faker. So I believe that if we cannot feel for our brother, who is right here beside us, and we cannot give him a helping hand, then we can't do anything, we lose everything. To me, this is how to cooperate as a church. Because you are church and I am church. Doing your work you are making the church. This is the church we make as we work. You go about working not only for yourself but also for the community. What is the use of all this information? To learn about what is happening in the world, to get it moving. You are sent because someone sends you, there is one who moves you. If not, you can't see where you are. He is here with us both, guiding us and who knows where? So this is God's house and this is the church. For me, this is what it is. (V:123)

In the discourse of Latin American Catholicism, intellectual circles, publications, official statements, and everyday speech are filled with references to this notion of "being church." "Being church" is also a matter for lively discussion among popular groups, where one often hears that "we are all church [*todos somos iglesia*]." Popular groups distinguish clearly between the church as an institution and "being church" as a community of faithful, the most obvious sense in which "we are all church." Contrary to what both critics and proponents of a popular church occasionally pretend, the distinction between these meanings carries no sense of class or group struggle within the church. Members easily combine expectations of help from the church with affirmations that "we are all church." With growing independence and confidence in personal and collective abilities comes willingness to criticize the church itself and insist that the institution live up to its own norms. In a formulation we shall hear again later (that life is hell), one Cali woman suggests that, unless this happens, the church will disappear:

and it should disappear, because what good is that kind of church, what use is it for the poor? Just to tell us we are going to hell. We live through hell every day we face floods, scarcities, and all those needs. What more hell is there than that? ... I was raised with the idea of a God above the rooftops, that you couldn't see. But tell someone they serve God in a person, because God is there; that you are church because the church is there, not in that pile of cement. Things change, we learn, and people need to see this. (CR:182, 183)

The notion of "being church" provides the underpinnings for a practical ethic of group life. It serves as shorthand for common notions of good behavior, what a Christian person should do. Values of trust, sharing, solidarity, and honesty are prominent here. It also compresses understandings of the particularities of belonging, of arrangements for membership in the institutional church. Among these are the way groups are founded; leaders selected, trained, and validated; programs approved and set in motion. Finally, as noted, the repeated assertion that "we are all church" advances personal and collective claims to take the measure of the institutional church, evaluating programs and judging the adequacy of priests, sisters, and pastoral agents. Popular willingness to do this is reinforced by a decline in long-standing distances between clergy and ordinary people, manifest for example in speech, dress, or life-style. Men and women raised to regard priests or sisters as holy and semi-mystical figures, approachable only with exaggerated deference, now encounter individuals they call by first names, who live close at hand, who dress alike, shop in the same stores, and often go to work every day just like everyone else (Levine 1992). The following comment from Barrio Meléndez suggests that current critiques differ from the anticlericalism of the past. The words express sympathy and even a little pity.

One thing I would like is for nuns and priests to do things that get them into poor barrios, and make them feel the problems there. I say that seeing all those things they would be more conscious of what is going on. Because sometimes I think they aren't responsible for their mentality. From the moment they start to study they are shut up in convents, right? And there it is just brainwashing, brainwashing, so that when they finally get out, it's like getting out of jail. They come out different from everything that goes on around them. *They know absolutely nothing.* (CA:176–77)

Changing Popular Religion

Full understanding of popular religious groups requires taking church affiliation, belief, and practice seriously. Whatever else the groups examined here may claim to be, whatever other ends they serve, their original and continuing identity is religious. The continuing power of religious belief and commitment enables groups to build meaningful vocabularies of moral concern. For this reason, if for no other, close attention to the content of popular piety and spirituality is required. It is their characteristic transformation, not their abandonment for other ideals, that lies at the root of cultural, social, or political changes such groups may spur or legitimize. The whole effort is then organized and legitimized in characteristically different ways depending on the elements of structure, control, leadership, and democratization examined to this point.

In *We Drink from Our Own Wells,* Gustavo Gutiérrez (1985) argues that "it is a serious mistake to reduce what is happening among us today to a social or political problem." To the contrary, a new spirituality is emerging.

> The spirituality now being born in Latin America is the spirituality of the church of the poor . . . the spirituality of an ecclesial community that is trying to make effective its solidarity with the poorest of the world. It is a collective, ecclesial spirituality that, without losing anything of its universal perspective, is stamped with the religious outlook of an exploited and believing people, trying to make effective its solidarity with the poorest of the world. It is a collective, ecclesial spirituality. (1985:2, 29)

Gutiérrez suggests that it may be too early for precise details. "At present we are in the position of those trying to decide whom a newborn child resembles. Some will say the father, others the mother. . . . Better to photograph the child and decide later on whom it resembles" (1985:92). To assess this emerging spirituality, I explore issues that are commonly grouped together under the rubric of "popular religiosity": first, prayer; second, views of the saints, of pilgrimages, and of the Virgin Mary and Jesus; third, the use of holy water; and fourth, ideas about life after death.[7]

Despite otherwise notable variations in opinions or activism, all group members pray a lot—alone and in family gatherings, in churches and group meetings, and on many other occasions. Prayer is a powerful experience: individual and collective speech, action, and memory are worked together with tremendous force and plasticity. Marcel Mauss (1970) comments that prayer is infinitely flexible, and has assumed the most varied expressions, alternatively pleading and demanding, humble and menacing, dry and full of images, immutable and variable, mechanical and mental. It takes on the most diverse roles: here a brutal demand, an order, there a contract, an act of faith, a confession, a plea, a word of praise, a "hosanna"! (95)

Much prayer remains conventional, devoted to giving thanks or to requests for specifics like health, economic success or to physical safety (from storms, accidents, or violence). This dependent and request-focused pattern predominates when links to the parish are tight and groups are less focused on Bible study and collective action. Two men from conservative Quebradanegra comment:

Yes, one sends prayers to God and to the Holy Virgin who are, they are the heads that direct us. [And what do you pray for?] Well, prayer is to thank God for a day's work, for passing the night, for making the rain stop, or for whatever favor or miracle God has done. We thank God and also ask for the youth, for families, and for ourselves. (Q:123)

So that God will increase our faith, and also to ask for help with the needs of our family and of the whole world. There are many needs and so we must ask God for help. Some people say that you shouldn't ask God for material things, but I always ask God to let me have my own house some day. Father Jorge told me that no, you shouldn't be asking because God already knows everyone's needs. It makes sense that God knows all our needs, but I ask anyway. It is like knocking on the door, to make sure he remembers, that he does not forget. (Q:96)

Prayer gives many the strength they need to endure a difficult life, in the words of this man from San Isidro, "always hopefully, with patience, and to suffer patiently what has to be suffered. With patience and with intelligence" (S:68). Prayers for security are especially common in the violence-plagued region around Caparrapí. Thus, one man prays every night "to God and the Virgin. I thank God for all the help he gives me, I offer him my worries, my feelings, and I ask him to help me and my community, so that strangers [gentes raras] won't come. I don't want guerrillas here" (C:60).

The focus of prayer starts to shift as groups become more participatory and active. Setting prayer in community contexts in this way makes praying less a matter of asking for favors or even of thanksgiving (though these remain) than of identifying with others, and thus with God. Listen first to a man from Agua Fría, then a woman from Cali.

> Yes, I pray continuously to find myself with the Lord, when I get up, when I go to bed, and lately, for a year or so now, I have become aware that when I am with other people, at work, playing, resting, I am praying then too, because I am communicating with my brothers. (A:13)

> [I pray] to identify myself, identify myself a little with him. Not just to repeat a prayer, but to identify with the model he is, with being Christian. Identifying with one another we can help ourselves. (CR:222)

A neighbor in the barrio adds a sharp rejection of conventional external markers like tracing a cross on the forehead to mark Ash Wednesday. Authenticity is different; real conversion requires solidarity with others:

> What a farce, to go there and put on a nice face for others when nothing changes inside. To my mind the issue isn't my own conversion to God, it's my conversion to others. I am converted to the extent that I give myself to others. It's not just a matter of converting myself alone. That's too easy, too comforting. . . . The basic thing, what we need to see clearly, is that if we take no heed of others, if there is no love in what we do with others, that will be the final judgment on us. (CR:326)

These comments exemplify the flavor of religious reform and conversion that often attaches to CEBs. Members feel that their religious practice is more authentic; false or unnecessary accretions are stripped away, exposing the true core. This emerges with particular clarity if we ask to whom people pray. A library of studies has addressed the importance of saints in popular belief and practice. Saints appear as uniquely holy and powerful figures who can also be influenced or manipulated to intercede in one's favor before God. In this vein, one rural Colombian woman told me that "God gave them the power to help us. We ask, and they make God work miracles" (S:32).

In general terms, viewing the saints as agents or lawyers has fallen into disfavor and is of dubious orthodoxy to most CEB members. Excessive attention to the saints is also felt to turn one's eyes away from God. As one rural activist told me, "I used to make petitions to the saints, but then I saw that it was only a lever, that it was better to pray directly to Jesus" (C:71a). A woman from Meléndez concurred, noting also that "lawyers are very expensive. If you talk with God you don't need to pay" (CA:217).

As prevailing views of the saints begin to change, traditional practices like pilgrimages or making promises (to bind saints to their word) have also lost popularity (see Christian 1981:175–208; Obelkevich 1979; Turner and Turner 1978). Concerns for orthodoxy and the greater availability of religious practice remove much of the clientele for such devotions. Why go to a distant shrine, pay for travel, food and lodging, fight crowds and run the risk of robbery or accident when you can get the same thing at home? Improved access to health services has also reduced the appeal of pilgrimages, which were often undertaken to appeal for health or relief from illness. When I asked members to whom did they turn when health problems arose, without exception they responded by citing health post, hospital, and priest (in that order), depending on the gravity of the situation.

These comments are not meant to suggest that saints have been abandoned or wholly removed from popular discourse. Instead, they have been reconceived, appearing now as role models: good men and women whose example teaches us how to live well. One man from Agua Fría believes that "they cannot be powerful, because they are just apostles, like we can be" (A:89). His views are echoed first by a Venezuelan peasant, then a woman from Cali:

So there are saints, saints who were converted through their good works. And that is our goal, every person has a goal and I tell you again, you come for your work to our communities, to our brothers. . . . You work according to your own image, from your community. You are sure that you are following a goal, searching for God. You go with God always, that is how life is, and so God is with you, and that is what the saints were doing too. Many people became saints because of their good works, many. (V:129)

I respect them a lot, but there is no one I am particularly devoted to. To me they are people who managed to do something positive in their lives; I can do the same. Everything is according to its period. If they did to me what they did to Saint Teresa, I couldn't endure it. But really they were people like me, they lived in a particular time and place, and perhaps with problems and they were able to succeed. Well, can't I do it too? (CR:329)

From this point of view, sainthood is found in ordinary life: anyone can become a saint. The concept of sainthood is also occasionally stretched well beyond the church's formal canon. In Cali, for example, homes and public transport often display decals of the Virgin Mary next to saints and portraits of Che Guevara, Camilo Torres, or perhaps John F. Kennedy. A resident of Barrio El Rodeo takes Mary and the saints as role models in this way:

I don't share the view of Mary as pure, puritanical, no. To me she was a woman who was mother of Christ, and suffered like any mother, like any of our mothers who suffer so much every day. Not that sanctified image. And I think the saints were people who did things, Che could be a saint, Camilo could be a saint, because they gave their lives for others, for the community, for the people's liberation. (CR:226)

Popular use of holy water (water blessed by a priest for sacramental and ritual use) is interesting and complex. Water is, of course, significant in many cultures and religions. It is a common sign of life and closely associated with health and healing. Miracles commonly involve the use of water; shrines are often founded on the site of springs or wells. Water also has specific importance in Christian symbology and practices, arising, for example, from Jesus' well-known invitation: "If anyone thirst, let him come to me and drink. He who believes in me, as the scripture has said, 'Out of his heart shall flow rivers of living water'" (John 7:38). Water also has a visible and legitimate place in Catholic sacraments (e.g., baptism) and in ordinary church routines.

Popular recourse to holy water draws particular strength from all these sources and extends well beyond common views of orthodoxy. Indeed, of all the practices ascribed to popular religion, extensive use of holy water is the most resistant to change, declining only in the most rigorously orthodox and Bible-centered groups. People often bring bottles and jugs of water to be blessed and then use it in the most varied fashion. Medicines are taken with holy water to make them work better; spouses are kept faithful by sprinkling it on beds in the form of a cross; spills, falls, spirits, or witches are warded off by its application to corners, doorposts, and gates of houses. In one case I witnessed, peasants asked the parish priests (in Caparrapí) for holy water to spread on fields as a guard against locusts. The priests were caught between their belief that God does not violate natural law and a wish to avoid sending these men away empty-handed. A predictable compromise ensued: the priests blessed the water, accompanied with a lecture on its true meaning. As this incident suggests, popular attitudes to holy water raise thorny problems for the church and pose questions about dimensions of persistence and change in popular culture. In the last analysis, the matter hinges on the difference between faith and magic. Orthodox views stress that the holiness of holy water comes as an affirmation of faith. Its significance and possible efficacy thus lie in affirmation of the power of faith, not in powers inherent in the substance or magical manipulations achieved by working with them. I return to this issue in the conclusion.

Concepts of death and the hereafter constitute our last indicator of popular religion. Contrasting attempts to prepare for and make sense of death result in strong differences in how religions are lived. Unremitting emphasis on death's imminence can lead to a stern and gloomy attitude, focused on "getting right with God." Religions can also stress ethical rules and thus emphasize living well over suffering and inevitable death. Questions about what members expect after death elicit responses ranging from conventional hopes for bodily resurrection in glory to concern for leaving something behind in the community. The former view expects, as expressed by one woman, "to find myself face to face with Jesus" (C:48). Others cleave to religion from fear of condemnation. Thus, "I guess salvation, what else is there to expect, other than going to hell. That would be bad" (A:89). Less conventional responses address continuing life (e.g., in the community) more than death. A case in point comes in these comments by a man from Agua Fría. His words recall Archbishop Oscar Romero's famous phrase about living on in the Salvadoran people:[8] "I ask God to have pity on me, on my spirit, and that what I have managed to sow with my witness, that after I die, it may live on" (A:14).

Most respondents distinguish clearly between salvation and condemnation: Heaven awaits the saved; hell is for the condemned. Not everyone concurs: a substantial group of dissenters from Cali blurts out that, although they are not sure, in no way do they believe in hell. No hell compares with this life. To be sure, such views can make death a release, as with this comment from a woman in Barrio Meléndez: "I hope to rest in peace after all the tragedy this world causes. The heaven I see, that heaven is resting in peace from all these tragedies . . . hell is here in this world" (CA:222). As a rule, more radical conclusions prevail. Thus,

> I tell you sincerely that I don't think there can be any more hell than this world. That's right! What happens is that what you don't do right in this world, after death amounts to nothing. I believe two things: that there is no more hell than this world because in this world you live through everything; and that this business of arranging for masses and I don't know what—doing charity in the name of the dead [a noise of scorn]. If they didn't do it in life, much the less in death. So what is the good of all that? I think that what you have to do you have to do it in life. And you do it because it's right. You don't leave it for others to pay your debts. No! (CA:262–63)

This rejection of conventional notions about heaven, hell, and recompense needs to be set in context. Such views differ from ideas that make "this world" a vale of tears to be endured patiently and with resignation until the moment of personal salvation. The commentary is both more bitter and more sociological. These people are saying that day-to-day life in their communities is a living hell. Threats of hell therefore hold few terrors; they prefer to live as well as they can, not to avoid evil ends but, rather, as an expression of faith and solidarity with others. Salvation is taken as a promise, not a reward to be gained by appropriate actions or manipulations.

Conclusions

If religion is to change popular culture, religion itself has to change. The linked transformations in belief, practice, organization, and spirituality sketched out here are critical to such developments. The preceding analysis shows that success in the effort turns on the way individuals and communities see themselves in the process and on the links they build to key institutions. Experience with participatory and egalitarian group life is particularly important. By working together to understand religion and the world and acting together in ways that bridge the two, members assert themselves as capable, articulate, and confident people. Whether the topic is Bible study, cooperatives, or prayer, we come back to how people see themselves as autonomous and capable actors and acquire confidence in the value of their own critical reason. Max Weber's comments (1978) on the significance of congregational and ethical religion to broad sociocultural transformations are particularly relevant here.[9]

A congregational religion is what the name implies—a religion organized in small, self-managed groups of believers in which all have presumably equal rights and capabilities. As Weber saw it, the viability of congregational forms was strengthened by an emerging religious discourse built around a rationalized, ethical view of the world. Congregational structures gave new weight and dignity to the experiences and views of average members, who were enjoined to fuse religion with daily life through continuous, self-moved ethical practice in all aspects of life. In this context, the term *ethical* does not imply that such beliefs are better or their holders more virtuous than others. Rather, by reference to "ethical religion," Weber pointed to a pattern of belief and practice whereby ordinary men and women were charged with (or, more precisely, made themselves responsible for) following a common set of ethical rules. External interventions have little place here. If all believers have access to truth, all are responsible *on their own* for carrying out the precepts set down in the Bible each person is expected to read. The emergence of such a point of view encourages a sense of independence and responsibility that is at once individual and collective. Each person is expected to order behavior according to God's will. The community (here the popular groups) offers a medium for discovering that will through shared efforts at edification and the solidarity born of work in common. The mystical and semisacred status of clerics is undercut.

Ethical rationalization is manifest in the changing elements of spirituality and popular religion noted here. Groups also provide spaces (literally and figuratively) in which new religious sensibilities can be worked out. Consider again the examples of prayer, the saints, and life as hell. Refocusing prayer away from request and manipulation, and toward community and mutual help, pushes the center of religious sensibility from individual gratification to life in common. Seeing the saints as role models rather than intermediaries also throws the burden of action back on the individual, further enhancing the value and significance of one's own actions. Taking life as hell removes fear from the center of spiritual life and frees members to concentrate on this life, confident that salvation is God's free gift. In the process, magical practices and manipulations of the natural order are set aside. Just as all are equal before God, all are equal in nature. Nature itself is organized along rationally understandable lines. Interfering with these in a capricious or ad hoc way is close to sacrilege. Locusts are unlikely to be kept away by holy water.

Weber drew explicit links between religious transformation, intensified spirituality, and a sense of "crisis." At the outset I noted how recent economic, social, and political change in Latin America had spurred religious innovation and activism. Do such changes qualify as crisis in Weber's terms, and, if so, what of it? The word itself is clearly no exaggeration: impoverishment, displacement, pervasive violence, suffering, and death have brought crisis home to many. But the religious outcomes differ from what Weber had in mind. In his view, crisis was a likely occasion for charismatic leadership, structural upheaval, or for ideological substitutes in working-class mobilizations. He expected little basic change from Catholicism (too bound up in hierarchy) or from peasants (too dependent on nature to free themselves from magic) whose reputation for piety he regarded as a modern invention of dubious value.

Latin American experience clearly confirms some of Weber's notions but casts serious doubt on others. The current Latin American crisis has given only marginal place to charismatic figures, new religious movements, shrines, or miracles (see Della Cava 1973; Slater 1986). Despite notable expansion, evangelical Protestantism also remains peripheral; the central axis of religious involvement in the crisis has found expression within the Catholic church, through new grass roots structures, along with a host of institutional reforms and theological argument directed at changing religion's place in society and the place of ordinary people in religion.

The fact that change has arisen within Catholicism and has been centered on groups hitherto believed to be passive and ill disposed to change suggests the need for another look at the relation between crisis and religious change. To begin with, religious change is clearly more than a matter of ideas alone. Ideas never come in the abstract. The predominant ideas of a culture are closely linked to structures and forms of practice. Ideas also need audiences and mediators, groups of men and women who find the messages meaningful, spread them through time and space, and find the associated forms of practice logical in their own changing circumstances. One of the major impacts group formation can have is to establish traditions of sociability and links of solidarity that make the idea of forming groups (for any purpose) both legitimate and familiar (Kincaid 1987; Putnam 1987; São Paulo 1978; Sklar 1987; Vélez-Ibañez 1983). Bear in mind that most of the communities reviewed in this essay have only limited historical depth. Despite their long history as urban foundations, Cali and Barquisimeto have each grown so spectacularly in the postwar period as to be—for all practical purposes—new. Massive migration and land invasions have spurred vast expansions of the popular sector in each city, as in Latin America generally. The rural communities examined here are also relatively new. They arose in both countries only with the development of an export market for coffee in the mid- to late nineteenth century (Bergquist 1986; Palacios 1980; Roseberry 1983).

For these reasons, it is rare to find much in the way of established patterns of sociability on which to build. Traditional gatherings of the kind reported by Eugen Weber (1976) or Maurice Agulhon (1982) in their work on change in nineteenth-century France are not to be found. One finds no counterpart here to the rural *veillées* discussed by Weber nor to the *chambrées* that, according to Agulhon, laid a foundation for acceptance of democratic norms coming from the society at large. As Agulhon puts it:

> On the eve of 1848 the *spirit of democracy*, whether immanent or latent, was probably more important than the impact of democratic *ideas* from the *direct* influence of the "enlightened" minds of the village. But no less fundamental, even if less clearly detected, was the receptiveness that the *chambrées* showed—once again for structural reasons—to bourgeois influences both in the form of ideas and of modes of behaviour. (1982:150)

Making friends, sharing experiences, and simply getting together on a regular basis furthers a general growth in sociability. In this light, one of the most enduring contributions democratic and participatory groups make to shaping the general character of politics clearly lies in their role in demystifying authority by giving the tools of association to everyone, making the effort legitimate in religious terms and thus furthering the growth of a truly independent civil society. Successful development of strong associational life and the shift of popular culture from passive resignation, dependence, fatalism, and powerlessness to equality, activism, and organization would be a cultural and political change of major proportions.

The connection among changing ideas, audiences, and structures is made in ways different from those that some classical formulations suggest. For example, Latin American experience does not confirm Geertz's expectation (1968) that declining coherence of a religious worldview produces an ideologization of religion. To the contrary, inspection of the record reveals a search for a new coherence driven by men and women making themselves into different individuals and communities. Their new stance is no more "ideological" than what went before; what changes is their own sense of self and their capacity to act and to judge. The matter is also not well addressed simply by contrasting elite and popular outlooks and attributing the gap to diverging class interests. There are differences, to be sure, but these are mediated by connections of ideology and institutional affiliation that underscore synthesis and continued ties rather than simple demarcation.[10]

Ideas and group structures evolve together; neither takes the lead. It is important to realize that more than elective affinities are at issue here. The notion of elective affinity is too passive and relies overly on conjuncture for its dynamic. But these are active subjects—people out to create a new reality, albeit often on a limited stage. Mannheim's work on ideology and utopia puts the matter of how change can get started and endure in particularly useful terms. In his view, individuals alone cannot turn utopian dreams into reality:

> Only when the utopian conception of the individual seizes upon currents already present in society and gives expression to them, when in this form it flows back into the outlook of the whole group and is translated into action by it, only then can the existing order be challenged by the striving for another order of existence. (1936:207)

In a small and scattered way, this is what is happening in communities and groups across Latin America today. The long-term significance of these experiences lies in how the setting, process, and content of religious change spur ordinary people to draw links between personal life and collective circumstances. Making such connections in an explicit way contributes to the creation of a popular subject by helping people see themselves as independent actors working in and on the world. The transformation of popular images of self and community and the attendant reworking of core cultural norms about activism, passivity, hierarchy, or equality are an essential first step. This is what lays down a cultural foundation (no matter how tentative at first) for authority or for resistance to its claims. It is here that the human solidarities that make any action endure are built. Changing the theory and practice of ordinary life strengthens the impact ideas and institutions can have and makes changes in any aspect of life more meaningful and more likely to last.

NOTES

The author wishes to thank Phillip Berryman, Thomas Bruneau, Raymond Grew, Thomas Kselman, Phyllis Levine, Scott Mainwaring, Cecilia Mariz, and Ric Northrup for helpful comments and criticisms. The field research on which this article is based was supported by grants from the Horace H. Rackham School of Graduate Studies of the University of Michigan and by the National Endowment for the Humanities Basic Research Grant RO-20172-82. Earlier versions were presented at the Kellogg Institute, University of Notre Dame, and at the annual meeting of the Society for the Scientific Study of Religion, November 1988, Chicago.

1. For further details, see Levine (1992).

2. Methodological choices are more than simple matters of technique. They are theory laden and have important theoretical consequences. To be sure, this formulation is one of the clichés of today's social sciences; specification is therefore in order. This note outlines the methodological principles that underlie the research reported here. I also provide a few details on the interviews.

I take off from a phenomenological perspective, working insofar as possible with the categories people use in ordinary discourse. As a practical matter, this means taking statements of belief and action at face value. Although I checked statements of facts and descriptions of programs against one another, I resisted the temptation to explain away elements of religious belief or experiences like visions or encounters with spirits.

Working with the categories in people's heads rather than with externally derived issues can be tricky. Some element of distance and externality always remains and must be accounted for. Care is also needed to avoid taking categories of belief as frozen, once and forever the same. People think about these things, discuss them, and change in overt as well as unstated ways. It is therefore important to know the history of categories, to understand how styles of thought evolve. This can be done by asking directly about change and also by tracing the institutional rootedness of ideas and the organizational forms through which they diffuse and are maintained.

A related principle concerns the need to place belief and action in meaningful social contexts. Beliefs are not well addressed in abstract terms: they are learned and held by particular people in well-defined circumstances. I provided for meaningful contexts by stressing connections among communities, groups, and individuals and building these into the structure of the research. This is the logic of working from the national level to grass roots communities through dense institutional networks that match links maintained through churches (dioceses, religious orders, parishes, etc.) with parallel ties through cooperative groups, state agencies, marketing relations, and the like.

Drawing these overlapping connections with care clarifies a few key points. First, *lo popular* must be addressed in terms of ongoing links between popular sectors and institutions of power and meaning. Popular religion (and popular culture generally) is no "natural" product, springing untainted and full blown from the spontaneous acts of the people. Rather, popular groups find focus and meaning in a continually renegotiated set of ties to structures of domination. These connections provide critical organizational and symbolic ladders on which issues and resources move across social levels. Their persistence indicates that elites and masses both prize the connection. It also suggests that more than class alone is at issue in popular actions. Class shapes needs, expectations, and forms of expression, but the link between class and action is mediated by institutional connections, organizational strategies, and cross-cutting loyalties. A close look at the legitimation of commitment and action (for example, with reference to loving the brother you can see, discussed below) suggests that class is not enough.

These considerations point to the need to bring together what analysis often holds apart: elites and masses, institutions and expressions of popular culture. In practical terms, this makes for reliance on an eclectic but structured bag of tricks. Thus, I did not rely on narrative history or documents alone, although these helped set the stage. Instead, I devoted intensive effort to reconstructing local and personal histories through depth interviewing along with considerable archival and documentary research. Instead of a general survey, I combined elite and informational interviewing (at national and diocesan levels) with two standard questionnaires: one for members and leaders of groups; another for priests and sisters. I also collected life histories of members and pastoral agents, including priests and sisters.

The geographical and organizational relation of research sites to one another is given in figure 1. Citations from interviews are identified according to a code that denotes the site and specifies a page in the volume of transcript that contains interviews from that site. For example, CR:186 denotes an interview from Cali Rodeo and a passage found on page 186 of that volume. The interview transcript amounts to over twenty-three hundred pages. The following codes are used: G = General interviews for Venezuela and Colombia. *For rural Colombia*; F = Facatativá, C = Caparrapí, Q = Quebradanegra and La Magdalena, S = San Isidro, A = Agua Fría, T = Tabio, R = Rio Frío. *For urban Colombia:* CR = Cali in general and Barrio El Rodeo, CA = Barrio Meléndez. *For rural Venezuela:*

V = Villanueva and surrounding hamlets. *For urban Venezuela:* B = barrios in Barquisimeto.

In all, approximately 250 interviews were carried out over a three-year period. This number includes many informational interviews and reinterviews. I also did extensive observation of group meetings in all the sites. The formal questionnaire was conducted only after such extensive preliminary work and often involved reinterviews. The questionnaire was given to a total of 69 lay people (53 Colombians, 16 Venezuelans, 38 men and 31 women) and 13 clerics (6 Colombians and 7 Venezuelans, 5 priests, and 8 sisters).

3. To date there has been relatively little systematic work on the social composition of CEBs, but see Bruneau (1982, 1986) and Hewitt (1986, 1987) for similar analyses.

4. See Father Divine's comment that "I would not give five cents for a God who could not help me here on the earth, for such a God is not a God at hand. He is only an imagination. It is a false delusion—trying to make you think you had just as well go ahead and suffer and be enslaved and be lynched and everything else here, and after a while you are going to Heaven someplace. If God cannot prepare Heaven here for you, you are not going anywhere" (in Weisbrot 1983:186).

5. This discussion recalls Raboteau's critique of accounts of slave religion that underscore its supposedly otherworldly character. "It does not always follow," he writes,

> that belief in a future state of happiness leads to acceptance of suffering in this world. It does not follow necessarily that a hope in a future when all wrongs will be righted leads to acquiescence to injustice in the present. . . .
> The slaves believed that God had acted, was acting, and would continue to act within human history and within their own particular history as a peculiar people just as long ago he had acted on behalf of another chosen people, Biblical Israel. Moreover, slave religion had a this worldly impact, not only in leading some slaves to acts of external rebellion, but also in helping slaves to assert and maintain a sense of personal value—even of ultimate worth. . . . By obeying the commands of God even when they contradicted the commands of men, slaves developed and treasured a sense of moral superiority and actual moral authority over their masters. (1978:317–18)

6. Marjorie Becker's analysis (1987) of elite and peasant ideology in Mexico is apposite here. She shows how Mexican campesinos rejected elite views that focused exclusively on class in favor of a more nuanced portrait of social relations. In her evocative phrase, the former came black and white only, the latter in color. See Portes 1972 on popular economic rationality, Hochschild 1981 on the complexities of common notions about distributive justice, and Thompson 1978 for a historical perspective on the relevance of class discourse.

7. These dimensions were selected for further analysis from a number of questions posed to group members about religious upbringing and practice. Along with Bible study and understandings of group practice, attitudes on these dimensions point to the continuing incorporation of traditional religious concepts and practices in the construction of group life. Variations in the specific interpretation and weight given to each emerge from the daily interactions of members

and pastoral agents with texts and group circumstances. Together they help provide legitimate underpinnings for group solidarity and for any common action groups may undertake.

8. In an interview with the Mexican newspaper *Excelsior* two weeks before his murder, Romero stated: "I have frequently been threatened with death. I must say that, as a Christian, I do not believe in death but in the resurrection. If they kill me, I will rise again in the people of El Salvador. . . . A bishop will die, but the church of God—the people—will never die" (Sobrino 1985:50–51). For other perspectives on Msgr. Romero's life, see Berryman 1984, Brockman 1983, and Carrigan 1984.

9. I comment more fully on Weber's views in Levine 1985b.

10. On the contrasting character of elite and popular ideologies and views of one another, see Becker 1987, Levine 1992, Mainwaring 1986a, and Smith 1982.

REFERENCES

Abel, C. 1987. *Política, Iglesia, y Partidos en Colombia.* Bogotá: Universidad Nacional de Colombia.

Adriance, M. 1986. *Opting for the Poor.* New York: Sheed and Ward.

Agulhon, M. 1982. *The Republic in the Village.* New York: Cambridge University Press.

Americas Watch. 1986. *The Central-Americanization of Colombia? Human Rights and the Peace Process.* New York: Americas Watch Committee.

Amnesty International. 1988. *Colombia Briefing.* New York: Amnesty International Publications.

Ashcraft, R. 1981. "Political Theory and Political Action in Karl Mannheim's Thought: Reflections upon *Ideology and Utopia* and Its Critics." *Comparative Studies in Society and History* 23, no. 1 (January): 23–50.

Azevedo, M. 1987. *Basic Ecclesial Communities in Brazil: The Challenge of a New Way of Being Church.* Washington, D.C.: Georgetown University Press.

Bagley, B. 1989. *The State and the Peasantry in Contemporary Colombia* (Latin American Issues Monograph Series no. 6). Meadville, Pa.: Allegheny College.

Becker, M. 1987. "Black and White and Color: Cardinismo and the Search for a Campesino Ideology." *Comparative Studies in Society and History* 29, no. 3 (July): 453–65.

Bergquist, C. 1986. *Labor in Latin America.* Stanford: Stanford University Press.

Berry, A. 1978. "Rural Poverty in Twentieth Century Colombia." *Journal of InterAmerican Studies* 20, no. 4: 363–73.

Berryman, P. 1984. *Religious Roots of Rebellion: Christians in the Central American Revolutions.* Maryknoll, N.Y.: Orbis Books.

———. 1987. *Liberation Theology.* New York: Pantheon.

Brockman, J. 1983. *The Word Remains: A Life of Oscar Romero.* Maryknoll, N.Y.: Orbis Books.

Bruneau, T. 1974. *The Political Transformation of the Brazilian Catholic Church.* Cambridge: Cambridge University Press.

———. 1982. *The Church in Brazil: The Politics of Religion.* Austin: University of Texas Press.

———. 1985. "Church and Politics in Brazil: The Genesis of Change." *Journal of Latin American Studies* 17, no. 2: 271–93.

———. 1986. "Brazil: The Catholic Church and Basic Christian Communities." In *Religion and Political Conflict in Latin America,* ed. D. Levine, 106–23. Chapel Hill: University of North Carolina Press.

Carillo Bedoya, J. 1981. *Los Paros Cívicos en Colombia.* Bogotá: Editorial la Oveja Negra.

Carney, J. 1987. *To Be a Christian Is to Be a Revolutionary.* San Francisco: Harper and Row.

Carrigan, A. 1984. *Salvador Witness: The Life and Calling of Jean Donovan.* New York: Ballantine Books.

Castells, M. 1983. *The City and the Grassroots.* Berkeley: University of California Press.

Centro Gumilla. 1979. "Projecto Campesinos." Barquisimeto: Centro Gumilla. Mimeograph.

———. 1980. "Rescatando Campesinos Caficultores." Barquisimeto: Centro Gumilla. Mimeograph.

Childers, V. E. 1974. *Human Resources Development: Venezuela.* Bloomington, Ind.: International Development Research Center.

Christian, W. 1981. *Local Religion in Sixteenth Century Spain.* Princeton: Princeton University Press.

Davis, N. Z. 1974. "Some Tasks and Themes in the Study of Popular Religion." In *The Pursuit of Holiness in Late Medieval and Early Renaissance Religion,* ed. C. Trinkaus and H. Obermann, 307–36. Leiden: E. J. Brill.

Della Cava, R. 1973. *Miracle at Joaseiro.* New York: Columbia University Press.

Dodson, M. 1986. "Nicaragua: The Struggle for the Church." In *Religion and Political Conflict in Latin America,* ed. D. Levine, 79–105. Chapel Hill: University of North Carolina Press.

Drogus, C. 1988. "Reconstructing the Feminine: Gender, Class, Religion, and Politics in Brazilian Base Communities." Paper presented to the Northeastern Political Science Association, Providence, R.I., November 10–12.

Eckstein, S. 1979. *The Poverty of Revolution: The State and the Urban Poor in Mexico.* Princeton: Princeton University Press.

———. 1989. *Power and Popular Protest: Latin American Social Movements.* Berkeley: University of California Press.

Geertz, C. 1968. *Islam Observed: Religious Development in Morocco and Indonesia.* Chicago: University of Chicago Press.

Giraldo, J. 1985. *Paros y movimientos cívicos en Colombia.* Bogotá: CINEP, Controversia 128.

Grindle, M. 1986. *State and Countryside.* Baltimore: Johns Hopkins University Press.

Gutiérrez, G. 1985. *We Drink from Our Own Wells.* Maryknoll, N.Y.: Orbis Books.

Hartlyn, J. 1988. *The Politics of Coalition Rule in Colombia.* Cambridge: Cambridge University Press.

Hewitt, W. E. 1986. "Strategies for Change Employed by Communidades Eclesiais de Base (CEB's) in the Archdiocese of São Paulo." *Journal for the Scientific Study of Religion* 25, no. 1: 16–30.

———. 1987. "The Influence of Social Class on Activity Preferences of Communidades Eclesiais de Base (CEB's) in the Archdiocese of São Paulo." *Journal of Latin American Studies* 19, no. 1 (May): 141–56.

Hochschild, J. 1981. *What's Fair? American Beliefs about Distributive Justice.* Cambridge: Harvard University Press.

Inter-American Development Bank. 1986. *Economic and Social Progress in Latin America, 1986.* Special Section: *Agricultural Development.* Washington: Inter-American Development Bank.

———. 1987. *Economic and Social Progress in Latin America, 1987.* Special Section: *Labor Force in Employment.* Washington: Inter-American Development Bank.

Kincaid, D. 1987. "Peasants into Rebels: Community and Class in Rural El Salvador." *Comparative Studies in Society and History* 29, no. 3 (July): 466–94.

Kselman, T. 1985. *Miracles and Prophecies in Nineteenth Century France.* New Brunswick, N.J.: Rutgers University Press.

———. 1986. "Ambivalence and Assumption in the Concept of Popular Religion." In *Religion and Political Conflict in Latin America,* ed. D. Levine, 27–41. Chapel Hill: University of North Carolina Press.

Lang, J. 1988. *Inside Development in Latin America.* Chapel Hill: University of North Carolina Press.

Leal Buitrago, F. 1984. *Estado y Política en Colombia.* Bogotá: Siglo XXI de Colombia.

———. 1988. "Democracia Oligárquica y Rearticulación de la Sociedad Civil: El Caso Colombiano." Paper prepared for a "Seminario Internacional Sobre Perspectivas de la Estabilidad Democrática en los Países Andinos dentro de un Marco Comparativo," Villa de Leiva, Colombia, August.

Levine, D. 1973. *Conflict and Political Change in Venezuela.* Princeton: Princeton University Press.

———. 1980. *Churches and Politics in Latin America.* Beverly Hills: Sage.

———. 1981. *Religion and Politics in Latin America: The Catholic Church in Venezuela and Colombia.* Princeton: Princeton University Press.

———. 1985a. "Continuities in Colombia." *Journal of Latin American Studies* 17, no. 2: 295–317.

———. 1985b. "Religion and Politics: Drawing Lines, Understanding Change." *Latin American Research Review* 20, no. 1: 185–201.

———. 1986a. "Colombia: The Institutional Church and the Popular." In *Religion and Political Conflict in Latin America,* ed. D. Levine, 187–217. Chapel Hill: University of North Carolina Press.

———. 1986b. *Religion and Political Conflict in Latin America.* Chapel Hill: University of North Carolina Press.

———. 1986c. "Religion and Politics in Comparative and Historical Perspective." *Comparative Politics* 19, no. 1: 95–122.

———. 1987. "Holiness, Faith, Power, Politics." *Journal for the Scientific Study of Religion* 26, no. 4: 551–61.

———. 1988. "Assessing the Impacts of Liberation Theology in Latin America." *Review of Politics* 50, no. 2: 241–63.

———. 1989. "Venezuela: The Origins, Nature and Prospects of Democracy." In *Latin America,* vol. 4 of *Democracy in Developing Countries,* ed. S. Lipset, J. Linz, and L. Diamond, 246–89. Boulder: Lynne Rienner.

———. 1992. *Popular Voices in Latin American Catholicism.* Princeton: Princeton University Press.

Levine, D., and S. Mainwaring. 1989. "Religion and Popular Protest in Latin America: Contrasting Experiences." In *Power and Popular Protest: Latin American Social Movements,* ed. S. Eckstein, 203–40. Berkeley: University of California Press.

Levine, D., and A. Wilde. 1977. "The Catholic Church, 'Politics,' and Violence: The Colombian Case." *Review of Politics* 39, no. 2: 220–49.

Mainwaring, S. 1986a. *The Catholic Church and Politics in Brazil, 1916–1985.* Stanford: Stanford University Press.

———. 1986b. "Brazil: The Catholic Church and the Popular Movement in Nova Iguaçu, 1974–1985." In *Religion and Political Conflict in Latin America,* ed. D. Levine, 124–55. Chapel Hill: University of North Carolina Press.

Mainwaring, S., and E. Viola. 1986. "New Social Movements, Political Culture, and Democracy: Brazil and Argentina in the 1980s." *Telos,* no. 61: 17–52.

Mainwaring, S., and A. Wilde. 1989. *The Progressive Church in Latin America.* Notre Dame: University of Notre Dame Press.

Malavé Mata, H. 1987. *Los Extravíos del Poder: Euforia y Crisis del Populismo en Venezuela.* Caracas: Universidad Central de Venezuela.

Mannheim, K. 1936. *Ideology and Utopia.* New York: Harcourt, Brace, and World.

Mauss, M. [1909] 1970. "La Oración." In *Lo Sagrado y Lo Profano, Obras I.* Barcelona: Barral Editores.

Mignone, E. 1988. *Witness to the Truth.* Maryknoll, N.Y.: Orbis Books.

Morris, A. 1984. *The Origins of the Civil Rights Movement.* New York: Free Press.

Obelkevich, J. 1979. *Religion and the People, 800–1700.* Chapel Hill: University of North Carolina Press.

Palacios, M. 1980. *Coffee in Colombia, 1850–1970: An Economic, Social and Political History.* Cambridge: Cambridge University Press.

Pásara, L. 1986. *Radicalización y Conflicto en la Iglesia Peruana.* Lima: Ediciones Virrey.

———. 1989. "Peru: The Leftist Angels." In *The Progressive Church in Latin America,* ed. S. Mainwaring and A. Wilde, 276–327. Notre Dame: University of Notre Dame Press.

Pearce, J. 1986. *The Promised Land: Peasant Rebellion in Chalatenango, El Salvador.* London: Latin America Bureau.

Perlman, J. 1976. *The Myth of Marginality: Politics and Urban Poverty in Rio de Janeiro.* Berkeley: University of California Press.

224 / *Constructing Culture and Power in Latin America*

Piven, F. F., and R. Cloward. 1979. *Poor Peoples' Movements: Why They Succeed, How They Fail.* New York: Vintage.

Portes, A. 1972. "Rationality in the Slum: An Essay on Interpretive Sociology." *Comparative Studies in Society and History* 14, no. 3 (June): 268–86.

———. 1985. "Latin American Class Structures: Their Composition and Change during the Last Decades." *Latin American Research Review* 20, no. 3: 7–40.

Portes, A., and J. Walton. 1976. *Urban Latin America: The Political Condition from Above and from Below.* Austin: University of Texas Press.

Putnam, R. 1987. "Institutional Performance and Political Culture: Some Puzzles about the Power of the Past." Paper presented at meeting of the American Political Science Association, Chicago, September 1987.

Raboteau, A. 1978. *Slave Religion.* New York: Oxford University Press.

Relensberg, N., H. Karner, and V. Kohler. 1979. *Los Pobres de Venezuela. Autoorganización de Los Pobladores: Un Informe Crítico.* Caracas: El Cid.

Romero, C. 1989. "The Peruvian Church: Change and Continuity." In *The Progressive Church in Latin America,* ed. S. Mainwaring and A. Wilde, 253–75. Notre Dame: University of Notre Dame Press.

Romero, O. A. 1985. *Voice of the Voiceless. The Four Pastoral Letters and Other Statements.* Maryknoll, N.Y.: Orbis Books.

Roseberry, W. 1983. *Coffee and Capitalism in the Venezuelan Andes.* Austin: University of Texas Press.

———. 1986. "Images of the Peasant in the Consciousness of the Venezuelan Proletariat." In *Proletarians and Protest: The Roots of Class Formation in an Industrializing World,* ed. M. Hanagan and C. Stephenson, 149–69. New York: Greenwood Press.

Sánchez, G., and D. Meertens. 1983. *Bandoleros, Gamonales y Campesinos: El Caso de la Violencia en Colombia.* Bogotá: El Arcora.

Santamaría Salamanca, R., and G. Silva Lujan. 1986. "Colombia in the Eighties: A Political Regime in Transition." *Caribbean Review* 14, no. 1: 12–15.

Santana, P. 1983. *Desarrollo Regional y Paros Cívicos en Colombia.* Bogotá: CINEP, Controversia no. 107–8.

São Paulo, Archdiocese of. 1978. *São Paulo Growth and Poverty.* London: Bowerdean Press.

Scott, J. 1985. *Weapons of the Weak: Everyday Forms of Peasant Resistance.* New Haven, Conn.: Yale University Press.

Segundo, J. L. 1985. *Theology and the Church.* Minneapolis: Winston Press.

Sheahan, J. 1987. *Patterns of Development in Latin America.* Princeton: Princeton University Press.

Sklar, R. 1987. "Developmental Democracy." *Comparative Studies in Society and History* 29, no. 2: 686–714.

Slater, C. 1986. *Trail of Miracles: Tales from a Pilgrimage in North East Brazil.* Berkeley: University of California Press.

Smith, B. 1982. *The Church and Politics in Chile: Challenges to Modern Catholicism.* Princeton: Princeton University Press.

Sobrino, J. 1985. "A Theologian's View of Oscar Romero." In *Voice of The Voiceless,* ed. O. A. Romero, 22–51. Maryknoll, N.Y.: Orbis Books.

Thompson, E. P. 1966. *The Making of the English Working Class*. New York: Vintage.

———. 1978. "Eighteenth Century English Society: Class Struggle without Class?" *Social History* 38, no. 2: 138–65.

Tocqueville, A. de. 1961. *Democracy in America*. New York: Schocken.

Turner, V., and E. Turner. 1978. *Image and Pilgrimage in Christian Culture*. New York: Columbia University Press.

Urrutia, M. 1985. *Winners and Losers in Colombia's Economic Growth of the 1970s*. New York: Oxford University Press.

Vélez-Ibañez, C. 1983. *Rituals of Marginality: Politics, Process, Culture Change in Central Urban Mexico*. Berkeley: University of California Press.

Walton, J. 1977. *Elites and Economic Development: Comparative Studies in the Political Economy of Latin American Cities*. Austin: University of Texas Press.

Walzer, M. 1985. *Exodus and Revolution*. New York: Basic Books.

Weber, E. 1976. *Peasants into Frenchmen: The Modernization of Rural France, 1870–1914*. Stanford: Stanford University Press.

Weber, M. 1978. *Economy and Society,* 2 vols. Berkeley: University of California Press.

Weisbrot, M. 1983. *Father Divine*. Boston: Beacon Press.

Wuthnow, R. 1988. *The Restructuring of American Religion*. Princeton: Princeton University Press.

Zamosc, L. 1986. *The Agrarian Question and the Peasant Movement in Colombia*. Cambridge: Cambridge University Press.

Zaret, D. 1985. *The Heavenly Contract: Ideology and Organization in Pre-Revolutionary Puritanism*. Chicago: University of Chicago Press.

Organizing, Ideology, and Moral Suasion: Political Discourse and Action in a Mexican Town

Michael W. Foley

Recent scholarship on peasant protest has shifted from the speculative analysis of large-scale historical trends to the limited testing of hypotheses to a preoccupation with micro-level analysis of peasant consciousness and decision making. That shift has been salutary, sharpening our attention to the role of people's perceptions in shaping behavior and to the subtle ways in which people act out their discontent, but we still understand too little about the origins of these perceptions and about the ways in which everyday discontent gets transformed into politically viable action. The present article argues that, while people's perceptions are grounded in their material and social situations and in past experiences, they are continuously reshaped in interactions with new experiences and with the claims of others. Understanding the role of political discourse in such interactions is essential to understanding popular mobilization.

This article analyzes an organizing effort in a Mexican community to show how the terms with which villagers and organizers represent their situation might succeed in transforming generalized discontent into a concrete program of action—and how efforts to do so might fail. The first section assesses recent work on peasant resistance and protest and argues the need for a fresh approach. Sections 2 and 3 describe the setting of the study and analyze the discourse of peasants and organizers in the midst of an organizing project. The fourth section discusses the exigencies of organizing in the town and focuses attention on moral appeals in the efforts of organizers to generate solidarity. In the conclusion I draw out some of the practical and theoretical implications of the study.

Resistance and Political Discourse

Scholarly attention to peasant politics, at least in this country since the 1960s, has focused disproportionately on one fashionable question: Why do peasants revolt? The standard answers are by and large cast in terms of motivation. Peasants revolt when their way of life is threatened, demands exceed expectations, or exactions undermine peasant notions of a just portion. Others add opportunity to the mix: peasant revolts arise when traditional mechanisms of social control begin to crumble, distant elites with limited coercive powers step up their demands, or the state is weakened by external threats.[1]

Peasant revolts, however, are forms of collective action, and all forms of collective action face tremendous obstacles in peasant communities. Isolated from centers of power, with poor communication among communities and with barriers of suspicion and distrust both among and within communities, peasants lack many of the opportunities and supports urban activists take for granted. Insofar as peasants are politically incorporated, the political structures that surround them generally serve more to subject and quiet them than to facilitate the full expression of their grievances.[2] Political clientelism, the co-optative role of populist parties, even the cooperative structures of the closed corporate village serve to diffuse discontent and disarm protest and, often enough, to suppress organized resistance.

The question of peasant revolt, then, raises larger questions of collective action[3]—not simply why and under what circumstances peasants might mobilize in common defense or in pursuit of common aims but, more specifically, how peasants overcome the very considerable obstacles they face to common action. One important class of obstacles is ideological. Agents of political control do not simply repress peasant responses; they attempt to structure them in at least two ways: on the one hand, they attempt to shape the actual opportunities peasants face in coping with their situation; on the other, they attempt to impose an ideology or a set of understandings that in effect shape the perceptions peasants have of those opportunities. The latter is of special interest to us here, and it is important to note from the outset that this is not a one-way street. Ordinary people, their leaders, and "outside agitators" of various stripes all respond to official initiatives in both deeds and words. The political discourse that emerges in the struggle between rich and poor, insiders and outsiders, representatives of the official order and their opponents defines peasant interests, the alternatives they face, the costs of action and inaction, and the norms they bring to bear in judging their situation and the action of others.

Material interests, as Ernesto Laclau has pointed out, are not simply "given"; they are a product of a larger social construction of reality, and often of a specifically political construction of reality, which establishes distinctive "positionalities" in large- and small-scale struggles.[4] But as James Scott has so eloquently argued, these "positionalities" are not themselves "givens" but, rather, emerge in the course of an ongoing struggle.[5] With these observations, research on popular movements shifts from mapping the conditions that provoke popular uprisings to a concern with the perceptions that mediate these conditions and mold people's positions.

Scott's work, in both *The Moral Economy of the Peasant* and *Weapons of the Weak,* can be interpreted as a study of the character and origins of such "positionalities" among peasants. For Scott peasant resistance, whether "silent" or voiced, is always rooted in the realities of peasant life—in the variety of ways in which peasants find their surpluses drained, their opportunities constricted, their very lives threatened. Peasant notions of "justice" are founded on standards of survival very closely tied to sheer physical survival. They assume the form of a "subsistence ethic" whose bedrock is "safety first."[6] Poor peasants, moreover, are adept at finding ways of twisting a so-called hegemonic discourse to their own ends, ends that are founded on an elemental class struggle between those with and those without sufficient resources.[7]

In mapping the implications and dynamics of this struggle in peasant discourse, Scott calls attention to the active role ordinary people play both in confronting their situation and the claims of their exploiters and in attempting to reshape the situation and the terms of discourse according to their own standards. That peasants, and the poor in general, are often unsuccessful in these attempts is beside the point. What Scott underlines so well is that people are not simply pawns of larger forces—least of all of some "hegemonic discourse" that forecloses all opportunities for protest—but are, rather, active participants in an ongoing struggle, even in defeat. This is an important lesson, one that is only now being recognized at more abstract levels in current efforts to rebuild social theory and resolve the "macro-micro problem" with a recognition of the active role people play both in reproducing and in altering the social structures within which they act.[8]

Scott's work is a rich and nuanced exploration of the ways in which positions are maintained, defended, and negotiated in the course of everyday class struggle, yet his insistence on grounding the expressions of peasant resistance in the concrete requirements of day-to-day survival is ultimately unsatisfying—and oddly at variance with his portrait of peasants as actors and not simply re-actors. As critics have pointed out in response to the formulations of *The Moral Economy of the Peasant,* it is by no means obvious what *subsistence* means, above a certain biological minimum, or why it is set at different levels by different groups. Similarly, in *Weapons of the Weak* Scott explains that the moral discourse of the village of Sedaka was developed under earlier relations of production, in which reciprocity and generosity on the part of the rich made sense for both rich and poor. This may be so, but it is obvious that specific forms of moral obligation in this village stem from Islam and that there is a readily available radical Islamic ideology in favor of social and economic leveling that the poor of Sedaka could bring to bear in their negotiations with their "betters."[9]

Scott's analysis thus illuminates only a part of a larger problem. Like the rational choice theorists who have attacked him (in an almost willful blindness to his intentions), Scott attempts to ground peasant choices in rational response to the circumstances and opportunities peasants face,[10] but neither Scott nor his critics can adequately account for the way in which those circumstances and opportunities are perceived and construed in the first place. His work explores with great subtlety the ways in which peasant discourse reflects and mediates the concrete conditions of class struggle. But the question remains: How are the terms of discourse set?

It is tempting to put this as a question of "political culture" or of "cultural materials," but this suggests that the answers lie in a realm over which most people have little control—some "synchronous" system of symbols—and that the political manipulation of such symbols is primarily the work of cynical political entrepreneurs. No doubt, symbol systems with deep resonances and unsuspected networks of meaning and response play a role in how people construct their everyday responses to their world, but such systems are widely open to dispute, their meaning subject to negotiation in ways Scott has demonstrated. Moreover, much political discourse centers on questions of fact, a surprisingly straightforward ordering of priorities and a less than primal appeal to varying loyalties.[11] Here persuasion, negotiation, vocal and silent amendment play a role in the rise and fall of political perceptions and commitments.

How do we get at these processes? How shall we come to understand what goes into the adoption or rejection of a new view of reality, of new terms of discourse? Scott himself, in attempting to unravel the dynamics of class struggle at the village level, looks at "ideology at work where it really counts—in the rationalization of exploitation and in the resistance to that rationalization."[12] Similarly, if we are to do justice to the role of "ideology" in political mobilization, if we wish to understand the development of new terms of political discourse,[13] we might turn to a situation in which political discourse is more or less explicitly at stake, to the interactions of organizers and their listeners, and to the language and appeals that each employs in describing the situation that all face.[14] The present article focuses on organizing because it provides a privileged moment in which to examine discursive change.

In the pages that follow, then, we will look at a contemporary organizing effort in "El Lago" (as I will call it), a populous village in the heart of peasant Mexico. The focus will not be so much on the process of organizing as on the language of organizing, or, better, the political discourse that organizers employed and peasants adopted or reshaped in responding to it.[15] Though any full account of popular mobilization would touch on such factors as economic interest, social networks, the quality of leadership, and the kinds of threats and opportunities that both individuals and groups face,[16] the focus here is on these realities as they are mediated discursively and in particular on the success and failure of various discursive strategies.

What do we get at when we examine "discursive strategies" or "discourse" or "the terms of debate"? To start, we do not necessarily get at people's perceptions, still less at their motivations. People are capable of all sorts of dissembling—in everyday conversation as well as in considered composition. Indeed, there is considerable evidence that we do not have particularly accurate access to our own motives;[17] nevertheless, our words generally signal our intentions and reflect our actions—and when they do not, they permit others to call us to account. On the other hand, people adapt and utilize terms of debate in a variety of ways and for a variety of purposes: confirming their own earlier views, managing relations with others, rationalizing their choices, and providing themselves with the means to organize their own motives.

An analysis of discourse and of discursive change thus cannot tell us much about why people act in defense of their interests or choose to remain in the background, but it can tell us how these interests are framed and to some extent, therefore, why certain kinds of action are relevant and others ignored. It can also suggest why certain targets and certain alternatives, and not others, came to be identified. Further, people will struggle over the definition of their situation and of their alternatives, and both the initial terms of that struggle and its outcome can have a profound impact on people's choices and on the success or failure of an organizing effort. The case material that follows broadly confirms this view of political discourse and illustrates an approach to understanding the emergence and character of popular movements through an analysis of the exigencies of discursive change. And this in turn, I would argue, will help us answer the difficult question how, despite all the obstacles, the powerless sometimes manage to take hold of their own destiny and, if only for a moment, gain the attention of the powerful—and occasionally of their historians.

The Setting

El Lago

The town of El Lago is an agricultural community of roughly ten thousand people in the Mexican state of Morelos, regional stronghold of peasant leader Emiliano Zapata during the Mexican Revolution.[18] There are still people in the town who remember the revolution, how Huerta's *federales* came through and burned the homes and fields, slaughtered the cattle, and raped the women; how the men and some of the women (there was a *generalisima* from El Lago) took to the hills and fought alongside of Zapata; how they had to rebuild everything after the fighting stopped, leaving but half the prerevolutionary population, the others dead or relocated. But these are ancient memories and have less political significance today than one might think; the coinage of the revolution has been debased: everyone draws on the common currency, but it buys little in specific commitments.[19]

More important are the economic and political structures established in the wake of the revolution. Morelos was the only state to benefit immediately from the land reform provisions written into the Constitution of 1917 at the behest of Zapata's representatives, but even here reform came slowly. The first repartition in El Lago was in 1928. Some five hundred heads of families received parcels within the *ejido* of El Lago. Another two hundred to three hundred chose to retain their private holdings. Though most of the latter were swallowed up in the eventual expansion of the town itself, the division was a significant one, for it established a large group of peasants with access to neither the economic guarantees of the reform nor the really important political posts in the town. The lack of further lands to partition and the limitations on formal fragmentation of land in the *ejidal* system mean that today fewer than five hundred *ejidatarios* (as official beneficiaries of the reform are called)—out of a population of roughly ten thousand—hold formal control over the bulk of the town's arable land. Because governmental support to the peasant sector is channeled largely through the *ejido* (in the form of subsidized credit, fertilizer, pesticides, even agricultural extension services), *ejidal* posts are the crucial political vehicles in distributing economic support to peasant farmers. They are also avenues to other posts within the local organs of the official Institutional Revolutionary Party (PRI) and on committees administering government funds for community improvements. Only a small minority of El Lago's peasants have access to these posts.[20]

Ejidatarios, however, do not themselves farm the bulk of the land. *Ejidal* plots, distributed in the beginning according to the farmer's resources to work them, have long since been unofficially divided up among the sons and grandsons, daughters, nieces, and nephews of the official usufructuaries. Many *ejidatarios* rent out parcels to nonkin, and most smallholders combine a bit of private property, some *ejidal* land "given" them unofficially (and therefore illegally) by a relative, and some rented land. A great many families, on the other hand, perhaps half the population, own no land whatsoever (legally or illegally). These are the *jornaleros*, or day laborers, who piece together a living from agricultural work for the state-run sugar cooperative in Zacatepec or neighboring smallholders; their sons and daughters commute to neighboring cities to work as vendors or in shops and factories. *Jornaleros* may also rent a small parcel to produce maize for home consumption. Economically, these represent the lowest strata in a largely homogeneous peasant community.

Coping with Change

Like many villages throughout Mexico, El Lago has seen considerable changes in the last few decades. Thirty years ago, the land was better, people claim. It was, nonetheless, under heavy pressure: maize prices had not risen substantially in close to forty years, yet peasants even in remote towns like El Lago had long relied on sales of surplus maize to provide cash for household extras, occasional emergency runs to the hospital, school supplies for those children who went to school, and planting expenses. As the population grew, pressure on the land increased, and by the 1960s farmers found that they could not do without fertilizer, which was soon followed by pesticides, and eventually, within the last five to ten years and at the behest of the mills, improved see\ varieties. Both urban growth and the demand for farmland also meant a reduction in the "wastelands" previously reserved for grazing, firewood, and building materials. People today do not build with sticks and thatch in part, at least, because they cannot: there is simply not enough available.[21]

"Rising expectations" thus kept pace with rising needs for cash, and it was in this context that Lagueños witnessed government efforts in the 1960s and 1970s to draw backcountry villages like El Lago into the national economy through improvements in roads, marketing facilities, health care, and education. None of these efforts quite hit the mark. Though hundreds of young Lagueños are now able to commute to Cuernavaca and Jojutla for urban jobs, their earnings scarcely make the trip worthwhile. Though the marketplace in town is booming and access to outside markets has improved, prevailing prices and the control exercised over outside marketing by rich local buyers and commercial intermediaries known as *coyotes* have prevented peasant farmers from advancing. In general, they are out from under the thumb of local moneylenders, but they are still lucky to break even. Though birth control is now widely accepted in principle, sizable families remain an economic necessity.[22] Moreover, such government efforts as improved roads, electrification, piped water, the new marketplace, and reorganized credit and farm support programs generate mixed reactions among local people, who have come, over the last twenty-five years, to expect more from government while distrusting both its promises and intentions. On the other hand, the many people who have benefited, directly or indirectly, from governmental programs are open to being persuaded that loyalty is a better lever than dissent.

The economic changes of the last quarter century, and the political efforts that have accompanied them, have thus set the stage for opposing interpretations of the classic political question "What is to be done?" On the one hand, peasant livelihoods have deteriorated, as they have all over Mexico. On the other hand, the question of survival has been politicized to some extent by government efforts to meet peasant needs, ranging from programs to sustain prices for farm goods to health, education, and developmental efforts aimed at integrating peasants into the national economy and providing for basic needs.[23] Throughout Mexico these two factors—the structural changes in the agricultural economy and the direct insertion of the state in the peasant economy—have prompted the emergence and growth over the last twenty years of an independent peasant movement pressing for change on various fronts.[24] The situation in El Lago, as we shall see in more detail shortly, is not particularly conducive to organized protest. Focused "enemies" are few, though the grip of the PRI and of corrupt local bosses, or caciques, on politics provides one target. The issues, moreover, are diffuse and center on the general sense that, despite all the material modernization, everyone is worse off than in the past. The questions that face us, then, are, first, how Lagueños have been brought to the level of mobilization they have reached; and second, why, in contrast to similar communities that have joined the current wave of protest, organizers in El Lago have not succeeded in more fully politicizing discontent and linking the local movement to larger national concerns. The answer proposed here focuses on "who organizes whom under what banners." That phrase captures well the union of ideological and structural factors necessary to explain divergent outcomes. We begin with the "banners," but we will return eventually to the "whom," to the structural differences among Lagueños and the circumstances that constrain mobilization in the town.

Organizing El Lago

In 1976 a young couple, recent graduates of the National Autonomous University of Mexico and enthusiasts of the educational philosophy of Paulo Freire, asked the Diocese of Cuernavaca to suggest a village in which they might work. The diocese, under the direction of then bishop Don Sergio Mendes Arceo, had long been a center for experimentation in social change and church renewal. Ivan Illich had his center there, and the diocese's base Christian community (BCC) program[25] was the largest in Mexico and had already gone a long way toward awakening a new form of popular piety and popular participation in local communities. Cristina and Eduardo were offered a choice of two villages; they took El Lago.

Originally working as school teachers in the town, the two spent their spare hours in meeting people and creating groups. Cristi worked at first through the local Legion of Mary, a traditional women's group. Her goal was to rejuvenate a moribund base Christian community. Today the Legion of Mary, an odd collection of pious older women and rather fiery young mothers, remains at the center of the organizing efforts in El Lago. Eduardo devoted himself to the men, meeting campesinos in their homes and fields, offering to give classes in literacy and agricultural production, convincing and cajoling men to join him for weekly meetings. These efforts resulted in the irrigation cooperative that still plays an important role in the movement.

Freirean theory enjoins the educator to listening as the fundamental starting point for adult education and community organizing. Both Eduardo and Cristi listened a good bit, concluding that the twin problems obsessing Lagueños were water and credit: the one a fundamental resource needed for any further effort to increase production, the other because the constant quest for financing tied people to the moneylenders and thus deprived them of all opportunity to enjoy the fruits of added labor. Fulfilling these two wants would decisively release Lagueños from the cycle of poverty, a cycle that was already a downward spiral in the generalized decline of the peasant economy in Mexico. The effort to meet these needs, moreover, would give them the two tools that they needed above all else to meet future difficulties: consciousness and organization.[26]

Freirean theory insists that insight and solutions must come from the people themselves; the Freirean educator's role is that of facilitator. This is a hard row to hoe, however, especially when one has the authority of the teacher and the catechist at one's disposal; Eduardo and Cristi, at any rate, did not hesitate to make suggestions. On the men's side, the project would be an irrigation scheme, collectively organized and maintained; on the women's side, it was a savings bank, or *Caja popular.* On the men's side, Eduardo acquired the assistance of a foundation set up by a group of priests and religious to do Freirean-style community development; they helped the men, some twenty-four smallholders with contiguous or nearly contiguous land, organize. The foundation also contacted a Dutch charity to help finance drilling, the purchase of the pump, and the construction of a cement canal to join the plots. The men themselves had to negotiate with one of the land-rich peasants through whose property the canal had to pass, and they had to deal with the rumors he spread that they were "Communists."

On the women's side, Cristi drew out a few leaders, put them in contact with representatives of the *Caja popular* movement in Cuernavaca, and began getting them to classes on accounting and organization.

These contacts provided long-term links with the *Frente Auténtico del Trabajo* (Authentic Labor Front, FAT), a leftist but nonpartisan organizing effort based in Cuernavaca with a strong interest in the Cuernavaca Caja. Later Cristi would bring in friends to show a group of women how to make cement blocks in a short-lived manufacturing project and, on another occasion, nurses to teach hygiene and medicine and promote the revival of herbal lore. Out of the latter effort came a group of "barefoot doctors," who continue to meet regularly for classes, preparing herbal medicines and helping one another deal with unfamiliar cases.

Eventually, the men and the women merged their movements as the result of their combined leadership of the base Christian communities; the educational sessions sponsored by the diocese (the bishop himself visited the village for the fiesta celebrating the drilling of the well); and the joint effort that built the community center in which the Caja is housed, literacy classes held, and the irrigation association meets. When Eduardo and Cristi separated and left El Lago in 1980, they left behind a handful of leaders with strong ties to the diocesan movement, FAT, and numerous smaller cooperative ventures in central Mexico. The development foundation that Eduardo had introduced to the community continued to offer support, and another Cuernavaca-based team of consultants offered their services as well.

Besides such helpful contacts, they left a wide-ranging ideology of social change. The BCC movement provided the spiritual foundation, underlining the coincidence of personal and social sin and the need for collective action to heal both. Individualism, *egoismo,* so the literature of the movement teaches, underlies personal sins such as adultery, drunkenness, and jealousy, which in turn "obstruct and destroy communal life." Communities are divided; some people lack the confidence to "participate, others abuse their authority. Evil, however, is not solely within each one of us. Evil is also in society, and for this reason we want to convert ourselves and change society." The capitalist system reinforces *egoismo,* divides communities, and introduces wants that undermine people's efforts to support one another. The remedy is faith and organization "for the good of all."[27]

The message of the BCC movement is complemented by that of the FAT, whose efforts were directed toward the formation of an independent cooperative network:

The cooperative movement from its birth forms part of the movement of the workers; one of its principal objectives has always been to show that people can live in harmony, without misery, sharing without exploiting one another, mutually protecting one another, sharing with justice the riches produced by human hands. The cooperative movement as an instrument of the workers is born to construct a new society.

Cooperatives, unions, and other organizations of the workers are permanently in danger of being undermined by the servants of capitalism, in an attempt to deprive them of their combativity, or even use them against us. Cooperativists should maintain a permanent vigilance to keep ourselves independent and democratic; they should not subordinate themselves to the state, nor to other interests foreign to the cause.[28]

The combat against "capitalism" and "egoism," the call for collective action, and the insistence that peasants learn to participate in democratic and independent organization; the identification of the vast majority, irrespective of land tenure, as the "poor" and the "community"; and the hostility to state control are common to both movements and provide the moral, ideological, and practical frames for the organizing effort in El Lago.

Political Discourse in El Lago

How do Lagueños respond to such claims, to the new political discourse? At the time of my research the movement touched perhaps four hundred families, recruited from among neighbors, friends, and relatives in all the barrios of the town. It was actively opposed by local leaders of the PRI, the chief of whom was the uncle of two of the movement's leaders. Though he and other opponents had some impact on people's attitudes, most of the participants did not see their involvement in political terms and, indeed, had only a very partial sense of the movement's larger agenda.

Consider Felipa, a housewife whose unquestioning devotion to her husband's leadership only breaks down when it is a question of her participation in the Caja and the BCCs, a commitment that he is "only just now beginning to understand."[29] Her cousin Tomasa, she says, talked her into asking her husband's permission to come to meetings; he reluctantly agreed. "Before, I was a dummy [*tonta*]," she says. "I was shut up in the house all day; I didn't do anything but chores. I didn't think about anything. Now that I am waking up [*despertando*], I feel better because I look forward to the meetings; I do my chores thinking this is what I have to do to go to the meeting." As in many such conversions, Felipa's awakening involves as much a change of venue as a change of mind, but the new activities also bring a new sense of self: "Now I feel different. I'm doing more. I'm waking up bit by bit to life as it is today. I feel different, more capable of doing more and doing different things."

What is she awakening to, and what does she want to do? Two problems preoccupy her: the people of El Lago need to unite "to go and cry out—cry out because the poor *jornalero* is killing himself in his sweat and they give him practically nothing. That those who have studied a lot earn a great deal, but the *jornalero* nothing, that they don't give us justice." When low pay and the high cost of living are coupled, they spell out injustice for the poor, and Felipa lays both of these complaints at the door of the government. But to whom she is going to cry out and in what forum remain vague. Her other concern is equally close to home—that the men and youth of El Lago go around in drunken brawls "killing our brothers *injustamente*," unjustly (we will return to this use of *justice* shortly). The problem is that parents haven't raised their children well: "All the time it's work, work, work, and nothing's been given to them in the way of instruction." The answer, then, is religious education, to teach the "right road" to their children and young adults, and secular education, to give them opportunities that the adults never had, "because we don't want to let our children end up the way we are."

Felipa's new sense of purpose scarcely constitutes a political program. There are respects, indeed, in which elements of her "awakened" consciousness block effective political action, but in order to see how activists such as Felipa—for that is what she is in the context of the movement in El Lago—interpret and adapt a political language, and to see more generally how the claims of organizers may succeed and fail, be blocked, amended or transformed, let us look more closely at the way Lagueños handle the three themes stressed in Felipa's accounting and around which people commonly organize their discussions of public matters in El Lago: justice, politics, and education. This last topic will lead us to a consideration of the role of women in the movement and in local politics and, finally, to a discussion of the terms of moral discourse that characterize the movement. These themes will also lead us, not coincidentally, to the heart of our question—how and why concrete concerns come to be interpreted politically; or how and why, conversely, "political" concerns may be muted as they cross paths with the everyday concerns and preconceptions of ordinary people.

Justice

People in El Lago have a number of colorful terms with which to describe themselves and their situation: *aplastados* (flattened), *apurados* (pressed), *amolados* (ground down), *atados* (tied up), *recortados* (cut short). They are constantly short of money, prices go up every seven days, and there is no work. People have to scramble for jobs, for income of any sort, and when they find a job they work ten and twelve hours a day and earn six hundred pesos—about two dollars at the time of my interviews. "Six hundred pesos! What can you do with six hundred pesos? Nothing," exclaimed one *jornalero*'s wife.

Like Felipa, people often put these and other complaints about life in El Lago in terms of justice. These claims of justice, however, are based in general not so much on traditional expectations about the proper roles of various members of the community or notions of reciprocity as on rather more straightforward judgments of equity and reflections of recognized standards of official probity. *Jornaleros* especially are eloquent about injustice, whether it be in regard to the opportunities for *engaño,* or trickery, in the weighing of sugarcane by refinery representatives (workers are paid by the ton, with adjustments made for quality); the benefits proffered by government agents or the refinery; or community affairs and the general terms of life that the society offers to them.

Thus, Arnulfo, whose sons have worked as cane cutters, argues that the only thing they got out of it was Social Security, and that, he notes, is available to cutters only while they are working. The refinery cheated them consistently on the tonnage, and the housing subsidies that the government offered through the refinery ultimately came out of workers' wages. In the end they were left with nothing. The behavior of *el rico,* the rich owner of the local construction materials outlet, an individual known as a moneylender and local political boss (cacique), likewise calls up questions of justice.

> Out of pure necessity—at times because of sickness, at times for lack of food—we would go to *el rico,* and he would give us maize—but

in exchange for the peanut crop. Even though the prices differed, he would treat them the same.... Or he would offer credit, and at the time of the harvest, even if it weighed out more, he'd take the crop. And there we were, our hands tied. They'd give us nothing.

Arnulfo's evaluation of various improvements introduced by the government links state action and the overall economic situation with questions of equity. "Sure, they have built schools, paved the streets, built the market. They've spent millions on electricity and potable water. But what good does it do us when they do nothing for the farmer and prices rise and rise while the price of our products stays the same?" Arnulfo, like Felipa, finds an obvious contradiction between the inflation peasants face when they make everyday purchases and the price of the farm products on whose sale they depend for their livelihood. Like Felipa, he lays the blame at the government's door.

Though many speakers associated with the organizing effort claim that people have been deceived by the rhetoric of the PRI and by the government's largess, this tendency to link the plight of the peasant to government neglect is not restricted to movement members. A *jornalero* with no ties to the movement makes the political connection still more explicit, even if he treats it, overall, in narrower terms: to recover its stolen lands,[30] El Lago would need the help of the president, but no one expects that to happen. Why not? "Because we don't have the money.... When a president or governor takes office, it's always the same as far as we're concerned. Instead of looking after the poor, they look after the rich." In those circumstances "there's no point in voting. Why sell ourselves when the prices of our products don't rise?" "And other things do go up," adds his wife. What about the government's price guarantees (which had just gone up)? "Here, it's dead. Here, there's no guarantee.... Sure, for the rich, for the [factory] worker, for these there are guarantees, but for the poor *jornaleros,* no, there's nothing."

For all of these speakers equity is a principal criterion—equity in prices and wages, equity in treatment of rich and poor—but certain notions both of probity and of what the government owes the poor as poor also appear in these and other discussions about the current situation. Local leaders especially are targets for attack from all sides for their persistent failure to work "for the good of the village." "They're here for their own benefit and that of their allies, nothing more." This is the repeated refrain from all strata and all the political factions of El

Lago. The *jornalero* quoted above puts it most colorfully: "The *comisariados* [ejidal officials] here were, so we'd say, good and hungry. They wanted money and used their positions for themselves, to sell off El Lago's land. . . . Here the tinkle of coins does the trick [*aqui cayendo los centavos son felices*]." His wife agrees: "Yes, it's just that here a lot of people are 'hungry.' These are the ones that get the help." We will come back shortly to the bad name that politics has acquired in El Lago; here we need only note that despite this *mala fama,* people judge *ayudantes* (mayors) and *comisariados* by standards of probity, fairness, and community mindedness. Their duty is to look out for the good of the community ("as they're supposed to," as Lagueños often observe) and not for that of themselves and their friends.

As we have seen, there are Lagueños who demand more than equity and probity of the government and its officials. Tomasa, one of the leading activists trained by Cristi, is quite clear about this, despite all of her misgivings about governmental intentions and promises: the government has the power and therefore the responsibility to do something for the community. Nora, a local woman who is community organizer for INEA, the National Institute for Adult Education, is very careful to assure people that her projects are funded with money that belongs to them: they will not owe the government anything in return—not votes, special allegiances, nor favors. Indeed, it is only a part of the money the government has drained from the people—a lot more is owed. These are broad and rather "modern" claims. Though sometimes grounded in notions of equity, as in Nora's position, they also echo broader arguments about government's role in the economy, arguments that government rhetoric and action since the revolution have only contributed to expanding. Although organizers have taken up and sharpened these arguments, usually against the government, they are by no means restricted to speakers influenced by the movement in El Lago.

Before we turn to investigate why such claims to justice do not materialize more readily in political action, however, we should consider one more form that the notion of "justice" takes in El Lago. We noticed earlier Felipa's remark about the contribution of alcohol to the "unjust" killings that plague the town. Her usage reflects, besides the extended meanings of the Spanish root *just-*, notions of justice common to Catholic social thought and readily apparent in the literature of the BCC movement. As in the classical tradition on which it draws, Catholic social thought teaches that justice is "giving each his or her due" in the broadest sense of the term *due*. Justice is nothing more nor less than doing right. Thus, Tomasa seems to have in mind a standard of justice in accusing her father of "egoism" for his failure to send her to school: "'No,' he says, 'I thought to myself you were going to marry one day, and the money you would get was going to be for your husband. . . . ' Perhaps it's egoism" she reflects, "because egoism is not giving what you have to give. It had to be either for me or for himself." Note that these terms parallel those with which the local officials are judged: they are acting "for themselves" versus "for the community." In contrast to the Anglo-American tradition, according to which justice is largely confined to the public realm, justice clearly begins at home for the BCC movement.

This ideological twist, in fact, has permitted a peculiar bifurcation in the movement in El Lago. On the one side stand the cooperativists associated especially with the irrigation project and other cooperative production schemes. On the other, there is a large group of women, together with a scattering of *jornaleros* and campesinos like Arnulfo, whose primary concerns are spiritual and moral, including the religious education of children ("so they won't go around drinking and killing one another like the young men today"); an end to drunken brawling and alcoholism; and, to achieve this end, the closing of the cantinas. On both sides the politicization of economic concerns sketched earlier finds no outlet. It is maintained as an item of discourse, even a central item both by organizers and participants, but the movement, as we shall see, provides no avenue for its active expression.[31]

The prevailing notions of justice, then, reflect ample room for judging the behavior of officials, the local rich, the government itself, even neighbors and family. There is not a great deal of evidence here of the norms of reciprocity that characterize Scott's "moral economy," but there is considerable stress on equity, and the claim that those in authority owe certain considerations to those below them is clearly present, particularly in the discourse of community activists. All of these claims could have political bearing, though the broadly moral notion of justice articulated by Catholic social doctrine also means that efforts to achieve "social justice" might well be confined to home and neighborhood.

The notion of justice thus plays a large role in political and moral discourse in El Lago. The Lagueños are clearly discontent, and they have particular targets for their discontent, among them the government itself. This is not the passive and befuddled peasantry of older stereotypes. Nevertheless, the judgment that a situation is unjust does not automatically lead to efforts to change it,[32] and as we have just suggested, the movement in El Lago has thus far hesitated to give its efforts a distinctively political cast. It is important to ask why not. One reason, we shall see, lies in the movement's agenda, or, rather, in its lack of an agenda for explicitly political action. Behind this, however, lie distinctive attitudes toward politics, and partisan political activity in particular, fostered in part by an objectively narrow array of possibilities yet also reinforced in both popular wisdom and movement ideology.

La Política

We have already noted the bad name that politics has acquired in El Lago. Those in charge of village affairs, says Tomasa,

> are grabbing the money for these projects, stealing it, and for that reason don't finish them or finish them badly, and the money is lost. The government is bothered by these things, and they're right. . . . Often it's we ourselves, people from here, who don't want the village to advance but to go backward . . . who want to go on beating it down to their own advantage.

These remarks are obviously rooted in reality, but they also reflect a suspicion of politics not only endemic to El Lago but confirmed and reinforced in the critical position that the organizing effort has articulated.

In general, politics—and organization of any kind—are suspect in El Lago. Most people note the conflict between two, sometimes three groups, for control of village posts, and they regard these struggles as "divisive" and unhealthy. Most agree that no one in office ends up working "for the good of the village," that everyone in politics is in it for himself. Most refuse to have anything to do with politics. "It's an affair for *ejidatarios*," one *jornalero* said. "They don't want anyone else to vote, and they wouldn't let me if I came." "It's an affair of men," the women say. "Our husbands don't let us vote, and when the women came to vote last time, the men jeered at them and told them 'This is a matter for men, not women. Go back to cooking your beans. . . . You belong in the kitchen.'" Felipa's husband says, "What's the use of voting? The prices still rise." Others see voting, not to mention getting involved, as dangerous: "It's better if I try not to associate with anyone. That way I don't harm [*perjudicar*] anyone, and no one harms me. Better if I just take care of my own work—for me *'solo Dios'*—and say nothing. I just listen." There are, in fact, larger dangers than being *perjudicado*, put in a prejudicial position in one's social and economic relations. People have been killed in village politics, and Tomasa admits that she fears for her husband and children if she ever became involved.

Most people are suspicious of any form of organization and will say that there is no group in the village working for the common good. Many can recount stories of cooperatives set up under government auspices that have failed because the leadership walked off with the funds or people got into arguments refusing to help, accusing the others of theft, or disputing the leadership of the group. People have come to expect such outcomes in any common endeavor.

Leaders in the organizing effort thus have to work against powerful prejudices rooted in a long experience with village politics and organizational efforts. In this struggle, they bring to bear a religiously sanctioned moral language, identifying the "sin" of individualism—of *egoismo*—at the heart of both popular resistance and the corruption of local politics. This may well be overkill, as the very language with which organizers condemn the conduct of village affairs reinforces people's perception that, indeed, no one can be trusted. The damage, however, goes further: both the BCC movement and the FAT are fundamentally anarchist in their approach to politics. BCC leaders in Cuernavaca, despite their leanings to the left and their anticapitalist analysis, shun partisanship, seeing in the parties of the Left either co-opted instruments of the PRI or a futile diversion from the real task of wresting justice from an all-powerful political machine. The FAT focuses its efforts on community organizing and is likewise militantly nonpartisan, even abstentionist in regard to electoral politics. Both promote the notion of a distinctive path not corrupted by electoral politics nor co-opted by the state.[33]

In practice, such notions, which echo on the lips of leaders in El Lago, go a long way toward maintaining the integrity of the movement in the town, which has resisted several attempts by both local party members and the bureaucracy to gain the group's support. But the rhetoric of independence, and the accompanying critique of politics, also makes it difficult for leaders to justify any insertion into politics, whether national or local. As one leader put it: "We want to move [into local politics] eventually, but it's not time yet. We would just become another faction." Factionalism—the very stuff of real politics—is out of the question here, because the fundamental critique both movement leaders and ordinary people advance against politics in El Lago is that it is divisive, while the one remedy Lagueños endorse is "unity."

The movement's rhetoric thus fails to provide specific political remedies to the grievances that Lagueños lay at government's door precisely insofar as it echoes the political language in common use. But the movement has also capitalized on an important contradiction in the complex of terms surrounding politics: even as Lagueños echo the prevailing individualism in a resigned "Here, it's everyone for himself [*cada quien*]," they condemn the practice of *egoismo* in both their political leaders and parents. The organizing effort in El Lago has made the attack on prevailing practice—on "individualism" in economic organization, the home, and politics—its central mission and does so using a prevailing (but by no means unequivocal) moral judgment.

If notions of justice and injustice have not been fully exploited by movement leaders, then, it is because they themselves share popular attitudes about politics and political action that block the politicization of the movement. Their own critique of local politics, moreover, has reinforced these attitudes. Nevertheless, the rhetoric of organizers is not paralyzed in front of such seemingly "given" aspects of popular discourse. Organizers have turned prevailing moral judgments on the speakers themselves, making them the basis, as we shall see later, for a central organizational appeal, the call to solidarity and community service. The movement thus has gained some ground and lost some in its dialogue with the population it is recruiting. In order to understand more fully its successes, and the discursive and structural roots of its failures, we should turn to two areas in which it has found particular resonance and had particular impact: education and the role of women.

Education and the Liberation of the Women

A broad current of opinion in El Lago has apparently turned against the wisdom of their fathers, that education was for *los ricos,* that *los pobres* had no need of it. People of all sorts speak fervently of their conviction that their children should be educated, "at least, as far as we're able." A good many people speak of their struggle to learn to read and to use numbers through the various adult education programs sponsored by Tomasa's group in the Caja. Lack of education is widely perceived as the major obstacle people from El Lago face in getting jobs, doing business with the *acaparadores* and *coyotes* who control the money and markets of peasant producers, and dealing with the government. Felipa tells her husband: "They don't help us, even though you vote; precisely because you don't know how to read, you don't know anything." She is learning, and so she sees herself "leading the way for my husband and children."

Another woman dwells a good deal on the *tontería* ("idiocy") of people in the past. She considers herself "a dummy" (*tonta*) in part because she doesn't know how to read. Learning was important even thirty years ago, when she was growing up. "If you didn't know how to read, didn't know numbers, you'd take your crop to *el rico* to pay off your loan, and he'd bilk you, every time. People were stupid (*tonta*) then." She herself, like a good many others, is "waking up, opening my eyes." Without such an awakening and without education, one is a "dummy," someone who "doesn't know anything." Tomasa's sister says of her own husband: "He doesn't understand a thing. It's because he grew up not learning to read or write, not knowing anything. That's why I think he doesn't take care of anything. Him? No, he lives like some animal." In respect to education, then, one's "awakening" may come too late, when one is already tied to a difficult situation or little able to acquire new skills. Still, people see their own "waking up" as their best substitute, and it alerts them to the needs of their children.

Some attribute their awakening to the changing times or to new opportunities, to "getting out" of El Lago. Sometimes it is attributed to the BCCs, the cooperatives, or the work of Eduardo and Cristi or Tomasa and the others. In any case, it is first of all, in the eyes of movement people and others, a waking up to "reality," to "the truth" that without education people are at the mercy of the forces presently making life miserable in El Lago, and parents are convinced in increasing numbers that education will provide that awakening for the young.

But education will also provide training; it is essential for getting a job and to "advancing," according to Lagueños. The last term calls attention to the fact that Lagueños in general do not hark back to an idealized past in their critique of the present; rather, they have adopted, with only a little ambivalence, the prevailing culture's approval of progress and "advancement." Above all, they think, education will change the level of life in El Lago. The neighboring towns have their architects, doctors, engineers, lawyers, and teachers. Why, people have begun to ask, has El Lago remained behind? Because the others have "prepared" their children, comes the answer, and Lagueños have not. Now that such preparation is under way, people often imply, life in El Lago itself will improve. Some people, nevertheless, doubt that the effects will amount to much. On the one hand, there remains considerable resistance among older people, especially the men, and the best students quit in the face of it or leave. On the other hand, everyone notes, opportunities are few in the area. There is an abundance of unemployed teachers in the town, and young women trained as secretaries must find work elsewhere, as nurses, skilled artisans, and the university educated also must do.

Aside from such practical doubts, moreover, there remains an undercurrent of distrust that owes much both to older attitudes and to long-standing experience with the educated. "I don't know how to read," says Felipa's husband, "but I know how to defend myself, to feed my children. . . . And I've done better, I think, than those who know, because those who know end up in drink. They end up lost, and those who don't know are better workers." If this smacks strongly of the defensiveness of the uneducated, Marcelino, a cooperativist and himself a graduate of a secondary school in the days when it took some effort to get to one, finds much to be suspicious of in schools: "In the past people were more open. . . . As if when people did bad things, everyone could clearly see what was going on. . . . And now, no, you don't notice, and it seems to me that's the first thing they teach you in school, not directly but by the way they go about things. They teach you how to rob from your own." And Arnulfo, speaking of the disorder in the irrigation society, argues that "the one who speaks best [*tenía mas palabras*] was the one who destroyed the unity of the society. He didn't want to do anything but order people around. . . . The one who was more intelligent, he got more out of the society, and that just made the others angry." The critique of *la política* and a certain suspicion of verbal powers associated with education here come together, a double association we will come back to shortly.

The BCC movement has promoted the view that education is not just another path to personal advancement but rather a solution to community problems. In the face of the spread of alcoholism and violence among the youth, many movement members place as much hope in the work of the BCCs and the catechists as in secular education. Several women involved in the catechetical program feel that this work was the only way to counter alcoholism and violence in El Lago: "I would really like my children to continue studying," said one woman, "so they can learn to follow the Word of God, so they don't go around fighting to the point of killing one another." "Even little ones start to drink here. Why? Because they haven't learned anything, and they don't study because there's no money. . . . There's no work here . . . and for what there is, they pay almost nothing." Lack of work, lack of education, and drinking: They all add up, according to these women. The answer is biblical education, "because the nuns explain the words to us really well—that they shouldn't fight, they shouldn't drink, because that way they end up killing one another."

Education, finally, is associated for many people with experience, with "getting out" (*saliendo*) in the world, and this getting out shares some of the ambiguities of education itself. "People who don't get out [*no sale*] of El Lago don't understand anything," Tomasa's sister told me. "I never get out. I'm ignorant." Tomasa, on the other hand, has gotten out a lot, "and because she has, she's gained a lot." Augustina's big disappointment is that her sons refuse to leave El Lago. They would rather scramble for agricultural work with their father than venture out into the wide world. Young women, in fact, "get out" increasingly more often than the men, and in doing so they test more opportunities and gain more experience. And to people like Augustina that's all to the good. Chema, the woman with so much scorn for the stupidity of the past, puts it this way: "Times are changing. . . . Women can't sleep on. . . . Women have their freedom, and they have the right to speak up." In pursuit of these rights, she is seeing to it that her own daughters go to school in Cuernavaca. Her other hope, a hope shared by other women whom I interviewed, is that, by gaining an education, the young women will be able to support themselves and avoid an early marriage, because "*el matrimonio es trabajoso,*" marriage is difficult.

Education is primarily, but not exclusively, a woman's solution. Mothers hope that their sons will take advantage of it, but if they lose their grip on them, then they are the more determined that their daughters shall "advance." In the eyes of many of the men, however, education shares the defect of politics: it is the realm of the fast talker. To deal in politics you need to be a good talker—indeed, a child who shows any fluency or forwardness is said to be bound for politics—and a good talker is someone who can fool people. Politics is talk. In some eyes it is nothing more than "women's gossip," not fit for men who have to go out and work; those who participate are drunkards who spend their time in empty disputes over land titles and stolen credit but drink the money away once they get it. In the eyes of most men, moreover, it requires dealing with *ingenieros* (engineers) and *licenciados* (licenciates), the awesome titles with which university graduates establish their authority over the uneducated. Suspicion combined with awe is enough to silence most people in El Lago.

Politics is talk, but people in El Lago are self-conscious before strangers, convinced they speak badly, suspicious of good talkers, unsure what good their words will do anyway: "We don't have the money you need to get things done." For a great many of the men, moreover, the educational and organizational activities of the women are bewildering. Again and again, women active in the Caja or the BCCs reported that their husbands did not "understand," were "only just now beginning to understand a little." Many of the men refused to permit their wives to go to meetings. At times the women went in defiance of such restraint, and the men had to accommodate themselves to the liberation of their wives. "He doesn't say no, he doesn't say yes, he doesn't say anything [*ni no, ni si, ni nada*]," said one young mother in disgust. The men go to work and come back late; they don't discuss politics; they don't take an interest in the community; if they go out, they go out to drink and, too often, brawl—that is the view of many women in El Lago, and to a large degree it appears to correspond to the facts. Next to the women, few men have anything to say. They have retreated into work and drink— into a culture of silence from which both wives and organizers have difficulty extricating them. This "culture of silence" reverberates in the discourse of the women, as the comments just quoted suggest. Some, like Chema and Augustina, have given up in disgust, but they remain tied, tenuously at times, to their marriages. Others have worked out a silent truce, like the young woman quoted earlier. Others still, like Felipa and Tomasa, have negotiated larger or smaller areas of independence, from whose relative safety they continue to try to educate their menfolk and expand their scope for action.

The resistance of the men appears to have both practical and ideological effects. As we have seen, women have to negotiate their freedom simply to attend meetings; some win it by pure willfulness; all have to struggle; and all have to justify the sacrifice of household duties to new responsibilities.[34] Ideologically and practically, the resistance of the men means that the cooperativist nostrums of the movement are out of reach for most of the women: much as they would like their families to join the cooperative ventures, they cannot commit economic resources that they do not control. The one exception is the Caja, which is widely regarded as the "women's bank," because women are the major participants. It is a tool of economic independence for many women, though of a very minor sort. It is also a source of family conflict, the men sometimes insisting that money would be better spent or invested in chickens or pigs or arguing that some day the directors will simply walk off with the money. ("One day," Chema reported with some disgust, "my husband said, 'you're saving—how much do you have?' I said to him, 'Very little,' He says, 'They're not going to lend you any?' I said, 'If you want to borrow, you'll have to put some in yourself....' And yeah, he joined," but without understanding, she implied, the cooperativist principles of the group.)

The Caja provides its members with a limited financial independence but no basis on which to build a cooperative movement, certainly not without the participation of the men, who remain, in most cases, the chief breadwinners; nor does it give the landless *jornaleros* much hope of investing in a cooperative venture: their incomes remain more or less hand-to-mouth, the Caja offering only a bit of security. Women who have been touched by the movement thus gravitate all the more easily to "women's issues," the problems of child rearing and community safety. The BCC movement provides ready ideological support: "sin" manifests itself in personal life and communal life equally; the two, indeed, feed into one another. By raising one's children properly, making sacrifices for their education, and mastering alcoholism in the home, one simultaneously contributes to the struggle against the glaring problems of poverty, lack of opportunity, and alcoholism and violence on the streets. The women's attention thus focuses on the familiar domain of home and streets and on the relatively inexpensive solution of education, both secular and moral.[35]

In this way the movement in El Lago neatly bifurcates between the two dozen families whose male heads have been drawn into the coop-

erative movement and who have the resources to pursue the cooperative
strategy and a much larger assemblage of women and mostly older men
who have been drawn into the BCCs and whose work, if they work at
all, centers on education—health education (the barefoot doctors), literacy work (there are classes for both children and adults at the community center), or religious education. This bifurcation follows the lines
of a twofold division of labor: on the one side, male smallholders; on
the other, a few older *jornaleros* and women whose husbands are
jornaleros.

The emphasis on education evident throughout the movement reflects
both the current circumstances of rural Mexico and the ideological predispositions of the movement. With the peasant economy faltering and
new opportunities opening up for women, education has become the
route by which both men and women might hope to break away from
the limited opportunities hitherto available in El Lago. Both fear of
losing their independence and the traditional distrust of the educated,
however, have held men back from embracing education. Women, on
the other hand, tied neither to the land nor to their traditionally subordinate status, have taken readily to the message that education might
free them from the various ills that beset their community, and their
efforts have been molded accordingly. Organizers have encouraged educational projects and the quest for a better education both out of a
devotion to education per se and because of the congruence between this
and their own message of personal empowerment. People can only advance, they teach, when they "wake up," "open their eyes," and grasp
the "truth" of their situation.

The material limitations most participants in the movement face,
however, and the structural divisions between the interests and concerns
of the men and the women mean that the movement's primary vehicle
for self-improvement—the cooperative—remains beyond the reach of the
majority. Unwilling to tackle political solutions to the community's problems and unable to offer economic solutions, the movement is left with
stressing the more personal side of its message, one to which the women
of the community in particular can best respond.

Organizing, Ideology, and Moral Suasion

Organizing in El Lago thus continues to confront formidable barriers,
which are both discursive and practical. Ideologically, the movement has

been hampered not only by the limited and limiting character of the proposals it offers (cooperatives, literacy programs, moral education) but by its very adherence to accepted judgment on the political process: the movement has not had a political impact because it has shunned politics as divisive and corrupting. It has been constrained practically as well by the limited resources of local people, especially *jornaleros,* for participation in its project; the continued resistance of the men to organization; and the narrow range of opportunities for political action in the town.

The organizing effort, moreover, has bifurcated along class and sex lines, reflecting both divergent material interests and divergent resource bases, both structural and practical differences among members of the community. That the latter is in many cases the more important determinant of participation seems clear from the several failed attempts, on the part of groups of women and occasionally young men, to establish production cooperatives of one sort or another. Cooperativism, though it tends to favor those who already have superior resources, is by no means inherently incompatible with the interests of the dispossessed, if they can assemble the requisite resources. By and large, interested women in El Lago have not been able to do so.

That the discourse of movement members and leaders nevertheless attempts to transcend important differences in the division of labor is both the source of a fundamental weakness and a significant strength whose character we will examine in closing. The case presented here shows that organizers do not just attempt to rearrange the way people see their situation; they also appeal to people on various grounds to do something about it. One such appeal stands out in the discourse of Lagueños—a call to solidarity and service to the community.

The undifferentiated appeal to "the poor" by the movement, its calls for "unity," and its condemnation of factionalism in local politics all gloss over important differences in the structure of economic and political relations in the town, which enforce a differentiated program even on a movement desiring to promote a common vision. The movement's moral language nevertheless is essential to generating the sort of action that organizers demand. Wives must justify their participation in understandable, if not invariably acceptable, terms; leaders must explain the sacrifice of personal and family concerns in ways that attest to their probity and capacity to lead; and organizers must convince an individualist peasantry that cooperative action is worth the risk. The language of unity, the praise of community service, and the condemnation of *egoismo* serve these purposes.

All of the above themes, as we have seen, echo one side of current discourse: the prevailing condemnation of politics as practiced. They also provide the broader moral basis for claims against the dominant solution: withdrawal. To her husband's objections that she was abandoning home and duty for her organizing work, Tomasa responded (so she reported):

> "On the one hand, maybe I am hurting you [*te hago daño*], but on the other hand, what does it matter if one person is hurt and everyone else benefits?" He said, "Why should other people interest you? They're not going to thank you. People are bad, they're perverse. Besides, you have your home, your kids." I said to him, "But it interests me a lot—I want to help people.

Persistence, pure willfulness, and Cristi's help probably contributed more to winning her husband's tolerance than moral suasion, but Tomasa needed the justification herself: she found she liked the work, but that was hardly a legitimate argument. Moral discourse helped her to order her priorities and rationalize her choices while pushing others to re-evaluate their own.

Ricardo, a young man who withdrew from the movement after the failure of one of the manufacturing schemes, still believes in cooperative action and finds the best possible example in Eduardo: "I always watched the way he helped us. He created the irrigation co-op disinterestedly, and out of that came all the rest." In a similar vein, participants in the movement echo the phrase "for the good of the community" over and over again. Disinterestedness, the sacrifice of familial to communal needs, community mindedness—these are elements of an appeal intended to open up space in the moral universe of Lagueños for action of a new sort.

Some such moral appeal is apparently essential to organizing, whatever the claims of justice or self-interest that a movement also provides. Appeals of this sort suppose a community of meaning, of common understandings and norms.[36] Their hortatory character, however, suggests that they are also ways of adapting that moral universe directly to particular needs. At times adaptation may expand choices, as in the case just sketched: "If you condemn the pursuit of selfish interest in public office, the solution is to adopt the public interest as your own," they seem to say. In other settings such adaptation may be restrictive, confining people through invocation of traditional norms.[37] In either case it is an attempt to link private choice with public purpose, and its effect is to provide a rationale for actions that leaders or organizers cannot simply assume will be taken by people on their own initiative.

People remain free, however, to accept or reject such moral arguments, and silence may play a larger role in their response than any explicit attempts at counterargument. In this respect silence is as crucial a feature of the negotiation of ideological change as it is of peasant resistance generally. Confronted with the moral appeals of activists and organizers, people might well argue the virtues of the selfish, the risks of community spiritedness, and the prior claims of family and kin, but by and large, the most effective argument is silence, and women as well as men retreat into silence in El Lago when the call for solidarity imposes too clearly on their own preferences or abilities to respond. In this way, too, silence shapes debate in El Lago, allowing people to set limits on their action, even when they are unable to limit their verbal adhesion to the principles of the movement.

Conclusions

Why people join in collective defense or pursuit of common goals is rarely clear. Some join movements for the sake of their children; others refuse because "my family comes first." Some rise up in outrage at an injustice visited upon their community; others follow a brother or an uncle or a friend to the front lines. The usual explanations of peasant revolt look for general reasons for peasant unhappiness or outrage, glossing over such individual variations—and at the macro-level they are correct to do so. As Anthony Oberschall observes, if only 20 percent of a population joins in a revolt, we still have a revolt. What we are usually interested in are the conditions that provoke these 20 percent, even if some of them may have been "bullied and coerced into choices that are contrary to their predispositions."[38] Nevertheless, a mere listing of the conditions likely to produce widespread discontent and common action—spontaneous or organized, violent or nonviolent—does not tell us anything about how people come to see their situation as both intolerable and changeable or how they manage to join together in common action to change it.

The case we have just examined illuminates major aspects of that transformation as well as significant pitfalls in the organizing process. We have focused in particular on ideological shifts, that is, on change in the ways people commonly talk about their affairs and on the manner in which such change may emerge from the interactions of organizers, local leaders, and ordinary villagers. The organizing effort in El Lago demonstrates, first, the extent to which collective action neither rises spontaneously from material conditions nor even from widespread feelings of "relative deprivation" or perceptions of injustice but, instead, depends upon and is shaped by people's understandings of their situation, their options, and their obligations. Prevailing discourse, for instance, may highlight elements of experience in ways that systematically impede concerted action, as in the suspicion of politics in El Lago. Organizers themselves may feed such suspicions, as they have in El Lago, and consequently find certain avenues for action blocked; on the other hand, they might devise appeals that effectively counter popular resistance and overcome popular timidity. The irony in this particular case is that the prevailing condemnations of politics and *egoismo* cut both ways: organizers found no way to mount political solutions to the ills townspeople face, but they did make use of Lagueños' critique of individualism in a sometimes successful effort to create solidarity and further the movement.

Second, while prevailing discourse and the efforts of organizers jointly frame and shape the problems and the answers people debate, this negotiation of the terms of debate is not carried on in a vacuum. In El Lago structural and material differences between *ejidatarios* and *jornaleros* and between men and women profoundly affect the relative ability of members of each group to respond to the organizers' program of action. In the face of resource scarcities, the women in particular chose two paths: they joined the Caja, or savings bank, to enhance their resources (and incidentally their independence); and they developed their own version of the organizers' vision, in which the education of the children and the spread of religious teachings would resolve what they came to see as the most pressing problems—the risk of the streets and the lack of opportunity for their children. The latter nicely fit prevailing conceptions of the women's concerns, but many women demonstrated their longing for more positive, economically meaningful measures. The lack of resources made "women's concerns" their primary outlet. The prospect of violent rejection of any challenge to the prevailing political arrangement apparently constrained people in the movement in other ways, thus shifting attention, again, to self-help and education as primary outlets for their commitment. Ideological change, no matter how profound, is bound to be constrained in significant ways by a lack of resources and by the prevailing distribution and use of power.

Third, ideological or discursive change is not the simple transmission of new ideas to a passive population. The claims of organizers on people's attention, adherence, and energy are actively negotiated—as are the claims of politicians, church people, schoolteachers, and other "influentials." As we have seen, people's responses, even when they are positive, often involve the selective adaptation of organizers' arguments. This is especially so when material or political constraints block full adoption, but it is also true in subtler ways, as attempts to integrate what they already "know"—for instance, about the arrogance of the educated—with what they are learning about the benefits of education. The fit is seldom complete, and that incompleteness provides the basis for the tensions that people may exploit in dragging their feet or launching counterattacks as organizers demand more and more of their time and energy. People may also respond, as we have seen, with silence or a refusal to engage in debate because, perhaps, to do so would already concede too much—the appropriateness, for instance, of women's taking an active role in community affairs and the decisions of men. In this process the direction and scope of an organizing effort may be altered, the character of its appeals narrowed or broadened, and its hopes for success dashed or bolstered.

Any adequate account of mobilization must take such facts into account. The organizing effort in El Lago, moreover, displays three key facets of any attempt to mobilize participation: organizers offer an interpretation and evaluation of a situation or of events; they offer programs and promises for action; and they employ exhortations to action grounded in solidarity.[39] All three are ways of creating space for action, of reconstructing reality in such a way that people can be moved to act. Why people join movements is, once again, another question, but the terms under which they join are set, at least provisionally, by the construction of reality they adopt, and this, finally, is not simply a matter of organizers' claims and arguments—their own political discourse—but of the responses of their listeners.

All three facets of political discourse must be taken into account in evaluating the relationships between language and action. Political discourse links motives and action. It provides people with a way of interpreting their situation, an agenda or a vision of alternative courses of action, and both the reasons and rationalizations for adopting one or another course. Political discourse is thus something more than an "intervening variable" between motives and action, for it provides the context, the reasons, and the rationalizations that select among and organize motives, arranging priorities, masking certain interests and reshaping still others. It should go without saying that the discourses that organizers introduce, ordinary villagers commonly employ, and participants and leaders of a movement adopt have varying limitations and strengths; that each leaves as much unsaid as said; and that the very saying circumscribes the field of vision and the possibilities for action that people may enjoy.

The above discussion suggests, fourth, that the success of organizers in tapping local attitudes does not necessarily guarantee the success of the movement that they set out to create. In the case of El Lago the organizers' own anarchist bent contributed to a fateful analysis: if government was part of the problem, it must not, reasoned the organizers, be part of the solution. Independent cooperativism, whatever its virtues, proved, however, too narrow of a platform to either reach the most needy of El Lago's peasants or penetrate the local political system. The organizers in this case had not failed to appreciate local problems or take into account local attitudes. On the contrary, Eduardo and Cristi not only pinpointed crucial bottlenecks in the local economy, but they also spoke directly to peasant perceptions about politics and the political process. Here was the rub. On the one hand, they could readily convince at least a portion of their interlocutors that the global system linking national and international capitalism and the Mexican state was ultimately responsible for the declining fortunes of peasant Mexico. However radical the language, though, the critique of capitalism that both FAT and the BCC movement shared had no particular consequence. Peasant producers dealt not with "capitalism" but with the local moneylender, the buyers for the mills and marketing firms, and the agencies of the state, and they had little leverage with any of these. On the other hand, the peasants of El Lago could easily agree that the state was corrupt and local politics even more so, that agencies of the state accommodated the rich while grinding down the poor, and that it was best therefore to stay as far from government and politics as possible. While this consensus provided easy commonality between organizers and peasants, however, it scarcely contributed to widening the scope or enhancing the effectiveness of the movement.

Finally, moral discourse of a rather specialized kind appears to be essential to an organizing effort. Thus, while the analysis and the solution organizers offered to the peasants of El Lago had the effect of narrowing the movement, the sorts of moral appeals they employed extended it beyond the limited confines of cooperativism and bridged the gulf between "middle peasants" and *jornaleros*. James Scott's work, especially in *The Moral Economy of the Peasant,* has been focused on the basic notions of justice rooted in the conditions of peasant life. Such notions certainly play a role in the discourse of Lagueños and in their judgments on merchants, local officials, and the system in which they are enmeshed. Some of their judgments could no doubt be traced to a "subsistence ethic" and theories of reciprocity that imply an obligation of the community to look after its own. But there is little sense in El Lago that some threshold of injustice might be crossed, precipitating an outraged outburst; rather, injustice and *egoismo* describe the very texture of life in the town, out of which Lagueños hope somehow to advance. What is crucial for organizing here, therefore, is not so much a sharpening of the sense of injury and injustice as a call to solidarity in defiance of prevailing practice—though not, as we saw, of prevailing judgments on practice.

Such a sense of solidarity is a crucial element of mobilization, I would argue, and not just in situations like that of El Lago. If people are to take common action, they need not just a sense of injustice but also, as Barrington Moore points out,[40] a sense that they can do something about it. That is partly a matter of people's perception of external circumstances—of the opportunities for action and the threat of reprisal. It is also a matter of trust and moral commitment, however. The judgment that a situation is unjust carries no commitment to act with it: frustration and anger, as Ted Robert Gurr admits, may lead to apathy and submission, avoidance behavior, or aggressive action.[41] Protest, revolt, and collective action in general are forms of social activity. Individual participation may depend upon a host of factors, subjective and objective, but collective action hinges in part, at least, on the ability of leaders to elicit and to some extent direct a sense of solidarity. They must be able to employ moral language. They must wield a distinctive sort of moral appeal as an essential part of their repertoire.[42]

To understand peasant revolts (or mobilization more generally) in sum, it is not enough to pin down the sorts of conditions likely to provoke discontent and protest. We need also see how those conditions are transformed into reasons and rationalizations for collective action. Part of the answer, of course, lies in the skills of leaders, the kind of situation people actually face, the social and political and economic networks among them, and the sorts of responses they can expect from the authorities and from their neighbors. But the transformation in question depends to a large degree on the terms of debate, and we must look to discourse—and to the links between discourse and practice or experience—to understand a major part of the considerable variation among cases.

Interpretations and evaluations of a situation, proposals for action, and appeals to solidarity are the basic elements of such discourse. Ideological change—the alteration, that is, of the terms of political discourse—is the outcome of continuous, if often only implicit, negotiations between ordinary speakers and the bearers of new terms of exchange. In these negotiations the meaning and content of class relations may be decisively altered, as Laclau suggests, but insofar as people's resources are affected in the outcome, it seems clear that differential access to resources—including those based on a sexual division of labor—will play an important role in where people stand and how they argue. Peasant silence, finally—the silence born of powerlessness and isolation, a "hidden injury of class,"[43] but also, no doubt, a defensive tool for life at close quarters—may likewise affect the outcome by limiting the effectiveness of organizers' appeals, restricting the agenda for action, and asserting the virtues of caution and self-interest in an uncertain struggle. Like the appeals of organizers, the silence of their listeners provides the scope for both action and taking stock. "He's waiting to see," said one of the women about her husband. "If things go well, if the Caja is not robbed by its directors, if I manage to save some cash and he sees the new cooperative working, he'll come around. But he has to see first. He's waiting to see." What he sees will depend, no doubt, on the material success of the cooperative project, but whatever its success, his vision will be importantly altered by the questions and the answers that the fledgling movement and his own wife have brought to bear on the circumstances of his life.

NOTES

The fieldwork on which this article is based was conducted between June 1984 and July 1985 and was supported in part by a dissertation fellowship from the Institute for the Study of World Politics and Graduate Research Grants from the University of California, Davis, for whose assistance I am grateful. I would also like to thank Gretchen Casper, Manochehr Dorraj, David Laitin, Ben Orlove, and James Scott as well as the editor and an anonymous reviewer for *Comparative Studies in Society and History,* for their very helpful critical readings of earlier versions of this article.

1. The critical studies are Barrington Moore, Jr., *Social Origins of Dictatorship and Democracy: Lord and Peasant in the Making of the Modern World* (Boston: Beacon Press, 1966); Eric R. Wolf, *Peasant Wars of the Twentieth Century* (New York: Harper and Row, 1969); Theda Skocpol, *States and Social Revolutions: A Comparative Analysis of France, Russia, and China* (Cambridge: Cambridge University Press, 1979); Jeffrey M. Paige, *Agrarian Revolution: Social Movements and Export Agriculture in the Underdeveloped World* (New York: Free Press, 1975); and James C. Scott, *The Moral Economy of the Peasant: Rebellion and Subsistence in Southeast Asia* (New Haven: Yale University Press, 1976).

2. The Mexican case has been particularly well documented. See Gustavo Esteva, *The Struggle for Rural Mexico* (South Hadley, Mass.: Bergin and Garvey, 1983); Merilee Grindle, *Bureaucrats, Peasants, and Politicians in Mexico* (Berkeley: University of California Press, 1977); Rosa Elena Montes de Oca, "The State and the Peasants," in *Authoritarianism in Mexico,* ed. José Luis Reyna and Richard S. Weinert (Philadelphia: Institute for the Study of Human Affairs, 1977), 47–66; Clarisa Hardy, *El Estado y los campesinos: La Confederación Nacional Campesina (CNC)* (Mexico City: Nueva Imagen, 1984).

3. Indeed, I take it that peasant revolt, and political violence generally, is but political action by other means and not a phenomenon sui generis that demands explanation in its own right. Cf. William A. Gamson, *The Strategy of Social Protest* (Homewood, Ill.: Dorsey Press, 1975), 39.

4. Ernesto Laclau, "Tesis acerca la forma hegemónica de la política," in *Hegemonía y alternativas políticas en América Latina,* ed. Julio Labastida Martín del Campo (Mexico City, Siglo Veintiuno, 1985), 19–44.

5. James C. Scott, *Weapons of the Weak* (New Haven: Yale University Press, 1985).

6. Scott, *The Moral Economy of the Peasant,* chap. 1.

7. Scott, *Weapons of the Weak,* especially chap. 8.

8. See Pierre Bourdieu, *Outline of a Theory of Practice* (New York: Cambridge University Press, 1977); Anthony Giddens, *The Constitution of Society: Outline of the Theory of Structuration* (Cambridge: Polity Press, 1984). See also the stimulating, if overly schematic, review of recent social theory in Alexander E. Wendt, "The Agent-Structure Problem in International Relations Theory," *International Organization* 41, no. 3 (Summer 1987): 335–70.

9. Scott recognizes the difficulty here. "There is no way," he writes, "in which the participants' interpretations of the impact of the green revolution in the [the region of] Kedah can be deduced from the crude economic facts" (*Weapons,* 180). As it happens, these facts are interpreted by the inhabitants in largely personalistic terms, outcomes as the result of the personal choices of local actors. This is a strategic choice on the part of the poor, Scott argues, because local actors are the ones these poor can confront. But, he admits, "if there were a movement or political party that supported security of tenure, land reform, or full employment in rural areas, the realm of plausible action might be appreciably widened" (*Weapons,* 183, n. 87).

10. But, it should be noted, in a rational response that is socially constructed. Scott is, in this respect, several steps ahead of his critics, who deny the social character of the individual's construction of his or her choices even as they attempt to explain it. See Samuel L. Popkin, *The Rational Peasant* (Berkeley: University of California Press, 1979).

11. David Laitin has demonstrated, for instance, how even "primal" religious cleavages, with considerable resonance in ongoing patterns of economic competition and strife, have been overlooked, and sometimes actively suppressed, in Nigerian politics as a result of the dominance of other sorts of cleavages in ordinary political discourse. See David D. Laitin, *Hegemony and Culture* (Chicago: University of Chicago Press, 1986).

12. Scott, *Weapons,* 204.

13. Ideology in practice, whatever that term might mean when used to describe a tool of analysis or a system of ideas, is first of all discourse, language in use. Analysts systematize it only at their own risk, always in danger of rigidifying what is in reality a constantly changing usage and distorting thereby the real meaning of ideology in everyday affairs. I speak by preference, therefore, of discourse rather than ideology.

14. This is not to suggest that discursive change must originate outside the village; on the contrary, we will see that peasants are active in altering the discourse organizers introduce, and some, of course, play the role of organizer in their own community.

15. I am drawing here on the distinction developed by Paul Ricoeur between language (or *langue*) as a self-contained system of signs and discourse as language in use, language as attempt to make sense of the world. See Paul Ricoeur, *Interpretation Theory: Discourse and the Surplus of Meaning* (Fort Worth: Texas Christian University Press, 1976).

16. For a comprehensive inventory and anatomy of such factors, see Charles Tilly, *From Mobilization to Revolution* (Reading, Mass.: Addison-Wesley, 1978).

17. See Richard E. Nisbett and T. D. Wilson, "Telling More than We Can Know: Verbal Reports on Mental Processes," *Psychological Review,* no. 84: 231–59.

18. See John Womack, Jr., *Zapata and the Mexican Revolution* (New York: Random House, 1968), for the best general account of this element of the Revolution of 1910–20.

19. Even the rightist National Action Party (PAN) claims Zapata, whom they

represent as a peasant smallholder who rose to defend private property and who today would favor dissolution of the *ejidos,* the communal landholdings of the agrarian reform sector created after the revolution.

20. Town government, though formally more open to popular control, is severely restricted in scope. Despite its size, El Lago is but a satellite of the neighboring *cabecera municipal* (equivalent to the county seat), a smaller but richer community that has effectively controlled politics in the area under its control since time immemorial. (There is some evidence that this town was the *cabecera,* the head, of this region even under the Aztecs.) With plentiful irrigated land, the cabecera's inhabitants have been able to raise their standard of living, educate their children, and maintain political power. With political power at their disposal, they have been able to channel taxes into improvements in their own town while leaving other towns in the *municipio* to beg the state and federal governments for aid.

21. For a similar story of the depletion of natural resources and their replacement with commercial products, see Steven Gudeman, *The Demise of a Rural Economy: From Subsistence to Capitalism in a Latin American Village* (Boston: Routledge and Kegan Paul, 1978).

22. The easy acceptance of family planning ideas in El Lago is probably a sign of the precariousness of the economic balance. Some families find security in numbers; others have decided it makes more sense to invest heavily in a few children. The heightened prestige of education in the town supports the latter strategy; the difficulties that the educated encounter in procuring work close to home supports the former. Family size, education, and work opportunities for the children are the subjects of constant conversation.

23. See Merilee S. Grindle, *State and Countryside: Development Policy and Agrarian Politics in Latin America* (Baltimore: Johns Hopkins University Press, 1986), on the changing ideology and politics of agricultural and agrarian policy in Mexico since 1940.

24. See Esteva, *Struggle.* Blanca Rubio, *Resistencia campesina y explotación rural en México* (Mexico City: Era, 1987), traces both the changing locus of protest over the last twenty years and its content to distinctive changes in the agricultural economies of the various regions of Mexico. It is worth noting that the agrarianist ideology of the Mexican state, and its shifting interpretation by successive administrations, provides both opportunities and incentives for peasant groups to mount their protests. See Michael W. Foley, "Agenda for Mobilization: The Agrarian Question and Popular Mobilization," *Latin American Research Review* 26:2 (1991): 39–74.

25. The so-called base Christian community movement, from the Spanish *comunidades cristianas de base,* or "base ecclesial community" (CEB, comunidades eclesiales de base), grew out of attempts to create social action "cells" in the barrios and villages of Latin America in the late 1950s and early 1960s. Originally under the auspices of the Catholic church and vehemently anti-Communist in orientation, the movement's techniques and focus on organizing the poor for community action soon spread to Protestant denominations as well, and in Chile, Brazil, Central America, and elsewhere, BCC leaders drew

closer and closer to parties of the Left and occasionally to revolutionary move-ments. Today the movement is widely known as a leftist-populist challenge both to national authorities throughout Latin America and in many cases to local church hierarchies as well. For an informal introduction to the movement, see Penny Lernoux, *Cry of the People* (New York: Doubleday, 1982), 389–408. David E. Mutchler, *The Church as a Political Factor in Latin America* (New York: Praeger, 1971), provides an "inside look" at the origins of the movement in Chile and Colombia, and Brian H. Smith's *The Church and Politics in Chile: Challenges to Modern Catholicism* (Princeton, N.J.: Princeton University Press, 1982) is an important study of the shifting strategies of the Catholic church in Latin America. Finally, Daniel H. Levine and Scott Mainwaring provide im-portant insights into the different ways in which national church hierarchies have shaped the movement; see their "Religion and Popular Protest in Latin America: Contrasting Experience," in *Power and Popular Protest,* ed. Susan Eckstein (Los Angeles: University of California Press, 1989).

26. See Paulo Freire, *Pedagogy of the Oppressed* (New York: Continuum, 1983); and *Cultural Action for Freedom* (Cambridge: Harvard University Press, 1970).

27. *Manual de la Communidad Eclesial de Base* (Tabasco, Mexico: n.p., n.d.), 35–36.

28. *Estatutos Cajas Populares de la Unidad Cooperativa Independiente— Frente Auténtico del Trabajo* (Cuernavaca: January 31, 1984).

29. Unless otherwise indicated, all quotations from villagers are drawn from the author's interviews conducted between May 5 and June 30, 1985, which were tape-recorded on site in El Lago and subsequently transcribed. Translations are my own.

30. There is widespread agreement that *ejidal* officials in the past have overseen the illegal sale of communal properties to landlords in neighboring towns, but, when people refer to stolen lands, they also have in mind accusations that people from neighboring towns have rented land from poorer Lagueños, or taken *ejidal* plots as security for loans and then held onto the land in question, claiming rightful title.

31. I would not want to suggest that the linkage between "personal" and "social" morality implied in Catholic usage blocks social action or would in-evitably move it in more conservative directions. "Socialist morality" plays a similar linking role in many secular movements of the Left, lending both the appearance and the reality of moral probity to a leadership dependent on popular approbation. "Justice" conceived as Felipa conceives it, however, allows her and other members of the BCC movement in El Lago to focus their energies on largely "spiritual" and educational efforts, perhaps at the expense of their po-litical energies.

32. Moral psychologist Lawrence Kohlberg has recently wrestled with the question. See Lawrence Kohlberg and Daniel Candee, "The Relationship of Moral Judgment to Moral Action," in *Morality, Moral Behavior, and Moral Development,* ed. William M. Kurtiness and Jacob L. Gewirtz (New York: John Wiley and Sons, 1984), 52–73. Barrington Moore observes that, for people to

take action, they need not just a sense that they are suffering an injustice but also the sense that they can do something about it. See Barrington Moore, Jr., *Injustice: The Social Bases of Obedience and Revolt* (White Plains, N.Y.: M.E. Sharpe, 1978), 459.

33. This was written before the dramatic shift in Mexican politics in the elections of 1988, but the emergence of a unified leftist opposition has only exacerbated the divisions among groups like those being considered here over the question of partisan alignment.

34. It appears that women can more readily do this since the appearance (in the 1960s) of *molinos de nixtamal*—commercial mills for the grinding of maize. A task that formerly took most women as much as four hours a day can now be accomplished by sending a youngster of ten to the mill with a bucket of maize. University of California, Davis, historian Arnold Bauer (in personal conversations, July 1988) suggests that the exigencies of tortilla production before the appearance of the mills must have shaped a great many aspects of life, including even the conduct of military affairs; one recalls Zapata's soldiers reduced to begging in the streets of Mexico City because they had been cut off from the Morelos villages, which supplied them with their daily tortillas.

35. Elsa Chaney has observed that throughout Latin America such issues and solutions tend to constitute the parameters for political action by women and that even women deeply involved in politics tend to take on the role of *supermadre,* thus defining their "public activity as an extension of their traditional family role to the public arena," in *Supermadre: Women and Politics in Latin America* (Austin: University of Texas Press, 1979), 159 passim. That the reasons for this are material as well as "cultural" is apparent in the case of El Lago. Whether and how far these parameters might be breached is being tested at this moment in the town, as the silence of the men has had another, more paradoxical effect: it has driven some of the women into the streets, into politics, to occupy the place that the men have left vacant. That women turned out at all for the municipal election of 1984 was something of a revolution in local politics. The jeers of the men did not keep them away, in part because they had organized to elect their own candidate, the nephew of their leader, as *ayudante,* or mayor. In fact, the women carried the day, as did the "reform" candidate in the *ejidal* elections, and, when the previous incumbents refused to release records to the new authorities, the women stormed the *ejidal* warehouse where the records and sacks of fertilizer illegally hoarded by their opponents were stored. One of their leaders engaged in a gun battle with one of the caciques, while her companions chased off his confederates with a rain of stones and insults.

For all the excitement, the capture of power has not been very satisfying, and women were talking of running one of their own in subsequent elections. It is not at all clear, however, what the women's party (which includes both movement participants and others, but none from the leadership of the BCC and cooperative movement) stands for, apart from "reform" and an end to the old factionalism and corruption. Their leader, who participates in the BCC movement, is also local president of Campesino Women, the women's organization of the PRI's National Confederation of Campesinos—from which leaders in the organizing effort have kept a studied distance. Her nephew, who was a member of the "socialist" faction in town (from the old PPS, Popular Socialist Party), switched allegiance to the PRI halfway through his term, when it became clear that state and federal aid flowed more readily through the channels of the official party. Local power, finally, is severely circumscribed, and the capture of town posts by no means ensures results even on the level of the municipio.

36. John R. Searle, *Expression and Meaning* (Cambridge: Cambridge University Press, 1979), chap. 5; J. L. Austin, *How to Do Things with Words* (Oxford: Clarendon Press, 1962).

37. See David Parkin's very illuminating discussion of such a case in *The Cultural Definition of Political Response* (London: Academic Press, 1978).

38. Anthony Oberschall, *Social Conflict and Social Movements* (Englewood Cliffs, N.J.: Prentice-Hall, 1973), 28–29.

39. James Q. Wilson develops the notion of "solidary incentives" in *Political Organizations* (New York: Basic Books, 1973), 33–45. See also Bruce Fireman and William A. Gamson, "Utilitarian Logic in the Resource Mobilization Perspective," in *The Dynamics of Social Movements,* ed. Mayer N. Zald and John D. McCarthy (Cambridge, Mass.: Winthrop, 1979). For a more extended discussion of the role of moral appeals in political mobilization, see Michael W. Foley, "The Language of Contention: Political Language, Moral Judgment and Peasant Mobilization in Contemporary Mexico" (Ph.D. diss., Department of Political Science, University of California, Davis, 1986).

40. Moore, *Injustice,* 459.

41. Ted Robert Gurr, *Why Men Rebel* (Princeton: Princeton University Press, 1970), 33–34.

42. This suggests the fundamental weakness in Lawrence Kohlberg's attempted resolution of the disjunction between moral judgment and the decision to act on that judgment. In keeping with his Kantian, decidedly atomistic, conception of human behavior, Kohlberg sees the second moment as the product of a certain "judgment of responsibility" toward oneself and one's principles, but such a judgment of responsibility may equally well be motivated by social criteria, ranging from fear of ostracism to a broader or narrower sense of obligation to others. See Kohlberg and Candee, "The Relationship of Moral Judgment to Moral Action"; the critiques by Norma Haan, "Two Moralities in Action Contexts: Relationships to Thought, Ego Regulation, and Development," *Journal of Personality and Social Psychology* 36, no. 3 (1978): 286–305; and Carol Gilligan, *In a Different Voice: Psychological Theory and Women's Development* (Cambridge: Harvard University Press, 1982). Michael Hechter's rational choice theory of group solidarity, *Principles of Group Solidarity* (Berkeley: University of California Press, 1987), is a subtle but ultimately unsatisfactory attempt to subsume an important variant of moral choice, the sense of obligation to a larger community, under the narrow rubric of "self-interest."

43. Jonathan Cobb and Richard Sennett, *The Hidden Injuries of Class* (New York: Random House, 1973).

To Be in Between:
The *Cholas* as Market Women

Linda J. Seligmann

When I did my first field research in Peru in 1974, I was struck by the forceful, energetic, and at times bawdy market women known as *cholas*. They stood out because they appeared fearless, astute, different, and unpredictable. I could not find a counterpart among Peruvian males. The *cholas* feigned neither humility toward rich white foreigners nor unbridled admiration for their ways. They inhabited a world distinct from that of either the Quechua peasantry or the Westernized mestizo but easily interacted with both campesinos and mestizos. They freely insulted whom they pleased; they engaged in wheeling and dealing and stood their ground—but they could also be surprisingly generous, almost religiously so.

Returning in the 1980s, I found that a new kind of lively popular music, a mix of African and traditional Quechua highland and criollo coastal rhythms, was being played all over the streets of Peru, especially in the closed and open-air markets. Its themes focused primarily on the lives and activities of those who inhabit the informal sector—truck drivers and market women selling their wares, migrating, transporting people and things, celebrating fiestas, drinking in *chicha* bars (often *cholas* tend or own these bars, which serve an indigenous maize beer); it protested the injustice of the government and the economic plight of urban dwellers. It seemed to me that the music itself acknowledged the growing number and power of those who constituted the informal sector, including the *cholas*. They had created their own music and were using it as a form of political expression, despite efforts of the state to control and sometimes co-opt them. (See Matos Mar 1988:83–86; and Stein and Monge 1988:144–58, for an extended discussion of *chicha* music as foundational to popular Peruvian urban culture.)

Between 1960 and 1980 Peru's urban informal sector increased a notable 60 percent (PREALC 1982). Between 1975 and 1984 alone it increased 80 percent (Stein and Monge 1988:30). The *cholas* continued to dominate the marketplace, the bills bulging in their purses barely keeping up with inflation. Violating both theoretical and social expectations (see, for example, Bourque 1971; Bourricaud 1970; Escobar 1964; Fried 1961; Fuenzalida 1971; Pitt-Rivers 1965; and Varallanos 1960), they have not disappeared from the urban landscape either by returning to the country-side or by becoming assimilated into the urban labor force and mestizo culture. They have become central to Peru's economy, and their political power as potential adversaries to the status quo is slowly gaining rec-ognition. A similar phenomenon has occurred in other nations comprised of multiple ethnic groups, whose economies are weakly developed (see Davies 1979; MacEwen Scott 1979; and Portes 1981, 1983, 1988).

Physically, the *cholas* are located in the marketplace, the crucial in-tersection between rural and urban sociospatial environments. As Ray Bromley and Richard Symanski (1974:23) have remarked, they are both "media and mirror" of the institutional fabric of society and of social relationships. Structurally, the *cholas* represent a crucible between the international and national economy, on the one hand, and between local and national socioeconomic organization and mores, on the other hand. Their unique position and their remarkable capacity to travel cultural and trade routes between rural and urban centers provide us with an opportunity to examine why they have not been fully acculturated or assimilated into national society, instead forming ties of solidarity among themselves and with rural communities of indigenous peasants.

This article is about *cholas* who are market vendors. It seeks to locate them both within the global economy and the national cultural, political, and ideological consciousness, relying upon historical accounts, system-atic and informal interviews, the autobiography of a market woman, literary representations of *cholas,* and other ethnographic reports that provide a basis for comparison (see, for example, the comprehensive bibliography on marketing and marketplaces compiled by Mott, Silin, and Mintz [1975]; Mintz 1964; and Bromley and Gerry 1979). It also examines how *cholas* have become intermediaries who broker not only economic goods but also cultural values and political power; in what ways issues of gender have contributed to that process; and why the position the *cholas* occupy, in turn, makes them a substantial political and economic threat to certain sectors of Peruvian society.

The Social Category *Chola:* Historical Processes

Peruvian market women have not been discussed more because of their very nature as brokers who belong to the social category *chola*. The boundaries of this social category are ill defined in terms of race, class, ethnicity, or geographic locus alone (cf. Pitt-Rivers 1965:41–49). Manipulating the term *chola* and the social category to which it refers began after the Spanish Conquest and has continued ever since. At that time one fascinating attribute of the position of *cholas* emerged and eventually took root in the social and national consciousness of Peru. The name *chola* acquired multiple meanings because the individuals to whom the term referred were situated in the middle, the result of processes of both social and racial miscegenation. These early processes, which were contentious and litigious, involved the conscious denial or appropriation of identity. A brief look at how this category emerged historically helps to explain the position of market women today and the political and cultural controversy that continues to surround their position and functions.

The category *cholo* originated in sixteenth-century Spanish colonial legal tenets and was designed to classify the indigenous population of Peru within a caste system according to racial characteristics (Varallanos 1962:21–66).[1] Gregorio de Cangas explains the general criteria upon which these caste categories were based: "From the male spaniard and female indian results a royal mestizo; from the royal mestizo and female indian, a *cholo* is born; from a *cholo* and female indian, a common mestizo" (1762–66:331). Legally, any individual whose blood was more than half-Indian was considered to be an Indian and forced to pay tribute to the Crown. The problem, however, was that, due to the lack of Spanish peninsular females in the colony, intermarriage or illicit unions between Spaniards and female Indians became a necessity.[2] Hispanic colonists considered intermarriage suitable between native female nobility and male Spaniards mainly because it gave members of the Conquest society further access to indigenous lands and economic resources (Burkett 1975: 203–5; Varallanos 1962:55). Parallel inheritance had been customary in Incaic Peru, and native women had wielded considerable economic and political power (Silverblatt 1987). While Hispanic colonists and the Crown condoned and even encouraged legal marriages between Indian nobility and Spaniards, they disparaged and begrudgingly tolerated illicit unions between male Spaniards and low-status indigenous females, which resulted in the formation of numerous matriarchal units.

The offspring of marriages between peninsular Spaniards and Indians were alternatively called mestizo or *cholo,* depending upon how much non-Indian blood they could claim. Biological distinctions between Indian and non-Indian became impossible to maintain, and *cholos,* who belonged neither to a pure Indian nor to a pure Spanish caste, constituted a thorny problem for colonial bureaucrats. Cases were fought to determine when persons of mixed blood were legally exempt from tribute. If they could escape from the caste of indigenous tribute payers, often they could eventually reject their indigenous heritage altogether. Bureaucrats and the Crown, on the other hand, had a vested interest in keeping them within the caste of Indians in order to collect economic revenues from them and have access to their labor (Kubler 1952).[3] Offspring of subsequent marriages between either *cholos* or mestizos and female Indians were also called *cholos* (Varallanos [1962:66], citing Cangas 1762–66). In addition, for the first five years of colonial rule female children were often given to Spaniards as a form of tribute, thus fostering the tolerance the latter demonstrated on occasion toward their illegitimate children, better known as *hijos naturales,* which resulted from these unions.[4] The social category of *cholo* began to be considered perjoratively within colonial society only after the proliferation of offspring from these mixed marriages threatened to undermine the purity of the castes and the protection of economic and cultural privilege (Burkett 1975:222; Varallanos 1960:81).[5]

During the colonial period in the highlands and later in the capital itself, *cholos* came to engage in service occupations as domestics, street cleaners, and nursemaids. Many women who were *cholas* came to reside in urban rather than rural areas since that was where their lovers or husbands lived. The distinctive socioracial category of *cholo* based upon ratios of Indian to non-Indian blood underwent changes due to extensive intermarriage and the emergence of a market economy and class structure that cross-cut ethnic affiliation. Since the colonial period, *cholos* have gradually become identified with various occupations within the urban service sector, particularly those characterized as "casual work" within the informal sector (cf. Bromley and Gerry 1979). One of the main occupations that females in this category have filled is street vending.

The *Chola* as Market Woman

Market women are called *cholas* because of the isomorphism between their functions as brokers and their social heritage as members of an intermediate "mixed race." François Bourricaud (1970:58) states that the denomination *middle* indicates that those who apply the term to themselves or to whom it is applied are primarily concerned with their relationship toward those above and/or below them. Richard Adams

(1975:88) adds that "power brokers link units or actors at different levels where the difference in power is such that the inferior has no real chance to confront the superior." In keeping with this description I would argue that any market dominated by brokerage represents the absence of full capitalist development and, as such, is a corollary to underdevelopment. In the case of Peru the conditions that make land ever scarcer leave little room for mobility or direct access to channels and institutions reserved for mestizos, and the progressive debilitation of the patrimonial state's capacity to provide services to its growing urban population create a role for market women as brokers (see Stein and Monge 1988). They fill a needed function, yet they are also situated in an "exposed" position, confirming Eric Wolf's much earlier description of brokers:

> Janus-like, they face in two directions at once. They must serve some of the interests of groups operating on both the community and national level, and they must cope with the conflicts raised by the collision of these interests. They cannot settle them, since by doing so they would abolish their own usefulness to others. . . . The study of brokers can provide unusual insight into the functions of a complex system through a study of its dysfunctions. (1965:97–98)

The diversity of market women's activities as intermediaries prohibits their characterization solely as petty commodity producers who no longer rely on ties with their place of origin in the countryside for their livelihood or as proletarians who have completely lost control of their means of production (see MacEwen Scott 1979; and Babb 1985:291–95; 1989). Even specifying their relations of production may not fully account for their class position, though it is a more fruitful approach. Many of them work for wages; others produce, process, and contribute to the circulation of commodities; some work on a consignment or putting-out basis; and still others combine barter and monetary exchanges in their transactions. In short, *cholas* can be market women, but some are not. The label *chola* is applicable to market women because of the identity between salient characteristics of the more general social category, *chola,* and the relations of production and exchange of market women. Just as the *chola* is a social category that originally emerged because it could be uniquely characterized as lying between the castes of *indio* and mestizo, market women are called *cholas* because they mediate between those considered as indigenous and nonindigenous people in the marketplace. The market-place itself, be it in the capital city or in smaller provincial centers, constitutes the border marking the separation between the urban and rural spheres and the nexus where they intersect. A more or less deliberate play is made upon the mediation of market women and the mediation of the market itself, particularly between classes and ethnic categories, lending an indefinite symbolic ambiguity to the meaning of market woman when *chola* applies metaphorically to her.[6]

Questions of Gender and Division of Labor

Being a market woman is only one female counterpart to the occupations *cholos* may hold, but in general the respective socioeconomic activities of *cholos* and *cholas* in connection to the market differ markedly. Only market women operate directly in the marketplace, where male *cholos* tend to be long-distance traders, wholesalers, or factory workers in urban or provincial centers. Sometimes the latter are also linked to market activities as street porters or as truck or bus drivers who transport both produce and market women to the market.

Market women's dress, over time, becomes highly distinctive compared to that of other groups, whereas the *cholo's* resembles a poorer version of the mestizo's dress (Nash 1979:312). Even in a sea of people the market women stand out in their tall, white stovepipe hats with a wide, black or colored band, their many cotton or velveteen *pullera* skirts and brightly colored polyester sweaters, their dangling earrings sparkling with rhinestones, and their money purses, bulging beneath their skirts.

Rondi Ericksen (personal communication, 1979) asked people living in rural communities surrounding Sicuani, an enormous market town in southern Peru, how they identified market women. All of them agreed that the white stovepipe hat was a feature associated only with market women. In Bolivia another style of hat, the bowler, distinguishes market women. Shirley Christian reports that, for "Bolivia's clothes-conscious *cholas*—urban women whose ancestry is mostly Aymara Indian but some Spanish—the bowler hat, more formally known as the derby, is their crowning glory. Owning a selection of them in various colors is a must, and ideally, one has an Italian-made Borsalino for special occasions" (1980). The distinctiveness of the dress of market women is primarily visible in the marketplace and in the travel routes they take for their business. Although strangers may no longer label them as *cholas* once they change into indigenous or mestizo dress and engage in activities not associated with street vending, their clients, friends, and relatives will still recognize who they are and what they do.[7]

The imperfect correspondence between male and female *cholo* has its roots in colonial law and custom.[8] Historically, intermarriage gave both a female spouse and her daughters access to resources unavailable to Indian husbands and their sons. Illicit unions, though they were associated with low status, prostitution, and promiscuous behavior, gave women the opportunity to learn crucial survival techniques, including autonomy and independence as matriarchal units.[9] Female advantage in the urban colonial system was offset by inheritance patterns in rural communities. Multiple reasons account for why women rather than men become street vendors. Skewed inheritance patterns in rural areas push women from the countryside (see Buechler 1978:351); the traditional division of labor in the countryside encourages and prepares women for this occupation—handling, processing, and serving food and controlling the outflow of cash (see Andreas 1985; Mintz 1971:248–49; Nash 1979; Silverblatt 1987; and Wolf 1965); women may be more successful than men as vendors since the majority of purchasers are also women (see Burkett 1975:245); and many women choose to be vendors rather than domestics or factory workers because of the greater autonomy it gives them, including the ability to care for their children during work hours.

Women also become market vendors often as a result of existing patriarchal values. In the domestic sphere negotiations take place frequently between a woman who wants to seek remunerative labor and her husband. Although economic necessity may ultimately determine a woman's motivation to enter the labor market, machismo within households encourages women to search for flexible kinds of occupations that will permit them to fulfill unremunerated household tasks while engaging in remunerative labor that is different from but similar to their household functions. Especially if a woman is married and her husband provides the bulk of the household income, women have the option of acting upon and, to a certain degree, manipulating this ideology of domesticity (see Benería and Roldán 1987). These conditions, along with the occupational structure in urban areas, lead women to take these jobs. The small size and low absorptive capacity of industry in Peru keep women from easily entering other urban occupations. Male migrants occupy most positions in formal sector factories and in the better-paid, more secure jobs within the informal sector (see Babb 1985; Bourque and

Warren 1981:196; Bunster and Chaney 1985:45; and MacEwen Scott 1979). Finally, this division of labor perpetuates itself because these vendors, in turn, also socialize their female offspring to become market women (Bunster and Chaney 1985:91).

Market women experience some benefits and advantages due to their position, a point Sidney Mintz (1971) makes. These are, however, primarily short-term and equivocal. They are independent of their husbands and of the wage labor market to some degree. Their husbands do not have direct access to their wages, and their activities are not contingent upon a mandatory extraction of surplus value by an employer who underpays them for their labor in order to turn a profit and also forbids them any mobility in both the physical and economic sense. In addition, married women who become market vendors may experience a shift in the balance of power between them and their spouses. If the woman is single, the shift may be more dramatic. In the first case, remunerated labor can bring women a sense of self-esteem. In the second case, women may entirely control cash flow and escape the kinds of implicit authority relations that normally operate between spouses in the domestic sphere. Nevertheless, though their position may give them greater autonomy from their husbands, my data show that often female vendors obtain their wares from male wholesalers, thus reinforcing a relationship of domination and subordination between men and women within a capitalist social formation.

Furthermore, as is true of most informal sector activities, many activities market women perform directly serve the purposes of the capitalist social formation without providing them with long-term opportunities for upward mobility. Mintz (1971:248–49) enumerates these activities: (1) transporting goods from rural producers or import houses to the consumer; (2) bulking produce and breaking bulk to facilitate exchange at quantity and cost levels appropriate to the scale of production; (3) processing items; (4) preserving capital in liquid form by serving as credit sources to their buyers and sellers; (5) breaking down the polarization between the rural and commercial sectors; (6) contributing to the national economy by paying taxes and market fees; and (7) making economic use of waste materials from Western society, which acquire use value for the peasantry.

Since market women do not usually control the means of production that generate their economic activities, they rarely accumulate capital for themselves (see Babb 1985:294–99; Nash 1979:293; and Mintz 1964).

If they make a profit, they tend to invest it, not in the expansion of their economic activities but, rather, in the education of their children. Education thus becomes a form of social capital for them. These children, once educated, theoretically have access to upward mobility and can seek lower-level wage labor occupations in factories or as salaried petty bureaucrats. Given the state of the Peruvian economy, however, few such positions are available, and with the continuing exodus from the countryside exacerbated by the guerrilla war Sendero Luminoso is waging, there will be fewer still. Thus, the education children receive is often to no avail in providing them with additional economic opportunities. The ambitions and aspirations of educated children also make them more fully removed from affiliation with their community of origin, which, as I shall discuss later, becomes critical if they decide to take political actions rejecting the legitimacy of national political leaders or governments.

Becoming a Market Woman:
The Art and Politics of Buying and Selling

The position of market women as successful economic, political, and cultural intermediaries depends upon their ability to establish themselves in the marketplace, the skills they can acquire to survive in the marketplace, and the specific kinds of activities they can perform. In her autobiography, narrated in Quechua and transcribed into Quechua and Spanish, Asunta tells how she decided to leave the countryside, eventually to become a market woman:

> I went to the fields to harvest some broad beans, which I picked from our field; at that moment, I decided to walk to Cuzco, just as anyone in the bean-selling business would do.
> In that state, I reached Cuzco for the first time, escaping from all my suffering, thinking that I would be better off there. When I arrived to Cuzco, I sold the broad beans in the central market but afterwards, I didn't know what to do or where to go. (Quoted in Valderrama and Escalante 1977:95)

Asunta only became successful as an independent market woman several years after she left her village. She traveled from place to place during that time and worked as a domestic servant, finally rebelling against the treatment she received from her employers. Juliana Cáceres Vera, a single mother with one child whose husband had died in a truck accident, sells vegetables without a license outside Cuzco's central market, San Pedro. She explains how she became a market woman:

> I lived in San Sebastian. My parents died when I was nine. I went to live with my aunts. They sent me to the market to sell vegetables and little by little I grew to enjoy it. I had to start selling out of necessity. I didn't have any money for clothes because my aunts would not give me any.

Magdalena Puma de Raymi sells oranges on the Avendia del Ejercito railroad tracks, one of the biggest sections of informal vendors in Cuzco. She purchases directly from wholesalers. A single mother with seven children whose husband had abandoned her, she is from the rural community of Acomayo. Her relatives brought her to Cuzco when she was seven years old, after her parents died. They arranged for her to work as a domestic servant for a couple from Lima. The couple made her work very hard and paid her very little. When she decided to marry the couple fired her. She decided to work as a vendor because she finds it more tranquil and receives assistance from other vendors, who help her find good products and watch her children. Juana Huaman sells cooked food on the Avenida del Ejercito railroad tracks. Abandoned by her husband, she has two young children. Her parents worked on a hacienda in the rural community of Anta. She was sent to Cuzco as a young girl because a lady from Anta recommended her to a family as a domestic servant. She worked fifteen years as a servant and described the work as grueling and her patrons as bad people who made her do everything. She was forced to leave after she gave birth to her first child. The mistress of the house suggested that she sell food because: "Sometimes you'll make money. When you sell, you'll make money. Whatever you don't sell, you'll be able to eat." She purchases the ingredients for her meals from people she knows in the informal sector of the San Pedro market.

To obtain the most advantageous position for processing, sale, and purchase purposes, the *chola* as market woman must learn to activate an elaborate network of kinship ties both in her rural community and in urban areas. When she first comes to the urban marketplace she usually stays with relatives, who are quick to inform her of how best to establish herself. She relies upon her relatives to introduce her to clients and to show her how to confront the language and demands of the bureaucracy and of local authorities. Once established, she cultivates her ties in rural areas to obtain primary products from her relatives there. Often these relatives (or her immediate family) take care of her land and eventually send their children to the city, where they are then able to stay with her. They may also be her clients on occasion when she sells nonagricultural products she has obtained from the urban commercial wholesale or retail sector.[10]

A market woman's success does not depend upon her connections, resources, and political skills alone. It also depends upon the larger economic system of which she is a part. One obvious question that arises is why rural peasants do not directly sell to urban residents, instead making their transactions through the market women. Peru's industrial sectors remain disarticulated from its agricultural sectors, and the necessary scale, communication and transportation infrastructure, and balance of foreign exchange do not exist to link them. Given these conditions, market women become essential to the circulation of primary products from the countryside to the cities. The burgeoning urban proletariat and the mestizo elite create the demand for cheap and plentiful agricultural products. In contrast, the indigenous rural population has more possibility of subsisting (albeit with increasing difficulty) without access to the market. The low wages workers receive combined with the explosion of Peru's informal sector and the primitive transport systems connecting agricultural peripheries to Peru's few but densely populated urban centers perpetuate the growth of market women as crucial nodes of the national economy (see Bourque and Warren 1981:196).

My interviews with household members in indigenous communities revealed that they clearly understood the disadvantages of selling their agricultural produce through market women but that the advantages outweighed the disadvantages. Many peasants take their produce to market, but others do not have the time, experience, or volume to make it worthwhile. The abysmal transportation networks, the high tariff they would have to pay truck drivers, and their fears of being robbed or taken advantage of in the city dissuade many peasants from marketing their agricultural products directly. The arrival of a truck is a frightening moment, even for the seasoned traveler. The *chola* is tough in her own right and has the contacts to help her out. Pierre Van den Berghe's (1974:135) and Gordon Appleby's (1976) research shows that market women rely heavily upon communication and intelligence networks for their success. This, in turn, serves them well in cultivating a rural clientele and helps to explain their predominance not only in urban industrial centers but also near or in towns that have mushroomed due to the presence of extractive resources such as minerals, which require transport and communication facilities.

The market women, who represent a critical juncture for the smooth functioning of the economy as well as a symbol of passive resistance and a threat to mestizos, are regarded ambivalently by the mestizos themselves, a sentiment that is reflected in the ways that the latter manipulate racial labels in social situations to correspond to their own vision of an ideal status hierarchy. As Linda Belote quips, the underlying truth of the oft-repeated adage that "the Indians don't produce, and they don't consume," is really: "The Indians don't produce, and they don't consume in a way that is directly beneficial to town whites" (1978:134). Even when a town is surrounded by productive fields, mestizos are still likely to be forced to purchase their goods indirectly from market women or itinerant peddlers. Because of the mestizos' relative dependency upon both market vendors and peasants who produce agricultural goods, many mestizos attempt to reinforce their power and sense of security by encouraging the use of distinct labels for those members of Andean society whom they wish to keep at a distance. Thus, mestizos frequently use the term *cholo* in denigrating fashion in order to keep aspiring "Indians" at a distance. Yet, as Anibal Quijano (1980:58–61) has pointed out, today there is no racial qualification for receiving the label "cholo," since it would postulate the existence of a sector of pure Indians. In fact, within contemporary Peruvian society great ideological emphasis is placed upon the unique social category of Indian, in turn provoking an awareness among so-called Indians of the kinds of goods and services to which they could have access were they not labeled as Indians. That is, by calling people Indians, who by all accounts share the same racial heritage as mestizos or *cholos,* at once calls attention to the deliberate hegemonic ideology that curtails the Indians' political and economic power (see also Stavenhagen 1975). Obversely, this kind of manipulative labeling can lead to countercultural demands for autonomy, justice, and the re-creation of a sector of pure Indians. Thus, so-called Indians and *cholos* turn this labeling on its head so that it becomes a political weapon of resistance to assimilation and integration.

The complexity and tension of daily class and interethnic relations between urban Hispanized mestizos, *cholos,* and peasants is reflected dramatically in the kinds of verbal exchanges that take place in exchanges in the marketplace. One can see how these exchanges make explicit mestizos' underlying fears and prejudices as well as the *cholas'* adamant rejection of the mestizos' efforts to use manipulative and denigrating labels. The following is an example of an exchange between a market woman selling potatoes and her client, an upper middle-class woman. The client begins the exchange:

"How much are your potatoes?"

"Five hundred, little mother. Buy some. They're delicious. Buy them now."

"Do you really think I'll buy them at such an exorbitant price? You who are from the countryside should sell them more cheaply."

"Buy them, little mother. We also need money so that we can continue selling. I have eight children I have to buy things for and to cook for."

"So you say, smelly *chola*. Who do you think I am to be telling such stories to? Do you think that money simply rains from the sky?"

"But, little mother. I am selling potatoes. I'm not asking you to lend me money. Go somewhere else if you want. Go somewhere else. Why did you ask me for potatoes? If you think you're so rich, buy from the wholesalers. Go ahead and get the potatoes from them."

"But, who do you think you are, vulgar *chola,* to make me beg in this way? I'll make you close down in a minute because of how you have offended me. You have no idea who I am."

"But, Señora, who do you think I am? Send whomever you like. Bring whatever shit you want. Because I'm poor, you think you can insult me. Do you think I should give away my potatoes? I also work. These are not stolen goods I'm offering."

"Now you'll see, you insolent Indian. You're making me very angry. I'll be back soon."

In the original text, as tensions rise between the mestiza buyer and the *chola* vendor, the language itself undergoes subtle but significant shifts. Whereas the vendor began by addressing her client with a Quechua term of endearment, *mam'tay,* by the end of the exchange she has shifted to using formal Spanish, addressing the woman as "Señora." In similar fashion the client, who speaks Spanish throughout, begins resorting to ethnic slurs. She first begins by addressing the vendor informally as *"tu,"* then as "smelly *chola*" and "vulgar *chola*" and, finally, as "insolent Indian." Also underlying the exchange are assumptions that each makes about the other. The client suggests that the vendor is taking advantage of her because the *chola* has access to agricultural products and invests her labor and knowledge in acquiring them. She becomes defensive, decrying the *chola*'s awareness that her client does not work and does not have the information to buy from wholesalers. In frustration, the client threatens to call the authorities, but the *chola* holds her own, daring her to do so.

In another, even more complicated exchange, an upper-class mestiza client, accompanied by her peasant servant, comes to buy meat in the butcher section. Women who sell meat in the market are among the most powerful and well-established vendors. The mestiza begins the exchange:

"Señora, how much is your kilo of meat?"

"Very cheap, little mother. Buy some. The meat is fresh."

"Then why is it so dirty? It's covered with dirt."

"But, little mother, all you have to do is wash it."

"But, Señora, don't you understand that the meat is already contaminated? Why do you [plural form] sell in these conditions? How horrible. The municipal agents should come and control this. How can you sell in this manner?"

"But you, who do you think you are to reject the meat I'm selling in this manner? If you are such a clean lady, then go buy somewhere else. You shouldn't buy in the market."

"But who do you think you are, refined *chola,* that you can tell me where I should buy? I can buy wherever I want."

"And you, who are you? Who do you think you are, stinking lady? You don't remember where you are from, who your grandparents are. Maybe they were worse *cholas* than I. And you, now you come calling us *cholas* without knowing who you are. Now you dress in pretty clothes, elegant clothes, you use makeup. With that, you think you are superior to us."

"But you, such an insolent Indian. You don't even know how to treat your clients. As if you ever set foot in a school. You have neither education nor culture."

"So, maybe you've gone to school or maybe you haven't. Maybe you're refined. Lady of high heels, go away. You're making me furious. Be careful or I'll throw this piece of meat at you."

"Go ahead and throw it, greedy Indian queen bee [a Quechua metaphor to describe those who accumulate money for themselves]. You don't know what I'll do to you."

[The *chola,* speaking loudly so her fellow vendors will hear]: "Lady, perhaps you're a millionaire who made your money as a prostitute. Go to your house. Don't fuck me over here."

[The client turns to her servant.] "What did she say?"

[The servant, smiling, responds.] "I have no idea."

[The client speaks to her servant]: "But you know Quechua. What did this woman say to me? I won't leave things this way. I'll denounce her to the authorities."

"Go ahead, bring your husbands and your lovers. What are they going to do? Go ahead and bring them. If you like, I'll go with you. You're a lady like a pig with lice eggs between her thighs."

"You'll see, foul-mouthed *chola.* Perhaps you don't realize the kind of power I have to do something about this. I'll come back tomorrow."

"Go ahead, stinking lady. I'm not scared of you. Bring whomever you like. How entertaining! Surely you wanted me to give away the meat to you. You say you have money and you still look for the best. If you want the best, you should buy imported meat and not come here to try my patience."

In this encounter, again, linguistic shifts take place. Both the client and vendor shift from formal to informal terms of address. In addition, whereas the client began by addressing the *chola* as "Señora," and the *chola* addressed the client as "little mother," by the end the client is calling the *chola* "Indian," and the *chola* is calling the client "stinking lady" and "prostitute." The *chola* forces her client to recognize that they probably come from similar backgrounds and that, whereas she works, the client does not, except perhaps by prostitution. The *chola* also creates ties with the domestic servant and other meat vendors by hurling her invectives at the client in Quechua that everyone but the client can understand. This serves as an effective rebuttal to the client's accusation that the *chola* is not cultured and does not have an education and highlights the fact that fancy clothes and makeup are not the only skills necessary for buying meat from the *cholas.* Finally, the vendor displays her gendered identity by displaying that she will not be intimidated if the client returns with "all her husbands and lovers."

Jean Comaroff refers to dynamics that take place among the Tschidi of South Africa as they seek to control the process of reproduction and establish and reestablish the coherence of their local social order in its interactions with the global system. Both the local and global orders are "at once systemic and contradictory." Comaroff states:

> It is in practice that the principles governing objective orders of power relations take cultural form, playing upon the capacity of signs—their polysemic quality, for instance, and the meaning they acquire through their positioning in relation to each other in sequences or texts. But this process of construction is never totally witting or unwitting. It involves the reciprocal action of subjects and their objective context; and it may serve both to consolidate existing hegemonies (ruling definitions of the "natural") and to give shape to resistance or reform. (1985:3–6)

In "signifying practice," Comaroff points out that the Tschidi are communicating with signs that are "elements in *systems* of signification [that] might have a meaningful logic of their own and hence can serve as the meeting ground of two distinct orders of determination—one material, the other semantic."

Most market women come from Quechua-speaking indigenous communities. They are well grounded in the principles of reciprocal exchange that continue to form the basis for complex interrelationships and the etiquette of working between and among members of rural communities (Alberti and Mayer 1974). However, as Billie Jean Isbell points out, the *cholo*[a] "might be called the 'bricoleur' of traditional concepts and symbols; [s]he takes the elements at hand and rearranges them for his[her] own purposes" (1978:180). Thus, whereas the indigenous population uses reciprocity for the maintenance of their subsistence level, for ritual and religious balancing acts with natural forces, for forging, perpetuating, and dissolving the ties among kin that make labor relations function, or for defending their autonomy, the *chola,* as market woman, manipulates reciprocity to obtain commodities for market exchange. The quote below, transcribed from a Quechua resident of Pinchimuro, a highland community in southern Peru, reveals the socially calculated efforts of different sectors of the indigenous population to create the conditions for both reciprocal and unequal exchange simultaneously:

The Collas always dance because they want to have money. The Colla is called *compadre* [coparent]. They dance because they want to have animals and be entrepreneurs. That is why they bring cheeses. They bring *cañehua* flour, they bring dried llama meat.

We take alcohol. When they ask us, "Alcohol, compadre?" we pass them the alcohol. I also always took a bottle of alcohol for the dance. I prepared flour with sugar. That was to give away. Before we also used to make roast pork. We made dried meat with salt too. Dividing it into pieces, we would invite the *chunchus* [highland dancers impersonating their feathered ancestors from the jungle] and our companions from the Colla. They made us try a little mold of cheese, saying, "Compadre, take this cheese. Only this am I bringing from my village, from Pantisera, from the village of the Collas.

All this we did because we wanted to be entrepreneurs. (Gow and Condori 1976:91)

The position of market women allows them to articulate two differing social formations, the peasant economy dominated by a capitalist one, which, in turn, remains inextricably a part of a larger global system. Market women are a product of the dominating relationship necessary between the smallholding peasantry and the national economy, composed of rural landed estate owners, agribusiness, the military, and industry, mining, and real estate. Although they control two "actors" in a vertical relationship of power, they do not hold enough power either to become mestizos or to rupture their ties of dependency with the indigenous, rural peasantry. In short, unlike Susan Bourque (1971:22), I refrain from associating the *cholas,* and specifically the market women, with real upward mobility. As Mintz (1971) states, there is a difference between facilitating the operation of an economy and making it grow or change to the market women's advantage. They serve to link the peasant community to the national market (they, themselves, are examples) yet strive to protect the autonomy of the community simultaneously. Their economic goals are at odds with their desire for upward mobility and personal success (Isbell 1978:21).

June Nash (1979) describing the perspective of one *chola,* who sympathized with the plight of miners but wanted her daughter to identify with the *gente de vestido,* dressing like them and establishing *compadrazgo* ties with them, brings home this paradox. In her words this represents "the alienated *chola* view of what the *chola* culture is like. . . . [The *chola*] embraces self-hatred along with strong mobility drives" (80–

81). This paradox is also reflected in market women's desires to establish themselves as a distinct social group while being accepted as full citizens, released from the ethnic prejudice peasants experience. One market woman, for example, explained to me that her mother, also a market woman, dressed in traditional *chola* garb because she wanted to be seen as "a mestiza" and as "a little superior to the peasants." The daughter, in contrast, prefers to purchase and wear Western dress so that she will be seen as "normal" and "not stand out." The general description of the attitude of *cholas* is equally valid for market women. Although the worlds of rural-based peasants and urban-based market women meet frequently, conflicts and tensions mark these meeting points because of differences in values within both worlds. Many peasants and market women experience conflicts between their desire to be treated as national citizens and their longing to establish and maintain ethnic autonomy. In order to become accepted as national citizens, they often emulate the values of urban mestizos. Some successfully achieve upward mobility, but the majority, whose dreams remain unfulfilled, begin to seek other means of establishing their identities.

I would argue that the brokerage of power and of cultural values and practices are more often than not inseparable. To negotiate access to political power or spoils usually involves a negotiation of the cultural meaning of power. Of course, it is possible that in a given situation one role may take precedence over another. However, the successful gaining of control over some resource of importance to the individuals or parties between whom *cholas,* for example, mediate frequently necessitates a simultaneous reevaluation of a constellation of cultural meanings and forms that alter the parties' worldviews. In short, through a close examination of the *cholas'* position and activities, one can gain a better understanding of the complex articulation of two very different and dynamic modes of production.

Adams offers a summary definition and discussion of a broker as "a central figure . . . who is granted, allocated or delegated power by one or more parties" (1975: 50–52). The broker's success, according to Adams, depends upon whether or not the third party consents also to transfer power to the broker so that he or she may then negotiate with the first party. The broker, to continue his or her activities, must finish such a negotiation with advantages to her- or himself and to the satisfaction of the other parties so that they will seek her or him out again. Adams also argues that brokers do not constitute a type of patron-client relationship, giving examples to the contrary. In this respect, he differs with Wolf's early classic definition of brokers as "standing guard over crucial junctures or synapses of relationships which connect a local system to the larger whole" (1965:97), by placing more emphasis on the articulation of relationships within a single, open system.

Adams also formulates an extremely interesting idea, that of the Janus, or brokerage, point in any social system. He defines this as the point below which brokers will favor the interests of those who hold less power than they do. It is clear that some members of the informal sector, such as the *cholas* of Peru, have a greater propensity than others to mobilize politically or to negotiate in ways that favor the lower rather than the upper classes and that this propensity is determined overwhelmingly by their perception of cross-cutting ethnic ties as well as by certain structural conditions, including degree of economic control. Adams's systemization of the shifting position of brokers with respect to the dominant or more powerful classes resembles Quijano's efforts to explain sociologically the shift in Peru among indigenous peoples away from acculturation as the sole option for upward mobility to that of "cholification," which is the actual constitution of an alternative cultural system with economic and political consequences. This alternative has been greatly enhanced due to the expansion of the service sector, the flood of migrants from rural areas who have steadily "Andeanized" urban space, and the diversification of economic opportunities as urbanization has increased. At the same time, successful political mobilization by market women is constrained by their need to perpetuate their role as brokers.

For analytic purposes it is possible to distinguish between different kinds of mediation that involve market women. Economically, they transform products with use value into commodities for exchange and must do so in order to perpetuate their role as economic brokers. As economic brokers who maintain alliances with the peasantry, they must also seek a profit for themselves. Thus, the economic exchange of products creates a degree of competition among market women themselves and between rural-based peasants and market women. At the same time, however, a process of segmentary opposition gradually develops in the practical course of exchange, potentially creating alliances among market women and between market women and peasants, as they confront structural impediments to upward mobility, the failure of the state to provide urban services, and the daily abuses of urban mestizos and authorities that are grounded in racial prejudice. As Michelle Rosaldo states: "It now appears to me that women's place in human social life is not in any direct sense a product of the things she does, but of the meaning her activities acquire through concrete social interaction" (1980:400). Although the structural position of market women has been created by the needs of Peru's weakly developed economy, market women can use their position to accumulate power for themselves. They do so politically in the ways they confront authorities and their participation in collectively based organizations such as unions and neighborhood clubs. They do so culturally in their use of language, rituals, music, and participation in confraternities for particular saint images in the countryside and city (see also Matos Mar 1988). Finally, they do so by the way they engender public space. Their self-conscious choice of clothing marks a particular terrain of ethnicity. They enter the marketplace, an urban public sphere, from the isolation of rural space, where they are consigned to patriarchal subordination. Within the market they exhibit collective behavior as hybrid females and miscegenated Indians whose aggressive character traits are usually associated with men; as miscegenated Indians, they refuse to broker ethnic slurs or insults and wield economic power ideally belonging to mestizos. They appear to mestizos as particularly threatening Indians who are acting in urban ways and contaminating the public sphere with an alternative construction of gendered, class, and ethnic identity. They do not fit the abstract model that mestizos have incorporated of ideal femininity or of Indians.

In summary, the position market women occupy as brokers has been created by the unequal exchange relationships between town and countryside, between the indigenous peasantry and nonindigenous mestizo, and between the informal and formal sectors. The indigenous origins of many market women and their ability to skillfully manipulate values of importance to mestizos and the indigenous peasantry alike also define and perpetuate their position. The contradictions that define their position make it highly unlikely that within existing structural conditions of Peruvian society they or their children can achieve substantial, real, upward mobility. Outside that structure the story is a different one.

Political Action among the Market Women

Market women may acquire a growing sense of class consciousness, leading them to mobilize politically. Class consciousness alone, however, is an insufficient condition for resistance among market women. Rather, it is consistently linked to their sense of shared ethnicity with the indigenous population and to their recognition that the lack of economic and political power among themselves as well as among rural peasants is due to status discrimination based on ethnic distinctions. Abstractly, market women operate between two paradigms. By this I mean that they operate according to "sets of 'rules' from which many kinds and variations of sequences of social action may be generated, but which further specify what sequences must be excluded" (Turner 1974:17). These sets of rules are as much economic as cultural. Although market women may not necessarily confront contradictions in their daily activities as they mediate between rules of conduct (some of which are determined by economic class; others by ethnicity) that make sense to the rural peasantry on the one hand, and to mestizos on the other, they can become aware of these contradictions through their fulfillment of certain economic functions. Frequently they resolve these contradictions over "exclusion rules" through political action or cultural spectacles. At the same time, because market women occupy an intermediate socioeconomic and cultural position, indigenous Quechua-speaking peasants perceive them in contradictory ways, just as mestizos do.

Michael Taussig, using a very different case, makes reference to this same kind of ambivalence by contrasting traditional healing methods with curing done by nontraditional shamans in Colombia. He shows how nontraditional shamans are regarded ambivalently because of "the uneven inscription into the social body of the meaning of being able to buy in a market" (1987:261–62). Here Taussig juxtaposes the "commoditization of magic" (spells in books rather than the long training and initiation process that traditional curers undergo) with the "magic of commoditization." He adds:

What is fascinating and not just complex here is the way that this uneven inscription into the social body of the meaning of buying in a market entails a discussion from various perspectives, the most important of which is the perspective immanent in colonial discourse with the views of whites, on the one side, and Indians' views on the other.... What is important here is not only the way that *magia* is identified by Indians as intrinsic to colonial culture, but also how what is in effect obtained through the purchase of magic books is the magic of the printed word as print has acquired this power in the exercise of colonial domination with its fetishization of print.

Likewise, market women and mestizos signify to the indigenous population the magical mystery and danger of purchasing and selling power; at the same time, both market women and the indigenous population recognize that this very power may permit them to defend themselves against the creators of the spell of commodities and the political clout that accompanies it. Commodities, then, have contradictory powers for both market women and peasants. Comaroff explains that, "for peoples relatively new to wage labor and the commodity economy," the twofold character of commodities that are at once depersonalized and severed from the social relations that produced them and reinvested with an autonomous life "presents itself as a paradox which is often addressed through ritual means" (1985:128–29).

One common ritual occasion that brings together mestizos, *cholos,* and peasants and re-creates the paradox that the power of commodities means to different sectors of societies is Carnaval. In the countryside Carnaval is a feast day intimately associated with fertility rites for live-stock and courtship. In market towns, however, rural concerns with increasing productive fertility through ritual exchanges with indigenous deities and through ritual battles in which blood is shed to feed the earth are replaced by urban concerns to increase fertility and multiply commodities through the exchange of commodities between those who have many and those who have few or none and through the accumulation of prestige and social ties activated by those who sponsor the festivities.

In the market town of Siccuani preparations for Carnaval are made a year in advance. *Cholo* couples are festival sponsors who finance their purchases of beer, brass bands, and costumes for the occasion through support from fellow *cholos* and mestizo godparents who are their clients. On the first day of Carnaval the market bustles with a flurry of buying, selling, trading, and verbal repartee between *cholos,* peasants who have traveled from rural communities, and mestizos. In the afternoon all flock to the Pumacahua Plaza, the *cholas* leaving their market stalls empty and covered with flapping plastic. The audience of mestizos seats itself on the terraced steps of the immense church of Santa Ana, which towers over the plaza. The plaza is hemmed in by trucks on all sides. Peasants from neighboring communities pile into the trucks to watch the festivities. The spectators on the steps of Santa Ana face the *llunsa,* which is a eucalyptus tree that has been chopped down and replanted in the plaza. Fruit, boxes of cookies, masks—many with horns representing the devil, others mocking white-faced mestizos—hang from the tree. The dancers arrive in couples, brightly colored serpentines flowing from their shoulders and confetti sprinkling their hair. They circle the tree, dancing. Throughout the festivities water balloons, flour, mud, small stones, and shaving cream are hurled at the onlookers, including authorities such as the police, inciting great laughter from the spectators. Male dancers wear costumes that combine accoutrements associated with large landholders, rich merchants, and foreign tourists—wool ponchos, dark sunglasses, black top hats, brightly colored scarves, suits, and false mustaches. Female dancers dress in silk and gold brocade skirts, carrying cloths of striped design, typical of the region, and elaborately embroidered silk shawls from the contraband market of Bolivia.

While a brass band plays, the couples dance counterclockwise, then each pair dances toward the tree, and the man, with axe in hand, eventually takes a hard whack at the trunk then returns to the circle and passes the axe to the next couple. After resting and drinking beer, the process resumes until one couple finally fells the tree. Everyone then makes a mad rush toward the tree to gather whatever goods they can. The couple who brought down the tree is now responsible for providing dancers, costumes, beer, the tree, and gifts for the next year's celebration.

On the second day of Carnaval the same event is repeated, this time in the main Sicuani market. On the third day Carnaval is ushered out by a *gacharpari,* or farewell, which takes place in the nearby rural community of Tinta. Here the main dancers are peasants rather than *cholos.*

For Carnaval, then, the *cholos* are the participants and sponsors. They engage in forms of generosity that require cash and an extensive social network. These relationships differentiate those who have had relative success in a cash economy from those who have not. Sponsorship of Carnaval requires individual wealth, accumulation of capital, and access to credit that cannot be supplied through traditional reciprocity alone. It therefore becomes an expression of active participation in the market economy and in the capitalist values that accompany that participation.

Although *cholos* elaborate a traditional symbolic expression of generosity during Carnaval, they resituate it in order, as Isbell remarks, "to construct literally an 'upper class'" (1978:190). An obvious example of this is the attire of the *cholos,* which imitates the dress of those whom they perceive to constitute the "upper class." The attire of the *cholas,* in particular, is also directly associated with the lucrative contraband trade between Peru and Bolivia and the traditional dress of upper-class

Limeñans in the nineteenth century. The contraband trade is one of the few in which market women may accumulate capital. Those who are successful at it may become wealthy. Thus, the *cholos,* in their exaggerated display of wealth, costume, and generosity, consciously use Carnaval to construct a class structure that simultaneously places a socioeconomic distance between themselves and the peasantry and threatens the position of the real upper class.

Once the tree is felled, those who are least successful, with little or no wealth, vie for the commodities that fall "from the heavens." They are mostly peasants who are closest to the ground, crowd around the spectacle, or sit in trucks. The mestizos among the audience, who observe from the steps of the church, do not participate in the scramble for goods or lower their dignity by abusing the authorities. In fact, little interaction takes place between the mestizos, on the one hand, and the *cholos* and peasants, on the other. Nevertheless, the entire event could not have taken place without the activation of patron-client ties between mestizos and *cholos,* which permit the latter to obtain economic goods for the occasion.

The sequential spatial structure of Carnaval must also be taken into account. The first two days of Carnaval occur in the marketplace, which, as Da Matta observes, "during the ritual period, ceases to be dehumanized" and becomes transformed "from the locale of impersonal decisions to the meeting place of the people" (1977:246). Indeed, the political and cultural boundaries and conflicts between *cholos* and peasants, on the one hand, and mestizos, on the other, become explicit during Carnaval's first two days, while the economic boundaries and conflicts are masked. The celebrations in the Pumacahua Plaza and the marketplace differ only in locale. In both places the mestizos are indirect providers of goods for the festivities, while the *cholos* organize the occasion, furnish the music, dance, and liquor, and shower other *cholos* and peasants with gifts.

The third day of Carnaval exemplifies the gradual return to daily life. Peasants from different rural communities play native instruments as they dance in indigenous costume around the Tupac Amaru Plaza. (Tupac Amaru was a colonial Indian resistance leader whose name has been taken up repeatedly by subsequent resistance movements.) *Cholos* attend the festivities, selling food and drink, and the audience is almost wholly composed of mestizos who have organized the event. The farewell lacks the intensity of the first two days, yet it powerfully expresses the socio-economic and interethnic relations as they are actually perceived by the mestizos as an economic and political elite. Whereas the first two days permitted the *cholos* to manipulate their identity, express their solidarity with peasants in opposition to mestizo and authority figures, and to feign more economic power than they really have, the farewell reiterates the exploitative relationships between mestizos, peasants, and *cholos* without inverting their thwarted aspirations or artificially marking boundaries between "insiders" and "outsiders." The peasants dance in native Indian costume, the *cholas* sell their wares, and the mestizos sponsor and supervise the event, thus replicating a "true" view of Andean society from a dominant mestizo perspective.

The role of *cholos* in Carnaval demonstrates their capacity for creating a new symbolic order through "a process of reorganization." This reorganization, or bricolage, "alters existing relations between signs but also integrates them with others bearing forms and forces of external origin. Complexes of signs are thus disengaged from their former contexts and take on transformed meanings in their new associations" (Comaroff 1985:119). At the same time, this new symbolic order by no means constitutes a temporary interlude, or safety valve, that, once activated, permits sociopolitical relations to return to their former equilibrium. As Comaroff points out:

> Ritual is never merely univocal and conservative, papering over the cracks in the cause of hegemonic social forces.... It is always the product of a more or less conflicted social reality; a process within which an attempt is made to impress a dominant message upon a set of paradoxical or discordant representations. Indeed, the power of ritual may come to be used, under certain conditions, to objectify conflict in the everyday world, and to attempt to transcend it. (1985:119)

The efforts of market women to mobilize politically combines practical knowledge and a reliance upon powerful multiplex symbols and metaphors. When market women take political action they often join forces with other *cholas* and *cholos* as well as with peasants. The following quote, taken from the autobiography of Asunta, typifies the kinds of problematic situations market women must confront daily that may eventually provoke their efforts to mobilize politically.

> One day when all was going well with my food business, the employees of the city council arrived in uniform, as police, and began to demand municipal licenses. I didn't know what this business about a municipal license was and continued to sell until one day these same municipal officers demanded our pots and plates. Those who had their documents were able to retrieve their things from the council by paying a fine, but since I, at that time, had no documents, I could not recover my pots or plates and was never able to. I still feel pain because of the loss of my six metal plates. They cost a lot. After that happened, I continued selling food but hid from those municipal dogs. But one day, just after arriving, as I was waiting for some buyers, a policeman appeared at the corner and I didn't even have time to escape with my pot. He said to me, "God damn it. Are you deaf, you Indian whore?"
> *Pun . . . pun.* . . . He kicked over my bucket of food and stomped on my ceramic plates. Seeing all the food on the ground and all the broken plates, and out of sheer anger and hatred for the municipal police, I began screaming and calling for help. (Quoted in Valderrama and Escalante 1977:193–94)

Eutrofia Qorihuaman describes a similar state of affairs: "The municipal agents abuse us, herding us like sheep, throwing our hats on the ground. They don't help us and they usually try to fine us just to keep a little money for themselves. We try to defend ourselves when they abuse us. We don't let the agents take anything away from us. We all help each other. As a political leader, I would like to make sure that all my companions had a good place to work."

Because market women are situated at the node between the larger, national society and the rural countryside, they begin to witness and experience the system of power that controls their very existence. To be successful, they must learn to deal with authority figures who demand that they fix prices and who force them to pay increasingly higher fees and taxes to keep a permanent market stall. They must learn how to deal with or avoid government officials, the men of law and order. They become more analytic in their understanding of their former lives as peasants. In short, they must go beyond *feeling* domination to *comprehending* some of its roots. In this way they begin to develop a sense of class and ethnic consciousness.

Their class consciousness remains embryonic rather than fully developed. Structurally and practically speaking, the degree of economic competition among market women and between market women and peasants prevents them from forming a united front. Furthermore, market women remain ambivalent about whether to seek acceptance among mestizos or to reject mestizo society altogether and constitute their own culture and social mores. Nevertheless, many of them are acutely aware of these contradictions, and they strive to resolve them, often by informal political action on a daily basis. It is both sobering and astounding, for example, to witness the degree of violence and coordinated action when municipal agents make their rounds, attempting to rout all the informal vendors. While not always successful, the market women will, on these occasions, form a united front. Some assist the victim to hide her products, screaming and creating confusion; others run ahead, warning other vendors that the agents are on their way. Still others will physically attempt to prevent the agents from seizing the products, jumping on the truck and trying to retrieve the products. Other more subtle tactics include using inaccurate scales and switching them when they hear that the municipal agents are making their inspection rounds. Union meetings and neighborhood organizations serve as significant forums for alternative strategies to be developed, for common problems to be aired, and for the organization of protest marches and strikes, often in conjunction with workers and peasants.

Since the market has penetrated rural areas along with a diverse and fascinating set of commodities, indigenous rural residents have an interest (which often becomes a need) in acquiring them. In other words, as a matter of course, their level of subsistence now includes such commodities as plastic items, kerosene, sugar, rice, noodles, and alcohol. Market women tend to sell such goods at lower prices to indigenous peasants with whom they have an established relationship, whereas in a show of collective solidarity, they will often raise the price for urban mestizos, frequently inciting a vicious backlash from local authorities. As one peasant client explained to me: "My market woman always lowers the price a little for me, more so than for the others, and I always buy from her. We have something like a friendship." Though fixing prices is disadvantageous to peasants and market women, who are well aware of the vicissitudes of the harvest, it is a policy that serves the interests of the industrial sector, which prefers to keep wages low, a defining characteristic of petty commodity production. Market women, prior to the economic crisis, also frequently offered credit to their rural kin.

Private mestizo merchants bitterly react to the competition from market women and from the informal sector in general. Tensions within the informal sector itself exacerbate the conflicts between informal sector market vendors and formal sector merchants. There are now a dizzying array of levels of control over processing and distribution. Those with permanent stalls in the artisan markets, for which they paid a high fee, resent the equally enterprising but less well endowed and greater numbers of artisan vendors who wander the plaza, selling their wares.[11]

There are many examples of these ongoing and underlying conflicts that erupt into violence periodically. In early summer of 1981 the established merchants of Lima formed an alliance with the government of Fernando Belaúnde to oust all street vendors from the most traveled routes in the city. Despite protests and demonstrations from approximately five thousand street vendors, led by Hugo Blanco, leader of the Leftist Revolutionary Front at the time and elected representative to the national Congress, the government-merchant alliance, with the use of repressive force, successfully confined all street vendors to Polvos Azules, an area of the city removed from the traditional routes of both tourists and resident shoppers in Lima (see Osterling 1981, for a detailed account). This pattern was also seen more recently in 1984 when the police made periodic nightly sweeps of the Plaza de Armas in Cuzco, a place where vendors sell their artisan wares to tourists and young children sell postcards. Those caught were arrested and spent a night in the already crowded jails.

Florence Babb (1985:300) and Carol Andreas (1985:142–46) suggest that the outcry against intermediaries, which has cyclically arisen in Peru, is a rhetorically engineered movement on the part of a government that must justify itself in the face of worsening economic conditions, a skyrocketing external debt, and increasing inflation. I would argue that economic rationalization alone does not explain the cyclical response of the state and dominant classes to street vendors. The confrontations between street vendors, on the one hand, and established merchants, mestizos, and the repressive forces of the state, on the other, represent a continuation of the litigious and contentious tradition in which a system of social stratification based not on relative class position but, rather, on racial and cultural heritage is used instrumentally to diminish competition within the dominant sector or to restrict it to members who are considered to have the same status requirements. Instead of protecting class interests per se, the state becomes more concerned with maintaining the law as the instrument of a dominating ethnic (postcolonial) group and with manipulating a hegemonic ideology to protect dominant positions within the existing status hierarchy (see also Portes 1988, especially his discussion of state policies toward the informal sector and Vargas Llosa's depiction of "well-to-do" attitudes toward the increasing lack of residential distinctions among those of different statuses in urban areas). Rodolfo Stavenhagen describes this dynamic well, stating that "there is no contradiction in considering stratification as a social reality (when it implies certain forms of behavior and determines standards of living), as a hierarchy of values, and as an ideology (in the sense of a moral, political, religious, or philosophical evaluation or interpretation of a social situation)" (1975:239).

Because of their progressive alienation from mestizos and because of their social origins in indigenous, rural communities, where they still maintain extensive ties, *cholas* begin to participate in political activities, sometimes geared toward the mobilization of the peasantry (Cotler 1978:37). In the marketplace they actively cooperate with each other, despite a degree of competition. They pool together their resources for lodging, and they use common strategies to gain access to clients. They engage in subterfuges to escape the police, and they share knowledge of how to avoid conflict with the authorities. This, in part, becomes their impetus for trying to form syndicates, unions, branches of political parties, and mutual help associations (see Bromley and Symanski 1974, citing Buechler and Buechler 1977; and Lessinger 1985:312–14, for similar explanations of political mobilization among vendors in Bolivia and in Madras City, southern India). There are instances when they begin to consolidate as a group, united by similar experiences and their awareness of the untenability of reconciliation between conflicting rules of conduct in their day-to-day activities. They begin to recognize that these "rules of conduct" are parts of larger ideological systems, and one of them is hegemonic. They may mobilize in the marketplace, or they may instigate land litigations, seizures, and uprisings in their home communities, along with other *cholos*. The peasants participate in these uprisings, but *cholos* frequently become political leaders in regional clubs, peasant confederations, or within the political hierarchy of their home communities, particularly because they have many contacts in urban areas and are better able to confront the bureaucracy.

Nash (1979:294) recounts how the better education *cholas* receive in Bolivia combined with the restrictions placed upon their upward mobility fuels their formation as radicalized leaders within the labor movement. Various authors (Quijano 1980; Handelman 1975; Cotler 1978) have confirmed that the impetus for political mobilization among the peasantry comes from those who are both "inside" and "outside" their home communities. Isbell (1978:22) points out that the *cholos* may be at the bottom of the urban class structure, but they dominate the direction of social change in their communities. They have been responsible for improving education and health care and for achieving the extraordinary magnitude of peasant mobilization during the 1960s in Peru and during the 1953 agrarian reform in Bolivia. Today more evidence has accumulated that their children are among the vanguard of activists and sympathizers working behind the scenes within Sendero Luminoso (the Shining Path movement), a guerrilla movement that is both urban- and rural-based (see, for example, Degregori 1990; Gorriti 1990; and Lowenthal 1988). Carol Andreas (1985) and Cecilia Blondet (1991) also report that the aggressive individualism of market women has been tempered by the local organizations that have formed in squatter settlements where many market women live. There they have established innovative mothers' groups and community kitchens, creating new forms of solidarity in response to the failure of the national government to assist them. These organizations have, in turn, encouraged a political consciousness that, in some cases, has led to active sympathy with, or participation in, the Sendero Luminoso movement.[12]

In José María Arguedas's *Deep Rivers* Ernesto, a "mixed-blood" himself, describes an uprising of *cholas,* led by Doña Felipa, owner of a *chicha* (maize beer) bar. Arguedas, always closely attuned to the contradictions of his own society, saw the *cholos* consistently as the potential saviors of indigenous society, though his vision was darkened by his knowledge of the swift violence with which their uprisings were met.[13] In this novel the *cholas* revolt to protest against merchants who are hoarding salt, a government monopoly:

> There were no men in sight. With their bare feet or high-heeled boots the women crushed the delicate park flowers, breaking off rosebushes, geraniums, lilies, and violets. They shouted in Quechua, "Salt, salt! The robbers, the thieving salt dealers!" . . .
> . . . I was excited by the women's violence. I felt like rushing at somebody, like fighting.
> The women occupying the terrace and the wide sidewalk that ran

along the front of the church carried big bags of stones in their left hands.

From the edge of the park we could see the woman who was speaking in the arched entrance to the tower. . . . The women were sweating; earrings made of silver and of gold coins glittered in the sunlight. The woman who occupied the tower archway was a well-known *chicha* bar owner; her stout body completely filled the arch; her blue silk bodice, trimmed with beads and velvet ribbons, shimmered. The ribbon on her hat shone even in the shade; it was satin and stood out in high relief from the extreme whiteness of her hat, which had recently been painted with white lead. . . . She was speaking in Quechua. . . .

"Manan! Kunankamallam suark'aku, . . ." she said. "No! No longer shall they steal our salt! Today we're going to throw all the thieves out of Abancay. Shout, women; shout loudly so that the whole world can hear you! Death to the thieves!"

The women shouted, *"Kunanmi suakuna wañunk'aku!* (Today the thieves shall die!). (1978:91)

The attempts of *cholas* to bring about change through political mobilization have usually been unsuccessful. The uprising of the *cholas* in *Deep Rivers* is put down by the police and army, though some of the *cholas* are able to escape to an indigenous peasant community, further inciting the fury of the forces of law and order. In the case of the July 17, 1980, coup in Bolivia, extensive uprisings of peasants, miners, and *cholas,* who engaged in battles and built blockades to prevent the flow of goods to and from rural areas, weakened the power base of the new military junta. The junta, however, put down the uprising with sophisticated arms. When the *cholas* decide to whom they will swing their political support or to whom they might consider offering a bargain, it is almost always to the peasants and workers. The risk involved in making such a decision is frightening. *Cholas* who decide to take a stand in peasant rebellions are portrayed without optimism. In *Deep Rivers* two schoolboys exchange their opinions about the possible outcome of the *chola* uprising: "'A regiment, against the *cholas?*' asked Valle. 'The *chicheras* are worse than men, even worse than soldiers,' answered Chipro. 'The myth of the race! The *cholas* will die like Indians if they're machine-gunned'" (Arguedas 1978:133). In fact, *cholas* and their offspring have been the target, repeatedly, of repressive violence during the current civil war.

The police forces and army rapidly resort to violence to squelch these uprisings because the state needs to maintain existing class and ethnic relations, whose structure the *cholas* severely threaten because the latter are at once economically necessary but also represent an important challenge to the existing social order, particularly as their numbers increase in urban areas. These movements also fail due to the number and kinds of political parties ostensibly engaged in educating both *cholas* and peasants for their own good. In fact, these parties manipulate their supposed constituents for personal gain and underassess the strength of the forces against which they encourage struggle. In addition, at the same time that mestizos use distinct labels for *cholas* to keep them at a distance, they also overemphasize the significance of *cholas* to the national society, depicting them as enterprising individuals who are the hope of a nascent middle class (see De Soto 1987). This ideology makes it more difficult for *cholas* to recognize that they are subordinated to the needs of an underdeveloped capitalist economy; it undercuts their efforts to genuinely increase their power and autonomy and therefore undermines their potential as a substantial political threat. *Cholas* who buy into the ideology of upward mobility and assimilation may downplay their need to coordinate with peasants and therefore their efforts become doomed to failure. A case in point has been the election of Alberto Fujimori as president of Peru in 1990. Fujimori came to power by campaigning as a representative of the popular classes, tapping into the power and potential threat to the existing order that the members of the informal sector have come to signify to the dominant classes. Market women voted overwhelmingly for him. Once in power he passed a series of severe austerity measures, and none of his policies has favored the popular classes.[14]

Whether or not market women achieve structural changes through mobilizing politically, in all cases they question and challenge the imposed hegemonic ideology that reinforces a stratification system that no longer corresponds to its economic bases. Until the 1980s *cholas* often reoriented their focus to seizing control over the means of production.[15] In many instances this meant regaining access to agricultural lands. Land thus became one of the primary symbols for those who rebel. One may question why this is the case for market women. The latter recognize land's importance to the peasantry in every sphere of their lives, and, likewise, land and labor stand out as key factors in the domination of the peasantry throughout the entire history of conquest and colonization.

Finally, more land signifies wealth and relative autonomy, not only to peasants but also to the market women. A number of other material objects that represent colonial cultural, economic, and political power also serve as symbols of rebellion (see, for example, the use of the bull in Arguedas's *Yawar Fiesta* [1985] or a discussion of the curious political meanings and symbolism of chickens [Seligmann 1987]). Since the 1980s, because of the overwhelming flood of migrants to the cities, due to worsening economic conditions and the civil war, the focus on regaining access to rural land is no longer common. Rather, it has shifted to acquiring urban lands, services, and rights for peasant migrants and established *cholas*.

The political actions of *cholas* and peasants do not always end tragically. In *Deep Rivers* the *cholas* make their point by distributing salt to all the peasants of the indigenous community of Patibamba. The priest intervenes, admonishing them not to "offend God." The leader, Doña Felipa responds simply with a question: "And who sold the salt to the haciendas for their cows? Do cows come before people?" (Arguedas 1978:92). Though the uprising of the *cholas* is put down and Doña Felipa's orange shawl is found hanging from a stone cross at the entrance to Patibamba, her body is never discovered. Although this is a fictional account, the same resurgence of struggle, despite actual repression, appears again and again, in the marketplace itself, in demonstrations and strikes, in the illegal establishment of squatter settlements, and finally, most recently, in the form of extreme violence perpetrated by Sendero Luminoso against the state, its "neocolonial" bureaucratic apparatus, and "representatives of imperialism."

The capacity of the *cholas* to speak and understand the language and behavior of the peasants, withdraw the services they provide to the mestizos, and ally themselves with the indigenous peasantry increases their prospects for successful political resistance to the existing economic and social order. These abilities moderate the tendency for power to flow to the top of the pyramid and become centralized, as Adams (1975) suggests. They also offset the probability that brokers will ally themselves with those social groups or actors who exert more power (or whom they see as exerting more power) over them (Adams 1975).

The civil war raging openly in Peru since 1980 is one that will probably continue for some time to come and involves the *cholas* directly. Between 1980 and 1991 human rights organizations who are monitoring the situation have reported thirty thousand deaths (most of them peasants or supposed subversive members of Sendero). Though Sendero began its activities in rural areas, it is now operating in urban regions, forcing the president to enforce a state of curfew for long periods of time in Lima itself and placing much of the country under emergency law. Many of the known leaders of the movement were educated in provincial universities in the central highland regions, and both leaders and participants are the sons and daughters of either wealthier peasants or urban-based *cholas* who were unable to fulfill the dreams and aspirations of their parents. By no means do they remain anonymous individuals in an urban setting, unprotected by their kin and without ties to their home communities. Instead, they have sought a different course from that taken by *cholas* in the past. (See Degregori 1990 for a detailed account of the participation of *cholas* and their offspring in Sendero Luminoso.) They are committed to long-term and clandestine guerrilla warfare outside the usual legitimate avenues taken to acquire political power, and they are well aware of the need to link urban and rural sectors and concerns in their ideological and military tactics and strategies. (See Walton 1984 for a discussion of revolution and its dependence upon both rural- and urban-based groups and their actions.) In fact, their military tactics of easily moving between, and adapting to, both rural and urban environments play on the very fears that their social position and economic activities have always inspired in mestizos.

Conclusion

The clash of two competing ways of living, that of the peasants, who live close to the land and to a cosmogony from which they obtain and to which they attribute all their energy (mountains, rivers, rocks, earth, stars, sun, and moon) and that of the mestizos, who live the power myth of capitalism and the commodity fetish—obtaining from, and attributing all their energy to, commodities—come together in the *chola* as market woman without resulting in a fundamental restructuring of power relations in socioeconomic and political terms.

Within Peruvian society the *cholas* are members of an imposed social category whose historical antecedents lie in the establishment of the Spanish colonial caste system; they also belong to a constructed social category that all Peruvians consciously manipulate. The definition of the social category *chola* can only be arrived at contextually and situationally with respect to other socially created categories such as *indio* and mestizo. The category itself is defined by ambivalence—for example, one is neither exactly a mestizo nor altogether an *indio,* and the category does not preclude the foregrounding of class consciousness or ethnicity.

With respect to their sense of class consciousness and their actual class relations, *cholas* as market women perform certain activities, some of which they can embellish and many of which are created by the economic and political structure that characterizes Andean society. Market women find themselves in an opportune position to obtain a sense of class consciousness, which may lead them to mobilize politically and to ally themselves with peasants. Their position and power are both created and limited by the penetration of capitalism and capitalist values into the peasant mode of production. The inherent contradictions of a market economy encourage the entrance of petty entrepreneurs from rural areas into the market to facilitate the circulation of commodities otherwise difficult to obtain. At the same time that the market women are necessary to the mestizo economy, providing ties with rural agricultural producers, they also constitute a threat to the mestizos, who perceive them perjoratively as *india* and who experience them as competition to their own commercial ventures. Although the aspirations of the *cholas* for upward mobility are clearly evident, the economy prohibits real fulfillment of their expectations, except in rare instances. Their economic success requires that they maintain links to different small rural communities; this also means that these preexisting linkages can be fairly easily subverted for purposes of political resistance. Likewise, the social and economic networks among *cholas* in urban areas permits them not only to coordinate with each other but also to coordinate the activities of the different small communities with which they are individually linked.

Although the meaning of the term *chola* has changed over time, becoming necessarily a multivalent category, it will only cease to exist when the entire structure of Andean society within a world system changes qualitatively and comprehensively. Given the historically engendered ideological and economic conditions and the nature of interethnic relations that have given rise to these brokers of values and resources, it is conceivable that they and their offspring will be in the vanguard of attempting to refashion Peru's social and economic fabric. Meanwhile, we must at least reassess the ideologies of modernization, development, and homogenization that have led to the perception of *cholas* as transitional beings who will eventually disappear in the process of assimilation. The reality of a global economy that is neither fully proletarianized nor agriculturally self-sufficient has created a position for the *cholas* as a politically radical and distinct economic and cultural group as well as a socioeconomic and cultural category that Peruvians continue to manipulate for their own purposes.

Epilogue

I returned to Peru in 1991 to find that, not surprisingly, the generalized severity of the economic crisis and unabated civil war have dramatically affected relations among market women, peasants, and mestizos. The war has caused increasing numbers of peasants to flock from the countryside to the cities. Many of them have no alternative but to sell whatever products they can obtain. Conflicts and competition between established and itinerant vendors have become extreme, hindering the capacity for collective action on a daily basis. President Fujimori's austerity measures, the precipitous decline of people's earning capacities, and the erosion of the value of currency due to inflation have seriously jeopardized the vendors' abilities to survive. Kin ties, which had facilitated mutual support and information sharing among market women, have become debilitated. In contrast, urban mestizo clients, also affected by the economic crisis, have begun relying upon mutual support networks. Frequently, one member of an extended family will pool funds from their kin, purchase products in bulk from wholesalers, then distribute them to the family, thereby avoiding the extra cost of purchasing from intermediaries. Furthermore, since market women's major occupation has become survival, they work longer hours, and many of them who previously traveled periodically to the countryside no longer do so, claiming that they do not have the time or money.

Counterbalancing the proliferation of petty conflicts among vendors is a clear recognition on their part that the government is responsible for their misfortunes. The contrast between Fujimori's promises to improve the lot of members of the informal sector and his actual policies has led market women to abandon their faith in all institutionalized politics or electoral channels. In their words: "All of us voted for 'El Chino.' With Vargas Llosa it would have been worse. They're all the same though. None of them fulfills his promises. What's the point of voting in the future? What will change?" In the words of another vendor: "This government is killing us with hunger in order to pay the foreign debt. Because of the lack of money, there is no work. Public employees are badly paid and this affects us. With their miserable salaries, they can no longer buy anything. They can only meet their most basic needs. The government has taken advantage of us. We thought it would favor the poor but it hasn't turned out that way. I voted for that dog but now I regret it."

It remains to be seen how many of the market women will turn their support, however reluctantly, to the guerrilla movement, simply due to the lack of alternative means of improving their welfare. The majority of established vendors and even many itinerant ones are members of unions that belong to the Cuzco Departmental Federation of Workers. Nevertheless, unions have never been weaker, due to fear of governmental reprisals and to violent attacks from the Shining Path, which will not tolerate "revisionist" organizations or activities. Numerous interviews with market women revealed that they placed the blame for current conditions squarely upon the shoulders of the government.

Clearly, the market women's capacity for active, organized resistance to the state and dominant classes is far less viable than ever before. They continue to perform crucial economic functions, but the impact of national economic policies has burdened them more than ever before with the need simply to survive day by day. Walking the streets of Cuzco and Lima, the isolation of the middle and upper middle classes is palpable. Almost all available urban space has been surrendered to vendors, hawking their wares. The outlines of the crucible linking the market women to the countryside and city has dissolved into more pervasive but dispersed linkages among members of the popular classes in which the formation of an alternative constitution of cultural identity and political force continues to take place but now may take the form of increasing alienation and direct violent attacks upon a disintegrating state.

NOTES

I am grateful to Daniel Levine, the members of his graduate seminar at the University of Michigan–Ann Arbor, and my two research assistants, Edgar Galdos and Teófila Huaman, both of whom were children of market women. Their detailed comments, suggestions, and criticism clarified my own ideas and made this a far better article. Part of the research for this project was made possible by the Wenner-Gren Foundation for Anthropological Research and the Nave Bequest of the University of Wisconsin–Madison. This article is dedicated and indebted to the *cholas* of good humor and fighting spirit whom I encountered in my many trips to market and interminable and uncomfortable truck rides.

1. The term *cholo* refers to the general linguistic category of both males and females; however, the social, economic, and cultural characteristics of females (*cholas*) and males (*cholos*) differ markedly.

2. These unions were more common in the highlands than along the coast or in the Spanish colonial capital of Lima. There were several reasons for this. Mixed marriages were more frowned upon in Lima than in the highlands. More women of Spanish descent were available along the coast, and the center of Spanish administrative and legal authority was located there. Although Hispanic women were scarce in the highlands, the majority of females who belonged to the Inca nobility and were considered suitable and useful for mixed marriages were found in the highland Inca capital of Cuzco.

3. Widows, in particular, migrated to seek jobs in urban areas in order to avoid the harsh tribute and labor demands levied upon them in their rural communities (Burkett 1975:209; Bourque and Warren 1981: 146–49). The number of widows who are market women today remains very high.

4. This practice became institutionalized in the form of the *serviñakuy,* often considered to be a peculiarly indigenous form of trial marriage. However, Varallanos (1962:63) argues persuasively that *serviñakuy* originated in the practice of *encomenderos* who took in female servants and used them as permanent or temporary concubines without marrying them.

5. A negative view of mixed marriages was not confined to *mestizos*. It extended to such indigenous persons as the remarkable native chronicler, Felipe Guaman Poma de Ayala (1980 [1583–1615]: 421, 498, 504–5, 578, 707), who, in the sixteenth century, wrote bitterly of these mixed marriages, bemoaning the disappearance of pure Indians. Interestingly, when he speaks of the danger of intermarriage, he almost always refers to those between Hispanic males and indigenous females. Rather than invent new categories or castes, he insists that it would be in everbody's interests if the offspring belonged to the lower ranking caste of the couple in question. An example of his view of "cholification" follows:

> Que el *cholo* y sanbahigo pague el pecho y tributo y a de acudir a todos los servicios personales en este rreyno. Porque del todo es yndio fino, que no se a de entender de la casta de prencipal de título, que el *cholo* ya no tiene cosa de español. Y en esto tiene la culpa y pecado su padre, maldición de Dios, hijo en el mundo de mala fama, *mestizo, y cholo,* mulato, zanbahigo.

> Para ser bueno criatura de Dios, hijo de Adán y de su muger Eva, criado de Dios, español puro, yndio puro, negro puro.

> Estos y sus desendientes *mestizos* y mulatos o mestizas, mulatas, *chola,* zanbahiga, uno ne nenguno no queden en los pueblos de los yndios, que an de estar en las ciudades y uilas, aldeas deste meyno. Y las justicias que consentieren, sean castigados y penados para la cámara de su Magestad en este rreyno. (Guaman Poma de Ayala 1982: 498)

6. Carrying this a step further, indigenous women became the focal point

of social and economic mediation in the colonial period. Burkett (1975:181–82) elaborates upon the economic functions of market women during that time: "Their economic activities led them to create perhaps the most inclusive social networks of any group of colonial society; from the wealthy men who supplied them with products or arranged their licenses, to their host of customers of all races and both sexes. They tended to live on the dividing line between the best Spanish neighborhoods and the mixed Indian and black districts of town, thus maintaining connections and proximity to both groups."

7. Informal surveys and observations show that the term *chola* is rarely used as a form of self-identification except in joking exchanges, where it is a form of endearment (combined with condescension), or in exchange of insults. In the Cuzco region, market women who dress distinctively identify themselves not as "cholas" but as "mestizas." In interviews, market women diverge in their perception of themselves as "campesinas" or "mestizas" depending upon factors such as place of origin, generations that have lived in the city, education, literacy, or economic status. Their determination of self-labeling, often assessed through daily interactions, always incorporates a comparison to others of distinct social and ethnic status. In fact, no single encompassing term of self-identification for this diverse and intermediate social category exists, as far as I know.

8. In a survey of literature on *cholas*, Burkett (1975:234) consistently found that a "chola" was described in the literature as "strong, willful woman, either Indian or mestiza, aggressive economically and socially. She stands in sharp contrast to her "cholo" brother, who is seen as drunk, bumbling, meek, and not very bright." Few convincing analyses of this curious contrast have been offered. The most frequent explanation is that the *chola* is a product of forces of modernization. Burkett, however, found in her review of archival documentation that the same picture of the *chola* had already been drawn in the early colonial period.

9. Burkett (1975:235–45) documents that the Spanish conquest amplified the role opportunities available to indigenous women in colonial society. Unlike indigenous men, the relationships of indigenous women to Spanish households were more intimate; they rapidly familiarized themselves with Spanish mores; many of them learned Spanish; and, though it was primarily religious in nature, they were granted an education, a privilege only available to indigenous males who were political leaders or connected to the church. Nash (1979:313) points out that the early deaths of male heads of households who worked in the Bolivian mines also encouraged women to enter assertively into market vending activities to support themselves and their children.

10. The linkages between urban market women and rural communities vary. Second- and third-generation market women often have few ties to rural areas. If market women are successful in their activities, they may prefer to buy directly from wholesalers rather than make the arduous journey to the countryside to acquire products.

11. These different levels of marketing had already begun to crystallize in the colonial period when nonelite Hispanic women were able to go into business and establish permanent stores. They resented the competition from indigenous and

306 / Constructing Culture and Power in Latin America

"mixed-blooded" itinerant hawkers who did not have to invest as much in licensing, etc. (Burkett 1975:222).

12. Despite Andreas's assertions, it is still unclear how many market women, and at what economic level, are welcomed into the ranks of Sendero, since one of the movement's principles is a movement away from the market economy back to one of subsistence.

13. Arguedas spent his entire life trying to write in a way that would convey to a literate audience the reality of being Quechua within the Peruvian nation-state. His novels and short stories, though they are eloquent but difficult reading for one unfamiliar with Andean society, are a supreme example of the challenge and potential of "intermarriage." As he himself explains (1985:xi), his novel *Yawar Fiesta,* represents:

> The search for a style in which the ancient Quechua language could pass over into Spanish and become an instrument of expression free enough to be able to reflect the heroic deeds, the thoughts, the loves, and the hatreds of the Andean people of Hispano-Indian descent-heirs of the Spanish conquerers, who for centuries have been influenced to the core by the Andean universe that is alive and pulsing in the native language.

14. Although it does not appear to be the case in Peru, Heath (1969:205–6) reports that peasant resistance in Bolivia has been hindered by alliances that middlemen form with mestizos against peasants, reiterating traditional hacienda patron-client relationships.

15. Stavenhagen (1975:33) discusses stratification systems in which the secondary factors of race, ethnicity, cultural traits, religion, etc., "at times become legally codified and in any case psychologically internalized, as reflections of certain social relations of production as expressed in class relations. . . . At the same time these factors perform the sociological function of "liberating" the stratification from its ties to the economic base. . . . As a result, stratifications may also be considered as justifications or rationalizations of the established economic system, that is, as ideologies."

REFERENCES

Adams, Richard N. 1975. *Energy and Structure.* Austin: University of Texas Press.

Alberti, Giorgio, and Enrique Mayer, eds. 1974. *Reciprocidad e intercambio en los Andes Peruanos.* Lima: Instituto de Estudios Peruanos.

Andreas, Carol. 1985. *When The Women Rebel: The Rise of Popular Feminism in Peru.* Westport, Conn.: Lawrence Hill.

Appleby, Gordon. 1976. "The Role of Urban Food Needs in Regional Development, Puno, Peru." In *Regional Analysis. Vol. 1: Economic Systems,* ed. Carol Smith, 147–78. New York: Academic Press.

Arguedas, José María. 1978. *Deep Rivers.* Trans. Francis Barraclough. Austin: University of Texas Press.

————. 1985. *Yawar Fiesta*. Trans. Francis Barraclough. Austin: University of Texas Press.

Babb, Florence. 1985. "Middlemen and 'Marginal' Women: Marketing and Dependency in Peru's Informal Sector." In *Markets and Marketing, Monographs in Economic Anthropology,* ed. Stuart Plattner, 4: 287–308. Lanham, Md.: University Press of America.

————. 1989. *Between Field and Cooking Pot: The Political Economy of Marketwomen in Peru.* Austin: University of Texas Press.

Belote, Linda S. 1978. "Prejudice and Pride: Indian-White Relations in Saraguro, Ecuador." Ph.D. diss., University of Illinois.

Benería, Lourdes, and Martha Roldán. 1987. *The Crossroads of Class and Gender: Industrial Homework, Subcontracting and Household Dynamics in Mexico City.* Chicago: University of Chicago Press.

Blondet, Cecilia. 1991. *Las Mujeres y el poder: Una Historia de villa el Salvador.* Lima: IEP.

Bourque, Susan. 1971. "Cholification and the Campesino: A Study of Three Peasant Organizations in the Process of Societal Change." Ph.D. diss., Cornell University.

Bourque, Susan, and Kay Warren. 1981. *Women of the Andes: Patriarchy and Social Change in Two Peruvian Towns.* Ann Arbor: University of Michigan Press.

Bourricaud, François. 1970. *Power and Society in Contemporary Peru.* Trans. Paul Stevenson. New York: Praeger.

Bromley, Ray, and Chris Gerry. 1979. "Who Are the Casual Poor?" In *Casual Work and Poverty in Third World Cities,* ed. Ray Bromley and Chris Gerry, 3–23. Chichester: John Wiley and Sons.

Bromley, Ray, and Richard Symanski. 1974. "Marketplace Trade in Latin America." *Latin American Research Review* 9, no. 3: 3–38.

Buechler, Judith-Maria. 1978. "The Dynamics of the Market in La Paz, Bolivia." *Urban Anthropology* 7, no. 4: 343–59.

Buechler, Hans, and Judith-Maria Buechler. 1977. "Conduct and Code: An Analysis of Market Syndicates and Social Revolution in La Paz, Bolivia." In *Ideology and Social Change in Latin America,* ed. June Nash, Juan Corradi, and Hobart Spalding, 174–84. New York: Gordon and Breach Science Publishers.

Bunster, Ximena, and Elsa M. Chaney. 1985. *Sellers and Servants: Working Women in Lima, Peru.* New York: Praeger.

Burkett, Elinor. 1975. "The Urban Female Experience." Ph.D. diss., University of Pittsburgh. Ann Arbor: University Microfilms.

Cangas, Gregorio de. 1762–66. *Compendio histórico, geográfico, genealógico y político del Perú.* MS.

Christian, Shirley. *Chicago Tribune,* December 29, 1980.

Comaroff, Jean. 1985. *Body of Power, Spirit of Resistance: The Culture and History of a South African People.* Chicago and London: University of Chicago Press.

Cotler, Julio. 1978. *Clase, estado y nación.* Peru problema 17. Lima: Instituto de Estudios Peruanos.

Da Matta, Roberto. 1977. "Constraints and License: A Preliminary Study of Two Brazilian National Rituals." In *Secular Ritual,* ed. Sally F. Moore and Barbara Meyerhoff, 244–64. Amsterdam: Van Gorcum.

Davies, Rob. 1979. "Informal Sector or Subordinate Mode of Production? A Model." In *Casual Work and Poverty in Third World Cities,* ed. Ray Bromley and Chris Gerry, 87–104. Chichester: John Wiley and Sons.

Degregori, Carlos Iván. 1990. *El Surgimiento de Sendero Luminoso.* Lima: IEP.

De Soto, Hernando. 1987. *El Otro Sendero.* Buenos Aires: Sudamericana.

Escobar, Gabriel. 1964. *Sicaya: Cambios culturales en una comunidad mestiza de la sierra central del Perú.* Lima: n.p.

Fried, Jacob. 1961. "The Indian and Mestizaje in Peru." *Human Organization* 20, no. 1: 23–26.

Fuenzalida, Fernando. 1971. "Poder, etnia y estratificación en el Perú." In *Perú hoy,* ed. José Matos Mar. Mexico: Siglo veintiuno.

Gorriti, Gustavo. 1990. *Sendero: Historia de la Guerra Milenaria en el Perú.* Lima: APOYO S.A.

Gow, Rosalind, and Bernabé Condori. 1976. *Kay Pacha.* Cuzco, Peru: Centro de Estudios Rurales Andinos Bartolomé de Las Casas.

Guaman Poma de Ayala, Felipe. 1980 [1583–1615]. *El Primer nueva cronica y buen gobierno.* Ed. John V. Murra, Rolena Adorno, and Jorge Urioste. Mexico: Siglo veintiuno.

Handelman, Howard. 1975. *Struggle in the Andes: Peasant Political Mobilization in Peru.* Austin: University of Texas Press.

Heath, Dwight B. 1969. "Bolivia: Peasant Syndicates among the Aymara of the Yungas: A View from the Grass Roots." In *Latin American Peasant Movements,* ed. Henry Landsberger, 170–209. Ithaca: Cornell University Press.

Isbell, Billie Jean. 1978. *To Defend Ourselves: Ecology and Ritual in an Andean Village.* Austin: University of Texas Press.

Kubler, George. 1952. *The Indian Caste of Peru, 1795–1940: A Population Study Based upon Tax Records and Census Reports.* Washington, D.C.: Smithsonian Institution, Institute of Social Anthropology.

Lessinger, Johanna. 1985. "Nobody Here to Yell at Me: Political Activism among Petty Retail Traders in an Indian City." In *Markets and Marketing,* ed. Stuart Plattner, 309–31. Lanham, Md.: University Press of America.

Lowenthal, Abraham. *Los Angeles Times,* October 23, 1988.

MacEwen Scott, Allison. 1979. "Who Are the Self-Employed?" In *Casual Work and Poverty in Third World Cities,* ed. Ray Bromley and Chris Gerry, 105–29. Chichester: John Wiley and Sons.

Matos Mar, José. 1988. *Desborde popular y crisis del estado: El nuevo rostro del Peru en la decada de 1980.* Lima: CONCYTEC.

Mintz, Sidney. 1964. "The Employment of Capital by Market Women in Haiti." In *Capital, Saving and Credit in Peasant Societies,* ed. Raymond Firth and B. S. Yamey, 256–86. London: George Allen and Unwin.

———. 1971. "Men, Women and Trade." *Comparative Studies in Society and History* 13:247–69.

Mott, Luis, Robert H. Silin, and Sidney W. Mintz. 1975. *A Supplementary*

Bibliography on Marketing and Marketplaces. Council of Planning Librarians, Exchange Bibliography, 792, May.

Nash, June. 1979. *We Eat the Mines and the Mines Eat Us: Dependency and Exploitation in Bolivian Tin Mines.* New York: Columbia University Press.

Osterling, Jorge P. 1981. "La Estructura socioeconómica del comercio ambulatorio: Algunos hipótesis de trabajo." *Revista Económica* 4, no. 8:65–102.

Pitt-Rivers, Julian. 1965. "Who Are the Indians?" *Encounter, Rediscovering Latin America* 25, no. 3:41–49.

Portes, Alejandro. 1981. "Unequal Exchange and the Urban Informal Sector." In *Labor, Class and the International System,* ed. Alejandro Portes and John Walton, 67–106. New York: Academic Press.

———. 1983. "The Informal Sector: Definition, Controversy, and Relation to National Development." *Review* 7:151–74.

———. 1988. "Latin American Urbanization in the Years of the Crisis." *Latin American Research Review* 24, no. 3:7–44.

Programa Regional de Empleo para América Latina y el Caribe (PREALC). 1982. *Mercado de Trabajo en Cifras, 1950–1980.* Oficina Internacional del Trabajo.

Quijano, Anibal. 1980. *Dominación y Cultura: Lo cholo y el conflicto en el Perú.* Lima: Mosca Azul Editores.

Rosaldo, Michelle. 1980. "The Uses and Abuses of Anthropology: Reflections on Feminism and Cross-Cultural Understanding." *Signs* 5:389–417.

Seligmann, Linda J. 1987. "The Chicken in Andean History and Myth: The Quechua Concept of *Wallpa.*" *Ethnohistory* 34, no. 2:139–70.

Silverblatt, Irene. 1987. *Moon, Sun, and Witches: Gender Ideologies and Class in Inca Colonial Peru.* Princeton, N.J.: Princeton University Press.

Stavenhagen, Rodolfo. 1975. *Social Classes in Agrarian Society.* Trans. Judy Hellman. Garden City, N.Y.: Anchor Press/Doubleday.

Stein, Steve, and Carlos Monge. 1988. *La Crisis del estado patrimonial en el Perú.* Lima: IEP and the University of Miami.

Taussig, Michael. 1987. *Shamanism, Colonialism, and the Wild Man: A Study in Terror and Healing.* Chicago: University of Chicago Press.

Turner, Victor. 1974. *Dramas, Fields, and Metaphors: Symbolic Action in Human Society.* Ithaca: Cornell University Press.

Valderrama, Ricardo, and Carmen Escalante. 1977. *Gregorio Condori Mamani, autobiografía,* 92–116. Biblioteca de la tradición oral andina 2. Cuzco, Peru: Centro de Estudios Rurales Andinos Bartolomé de Las Casas.

Van den Berghe, Pierre. 1974. "The Use of Ethnic Terms in the Peruvian Social Science Literature." *International Journal of Comparative Sociology* 15, nos. 3–4:132–42.

Varallanos, José. 1960. *Historia de Huánuco: Desde la era prehistórica a nuestros días: Introducción al estudio de la vida social de una región del Perú.* Buenos Aires: Imprenta López.

———. 1962. *El Cholo y el Perú: Introducción al estudio sociológico de un hombre y un pueblo mestizo y su destino cultural.* Buenos Aires: Imprenta López.

Walton, John. 1984. *Reluctant Rebels: Comparative Studies of Revolution and Underdevelopment.* New York: Columbia University Press.

Wolf, Eric. 1965. "Aspects of Group Relations in a Complex Society." In *Contemporary Cultures and Societies of Latin America,* ed. Dwight B. Heath and Richard N. Adams, 85–102. New York: Random House.

Regarding the Philanthropic Ogre: Cultural Policy in Brazil, 1930–45/1964–90

Randal Johnson

> The Ministry of Culture should be replaced by a Ministry of Supplies that would simply give ink and paper to writers, canvas and paint to artists, film to cinéastes, and instruments to musicians.
>
> —Eugene Ionesco

This essay will discuss contradictions and paradoxes that permeate attempts by the Brazilian state to preserve, support, stimulate, shape, and control diverse aspects of the nation's cultural production in two key periods of its recent history, 1930–45 and 1964–90. During the first, from the Revolution of 1930 until the fall of the Estado Novo, Getúlio Vargas established the legal precedents and the fundamental institutional framework of Brazilian cultural policy. During that same period, and more specifically between 1935 and 1938, the city of São Paulo provided a fruitful alternative model for state/culture relationships through the activities of the municipal Departmento de Cultura.

During the second period, from the military overthrow of João Goulart until the 1990 inauguration of Fernando Collor de Mello as Brazil's first democratically elected president in almost thirty years, the government's cultural policy and its institutional framework expanded through the creation of new agencies and an extension of policy objectives. Added to what might be called a "patrimonial" orientation, concerned primarily with the preservation of the nation's cultural and historical patrimony, which had long formed the backbone of Brazilian cultural policy, was an "executive" orientation designed to support different forms of cultural production, especially in sectors with a small market potential.[1]

These two time frames merit primary focus because they represent the two periods in Brazilian history when state intervention in the cultural arena has been most intense and when the state's major institutions of cultural activity were established. In contrast, the democratic "interregnum" of 1945–64 was a period of consolidation and continuity rather than policy development and institutional construction. Some reorganization of the Ministry of Education and Culture's cultural component did occur during this period, but with the exception of the Conselho Nacional de Pesquisas (CNPq), established in 1951, which funds much scientific and academic research in the country, no truly significant new initiatives occurred until after the coup d'état of 1964.[2]

Chronologically, the situation in Brazil parallels that of much of the rest of Latin America, where cultural policies began to take shape in the 1930s with the organization of agencies to protect national cultural and historical patrimonies, among them the Instituto Nacional de Antropología e Historia (Mexico, 1938), the Consejo Nacional de Preservación y Restauración de Monumentos Históricos (Peru, 1939), and the Comisión Nacional de Museos, Monumentos y Sitios Históricos (Argentina, 1940). As in Brazil, such policies expanded considerably in later years with the creation of additional forms of support for the arts and different modes of cultural production.[3]

After summarizing some of the underlying theoretical issues, the study will examine the process of institutional construction in the cultural field during the Vargas period, focusing first on the federal level then on the very different experience of São Paulo's municipal Department of Culture. In the first case the study will show how the co-optation of artists and intellectuals constituted an important part of Vargas's cultural policy. In the second, it will discuss the paradoxes of state cultural activity at the municipal level, contrasting its more open, democratic notion of culture with the authoritarian paternalism implicit in many of its actions.

Turning to the post–1964 period, the essay will delineate the military government's cultural offensive and describe changes in cultural policy under different regimes, changes that involve distinct notions of culture and different views of the cultural role of the state as well as the composition and political connections of individual ministers of education and culture. The essay will close with a case study of state policy toward the film industry, which is perhaps the sector that has benefited most and, subsequently, suffered most from state intervention.

Cultural Policy: Introduction and Theoretical Issues

One of the first actions Fernando Collor de Mello took after his March 15, 1990, inauguration was to reverse a governmental cultural policy that had been evolving irregularly in the country since the 1930s. He reduced the Ministry of Culture, which had been created five years earlier by José Sarney, to a secretariat in a reorganized Ministry of Education and Culture; he eliminated, radically altered, or suspended virtually every state agency that dealt in some way with Brazilian culture; and he abolished fiscal benefits for private sector investments in the arts under what had become known as the Lei Sarney. In consonance with the antistatist agenda announced throughout his campaign, he did all of this in the name of a free market economy, the withdrawal of the state from nonessential sectors, the shrinking of a bloated bureaucracy, and, concomitantly, the reduction of the government's budget deficit. Underlying Collor's action—and its apparent lack of criteria, which, more than anything else, provoked strong opposition from virtually all cultural sectors as well as from economists such as former minister of planning João Sayad and former minister of finance Luiz Carlos Bresser Pereira— is the implicit notion that the state has no legitimate role in the cultural field beyond the preservation of the nation's historical patrimony.

In fact, government support of various modes of cultural production has existed for centuries and continues to exist throughout the world, including advanced industrial democracies. Rationales for such support are generally cast in terms of the notion that culture is an integral part of development and that, as the ultimate guarantor of a nation's cultural unity and identity, the state has a responsibility to protect society's cultural memory and heritage, to defend its cultural values, to stimulate cultural production, and to ensure that culture is not defined exclusively by market criteria.

Cultural policies represent one of the least studied aspects of the state/society relationship, despite increased recognition of their importance. The United Nations Educational, Scientific, and Cultural Organization (UNESCO) defines cultural policies as "a body of operational principles, administrative and budgetary practices and procedures which provide a basis for cultural action by the State" (Herrera 1981:73–74). In the broadest sense, they may be formal or informal, explicitly codified in legislation or implicitly manifest through diverse governmental practices, and may include the state's activity in relation to virtually any aspect of culture, ranging from support for different modes of elite and popular artistic production to the preservation of historical monuments and documents, the operation of museums and libraries, and the subvention of folk festivals, carnivals, and sports activities.

314 / Constructing Culture and Power in Latin America

Cultural policies in different countries by necessity vary according to the set of cultural and social values at stake. Policies involving archaeology naturally have a greater weight in Mexico, Peru, and many Arab states than they do in Brazil. Language policy also takes on greater importance in some national contexts. In pre-independence Algeria, for example, two separate, though often related, cultural and intellectual traditions developed over time, one deriving from the nation's Arabic roots, the other of a more distinctly French orientation, a distinction related directly to colonialism. After the revolution this situation obviously created certain problems when it came to structuring a cultural policy or even staffing a bureaucratic institution in the cultural field. The question of language itself became an essential element of the Algerian government's cultural policy as it undertook a program to limit the usage of French in government affairs and to increase the country's *arabité* (Arabness). Laws were passed determining that all government posters and billboard had to be in Arabic, that Arabic should be the official language of the country's televisions, and that judges could speak only Arabic in the courtroom. The sociopolitical struggle thus entailed the linguistic struggles incorporated in Algerian cultural policy (Haddab 1983:5–9, 14).

This brief example reveals the complexity and the clear political importance of cultural policies in certain contexts. Brazilian cultural policy has never reached the same level of immediate political import, which is not to say that the situation there is not complex. Rather, the stakes and the strategies are necessarily different, deriving from distinct sociohistorical conjunctures. The question of language has not been an important one in Brazil, although it may well be much more central in countries such as Bolivia and Peru, with significant non-Spanish-speaking populations.

Most cultural policies, regardless of specific context and content, have two elements in common. They are designed first and foremost to preserve the nation's historical and cultural patrimony and thereby safeguard its cultural identity and values, regardless of how such values are defined. Secondly, cultural policies are frequently conceived as a means to mitigate what many policymakers see as the deleterious effects of mass media and the culture industry.

The relationship between culture and the state has rarely if ever been free of tensions and contradictions. As Jacques Rigaud has written in relation to France: "For the state, the creator is the most prestigious among its constituents and the most elusive of its agitators. For the creator, the state is the revered protector and the dreaded oppressor. If the state supports him, the creator cries out at the humiliation; if it doesn't, he denounces its indifference" (1975:167). To say that the state has a legitimate role to play in relation to culture is a far cry from reaching a consensus about its nature and goals.

A perfect example of the tensions engendered by cultural policies appeared recently in the United States in the wake of the National Endowment for the Arts' (NEA) support of the Robert Mapplethorpe exhibit. Episodes such as this call into question the precise nature of the state's cultural role. Should the state fund any kind of art or only that which does not offend what are taken to be the moral standards of some vaguely defined social segment? How does one determine the social legitimacy of art—and thus the justification for public expenditures— and who should be the arbiter? Can government refusal to fund certain modes of artistic expression be considered a form of censorship? These are complex and often controversial questions for which there is no simple answer.

In *El Ogro filantrópico,* a book whose title goes a long way toward describing the state's relation to cultural production, Nobel laureate Octavio Paz discusses the role of artists and intellectuals in Mexican society. He says that, as a writer, his duty is to maintain a marginal position in relation to the state, to political parties, to ideologies, and to society itself. At the same time, Paz echoes many official statements on cultural policy when he affirms that the state should increase its support of cultural production but with no strings attached. He cites as a negative example the case of Mexican muralist art, which lost energy following state intervention (1979:306, 314). In fact, the state, especially in developing countries, is rarely "neutral" with regards to art and culture.

The Brazilian state historically has acted as a sort of philanthropic agent and patron of the arts, frequently supporting artists and intellectuals through bureaucratic positions, donations, awards, and sinecures. More recently, it has intervened in one way or another in virtually every sector of cultural production and has created state enterprises, institutes, foundations, agencies, or commissions to regulate or support the plastic arts, dance, music, theater, soccer, carnival, folklore, Afro-Brazilian religious cults, television, tourism, and the cinema. At least partially because of the state's centrality in the cultural field, many artists have come to expect state support as a natural benefit of their profession. At the same time, since such support has more often than not been granted by authoritarian regimes that many artists and intellectuals viscerally oppose, the specific shape and nature of state support frequently tends to be much more controversial and rife with contradiction than in the United States, the Helms amendment notwithstanding.

Underlying the present study are a number of theoretical assumptions concerning the nature of the Brazilian state and the regimes that have held power since the 1930 period as well as of the specific configuration of the relationship between state and society in Brazil. They include the corporatist nature of the Brazilian state, its clientelistic relationship with civil society, co-optation as a strategy of manipulation and control, the essential role of elite groups in the decision-making process, and diverse notions of culture, including the relationship between popular and elite culture.

Since at least 1930, and thus throughout the period under consideration, the Brazilian political system has been characterized by the "historical persistence and continuity"[4] of what have been called "corporative regime types," in which individuals participate in the political and social process through state-approved and regulated organizations, which themselves have varying degrees of autonomy from the central government.[5] Society is thus organized horizontally into classes and vertically into state approved or even state-created organizations. That is, society is "organized along both *class and corporate lines*" (Wiarda 1981:34). Within these organizations, as with the rest of civil society, the state maintains patron-client relationships.

The corporative structure of Brazilian regimes has shown relative permanence over time, adjusting to change without significantly altering its fundamental design. At different times in modern Latin American history, corporative states have had to adjust and expand to encompass new rising groups, but "the structure of society [has] remained hierarchical, authoritarian, elitist, corporative, and closed" (Wiarda 1981:47). Alfred Stepan distinguishes between "inclusionary corporatism," which characterized Vargas's Estado Novo, and "exclusionary corporatism," which describes the Brazilian political system under post-1964 military regimes (1978:47). In short, the Brazilian state has grown out of a strong patrimonial tradition and has remained, at least since the 1930s, a state supported by corporative regimes.

In practical terms—and this is particularly significant for a discussion of the relationship between state and culture—the state has become not only a site where opposing social forces struggle unequally for domination but also a site and source of legitimation. In some instances, such as the film industry in the post-1964 period, the state has even become a marketplace where individuals compete for recognition and, in a more immediate sense, financing. The Brazilian state historically has had a propensity to intervene in virtually all areas of society, and society, on the other hand, tends to see the state as the supreme source of legitimation.

In this regard, it is important to distinguish between two forms state support, or patronage, of artists has historically assumed: clientelism, in which an artist rendered services in exchange for some sort of benefit, and the *mécènat* system, in which a wealthy or powerful person (or the imperial court) supported an artist in a rather more disinterested manner. Alain Viala has suggested that the difference between clientelism and *mécènat* is that the former obeys a "logic of service" while the latter reveals a "logic of recognition."[6] Clientelism in the cultural field, which derived from medieval social structures, instituted fidelity as a virtue of the social organism and was, as late as the eighteenth-century, considered both normal and obligatory in the life of the higher social strata. Many well-known writers and artists served as preceptors, secretaries, intendants, and confidants of the powerful. They derived multiple benefits from the relationship but were never free of the demands it entailed (Viala 1985:52–53).

In the *mécènat* system, benefits were frequently the same, but services were often of a symbolic nature. Support of the artist was not necessarily disinterested, for the Maecenas often stood to gain prestige through a logic of mutual recognition. By offering him his work, the artist recognized his patron's grandeur and good taste, thus legitimizing his power or wealth. The patron, on the other hand, offered public recognition of the author's talent. Unlike clientelistic relationships, here the utilitarian nature of the exchange remained hidden: the rich symbolically masked their fortunes, and artists their dependence, through the practice of art itself (Viala 1985:54–55). Our discussion of the relationship between intellectuals and the state in the 1930s and of state policy toward the film industry in the 1970s will reveal the essentially clientelistic nature of state/culture relationships.[7]

In the cultural field clientelism functions through diverse mechanisms of co-optation, ranging from the granting of posts in the cultural bureaucracy, which was characteristic of the Vargas period, to the granting of financing for individual projects of a cultural nature, which exemplified post-1964 regimes. In both periods intellectuals and artists were "incorporated" into government policy, albeit in different ways, and granted limited autonomy within a framework aimed at reinforcing mechanisms for state control. The relationship reveals both the uneasy dependence of artists/intellectuals on the state and the transformation of the state into an agent of cultural legitimation.

Cultural policies, normally formulated by social and political elites, tends to reflect the structure and concerns of the intellectual field of which they are a part. This often makes for a primary focus on support of elite cultural practices along with a paternalistic conception of popular culture. Seen in these terms, even the seemingly noncontroversial question of patrimonial preservation is fraught with contradictions, paradoxes, and ambiguities. A study of a nation's cultural patrimony immediately raises the problems of canonicity and access. In most societies, with a multiplicity of modes of production and consumption of culture, canonicity involves the question of *whose* cultural identity and historical patrimony are to be preserved, informed by *which* concept of the nation? *Whose* cultural projects are to be financed? Based on what criteria? What degree of access do different groups have to society's collective cultural capital?

In an empirical study of museum attendance in Europe, Pierre Bourdieu has shown that, although everyone has the theoretical possibility of taking advantage of works of art exhibited in museums, only a minority have a *real possibility* since, as he puts it "the work of art considered as a symbolic good exists as such only for those who have the means to appropriate it, that is, to decipher it," and that "access to cultural works is the privilege of the cultured class . . . a privilege with all the outward appearances of legitimacy . . . [since] the only ones who are ever excluded [from participation] are those who exclude themselves." Bourdieu argues that inequalities in relation to works of culture are merely one aspect of inequalities of an educational system that creates "cultural needs" while at the same time developing unequal means of satisfying those needs (1969:69). The question of access is thus a complex one that goes beyond mere availability of cultural works.

The ability to implement policy decisions in the cultural field, regardless of their specific orientation, also tends to correspond to the specific weight of individual ministers of education and culture—and thus of their ministries—in their respective regimes. In this regard, the significant advances made during the tenure of Gustavo Capanema (1936–45) and Ney Braga (1974–79) are exemplary.

Finally, one should ask why cultural policies have tended to expand during periods of authoritarian rule and lapse—or at least either remain steady or decline—during periods of greater democratization. Although further research is needed to arrive at a definitive conclusion, we can speculate that it has something to do with the desire for increased social control during authoritarian periods. This control, guaranteed by the state's coercive apparatus, is intertwined with attempts to construct a hegemonic relationship with civil society. During periods of authoritarian rule, a regime's legitimacy does not derive from an electoral mandate and must be constructed on various levels. One such level is the granting of favors (or bureaucratic posts, sinecures, or financing), which in many cases constitutes what Philipe Schmitter might call "preemptive co-optation" (1971:72–73). This has been particularly characteristic of the Brazilian state's relationship to the intellectual and artistic fields, which often have a significant role in the shaping of middle-class public opinion.

In short, the state has a monopoly on institutional coercion, which inevitably functions as a component of its policy toward culture. Although it can and often does control the distribution of cultural goods through censorship and repression, it would rather control by indirect constraints and consensus rather than coercion. This at least partially explains the creation of numerous governmental bodies designed to oversee or subsidize different cultural areas, the co-optation or incorporation of intellectuals into the state apparatus, and the expansion of cultural policy initiatives during periods of authoritarian rule.

Culture as the State's Business, 1930–45

The Estado Novo

The Brazilian state first systematically turned its attention toward the cultural field only after the revolution of 1930, which swept Getúlio Vargas to power, and especially after the November 1937 decree of the authoritarian Estado Novo (1937–45). Shortly after taking command of the provisional government, Vargas began to take a more aggressive role in the defense of national industry and in the creation or reform of social institutions, political structures, and administrative systems. Among governmental bodies created during Vargas's regime were the Ministério de Trabalho, Indústria e Comércio (1930), the Conselho Nacional do Café (1931), the Ministério de Educação e Saúde Pública (1932), the Instituto de Açúcar e Álcool (1933), the Conselho Federal de Comércio Exterior (1934), the Conselho Nacional de Petróleo (1938), the Instituto Brasileiro de Geografia e Estatística (1938), and the Companhia Siderúrgica Nacional (1941). These organizations, along with many others, were not necessarily the result of a carefully planned program of institutionalization but, rather, were often governmental responses to crises and problems that arose in the course of administering the nation's economy and political system (Skidmore 1967:15).

The Estado Novo put its own particular stamp on cultural production and debate in at least three major ways, each reflecting a different aspect of its overall cultural policy: coercion, orientation, and co-optation of cultural producers. First, it institutionalized forms of political and cultural repression paralleled only by the excesses of more recent military regimes. Books were banned, seized, and burned, and writers were imprisoned, exiled, or otherwise persecuted for "ideological offenses." The government took over and in some cases permanently expropriated selected newspapers, magazines, and publishing houses, while censorship forced numerous small presses out of business and ultimately caused a decrease in the number of Brazilian authors published (Hallewell 1982:272). Theater and film were tightly controlled by censors. In fact, Vargas's first measure concerning the film industry (decree 21,240, April 4, 1932) was the creation of a censorship commission in the Ministry of Education and Public Health.

Second, the regime's sophisticated propaganda agency, the Departamento de Imprensa e Propaganda (DIP), used multiple forms of cultural expression to further its ends. DIP attempted to control the dissemination of information not only through rigid censorship but more fundamentally by transforming civil society's channels of expression—especially radio and the press—into spaces for the transmission of state ideology. Radio was particularly important, for it had a greater power of penetration than the other media, but film and popular music were also used. The government viewed free broadcasting and a free press with suspicion, since they could potentially undermine its pedagogical objectives (Velloso 1987:22, 29). It thus attempted to devise mechanisms for the control of diverse fields of cultural expression, ranging from traditional elite forms to new or emerging modes of mass culture.

The regime saw the homogeneity of the cultural field as important for assuring the regime's organization and the defense of what it saw as the national interest (Velloso 1987:24). A fascinating example of the regime's intervention in the cultural arena involves its effort to manipulate samba lyrics to discourage bohemian life-styles and create a work ethic in the populace.

Sambas such as Jorge Faray's "Eu trabalhei," Luís Antônio and Brasinha's "Zé Marmita" and Ataúlfo Alves and Wilson Batista's "Bonde de São Januário" participate in this effort. Antônio Pedro has called such compositions "sambas da legitimidade" (sambas of legitimacy).

> Eu trabalhei
> Eu hoje tenho tudo, tudo que um homem quer
> Tenho dinheiro, automóvel e uma mulher
> Mas pra chegar até o ponto em que cheguei
> Eu trabalhei, trabalhei, trabalhei
> Eu hoje sou feliz
> E posso aconselhar
> Quem faz o que eu já fiz
> Só pode melhorar
> E quem diz que o trabalho
> Não dá coisa a ninguém
> Não tem razão, não tem, não tem.

It might also be noted that it was during the Estado Novo that carnival festivities were "officialized" and began to be organized by DIP's tourism sector. Themes of national exaltation in carnival sambas became obligatory.[8]

Elite cultural forms were not immune to such attempts at manipulation. In a speech delivered on February 19, 1942, Vargas's minister of labor, industry, and commerce, Alexandre Marcondes Filho, announced a literary contest with the express goal of stimulating the production of literary works that would "take an educational message to the men who toil in the factories." Through this contest the Estado Novo attempted to co-opt and redefine the "proletarian novel," which was then much in vogue in Brazil as elsewhere, in accordance with Vargas's concept of *trabalhismo* (Marcondes Filho 1942: 7–10).[9]

Finally, Vargas's program of institution building included a strong, explicit cultural component.[10] Vargas cast himself indirectly in the role of patron of the arts, greatly expanding the state bureaucracy and creating numerous governmental agencies that in various ways subsidized, incorporated, or co-opted intellectuals and cultural production. By way of a single law (law 378, January 13, 1937), his government created the Serviço de Radiodifusão (Radio Broadcasting Service), the Instituto Nacional de Cinema Educativo (INCE; National Institute of Educational Cinema), and the Serviço do Patrimônio Histórico e Artístico Nacional (SPHAN; Service for the National Historical and Artistic Patrimony). Later that same year he founded the Serviço Nacional de Teatro (SNT; National Theater Service) and the Instituto Nacional do Livro (INL; National Book Institute).[11] In 1941 he formed the Conselho Nacional de Desportos (National Sports Council) and in 1942 the Conservatório Nacional de Canto Orfeônico (National Conservatory of Choral Music).

The most important of these institutions from the cultural policy perspective was without doubt SPHAN, which constituted the most successful example of the state's cultural action from its creation until the 1960s, partially because of the leadership of Rodrigo Mello Franco de Andrade, who directed the agency from 1937 until 1967 and who brought together a highly competent team of architects and technicians dedicated to preservation. SPHAN, according to Sérgio Miceli, "is a chapter of the intellectual and institutional history of the modernist generation, a decisive step of governmental intervention in the field of culture and an effective action of an authoritarian regime engaged in the construction of an enlightened 'national identity' in the dependent tropics" (1987:44).

Despite its undeniable success in the patrimonial field, the activities of SPHAN are not without their contradictions and thus reflect the general problematic of state intervention in the cultural field. Critics like Joaquim de Arruda Falcão and Dalton Salla have criticized SPHAN's emphasis on the preservation of what are frequently called *"monumentos de pedra e cal,"* arguing that such monuments reflect only the historical experience of dominant social segments. Based on a survey of the social origin of monuments protected since SPHAN's creation in 1937, Falcão has shown that most derive from the "victorious experience of white Brazilians," from the "victorious experience of the Catholic church," from the "victorious experience in the State (palaces, forts) and society (*fazendas,* urban houses) of the country's political and economic elite" (1984: 28). Along the same lines, Miceli has suggested that underlying SPHAN's policy of historical restoration is a logic of the "embellishment of style and the consequent dilution of social markers" (1987:44). This again brings to the fore the specific conception of culture underlying the state's cultural policy. For the Estado Novo the nation's cultural and historical patrimony worthy of preservation was that of the elite. More popular forms were to be "oriented" and controlled.

All of the major cultural organizations created during the Vargas years have continued to exist in one form or another until the present—or at least until March 1990—and collectively they represent the backbone of Brazilian cultural policy.[12] Their importance is twofold. First, they created the institutional framework for government initiatives in the cultural arena, officially transforming culture into the state's business. Second, they provided the means for incorporating artists and intellectuals into the state apparatus—exemplary of "preemptive co-optation"—and, consequently, making the state an agent of cultural and intellectual legitimation. Given the small market for the dissemination of elite culture products, the state has traditionally been a locus for social recognition and legitimation as well as, in a more immediate sense, employment. Carlos Drummond de Andrade once wrote, in fact, that Brazilian literature is a literature of "public employees." This was as true of the First Republic as it was of the Estado Novo, although the latter period saw a marked change in the scale and degree of co-optation.

The roots of Vargas's cultural policy can be traced indirectly to the modernist movement of the 1920s. Vargas often called on intellectuals and writers to abandon the ivory tower they frequently occupied during the Republican period and to participate actively in the task of nation building. Speaking on the occasion of his induction into the Academia Brasileira de Letras in 1943, Vargas criticized the previous role of the academy and the isolation of intellectuals from the rest of society, advocating instead the "necessary symbiosis of men of thought and men of action," which had begun to take shape in the 1930s. Vargas's entrance into the academy, engineered by poet and Estado Novo ideologue Cassiano Ricardo, personified, on a purely symbolic level, this symbiosis (Velloso 1987:8–12).

On other occasions Vargas recognized the importance of the Brazilian modernist movement for the Revolution of 1930 and the Estado Novo. In a speech delivered at the Universidade do Brasil in 1951, Vargas recalled the significance of the relationship between literature and politics.

> The collective forces that provoked the revolutionary modernist movement in Brazilian literature . . . were the same ones that precipitated the victorious Revolution of 1930 in the social and political field. Brazilians were disquiet, . . . searching for something new, something more sincerely ours, more viscerally Brazilian. . . . The renovation of literary and artistic values, on the one hand, [and] the renovation of political values and institutions [on the other] . . . fused into a broader, more general and complex movement that was simultaneously reformist and conservative. (cited by Oliveira 1982:508)

According to Vargas's retrospective interpretation, the literary and political fields had converged in their desire for modernization ("renovation," in Vargas's speech) and in their nationalism. In fact, the tension between cosmopolitanism and cultural nationalism that structured modernism— its "contradictory modernity," to use Daniel Pécaut's expression—is at the core of many of the political questions raised in the 1930s (1989:21).

Vargas's dual emphasis on modernization and tradition ("reformist and conservative") quite precisely characterizes both modernism and the ideological foundations of Vargas's corporatist regime, which made concerted efforts to delineate and establish its cultural roots and intentions (Oliveira 1982:508). Working with this coincidence of national(ist) purpose, the Vargas regime was successful at co-opting and incorporating intellectuals of all stripes on a fairly large scale. Its definition of its cultural mission—constructing a sense of nationality and cultural unity through the rediscovery of the nation's cultural roots—fit well with that of many intellectuals (Pécaut 1989:72–75, 90–96; Velloso 1987:17–18).

In his expression of the proper relationship between the intellectual and political elite, Vargas adopted an idea that had been advocated since the mid-1920s by the intellectuals associated with the conservative Verde-Amarelo, or Anta, subcurrent of literary modernism, most of whom were actively engaged in the ideological justification of the authoritarian/corporative state as well as in various facets of the Estado Novo's propaganda efforts. Menotti del Picchia, Cassiano Ricardo, and Cândido Motta Filho successively served as director of the São Paulo division of the government's propaganda agency, the Departamento Estadual de

Imprensa e Propaganda (DEIP). Ricardo subsequently directed the government newspaper *A Manhã*, Menotti del Picchia *A Noite*.

But they were not the only modernists incorporated into the state apparatus. Gustavo Capanema's ministry of education became a new Maecenas for many intellectuals. Throughout the Estado Novo Carlos Drummond de Andrade served as Capanema's chief of staff. Rodrigo Melo Franco de Andrade served as director of SPHAN. Mário de Andrade elaborated the first draft of the law creating SPHAN, collaborated closely with the agency, and elaborated a project for a Brazilian encyclopedia for the Instituto Nacional do Livro. Composer Heitor Villa-Lobos wrote the "Hino da Revolução de 1930" and directed the movement of choral music for the ministry. Architects Lúcio Costa and Oscar Niemeyer, originators of Brasilia's ultramodern architecture, designed the ministry's new building, and Costa directed the Escola Nacional de Belas Artes. Plastic artist Cândido Portinari was commissioned to do murals. Sculptor Bruno Giorgi undertook the construction of a monument to youth. Augusto Meyer served as director of the Instituto Nacional do Livro, Prudente de Moraes Neto and Vinícius de Moraes on the government's film censorship board. Ronald de Carvalho, Ribeiro Couto, Murilo Mendes, and Raul Bopp served in the diplomatic corps. Sérgio Buarque de Hollanda and Rubens Borba de Moraes held high-level positions in the Biblioteca Nacional. Manuel Bandeira was a member of the Consultative Council of SPHAN and, along with Jorge de Lima, professor at the federal Faculdade de Filosofia. Rosário Fusco, Marques Rebelo, and Graciliano Ramos all contributed to the DIP's journal *Cultura Política* (Candido 1984:27–36; Martins 1987:84; Miceli 1979:129–97).

Sérgio Miceli suggests that in many cases intellectuals served in posts having little if anything to do with their intellectual work as such, which they continued to develop as parallel activities, while in others there existed a close connection between the two spheres of activity. He thus outlines the hierarchical structure of bureaucratic positions themselves, distinguishing between "escritores-funcionários" ("writer-employees"), such as Mário de Andrade, Drummond, and other modernists, who entered the state apparatus at a rather high level due to their capital of social relations (e.g., Drummond's long-standing friendship and collaboration with Gustavo Capanema, Andrade's with both Drummond and Capanema), and "funcionários-escritores" ("employee-writers"), such as Oswaldo Orico, who lacked such social capital, entered the bureaucracy at a lower level, often through public competition, and worked their way up the bureaucratic ladder with varying degrees of success. The latter, Miceli suggests, had to subject themselves to the regime's political directives while the former could "take refuge under the posture of a benevolent 'neutrality' in relation to the state, which permitted them to save many of their works from the heat of political struggles" (1979:178-87).

Nevertheless, Miceli suggests that, in both instances,

> a situation of material and institutional dependence is created which begins to determine the relations that the intellectual clienteles maintain with the public sector, whose subsidies support initiatives in the area of cultural production, free intellectuals from the oscillations of prestige, immunize them from the restrictions of the marketplace, and define the [nature] and volume of benefits for both.
>
> For all of these reasons, the writers employed by the cartorial state find themselves in a contradictory situation in relation to their intellectual production. Operating in an extremely complex politico-ideological conjuncture, if compared to that of the generation of 1870, they end up negotiating the perspective of completing their individual intellectual work in exchange for the collaboration offered in the task of "institutional construction" then underway, remaining silent about the cost of this work indirectly subsidized by the state. As captives of the state apparatus and, at the same time, desirous of freeing themselves from the constraints that normally fall on practitioners of official art and literature, they resolve the dilemma by resorting to the charm of idealistic justifications. (1979:158)

Perhaps the most common of these justifications was their nationalism, their attempt to create a more authentically "Brazilian" culture, which had led to their approximation with the authoritarian state to begin with.

The relationship between artists/intellectuals and the state during the authoritarian Estado Novo was clearly clientelistic and mutually beneficial. The participation of leading intellectuals in the government's cultural project lent it a legitimacy it might not otherwise have, and their selection by the government afforded them an additional instance of recognition and consecration. No matter how indirect and refracted, their contribution to the state's cultural project served to reinforce and reproduce the intellectual field's position within the broader field of power and to reinforce the state's role as an agent of intellectual and cultural legitimation.

The Departamento de Cultura of the City of São Paulo

The 1930s provided an important alternative model of cultural action on the municipal level in São Paulo's Departamento de Cultura. It had a more activist and arguably more liberal orientation than that of the federal government, and although numerous commentators have tended to idealize its efforts, it reveals contradictions of a different sort from those that permeate the Estado Novo's cultural policy.

The Department of Culture, conceived by state legislator Paulo Duarte, was established by Municipal Act 861, on May 30, 1935, during the administration of mayor Fábio Prado (1934–38). It was an essential component of a number of cultural, educational, and intellectual initiatives taking place in São Paulo in the early 1930s, including the creation of the Escola Livre de Sociologia e Política (1933) and the Universidade de São Paulo (1934), both of which were designed to participate in the transformation of society through the formation of new elites (Pécaut 1986:26; Sandroni 1988:84; Limongi, 1989a:218). The department's importance is that it preceded and in many ways provided the impetus for the federal government's cultural initiatives and that more recent cultural planners have looked back at its activities as a possible model to follow in the reelaboration of the state's cultural policy.[13]

All three institutions were formed by people formerly associated with the Partido Democrático (PD)—created in 1926 in opposition to the traditional party of São Paulo's oligarchy, the Partido Republicano Paulista—and under the general leadership of Armando de Sales Oliveira (1887–1945), the founder of the Partido Constitucionalista (1934), who had been appointed state interventor in 1933.[14] Antônio Candido sees these initiatives, and especially the Department of Culture, as a conscious attempt on the part of a "moderate Left" within the PD—a "cultural vanguard in the shadow of a ruling oligarchy that accepted and supported it"—to take culture from the privileged and "transform it into a factor for the humanization of the majority through planned institutions" (1985:xiv–xvi). Claude Lévi-Strauss, who was one of the European professors hired to form the university's initial faculty, offers a slightly different perspective when he writes, in *Tristes Tropiques,* that "it was because the oligarchy felt the need of a civic and secular public opinion to counterbalance the traditional influence of the Church and the army, as well as personal political rule, that they undertook to make culture available to a wider audience by creating the University of São Paulo" (1975:101–2).

To understand the fundamental differences between the activities of the Department of Culture and those of the federal government— differences based on strikingly dissimilar notions of culture—one would do well to compare Mário de Andrade's draft (*anteprojeto*) of the law that created SPHAN with the version that was finally enacted and with the general orientation of the agency's activities after its creation.[15] Rather than focus on *"monumentos de pedra e cal,"* as does the Estado Novo's version of SPHAN, Andrade's conception of cultural patrimony was broadly based, including forms of cultural expression ranging from elite art to Indian and popular art and cultural artifacts. His draft would have included such things as indigenous tools, habits, legends, folklore, music, and superstitions, as well as urban slums and Indian dwellings, as an integral part of the nation's cultural patrimony. It was for this reason that cultural planners in the 1970s such as Aloísio Magalhães looked back at Andrade's draft—as well as his other activities in the cultural field—as a possible model for the transformation of Brazilian cultural policy.

The DC constituted an attempt, on the part of an enlightened bourgeoisie, to institutionalize, rationalize, and organize certain aspects of cultural production, leisure activities, and historical preservation in the city of São Paulo. Its creators conceived it as the embryo of a future Instituto Paulista de Cultura, which would be expanded on a national scale, through an Instituto Brasileiro de Cultura, after Armando de Sales Oliveira's hoped-for election to Brazil's presidency in 1937 (Duarte 1985:61).

The department comprised four divisions: Cultural Expansion, Libraries, Education and Recreation, and Historical and Social Documentation.[16] Modernist writer Mário de Andrade was named director of both the Division of Cultural Expansion as well as of the department as a whole. According to its founding legislation, the department was charged with stimulating and developing all sorts of educational, artistic, and cultural initiatives, ranging from support of music, theater, and cinema to the organization of libraries and the creation of children's parks and recreational facilities. Its responsibilities also included the collection, restoration, and publication of documents concerning the city's history.[17]

The creation of the Department of Culture came at a moment (1934–37) when there was a political rapprochement between the federal government and the more liberal wing of São Paulo's political leadership, that is, with elements previously associated with the PD, most of whom had followed Armando de Sales Oliveira into the Partido Constitucionalista. Mário de Andrade, Rubens Borba de Moraes, and Sérgio Milliet, directors of the department's major subdivisions, had all been affiliated, not coincidentally, with the PD.

The breadth of activities undertaken by the department's various divisions is indicative of the energy and creativity of its founding group. The following represents only a sampling:

Libraries. The department laid the groundwork for the construction of a municipal library, inaugurated on January 25, 1942, and subsequently renamed the Biblioteca Municipal Mário de Andrade. It also established "popular" libraries in working-class neighborhoods, children's libraries, and a bookmobile in which Mário de Andrade himself would drive a specially equipped Ford to city parks and lend books to passersby (Dassin 1978:109).

Music. The Division of Cultural Expansion was responsible for São Paulo's musical education. To that end, it worked on several levels. First, it attempted to make erudite music more accessible to a broad, socially and economically diversified audience by sponsoring free concerts in public parks and squares as well as in the municipal theater and on the radio. Second, it established a record library and recording service, with a number of different functions and services: recording Brazilian musical folklore, São Paulo's erudite music, and the voices of Brazil's most illustrious men as well as those of Brazilians from different regions and social classes for the purpose of phonetic study; the establishment of an ethnographic and folklore museum, specially designed for the collection of popular Brazilian musical instruments; the maintenance of an archive of recorded folk music; the development of a record collection for public consultation, a library of scores and technical publications, and the organization of public concerts using records in the library's collection (Dassin 1978:111; Duarte 1985:62).

Parks and Recreation. The department opened or operated children's centers in Parque Dom Pedro II, Lapa, and Ipiranga. The centers were designed to support the education and health of less-privileged children, providing them with directed games and educational activities, medical and dental care, and notions of hygiene and nutrition. They were also intended to "keep poor children off the streets." In the evening the children's centers were used as "clubs for minors" designed to provide working-class adolescents with a supervised place to gather at night (Dassin 1978:108-9; Duarte 1985:81-82).

Documentation. The Division of Historical and Social Documentation was responsible for collecting, restoring, preserving, and publishing historical documents and making such documents available to researchers. As part of its program, it published the *Revista do arquivo municipal*. The division also undertook research concerning the social situation of the working class with the intention of providing rational solutions to problems such as cost of living, transportation, and housing (Dassin 1978:114).[18]

Other. In 1937 Andrade developed plans for a series of Casas de Cultura Proletária (Houses of Proletarian Culture), which would include lecture halls with stages for theatrical rehearsals, game rooms, reading rooms, space for choir rehearsals, and libraries for adults and children.[19]

Also under the department's auspices, in July 1937 Andrade organized the Congresso da Língua Nacional Cantada, with the purpose of establishing norms for the pronunciation of Portuguese in lyrical singing.

The lofty designs and good intentions of the department's programs cannot efface an element of paternalism expressed in the idea, widely accepted at the time, that intellectual elites have ultimate responsibility for the cultural and educational well-being of the masses and that elite culture is naturally superior to popular culture. Based on an analysis of mayor Fábio Prado's description of his own administration's accomplishments, Joan Dassin writes that "a sense of the new and progressive was mixed with an attitude of protectionism toward the *povo,* often expressed in a rather patronizing way" (1978:108, 110).

Carlos Sandroni's discussion of the implications of the department's activities and Magali Alonso Lima's analysis of children's centers and clubs for minors are more incisive in their critiques. Borrowing largely from Michel Foucault's *Discipline and Punish,* Sandroni sees the Department of Culture as an important element in an effort to "advance the process of disciplining society" and to increase the state's governability in Brazil by participating in the attempt to "re-create" social institutions and "construct" society on a more rational basis (1988:83; Pécaut 1986:14). This rationality included improved methods of gathering and storing information, investigating diverse aspects of Brazilian society, and experimenting with new techniques of social organization. While on the one hand such techniques were essential for the process of modernization, on the other they provided more efficacious methods for social surveillance, discipline, and control (Sandroni 1988:89–92).

The idea behind the program for developing children's parks, located in poor or working-class districts, was to provide children with "healthy and attractive" places for recreation and exercise "under the control of public powers" and far from the "foci of bad habits, vices, and criminality" that surround them. Poor neighborhoods and homes are thus seen as atmospheres that serve only to corrupt childhood innocence. State control is needed to provide the child's "adequate moral and material formation." Sandroni ironically recalls Paulo Duarte's suggestion that the policy behind the children's parks was inspired by sixteenth-century Jesuit priest José de Anchieta, "who ingeniously understood the method of conquering adult savages through the children he catechized" (Sandroni 1988:94–95; Duarte 1985:86).

Lima discusses the parks within the broader context of the Estado Novo's attempt to discipline society through the construction of a "new Brazilian man."[20] Seen as part of the state's program of physical education, which was designed to form strong, healthy bodies that would serve to increase their economic productivity, children's parks in São Paulo and elsewhere in the country differed from normal parks in that they included a fairly rigorous schedule of programmed activities designed to structure and organize leisure hours in such a way as to keep children away from the more negative atmospheres of the home—especially in those cases in which both parents work—and the street (Duarte 1985:87–98).

Nicanor Miranda, director of the department's Division of Education and Recreation, is explicit in his outline of the parks' function:

The children's parks are, in the final analysis, a form of social assistance and popular education. It is thus impossible to separate their mission from their higher responsibility as an element in the formation of the state, which should be, in our opinion, essentially democratic.

To provide the means necessary for new generations to be blessed with aptitudes to exercise active functions in the collectivity; to stimulate the formation of a national consciousness; to struggle toward the realization of the ideals of a true human solidarity; for obedience to be always present in the spirit . . . these are the mediate objectives of a form of popular education that seeks the supremacy of truth and freedom!

But without the child's preparation this is a mere utopia. For this reason, let us make children accustomed to the law, to objective and social norms so that they will voluntarily and freely obey with noble and human discipline. (Cited by Lima 1979:91–92)

In the guise of democratic principles, Miranda is proposing what Foucault calls a "disciplinary society" through the organization, structuring, supervision, and control of what might otherwise be a purely recreational social space. The parks function not only in such a way as to control children's time but also, and perhaps more important, to control and shape their bodies as potential productive agents (92–93).

The parks, as well as their evening extensions, the Clubes de Menores Operários (Clubs for Working-Class Minors), clearly had control through observation and prevention of delinquency as one of their implicit, and at times explicit, goals. As Sandroni describes their purpose, "instead of putting [minors] in jail, it put them in the children's parks; instead of segregating them, it circumscribed the spaces where it would be possible, in fact, to establish a permanent, observing gaze, taking in all aspects of their lives. Spaces which were, to use Foucault's words, 'minute social observatories that penetrate even to the adults and exercise regular supervision over them'" (1988:97; Foucault 1979:211; Lima 1979:58–61). In short, although the children's parks and clubs for minors no doubt originated with good intentions, those intentions themselves are permeated with an authoritarian paternalism implying a desire for increased social control and, perhaps more important, increased control over the shape and process of social reproduction.

Through the inclusion of "public diversions"—ranging from movie theaters to circuses to soccer fields—under the DC's aegis, leisure activities legally became an area of social life subject to state surveillance and control, exercised through the mechanisms of obligatory registration with the government and regular inspection. One should recall, in this regard, that among the attributes of the department's Division of Cultural Expansion was the formulation of municipal censorship laws in the area of public entertainment. The creation of the category of "public diversion" as an area of legitimate state concern had two basic results: (1) it directed the attention of the state's "controlling gaze" toward areas with which it had previously not been involved; and (2) it brought together under a single category a number of activities that had previously been considered totally disparate, such as popular dance halls and the luxurious municipal theater, thus broadening the official definition of *cultural event* and expanding areas of state intervention (Sandroni 1988:104–6).

The alternative model of state/culture relations provided by the DC— which was much more activist (in a positive sense) in its immediate social relations than was the federal government—is thus not without its contradictions and is not totally unrelated to the authoritarian paternalism that tended to dominate elite debates about the production, circulation, and consumption of cultural goods. It attempted to expand access to culture but often in an authoritarian manner. One final example along these lines should suffice. According to Mário de Andrade, the DC's director, the state's pedagogical action should take place on multiple levels, although especially through museums and cultural institutes. Museums should be open to all forms of culture, ranging from folklore to industrial design. Visits by workers, students, and children would be obligatory and accompanied by trained guides, resulting in the visitors' enlightenment (in Duarte 1985:152).

Although Andrade's view of the role and nature of museums is broadly based, reflecting an openness of spirit and a recognition of the inherent value of different modes of cultural expression, it is also authoritarian in its desire to *impose,* through obligatory visits, a specific notion of culture on the working class, students, and children. Implicit in this conception is a utilitarian, intentional notion of change through the pedagogical action of the state, oriented by intellectual elites such as those who took on the task of developing the Department of Culture.

Between the Sickle of the State and the Hammer of the Cultural Industry, 1964–90

The Military's Cultural Offensive

When the military overthrew the government of João Goulart in 1964, it brought with it an implicit promise to reverse the wave of state interference in the free enterprise system that had characterized the administrations of Jânio Quadros and, especially, Goulart. Despite their ostensible ideological support of economic liberalism and an ever-present laissez-faire rhetoric, the military takeover led not to a decentralization but, rather, to an increasingly centralized process of economic decision making.[21] Increased state participation in the economy did not derive, however, from an explicit statist ideology but, rather, from the military's national security doctrine or from the inability to convince the private sector to invest in areas in which prices were held down and return was slow.

The military, for example, felt that the ability to produce its own planes was essential to the country's security, so it created the state enterprise Embraer. In the field of telecommunications, Telebrás and Embratel, responsible for the implantation of microwave relay systems and satellite hookups, which proved to be essential for the development of the country's highly successful television industry, were created for the second reason (Evans 1979:216–19). Through the military's actions the state became more deeply involved in the national economy than ever before.

State intervention in the cultural arena also increased dramatically in the 1960s. Like state activity in the economic sphere, support for cultural production forms part of the military's ideology of national security, which saw development as including psychological, social, and cultural factors as well as economic considerations. According to this ideology, the state should stimulate cultural production as a means of national integration but at the same time should maintain that production under state control. Attempts were made to create what has been called a "National System of Culture," much like the National System of Tourism (consolidated in 1967) or the National System of Telecommunications. The centralization of cultural activities under the aegis of the state thus became an implicit if not explicit goal of the military government (Ortiz 1985:80–87).[22]

The question of centralization and control serves as a backdrop for a discussion of Brazilian cultural policy in the post-1964 period, which necessarily obeys a somewhat different logic than that of the 1930s, especially because of the emergence of powerful new media and culture industries. After 1964 there occurred an irreversible division in the market of symbolic goods in which lucrative areas (such as television, FM radio, records, tapes, video cassettes, and mass publishing) were in effect yielded to the private sector, while activities and genres with small or declining publics—activities ranging from film and theater to opera, classical music, dance, and the plastic arts—came to depend on official protection. In this sense the state became a new Maecenas in the 1970s through its disposition to subsidize intellectuals and artists without a market potential for the goods they produce. In other words, the presence of the state in different fields of artistic activity became proportional to the inability of each sector to be self-sufficient in market terms. The less marketable a sector is, the more pressure it exerts for increased state support. Under such conditions the state developed what might be called a clientelistic "social security system for the arts" (Miceli 1979:99).

This situation is not exclusive to Brazil and can be found even in the United States and such organizations as the National Endowment for the Arts. In *Le Paradoxe du musicien,* Pierre-Michel Menger describes a similar situation in relation to the field of avant-garde music in France, whose only market is comprised of other composers and specialized critics. Thus, its absolute dependence on the state, which, through various forms of subvention, ranging from commissioned works to the sponsorship of festivals, virtually created a "market" for such music and became its sole source of financial support (1983:242–49). As in the case of Brazilian cinema, to use an example that will be discussed below, one of the primary arguments for such support is that an increase in production will lead inevitably to an increase in demand. Menger shows, and I think his analysis is equally valid for Brazil, that the expansion of the market for such music is in fact due not to increased public demand but, rather, to increased subvention and intervention by the state (254).

The military regime's initial proposal in the cultural field came in 1966 when a commission was formed in the Ministry of Education and Culture (MEC) to study and reformulate the government's cultural policy. The commission recommended the creation of a council along the lines of the Conselho Federal de Educação, which had been created in 1962.

The result of the commission's recommendations was the creation of the Conselho Federal de Cultura (CFC) on November 21, 1966, an essentially normative body designed to provide information and recommendations to MEC on policy matters (*Legislação* 1976; Filho 1978:3). Although other agencies, such as Embratel, had been created previously, the formation of the CFC marked the beginning of a virtual cultural offensive by the military government. Even a cursory view of the list of organizations created since the military coup asserts the breadth of the state's activity:

1965: Empresa Brasileira de Telecomunicações (Embratel)
1966: Conselho Federal de Cultura
       Conselho Nacional de Turismo
       Empresa Brasileira de Turismo (Embratur)
       Instituto Nacional do Cinema (INC)
1967: Ministério de Telecomunicações
1969: Empresa Brasileira de Filmes (Embrafilme)
1970: Diretoria do Patrimônio Histórico e Artístico Nacional
       (1945) becomes an institute (IPHAN)
1972: Departamento de Assuntos Culturais (DAC)
1973: Programa de Reconstrução de Cidades Históricas
       Programa de Ação Cultural (PAC)
       Conselho Nacional de Direito Autoral
1975: Campanha de Defesa do Folclore Brasileiro (CDFB)
       Centro Nacional de Referência Cultural
       Fundação Nacional das Artes (Funarte)
       Política Nacional de Cultura
       Embrafilme reorganized, extinction of INC
1976: Conselho Nacional do Cinema (Concine)
       Radiodifusão Brasileira (Radiobrás)
1978: Secretaria de Assuntos Culturais (SEAC)
       CDFB incorporated into Funarte as Instituto Nacional de
       Folclore
1979: IPHAN becomes Secretaria do Patrimônio Histórico e Artístico Nacional (SPHAN)
       Fundação Nacional Pró-Memória
       Secretaria de Cultura (SEC)
1985: Ministério da Cultura

1986: Lei Sarney (provided fiscal benefits for private sector investment in the arts)

1987: Embrafilme divided into Embrafilme Distribuidora de Filmes and Fundação do Cinema Brasileiro

1990: Ministry of Culture replaced by Secretaria de Cultura in MEC

Embrafilme extinguished

Fundação do Cinema Brasileiro extinguished

Funarte extinguished

Fundação Pró-Memória and SPHAN suspended pending reorganization

Instituto Brasileiro de Arte e Cultura

A thorough study of Brazilian cultural policy in the post-1964 period would require differentiation of specific orientations under successive regimes, since their respective ministers of education and culture had different conceptions of what shape policy should take and different relationships with central decision-making authorities. Their ability to implement their programs derived not only from the importance granted to culture by successive governments but also, and perhaps more important, from their own position in the power structure.

The most intense period of state initiatives in the cultural field came during the regime of Ernesto Geisel (1974–79) with retired general Ney Braga as minister of education and culture. It was during this period that a cultural policy was formalized with the publication of the *Política nacional de cultura*.[23] The Geisel regime also expanded the institutional framework of Brazilian cultural policy with the creation of Funarte, the revitalization of the Serviço Nacional do Teatro, and the reformulation of state policy toward the film industry, including the restructuring of Embrafilme and the creation of Concine. In addition to a longstanding patrimonial orientation, which continued to exist in IPHAN, the cultural offensive in the mid-1970s focused primarily on those areas—the plastic arts, music, theater, and the cinema—with a reduced market potential and a more personalized or even artisan mode of production (Miceli 1979:64). In other words, with some significant exceptions, its offensive focused largely on elite cultural forms.

Renato Ortiz sees increased state investments in culture during the 1973–75 period as one result of the economic optimism produced by the

"miracle" of 1967–73 as reflected in the II Plano Nacional de Desenvolvimento (1974). Previous governments had focused primarily on economic aspects of development, although they had given lip service to
the need for the "humanization of development" or for "psychosocial
development" to accompany economic development. The Geisel regime,
according to this analysis, attempted to put such ideas into action and
thus gave more attention to the area of culture (Ortiz 1985:82).[24]

Although there is no doubt some truth in Ortiz's interpretations, other
factors are clearly of equal or greater importance. The years between
1969 and 1975 were the most repressive of military rule. Sparked by an
impasse in its constitutional relationship with Congress, on December
13, 1968 the Costa e Silva regime decreed the Fifth Institutional Act,
which led to the imposition of the harshest censorship yet known in
Brazil and forced a number of political leaders, intellectuals, and artists
into exile. The appearance of armed movements in opposition to the
regime led, in turn, to the institutionalization of torture and a national
campaign by the military against "subversion."

This period of repression and censorship exacerbated the military's
crisis of legitimacy,[25] especially in relation to the intellectual/cultural
field, and the increased activity in the cultural arena can be interpreted
as one response to this crisis. In August 1973 General Médici's minister
of education and culture, Jarbas Passarinho, initiated a Program of
Cultural Action (PAC), which, according to Sérgio Miceli, was designed
to provide financial (and political) credit to some areas of cultural production that had previously been ignored by the government and which
constituted an official attempt to improve relations with artistic and
intellectual circles (Miceli 1984:56). Film producer Luiz Carlos Barreto
has explained that the reformulation of Embrafilme's program of production financing, which will be described in the following section, grew
out of conversations he and other film industry professionals, especially
those associated with the Cinema Novo group, had during this period
with Jarbas Passarinho (in *Jornal da Tela* 14).[26]

Geisel's minister of education and culture, Ney Braga, managed to
recruit cultural administrators who were either identified with the Left
of the cultural field or who had the confidence of the Left (Roberto
Farias and Gustavo Dahl in Embrafilme, Orlando Miranda in the SNT,
Manuel Diegues, Jr.—filmmaker Cacá Diegues's father—in the Departamento de Assuntos Culturais, which functioned as an umbrella agency
within MEC with the responsibility of overseeing all of the government's

cultural activities). The optimism that reigned in the cultural field at this time, despite the repression, was due in part to the feeling among different cultural sectors that they not only had the support of the government but that they were finally able to influence the shape of state policy toward their respective areas.

Miceli correctly points out that the success of this cultural offensive would have been impossible without a strong minister of education and culture with legitimacy in both the government and the cultural field. A retired army general, Ney Braga's political career was consolidated through successive electoral victories in the state of Paraná (mayor of Curitiba [1954], federal deputy [1958], state governor [1960]) and service in nonmilitary positions of the post-1964 period (he was minister of agriculture under Castello Branco). In Paraná his political legacy included many important cultural initiatives, including the Fundação Educacional do Paraná, the Teatro Guaíra, and the Companhia Oficial de Teatro.

In addition, he was the central figure in what was then considered to be one of the strong civilian political "clans" in the country, which included such government officials as Karlos Rischbieter (president of the Banco do Brasil), Reinhold Stephanes (director of the Brazilian social security system), and Maurício Schulmann (director of the Banco Nacional de Habitação). Together Braga's group was said to control almost half of the national budget. The group also counted on the support of then secretary of planning, João Paulo dos Reis Velloso, who was seminal in obtaining increased funding for Embrafilme (Miceli 1979:64–66).[27] This strong government support led to the remarkable success of the Brazilian film industry in the late 1970s.

The Film Industry and the State, 1964–90

No sector of cultural production has been more negatively affected, as journalist José Neumanne Pinto has put it, by the sickle of the state and the hammer of the cultural industry, or, in other words, by a misdirected state policy and the exigencies of the market, than the film industry. The Brazilian film industry today faces the most severe crisis of its history, a crisis that threatens its very existence. In the late 1970s it seemed that Brazilian cinema, supported by the state through Embrafilme, would finally take off and reach an unprecedented level of stability and prosperity. Between 1974 and 1978 the total number of spectators for Brazilian films doubled from thirty million to over sixty million, and total income increased by 288 percent, from $13 million in 1974 to over $38 million in 1978. Brazilian cinema's share of its own market increased from around 15 percent in 1974 to over 30 percent in 1978.

Despite such success, the last decade has witnessed a downturn, which reversed the economic growth of the previous decade. The number of theaters in the country dropped from 3,276 in 1975 to slightly over 1,500 in 1984 to less than 1,100 in 1988. Attendance figures for Brazilian films dropped from the 1978 high of sixty million to less than twenty-two million in 1984 (the figure for 1988 was under twenty-four million). In 1986 films distributed by Embrafilme—which came to handle virtually all nonpornographic national films in Brazil—drew only eleven million spectators, a figure representing an increase of almost 100 percent over the previous year. The occupancy rate for all theaters dropped from 19 percent in 1978 to a mere 12 percent in 1984, and annual attendance per capita went from 2.6 times in 1975 to 0.8 in 1983. National film production, in turn, declined from 102 films in 1980 to 84 in 1983. But the crisis is less apparent in the number of films produced than in their quality. Between 1981 and 1985 pornography accounted for an average of almost 73 percent of total production, a trend that continued at least through 1988, a year in which twenty of the thirty top-drawing Brazilian films were pornographic.

The crisis of Brazilian cinema in the 1980s reflected the larger crisis of the national economy in a period when the so-called economic miracle of the 1967–73 period, characterized by high growth rates and relatively low inflation, was replaced by an economic nightmare with a $100 billion foreign debt and near hyperinflation. The economic crisis forced the government to impose severe restrictions on imports, making film production costs rise dramatically and accentuating what is often called the "dollarization" of the film production process. Film production costs increased rapidly at a time when the market was shrinking, thus accelerating the process of decline, and ticket prices, which have long been controlled by the government, have not kept pace with inflation, further reducing the industry's income.

There are many additional reasons for the decline of the Brazilian film industry in the first half of the 1980s. High inflation rates have made film going a luxury for much of the Brazilian population. Television, which has been so successful during this same period (due in

part to considerable infrastructural public sector investments in the telecommunications industry), has provided Brazilians with inexpensive yet
generally high-quality entertainment in the comfort of their homes. At
the same time, unlike the United States and Western Europe, television
has not provided the national film industry with a significant additional
source of income, since historically there has been little integration between the two media. In 1984, of 1,967 feature-length films shown on
Brazilian television stations, only 82 were Brazilian.

But the crisis goes beyond mere economic considerations. It represents
the bankruptcy of the state-supported model of film production that led
Brazilian cinema, in the mid-1970s, to truly remarkable levels of success.
It is a crisis of a questionable policy that did not derive from a far-
sighted vision of the future of Brazilian cinema and that was authoritarian in many of its particulars, especially in relation to the exhibition
sector. Although the policy made viable many important film projects,
including most of the Brazilian films distributed in the United States in
recent years, it ultimately failed to reconcile the state's cultural and
industrial responsibilities vis-à-vis the cinema and led to the meteoric
fall of the Brazilian film industry during the last several years.

In this section I will discuss the reasons for this failure, focusing on
the shift in state policy toward the cinema in the early 1970s within the
context of the regime of Ernesto Geisel (1974–79) and, in a broader
sense, the political conjuncture that contributed to the shift. The policy
failed largely because of its clientelistic nature, which led it to respond
to the demands of clients who occupied dominant positions in the cinematic field rather than provide infrastructural support, which could
have strengthened the industry as a whole.

Although the state claimed that its goal was to make the cinema more
competitive in its own market, the screen quota and the various forms
of financial assistance it provided in fact suspended the rules of the
marketplace for national films, which ceased to compete against foreign
films in the domestic market and began to compete against each other
in the reserve market. Embrafilme became the major source of production
financing and itself became a marketplace in which filmmakers competed
against each other for the right to make films, thus exacerbating tensions
within the industry and creating a situation in which the play of influences
was often more important than the talent of the filmmaker or producer.[28]

To put the discussion in context, a brief overview of the historical development of state policy toward the film industry is in order. Like Brazil's cultural policy in general, state intervention in the film industry dates from the early 1930s, when Getúlio Vargas implemented the first of what would turn out to be a long series of protectionist measures, most in the form of a screen quota for national films, designed to give the industry a modicum of stability for future development in a market long dominated by foreign cinemas.[29] Since the 1930s, and especially after 1964, the state role evolved from that of regulator of market forces to active agent and productive force in the industry, especially through its various programs of film production financing (low-interest loans, advances on distribution, and coproduction with private companies).

The state began its direct financial support of the film industry in 1966 with the creation of the Instituto Nacional do Cinema. The institute, created by an executive degree of the Castello Branco regime, was the result of a long struggle by most sectors of the film industry (Johnson 1987:107–12). It administered three major programs of support: first, a subsidy program providing all national films exhibited with additional income based on box office receipts; second, a program of additional cash awards for "quality" films, selected by a jury of critics and film industry professionals; and third, a film financing program in which the institute administered coproductions between foreign distributors and local producers using funds withheld from the distributor's income tax.[30] These three programs were available to all interested filmmakers and thus tended to support the production sector as a whole.

The coproduction program ended in 1969 with the creation of Embrafilme, which was originally intended to promote the distribution of Brazilian films in foreign markets, and the funds withheld from the distributor's income tax became a major source of the agency's budget. As early as 1970, Embrafilme began granting producers low-interest loans for film production financing. Between 1970 and 1979, when the loan program was phased out, Embrafilme financed over 25 percent of total national production in this manner. Carlos Diegues's *Bye Bye Brasil* (1980) was the last film financed under this program.

As initially formulated, decisions to grant production financing were ostensibly made on purely technical grounds, taking into consideration the size of the company, its production history, the number of awards it had won in national and international festivals, and its experience. Such a policy may seem reasonable for most economic sectors or most industries, but the film industry is different in that its product transmits cultural, social, and ideological values, and such "neutrality" was seen as unacceptable by many segments of Brazilian society. *O Estado de São Paulo,* for example, editorialized on January 28, 1972, that Embrafilme should *not* be a merely technical agency but, rather, should finance only films of high quality that contribute to the "moral foundations" of Brazilian society. Since a "neutral" policy designed to foster Brazilian cinema as a whole led to the production of films deemed undesirable by many social sectors, including the military—and here I am referring to the rash of *pornochanchadas* (erotic comedies) that began to appear in the early 1970s, many partially financed by the state—a reformulation of Embrafilme's production policy became inevitable.

In 1975, during the Geisel regime, Embrafilme was reorganized and at that time absorbed the executive functions of the now defunct INC. The Conselho Nacional do Cinema (Concine) was created the following year to assume INC's legislative role.[31] In 1973 Embrafilme had created its own nationwide distributor, long a goal of Brazilian producers, and in 1974 it initiated a program of coproduction financing that gradually replaced the loan program. As initially formulated, the enterprise participated in selected film projects with up to 30 percent of total production costs. With an advance on distribution of another 30 percent, the state could cover up to 60 percent of a film's production costs. In the late 1970s Embrafilme began providing up to 100 percent of a film's financing in some cases.

The coproduction program described above marked a fundamental redirection in state policy toward the industry, much in line with what producers had proposed to Jarbas Passarinho in 1972. This new orientation intensified under the ministry of Ney Braga. With this program, the granting of production financing became much more selective. When the state decides to coproduce a limited number of films, it must inevitably decide *which* Brazilian cinema it will support. This causes the state, on the one hand, to enter into competition with nonfavored sectors of the industry and, on the other, to become a site of contention for competing groups. The reorientation of the state's financial assistance to the industry exacerbated conflicting positions among filmmakers (Bernardet 1983; Ramos 1983:chap. 4).

Another effect of the shift in policy was, it is often said, to "socialize losses and privatize profits" (Schild 1986). Since the state assumed the lion's share of the financial risk involved in film production, many directors and producers tended to be less concerned with keeping costs down and, at least to some extent, with public acceptance of their films. Embrafilme's coproduction program undeniably improved the technical quality of Brazilian cinema—virtually all of the Brazilian films exhibited in the United States during the last decade were produced under such programs—but by doing so it allowed production costs to be inflated to levels far above the market potential for return in the domestic market. At the same time Embrafilme did little to improve and strengthen the industry's infrastructure. Its focus, at least in terms of financial support for the industry, was almost exclusively on production and its own distribution sector.

By the mid-1980s it became clear that the existing mode of state-supported cinematic production was obsolete and that transformation of the relationship between cinema and the state was necessary. The urgency of the restructuring became clear, and Embrafilme once again became the object of severe public criticism and debate, when the *Folha de São Paulo* published, in early 1986, a series of articles on the enterprise's management.[32] In an editorial entitled "Cine catástrofe" (March 20, 1986), the newspaper referred to Embrafilme's activities as a "moral, economic, and artistic disaster." Increasing numbers of film industry professionals recognized the need for a reevaluation of the relationship between cinema and the state.[33]

Although minor changes in policy had occurred throughout the late 1970s and early 1980s, the next major attempt at transformation took place during the Sarney administration, with Celso Furtado as minister of culture. Sarney restructured Embrafilme, separating its cultural and commercial activities, by creating a mixed-ownership enterprise (Embrafilme—Distribuidora de Filmes S.A.) housing all of the firm's commercial activities and transferring its other sectors into a foundation (Fundação Brasileira de Cinema).[34] Even under this new structure, Embrafilme's fundamental orientation—the clientelistic support of individual film projects rather than of the industry as a whole—remained unchanged, and the general situation of the Brazilian film industry continued to deteriorate.

One result of this orientation, and consequently one of the major reasons for the current crisis, is the tension, if not outright antagonism, between the state-supported production sector and the private exhibition sector. This antagonism goes back to the very beginnings of Brazilian cinema. In the early 1900s producers and exhibitors were normally one and the same. The development of independent distributors drove a wedge between producers and exhibitors, and the exhibition sector began to function almost exclusively for the benefit of foreign cinemas. In the 1930s exhibition groups fought legislation initiating a timid screen quota for Brazilian short films, just as they have fought every attempt to expand the quota until today, arguing for free trade and open markets in opposition to state intervention and manipulation of the rules of the marketplace.

Without a screen quota and other protectionist measures, Brazilian cinema very likely would exist only on the most crass, commercial basis. At the same time state policy toward the film industry has clearly led to a loss of profits for exhibitors and is at least partially responsible for the current decline of the exhibition sector, which is pernicious for the Brazilian film industry as a whole. It is thus a difficult question to deal with, for both sides are obviously correct in their arguments.

The relationship between the state and the exhibition sector deteriorated steadily over the last two decades and especially since the reorientation of state policy toward the industry described above. In 1974 *O Estado de São Paulo* ran an article with the headline "The Great Duel of National Cinema," referring to the duel between exhibitors and state-supported producers as analogous to a Western movie, with the producer as hero, the exhibitor as villain, and the state as sheriff. The "duel" would by 1980 become a "war," fought largely in the courts, as exhibition groups, sometimes in conjunction with distributors, continually filed suit and frequently obtained at least temporary injunctions against various aspects of state policy, especially the compulsory exhibition law (screen quota). In its report for the second half of 1988 Concine lists suits filed by thirty-two exhibition companies (not counting multiple colitigants) representing over 10 percent of the total number of theaters in Brazil (Concine 1989:314–17).

The war between exhibitors and producers was fought not only in the courts but also in the theaters. Jorge Schnitman suggests that, "historically, whenever exhibitors were forced to exhibit a large number of national films, they attempted to produce their own" (1984:67, n. 1). As early as 1971, exhibition groups began joining together to form production companies with the expressed intention of making films to meet the requirements of the compulsory exhibition law. The result was the rash of poor-quality *pornochanchadas* (soft-core sex comedies) that began to flood the reserve market in 1972–73, leaving even less room for more culturally serious films. In the 1980s such production would become even more noxious as the soft-core *pornochanchada* was replaced by hard-core pornography. Table 1 not only indicates the astonishingly high percentage of pornographic films after 1980 but also the nonexistence of independent sources of film production financing and the almost total dependence of the production sector on either exhibitors (i.e., pornography) or the state.

Rather than go into more detail or discuss the merits of exhibitors' arguments, it is important to summarize legislation regarding the exhibition sector to attain an at least partial understanding of its situation. Brazilian cinematic legislation stipulates that exhibitors must show national films at least 140 days per year, regardless of the number of Brazilian films produced in a given year or the quality of those films. Although exhibitors negotiate with distributors of foreign films, they are obligated to pay a minimum of 50 percent of net income for Brazilian films, and they must make payment within fifteen days of exhibition. They must show a national short subject as part of each program of foreign films, purchase standardized tickets and box office income recording sheets from Embrafilme at inflated prices, and keep Brazilian films in exhibition as long as the average of total spectators for two weeks or more equals 60 percent of the previous year's weekly average.

In return, exhibitors have received virtually nothing from the state except the disdain that has long characterized producer's attitudes toward the exhibition sector. Although it was among Embrafilme's attributes to attend to the needs of the sector, it has refused to divert funds from production and has not even provided subsidies or low-interest loans to help them renovate their equipment and theaters. The authoritarian imposition of such unwelcome measures has resulted in a decline in income and an overall deterioration of the sector, which has led to the closing

TABLE 1. Brazilian Film Production, 1978–84

Year	Total	Pornographic	Embrafilme	Others	Percentage Pornographic
1978	100	15	13	72	15
1979	93	07	16	70	08
1980	103	32	18	53	31
1981	80	63	16	01	79
1982	85	59	22	04	69
1983	84	62	18	04	74
1984	90	64	22	04	71

Source: Embrafilme, *Jornal da Tela,* Edição especial ("Proposta para uma política nacional do cinema") (March 1986): 3.

of many theaters, especially in the interior of the country, and to the current crisis of Brazilian cinema. The proof of the failure of state policy toward the exhibition sector—and toward Brazilian cinema as a whole— is the dramatic decline in the number of theaters in operation in the country, now slightly over one thousand for a country of 140 million. Today the only films that can cover costs in such a small market are children's films using popular television stars as actors (Xuxa, Sérgio Malandro, the Trapalhões). State support of the film industry, in short, has had consequences diametrically opposed to its original intention of providing stability for future development.

Conclusion

Cultural policy studies are now in their infancy. For a thorough analysis one would need to examine the functioning of individual state cultural agencies, institutes, enterprises, foundations, and commissions over time and both within the specific contexts of the different political regimes under which they exist and in a comparative framework. This would include an examination of specific programs and activities, budgets, degree of autonomy from the central administration, relationship to the cultural field under consideration, and the primary actors in decision-making positions.

In other words, one would need to analyze the functioning of cultural administration as a whole, its mechanisms of expansion, its relations with a growing clientele, the expansion of its prerogatives, and the actions of its directors. One would also need to examine the modalities and characteristics of its process of recruitment, its place in the hierarchy of public administration, as well as its circles of influence and its social or political affinities with its "clients" in the cultural field (Menger 1983:256–57). All of this varies according to the specific agency and the specific national or regional context involved.

Integrated within the state apparatus, cultural action (or action for or against culture) becomes one of many modes of social regulation that all modern states have at their disposal to guarantee social reproduction. Sociocultural institutions frequently become a terrain—as I have attempted to show in the case of state/cinema relations—for confrontation where different cultural practices contribute to assuring the status of specific social groups, especially those associated with intellectual fractions of the middle class (Rétaine 1983:70–71).

Contradictions similar to those that have affected (and afflicted) state cinematic policy permeate Brazilian cultural policy in general. Since 1930 the Brazilian cartorial/patrimonial state developed an increasingly comprehensive approach to culture, taking under its wing areas ranging from education to sports and leisure and from carnival and popular religion to elite forms of artistic expression, although it is clear that it has attended primarily to the needs of cultural elites. Although it has supported cultural production in different ways, it has done so in such a way as to make the state itself the ultimate site of cultural legitimation. Through its clientelistic co-optation of artists and intellectuals, either through direct employment, as in the 1930s and 1940s, or through the financing or subvention of specific cultural projects, as in the post-1964 period, it has made much cultural production directly dependent on the state.

The state has become, in this sense, what is often called the *Grande Mãe* of Brazilian culture and society. By doing so, it has created a situation of distortions in which the true social role of culture—or, at least, elite culture—is no longer clear, for on the logic of the cultural field per se has been imposed a logic of administrative action and political imperatives. In other words, many fields of cultural expression have ceased to have an autonomous life of their own, and their modes of production, distribution, and consumption have become mediated and bureaucratized by the state.

A reformulation of the Brazilian government's cultural policy and a rethinking of the relationship between culture and the state—in conjunction with a broader discussion of the role of the state in the society—is in order. In reference to France, possibly the most culturally "statist" country in Europe, Jacques Rigaud has suggested that the state should enter only those areas in which no other institution is capable of assuming responsibility. He further suggests that its mode of intervention should have its own disappearance as a goal, creating the conditions for autonomous cultural development (1975:156). After Collor's at least temporary dismantling of the state cultural apparatus, Brazilian culture is faced with the task of redefining both its relationship to the state and its position in the broader field of social relations.

NOTES

1. I am fully aware of the ideological baggage accompanying the widely used term *patrimony*. However, given the fact that much of what has been

preserved through the Brazilian government's "patrimonial" policies reflects the historical experience of dominant, white, male social segments, the term seems exceedingly appropriate.

2. Two examples of state activity in the democratic period should suffice. First, in the preservational area SPHAN, originally created in 1937, was transformed in 1946 into a directorate (Diretoria do Patrimônio Histórico e Artístico Nacional) with four regional subdivisions (Belo Horizonte, Recife, Salvador, and São Paulo) but still under the jurisdiction of the Ministry of Education and the directorship of Rodrigo Melo Franco de Andrade, who headed the agency from 1937 until 1967. This change did not alter its attributes, responsibilities, or functions.

In relation to the film industry, the period between 1945 and 1964 was marked by the formation of a series of commissions designed to make recommendations regarding industry development and the possibilities for state support: Comissão Nacional de Cinema (1951), Comissão Técnica de Cinema (1954), Comissão Federal de Cinema (1956), Grupo de Estudos Cinematográficos (1958), and Grupo Executivo da Indústria Cinematográfica (1961). The first of these commissions, formed, significantly, by Getúlio Vargas and commonly known as the Cavalcânti Commission, developed a proposal for an Instituto Nacional de Cinema but was unable to obtain congressional approval. The institute would finally come into being—by an executive decree of the military regime—in late 1966.

Philipe Schmitter describes such commissions as "institutional devices" used "in keeping with the general propensity for paternalistic corporatism" as a means of co-opting and manipulating certain social sectors. They are "important institutional mechanisms for the capturing of new signals, the drafting of future proposals, and the negotiation of new projects" (1971:255). The existence of these commissions during the 1945–64 period supports the suggestion, made in the next section of this study, concerning the "historical persistence and continuity" of corporative regime types in Brazil from at least 1930 to 1990.

3. Some state cultural agencies in other Latin American countries are the Instituto Nacional de Bellas Artes y Literatura (Mexico, 1946), Instituto Nacional de Cultura e Bellas Artes (Venezuela, 1960), Casa Ecuatoriana de Cultura (Ecuador, 1966), Instituto Cultural Colombiano (Colombia, 1968), and the Instituto Nacional de Cultura (Peru, 1972), among many others. For a description of these and subsequent agencies throughout Latin America, see Herrera 1981:103–26.

4. I borrow the expression "historical persistence and continuity" from the editors of *Bringing the State Back In,* who suggest that "basic patterns of state organization and of the relationships of states to social groups often persist, even through major periods of crisis and attempted reorganization or reorientation of state activities" (Evans et al. 1985:348).

5. I am using the term *state* in concrete, rather than abstract, terms, that is, as an institutional framework—a state apparatus—with very specific characteristics embodying the "historical and social processes that have most influenced the formation of the nation or the society. In this role the state is greater than the sum of regimes over time" (Roett 1972:51). Other analysts have referred to this or similar states as bureaucratic-authoritarian (O'Donnell 1973), as a cartorial state (Jaguaribe 1958), and as a patrimonial state (Roett 1972).

6. Although Viala's study (1985) focuses on the French literary field in the seventeenth century, his discussion of the relationship between writers and the powerful is of obvious relevance to the current study.

7. One could argue that *mécènat* has continued to exist during the period in question in the form of government-sponsored financial awards and prizes (e.g., the Golfinho de Ouro).

8. For an expression of the official line taken toward samba, see Meireles 1942; also Velloso 1987:34–35.

9. The "contest" was won by *O Futuro nos pertence,* written by DIP director Amílcar Dutra de Menezés. For brief comments on this work, see Johnson 1988.

10. The Constitution of 1934 was the first to recognize culture as a legitimate area of governmental concern. Title 5, chapter 2, article 148 states that "Cabe à Uniao, aos Estados e aos Municípios favorecer e animar o desenvolvimento das ciências, das artes, das letras e da cultura em geral, proteger os objetos de interesse histórico e o patrimônio artístico do país, bem como prestar assistência ao trabalhador intelectual."

11. The SNT was created by decree-law 92 and the INL by decree-law 93, both of which were promulgated on December 21, 1937.

12. The Serviço de Radiodifusão, designed as a government broadcasting service, would later be transmuted into Rádio MEC; the INCE, which was created, according to the law which gave it birth, "to promote and orient the utilization of cinematography ... as an auxiliary process of teaching and as a means of education in general," planted the seeds for the future Instituto Nacional do Cinema; SPHAN, charged with the preservation of the national historical and artistic patrimony, existed under slightly different names at least until March 1990; the SNT, formed to subsidize theatrical productions, later became the Instituto Nacional de Artes Cênicas (INACEN); the INL exists until today; and the Conservatório Nacional de Canto Orfeônico later became part of the Instituto Nacional de Música.

13. See, for example, Magalhães 1985:18, 22.

14. On the ELSP see Limongi 1989a; and on USP, see Limongi 1989b. In the former Limongi also notes the predominance, in the creation of the ELSP, of engineers and physicians associated with the Instituto de Organização Racional do Trabalho (IDORT [Institute for the Rational Organization of Labor]), created by Armando de Sales Oliveira and others in 1931, "a society that subscribed to an updated version of F. W. Taylor's scientific management as a solution to Brazil's economic depression" (Love 1980:173; Limongi 1989a:220–21).

15. The complete text of Andrade's *anteprojeto* can be found in Andrade 1981b:39–54.

16. In *Mário de Andrade por ele mesmo,* Paulo Duarte refers to a fifth division, Tourism and Public Diversions, created as a separate division by law 1146. According to act 861, it was to function as a subsection of the Education and Recreation Division (1985:62; see also Dassin 1978:106).

17. For a more detailed account of the department's attributes, see Dassin 1978:106–7.

18. In the 1937 issue of the *Handbook of Latin American Studies,* Paul

Vanorden Shaw wrote that "if there is any real difference between the historical and archival work of the Departamento de Cultura and that done by the ordinary Latin American archivists and archives it lies in the fact that the Departamento de Cultura, though definitely a political organism, has been directed by people who are primarily scholars interested in scholarly work. Though the Historical Section is not a research institution, its two main chiefs [Sérgio Milliet and Nuto Sant'Anna] are research historians who look upon the archive they are organizing from the point of view of the student who wishes to use and handle documents rather than from that of the public official whose main concern is to store the documents away as economically and inaccessibly as possible" (452).

19. The department also sponsored a Contest for Proletarian Furniture, which was apparently opposed by elements of the Left who argued that it was impossible for a proletarian art to flourish under a bourgeois regime. Mário de Andrade, however, understood the proletariat in more complex and diversified terms. In a letter to Murilo Miranda (n.d., 1936), he writes that "to fail to recognize that even in Brazil there exist diverse levels of proletarian life, and that in these levels there are different kinds of furniture, curtains, carpets, radios (even pianos!), is simply . . . a lie" (1981b:33–34).

20. For a discussion of the Estado Novo's attempts to create a "new Brazilian man," see Gomes 1982.

21. Maria Helena Moreira Alves has shown that the military's economic model, developed by national security theorists of the Escola Superior de Guerra, was considerably closer to state capitalism than to laissez-faire capitalism (1985:27).

22. For a description of the proposed "National System of Culture," see Diegues 1976 (esp. 22–23).

23. According to the *Política Nacional de Cultura,* the Brazilian government's cultural policy is founded on a number of basic principles that reflect the historical, social, and spiritual values of the Brazilian people. The document says explicitly that the state role includes support of spontaneous cultural production and in no way implies that the state has the right to direct such production or to in any way impede freedom of cultural or artistic creation. The state's responsibility, in other words, is ostensibly to support and stimulate cultural production, not control it. The document is infused with a nationalist sentiment that is broad enough to include virtually all Brazilian cultural production. It formulates a desire to construct a harmonious "national identity" on a symbolic level based on respect for regional and cultural diversity and the preservation of the nation's cultural and historical patrimony.

24. Geisel's minister of Education and Culture, Ney Braga, made frequent pronouncements on the role of culture as an integral part of development. In "Integração cultural," for example, he affirms that "it is never too much to repeat that development is not a fact of a purely economic nature but rather has a cultural dimension which if not respected will compromise the whole" (1976:10). See also Braga 1975 (esp. 45–49).

25. Maria Helena Moreira Alves has argued that a constant crisis of legitimacy is one of the characteristics of the "national security state" created after 1964:

"because it is unable to eliminate the causes of dissent, and thus to control and contain the opposition, the national security state is haunted by contradictions, which produce a situation of ongoing institutional crisis. In addition, the shifting control mechanisms and the application of physical violence create a gap between the language of legitimation by means of democracy and the reality of oppression. Ultimately, the deep legitimacy crisis that results from this gap, together with the institutional crisis, undermines the stability of the state" (1985:10).

26. Barreto and other producers formulated and presented to Passarinho a five-point program proposing, among other things, the restructuring of Embrafilme (Johnson 1987:150).

27. Velloso, who was an avid film fan and a friend of Cinema Novo veteran Nelson Pereira dos Santos, has explained the Geisel regime's support of the film industry in the following terms: "Our objective was not to make an experimental, formally sophisticated and hermetic type of cinema. Not that that was excluded, but it wasn't our primary objective. We had to make a kind of cinema that really reached the people, a culturally dignified cinema. . . . From the beginning there was an understanding that the government would not culturally restrain anyone. The filmmaker would have artistic freedom to make his film, but at the same time I warned them that although political cinema is certainly legitimate, they should not make a doctrinaire, propagandistic cinema" (in Tendler 1982:164).

28. In this sense, the situation in Brazil has become remarkably similar to that of Mexico. Alberto Ruy Sánchez has convincingly written that state support of the Mexican film industry, sustained by a complex play of personal and political interests, is essentially pernicious, creating a situation in which the film itself is the least important aspect of the industry (1981:46).

29. The evolution of the screen quota was the following: 1932: One short for each program of foreign films; 1939: one feature per year; 1946: three features per year; 1951: one feature for every eight foreign films; 1959: 42 days per year; 1963: 56 days per year; 1969: 63 days per year (provisional); 1970: 77 days per year (provisional); 1970: 112 days per year (not implemented); 1970: 98 days per year (not implemented); 1971: 84 days per year; 1975: 112 days per year; 1978: 133 days per year; 1980: 140 days per year (Johnson 1987:185).

30. Among films financed under the coproduction program were Joaquim Pedro de Andrade's *Macunaíma* (1969), Carlos Diegues's *Os Herdeiros* (1968), and Nelson Pereira dos Santos's *Como era gostoso o meu francês* (1971). For a complete listing, see Johnson 1987:202–4.

31. The texts of the decree-laws that founded and subsequently reorganized Embrafilme and founded Concine are in Mello 1978: vol. 1:11–29, 53–58.

32. See, in the *Folha:* "L. C. Barreto diz que é credor da Embrafilme," March 17, 1986; Renata Rangel, "Co-produção aumenta déficit da Embrafilme," March 18, 1986; "Nova declaração de Massaini," March 18, 1986; "Cineastas pediram o fim da correção," March 19, 1986; Carlos Diegues, "De quem é mesmo o dinheiro da Embra," March 20, 1986; "Calil investe no cultural e comercial," March 21, 1986; Sérgio Santeiro, "O modelo cinematográfico opressor," March 21, 1986; "Furtado quer mudar Embrafilme," March 22, 1986; "Embrafilme

responde à reportagem da *Folha,*" March 23, 1986; Luiz Gonzaga Assis de Luca, "Embrafilme, o consumidor é quem paga," March 23, 1986; "Decreto de Sarney determina o que é o filme brasileiro," March 25, 1986; Sérgio Toledo and Roberto Gervitz, "Embrafilme é um antídoto," March 30, 1986.

33. Cinema Novo veteran Carlos Diegues (*Bye Bye Brasil*), for example, referred to the enterprise as a "cultural Medicaid system that treats cancer with bandaids," and Embrafilme director Carlos Augusto Calil (1985–87) asserted that the state could no longer attempt to substitute for private enterprise and that the existing model was simply no longer viable. Diegues's remark came in an interview to the *Jornal do Brasil,* February 23, 1985, and Calil's in an interview to that same paper on March 23, 1986.

34. In the past, some 15 percent of Embrafilme's capital has been designated for nonprofit cultural activities, creating what many feel to be a financial burden on an enterprise designed to engage in entrepreneurial activities in support of the national industry qua industry.

WORKS CITED

Adonias Filho. 1978. *O Conselho federal de cultura.* Brasília: MEC.

Alves, Maria Helena Moreira. 1985. *State and Opposition in Military Brazil.* Austin: University of Texas Press.

Andrade, Mário de. 1981a. *Cartas a Murilo Miranda: 1934–1945.* Rio de Janeiro: Nova Fronteira.

———. 1981b. *Cartas de trabalho: correspondência com Rodrigo Mello Franco de Andrade (1936–1945).* Brasília: MEC/SPHAN/Fundação Pró-Memória.

Bernardet, Jean-Claude. 1983. "Cinema e Estado." *Folha de São Paulo (Folhetim)* (September 4).

Bourdieu, Pierre, Alain Darbel, and Dominique Schnapper. 1969. *L'amour de l'art: Les musées d'art européens et leur public.* Paris: Editions de Minuit.

Braga, Ney. 1976. "Integração cultural." In *Conclusões do encontro de secretários de cultura: Subsídios para um programa de integração cultural,* 9–11. Brasília: MEC/DAC.

———. 1975. *Política da educação, da cultura, e do desporto.* Brasília: MEC.

Candido, Antônio. 1985. "Prefácio." *Mário de Andrade por ele mesmo,* by Paulo Duarte. São Paulo: Hucitec.

———. 1984. "A Revolução de 1930 e a Cultura." *Novos Estudos CEBRAP* 2, no. 4 (April):27–36.

Cardoso, Fernando Henrique. 1979. "On the Characterization of Authoritarian Regimes in Latin America." In *The New Authoritarianism in Latin America,* ed. David Collier, 33–57. Princeton: Princeton University Press.

Concine. *Relatório de atividades.* 1989. Segundo semestre 1988. Rio de Janeiro.

Conclusões do encontro de secretários de cultura: Subsídios para um programa de integração cultural. 1976. Brasília: MEC/DAC.

Dassin, Joan. 1978. *Política e poesia em Mário de Andrade.* São Paulo: Duas Cidades.

Diegues, Jr., Manuel. 1976. "Regionalização e inter-regionalização da cultura." In *Conclusões do encontro de secretários de cultura: Subsídios para um programa de integração cultural,* 17–23. Brasília: MEC/DAC.

Duarte, Paulo. 1985. *Mário de Andrade por ele mesmo.* São Paulo: Hucitec.

Embrafilme. 1990. *Jornal da Tela.* Edição documento: Embrafilme 20 anos. Rio de Janeiro.

————. 1986. *Jornal da Tela.* Edição especial: "Proposta para uma política nacional do cinema" (March).

Estado e Cultura no Brasil. 1984. Ed. Sérgio Miceli. São Paulo: Difel.

Estado Novo: Ideologia e poder. 1982. Ed. Lúcia Lippi Oliveira, Mônica Pimenta Velloso, and Angela M. C. Gomes. Rio de Janeiro: Zahar Editores.

Evans, Peter. 1979. *Dependent Development: The Alliance of Multinational, State, and Local Capital in Brazil.* Princeton: Princeton University Press.

Evans, Peter B., Dietrich Rueschemeyer, and Theda Skocpol, eds. 1985. *Bringing the State Back In.* Cambridge: Cambridge University Press.

Falcão, Joaquim Arruda. 1984. "Política cultural e democracia: A preservação do patrimônio histórico e artístico nacional." In *Estado e Cultura no Brasil,* ed. Sérgio Miceli. São Paulo: Difel.

Foucault, Michel. 1979. *Discipline and Punish: The Birth of the Prison.* Trans. Alan Sheridan. New York: Vintage Books.

Gomes, Angela Maria de Castro. 1982. "A Construção do homem novo: O trabalhador brasileiro." In *Estado Novo: Ideologia e poder,* ed. Lúcia Lippi Oliveira, Mônica Pimenta Velloso, and Angela M. C. Gomes, 151–66. Rio de Janeiro: Zahar Editores.

Haddab, Mustapha. 1983. "L'Arabisation, L'Islam et les strategies sociales des lettes arabisants en Algerie." In *Stratifications sociales et enjeux culturels dans la société algérienne,* ed. Mustapha Haddab, 1–20. Paris: Centre de Sociologie de l'Education et de la Culture, Ecole des Hautes Etudes en Sciences Sociales.

Hallewell, Laurence. 1982. *Books in Brazil.* Metuchen, N.J.: Scarecrow Press.

Herrera, Felipe. 1981. "Cultural Policies in Latin America and the Caribbean." In *Cultural Development: Some Regional Experiences,* 71–126. Paris: UNESCO Press.

Jaguaribe, Hélio. 1958. *O Nacionalismo na atualidade brasileira.* Rio de Janeiro: Instituto de Estudos Brasileiros.

Johnson, Randal. 1987. *The Film Industry in Brazil: Culture and the State.* Pittsburgh: University of Pittsburgh Press.

————. 1988. "*O Futuro nos pertence. E agora, que fazer?:* The Estado Novo and the Social Relations of Brazilian Literature." Paper presented at the Symposium on Luso-Brazilian Literature: A Socio-Critical Approach, University of Minnesota, October 21–22.

Legislação do Conselho Federal de Cultura. 1976. Brasília: MEC/CFC.

Lévi-Strauss, Claude. 1975. *Tristes Tropiques.* Trans. John and Doreen Weightman. New York: Atheneum.

Lima, Magali Alonso. 1979. *Formas arquiteturais esportivas no Estado Novo (1937–1945): Suas implicações na plástica de corpos e espíritos.* Rio de Janeiro: Funarte.

Limongi, Fernando. 1989a. "A Escola livre de sociologia e política em São Paulo." In *História das ciências sociais no Brasil,* ed. Sérgio Miceli, 1:217–33. São Paulo: Vértice, Editora Revista dos Tribunais, IDESP.

———. 1989b. "Mentores e clientelas da Universidade de São Paulo." In *História das ciências sociais no Brasil,* ed. Sérgio Miceli, 1:111–87. São Paulo: Vértice, Editora Revista dos Tribunais, IDESP.

Love, Joseph L. 1980. *São Paulo in the Brazilian Federation, 1889–1937.* Stanford: Stanford University Press.

Magalhães, Aloísio. 1985. *E Triunfo?: A questão dos bens culturais no Brasil.* Rio de Janeiro: Nova Fronteira.

Marcondes Filho, Alexandre. 1942. "O Governo e os intelectuais." *Cultura Política* 13 (March):7–10.

Martins, Luciano. 1987. "A gênese de uma intelligentsia: Os intelectuais e a política no Brasil, 1920–1940." *Revista Brasileira de Ciências Sociais* 2, no. 4 (June):65–87.

Meireles, Cecília. "Samba e educação." *A Manhã,* January 18, 1942.

Mello, Alcino Teixeira de. 1978. *Legislação do cinema brasileiro.* 2 vols. Rio de Janeiro: Embrafilme.

Menger, Pierre-Michel. 1983. *Le Paradoxe du musicien: Le compositeur, le mélomane, et l'état dans la société contemporaine.* Paris: Flammarion.

Miceli, Sérgio. 1979. *Intelectuais e classe dirigente no Brasil, 1920–1945.* São Paulo: Difel.

———. 1984. "O Processo de 'construção institucional' na área cultural féderal (anos 70)." In *Estado e Cultura no Brasil,* ed. Sergio Miceli, São Paulo: Difel.

———. 1987. "SPHAN: Refrigério da cultural oficial." *Revista do Patrimônio Histórico e Artístico Nacional* 22:44–47.

O'Donnell, Guillermo A. 1973. *Modernization and Bureaucratic Authoritarianism.* Berkeley: Institute of International Studies.

Oliveira, Lúcia Lippi. 1982. "As Raízes da Ordem: Os intelectuais, a cultura e o estado." In *A Revolução de 30: Seminário internacional,* 505–26. Brasília: Editora Universidade de Brasília.

Ortiz, Renato. 1985. *Cultura brasileira e identidade nacional.* São Paulo: Brasiliense.

Paz, Octavio. 1979. *El Ogro filantópico: Historia y política, 1971–1978.* Mexico City: Juan Mortiz.

Pécaut, Daniel. 1986. *Les Intellectuels au Brésil: De la construction de la société à celle de la démocratie.* Vol. 3 of *Le Role politique des intellectuels en Amérique Latine.* Paris: Centre d'Etude des Mouvements Sociaux. Portuguese language edition (1989): *Os intelectuais e a política no Brasil.* São Paulo: Atica.

Pedro, Antônio. 1980. "Samba da legitimidade." M.A. thesis, Universidade de São Paulo.

Ramos, José Mário Ortiz. 1983. *Cinema, estado e lutas culturais.* Rio de Janeiro: Paz e Terra.

Rigaud, Jacques. 1975. *La Culture pour vivre.* Paris: Gallimard.

Rétaine, Evelyne. 1983. *Les Strategies de la culture.* Paris: Presses de la Fondation Nationale des Sciences Politiques.

Roett, Riordan. 1972. *Brazil: Politics in a Patrimonial Society.* Boston: Allyn and Bacon.

Salla, Dalton. 1988. "O Serviço do patrimônio histórico e artístico nacional: História oficial e Estado Novo." M.A. thesis, Escola de Comunicações e Artes, Universidade de São Paulo.

Sánchez, Alberto Ruy. 1981. *Mitología de un cine en crisis.* Mexico City: Premia.

Sandroni, Carlos. 1988. *Mário contra Macunaíma: Cultura e política em Mário de Andrade.* São Paulo: Vértice.

Schild, Susana. 1986. "Embrafilme, um modelo falido." *Jornal do Brasil* (March 23).

Schmitter, Philipe C. 1971. *Interest, Conflict and Political Change in Brazil.* Stanford: Stanford University Press.

Schnitman, Jorge. 1984. *Film Industries in Latin America: Dependency and Development.* Norwood, N.J.: Ablex.

Shaw, Paul Vanorden. 1938. "The Division of Historical Documentation of the Department of Culture of the Municipality of São Paulo, Brazil." In *The Handbook of Latin American Studies,* ed. Lewis Hanke, 450–55. Cambridge: Cambridge University Press.

Skidmore, Thomas E. 1967. *Politics in Brazil, 1930–1964: An Experiment in Democracy.* New York: Oxford University Press.

Stepan, Alfred. 1978. *State and Society: Peru in Comparative Perspective.* Princeton: Princeton University Press.

Stratifications sociales et enjeux culturels dans la société algérienne. 1983. Ed. Mustapha Haddab. Paris: Centre de Sociologie de l'Education et de la Culture, Ecole des Hautes Etudes en Sciences Sociales.

Tendler, Sílvio. 1982. "Cinema e estado: Em defesa do miúra." M.A. thesis, Pontifícia Universidade Católica, Rio de Janeiro.

Velloso, Mônica Pimenta. 1987. *Os Intelectuais e a política cultural do Estado Novo.* Rio de Janeiro: CPDOC, Fundação Getúlio Vargas.

Viala, Alain. 1985. *Naissance de l'écrivain.* Paris: Editions de Minuit.

Wiarda, Howard J. 1981. *Corporatism and National Development in Latin America.* Boulder: Westview Press.

The Function of the Form: Power Play and Ritual in the 1988 Mexican Presidential Campaign

Larissa Adler Lomnitz,
Claudio Lomnitz Adler,
and Ilya Adler

This essay presents some findings and ideas that are suggested by an ethnographic study of the 1988 presidential campaign of the Partido Revolucionario Institucional (PRI) of Mexico. In the pages that follow we will discuss the fundamental elements of the organization of public acts of the Salinas campaign as well as their possible origins and reasons.[1] Much of the recent literature on politics and elections in Mexico suggests that the country is at a crossroads. One path is to democratize and abolish the corporatist, or "traditional" authoritarian, forms of politics; the other is to maintain a system that has been described as "presidentialist" corporatist, or authoritarian, and which is already very decrepit and destined for extinction.

These notions are shared by a wide spectrum of political society: they may be found in the modernizing ideas of President Carlos Salinas de Gortari, in the Liberal criticism of the PAN (Partido de Accíon Nacional), as well as in important sectors of *neocardenismo* and the Left. According to this view, Mexico today has a more educated population, which no longer supports nor seeks a corporatist government or a populist, paternalist ideology. The Mexican people demand democracy, and the crisis has weakened the material capacity of the system to co-opt or repress this demand.

Nevertheless, traditional Mexican political culture is still firmly rooted as much in the political practice of the parties as it is in the attitudes and actions of the population in general. This fact must be understood and taken into account in order to carry out a successful democratic transformation. Our intention in this essay is to present some aspects of this traditional system, as we have been able to observe it in the public acts of the presidential campaign of the Partido Revolucionario Institucional of 1988.

The Role of the Presidential Campaign in the Mexican Political System

We focus on the campaign as a privileged place for understanding Mexican political culture because it has been a crucial arena for the reproduction of the Mexican political system, even in periods in which there was no serious competition between political parties. This crucial arena, which we analyze below, is responsible for the ritualized organization of the campaign, since the campaigns occupy—like the famous rites of passage explored by Arnold Van Genneph and developed theoretically and substantially by Victor Turner[2]—gray areas, border lines, potentially disruptive of the social order.

The Mexican political system has been, until now, essentially a one-party system.[3] Nevertheless, the party includes a great diversity of groups and organizations, which, in turn, generate leaders with different ideologies and interests. The only way to guarantee that each group represented in the PRI gets a position in the government has been to use the principle of non-reelection of the president combined with an extremely presidentialist system. Mexican presidentialism guarantees that a great quantity of posts will change hands every six years (*sexenio*),[4] in such a way that groups that do not get access in one *sexenio* may wait in the hope of entering during the next period.

Not everything changes, however, when a new candidate is designated. The continuity of the PRI is based not only on agreements between diverse groups in which each "waits his turn and his place." The continuity of the system has also been guaranteed by the fact that politicians are divided into two kinds: the men and women "of the system" and those tied directly to the president and his team (*equipo*).[5] Thus, when the new candidate appears on the scene he cannot simply appoint his personal supporters to important posts in the government: he must also appoint PRI supporters who can negotiate and maintain the support of less-favored political groups and also of PRI supporters who have control over important segments of the population. He also needs people who have expertise in certain specialized technical and political areas.

Understanding the distinction between "system men" and the "President's men" is fundamental to understanding presidential strategy. System men, who are always subject to the disciplinary rigors of the changes that come at the end of each *sexenio* are indispensable for presidential transitions and administrative continuity. They are the key means of communication between the incoming president and groups excluded from his immediate circle. Likewise, the number of places taken by the president's men are a sign of the president's own strength and of the political space he hopes to dominate.

At the same time, this type of analysis is made difficult by the fact that these categories—which were suggested in different forms in our interviews—do not exist as a fixed part of the political vocabulary. This fact permits a certain flexibility in the presentation of the different personalities in question: from the very beginning all president's men are publicly presented as system men: capable experts, seasoned public servants, and people with "party discipline."[6] For their part, system men try to achieve a closer relationship with the incoming president and may come to identify themselves with the new regime, at which point their status as system men is undermined. Looking from a more long-term perspective, one can observe the tendency for president's men to convert themselves into system men, at the time that the president is about to name his successor, as well as a countertendency for system men to emphasize their close relationship to the successor once he has been selected.

In the campaign of 1988 analysis of the events by the media and by the "political class"[7] took into account the existence, position, and disposition of these distinct types of politicians: it was commented in certain circles that the candidate was not able to select a campaign cabinet strictly of his choosing and that some principal positions had gone to those known to be system men. This was generally interpreted as revealing the weakness of the candidate and his need for support from other sectors of the party.[8] Nevertheless, when they tried to analyze the cabinet of the new president, some of the same analysts commented that many of the key posts ended up being held by president's men, leaving a second circle of system men. To explain the situation of a system man within one of the campaign's acts, our interviews generally emphasized his technical knowledge of the area he administered or his capacity to negotiate with groups distant to the candidate.

This method of analyzing distinct types of politicians is not the same as the traditional distinction between "politicians" and "experts," or "technocrats" (*técnicos*), since there are politicians and technocrats among both system men and president's men. The distinction technocrat and

politician is linked with the internal transformations of the state bureaucracy and thus is related to the government's handling of economic
policy and social forces. In contrast, the distinction between system men
and president's men reveals a tension between the politicians and technocrats who have a personal relationship with the president (of familiarity, friendship, or proven loyalty) and those politicians and technocrats
who do not have this kind of relationship with the president.

Because the president cannot be reelected, an internal split develops
between politicians and bureaucrats associated with the government.
With each *sexenio* new president's men surface, and relationships between
bureaucrats (and those who wish to be bureaucrats) and the highest
circles of state power are redrawn. The main part of the dramatic tension
of the *destape,* or selection of a new presidential candidate, is caused,
without a doubt, by the expectation of the fragmentation and reorganization of relations and positions of power. Usually, a large part of the
activity of the candidate in the campaign is directed at consolidating his
"group" (president's men) and negotiating positions and agreements with
system men.

On the other hand, the distinction between technocrats and politicians
sometimes does coincide with the distinction between system men and
president's men, since the president's men seek to form the policies of
the new government and leave its administration to system men. A well-
known example of this situation on a grand scale is the fragmentation
of the Ministry of the Treasury (Hacienda) and the creation of the
Secretary of the Presidency (now Programming and Budget). In this
transformation of the government's organizational chart, the space for
technocrats and system men in the treasury ministry was defined, and
the power of president's men was enhanced in the political and economic
setting under each president.[9] But note that the split between the ministries of the Treasury and Programming and Budget (or Presidency, as
it was known before) is not, strictly speaking, a split between politicians
and technocrats but, rather, a split between technocrats of the system
(administrators) and technocrats of the presidency (technocrats who make
policy). In sum, the distinction between president's men and system men
is directly tied to the exercise of power, while that of technocrat versus
politician is related with the kind of relationship of power that is established. For this reason, political scientists (notably Peter Smith and
Roderic Camp) have been concerned mainly with the ways in which
politicians are recruited: the exercise of power depends upon personal

relations. In contrast, the decision to put a technocrat or a politician in any given post depends upon which type of bureaucracy a president seeks to create (a decision that depends on economic and political considerations as well).[10]

While the president is still a candidate, the president's men are a vertical and horizontal net of subordinates and allies who ascend with him. These president's men form the major portion of the "campaign cabinet" and later occupy many of the principal ministries and top positions in parastatal enterprises. If the candidate is able to become a strong president, these president's men may very well succeed the president.[11] Each new candidate, however, must represent interest groups different from those of the previous president, since the ideology and social politics of the government may be, and frequently has been, transformed between *sexenios.*

The stability of the PRI regime has depended on this dynamic between system men and president's men (recall that this dichotomy includes the important category of those aspiring to enter or reenter the bureaucracy by way of their personal relationships with the president or with president's men). The catharsis created by the process of naming the PRI candidate (which includes aspirants to political positions) reveals this phenomenon with eloquence. This fracturing and internal recomposition of the bureaucracy—with all of the stress placed upon personal relationships and bureaucratic rationality—has been the very peculiar formula by which the PRI regime has guaranteed change within continuity: the PRI is one of the few political parties that can be called "audaciously traditional," "traditionally revolutionary," or, as it is known, "institutionally revolutionary."

In this light presidential succession has to be seen as an especially dangerous period for the system. It is the time when, at first, the power of the departing president is the greatest, at the designation of a successor. Further, it is a period of a relative power vacuum in that the designation of a successor marks the beginning of the fall of the departing president at a time when the candidate himself is not yet in power (a politically risky situation). In addition, the succession generates a process of renegotiation of positions within the PRI and the government, a process that must be successful to guarantee the continuity of the system. Finally, succession within the PRI is risky because (as happened in 1988) it can lead to the fragmentation of the party and demands for elections as a real alternative to the process of selecting a PRI candidate.

These three situations make the campaign a series of highly ritualized events that represent the drama of power in the Mexican political system: the acts of the campaign are places where the drama of presidential power is acted out. Moreover, conflicts and alliances that undergirded the old (and which will sustain the new) regime are ignited; the technocratic rules and myths of the national political system (the internal organization of the party, of the government, of the representation of these organizations and their origin myths) are affirmed; the president's image is constructed; and the forces that "move the country" find their expression. In this essay we will explore each of these aspects of the rituals of the campaign.

The Campaign of 1988 and the Structure of PRI Campaigns

The election campaign of 1988 unofficially began in October of 1987 and ended on July 6, 1988. In terms of our analysis of the campaign as ritual, the campaign is composed of a series of separate stages, each one made up of one or more rituals that are complete in and of themselves. Because no publications exist that permit us to develop a theoretical framework of the historical evolution of the stages of the campaign, we will center our description on the stages as they exist today and as they were organized for the 1988 campaign. Many of these stages— all of the principal ones—are common to the presidential campaigns following that of Lázaro Cárdenas (1934). In contrast, some of the minor stages are more recent innovations, which generally serve to bolster the general structure of the event. In this section we discuss the general organization of the stages of the campaign and not the internal structure of the discrete rituals that comprise each stage.

The first phase is that of the selection of the aspirant to PRI candidacy (which is, in reality, effectively the selection of the PRI candidate). In this period, whose duration is the object of political struggle, the declarations of the president, of leaders of sectors, trade unions, and businesses, and of public opinion leaders are all interpreted within a framework of "futurism," that is, with an eye to possible future presidential candidates. As with rituals of transitions, this first phase is marked by the establishment of an analysis of the situation of the country and its problems, which will be resolved by the selection of a candidate. This problem or situation is always a balance sheet of the present state of the country, which the new president will rectify. Analyses of "the problem" that the new president will solve are therefore also read as subtle allusions to the precandidates. If "the problem" is economic in nature, the candidate that analysts will favor will be an economic advisor. If the problem is order, he will belong to the Ministry of Government (Gobernacion). If the problem is to regain business confidence, he will be from the Right, and so forth. Along with this interpretive activity, which is played out in the media, this first stage is also marked by a large number of meetings of different sectors, by intense activity in ministries whose leaders are eligible to be candidates (candidatables), and by a great quantity of forums of discussion, organized above all by the Instituto de Estudios Politicos y Sociales (Institute of Political and Social Studies, IEPES). Together these activities prepare the terrain for the unbridled activity of the campaign.

The second moment of the cycle of rituals is the selection of the precandidate. This is the point of greatest drama and emotion, since out of all the possible candidates one is finally chosen, and then it becomes clear which positions will be occupied by which members of the political class in the next *sexenio*. It is understood who will make up the president's inner circle, which political groups will be completely out of power, and who will have to be negotiated with for key positions. This second moment occurs with the *destape,* the selection of a precandidate for the party. Although the style of the *destape* has varied significantly in different elections, in general terms the system consists of an announcement of support for the candidacy of a certain minister by one sector of the PRI, followed by similar announcements by the other sectors, trade unions, and different organizations within the PRI. In the case of the *destape* of 1988, this stage occurred in new ways.

The third stage is the precampaign. Here begins the fever of support and efforts by politicians to situate themselves on the side of the new candidate. There is a flood of propaganda from different groups in support of the new precandidate, at the same time that the central apparatus of the party (which now passes to the control of the pre-candidate) still lacks guidelines for the forms of propaganda as well as for the spirit of the campaign. The precampaign is also marked by a series of rituals of democracy: the official voting, in which the party converts the precandidate into the candidate; the semblance of "spon-taneous" enthusiasm for the candidate on the part of sectors and people who had supported other aspiring precandidates prior to the *destape;* and so forth.

In addition, in this precampaign stage the precandidate is building his *equipo,* or close circle of advisors, and begins to give them key positions in his campaign organization: as director of IEPES, director of information and publicity, director of logistics, and president and secretary of the PRI. In principle, these people are the president's men and will occupy many of the most powerful positions in the next *sexenio* (if things develop as planned in the campaign).

Finally, for the fourth stage there is what is formally called the campaign. This begins after a party ritual in which the state delegates officially ratify the candidacy of the precandidate. In this stage the National Executive Committee of the PRI and the IEPES together determine much of the organization, messages, and style of the campaign. They provide central themes of the campaign, regional strategies, and problems for discussion in the IEPES. The types of activities that define the campaign are the following: meetings of the Centros de Estudios Politicos, Economicos y Sociales (CEPES), and of IEPES; acts of partisan support; dialogues with special groups (farmers, business leaders, regional groups, miners, Indian groups, etc.); televised debates (which began with this past campaign), also carried by radio; and fairs and festivals. Through these different events, which generally determine the route of the candidate's regional trips, the state and groups, classes, and regions of the country come together in a series of concertations. At the same time the image of the country, and of the PRI, is revitalized.

If we consider the organization of the campaign through a wide-angle lens, we note above all two principal axes: campaign trips to the states and discussions of great national problems. The public for the first is basically regional, although the entire country has access to campaign materials through the media; the public of the second is explicitly national and is interested in general problems.

The fourth stage of the campaign centers on grand "closures of the campaign" in each state and the final closure, in the central plaza in Mexico City, in a crusade to get out the vote. This is the end of the campaign, and the stages that follow are not the object of study here. After the campaign come the elections. Frequently, this stage has been a simple formal ratification of what is already known to everyone and, in these cases, can be seen as another of the "democratic rituals" that occur throughout nearly all of the stages of the campaign. The insistence upon democratic forms permeates almost all of the stages of the campaign. The use of these forms generally serves to legitimate decisions that have already been made and at the same time are indispensable for the legitimacy of the traditional process.

These comments notwithstanding, in 1988 the contest for the presidency was a real competition, and therefore the phase of elections was, for the most part, marked by additional tensions reflected in the range of policies and declarations seeking to reaffirm confidence in clean elections, in the absence of fraud or pressure from the federal government, and so forth. It is as if, in the history of presidential campaigns, democracy has mostly appeared as a mere formal requirement of the legal system or of international relations, while at other times (or for other people) it appears as a sign of democratic longings (of a duty postponed) that, until now, has never been fulfilled in Mexico, at least not on the national level.

After the elections the political system enters a new phase. The winning candidate continues forming his plans for the new government and (silently) organizing his team. The winning candidate also influences the policies of the departing president, who, in turn, attempts to complete the principal projects of his government. The ritual process of the campaign concludes with the exchange of power. Now ambiguity over the real place of power ends, and a new period of national history begins. This same day the new president officially names his cabinet, which provides the final confirmation of the places different groups and persons have achieved in the new regime.

The 1988 campaign will surely be remembered as the most difficult that the PRI has undergone since its creation in 1929. Economic crises undermined the bases of the party's social consensus and its ability to co-opt. There was a split in the party, and the selection process for the presidency marginalized important sectors. The 1988 campaign also was remarkable for the expression of reformism and "modernization" on the part of the PRI candidate, Carlos Salinas de Gortari: the weakening that the party suffered due to the crisis was augmented by the distance between the candidate and some of the oldest leaders and members of the party. For these reasons it is important to note, although briefly, some aspects of the historical development of this campaign before entering into an analysis of the meaning of the rituals.

Perhaps due to the demands of the Frente Democrático (a dissident wing of the PRI led by Porfirio Muñoz Ledo and Cuauhtémoc Cárdenas, who later left the PRI and allied himself with a group of opposition parties) or perhaps because of the institutionalist and legalistic spirit of President De la Madrid, the PRI decided to modify its traditional strategy for selecting the presidential candidate. Instead of having one sector nominate a precandidate and the rest follow in support, the PRI named six official precandidates, and each of them publicly announced a political platform he would follow if he were selected as the candidate. In order to safeguard the special quality of the president's vote in choosing his successor, leaders were pressured to avoid revealing their preferences among the precandidates.[12] This appeal for silence about the political sympathies of leaders of sectors, confederations, and trade unions in the *destape* of the precandidate made the role of the president in naming his successor more obvious than ever. In this succession not even the leaders of the sectors seemed to know for certain who the PRI's candidate for the presidency would be.[13]

As a result, when the candidacy of Salinas was announced, he found himself in a weak situation within the party, since the sectors had used up their energies in making diverse alliances with the six official precandidates as an insurance policy.[14] The Corriente Democrática definitively separated from the PRI and formed an alliance opposing it, which eventually gained a great deal of popular support. Aside from these problems, Salinas's political position was strongly identified with the economic policies of the government of De la Madrid, associated in the minds of the majority with the most difficult period of the economic crisis.

The Salinas campaign thus had to gain strength within the negotiations of the campaign. Since his inaugural speech, Salinas has delineated what he considered to be the four principal challenges his government would confront: the poor economy, sovereignty, social problems, and democracy. Salinas dedicated himself to specifying and reformulating these grand objectives as the campaign transpired.

At the start of each campaign the candidate's team chooses a slogan and works on a logo that will represent its political line. The slogan of President Miguel De la Madrid, for example, who campaigned in a period of great disillusionment with politics because of the previous government's corruption and ineptitude, was "The Moral Renewal of Society" (*La Renovacíon Moral de la Sociedad*); that of López Portillo, who succeeded Echeverría's populist government, which had alienated business, was "Together, We Are the Solution" (*La Solución Somos Todos*);

and Echeverría, inventor of the grandest slogans, tried to rebuild alliances between the lower and middle classes after the repression of 1968 with the famous refrain "Straight Ahead" (*Arriba y Adelante*).

At the start of the Salinas campaign the slogan "Modern Politics" was used as a sign for the deepening of the economic and political policies of De la Madrid, increasing the international competitiveness of the Mexican economy, reducing the participation of the state in the mixed economy, and solidifying the system of parties and the strength of the legislative branch. Later, and perhaps as a result of the disorder that the concept of modernization caused the campaign, the slogan "Modern Politics" was replaced by "Let Mexico Speak," and the campaign was organized into a continuing series of "dialogues" between Salinas and representatives of different sectors and regions.

This slogan pointed to the need to go to the people after six years of crisis and began to be used in the campaign without any specific promises by Salinas. In effect, during the first months of the campaign Salinas insisted upon integrity with respect to his relationship to the then current president, and, perhaps for this reason, he did not respond to the party's pleas for concrete plans but simply continued affirming his good intentions.[15] Nevertheless, later Salinas decided to differentiate his position from that of the president, and he made a "declaration of independence" in Tlaxcala during the month of January.[16] From this point onward campaign tactics changed, and Salinas made a series of concrete commitments in the dialogues he held all over the country. These agreements were extremely important, since they demonstrated to members of the PRI that the candidate understood their problems and intended to solve them, even though in that particular moment he lacked the resources to do so.

In the final phases of the campaign the walls and billboards of the Salinas campaign were not only saying "Let Mexico [or Puebla or Yucatán] Speak," but they were also listing the concrete statements and promises that the candidate had made at different moments in his campaign travels. These statements and promises were taken by the campaign managers in each state and municipal district and turned into campaign publicity material. In the last few months of the campaign Salinas also made various speeches of special, ideological importance in which he spelled out in clear and specific terms the policies his government would follow—about the international debt, welfare spending, taxes and tariffs, the environment, education, parastatals, and democracy.

All of this process of change and accommodation was carried out through a long series of acts destined for the general public or restricted to particular groups that were directed by the party. We now turn to consider the nature of these acts and examine the candidate's campaign trips in general terms, since they help us trace a map of political society as perceived by the Mexican government and the PRI. Our description is taken from four different points of view: that of the public, which attended the rallies (as listeners and/or participants); the nature of the discourse used in these rallies; the "atmosphere" created at these gatherings; and the complementarity between any specific act and the group of acts as a whole.

Public Acts and Their Interpretations: The Triumph of Negotiation

Political scientists emphasize the differences between a democratic system and one that is corporatist or authoritarian. This contrast operates above all on the organizational level: the structure of the parties, the relationship between the party of the government, the relationship between corporatist groups and the government, the relationship between executive power and other authorities. Here we focus on the other side of the coin: the contrast between political systems founded on individualism ("democracy") where social representation is based on the sovereignty of the individual (through the vote and rights) as opposed to political systems based on what Louis Dumont calls "hierarchy,"[17] in which a vision of society as a complete organism prevails, composed of segments related in a hierarchical manner, and in which forms of representation are the product of negotiation between segments or persons who are recognized as having distinct natures. Our thesis is that the so-called traditional political system is a unique creation of the Mexican Revolution, which makes it possible to combine a hierarchical system with an individual one. This articulation privileges negotiation among diverse social groups over sovereignty of the individual (and of the law).

The idea that Mexican society lives a contradiction between democracy (individualism) and corporatism (holism, hierarchy) has been developed in a variety of ways by different authors. Among historians, Richard Morse has been one of the first to develop these ideas. He argues that the unification of Spain was achieved under the sign of the political philosophy of Saint Thomas Aquinas.[18] In these arrangements—an operative legal system created by Spanish neoscholasticism—the kingdom was composed of a group of diverse social segments, each with its own nature and area of autonomy. Social diversity was unified at the level of the king, so that each segment had a place within the whole. In scholastic philosophy the ideas of goodness and beauty are directly related to the notion of harmony: each thing has its place and its function within the whole. To occupy this place, to understand this function, is the essence of "the good," and to appreciate the harmony between the functions is beauty.[19] That is, the Spanish neo-Tomist state was a whole, dependent upon divine grace, which gave to each social segment a position specific to it that was proper and good. The operation of this political and cultural system has been explored in recent years by a number of historians.[20]

Before continuing with this historical argument about democracy and holism in Mexico, a socioanthropological interlude is necessary. The idea of hierarchical society comes principally from Louis Dumont, who laid out general characteristics of hierarchy as a concept in his monumental work on castes in India and who has since dedicated himself to tracing the development of individualism in the West. In addition, it is important to note that the contrast between holistic societies and modern democracies has been developed in various ways by a number of writers who, since Alexis de Tocqueville, have dedicated themselves to understanding medieval Europe and the beginnings of capitalism (e.g., Johan Huizinga, Norbert Elias, and Max Weber).

Dumont's suggestions with respect to hierarchical culture have influenced studies of the Socialist "totalitarian" state (cf. Claude Lefort and Cornelius Castoriadis),[21] and in recent years they have begun to have an impact on scholars of Latin America. Still, Latin American societies appear as a problem—since the majority are neither hierarchical (in Dumont's sense) nor individualistic societies. Thus, for example, in her works on the informal sector and the national bourgeoisie in the Mexican economy, Larissa Lomnitz has shown that there exists a kind of "moral economy" among modern classes in Mexico that parallels the kind of moral economy of traditional sectors (such as the peasantry or the aristocracy).[22] This type of conclusion has been affirmed in many case studies of modern sectors in Mexico.

Likewise, in his work on the national rituals of Brazil Roberto DaMatta concludes that Brazil is a society in which two types of sociability (as well as two types of discourse) compete: a "relational" discourse (holistic, hierarchical), which has the house and the family as its social reference point; and an individualistic and impersonal discourse, which takes "the street" as the source of its rhetoric.[23] DaMatta centers attention on the many points at which these two logics meet and the holistic system subverts and ultimately dominates, or at least degrades, the individualistic system. Faced with the hindrance of a law, two Brazilians negotiate a way out (*"um jeitinho"*); in the atmosphere of social equality produced by the anonymity of the street, a Brazilian says to another, "Do you know with whom you are speaking?" (*"¿voce sabe com quem esta falando?"*)

Likewise, the social anthropology of Latin America has begun to discover forms that coexist alongside and interpenetrate the relationships and social values rooted in Iberian culture, and the social relationships that, in theory, should better correspond to the requirements of production of capitalism as well as those of the international political system.

Inspired in good measure by the ethnographic descriptions of the moral economies (and the nondemocratic "sociability") of today's Mexico, François Xavier Guerra produced an important book on the "old regime" (the prerevolutionary regime).[24] Here Guerra, the first historian in Mexico to use Dumont's work, explicitly develops a minutely detailed portrait of society in the Porfiriato. He shows that in the Mexico of this era there existed "collective actors" (villages, haciendas, the church, the armies) forged from certain types of social relations (parenthood, *compadrazgo*—a system of artificially imposed kinship—friendship, loyalty). On the other hand, these collective actors—whose force, as Guerra shows, accounts for the absence of free elections throughout the nineteenth century—and the whole social order forged by them were subverted by new forms of sociability linked to liberal ideology: the *fraternité* and democracy of the political clubs, of masonry and the trade unions. Despite the fact that the Díaz regime (like that of Juárez and Lerdo) was founded upon an articulation of these two types of social organization, the very stability and development achieved by the Porfiriato caused an expansion of individualistic forms of sociability, which ended up undermining the control that Díaz exercised over social groups in the country.

Nevertheless, it may be problematic to describe the Porfiriato as the old regime, as Guerra does, since the problem of the articulation of holism (corporatism) and democracy can be found at the roots of the formation of the official political party of Mexico, the PRI, and survives to the present.

Some of the confusion arises because concepts such as "hierarchy" and "corporatism" are easily reified. It is true that some nineteenth-century "corporations" were eliminated by industrialization or the "institutionalization of the Mexican revolution." Guerra shows how capitalist investment in agriculture undermined traditional patron-client relations on Mexican haciendas, which eventually stopped functioning as "collective actors." A wealth of ethnographic studies demonstrates how many villages were changed into heterogeneous social entities that no longer function as "closed communities."[25] Moreover, it is possible that recent events in Mexico represent a tendency toward the dissolution of trade union corporatism. Nonetheless, traditional forms of sociability and their relation to economy and politics in Mexico have not disappeared. New corporations (pressure groups, professional associations, neighborhood associations, political groups, etc.) can surface, built upon the old principles of personal relations, loyalty, friendship, and kinship. This is what Lomnitz maintains in her work on "vertical" and "horizontal" relations in Mexico.[26]

So, on the one hand, we have an individualistic, democratic ideology that has not dominated Mexican political ideology since the nineteenth century, allied with the capitalist relations of production and the free market (promoted by different sectors in Mexico at different moments). But the tragedy of the democratic-individualist system is that it has never managed to impose itself completely on the system.[27] On the other hand, we have a system of social relations in Mexico that undermines the free competition of the market, equality before the law and democracy. The tragedy of the latter has been that it has never found a political ideology capable of giving this system of social relations a legitimate place in the political order.

Instead, there has been a series of accommodations between democratic-liberal ideology and "practical relations" (to use DaMatta's term). This is as visible in "Liberal" regimes of the past century as in the structure of postrevolutionary regimes or in the discourse and practice of *neocardenismo*. The party and its system of sectors are historical forms of this accommodation between Liberalism and holism. At the same time these accommodations are always contradictory, since their legitimacy is based on consent, not on law, and depends upon the capacity of the regime to give each sector and group a place of its own. This capacity has decayed notably since the onset of economic decline in 1982, a situation that has strengthened the position of liberalism in the Mexican economy, without constituting a fully Liberal political solution. Thus, we find ourselves in a situation very similar to that of the *Porfiriato;* changes in the economic system are in contradiction with the system of organization of power.[28]

Bearing the preceding arguments in mind, let us turn to examine the public events of the campaign. In Mexican politics actions are scarce, while interpretations proliferate. Our analysis of the rituals of the campaign will amply document this syndrome, and explain its reason for being and its profound importance.

Let us begin with concrete examples. In a recent study Gómez-Tagle provides data on the election of deputies in the last three national votes.[29] After examining cases in which the opposition raised charges of fraud, Gómez-Tagle concludes that:

1. There was definitely electoral fraud on the part of the PRI in some districts.
2. Nonetheless, this could not be proved before the electoral commission.
3. Despite the fact that the fraud was not proved, the electoral commission recognized irregularities in some cases and declared the elections invalid.
4. These annulments, which gave victory to the opposition, did not come as a result of direct pressure applied in particular electoral districts but, rather, from a general negotiation among all the parties.
5. In many cases of apparent irregularity on the part of the PRI, these did not seem to be necessary for the party's triumph; that is, fraud was carried out in cases in which the PRI would have triumphed anyway.

These findings coincide with those in our interviews, and it is worth dwelling on them for the moment. It is as difficult to document pressure or fraud by the PRI as to refute the legitimacy of accusations of fraud.[30] This would place the opposition parties (and the PRI candidates against their own party) in closed-door negotiations. The PAN, for example, cannot demand that its candidates be allowed to win in *x, y,* or *z* district. It can only pressure and negotiate for these victories. The PRI member of Congress who wins a seat cannot present his victory as a personal achievement; he or she must recognize that the debt is to the party (implying that it is necessary to establish relative positions for future negotiations). Thus, in the electoral process a system of accountability and verification of votes exists to guarantee that interpretations prevail over facts, and that negotiations prevail over the rights of individuals.

Another example of the importance of interpretation (and its link to political negotiation) is the role campaign rituals play in negotiations between the candidate and various leaders and sectors. All the public acts of the campaign contain symbolic expressions of conflict, alliance, and solutions to conflict: where the leaders sit with respect to the candidate; the speeches of leaders and candidate; the presence or absence of specific persons in the discussion of certain topics. All these may be interpreted in terms of the alliances and relations between the candidate and different national groups of the country.

In the 1988 campaign much of the interpretation generated around the campaign rituals came from the conflict between the group that supported the candidate and various traditional sectors of the party, such as the Confederacion de Trabajadores de Mexico (CTM) and the oil workers. These conflicts, which stemmed from the fact that Licenciado Salinas de Gortari was not the candidate of the workers' sector,[31] were expressed and "resolved" in diverse ways throughout the campaign. The CTM was late in sending its congratulations to the candidate after the *destape*. Fidel Velázquez was absent from the ceremony in which the party named Salinas the official candidate; he attended the closing ceremony of the Congress of the Oil Workers union instead. Hernández Galicia (alias "La Quina") gave speeches of support, which were interpreted as "aggressive" and only much later were reinterpreted as giving a clear "signal" (not so clear in the end) of support for Salinas de Gortari.[32] The lists of candidates for both houses of the Congress, which the PRI presented, were interpreted as being the result of negotiations between Salinas and the political groups within the party. The presence of TV stars in many of the PRI ceremonies was interpreted as part of the logistical support of the television consortium to the Salinas campaign—and not as spontaneous support by the stars. When conciliatory signals were given as part of the rituals themselves (e.g., the active presence of the oil workers in the campaign in Veracruz or speeches of support for Salinas given by Fidel Velázquez or by business groups) there was speculation about private negotiations having taken place prior to the ritual in which what had been agreed upon was formalized.

We have argued that in Mexican politics facts dissolve into interpretations. Moreover, the importance of these interpretations rests on the way in which they permit the construction of a system of political representation based upon negotiation—instead of the abstract rights of each individual—even at the highest levels.

These processes of negotiation, which take a privileged role in the campaigns (within the party) and in the elections (between parties), illuminate particular aspects of the problem of holism versus individualism in Mexico. If we return to DaMatta's work on Brazil, we find a pattern in which the world of relationships subverts the normative-legal order at the lower levels, at the roots of the system. The *jeitinho* and the *voçe sabe com quem esta falando* are not institutionalized solutions at the highest levels of national politics but are, rather, "improvised" solutions to unforseen situations (always temporary even though always present). In contrast, the one-party system of postrevolutionary Mexico has produced a political order in which negotiation at the margin of the law has been institutionalized at the highest levels of politics.[33] It is no accident that Liberal critics of Mexican politics have written books with titles such as *El Estilo personal de gobernar* (The Personal Style of Governing), *La Economía presidencial* (The Presidential Economy), and *Democracia sin adjetivos* (Democracy without Adjectives).

In addition, we have suggested that the campaign itself articulates, albeit in an inconvenient way, social relations with individual relations. The campaign is about an election, which forms part of the legally democratic system. But the campaign is also a mediating process in which the candidate places himself in negotiation with all important political groups in the country ("collective actors," according to Guerra). In this context it is worth asking how the system cannot help but abound in interpretations, and lack facts, when the system itself is split between two contradictory codes, individualism and holism. Due to this contradiction, the construction of "facts" in Mexico necessarily passes through a field of interpretations. Facts can only be established after the fact, after the interpretations—that is, if they manage to establish themselves. Sometimes there are facts that wander around the country without finding a consensus to give them shelter. They are argued over until they become irrelevant and are then best forgotten.

In the following sections we consider some of the practical consequences of this basic dimension of Mexican political culture.

The Socialization of the Candidate

One of the important functions of the PRI's campaign is the construction of the image of the president of the republic. During the campaign the candidate travels through Mexico and receives support, complaints, petitions, and praises from a great diversity of groups and individuals who claim privileged positions in negotiation with the candidate. In this process of identification and making demands to the candidate, his personal identity is manipulated to create an image that is simultaneously general and strongly identified with particular groups. Consider a few specific examples. In Tlaxcala, Carlos Salinas was called an honorary Tlaxcalan because he did fieldwork in this state. In Puebla the Pueblans considered him one of their own because he had once worked in a town there. In Veracruz he was Veracruzan because his mother was a teacher in that state. In one rally teachers displayed a banner with these words: "I sympathize with teachers: my mother was a teacher and I know her great sacrifices." Signature: Carlos Salinas de Gortari. On the day of the agronomist Salinas was named honorary member of the Society of Agronomists (Colegio de Agronomos) because he wrote a thesis about the problems of the countryside. In a meeting with scientists they referred to the candidate as Doctor Carlos Salinas de Gortari (and not as *licenciado*,[34] which is the title used by the rest in the tradition of politicians), claiming in this manner a special identification between the candidate and their sector.

The examples of this phenomenon are countless. Throughout the process of the campaign, the gestures, presences, and absences of the candidate are interpreted in terms of his relative proximity to persons, groups, and regions. To obtain a better negotiating position with him, each sector tries to place itself symbolically in a position of identification with the candidate.

At the same time this process also modifies the candidate's image itself, since his personal history is made a part of national history and society. The candidate's personal anecdotes and vital data are appropriated by the nation; each one is amplified and connected (metaphorically or metonymically) with "national" groups and sectors. The effort to negotiate positions with the candidate does more than modify or consolidate the situation of negotiating groups and persons. The process also changes the negotiator-candidate into the president of the republic—

Fig. 1.   Candidate Carlos Salinas Gotari with a constituent

that is, into a fetish whose special quality depends on the fact that the history of his personal relations become the same as the political (public) relations of the state. The fetishization of the president of the republic grows from his identification with each part of the nation. The role of the president is central to Mexican holism: the place of each group is determined by its position with respect to state power.

One of the people that we interviewed—who had worked on building the image of an earlier PRI presidential candidate—spoke of this fetishizing process from another viewpoint. As he saw it, politicians spend their lives "looking upward" (toward their immediate superiors, toward the presidency). But when a man finally becomes the PRI's candidate for the presidency, he has nowhere to look except "down" (in other words, toward the people). With this double movement the hierarchical structure completes the process of fetishization of the president. On the one hand, the truth of facts is established in a consensual manner, depending, in the last analysis, on how events turn out. In this way the place in the "whole" (in power, in the nation) is fundamental to the construction of reality. This is why everyone strives to know (or reaffirm) his or her place in the nation, a place that, in the end, is represented in the relationship between the actor and the president (whence the fetishization).

Parallel to this process, the verticality of the bureaucratic system of power impels the president to link himself with "society": for him there is nowhere else to look. This is the source of the populist sentimentalism of so many presidents, dramatically represented in the tears shed by Jose López Portillo in some presidential report but also traceable, to be sure, to all the presidents created by the institutionalized revolution. In the campaign this second process finds its expression in the trans-formation of the image of the candidate through the campaign. The candidate's growing security is a product of his metamorphosis from just a powerful man to representative man. This transformation is manifest in the poise and security of his public presentation, even in his posture and speech style. The media managers search for pictures and stories that will underline his identification with all sectors of the national population. The campaign strives to convert the candidate into a national symbol.

Language of Strength and Vertical Orientation

Analysis of the organization of the campaign's rituals underscores the fact that the public acts are organized first to impress the candidate and only secondarily the public. Thus, for example, in rallies the party works with two types of propaganda: that of "atmosphere" (placards, flags, banners, painted walls, and billboards) and that of useful and personal objects (purses, hats, pencils, pins, or stickers with the logo and the mottos of the campaign). The strategy of the propaganda of atmosphere is to cover first the routes that the candidate will follow in a city; second, to cover the roads through which the marchers will pass; and third, to

Fig. 2.   Carlos Salinas Gotari campaigning, already in
the role of future president

cover the city's main roads. Propaganda that is movable is transferred,
after the candidate's visit, to the popular barrios or residencies in the
city or sent to other places that the candidate will visit.

If the candidate notes some organizational defect on his route, this
can mean disaster for the organizers responsible. The organization of a
tour depends on negotiation among several levels: the state government,
electoral districts, and municipal governments; the state delegation of

the Comité Ejecutivo Nacional (CEN) of the PRI and the subsectors of logistics, information, and propaganda of the central PRI. In principle, what should happen is that the CEN of the PRI defines the form and core substance of the "line" that propaganda is to follow during the tour, along with the effect of the political situation in the state.[35] The campaign's organization, however, is primarily in the hands of the governor and members of the state delegation of the PRI, who have to coordinate the efforts of various local "leaders" and make sure that acts are well attended and successful. The campaign's resources should be raised primarily by the governor's efforts and also from the leaders and private people who want to have a role, and only secondarily do they come from the national PRI, even though it is in charge of the distribution of propaganda. In this manner the organization of a regional tour represents for the candidate not only the construction of alliances with the sectors and groups of the region but also a proof of the loyalty, power, and political efficacy of the governors and the regional leaders. If they fail, the CEN of the PRI steps in to organize the campaign with people and resources from the Federal District of Mexico (Mexico D.F.). Since these PRI personnel are the candidate's personal team, he immediately learns about the state of his alliances with the governors (as well as about their abilities and power).[36]

The mobilization tools used by the PRI, including the famous *acarreo,*[37] thus depend on distinct types of relationships among various leaders (each one with his personal power) and their social bases, or subordinates. In this sense the *acarreo* is a syndrome that forms part of a traditional power structure that permeates a good part of the power relationships in the country.[38] This also modifies a few myths about the *acarreo,* which present it as wholly manipulated from the center; instead, the *acarreo* now appears as part of a global process of negotiation among leaders, the candidate, and sometimes followers.

In some cases the relationship of followers with leaders is based on a long-term exchange of loyalty for economic resources. In others, control over subordinates is exercised in a bureaucratic manner (as in the cases of control of *acarreados* through prepared lists) with no relationships of loyalty between mobilizers and mobilized. Finally, there exists the practice of paying people to be present. Here the *acarreo* is not based on patron-client relationships or bureaucratic control but, rather, on a kind of remunerative power that has little to do with the ups and downs of the party politics. In the cases of loyalty relationships between leaders and followers, the presence of "followers" in public acts reflects the continuing existence of long-standing social ties. For this reason, an interpretation holding that *acarreo* of this type do not represent real support for the PRI misses the point. Bureaucratic control of *acarreados* is quite different, since the loyalty relationships between leaders and followers are not grounded on the medium- or long-term personal ties. Finally, in cases in which *acarreados* go to rallies in exchange for money or food, we suggest, following Etzioni,[39] these can be interpreted as an index of passivity or indifference by the *acarreados* themselves. In this way the *acarreo* phenomenon in reality comprises three different relationships: there are *acarreados* who really have a commitment to their leader (and, through him, to the PRI); there are *acarreados* who have been coerced to attend through the bureaucratic control of employment; and there are *acarreados* who simply offer their presence to the highest bidder.[40]

No matter what the case, the importance of these public attachments of *acarreados* remains great because, even though *acarreo* may not translate into votes for the party, it stands as living proof of the social strength and social roots of the PRI. And this is why the propaganda and material organization of campaign tours are oriented primarily toward the candidate and, at each level, to the immediately superior leader. This primary orientation to the candidate (and, more generally, upward) occurs not only on the organizational level (e.g., how many people the leader brought, the overall organization of the tour, the resources and support made available, etc.) but also in the very content of the meetings and in the form and substance of the campaign's rituals. In this way, for example, every meeting held to discuss basic problems of substance (CEPES, IEPES, and "popular dialogues") has its own organizer, generally a person familiar with the subject to be discussed and close to the candidate or to those closest to the candidate. His organizational role serves as a principal test that will likely have repercussions in the position he receives within the next government. This organizer is responsible for inviting speakers and for assuring that key persons are present as well as for making sure that relevant themes are discussed in an informed way. When key people are absent, or when the presentations and discussions fail to touch the central problems, the organizer looks bad (*le queda mal*) to the candidate, who has wasted his time in a meeting that does not achieve its core goal: contact with key persons and discussion of key subjects. This organizer probably will not get a prominent position in that candidate's government.

The content of this type of act is primarily directed toward the candidate, not to the national problem that ostensibly is being considered. If a meeting counts with the appropriate participants, it demonstrates the organizer's convocational and organizational capacities. If a meeting discusses the main problems and provides new perspectives on them, it shows the organizer's good nerve and strengthens his or her position in the candidate's eye. Finally, the organization of the ritual, in itself, reflects the fundamental importance of impressing the candidate at the same time that it reflects the differential importance the various classes and groups have for the PRI. Once more we find ourselves before the image of a hierarchical society, in which each person or group has a specific weight according to its place in the political structure. Last minute itinerary changes sometimes leave publics waiting during long hours; at other times the candidate never does get to visit towns that were already prepared for his arrival. Nonetheless, efforts are made to avoid irritating entire labor unions, entrepreneurial groups, or the intellectual community. The pep rallies that take place before the candidate arrives are intended to communicate to him the strength, organization, and enthusiasm of the group, sector, or region called to the meeting. This organization of cheering is not so much to sway the masses as to impress the candidate with the organizational capability of these same masses. The animators, or *jilgueros,* who warm up the group and keep them lively until the candidate arrives, always stress that they "will show" the candidate their importance, that they are going to tell him about their problems so that he will take them into account, and that he will see the enthusiasm with which their group supports the PRI.

It is this aspect (orientation toward the candidate) that—added to the three types of *acarreo* outlined above—makes the mass acts of the campaign more instances of group organization than examples of popular fervor for the candidate. We believe it is incorrect to see lack of enthusiasm by the masses as just a repudiation of the regime. It may well be repudiation, but it can also be a sign of indifference or, simply, a recognition that the rallies have nothing to do with electoral passions and everything to do with the negotiation of positions.[41]

A large part of the campaign's efforts are directed toward the candidate. The effect of this preoccupation with the candidate is to make the PRI's strength evident. As a group, the different events of the campaign bring together a good share of the main entrepreneurial, artistic, intellectual, and political figures of the country. The rallies are multitudinous; the propaganda is impeccable;[42] and the technical opinions frequently are of an acceptable quality. In all these ways the campaign's orientation toward the candidate communicates the PRI's strength to the public at large. On the campaign tours that we attended we were surprised by the people we found there: intellectual critics (of the Left and Right), prominent journalists, entrepreneurs of the Right or of known *panista* affiliation, (affiliation to the PAN party). The presence of such persons, who did not necessarily support the PRI, communicates and reiterates the party's strength, and it is this strength that, in the last analysis, is brought to bear. The language of strength thus combines with the highly symbolic and interpreted nature of politics to construct the legitimacy of the PRI and its triumphs.[43]

During the 1988 campaign, however, this traditional campaign logic was a source of conflict between the candidate and the party. The candidate began the campaign with a stance of political modernization, implying, among other things, that the campaign be directed primarily at acquiring votes, not showing the organizational strength of the party. This point was made so strongly that, when the candidate first pronounced himself against caciquism, there seemed to be some disagreement within the party about how far-reaching the new political culture Salinas was promising was likely to be.[44] This irritated the party's leadership, which continued to follow its traditional practices. According to some interpretations by the party's politicians, the conflict between candidate and party was felt primarily in the first weeks of the campaign; later, however, the candidate's position was modified, and an intermediate agreement was achieved in which the theme of modernization was replaced by a more innocuous kind of democracy: the slogan "Let Mexico Speak."

The final results of the elections have revived this conflict within the PRI as efforts are made to interpret "what happened." One line of interpretation asserts that the results of the elections affirm the urgency of Salinas de Gortari's modernizing reforms (particularly facing a multiparty situation), while the other holds that the fundamental mistake of the campaign was not using the traditional organization of the PRI.

The Image of the Nation

At the same time that the campaign impresses spectators with the PRI's strength, it also plays the chords of nationalism. This is not only because the PRI uses the colors of the Mexican flag. The PRI itself has created the nation's image, which is implicit in the whole institutional order of the country, in a large part of the daily political discourse, and in all educational materials. This image is converted into a living reality during the campaign.

We say "living reality" because the acts and presences that take place at each moment of the campaign not only express the situation of those who are there with the candidate but also stand for the situation of the group, sector, or region within the national order (which is made present in the symbol candidate/chief of state). In this way each act consolidates or reinforces what Benedict Anderson has called the "imagined community."[45] The imagined community here is the one that has been constructed together with the organization of the Mexican state: the federal entities and all the social categories that have been created by the state bureaucracies.

The nationalist effect of the campaign takes effect, then, by elevating each act into a hierarchy that converts all of them into events directed toward revitalization of the concept of the country. But the important nationalist effect of the campaign's acts is also supported by other aspects of the paraphernalia. Massive public acts are like parties, frequently with music bands that play before the arrival and after the departure of the candidate. There are street vendors, and all types of transactions take place (commercial, business, and personal) that, in the last analysis—for many because of the intensity with which they are concentrated—can come to symbolize "the life of the people covered by the national government." In the case of the 1988 campaign many of these massive acts were animated by known artists: from nationally famous artists like Juan Gabriel, Lola Beltran, and Luis Miguel to talents known only in cities and towns. The presence in the campaign of television stars (along with many important figures from the economy, politics, and culture) furthers the creation of a sense of "centrality" for the attendees, that is, a sensation of having a place in the imagined community.[46]

In regional tours the candidate's speeches generally begin by recognizing the importance, beauty, or strength of the state in question, along with a history that highlights events and characters of the state that have been of national importance (heroes, key political and social moments, important artists or writers, etc.). These events and characters are always presented as proof of the importance of the region to the country but also of the importance of the country for the region. One provides its best people to the other and finds its meaning in the recognition that it receives from the country. Chihuahua, for example, housed and protected Benito Juarez during one of his most difficult years. Puebla was the cradle of the Mexican Revolution; Guanajuato was cradle of Independence. The Tabascan Pellicer, the Veracruzans Diaz Miron and Reyes Heroles, the Jaliscans Juan Rulfo and Jose Clemente Orozco, all converted their regional values into Mexican values that now are recognized by the whole world. In other words, the candidate's speeches work in words what the rituals produce in events: a revitalization of the national myth, through which the parts of the imagined community that constitute the nation are recognized.

What is the national myth composed of? How, precisely, is it actualized in the rituals? The myth of the Mexican nationality has two principal sources: one, cosmogenical, provides unity to the country by explaining the origins of the present; another, cosmological, defines the groups that compose the nation and explains the relative places they occupy. There are, then, two dimensions of the national mythology: a myth of origins (that is explanatory) and a myth of social composition (which pretends to be descriptive). Both dimensions are activated in the campaign's rituals: the cosmological one is asserted in the organization of the event itself, where the strength of the different groups that compose the imagined community (of the country) are measured in a concrete manner;[47] the cosmogenical dimension is revitalized to explain and provide order to the events.

The historical, or cosmogenical, source has been more widely analyzed by social scientists than that of the order and structure of the imagined community (cosmological). It is the myth of the origin of the Mexican people: the conquest, the fusion of races, the struggle for independence and against the imperialist forces of the conservatives and the church, and, finally, the arrival in power of the new Mexicans, the mestizos, since the Mexican Revolution.[48]

Nevertheless, critics of the myths of the origin of the *mexicanidad* (and, in general, of *lo mexicano*) tend to trap themselves in new mythologies, since they tend to direct their criticism to a particular national myth, leaving untouched the cosmology, that is, the imagined order of the "national community," which is, after all, what the myths of origin search to legitimate. Success is so strong that even criticisms of the theory of origin leave the love for the national order in place. In this way the relations of inclusion/exclusion between "the country," "the classes," "the sectors," "the regions," and "the cultures" are maintained more or less constant, which propitiates the eternal construction of theories about the origins that legitimate these orders.

The PRI has shown more capacity to transform the myths of origin than the idea of the imagined (national) community, because this ideal construction is directly linked to the institutional organization of the country: workers, peasants, "popular groups," and entrepreneurs. For this reason the myth of the imagined community is indispensable for the proper function of the institution. Civil society is organized in terms of a perception of what is the national community, and in this way it integrates itself to different levels of government: the federal government with its different ministries, the state governments, electoral districts, municipal governments, parastatal industries, and so forth.

The relationship between concrete political strength and national ideology (as much on the side of "myth of origin" as on the side of "national order") provides the framework within which group and individual positions within or against the state are negotiated. There are groups with important organizational weight in the daily functioning of the national order, just as there are groups whose political weight derives from the symbolic place they occupy in the cosmogenical order (e.g., the Indians, the "Mexican woman," and, in general, the "dispossessed"). The latter, whose importance varies according to the cosmogeny in fashion at the moment, find places in the organizational order of the state, although the importance and strength of these places follows a different logic than that of the groups' positions, which are contested from a base of independent political strength.

With respect to the 1988 campaign's nationalism we can infer from the groups that were explicit ritual subjects the following important positions in the imagined community we call "Mexico": the three sectors of the PRI, the entrepreneurs, the large unions or federations of unions (Federación de Sindicatos de Trabajadores al Servicio del Estado [FSTSE], Sindicato Nacional de Trabajadores del Estado [SNTE], and oil workers), the states and municipalities of the republic,[49] intellectuals, state bureaucracy, Indians, young people, and women. If we consider these cosmological positions through analysis of the rituals, we can see that they conform to a three-dimensional map whose vertical axis is made up of the sectors, entrepreneurs, and large unions. In real political terms this vertical axis culminates in the federal government: there are lesser culminations in power in state and municipal governments.

On the horizontal order we find regional power groups. In the state of Morelos, for example, the CNC has traditionally controlled the majority of the municipal governments, although not the most important ones, along with slates for federal deputy. The fact, however, that these latter positions are held by the CNC (regardless of the real weakness of Morelean peasants compared to workers or popular sectors) reflects two things: first, the importance of the myth of origin in the political representation of Morelos before the federation (the seats of federal deputies go to the CNC because Morelos is the state of Zapata, not because of the real strength of the CNC in the state). Second, due to the weakness of Morelos within the federation, no single regional political elite can impose its people on the federal level. All this contrasts markedly with strong regional groups, like the Jonguitudistas in San Luis Potosi, the followers of Hernández Galicia in Tampico, the entrepreneurs in Monterrey, and the cattle raisers in Veracruz, who win positions in the government through their own independent power. Thus, the regional levels are the concrete places where the power of each sector exists; the weak regions or those with limited power are generally dominated within the cosmogonic logic.

The same happens to certain groups that lack the ability to first place important pressure on the state but who nevertheless hold an important place in the myth of origin or in the utopias of the regime. This is the case of Indians and of combatants of the revolution. These sectors of the population take on an importance in the imagined community that is constructed in the rituals of the campaign according to the place that is assigned to them in the myth of origin (and not vice versa).

In summary, there are two dimensions of the national mythology: that of origins, which is explanatory, and that of the social components of the country, which is descriptive. Both dimensions are activated in campaign rituals: the cosmological is asserted in the organization of the event itself, where the strength of the different groups that compose the imagined community is made manifest in concrete ways; the cosmogenic is revitalized to explain and provide order to the events and frequently appears in the speeches that are presented in the acts.

In this way the campaign's rituals, taken as a whole, provide a dramatization of the idea of the nation, as it has been crafted by the state. There are many persons who are situated, in various ways, in this national structure and who can feel a certain emotion of belonging during the campaign's rituals. Others can feel they are playing roles that have been put together especially for these dramatizations of the national power: women who are dressed in regional costumes they never otherwise use; construction workers disguised as peasants; or just people, who may not identify in any notable way with the categories assigned in the rituals ("youth," "women," etc.). Of course, there are also those who are not satisfied with the place assigned to them in the national cosmology or who feel that there is a large discrepancy between their place in ritual and their place in the country the rest of the time (e.g., Indians who are only visited during the campaigns). But regardless of the difficulties that the PRI has in placing all Mexicans within the "national whole," which this party has contributed so much to construct, there is no doubt that in the party's acts this whole is dramatized and vitalized and that this produces emotional effects, positive and negative, related to the nationalist proposal specific to the PRI.

The Role of the Press

In the organization of all the public acts of the campaign there are two main actors who strive to impress one another: the candidate and the public. The public, as noted, negotiates with its leaders (with varying degrees of success) a display of support that attempts to demonstrate to the candidate the strength, intelligence, and capacity of the leaders and groups. For his part the candidate attempts to secure his relationship with leaders and groups, giving them a well-defined place in the national order and, by implication, assuring them that he will look after their needs and interests when he becomes president. In all these acts, however, there also are two other publics that are relatively inconspicuous in the rituals. These are the only participants who authentically play the role of spectators: the "special guests" of the candidate and the press.

The special guests of the candidate generally include ex-governors; municipal ex-presidents of important cities in the region; intellectuals, journalists, distinguished actors or artists of the region; important entrepreneurs; figures from the party or the government; close collaborators of the candidate; and organizers of sectors or PRI groups who go to see or learn some campaign strategy. This group of spectators is, we believe, of great importance as much for the conformation of the future president's government as for the negotiation of regional alliances and strategies during the campaign itself.

The second group that occupies the position of spectator during the acts of the campaign are the journalists. The importance of the press in the campaign is a quite complex subject; we attempt here only to sketch out some considerations. As with the case of special guests, the passivity of the journalists in the public acts of the campaign contrasts in every way with its very active role in other spheres. The press presents public acts that are only attended by a small portion of the national population to a quite ample public. Newspapers and magazines also provide a point of comparison and a base for discussion for different interpreters of what happened at the acts. That is, they serve as vehicles of communication for the "political class." But before covering the functions of the press towards those two publics, we must begin by recognizing the fundamental importance of the campaign for the press.

A very important part of the campaign budget is directed to the press (25 percent according to some calculations).[50] This includes expenses for reporters in the campaign, official publicity, and the *gacetillas* (publicity that is published in the format of "news"), and so forth. The revenue that the press gains through the campaign can be vital for the newspapers as businesses as well as for the reporters.[51] At the same time the media also establish their relationship with the future president through their coverage of the campaign.

The great majority of publications offers unconditional support to the campaign from the beginning; however, the most important newspapers do not assure full support, and some of the most prestigious, such as *Excelsior* or *Siempre,* began the 1988 campaign with some quite severe critiques. Due to these factors, the press's action is in itself a subject of interpretation during the campaign. The press is viewed by the political class as a kind of mirror distorted by the forces of the campaign itself.

The role of the press in the relationship between the candidate and the "political public" is difficult to disentangle. On one hand, the reports surely have less nationalist effects than those we described in the live rituals, since readers of news, television audiences, and radio listeners do not participate directly in the group of relationships and situations that combine to produce the effect in the ordering of national myths that we discussed earlier. On the other hand, although this is difficult to measure, many opinions of characters related to the press who were interviewed for this research doubt the importance of mass media in swaying votes. Even the massive support of Televisa to the Salinas campaign appears to have had ambiguous, if not negative, imports on the "general public." What ever the case, considerable energy is dedicated, particularly in television but also at the graphic level in the newspapers, to presenting images of the candidate. These images are carefully studied in the party and tend to present a coherent front.

In our view the written press is fundamental particularly for the political class, including in this group political parties, government employees, and intellectuals. Only the press can include the enormous amount of information, opinion, and nuance that this class requires to make its own interpretations.[52] In this way, for example, newspaper pictures are always carefully evaluated: pictures of the candidate shaking someone's hand become clues about the state of negotiation between the groups. A photographer commented to us that frequently he is offered bribes from people who want to appear in the news shaking the hand of the candidate. Photographs that show the scale of public manifestations, lists, or pictures of special guests who attended are all sources of valued information.

This is how the role of the press is transformed into a great source of interpretations. Further, many journalists that we interviewed take for granted the importance of their principal role as interpreters:

> Frankly, the newspapers do not need to send reporters simply to cover the events [of the campaign]. We gather all the information, even with photos, directly from the PRI, so the only important thing that I need to do in this campaign is to report these subtle symbols that can reveal who is going to do what in the new government.

Due to the importance of the press in shaping the "facts," the press becomes an object of desire for those in power. From the moment of the *destape,* it is expected that the candidate will get favorable press treatment and, further, that he direct the form and substance of what the press will cover. Even more, it is expected that the candidate will stand out in the news. Thus, in the first weeks after the selection of the candidate Carlos Salinas de Gortari, the outgoing president Miguel De la Madrid continued to "dominate" the front page of the newspapers.

This was interpreted by specialists in the relationship between the government and the press as a signal of weakness on the part of Salinas. An expert of the government commented to us: "If [the candidate] cannot place his name in eight columns, he won't be able to do much." Dominating the press is understood by members of the political class to be a sign of strength and a fundamental tool for communicating government plans that form during the campaign.

In previous sections we discussed the relationship among the ambiguity of political facts, political interpretation, and negotiation. The performance of the press in the campaign allows one to see another dimension of this issue: the ambiguity is a source of power, since it maintains the opponents (or subordinates) in a situation of vacillation and uncertainty. Those interested in politics look toward the press to reduce their uncertainty. This is why political columnists have so much importance in Mexico, above all during the campaign and the period prior to the *destape*. These chroniclers form an elite within journalism, receive special treatment during the campaign, and frequently travel as special guests of the candidate. They are well known by all members of the political class. The political chroniclers dedicate all their energy to the selection and interpretation of the "revealing details" of the campaign. Through these hermeneutic exercises, political columnists help orient and shape "authorized" versions of the facts.

On the other hand, the fact that the press in itself is a field of forces that the various powers compete to appropriate means that the role of the press in reducing uncertainty is partial and that the press itself is the object of much speculation and interpretation. What are the personal relationships of the president of a newspaper and the candidate? To what group does the vice president belong? What sectors of the party are dominating the news, and why? Such questions surface continuously in the campaign, and there are varying evaluations of the position of each newspaper and of the major journalists with respect to the candidate and the different members of his team.[53]

Further, the strategies of the candidate and of the various politicians who figure in the press can include manipulation, intentional or not, of considerable ambiguity. Some reporters we interviewed, for example, underline the "contradiction" (ambiguity) in the candidate's speeches. One reporter, at various points, spoke "frankly" about how the one-party system was a phenomenon of the past. But on the other hand, he emphasized his adherence to the "goals of the Mexican Revolution," a phrase that was understood as a warning against a hasty interpretation of his reformism. This manipulation of contradictory messages exemplifies the use of ambiguity as a strategic weapon: it keeps all the groups that are potentially affected by the candidate's ideology uncertain and on the defensive. The press is a fundamental tool in the diffusion of these contradictory or ambiguous messages.

The analysis of the campaign as a ritual cycle requires a conceptualization, like the one we have begun to sketch here, of the role of the press and the media in the process. The press clearly provides a forum from which one can see a campaign that is very different from the campaign lived by participants in the public acts. The effects of the transmission of the campaign to the general public and its role in the determination of the vote cannot be analyzed in detail with our research methods. Still, the role of the press in the creation of the candidate's image, in the socialization of interpretations, and as a forum of negotiation among groups is fundamental. The fact that the only spectators in the campaign rituals are the press and the powerful special guests is very meaningful. These two groups are fundamental in the process of negotiating what will be the political reality of the upcoming regime.

Conclusions

The Institutional Revolutionary Party has forged a political time in Mexico: the *sexenial* order. Reproducing this order is problematic. As in many other cases, the problems posed by reproducing the political system are organized in time (delineate the phases of political time) and marked by the ritualization of alliances, of enmities, and of fundamental myths of the political system (the image of the country and its history). The crucial place of rituals makes it possible to apprehend fundamental aspects of the political system through their study.

In this overview of several aspects of the rituals of the PRI presidential campaign we have emphasized the following points. First, the internal conflicts of the party as well as the conflicts between the "candidate's people" and the "people of the system" are expressed, and attempts to resolve them are made, establishing change in continuity. Further, the process is intended to reaffirm the positions of the different groups and political regions before the presidential and federal institution. Third, the power of the outgoing president is at first reaffirmed (inasmuch as he chooses his successor), but from this point his power declines until he leaves office. Fourth, the image of the new president is socially constructed. Fifth, the strength of each person and interest group that participates in the party/government finds expression. And finally, attempts are made to revitalize national myths through the speeches and the organization of events.

The analysis of this group of effects permitted us to understand the means (the culture) through which vertical and horizontal nets of social relations are constructed and realized in the organization of the national state. In general terms, the campaign is organized upward, in that it operates based on the relationships between inferior and superior leaders. This means that the operational logic of the campaign is directed to the demonstration of strength of particular leaders and of the party in general, through the public mobilization of individuals and persons. The study of public acts (of the ritual cycle) of the campaign also lets us understand how and why nationalism operates as a central ideology of the political system. We thereby discover that the Mexican political system is not democratic (according to traditional definitions of *democracy*), since the fundamental unit of politics here is not the individual but, rather, the person—that is, the individual in his or her social role and place. The cultural system is not individualistic; it is, rather, a holistic and hierarchical cultural system with particular democratic and individualistic forces at its heart. We should not be too surprised, therefore, that the campaign we observed was not much oriented toward getting votes. That would go against the very nature of the politics taking place.

On the other hand, it is also important to be clear about what is not explained in this study of campaign's rituals. Our work does not concentrate on the historical transformations that explain, for example, the strength of the opposition movement in 1988. Instead, our analysis takes off from a general understanding of that history, which includes facts such as the formation of a power elite that links technical demands with inherited economic and political power, the accelerated growth of Mexican cities, and the economic "crisis" of the government and the role of the government in that crisis. It seems to us that political studies of conjunctures and the studies of economic and political development of Mexico are an indispensable complement of our work, particularly if the reader wishes to know what happened in the 1988 elections. Our study has not been directly aimed at that question. Instead, we have dedicated ourselves to studying the political culture, and the political system in general, that can best be seen from the viewpoint of the PRI's organization of public events.

This strategy permits us to reveal how politics in Mexico continues to operate within a framework that tries to reconcile a utopia of democracy (supported in the whole legal frame) with a holistic and hierarchical system. Our study also underscores the extent to which ambiguity and interpretation are cornerstones of the political system, without which the negotiation that is indispensable in the construction of the "national project" could not be generated.[54]

Moreover, our strategy permitted us to show, clearly and empirically, the vertical orientation of the campaign (and of the political system in general), which itself precisely reflects the holism of the system. Such holism emerges again in the ways in which the national cosmogeny and cosmology are utilized in the organization of the campaign. The PRI appears, in this context, as a seller of proper places within the national whole. Moreover, the very idea of what is "national" as a last instance of solidarity among the inhabitants of Mexico is, to be sure, a state creation. The different traditions of relationships in Mexico, founded in principles of kinship, friendship, loyalty, and rivalry contribute to the conformation of different types of collective actors; this communitarian tradition probably reinforces the use of nationalism as the last and main *raison d'état*.

We wish to reiterate that in this essay we do not explore the degree of success or failure that the campaign of 1988 had in its various specific objectives. Although the internal processes of negotiation appear to have been quite dynamic during the campaign, it cannot be forgotten that 1988 saw a redefinition of what was "internal" and "external" for the PRI, since an important constituency of *priistas* (PRI people) separated from the party and united with the Cardenist opposition. This situation created a partisan fight in which voting became important. Our impression is that the public acts of the PRI campaign continued to be oriented as we have suggested here, less to getting votes than to negotiating positions in the future government. The task of getting votes was left mostly to television[55] (which appears to have failed) and to traditional mechanisms of corporate control of votes (different unions and sectors promised the provision of several numbers of votes, as if their members voted collectively).[56]

In any case, our purpose has not been to diagnose what happened in the electoral struggle (although we have opinions in this respect) but, rather, to explain the form in which the PRI campaign is organized. This research has permitted us to point to a series of fundamental aspects of politics in Mexico. Too many years have already been spent with democracy presented as a goal in the face of a supposedly traditional system that, in reality, is much more dynamic and socially important than is usually recognized. The democratic transformation of Mexico begins with an understanding of these nondemocratic systems of social relationships and of how these social relationships coexist with the democratic juridical order (that is to say, it is necessary to understand how and why democracy gets "subtitled").

In 1910 there were many revolutionaries who thought that the only bad thing about Porfirio Diaz was that he had lived too many years. After the revolution a political system was created with presidential rotation but no rotation of the party—a system that guaranteed continuing coexistence between Liberal ideals and traditional practices (a coexistence that characterized many of the prerevolutionary regimes). Since the middle of the 1980s, many Mexicans have begun to imagine what before was unimaginable: the end of the PRI. But if the PRI is not understood, the major criticism that can be mounted against it will be that it has stayed too long in power, and perhaps the century will end with no more than this cry: "The PRI has died—long live the PRI."

NOTES

This essay was supported by the Universidad Nacional Autonóma de Mexico, El Colegio de Mexico and the Tinker Foundation. The authors are grateful for the helpful comments of Roberto DaMatta, Ilan Semo, Guillermo de la Peña, and Karen Kovacs. They also gratefully acknowledge the valuable contributions of Grisel Castro and Maria del Carmen Hernandez Beltran, to the fieldwork and bibliographic research. Finally, they thank the Partido Revolucionario Institucional, without whose cooperation the fieldwork for this study would not have been possible. The authors are completely responsible, however, for the project and the ideas presented herein. English translation by Sarah Hernández, Margaret Martín, and Daniel H. Levine.

1. In our fieldwork we were able to be present at campaign appearances by Carlos Salinas de Gortari in the states of Tabasco, Yucatan, Coahuila, Puebla, Veracruz, Jalisco, Chihuahua, and Hidalgo as well as at numerous events in the Federal District and in various provincial capitals. With respect to the news media, we studied the press systematically in *Excelsior, Proceso, Siempre,* and

Impacto and less systematically in *La Jornada, El Nacional,* the television networks and local radio stations, and magazines, during the time of the candidate's campaign trips. We hope to present our findings on this material in a more detailed manner in future publications: the present essay consists only of a summary of the main ideas that we have gathered from an initial analysis of the data.

2. See Arnold Van Genneph, *Rites of Passage* (New York: Johnson Reprint, 1969); and Victor Turner, *Dramas, Fields and Metaphors* (Ithaca: Cornell University Press, 1974). Turner's analysis of the rebellion led by Miguel Hidalgo and its links with religious pilgrimages was perhaps the first anthropological work to study the relationship between ideology, political practice, and dramatic representations in complex societies. In the last few years there have been a number of anthropological studies of political rituals in complex societies, among them: the work of Roberto DaMatta (on Brazil), Clifford Geertz (Bali), David Kertzer (Italy), Mona Ozouf (France), and Myron Aronoff (Israel). In this work we will not attempt to do a critical review of all of the ways in which political ritual has been studied. Nevertheless, we would like to at least mention here that an important diversity exists among theories that attempt to deal with the relationship between ritual and politics and that our position is opposed to that which treats politics as "a text" as an end in itself. (viz. Clifford Geertz, *Negara,* [Princeton University Press, 1981]). Cultural logic is related in a very complex way to social logics that are out of its control. In other words, the analysis of culture (and, as a privileged aspect, of rituals and mythology) cannot remain totally unconnected to its relationship with political economy. On the other hand, we are in agreement with Geertz in that politics must be understood by its relationship with social subjects who are formed in terms of a cultural logic. Finally, we want to emphasize that in this work we dedicate our efforts principally to the sociology of rituals; space does not permit us to detail the relationship that this sociology has to social change in Mexico in the last few decades.

3. In general, party politics has occurred above all on the local and regional levels, not at the presidential level. Nevertheless, there have been contested presidential elections: in the 1920s, before the formation of the party, there were military rebellions each time the president named his successor (that is, there were rebellions in 1920, 1923, 1927, and 1929). After the formation of the party there was a military revolt in 1939—related to presidential succession—and there were contested elections (which did not result in uprisings) in 1940 and 1952. These contests, however, were not partisan; rather, the opposition was organized around personalities who were disgruntled after not being chosen as the official party's candidate. These personalities separated from the party and ran for the presidency. The situation of *neocardinismo* in 1988 might have been understood as similar to these situations if a new party had not been formed after the election.

4. See Peter Smith's *Labyrinths of Power: Political Recruitment in Twentieth-Century Mexico.* (Princeton: Princeton University Press, 1979); and Roderic Camp, "El sistema político mexicano y las decisiones sobre el personal político," *Foro Internacional* 17, no. 65 (1976):51–81.

5. The distinction between "system men" (*hombres del sistema*) and "the president's men" (*hombres del presidente*) appeared clearly in the many interviews we had with campaign organizers, in the overall analysis they gave of who was responsible for which tasks and why in the campaign.

6. Rogelio Hernández Rodríguez presents a lucid and rich analysis of technocracy in the 1982–88 *sexenio* as a group of "president's men." See "Los hombres del presidente De la Madrid," *Foro Internacional* 28, no. 109: 5–38.

7. In this essay we use the term *political class* to refer to the segment of the population whose members are actively interested in national politics, be it because they occupy posts in government or because they seek to interpret governmental politics (this includes bureaucrats, intellectuals, and business leaders). We know that this definition (like *political class*) leaves a great deal to be desired in terms of the rigor that should define a group or class, but we feel that this is a sector that should be identified in some way. We will leave to others the task of defining this sector (and finding a better name); we believe that greater precision is not necessary here.

8. There are numerous examples of this type of speculation. See, for example, *Proceso,* no. 613: 16–17: "Madrugete de De la Vega a los Priistas: Sus lideres camerales, no modernos, pero habilidosos," *Excelsior* (October 7, 1987) ("Forjar consensos").

9. This is the theme of *La economia presidencial* by Gabriel Zaid (Mexico: Editorial Vuelta, 1987).

10. Various political analysts have noted the tendency for the Mexican government to give more importance to the bureaucratic apparatus, at the expense of the relationship between government and social groups outside of the bureaucracy. This tendency is very important in explaining what happened in the 1988 elections (the reader should recall that explaining the results of that election is not our purpose here). See, for example, Miguel Alvarez Uriart, "La politica economica y la economia politizada de Mexico," *Foro Internacional* 11, no. 41 (1982): 576; Sergio Zermeño, "De Echeverría a De la Madrid, ¿Hacia un régimen burocrático-autoritario? *Revista Mexicana de Sociología* 45, no. 2 (1983): 473–506; and, by the same author, "El fin del populismo mexicano," *Nexos* 10, no. 113 (1987): 30. It is interesting to note that, together with this wave of regimes that emphasize the role of the state apparatus, some authors discuss the "end of nationalism" in the government. (e.g., Carlos Monsivais, "Muerte y resurrección del nacionalismo mexicano," *Nexos* 10, no. 109: 13; Lourdes Arizpe, "El exilio de la cultura nacional," *Nexos* 10, no 117: 12. Later we will discuss the central role that nationalism has within Mexican political culture and within the political system under the PRI.

11. This was the case with Salinas de Gortari as well as Manuel Bartlett, both strong candidates to succeed Miguel De la Madrid, who occupied high-ranking positions in the campaign cabinet of De la Madrid.

12. For example, weeks before the official date of the selection of the pre-candidate, the leader of the CNC announced that the CNC had already chosen its candidate, which had the effect of letting loose a whole string of denunciations by PRI leaders; Fidel Velázquez for example, announced that "no one has a

candidate until the Party decides." Olivares Venura, the leader of the CNC was forced to admit that, although the CNC had its candidate, he would not divulge who that candidate was until the PRI designated him. See diverse declarations in *El Sol de Mexico,* September 24, 1987.

13. To the degree that, on the same morning that the precandidacy of Carlos Salinas de Gortari was announced, there was a "false *destape*": a radio station announced the precandidacy of Doctor Sergio García Ramírez. Various important PRI leaders rushed to congratulate García Ramírez; the identity of the precandidate of the PRI was not known until the minute that it was officially announced. See *Excelsior,* October 5, 1987. For a complete synopsis of this series of events, see Jorge Herrera Valenzuela, *La radio, el PRI, y el destape* (Mexico: Editorial Diana, 1988); this journalistic treatment focuses upon the intensity of the speculation and interpretations of the *destape.*

14. In its political analysis the magazine *Proceso* noted three different presidential candidates (in terms of ranked preference) for each politician.

15. For example, in a television interview with Salinas in Coahuila, on February 10, 1988, the candidate declared: "I am not going to make any promises that I cannot keep." This was a common theme in the first months of the campaign.

16. See *Excelsior*, January 9, 1988: Salinas declared: "I haven't made any agreements to continue any present policies." In the days that followed, political commentators speculated on what differences could have come about between the policies of De la Madrid and Salinas.

17. *Homo Hierarchicus* (Chicago: University of Chicago Press, 1970).

18. The ideas that Morse developed about Spanish political philosophy have been summarized recently in his book *El Espejo de próspero* (Mexico: Siglo XXI, 1982).

19. Umberto Eco, *Art and Beauty in the Middle Ages* (New Haven, Conn.: Yale University Press, 1986).

20. For example, Peggy Liss, *Mexico under Spain, 1521–1526: Society and Origins of Nationality* (University of Chicago Press, 1975); Colin Machlan and Jaime Rodríguez, *The Forging of the Cosmic Race: A Reinterpretation of Colonial Mexico* (Berkeley: University of California Press, 1980).

21. See, respectively, *The Forms of Modern Society: Bureaucracy, Democracy, Totalitarianism* (Cambridge: MIT Press, 1986); and *The Imaginary Institution of Society* (Cambridge: MIT Press, 1987).

22. Larissa Lomnitz, *Como sobreviven los marginados* (Mexico: Siglo XXI, 1975); *A Mexican Elite Family* (Princeton: Princeton University Press, 1987).

23. *Carnavais, Malandros e Herois: Para uma sociologia do dilema brasileiro* (Rio de Janeiro: Zahar, 1978); *A casa e a rua: Espaço, cidadania, mulher e morte no Brasil* (São Paulo: Brasiliense, 1985).

24. *Le Mexique de l'ancien régime à la révolution* (Paris: L'Harmattan, 1985).

25. See, for example, Guillermo de la Peña, *Herederos de promesas* (Mexico: Casa Chata, 1980); and Claudio Lomnitz, *Evolución de una sociedad rural* (Mexico: SEP / Fondo de Cultura Económica, 1982); and *Cultural Relations in Regional Spaces* (Ph.D. diss., Department of Anthropology, Stanford University, 1987).

26. Larissa Lomnitz, "Horizontal and Vertical Relations and the Structure of Mexico," *Latin American Research Review* 16:51–74.

27. We believe that one can interpret the affirmation of Paz in the sense that "Mexicans lack the same in the private sphere as in the public, to return to Montesquieu, that is, to know and recognize the limits of each person, that which is mine and my neighbor's" (*Vuelta* 127 [1987]: 63). The difficulties of imposing liberalism have been the center of attention of essayists associated with the magazine *Vuelta* (Octavio Paz, Gabriel Zaid, and Enrique Krauze), especially after 1985. The demands for democracy have been taken up by the opposition parties as well (including the Left), above all, through the political reform of Reyes Heroles.

28. In this sense, we do not think that there is a causality similar to arguments made by political commentators such as Lorenzo Meyer, Enrique Krauze, or Gabriel Zaid, who have begun to draw parallels between the present period and the end of the Porfiriato, even before the elections of 1988. See, for example, the political essays in the magazine *Vuelta* in 1985, 1986, and 1987.

29. "Democracia y poder en México: El significado de los fraudes electorales en 1979, 1982 and 1985," *Nueva Antropología* 9, no. 3 (1986): 127–57.

30. This is a basic element of political culture in Mexico: the accusations of fraud, like accusations of corruption, reflect social tension, political groups, and political strategies of any given moment. (Cf. Claudio Lomnitz, *Evolución de una sociedad rural* [Mexico: SEP / Fondo de Cultura Económica, 1982], chap. 3, in which accusations of corruption are compared to the uses of accusations of witchcraft in "primitive" societies.)

31. In the first few weeks of September (that is, a month before the *destape*), the CTM concentrated upon discussing its demands for the next *sexenio;* these included dropping De la Madrid's economic program, which meant that Salinas, who was heavily identified with it, was not the candidate of the CTM. See *Excelsior,* September 1, 1987; and September 1–15, 1987.

32. For an interpretation of the relationship between the oil workers and Salinas during the campaign, see *Proceso* no. 612: 26.

33. This comparison was suggested by Roberto DaMatta.

34. In Mexico there are two grade levels when completing the bachelors of arts (B.A.) degree. A "pasante" is a person who completes all course work but does not do a thesis, and a "licenciado" is somebody who completes both course work and a thesis. As in the United States, a person with a Ph.D. degree is sometimes called Doctor, in Mexico a person with a B.A. degree, having done a thesis, is called Licenciado.

35. This diagnosis includes analysis of the strength of the different parties in the location, their presence in the means of communication, their campaign strategies, and the groups in which they are stronger. It includes also diagnoses of the location's main problems and questions that would be pertinent to address during the candidate's tour.

36. Newspapers and critics of the PRI also noted the presence, in some acts, of "mobile brigades of *acarreados,*" that is, of people who were transported to rallies from remote localities. This type of mobilization took place when the local leaders failed in the campaign's organization.

37. *Acarrear* means "to bring along or carry along." *Acarreados* are the people who are carried along. *Acarreo* is the act of bringing someone along.

38. L. Lomnitz, "Horizontal and Vertical Relations."

39. *A Comparative Analysis of Complex Organizations: On Power, Involvement, and Their Correlatives* (New York: Free Press, 1975).

40. Although we could not do a systematic study of *acarreados,* we frequently saw that the payments were very small: five or ten thousand pesos (two to four dollars) and perhaps a little food. There is a joke from the time that Carlos Hank Gonzales was governor of the State of Mexico that reflects what is at stake for those *acarreados* who are paid to attend. It is said that some peasants in his campaign's rallies were yelling "Viva Juan Gonzales!" and, when a leader told them it was Hank Gonzales not Juan Gonzales, the response was: "For a sandwich and a soda, I do not learn German!"

41. Paul Camack has suggested to us that a "socialization" of the electorate takes place during the campaign, during which the electorate learns that its opinion is irrelevant to the development of the elections. Although there is a repressive side of the Mexican political system, it seems to us that this conclusion is applicable only to one part of the electorate: that which does not find a place in the groups organized within the PRI (or that finds itself very unhappy of its position within these groups). This aggregate of people could be large in some elections and small in others; without doubt it was large in the 1988 election. On the other hand, it is true that the elections are still a problematic institution in Mexico, inasmuch as there exists the contradiction (that we have been underlining in the whole of this essay) between the holistic-relational-hierarchical political organization and the individualist-democratic one.

42. The party places great emphasis on the order of placement of propaganda. This, it seems to us, is also part of the "language of the strength": it is about the unfolding of efficiency, planning, patience, and resources.

43. In one of the state tours of the campaign a public official of the PRI commented to us: "It will not be possible anymore to say that the PRI does not have support in this state: Salinas has filled all the plazas in all the cities he has visited."

44. For a speech by Salinas in which he defines the characteristics of this "new political culture," see the speech given in the *VII Convencion Ordinaria del PRI,* November 8, 1987. For a statement against *caciquismo,* see the speech to the petroleum workers, *Excelsior,* November 6, 1987, 5.

45. *Imagined Communities* (London: Verso, 1983).

46. In this context the type of charisma that the Mexican presidents develop could be researched. Let us remember that Geertz, following Edward Shils, links charisma with the idea of the "social centers" (see "Centers, Kings, and Charisma: Reflections on the Symbolics of Power," in *Local Knowledge* [New York: Basic Books, 1983]). This idea of centrality produced in the rituals of the campaign appeared to generate, as Shils wants, the candidate's charisma, who, even for us the researchers, seemed to become more good looking and more intelligent after each one of these acts.

47. One of the main logistical organizers of the campaign at the national

level commented to us that a key task they faced was to limit the attendance of persons to the different public acts of the campaign. In his view all the political spaces are occupied in a natural manner, hence the central PRI has to concern itself with which spaces are to be open to whom. (That is, the PRI's national leadership concerns itself with representation of the "cosmological" order in each public act.) This same organizer provided us with many examples in which the central PRI restricted the number of persons that a sector or organization could bring to some public act.

48. This myth has been discussed, reinforced, created, and criticized by Mexican intellectuals; see Roger Barta, *La Jaula de la melancolia* (Mexico: Grijalbo, 1987); and C. Lomnitz, *Cultural Relations.*

49. In the 1988 version of the PRI's nationalism, little space is given to the regions not contained by the administrative dimension of space (states and municipalities). This was so despite the fact that sub-regional and nonadministrative orders as Bajio, Laguna, Istmo, Huasteca, Mixteca, the northern border, and others are recognized and used for political analysis in the PRI's diagnoses and partisan work.

50. Bear in mind that calculations of the campaign's expenditures will always be interpretations—more or less informed but never 100 percent sure. The decentralized structure of campaign expenditure makes any precise accounting very difficult.

51. In this campaign there was some tolerance of opposition newspapers that achieved economic success in their coverage of the campaign through direct sales and publicity from unofficial sources. This is the case of *Jornada* (particularly toward the end of the campaign) and, especially, of *Proceso.* Most newspapers and magazines appear to have been effectively co-opted during the campaign.

52. For a more complete analysis of the issue, see the work of Ilya Adler: "Media Uses and Effects in a Large Bureaucracy: A Case Study in Mexico" (Ph.D. diss., School of Journalism, University of Wisconsin, 1986).

53. An interesting example of this occurred at the beginning of the campaign, when an editorial of the prestigious political magazine *Siempre* accused the candidate of being "inept." This behavior was so unusual that it was compared by a journalist with attacking the Virgin of Guadalupe or the armed forces. This attack got so much attention that it served as the opening theme of one issue of the *Proceso.* Some interpreted the event as an ideological demarcation between the president of *Siempre* and Salinas, others as a move to negotiate positions.

54. A similar idea has been proposed by Pablo Gonzales Casanova in *El Estado y los partidos políticos en Mexico* (Mexico: Ediciones ERA, 1986), 62–70. In that work Gonzales Casanova suggests that ambiguity has a double function: on the one hand, it serves to appropriate the discourse of others, and, on the other hand, it generates a feeling of common belonging to the national state.

55. We owe this suggestion to Soledad Loaeza.

56. In this way, for example, during the campaign the CNC promised to give ten million votes to the candidate (*El Nacional,* December 1, 1987, 2); the Federation of Unions of Workers at the Service of the State (Federación de Sindicatos

de Trabajadores al Servicio del Estado, FSTSE) promised two million votes (*Excelsior,* February 21, 1988, 27); and Jonguitud Barrio, leader of the teachers' union, promised to put a million teachers to work to get votes for the PRI (*Excelsior,* November 1, 1987, 1, 13).

Political Elites and State Building: The Case of Nineteenth-Century Brazil

José Murilo de Carvalho

The process whereby political independence came to the Spanish and Portuguese colonies in America has been the object of a rich body of scholarly interpretation. Although most of this literature concentrates on the causes of independence, several authors, particularly those concerned with the Brazilian case, have tried to explain also the reasons for the differences in the political evolution of the two colonial empires. Without denying the value of some of these explanations, this essay argues that they are not entirely satisfactory and that an alternative, or at least supplementary, explanation can be found in the nature of the political elites that emerged in the two colonies as a consequence of differing colonial policies.[1]

Some Traditional Explanations

The most striking difference in the political evolution of the Spanish and the Portuguese colonial possessions is the well-known phenomenon of the balkanization on the Spanish part, in contrast with the unified nation that emerged from the Portuguese domain. To put it in quantitative terms, at the beginning of the nineteenth century the Spanish colony was divided administratively into four viceroyalties, four captaincies-general, and thirteen high courts; by mid-century it was fragmented into seventeen different countries. In contrast, the Portuguese colony, of comparable size, which up to 1820 was still divided into eighteen captaincies-general, by 1825 had already been transformed into one independent nation.

Another important difference, although not as clear-cut as the first, regards the nature of the two political systems. Brazil managed to maintain a reasonably stable constitutional monarchy, and this for sixty-nine years, while most of the Spanish-speaking countries, Chile being the conspicuous exception, had to cope with constant political upheavals that ended frequently in civilian or military caudillistic types of government. My main concern here will be with the first type of difference, although it could easily be argued that the nature of the independence movement was closely related to the subsequent evolution of the emancipated countries.

One first explanation found in the literature is based on economic factors. Celso Furtado, for instance, argues that the early decline of the mining cycle in the Spanish colony in the seventeenth century, and the consequent reflow to agriculture, led to greater isolation among the units within the colony than occurred in the Brazilian case, where the mining cycle took place in the eighteenth century and provided greater integration. The argument is not convincing. The Brazilian gold rush had already begun to subside by mid-eighteenth century, and by the end of that century the same reflow to agriculture had taken place in the mining areas.[2] Moreover, even had the cycle been in effect in 1822, the year of Brazilian independence, only the center-south of the country would have been affected, leaving out part of the northeast and the entire north.

The more elaborate economic analysis of the colonial period undertaken by Osvaldo Sunkel and Pedro Paz turns out to be inconclusive regarding the impact of economic factors on the unification/fragmentation of the colony. According to these authors, important economic links developed among several units of the Spanish American empire, particularly after the introduction of the somewhat more liberal Bourbon reforms during the eighteenth century. But they also point out economic conflicts among these same units, which favored fragmentation instead of unity. The maintenance of the integrity of the Portuguese colony is attributed by Sunkel and Paz to the presence of the monarchy, a traditional political explanation that will be examined below.[3]

Some authors mention social factors as important explanatory elements. More specifically, the presence of slavery in Brazil is said to have been a powerful incentive for the dominant classes to adopt a monarchical solution in order to avoid the breakdown of social order, a likely consequence were the unity of the former colony to collapse.[4] It is certainly true that nowhere else in the Spanish American empire, except in Cuba, was slavery as important as in Brazil, both in terms of the number of slaves and of the economic weight of the slave sector of the economy. There is also no denying that sectors of the Brazilian elite were greatly concerned with the possibility of slave revolts. The events of 1791 in Saint Dominique were still remembered by the slave owners, and some of the rebellions of the colonial period had clear racial and social overtones.[5] But the fear of slave revolts varied a great deal in different parts of the colony. In Rio de Janeiro, where the major decisions regarding independence were made, it was barely expressed. In fact, the greatest resistance to the monarchical and unitarian solution came from areas where the perception of threat was strongest, such as Bahia and Pernambuco. Furthermore, the fear of popular mobilization was not a privilege of the Brazilian upper classes—it was present all over Spanish America among Creoles. And it did not prevent them from developing the factional rivalries that helped to create different nuclei of national identity.

Slavery certainly had an impact in restraining intra-elite conflict in Brazil, but it does not seem to have been a crucial element in keeping the country together at the time of independence. Members of the elite involved in the emancipation process did not consider the maintenance of the unity of the country as a necessary condition to preserve slavery. In the case of one of the most important among them, José Bonifácio, the perception was in the opposite direction: being personally and openly against slavery, he nevertheless resisted British pressures for a quick end to the slave trade lest the measure destroy the weak bonds that kept the provinces together.[6]

A third possible explanation can be traced to the colonial administrative policies of Spain and Portugal. It is known, for instance, that the Spanish policy under the Habsburgs was guided by a federal conception of the empire, in contrast to the more centralized Portuguese policy. One consequence of this difference was the establishment of thirteen high courts of justice—*audiencias*—in the Spanish colonies, as compared with only two on the Portuguese side. Some authors have remarked that the territorial limits defined by these courts formed in several instances the boundaries of the future independent nations.[7] But here again there are difficulties. First, in both the Spanish and Portuguese cases there was an initial phase of a more liberal colonial policy followed by a centralization effort during the eighteenth century, not to mention the fact that from 1580 to 1640 the two crowns were united. Second, despite the policy differences, the end result in terms of internal communication among the distinct units of the two colonies was similar, id est, the links were very weak in both cases. The authority of the viceroys within either side was more nominal than real outside their own territorial jurisdictions. The *oidores* (judges) of *audiencias* and captains-general were appointed by the Crown and could communicate directly with it, eschewing the mediation of the viceroys. Both the Portuguese and Spanish crowns played one colonial authority against another as a strategy of political control.[8] Third, the exclusion of Creoles from the most important positions in the Spanish colonial administrative bodies, a practice reinforced under the Bourbons, reduced the impact these bodies could have had in forming local centers of Creole power.[9]

Even assuming that the Portuguese policy led to closer contacts between the colony and the metropolis, it did not generate greater communication among the captaincies. It is almost consensual among historians that, at the time of the arrival of the Portuguese court in Rio in 1808, the captaincies were very much isolated from each other politically. Even after the arrival of the court, the northern part of the colony, which from 1624 to 1775 had been completely separated from the rest as a different state, continued to deal directly with Lisbon instead of obeying the Portuguese regent in Rio de Janeiro. The situation of the captaincies at the end of the colonial period was described in the following terms by the French botanist Saint-Hilaire, who had direct knowledge of several of them: "[the captaincies] hardly communicated with each other; frequently they even ignored each other's existence. There was no common center in Brazil: it was a huge circle the radii of which converged far from the circumference."[10]

The most common explanation points to a political factor. It argues that the flight of the Portuguese court to Brazil at the end of 1807 as a consequence of the invasion of Portugal by the Napoleonic troops and the settlement of the court in Rio de Janeiro at the beginning of 1808 made possible a smooth transition to independence under a monarchical system, and by doing so, reversed the centrifugal tendencies among the provinces and provided the basis for national unity.[11] Again, there is no denying the importance of this event. A monarchy was contemplated in several parts of the former Spanish colony, and a short experiment with it was made in Mexico, where a plebeian candidate proved unconvincing as king. Among the *libertadores,* San Martín was convinced that only a monarchical solution would avert anarchy after the wars of independence had been completed.[12] But the presence of the Portuguese court in Rio did not make a monarchy a necessary outcome in Brazil. The events of the years 1821 and 1822 show that the option for a monarchy under the Portuguese Prince Pedro was a decision of the national political elite, and one for which popular support existed, particularly in Rio. The option became clearer in 1831 when the now Pedro I of Brazil was forced to resign; instead of establishing a republican government, as all other independent countries in the Americas had done and as many Brazilians wanted, the national elite decided to proclaim as emperor Pedro's five-year-old son, who then became Pedro II of Brazil. The presence of the court in Rio certainly made the decision to keep the monarchy easier, but it did not make it a certainty, for there were strong tendencies, particularly in the northern areas of the country, toward a republican solution and secession from Rio.[13] If the decision was a political one, a look at those who made it would be useful in searching for a more satisfactory explanation.

The Political Elite as an Explanatory Factor

The political elites formed during the Spanish and Brazilian colonial periods confront us immediately with a major contrast. The great majority of the Brazilian elite at the time of independence and up to mid-century had three common characteristics: first, they were all trained in one university, Portugal's Coimbra; second, they were trained mostly in civil law; third, they were principally bureaucrats, especially magistrates or judges. Although there are, to my knowledge, no quantitative studies of the elites of the Spanish-speaking countries, from the evidence available it can be safely asserted that no group comparable to the Brazilian was present in any of them. Many elites were certainly highly educated, but not in one place and in one subject and not with practical experience in matters of government.[14]

This fact, I will argue, was due to a clear difference in the colonial educational policies of Portugal and Spain. Portugal refused systematically to allow the organization of any institution of higher learning in her colonies, not considering as such the theological seminaries. Only after the arrival of the Portuguese court were two medical and two military academies allowed. The reason for this policy was clearly stated by the Conselho Ultramarino (Overseas Council) in 1768 when it denied a request made by the still rich gold-mining captaincy of Minas Gerais to build its own school of medicine. The *conselho* answered that the question was a political one and that a favorable decision could lead to a further request for a law academy, and the whole process would end up in independence, since "one of the strongest unifying bonds that keeps the dependency of the colonies, is the need to come to Portugal for higher studies."[15]

As a consequence of the refusal, Brazilian students had to go to Portugal for their training. From 1772 to 1872 a total of 1,242 of them, coming from all captaincies, were enrolled at Coimbra, of whom 80 percent attended before 1828, when two Brazilian law schools were opened.[16] As it turned out, a substantial part of the leadership involved in the independence movement at the national level, as well as the majority of the national political elite in the three decades that followed, was drawn from this group of university graduates. As table 1 shows, all of the university-educated cabinet ministers during the first decade of independence were trained in Portugal, and by mid-century almost half of the ministers still belonged to this Coimbra generation.[17]

Nothing of the sort happened in the Spanish colony. It was the consistent policy of the colonial government to encourage the organization of universities under the aegis of the state or of the church. The royal universities were modeled after the University of Salamanca, the religious ones mostly after that of Alcalá. At the end of the colonial period twenty-three (or twenty-five, according to some authors) universities had

TABLE 1. **Place of Higher Education of Cabinet Ministers, by Period, 1822–1889 (in percentage)**

	1822–31	1831–40	1840–53	1853–71	1871–89	Total
Portugal						
Coimbra	71.8	66.7	45.0	—	—	28.5
Other	28.2	16.1	—	—	—	8.0
Total	100.00	82.8	45.0	—	—	36.5
Brazil						
Two law schools	—	3.3	45.0	75.0	84.1	49.5
Other	—	6.6	10.0	20.8	14.3	11.5
Total	—	9.9	55.0	95.8	98.4	61.0
Other Countries	—	6.3	—	4.2	1.6	2.5
Total number of ministers	(39)	(30)	(20)	(48)	(63)	(200)

Source: José Murilo de Carvalho, *A Construção da Ordem: A Elite Política Imperial* (Rio de Janeiro: Campus, 1980), 63, 66.

Note: The total number of ministers during 1822–89 was 219, so that only 19 had no higher education. The figures for senators are similar to the ones shown above. Senators were elected for a life tenure. Being among the first who were selected, the Coimbra generation lasted even longer among them. It made up 62 percent of the total in the third period and 9 percent in the fourth.

been created, the first ones, those of Peru and Mexico, as early as 1551. The geographical distribution of these universities presents a striking coincidence: there were universities in almost all of the regions that later became independent countries, except for some of the small Central American nations. The twenty-three universities were scattered in what eventually would become thirteen different countries.[18]

My contention is that the phenomenon was no coincidence at all. The Spanish colonial universities made possible the creation of numerous local educated elites, with little if any contact with the mother country or with other neighboring colonial subdivisions. When the struggle for independence began, few of these people had, as did the *libertadores,* the larger view of the whole colony in mind, the majority being limited by its parochial experience. But at the same moment, in the former Portuguese colony, there was a single elite, one which was, so to speak, a small club of friends and former classmates. Its members came from all parts of the huge colony, but they had gotten to know each other at Coimbra, where they had an organization of their own. The absence of universities in the colony had also the consequence of holding the number of graduates to a small group. As mentioned, only slightly over a thousand Brazilian students were enrolled at Coimbra after 1772. In clear contrast, the Royal University of Mexico alone graduated around 39,000 before independence, and it has been calculated that the total number of graduates for the entire Spanish colony was 150,000.[19] This greater diffusion of higher education also multiplied the chances for competing leaderships and for the spread of political conflict.

The ideological content of the education of the Spanish and Portuguese elites was another source of divergence. Since its beginning in 1290, the University of Coimbra had been under the intellectual influence of the University of Bologna, the major European center of study of Roman law at the time. Several of the Coimbra faculty had been trained at Bologna and were for this reason called "the *bolônios.*"[20] From the end of the sixteenth century until 1759 the Jesuits controlled the College of Arts and managed to reduce the emphasis on legal studies but did not eliminate them. In 1759 they were expelled from Portugal by the Marquis of Pombal, the powerful minister of King José I. As part of the marquis' overall policy to promote the economic recovery of the empire, the university was submitted to a drastic reform with new emphasis being put on the natural sciences, particularly zoology, botany, and mineralogy. The new rector to whom Pombal entrusted the reform was the Brazilian Francisco de Lemos. After the death of D. José and the fall of Pombal in 1777 there was a reaction against his reform, the emphasis on natural sciences was abandoned, and civil law regained its ancient prestige. But the reform movement, while it lasted, managed somewhat to bridge the gap between Portuguese education and the achievements of the European Enlightenment, and it trained an important group of scientists, among whom were several Brazilians who were still politically active at the time of independence.[21] But the majority of the Brazilian elite at independence had been trained at Coimbra after law degrees were again predominant. In the first two decades following independence, as table 2 shows, there was still among the cabinet ministers a considerable group of scientists and of persons with a military training. Military education was imparted at the Colégio dos Nobres (College of the Nobles), an institution created by Pombal; it, too, placed strong emphasis on the natural sciences and intended thereby to transform the scions of noble families into subjects more useful to the king.

The concentration of training in one place and in one discipline gave the elite a solid ideological homogeneity. The Romanist tradition was of particular importance. Although Roman law was used for various purposes after the revival of its study in Europe at the end of the eleventh century, in Portugal the *bolônios* had been using it consistently to help consolidate the power of the kings. As Teófilo Braga puts it: "The jurists were the theoretical organizers of this monarchical dictatorship; the transformation of the feudal regime under D. João I takes place by virtue of the predominance of Chancellor João das Regras, a legist of the

TABLE 2. Field of Higher Education of Cabinet Ministers, by Period, 1822–1889 (in percentage)

	1822–31	1831–40	1840–53	1853–71	1871–89	Total
Law	51.3	56.7	85.0	77.1	85.7	72.5
Exact sciences	20.5	13.3	5.0	2.1	—	7.0
Military	28.2	20.0	10.0	18.7	7.9	16.5
Medical	—	6.7	—	2.1	6.4	3.5
Religious	—	3.3	—	—	—	0.5
Total number of ministers	(39)	(30)	(20)	(48)	(63)	(200)

Source: José Murilo de Carvalho, *A Construção da Ordem: A Elite Política Imperial* (Rio de Janeiro: Campus, 1980), 68.

Note: The figures for senators are similar, with some minor variations. The importance of training in law is greater among them for the first two periods (61 percent and 71 percent, respectively); there is a substantial presence of religious education in the second period (28 percent); and the general presence of military education is less significant (8 percent).

school of Bologna."[22] The absorption of a centralizing, postclassical version of the Roman tradition was instrumental in infusing the future Brazilian leaders with a strong statist orientation, a firm belief in the reasons of the state and in its supremacy over church and barons.

At the same time Coimbra managed to isolate its students from the most dangerous aspects of the French Enlightenment, admitting only the reformist and Christian version of the *Lumières*.[23] It is noteworthy that several Brazilian students who went to France or England, and even some priests trained in the colony, were more influenced by the subversive ideas of the time and more willing to put them into practice through political action than were their Coimbra fellows. It might not be an exaggeration to say that it was easier to have access to the *philosophes* in the captaincy of Minas Gerais, four hundred miles to the interior of Brazil, than at Coimbra. The library of one priest who participated in a 1789 political rebellion that occurred in that captaincy was made the object of a study, the revealing title of which is "The Devil in the Canon's Library." The devil was *l'Encyclopédie,* Diderot, Voltaire, d'Alembert, Mably, and the like.[24]

From the studies available on the elites of the Spanish-speaking countries, it can be concluded that no such ideological homogeneity existed among them. For one part, as already noted, the greater diffusion of higher education favored wider diffusion of ideas. For another, although Roman law was also very influential in Spain, most of the colonial universities were controlled by religious orders and dedicated to religious training. Jesuits, Franciscans, Dominicans, and Augustinians competed for the control of higher education as a weapon of religious conquest. Even the state-controlled Royal University of Mexico put the emphasis of its training in theology, thus departing from its model, the University of Salamanca, where law had the upper hand.[25] This type of education was less likely to convey a concern with and knowledge of state building than was the training imparted at Coimbra.

The statist orientation of the Brazilian elite was further enhanced by the elite's third characteristic, its occupational composition. As can be seen in table 3, up to 1853 the overwhelming majority of cabinet ministers were public employees. A similar picture can be obtained for senators and deputies. And among these public employees the magistrates had a dominant position, be it among ministers, senators, councillors, or deputies, except during the first period when the military predominated among ministers.

Magistrates, as Stuart Schwartz has shown, were the backbone of the Portuguese state, over which they had made their influence felt since the fourteenth century. They were a surprisingly modern professional group with elaborate training and career patterns. They were made to circulate from colony to colony and from the colonies to the higher posts in Portugal. And since the exercise of judicial functions was always linked to public administration in general, the whole process transformed several of these magistrates into consummate statesmen. Another important point about this group, which was true also for the entire Portuguese bureaucracy, was that there was relatively little discrimination against Brazilian nationals. Brazilian judges served in different types of courts, both in Portugal and in the colonies of Asia and America.[26]

The Spanish bureaucracy was not very difficult from the Portuguese in terms of professionalization, and the magistrates—particularly the *oidores* of the *audiencias*—were its most important part.[27] The major difference here, and this has frequently been pointed out, was the much greater degree of exclusion of American-born Spaniards from the higher posts in the Spanish side. This fact has been singled out with reason as an important source of alienation of upper-class Creoles and of conflict with *peninsulares*.[28] And it must be added that the exclusion had also the consequence of preventing the development of a sizable group of

TABLE 3. Occupation of Cabinet Ministers, by Period, 1822–1889 (in percentage)

	1822–31	1831–40	1840–53	1853–71	1871–89	Total
Public employees						
Magistrates	33.3	45.7	47.8	30.0	12.1	29.7
Military	46.7	31.4	13.0	20.0	6.1	22.4
Other	6.7	5.7	—	4.0	1.5	3.7
Total public employees	86.7	82.9	60.8	54.0	19.7	55.8
Professions	6.6	14.3	26.1	40.0	65.1	35.1
Other	6.7	2.8	13.1	6.0	15.2	9.1
Total number of ministers	(45)	(35)	(23)	(50)	(66)	(219)

Source: José Murilo de Carvalho, *A Construção da Ordem: A Elite Política Imperial* (Rio de Janeiro: Campus, 1980), 79.

Note: The percentages of public employees among senators are, for the first three periods, 65, 67, and 57, respectively. The figures for magistrates for the same periods are, in percentages, 42, 53, and 43. Among deputies, public employees represented around 40 percent until the end of the fifties; magistrates accounted for about 30 percent of the total.

Occupation was used here as an indication of training and socialization, not of social origin or of class links. Many public employees, for instance, including judges, were sons or relatives of landowners if not landowners themselves. Available data on social origin, though, are not very complete and not very reliable.

Creoles with practical experience in government matters at the highest levels of public administration, that is, of state building proper. Participation in the *cabildos,* the local administrative bodies, was not likely to provide such experience.

In summary, I am arguing that the presence in Brazil by the time of independence of an elite that, by the place and content of training, by career pattern and occupational experience, constituted a closely united group of people, ideologically homogeneous, statist oriented, and practical in government matters, was a basic factor in the maintenance of the unity of the former colony and in the adoption of a centralized monarchical system. This could have been a not sufficient condition, but it seems to me that it was a necessary one. The great number of rebellions, some with secessionist tendencies, that took place in Brazil both before and after independence shows that the business of keeping the country together was a very difficult task indeed. Between 1831 and 1848 alone, more than twenty minor revolts and seven major ones broke out in different parts of the country. In three of the latter, the leaders proclaimed independent republican governments. Had there been numerous local and parochial elites, instead of a united national elite, the colony would most probably have broken apart into several different countries, just as happened on the Spanish side.[29]

It is significant, for example, that very few of the graduates of Coimbra, or of the military trained at the College of the Nobles for that matter, took part in the rebellions. A look at the list of persons indicted for participation in three of the preindependence rebellions shows that, aside from a few intellectuals trained in Europe outside of Portugal, the most conspicuous participants were priests and local lower-rank military.[30] Priests, in fact, provided the clearest opposition to the magistrates among the educated elite. Most of the lower clergy had been educated in Brazil and were both more parochial, in the sense of lacking concern for maintaining the unity of the country, and more influenced by politically subversive ideas, such as popular sovereignty and republicanism. Two years after independence, a rebellion, led mostly by priests, went as far as to proclaim an independent republican government in the northeastern part of the country. By mid-century, when the rebellions had ended and the monarchy was solidly established, priests had been completely eliminated from the national political elite.

One alternative explanation that has been put forward for the difference in political behavior between magistrates and priests points in the direction of their different class origins, priests being recruited among the lower strata of the population. There may in fact have been some difference in social origin, in general, between the two groups. Only families of substance could afford to send their sons to Coimbra. But on the other side, it is well known that to have a priest in the family was as prestigious as to have a magistrate or lawyer. It was also very convenient for rich families to have one of the sons become a priest since a noninheriting male heir made it easier to keep the family estate intact. And the fact is that almost all priests who took part in the rebellions were rich and the offspring of wealthy families. Some priests were usurers, some landowners, some even plantation and slave owners. In terms of social origin, therefore, there seems to be little or no difference between the rebellious priests and the magistrates. The major difference was in their ideology and training.

As far as the military are concerned, their participation in the rebellions was limited to members of the lower ranks or to officers of the militia corps. Most of the higher-ranking officers who appear among the national political elite during the first and second decades after independence were trained at Coimbra or at the College of the Nobles, and they did not differ very much in terms of political outlook from the magistrates, being also deeply involved in state affairs. Their number among the elite, particularly among senators and deputies, was progressively reduced in favor of magistrates and lawyers, reflecting the consolidation of the monarchical system. In the meantime, the training of the military took a more technical direction and was clearly separated from the training of the political elite. This fact, together with a change in the social composition of the officer corps and the influence of positivism, gradually helped to alienate them from the civilian elite and from the monarchy. They would come back to the national political scene at the end of the empire as allies of republican groups.[31]

The absence of a radical break in the Brazilian process of independence made it possible for the national elite to replicate the policy that had produced it. Only two law schools were established during the empire, and the members of the elite, as previously shown, continued to be drawn from the graduates of these schools. An elaborate system of advancement in the political career was also developed: starting as a municipal judge, the politician would slowly proceed up to the highest posts of ministers and state councillors in a further reinforcement of the ideological unity, statist orientation, and familiarity with public office that were found among their Portuguese antecedents.

The Political Elite and the Nature of the State

From the previous discussion it can be concluded that the presence of an elite such as the one found in Brazil at the end of the colonial period was no accident at all. It was the product of an explicit effort made by the Portuguese state. And this brings us to the problem of the nature of this state and of its relationships with society. The Portuguese state would and could train such an elite because it had itself benefited from an early consolidation, which dated from the accession to power of D. João I after his victory at the battle of Aljubarrota in 1385. D. João won with the support of the merchant class and this, according to Oliveira Martins, meant the end of the Middle Ages in Portugal, a final blow against the feudal barons, who were already weakened by the long struggle against the Moors.[32] But unlike the case in England, a modern market economy and a liberal society did not develop in Portugal at the same time that a modern state was being molded. With the overseas adventure, commercial capitalism developed under the protection of the crown, the king being the country's first and most powerful merchant. An independent bourgeoisie could not ascend to become a dominant social class as in other European countries. As a consequence, there was a predominance of the state and a weakness of the institutions of political representation, one characteristic of which was the pervasive overrepresentation of public employees among the political elite.[33]

In Brazil this predominance—and that of the magistrates in particular—led eventually to a reaction. In 1855 a House bill was introduced in the Brazilian Congress intended to establish restrictions on the eligibility of magistrates and other public employees to serve as legislators. In the illuminating debate that followed some deputies called attention to the consequences of the continued predominance of magistrates for the nature of political representation in Brazil. I quote one of them: "Can we say, Mr. President, that a House represents faithfully the interests of all classes in society when 82 of its 113 members are legists [magistrates]? Where are, Gentlemen, the representatives of the industrial classes, of the landowners, of the capitalists, of the merchants?" Another had voiced a similar concern: "In this House there are no merchants, no farmers, all are public employees, so to speak." The role of the magistrates in politics was forcefully defended during the debate, but the fact remained that political representation was impaired by the overwhelming presence of government employees in the legislature.[34]

In a parallel direction there was a constant complaint against the excessive size and influence of the central bureaucracy. One of the most perceptive politicians and social reformers of the last years of the regime, Joaquim Nabuco, attributed this overgrown structure to slavery. In his view the existence of slave labor prevented the majority of the free population from developing economic alternatives to public employment, to which the majority was forced to turn as a source of income; slavery made public employees, in his words, "the government's serfs."[35] Nabuco was, of course, overstating the case. But public jobs were certainly the aspiration of many, and the bureaucracy weighed heavily on the state's budget. By the end of the empire expenditures on personnel ate up 60 percent of the central budget, and almost 70 percent of the civil service was concentrated in the central government. This contributed to the high visibility of the national government, and the state in general, and led some observers to view the political system as stateful and the state as a leviathan dominating an inert society. On the other side, those who stressed the existence of a powerful land- and slave-owning class, in control of the export-oriented economy, concluded that the government was simply the representative of the interests of this class.[36] The present discussion of the political elite can help to reconcile such conflicting views.

The continuity that characterized the process of independence, and the centralized monarchical system that was established—in good part, as I have argued, because of the nature of the political elite—gave the state apparatus a significant weight of its own and made the government a major actor in the life of the country, as had been the case in Portugal. It made possible the partial fusion of the bureaucracy and the political elite, giving at times the impression that it was the government and not social groups and classes that was represented in Congress. But on the other side, unlike Portugal, Brazil had a strong landowning class highly dependent on slave labor. This class dominated the economy of the country, which was based mostly on exports of coffee, sugar, and tobacco. And the central government depended on the taxes levied on external trade, which amounted to 70 percent of the budget. So the stability of the government required an alliance between the bureaucracy and the landed classes.

But this was an unstable alliance. Several observers besides Joaquim Nabuco have pointed out how the slave system restricted economic opportunities for elements of the middle sectors, both rural and urban. Moreover, the long-term stagnation of the sugar economy in the northern part of the country contributed to the unemployment of members of landed classes also. In addition, the near monopoly held by foreigners on the commercial sector of the larger cities aggravated the situation. The bureaucracy became then one of the few alternatives for all those job seekers, and the scramble for public jobs was a widely recognized fact. Having been either expelled from the slave economy in its decadent sector, or denied channels of upward mobility by the general constraints of a slave society, many members of the bureaucracy had no strong commitment to maintain the slave system. They could support or even initiate social reforms once convinced that the fiscal basis of the state, that is, of their salaries, would not be threatened by such action. In fact, the major abolitionist law of 1871, that which declared free all children born thenceforward to slave mothers, was passed over the strong opposition of landowners, who bitterly attacked the government and the emperor. The approval of the law was made possible by the large number of public employees in the House.[37]

This was a complex situation indeed. The elite, and the state itself, were dependent on the slave economy and were in some sense the supporters of the slave society. But they were also able to detach themselves from the interests of slavery and become an instrument of reform. This contradiction was perceived by Joaquim Nabuco when he observed that the state was at the same time a shadow of slavery and the only force capable of putting an end to it. This was also the reason why the regime was, on one side, able to survive for sixty-nine years but also, on the other, very vulnerable. One year after his daughter, then regent, was enthusiastically applauded in the streets of Rio for abolishing slavery, the aging emperor was quietly sent into exile after being overthrown in a bloodless coup d'état engineered by a sector of the bureaucracy he had always overlooked, the military, and by the republican landowners of the most prosperous coffee areas.

A unified elite was instrumental in consolidating the political power of the dominant classes by neutralizing the consequences of their internal divisions and by keeping at bay political mobilization from below. But in view of the very lack of cohesion within these classes, and as a consequence of its own training, the elite could achieve this goal only by building a national state apparatus, which then became a major political actor in its own right. Now the major common interests between the state and the dominant classes were the maintenance of order and the control of political mobilization. When it came to specific issues that affected differently the economic interests of various sectors of the dominant classes, the elite, and particularly its bureaucratic component, was able to play one sector against the other and implement important reforms, even at the cost of the political legitimacy of the regime. So, instead of a dichotomic division of state versus society, or of the mechanistic representation by the state of the interests of the landowners, Brazilian political reality looked more like a field of dialectical tensions that did not lead to radical ruptures but was, nonetheless, dynamic enough to generate political and social changes.[38]

Political Elites and State Building

The case of nineteenth-century Brazil suggests some speculations on the role of political elites in general. The classical studies of political elites remain up to now the ones written by Vilfredo Pareto and Gaetano Mosca. But both authors are guilty in this subject of reductionist explanations, a psychological reductionism in the case of Pareto, a sociological reductionism in the case of Mosca. In Pareto's view elites appear and disappear according to the distribution of what he called the residues, particularly the residues of coercion and of persuasion. In the same vein, Mosca sees elites as a function of societal forces. If force predominates in society, an elite of warriors will emerge; if wealth, an elite of plutocrats; if religion, an elite of priests; and so on. Neither of the two have paid attention to the possibility of politically created elites, especially trained for the tasks of government, and to elites that could reproduce themselves and have a significant impact on the nature of the political systems.[39]

However, from the mandarins, or *literati,* who for more than one thousand years were carefully trained to administer and govern the Chinese agrarian society, to the professional revolutionaries of Lenin, history is full of examples of these elites.[40] Without going into the rather sterile discussion that involved many American scholars during the 1960s about the existence or nonexistence of power elites,[41] I shall assume as historically demonstrated the presence of particular types of elites that were especially important for the political evolution of some states and inquire into the nature of these groups and into the conditions of their emergence.

From the discussion of the Brazilian case, it is apparent that one basic characteristic of these elites is their homogeneity. The more homogeneous an elite, the greater its chances of being successful, ceteris paribus. But there can be different types of homogeneity. The most obvious one is social homogeneity, which is obtained by recruitment of the elite from one particular social class or social group. This type of homogeneity, it seems to me, is not always present in these governing elites and is seldom sufficient to produce a unified elite. The Chinese gentry, according to Chung-li Chang, had no such characteristic; the Portuguese magistracy also was not recruited from a single social group, and the same can be said of the bolsheviks. Even an elite as socially homogeneous as the British developed some additional means to reinforce its unity. Such was, for instance, in good part, the role of the education imparted at Eton, Harrow, Oxford, and Cambridge. In W. L. Guttsman's view, these schools were very efficient in providing the British elite not so much with a particular expertise but, rather, with a common ethos, an aristocratic style of life appropriate for a class that believed itself destined to rule.[42] In Latin America the best example of a socially homogeneous elite was the Chilean. Its homogeneity was also increased by higher education, although not as much as in the British case. And another important factor accounting for the exceptional homogeneity of the Chilean dominant class was its concentration in agriculture and in one geographical area, the Central Valley, where 60 percent of the population also lived.[43] The same homogeneity did not obtain among the dominant classes of other Latin American countries, not to mention other former colonies, such as those of Africa, where ethnic and tribal cleavages made almost impossible the formation of a socially homogeneous dominant class. In the Brazilian case it can be said that a substantial part of the elite, at least at the time of independence, was also recruited among the dominant class.[44] But—and this is true also for other countries of the area—recruitment in the dominant class was not sufficient to generate a unified elite because this class was itself divided into conflicting sectors, or at least into sectors that had no strong bonds to keep them together.[45]

It seems, therefore, that, if not instead of social homogeneity, there must be present, at the least as an additional factor, the element of ideological homogeneity. The latter can be generated through various means. Usually it comes about through a common worldview implanted by formal training, through common career experiences, through common political or life experiences, or through combinations of the above. In China there was Confucianism and the elaborate examination system, besides the career itself. In Portugal there was Roman law and Coimbra and the bureaucratic experience. In Russia there was Marxism and the party organization, besides the shared experience of a protracted struggle. The same can be said of modern China, where the Long March produced a closely united group of comrades that for a long time after victory provided the nucleus of the socialist state.[46]

In the Brazilian case it is my argument that social homogeneity alone would not have been sufficient to weld a unified elite, as the rebellions led by upper-class elements, including priests, demonstrate. The multiplication of these rebellions during the regency period, 1831–40, ended by providing a further element of unification of the national elite since its members read into them the threat to order and national unity, the materialization of which could be seen in their Spanish-speaking neighbors. In the latter, the fact that the elites existing at the end of colonial rule were not unified by a common view and a common experience favored their involvement in conflicts that resulted in further fragmentation and contributed to the breakdown of the political unity of the major colonial centers and to extreme political instability.

Finally, a third factor appears among the elites I have been talking about. Besides being homogeneous, these groups have a common training that, in addition to reinforcing their unity, provides them with a special capacity for the tasks of government and organization in general. This is evident among the elites that have a strong bureaucratic component, from the Chinese mandarins to the Turkish elite of the Ataturk period, with the Portuguese, Prussian, and Japanese elites in the middle.[47] But the bolshevik experience shows the possibility of training such an elite outside the state apparatus. Lenin's *What Is to Be Done?* argues cogently the need for special training. He states that the professional agitator and organizer should be carefully trained, under the party's supervision; should combine theory and practice; should expand his experience to different factories and eventually to the whole country; and should learn from the leaders of other parties. Without such men, he concludes, the proletariat could not sustain a steady struggle.[48] With the help of this trained and ideologically homogeneous group of people, he and other leaders were able to organize the masses in order to destroy the old regime and, particularly, to build a revolutionary state from the ashes of the old.

Since these elites are politically engineered, it is very difficult, if not utterly impossible, to establish a priori the conditions for their emergence. I shall observe only that they tend to have special importance during the initial phase of state building, which is characterized by the delim-itation of a territory, the establishment of a tax system, the organization of justice, the control of the means of physical coercion, and so on— that is, to paraphrase Marx, during the phase of primitive accumulation of power. This usually takes place in times of intense political change, such as liberation from colonial rule or revolutions, or in the type of situation that has been called conservative modernization.[49] But this observation is not of much help since, even in those circumstances, the elites I am talking about may or may not be present. If they were present in Brazil in 1822, they were not in other countries of Latin America; if they were present in Russia in 1917 and after, they were not in Mexico in 1910.

As a product of political decisions, the emergence of these elites must be left in good part to the uncertainties of historical contingency. The important point is that they represent a particularly strong example of human intervention in molding history and that this intervention is never an innocent one. In fact, these elites are especially effective in consoli-dating the political power either of divided socially dominant classes or of poorly organized dominated classes after the victory of a revolutionary movement. But however different is the social content of the policies implemented in these cases, one characteristic tends to remain constant. By usually operating from within the structure of state power, these elites seldom, if ever, favor the development of autonomous political partic-ipation. If they are efficient in accumulating power, they almost always fail when it comes to distributing it.

NOTES

This article was written while I was in Princeton as a member of the Institute for Advanced Study, whose support is greatly appreciated. I benefited from comments by several members of the institute, particularly Clifford Geertz and John H. Elliott. I am also grateful to Raymond Grew for his suggestions.

1. Many of the arguments and data presented here were developed in connection with the research done for my Ph.D. dissertation, "Elite and State-Building in Imperial Brazil" (Stanford University, 1975), and, in Brazil, *A Construção da Ordem: A Elite política imperial* (Rio de Janeiro: Campus, 1980).

2. Celso Furtado, *Economic Development of Latin America: A Survey from Colonial Times to the Cuban Revolution* (Cambridge: Cambridge University Press, 1970), 13–18. On the decadence of the mining economy, see, for instance, Kenneth R. Maxwell, *Conflicts and Conspiracies: Brazil and Portugal, 1750–1808* (Cambridge: Cambridge University Press, 1973). Caio Prado, Jr., recognizes that the bulk of colonial commerce was done with the metropolis. The only internal commercial link that, according to him, had some impact in terms of unifying parts of the colony was provided by the cattle trade. See Caio Prado, Jr., *The Colonial Background of Modern Brazil* (Berkeley and Los Angeles: University of California Press, 1967), 271–72.

3. Osvaldo Sunkel and Pedro Paz, *El Subdesarrollo latino-americano y la teoria del Desarrollo* (Mexico City: Siglo XXI, 1970), 275–343, esp. 300, 328.

4. See Hermes Lima, *Notas à vida Brasileira* (São Paulo: Brasiliense, 1945), 8–10, 136–40. For a similar view, see Emília Viotti da Costa, "The Political Emancipation of Brazil," in *From Colony to Nation: Essays on the Independence of Brazil*, ed. A. J. R. Russell-Wood (Baltimore and London: Johns Hopkins University Press, 1975), 70. A different view, arguing that slavery was favored by political decentralization, is presented by Manoel de Oliveira Lima, *The Evolution of Brazil Compared with That of Spanish and Anglo-Saxon America* (Stanford: Stanford University Publications, 1914), 51–52.

5. This was particularly the case of a frustrated rebellion that took place in Bahia in 1798. Several slaves were involved in it, and twenty-four of the thirty-four people indicted were either blacks or mulattoes. See Affonso Ruy, *A Primeira revolução social brasileira (1798)* (Rio de Janeiro: Laemmert, 1970), 114–17. The position of the Bahian elite is described in John Norman Kennedy, "Bahian Elites, 1750–1822," *Hispanic American Historical Review* 53 (August 1973):415–39.

6. On José Bonifácio, see Octávio Tarquínio de Souza, *José Bonifácio, 1773–1838* (Rio de Janeiro: J. Olympio, 1945). See also Leslie Bethell, *The Abolition of the Brazilian Slave Trade* (Cambridge: Cambridge University Press, 1970), 42–43. The idea of transforming the former colony into a "great nation," in a "vast empire," was almost an obsession among many leaders of the independence movement, as the minutes of the first Council of State, created in 1822, well indicate. One councillor, comparing D. Pedro to the Roman emperors, declared that it would be "the greatest pleasure of my life to see Brazil, from the Amazon to the Prata, united in one single kingdom." See Senado Federal, *Atas do conselho de estado*, ed. José Honório Rodrigues (Brasília: Senado Federal, 1973), 1:23.

7. See C. H. Haring, *The Spanish Empire in America* (New York: Oxford University Press, 1947), 137; and also John Leddy Phelan, *The Kingdom of Quito in the Seventeenth Century: Bureaucratic Politics in the Spanish Empire* (Madison: University of Wisconsin Press, 1967), 122–23.

8. For case studies on the relationships of colonial administrators among

themselves and with the metropolis, see Dauril Alden, *Royal Government in Colonial Brazil with Special Reference to the Administration of the Marquis of Lavradio, Viceroy, 1769–1779* (Berkeley: University of California Press, 1968), esp. chap. 16; and Phelan, *Kingdom of Quito,* esp. pt. 2. A recent argument in favor of a basically similar tradition can be found in Claudio Veliz, *The Centralist Tradition of Latin America* (Princeton: Princeton University Press, 1980).

9. The introduction of the more aggressive *intendentes* (intendents) during the Bourbon period, as substitutes for the *corregidores* (district magistrates), together with the continuing exclusion of Creoles, might have had the unintended effect of spurring local government represented by the *cabildos* (municipal councils). This was, according to John Lynch, what happened in the Rio de la Plata viceroyalty. See his "Crisis of Colonial Administration," in *The Origins of the Latin American Revolutions, 1808–1826,* ed. R. A. Humphreys and John Lynch (New York: Alfred A. Knopf, 1966), 122–23.

10. Quoted in J. F. de Almeida Prado, *D. João VI e o início da classe dirigente do Brasil* (São Paulo: Editores Nacional, 1968), 134. The same view can be found in J. M. Pereira da Silva, *História da Fundação do império Brazileiro* (Rio de Janeiro: B. L. Garnier, 1864), 135; Henrique Handelman, *História do Brasil* (Rio de Janeiro: RIHGB, 1930), 710; Viotti da Costa, "Political Emancipation," 66; and others.

11. See Pereira da Silva, *História da Fundação,* 275; C. H. Haring, *Empire in Brazil: A New World Experiment with Democracy* (Cambridge: Harvard University Press, 1969), 23–24; John Armitage, *The History of Brazil from . . . 1808 to . . . 1831* (London: Smith, Elder, 1836), 2:138; Tobias Monteiro, *História do império: A Elaboração da independência* (Rio de Janeiro: F. Briguiet, 1927), 851; Francisco Adolfo de Varnhagen, *História da Independência do Brasil* (Rio de Janeiro: Imprensa Nacional, 1917), 349–50.

12. See Carlos A. Villanueva, *La Monarquia en America: Bolívar y el General San Martín* (Paris: Libreria Paul Ollendorff, 1911), esp. 235–51. According to Villanueva, besides Mexico and San Martín's Argentina, the idea of a monarchy occurred also to elements of the elite in Venezuela, Chile, Peru, and Colombia.

13. It is interesting to observe that the Spanish American countries served as a negative example for the Brazilian elite. During the difficult years of the regency, 1831–40, troubled by constant rebellions, some of which with secessionist and republican tendencies, it was common for members of the national elite, liberals and conservatives alike, to insist on the maintenance of the monarchy as a way of preventing the evils of fragmentation and internal struggle that had befallen Brazil's neighbors.

14. Not by coincidence, the most specific and detailed study available deals with the Chilean elite, the most homogeneous of the Spanish-speaking countries. See Alberto Edwards Vives, *La fronda aristocrática en Chile* (Santiago de Chile: Ediciones Ercilla, 1936). Other useful works include Tulio Halperin-Donghi, *Revolución y guerra: Formación de una elite dirigente en la Argentina Criolla* (Buenos Aires: Siglo Veintiuno, 1972); Robert G. Gilmore, *Caudillism and Militarism in Venezuela* (Athens: Ohio University Press, 1964); D. A. Brading,

"Government and Elite in Late Colonial Mexico," *Hispanic American Historical Review* 53 (August 1973):389–414; and Seymour Martin Lipset and Aldo Solari, eds., *Elites in Latin America* (New York: Oxford University Press, 1967).

15. Quoted in Américo Jacobina Lacombe, "A igreja no Brasil colonial," in *História geral da civilização brasileira,* ed. Sérgio Buarque de Holanda, bk. 1, 2:72 (São Paulo: Difel, 1965–72).

16. See Francisco Morais, "Estudantes brasileiros na Universidade de Coimbra (1772–1872)," *Anais da Biblioteca Nacional do Rio de Janeiro* 62 (1940):137–335.

17. I am defining as the national political elite the persons who occupied the top positions in the political system. The core of this elite was formed by cabinet ministers, state councillors, and senators, a total of 342 persons. A total of 1,027 deputies, who served in ten legislatures, were also considered, although in less depth, due to the greater difficulty in finding information on them. State councillors were appointed for life by the emperor and in good part overlapped with ministers and senators. Senators were elected but also held a life tenure. Deputies were elected for a four-year term. For the sake of simplicity, I will present complete data only for ministers. There are no major variations for the rest. A parallel work independent of this study arrived at somewhat similar conclusions about the nature of the Brazilian elite: see Eul-Soo Pang and Ron L. Seckinger, "The Mandarins of Imperial Brazil," *Comparative Studies in Society and History* 14, no. 2 (1972):215–44. The importance of juridical training was also stressed by Roderick and Jean Barman, "The Role of the Law Graduate in the Political Elite of Imperial Brazil," *Journal of Inter-American Studies and World Affairs* 18 (November 1976):432–49.

18. On the colonial universities, see John Tate Lanning, *Academic Culture in the Spanish Colonies* (Folcroft: Folcroft Press, 1969), 3–33; and German Arciniegas, *Latin America: A Cultural History* (New York: Alfred A. Knopf, 1967), 151–52. Arciniegas lists twenty-five universities, which Lanning reduced to twenty-three, arguing that some were counted twice because of their transformation from minor to major universities.

19. Lanning, *Academic Culture,* 53.

20. For a history of the University of Coimbra, see Teófilo Brago, *História da Universidade de Coimbra nas suas relações com a instrução pública portuguesa.* 4 vols. (Lisboa: Tip. da Academia Real das Ciências, 1892–1902).

21. On Pombal's effort to revitalize the Portuguese and colonial economies, see Maxwell, *Conflicts and Conspiracies,* esp. chaps. 1–2. On his educational reforms, see Laerte Ramos de Carvalho, *As Reformas pombalinas da instrução pública* (São Paulo: USP, 1952). The activity of the reform generation in Brazil was studied in Kenneth R. Maxwell, "The Generation of the 1790s and the Idea of Luso-Brazilian Empire," in *Colonial Roots of Modern Brazil,* ed. Dauril Alden, 107–44 (Berkeley: University of California Press, 1973); and in Maria Odila da Silva Dias, "Aspectos da ilustração no Brasil," *Revista do Instituto Histórico e Geográfico brasileiro* 278 (January–March 1968):105–70.

22. Braga, *História da Universidade,* 1:126. On the general influence of Roman law and its instrumental part in strengthening the authority of the kings,

see Hans Julius Wolff, *Roman Law: An Historical Introduction* (Norman: University of Oklahoma Press, 1967), chap. 7. Its influence and the role of university-trained jurists is also stressed by Max Weber. See H. H. Gerth and C. Wright Mills, *From Max Weber: Essays in Sociology* (New York: Oxford University Press, 1946), 93. For a demonstration of a more diversified use of Roman law during the period of emergence of the modern state, see Myron Piper Gilmore, *Argument from Roman Law in Political Thought, 1200–1600* (Cambridge: Harvard University Press, 1941). The influence of Roman law, particularly the *jus civile*, on the Brazilian legislation, is described in Theresa Sherrer Davidson, "The Brazilian Inheritance of Roman Law," in *Brazil: Papers Presented in the Institute for Brazilian Studies, Vanderbilt University*, ed. James B. Watson et al., 59–90 (Nashville: Vanderbilt University Press, 1953).

23. See Cabral de Moncada, *Um "Iluminista" português do século XVIII: Luís Antônio Verney*, quoted in L. R. de Carvalho, *As Reformas pombalinas*, 26–27. Even Pombal's reform did not go so far as to accept authors such as Rousseau and Voltaire. It remained politically conservative, in line with the authoritarian views of the marquis. Many of the scientists trained under the influence of the reform were sent to Brazil, commissioned by the crown to explore the economic potentialities of the colony. The captaincy of Minas Gerais alone, rich in mineral resources, had thirty-four such scientists holding public office at the end of the colonial period. See José Ferreira Carrato, *Igreja, iluminismo e escolas mineiras coloniais* (São Paulo: Ediciones Nacional, 1968), 240–45.

24. See Eduardo Frieiro, *O Diabo na livraria do Cônego* (Belo Horizonte: Itatiaia, 1957); and also Alexander Marchant, "Aspects of the Enlightenment in Brazil," in *Latin American Enlightenment*, ed. Arthur P. Whitaker, 95–118. (Ithaca, N.Y.: Cornell University Press, 1961). The more progressive aspects of the activities of intellectuals in the colony are stressed in E. Bradford Burns, "The Intellectuals as Agents of Change and the Independence of Brazil, 1724–1882," in *From Colony to Nation*, ed. Russell-Wood, 211–46. Many of the more radical intellectuals, though, were priests or had been trained in France or England. Particularly active were physicians trained in France at Montpellier.

25. See Lanning, *Academic Culture*, 18, 33. For the general impact of the Catholic church, see Richard E. Greenleaf, *The Roman Catholic Church in Colonial Latin America* (New York: Alfred A. Knopf, 1971). On the influence of the Enlightenment in Latin America in general, see Whitaker, *Latin American Enlightenment*.

26. Stuart B. Schwartz, *Sovereignty and Society in Colonial Brazil: The High Court of Bahia and Its Judges, 1609–1751* (Berkeley: University of California Press, 1973). By the same author, see "Magistracy and Society in Colonial Brazil," *Hispanic American Historical Review* 50 (November 1970):715–30.

27. See Phelan, *Kingdom of Quito*, 119–46.

28. A selection of texts on the conflicts between Creoles and *peninsulares* can be found in Humphreys and Lynch, eds., *Origins*, pt. 7. M. A. Burkholder and D. S. Chandler challenge the traditional view of the exclusion of Creoles in their study of *Audiencia* appointments. But they recognize that after 1776 discrimination against the American-born increased. See Burkholder and Chandler, "Creole Appointments and the Sale of Audiencia Positions in the Spanish Empire

under the Early Bourbons, 1701–1750," *Journal of Latin American Studies* 4 (November 1972):187–206.

29. In a recent book Jorge I. Dominguez, after discarding several possible explanations for the political evolution of the Spanish colonies, also stresses the nature of the relationships between elite groups and the government as an explanatory factor, concentrating on the cases of Chile, Mexico, Cuba, and Venezuela. The difference from my approach is that he is dealing not only with the political elite but primarily with the economic and local elites, and he does not give particular emphasis to socialization factors. The specificity of the Brazilian case, it seems to me, was exactly the presence of a national political elite, that is, of an elite that could aggregate the interests of the dominant groups and protect them through the mediation of the state power. See Dominguez, *Insurrection or Loyalty: The Breakdown of the Spanish American Empire* (Cambridge: Harvard University Press, 1980).

30. See J. M. de Carvalho, *A Construção,* 145.

31. On the military, see John Henry Schulz, "Brazilian Army and Politics, 1850–1894" (Ph.D. diss., Princeton University, 1973).

32. Oliveira Martins, *História de Portugal* (Lisboa: Guimarães Editores, 1968), 158.

33. On the economic evolution of Portugal, see João Lúcio de Azevedo, *Epocas de Portugal econômico* (Lisboa: Livraria Clássica Ediciones, 1973). The development of a powerful bureaucratic stratum is described in Raymundo Faoro, *Os Donos do poder: Formação do patronato político brasileiro* (Porto Alegre: Globo, 1958), chaps. 1–3.

34. See J. M. de Carvalho, *A Construção,* 138. At the time the House had 77 members who held law degrees in a total of 113 members. Of the 77, there were 43 judges, and several others were also public employees.

35. Joaquim Nabuco, *Abolitionism: The Brazilian Antislavery Struggle,* ed. and trans. Robert Conrad (Urbana: University of Illinois Press, 1977), 128.

36. For the first view, Faoro, *Os donos do poder,* 262; for the second, Nestor Duarte, *A Ordem privada e a organização political nacional* (São Paulo: Editores Nacional, 1939). On the concept of stateful societies, see J. P. Nettl, "The State as a Conceptual Variable," *World Politics* 20 (July 1968):559–92.

37. The vote in the House showed a combination of political and economic pressures. Public employees voted overwhelmingly for the measure, but most of them came from the northern and northeastern parts of the country, where the importance of slave labor was becoming less pressing because of the lack of economic dynamism. The south had fewer public employees among its representatives, and its growing coffee economy depended heavily on its slave work force. Southern representatives voted overwhelmingly against the measure. See J. M. de Carvalho, "Elite and State-Building," 329–39.

38. For an elaborate analysis of the compromises between the central government and local power elites using the Weberian notion of patrimonial bureaucracy, see Fernando Uricoechea, *The Patrimonial Foundations of the Brazilian Bureaucratic State* (Berkeley: University of California Press, 1980).

39. See Vilfredo Pareto, *Sociological Writings,* sel. and intro. S. E. Finer

(London: Pall Mall Press, 1966), 51–71; and Gaetano Mosca, *The Ruling Class* (New York and London: McGraw-Hill, 1939), chap. 2.

40. On the Chinese literati, see Chung-li Chang, *The Chinese Gentry: Studies in Their Role in Nineteenth-Century Chinese Society* (Seattle: University of Washington Press, 1970). An interesting, although somewhat overdrawn, comparison between the Chinese mandarins and the Brazilian elite can be found in Pang and Seckinger, "Mandarins of Imperial Brazil," 215–44. On revolutionary elites, see Harold D. Lasswell and Daniel Lerner, eds., *World Revolutionary Elites: Studies in Coercive Ideological Movements* (Cambridge: MIT Press, 1966); and Robert A. Scalapino, *Elites in the People's Republic of China* (Seattle: University of Washington Press, 1972).

41. The debate involved sociologists and political scientists. For a critical evaluation, see John Walton, "Discipline, Method, and Community Power: A Note on the Sociology of Knowledge," *American Political Science Review* 52 (June 1958):463–569.

42. See W. L. Guttsman, *The British Political Elite* (London: Macgibbon and Kee, 1963), 151–58.

43. See Vives, *La Fronda aristocrática,* 15 and passim.

44. As mentioned, data on the social origin of the elite are extremely scarce and not very reliable. According to the information I could gather, around 50 percent of the elite had some sort of connection either with the landed or the commercial upper classes. The actual figure was probably higher. One sector of the elite that presented a clear change in its recruitment pattern was the military. From a more aristocratic origin at the beginning of the empire, the military elite began to recruit more and more from lower-middle sectors and from their own ranks. See J. M. de Carvalho, *A Construção,* 86–89.

45. Conflicts among sectors of the dominant classes in some Spanish-speaking countries are described by Dominguez, *Insurrection or Loyalty.* In Brazil landowners were involved in the rebellions of 1789, 1817, 1824, and 1848; they were the major actors of one republican rebellion that lasted from 1835 to 1845 in the south and of two rebellions in 1842 that involved two of the most important provinces close to the capital of the empire. When basic issues, such as slavery or land property, were debated in Congress, conflicts of the interests of different sectors of the upper classes became always apparent.

46. On China, see Scalapino, *Elites in the People's Republic of China.* An interesting negative example of the importance of socialization is provided by a study of the Algerian elite. According to this study, different political experiences, and not social or ethnic differences among the various sectors of the elite, accounted for the difficulties in establishing a stable political system. See William B. Quandt, "The Algerian Political Elite, 1954–1967" (Ph.D. diss., MIT, 1968).

47. On the Prussian elite, see Hans Rosenberg, *Bureaucracy, Aristocracy, and Autocracy: The Prussian Experience, 1660–1815* (Cambridge: Harvard University Press, 1958). On the Turkish elite, see Frederick W. Frey, *The Turkish Political Elite* (Cambridge: MIT Press, 1965). There is a striking similarity between the Brazilian imperial elite and the Turkish elite of the period between 1920 and 1954 in terms of education and occupational distribution. According to Frey,

the consolidation of the Turkish state under Mustafa Kemal was achieved by an elite heavily dominated by bureaucratic elements.

48. V. I. Lenin, *What Is to Be Done?* trans. S. V. and Patricia Utechin (London: Clarendon Press, 1963), 152–53.

49. On the role of elites in conservative modernization, see Rosenberg, *Bureaucracy,* for the Prussian case. The Meiji reform and the Ataturk revolution were analyzed by Ellen Kay Timberger in "A Theory of Elite Revolutions," *Studies in Comparative International Development* 7 (Autumn 1972):191–207.

The Cuban Revolution in Comparative Perspective

Susan Eckstein

How did Castro survive the "popular" revolts against Communist rule the world over in 1989? Is the reason rooted solely in his charisma or the repressive capacity of his regime, or have Cubans benefited from their country's political, economic, and social transformation?

The impact of the revolution can best be assessed by comparing contemporary Cuba not only with the prerevolutionary society but also with developments in other Latin American countries. Cuba shares with other countries in the region a common colonial heritage and common historically rooted ties to the world economy. No study has systematically compared developments in postrevolutionary Cuba with developments during the same period in the rest of Latin America.

The impact of revolution must be differentiated from the impact of evolutionary tendencies. It will be "teased out" by examining how Cuba's ranking among Latin American countries on quantifiable indicators of social and economic development has changed since the sociopolitical transformation. If Cuba registers change on a measure of development but its regional ranking on the indicator remains the same since the prerevolutionary period, either revolutionary forces have similar effects or the changes in postrevolutionary Cuba reflect forces not specifically rooted in the transformation; in either case the evidence suggests that revolution does not have a markedly distinguishable impact on the aspect of development under consideration.

The cross-national and cross-temporal analysis contributes to a better understanding of the ways in which revolutions are of consequence. The quantitative analysis will be supplemented, however, with a more in-depth qualitative discussion of developments in Cuba. The quantitative and qualitative analysis combined help to explain why Castro's Cuba is almost a solitary Communist survivor. Cuba will be shown not to be the "basket case" portrayed by the U.S. government.

The specific dimensions of development to be examined are: the expansion and diversification of the productive capacity of the economy;

trade vulnerability and foreign indebtedness; and health, welfare, and the distribution of land and wealth. These aspects do not exhaust all components of economic and social development, but they include the most important. Reasons why each factor has been selected for inquiry will be discussed. Before comparing developments in Cuba and the rest of the region, island conditions at the eve of the societal upheaval are described, for the revolution can only be adequately understood in historical context. The final section presents theoretical and policy implications of the findings.

Cuba at the Time of the Revolution

The Cuban revolution is Fidel Castro's revolution. Without his charismatic appeal modern Cuban history would be different. Yet he has influenced island developments under conditions not of his choosing. Castro marched triumphantly into Havana in January 1959. He led a nationalist and then socialist movement that defied the "Colossus of the North," in a region Washington considered its sphere of influence. Castro came to power with no clear blueprint for the future.

Hostile to a movement in its backyard that jeopardized its own business interests, Washington first tried to contain and then to subvert the revolution, only to contribute to its radicalization. When the U.S. government threatened to cut trade with the island, Castro nationalized U.S. firms, turned to the Soviet Union for trade and aid, and declared himself a Communist.

The revolution did not occur in one of Latin America's most backward countries. Available data must be viewed cautiously, but estimates summarized in table 1 show the island to have ranked ninth and tenth among Latin America's twenty principal countries in the mid-1950s in, respectively, gross domestic product (GDP) and GDP per capita.[1] Only two countries had manufacturing sectors that contributed more to the national product than Cuba's (see table 2), although much Cuban industry was sugar related. Also, capitalist dynamics shaped the organization and relations of production in the countryside to an extent found in few other countries in the region. Foreign capital, above all U.S. capital, played a major role both in agriculture and in industry. In 1958 U.S. investment in Cuba was possibly the second largest in Latin America (Mesa-Lago 1981:8). Its role in sugar production, the linchpin of the economy, had declined, and its role in industry had expanded in the years immediately preceding the revolution.

The economy was not without its problems. In particular, the economy centered very heavily around trade. Consequently, it tended to expand and contract with export opportunities. When Castro assumed power only three other Latin American countries had more export-oriented economies, and only three were more dependent on a single commodity for trade than Cuba (see table 3). In addition, unemployment and under-employment were chronic, especially during the so-called dead season, when labor demand in the sugar sector was low.

Aware of the island's dependence on trade in general and on sugar exports in particular, and of its extreme dependence on the U.S. for trade and investment, Castro sought, immediately upon assuming power, to regulate external economic relations and to diversify the domestic economy. His administration quickly established monopoly control over all import, export, and foreign exchange transactions, and it nationalized first the foreign- and then the domestically owned export-oriented sugar sector. Upon nationalizing enterprises producing for the local economy and, accordingly, entirely destroying the economic base of both the local and foreign bourgeoisie, it made a concerted effort to make the economy less trade dependent. It considered national autonomy more important than the cost of domestic production (relative to the cost of importing

TABLE 1. Cuban Gross Domestic Product and Gross Domestic Product per Capita in Selected Years: Value in Constant Dollars (U.S.) of 1980 and Ranking among Latin American Countries

	Gross Domestic Product (GDP)			
	Millions U.S. $	Latin American Ranking[a]	Per Capita U.S. $	Per capita Latin American Ranking[a]
1955	5,555	9	871	10
1960	6,235	8	887	6
1965	7,190	8	921	10
1970	7,414	8	867	12
1975	10,810	8	1,158	8
1980	14,159	8	1,455	9
1985[b]	22,549	8	2,199[b,c]	—

Source: Eckstein 1991:316–17 (and references therein).

[a]The rankings of countries for 1950, 1955, 1960, 1965, and 1975 are based on GDP data in 1970 dollars and for 1985 and 1986 on data in 1986 dollars (except Cuba).

[b]Constant 1981 pesos; peso conversion is based on 1981 year-end official exchange rate. Estimates based on gross social product data (larger than market economy GDP estimates).

[c]Economic data for 1985; population data for mid-1986.

comparable goods). Government capacity to direct and stimulate the growth process would be expected to improve with the increased role of the state in the capital accumulation process.

Postrevolutionary Economic Expansion and Diversification

Since World War II less developed countries (LDCs) have been particularly concerned with improving their productive capacities, above all in industry. Domestic industrialization, it came to be believed, would make a country less vulnerable to, and less dependent on, adverse foreign market conditions than their previous trade-based economies. Industrialization also came to be viewed as a sign of modernity. When it became recognized, beginning in the 1960s, that import-substitution industrialization in the region created chronic balance of payments problems, countries modified their economic priorities. They remained committed to industrialization but tried to turn industry (and other goods and services) into foreign exchange–generating export items as well.

TABLE 2. Cuban Manufacturing in Selected Years

	Value (millions U.S. $)[a]	Latin American Ranking Value of Manufacturing[g,h]	Manufacturing as Percentage of GDP/GSP[b]	Latin American Ranking, Manufacturing as Percentage of GDP/GSP	Metal and Machine Industry as Percentage of Total Manufacturing Production	Latin American Ranking, Metal and Industry as Percentage of Total Manufacturing Production[i]
1955	1,166.4	6	21	3[f]	—	—
1960	3,286.2[c]	4	45[e]	1	5.2	12
1965	3,575.4	4	43[e]	1	4.7	15[f]
1970	4,619.0	4	47	1	6.4	15[f]
1975	7,052.0	4	40	1	13.2	7
1980	8,425.4	3	41	1	8.8	12
1985	12,793.3	3[d]	44	1	9.8	7

[a]Includes mining and electricity; 1981 prices
[b]GDP = gross domestic product; GSP = gross social product
[c]1961
[d]Estimates based on first eleven months of 1985
[e]Includes mining, petroleum, and quarrying
[f]Tied in rank with one other country
[g]Latin American ranking: data for fifteen countries for 1960, fourteen countries for 1965, seventeen countries f[...] 1975, and twenty countries for 1970, 1980, and 1984. Countries without data for a given year are assumed to have t[...] same ranking as in the succeeding year with data.
[h]Value added by manufacturing for 1960, 1970, 1975, 1980, and 1985. Estimates for 1950, 1955, and 1965 are calculate[...] on basis of manufacturing as percent of GDP (in constant 1980 dollars).
[i]Latin American ranking: data for sixteen countries for 1950, seventeen countries for 1955, and twenty countries f[...] all other years. Countries without data for a given year are assumed to have the same ranking as in the succeedin[...] year with data.

In principle, the larger and more diversified a country's economic base, the higher the living standards of its people can be and the more influence a government can wield in the international as well as domestic arenas. Gross national production data, in the aggregate and by sector, provide a basis for evaluating how successful countries have been in expanding and diversifying their productive capacities.[2]

Table 1 reveals that Cuba's national product increased fourfold between 1955 and 1985.[3] The island was remarkably immune to a world recession in the early 1980s. United Nations (1983:11) sources estimate Cuba's 1981–83 growth rate (gross social product, GSP) to have been 23 percent, at a time when the average growth rate (GDP) for Latin America was negative (-2.8) and 11 percent in the fastest-growing capitalist economy in the region.

Cuba did less well later in the decade, partly because a mounting

TABLE 3. Role of Trade in Cuban Economy in Selected Years and Cuba's Latin American Ranking on Each Measure

	Main Export as Percentage of Total Exports	Latin American Ranking, Dependence on Single Export for Trade[h]	Exports as Percentage of GMP[g]	Latin American Ranking, Role of Exports in GDP/GMP[a,f,g]	Exports Manufactures as Percentage Total Exports of Goods	Latin American Ranking, Role of Manufacturing in Exports
1950	89.2	—	32	2	—	—
1955	79.6	4	27	4	—	—
1960	79.4	3	23[d]	6	—	—
1965	86.2	2	17	11	4.0	13
1970	76.8	2	25	5[e]	—	—
1975	89.1	2	33	3[e]	—	—
1980	82.7	1[b]	28	4	2.9	17
1984–86	73.9[c]	2	22	9	4.2	17

Source: Eckstein 1991: 326–27 (and references therein).
[a]GMP = gross material product; GDP = gross domestic product
[b]1980–82 data for all countries besides Cuba
[c]Preliminary
[d]1961
[e]Tied with one other country
[f]Information for seventeen countries for 1950, nineteen countries for 1955, and all twenty countries for other years. Countries with information missing for a given year are assumed to have the same ranking as in the succeeding year with available data. The higher the country rank, the higher the export/GDP ratio. The Cuban data refer exclusively to the value of commodity exports, whereas the data on the other countries refer also to the value of nonfinancial services.
[g]National product in current GDP or GNP prices for all countries besides Cuba. In Cuba, national product calculations are based on GNP estimates in current prices for 1950 and 1955 and on GMP estimates in current prices for all subsequent years. Since GMP is a conservative estimate of GDP, Cuba's export/national product ratio is higher than it would be were GDP estimates used.
[h]Insufficient data to rank countries in 1950; information for all 20 countries for all other years.

foreign debt compelled the government to initiate austerity measures that had a recessionary effect on the economy in conjunction with a so-called rectification process. The campaign was officially designed to "rectify errors and negative tendencies." The island appeared at the time to be going against world "liberalization" trends, including in the Soviet Union under the banner of perestroika. A renewed ideological emphasis on Marxist-Leninism aside, in practice the Cuban reforms appear to have been rooted in state concern with increased economic efficiency and budgetary belt tightening (see Eckstein 1990; and Mesa-Lago 1990, for contrasting interpretations of the rectification process).

While the growth rate in 1989, before the collapse of the Council for Mutual Economic Assistance (COMECON) was fully felt, was only about 1.5 percent, it exceeded the 1.1 percent growth registered by Latin America as a whole (Gunn 1990:133). In 1990, though, the changes in Eastern Europe, including Soviet domestic economic and political problems, resulted in delivery delays, import cutbacks, and declining terms of trade, all of which had a devastating effect on the island economy. The economy is believed to have contracted about 5 percent that year.

The positive impact of the revolution on overall output until the mid-1980s should not, however, be overestimated. For one, Cuba's per capita performance, from a regional vantage point, had been uneven over the years. The removal of "old regime fetters" and state commitment to economic development have not in themselves generated a continually high rate of growth or a rate consistently exceeding that of capitalist economies in the region. Second, Cuba's overall economic performance, relative to other countries' in the region, is not sufficiently great to conclude with certainty that the differences are real rather than a by-product of different bases of economic calculation. Indeed, Cuba's economic performance has been the subject of great dispute by specialists.[4]

Cuba's economic performance might also seem unimpressive given the amount of Soviet aid it has received. Cuba has benefited from substantial sugar and nickel price subsidies, technological assistance, and development and balance-of-payments aid. Official Western sources, however, overestimate the sugar subsidy (by comparing Soviet prices with world market prices, not with the subsidized rates at which most sugar is traded, and by using official peso-dollar exchange rates, which overvalue the ruble aid). Official estimates, furthermore, fail to take into account the costs of Soviet dependence. Most Soviet aid has been "tied aid." Cuba has had to buy overpriced, poor-quality Soviet products with the rubles earned for island exports. Also, its close relationship with Moscow cut the island off from U.S. aid and trade.[5] Cuba would like to "normalize" relations with the United States, Castro's continued anti-imperialist proclamations notwithstanding. The souring of relations between Washington and Havana were not Castro's own doing. In the early revolutionary years he sought to limit but not eliminate U.S. political and economic influence; by the 1990s Castro recognized how paramount it was to improve economic relations with the United States to "save the revolution," but Washington continued to enforce the embargo, even as its relations with Moscow improved.

Castro has attempted to improve not only the overall performance of the economy but also the performance of specific sectors. One such sector is industry. Available data suggest that the importance of manufacturing in the economy increased immediately after Castro assumed power and that it has remained important ever since. Table 3, for example, shows manufacturing to play a more central role in the economy in Cuba than in any other Latin American country; as previously noted, before the revolution two other countries on the continent had industrial sectors contributing a larger share to the national product. Industry, however, appears to be so dynamic in part because of changes in the bases of national product calculation under Castro. Industry's importance is exaggerated because: (1) Cuban gross material and gross social product (GMP and GSP) estimates exclude information on several dynamic non-manufacturing sectors; (2) complete data on the contribution of different sectors to the national product is available only for GSP estimates (since GSP calculations involve double counting [see n. 3], they overestimate the value of industrial output as measured by market economy value-added compilations); and (3) postrevolutionary pricing policy overvalues industrial and undervalues agriculture output (Mesa-Lago 1981:211–12), although Cuba is not the only country in the region to have such a pricing bias.

Because there is no uniform pre-/postrevolutionary measure for assessing the national product and industry's contribution to the national product, in turn, data on changes in output *within* the industrial sector are more enlightening. Available data suggest that the value of manufacturing output in general and of the metal and machine industries in particular have improved significantly since the revolution and that the island's regional ranking on both measures has risen under Castro.[6] The impressive improvement in Cuba's regional ranking resulted from heavy state emphasis on investment (versus consumption) in the late 1960s and then a rise in world sugar prices in the early to mid-1970s. Castro "seized the opportunity" that favorable world market conditions provided, investing the earnings and the Western financing to which the country gained access at the time in capital-intensive industry. Communist party rule and official commitment to socialism have not eliminated the importance of global market forces on domestic industrial and other prospects.

Cuban industrialization, however, is not attributable merely to clever use of a "market opening." Cuban industry also benefited from Soviet (and, to a lesser extent, other COMECON country) aid. According to available information, approximately three-fourths of Soviet technical and economic assistance for development during the first thirteen years of Castro's rule went to industry, and programs that the Soviets assisted in the early 1980s accounted for 10 percent of total Cuban industrial production.[7] The Soviets assisted the most technologically sophisticated sectors, including steel, machine building, sheet metal, and electric power.

Soviet industrial aid has actually been a mixed blessing. The Soviets, for one, have drawn on a variant of their own "heavy industry first" model in aiding Cuba, not giving priority to the consumer goods that people most want. Industrial output figures do not capture the politics of industrialization. Second, Soviet technology is not "state of the art" and internationally competitive.

Foreign industrial assistance does not distinguish Cuba from other countries in the region. Industry in other Latin American countries also has benefited from foreign investment, though it has been dependent on a different form of capital assistance. The market economies were heavily dependent on foreign direct investment until the mid-1970s then on foreign bank capital as well. Initially light industry and only recently basic industries received major foreign funding. In the market economies, moreover, foreign assistance, especially from private sources, has hinged on profit considerations, with profits typically repatriated. In Cuba, by contrast, profits generated by Soviet-assisted firms have not left the country, and the Soviets have not based their aid on enterprise profit-making criterion.

As impressive as Cuba's industrialization has been from a regional standpoint, the country is likely to experience deindustrialization in the 1990s. Like import-substitution industrialization elsewhere in the region, in Cuba it has been import dependent. Import-driven development will be contingent in the years to come on the island's hard currency–generating capacity. East European countries, including the still Communist Soviet Union, have joined other countries in insisting on the currency for trade. Also, East European countries have raised the prices of the goods they sell Cuba.

Both the more unfavorable terms of trade and the insistence on hard currency reduce Cuba's import capacity. The government has already closed factories, and enterprises remaining open suffer from cutbacks in supplies and spare parts. The import crisis even led the government, in the fall of 1990, to subordinate explicitly industrial to agricultural production. The so-called special period in peacetime gives priority to agriculture, formalized in the food program. Unable to count on former trade partners and with improved relations with the United States not on the horizon, the government is seeking to "save the revolution" by focusing on basic subsistence. Industry has become a luxury the government feels it cannot now afford.

In sum, until the crisis in international communism, Cuba expanded and diversified its economic base much more than the U.S. government and media have led Americans to believe. Production did not increase to the point that the country's regional national product ranking improved, but industrial growth was impressive by regional standards. Changes in the class structure and the state's role in the economy, together with changing state priorities and foreign aid and trade, spurred economic development.

Reduction of Trade Vulnerability

International trade is one of the most important elements of the world economy, and trade is one of the foremost mechanisms contributing to LDC vulnerability to external forces. The greater the diversity of exports, the less prey a country is to international price fluctuations of any single item, and the more a country moves out of the commodity into the industrial export market, the more stable its export earnings and the more favorable its terms of trade are likely to be. A country's import capacity, in turn, will depend on its export earnings. To the extent that domestic production requires foreign inputs, export activity is vital.

The revolutionary leadership quickly reduced the role of exports in the economy as it promoted import-substitution agriculture and industrialization (table 3). During Castro's first decade of rule exports contributed less to the national product than in the twelve preceeding years (LeoGrande 1979:6–7). However, the imported inputs that were needed to "deepen" import-substitution caused such a balance of payments problem, that by the mid-1960s the government began to emphasize exports, above all of sugar, Cuba's most favored product in international markets. The role of exports in the economy subsequently rose. The export/national product ratio has varied over the years, though, not merely with export emphasis but also with the price foreign purchasers have been willing to pay for Cuban goods. When world sugar prices reached a record high in the first half of the 1970s, for example, the importance of exports in the economy peaked, even though the political and economic failure of the late 1960s massive sugar campaign had led the government to reemphasize production for domestic consumption in the 1970s.

Regional comparisons reveal that Cuba remains one of the most mono-product economies in the region. Despite state ownership of most of the economy and state commitment to reducing the centrality of sugar in the economy, Cuba was the most (or second most) monoproduct-dependent trade economy in the 1980s; before the revolution it had ranked fourth. And it is dependent on one of the most price volatile commodities for trade. Its Latin American export/national product ranking improved in the 1980s, however, suggesting that its economy by then had reduced its trade dependence more than other countries in the region.

Owing largely to global geopolitical dynamics and Soviet trade policy, Cuba has failed to find export markets for its nonsugar products. Both Western and East European countries have been resistant to buying industrial goods from Cuba, though for somewhat different reasons: the United States, Latin America's principal importer, for political reasons and other countries for economic reasons (Western products typically being preferred for their quality and price). Until recently Moscow only wanted Cuban farm and mineral products, revealing that monoproduct primary product export dependence has not been a characteristic merely of the capitalist world, as "dependency" writers have suggested. Iron-ically, in 1989 and 1990, as the Soviet bloc disintegrated, the former superpower began to purchase Cuban biotechnology and pharmaceutical products, and it turned to Cuba to assemble its high-tech products (turn-ing Cuba into a *maquiladora* of sorts); its imports of Cuban manufac-tures, however, remain limited to date.

Other Latin American countries have more successfully expanded their industrial exports, not merely because they benefit from more favorable importing country trade policies but also because they benefit from multinational corporation (MNC) global strategies. Third World governments have been offering tax and other incentives to foreign investors to develop their export sectors, especially once faced with severe foreign debt crises in the 1980s. The Castro government has tried to do so as well, but its efforts in the industrial sector have thus far been to little avail. Accordingly, Cuba has not gained access to MNC international marketing networks. Washington import and export restrictions contribute to investor disinterest in Cuba (*New York Times*, December 25, 1983, 12; Zorn and Mayerson 1983).

Washington constricts Cuba's nickel as well as industrial export market. The island has successfully developed, with Soviet support, its nickel industry, but the United States refuses to purchase not only the mineral directly from Cuba but also industrial items that contain Cuban nickel from other countries (including from the Soviet Union, as of the 1990s). The U.S. restriction makes the Cuban product unattractive to countries seeking to sell nickel-based goods to the United States.

The "special period in peacetime" includes heavy emphasis on hard-currency exports as well as agriculture import-substitution. No longer assured of East European export markets and a victim of a deterioration in terms of trade with the former COMECON countries, Cuba is aggressively seeking to develop new export markets. Thus far with limited success, it is promoting competitively priced biotechnology and pharmaceutical products to countries besides the Soviet Union, including Brazil, Italy, and Spain. Exports of the Center of Genetic Engineering and Biotechnology rose from zero in 1988 to approximately $800 million two years later. Its exports include epidermal growth factor, which helps skin to regenerate, and vaccines for meningitis and hepatitis-B (*Cuba Business* [October 1990]: 3; *New York Times*, December 5, 1990, 18).

In light of its external sector needs and its failure to find sufficient markets for *goods* domestically produced, Havana is promoting "invisible" hard currency–earning tourism. It is doing so with foreign private investment assistance. In 1990 Cuba earned somewhat under $200 million from tourism. The government has attracted more foreign capital here than in industry. Economic exigencies have led the government to defy its earlier moral repugnance of tourism, tourism having contributed to the island being known as the brothel of the Caribbean under Batista.

Thus, the revolution has been no panacea to the island's historic trade dependence. COMECON long-term trade contracts and subsidies made the island less vulnerable to world market vicissitudes, until its disintegration in 1991, but even when in force Cuba's ties to the Soviet Union marginalized its ability to compete in international markets. Cuba has become less successful, *from a regional vantage point,* in negotiating favorable trade relations than was true before the revolution.[8] Faced with a need to generate hard currency, the government has been promoting since the 1980s tourism and foreign investment, activity previously proscribed on moral grounds. As the head of the chamber of commerce noted, "We have to think like capitalists but continue being socialists" (EIU no. 3 [1990]: 17).

Foreign Public Debt

LDCs rely on foreign capital to supplement and compensate for meager domestic funds. Foreign borrowing may, however, limit domestic development options. Foreign borrowing may have such an effect if: (1) creditors make loans contingent on a series of structural conditions that adversely affect production in certain economic sectors; (2) repayment obligations compel borrowers to subordinate production for domestic consumption to production for export; (3) loan repayments drain the country of scarce foreign reserves; and (4) high interest payments on debts significantly reduce the economic surplus available domestically for capital formation. Adverse effects of foreign borrowing are reflected in the size of the debt and, especially, the debt service/export ratio; foreign loans typically have to be repaid in foreign currency. The debt discussion focuses on the 1970s and thereafter, the period during which LDCs borrowed heavily in foreign financial markets.

Cuba has not escaped the debt problems of most LDCs. As of 1991 its debt to the Soviet Union was believed to amount to fifteen billion rubles. No country is as heavily indebted to a single creditor as Cuba is to the Soviet Union. Assuming the debt estimate to be correct, Cuba owed the former superpower twenty-four billion dollars at the official exchange rate, the real value in hard currency is much less: estimated to be somewhere between one to two billion dollars at the exchange rate then prevailing in Soviet hard-currency auctions (*Cuba Business* [June 1990]: 8).

Soviet politicians do not all agree that Cuba should continue to receive aid. "Liberal" reformers, most notably the leader of the Russian republic, Boris Yeltsin, favor slashing aid. The reformers depict Cuba as a Brezhnev-era police state. They also argue that aiding Cuba is a drag on the budget, exacerbating Soviet fiscal problems. "Conservatives," such as the Soviet ambassador to Havana (in 1990), Yuri Petrov, by contrast, argue that Moscow should continue offering military and economic aid as long as the United States refuses to normalize relations with the island. Future assistance accordingly will be contingent on political struggles six thousand miles away.

Soviet financing had its advantages. It was offered on concessionary terms. Moscow charged 2 to 2.5 percent per annum interest, and it offered an amortization period of ten to twelve years on credits to Cuba during the first decade of Castro's rule (LeoGrande 1979:20). In 1972, moreover, it extended new credits and agreed to allow the island to postpone debt repayments until 1986 and then to repay over twenty-five years interest free.

Despite the concessionary terms of Soviet loans, the financing has been a mixed blessing. According to Western sources, most Soviet funding covers Cuba's trade deficit with the former superpower (although, as previously noted, most funding earmarked for domestic development goes to industry). The funding therefore fails to address the root cause of the island's balance of payments problem: its inability to generate sufficient export revenue to offset import needs or to advance import-substitution to the point that trade is less vital to the economy. Cuba, in addition, had to purchase Soviet goods with Soviet ruble financing. Since Soviet products, as previously noted, are often inferior to and more costly than comparable Western goods, Cuba's ties to the former Soviet Union have driven up the island's import bill. Thus, the once superpower has contributed to the very debt burden that it is helping to alleviate.

Because of Soviet fund restrictions, Cuba drew on Western capital sources when they became available in the mid-1970s, long before access to new Soviet aid became questionable. The Western financing lacks the concessionary qualities of Soviet credits, but it allowed the island to acquire goods and technology then unavailable from COMECON. Western governments and banks extended financing to the island when world market sugar prices peaked; under the circumstances, Cuba was thought to be a good credit risk.

When sugar prices plunged in the latter 1970s, and Cuba's capacity to generate hard-currency export earnings accordingly declined, Cuba's

Western debt soared. The spiraling of Western interest rates compounded the amount of money owed to foreign banks. The island's hard currency debt and debt service/export ratios shifted from around the mean to one of the worst in the region (see table 4).[9] Since this debt must be repaid in hard currency and since Cuba has such difficulty generating hard currency goods and services, this debt has proven more burdensome than its Soviet debt.

The Western debt has had two very negative consequences on the domestic economy. First, it has pressured the government to subordinate production for domestic consumption to production for export: witness the preoccupation with hard-currency activity during the crisis-induced special period in peacetime. Second, much of the hard currency that Cuba does generate must be used for debt repayments rather than for purchases to stimulate local economic activity. Some Cuban factories operated at half their capacity already in the early 1980s, for lack of foreign exchange to buy such basic materials as synthetics and plastics (*Business Week* [September 20, 1982]: 56), and production has been more jeopardized since the collapse of COMECON.

Cuba's hard-currency crisis has been compounded by U.S. political hostility. Not only does Washington deprive Cuba of access to Latin America's principal export market; it also has pressured Western creditors to force Cuba to borrow on less favorable terms than other Latin American countries with higher risk profiles (*New York Times,* December 25, 1983, and January 9, 1984, *Espindola* [1983]: 70).

TABLE 4. Cumulative Outstanding Cuban Soviet and Western Debt

	Amount[a] (millions U.S. $)	Latin American Ranking, Size of Debt	Debt as Percentage of Exports[c]	Latin American Ranking, Debt as Percentage of Exports	Debt-Service Export Ratio	Latin American Ranking, Debt-Service as Percentage of Exports
			Western Debt			
1970	291.0	9	—	—	—	—
1975	1,338.0	7	117	11	9	13
1980	4,536.8	9	273	5	19	8
1985	3,566.4[b]	15	484	3	33	4

Source: Eckstein 1991: 330–31 (and references therein).
[a]Disbursed public debt
[b]Preliminary
[c]Total disbursed debt data for all countries in 1980 and 1985 and for most countries in 1975. The data for the other countries in 1975 refer only to disbursed medium and long-term debt, not to short-term debt.

Castro has been reluctant to defy the banks. He has argued for an LDC debtors' cartel and for a moratorium on debt repayments. Yet he has not dared, without the support of other countries, to act on the policies he preaches. His reluctance to do so reflects the precarious status of a publicly committed Third World socialist state in a capitalist world economy.

Thus, Cuba has turned to foreign sources of financing to supplement meager domestic funds, the nationalism of the revolution notwithstanding. The type of foreign funding on which it has drawn has depended less on its own predilection than on international credit options. Because Soviet funds were limited and for restricted use, Cuba sought Western financing already before the collapse of COMECON. And Cuba, as a consequence, fell into the same debt trap as capitalist LDCs. Meanwhile, U.S. discrimination against Cuba has made it more difficult for Cuba than other Latin American countries to generate hard currency to repay its debt, causing interest on the unpaid loan to spiral over the years.

Social Welfare

A revolution should be judged not merely in terms of aggregate economic improvements but also for its effect on people's well-being. Revolutions might improve living standards of previously deprived groups, independently of whether they expand and diversify production and restructure global aid and trade relations. Postrevolutionary regimes are likely to be more concerned with distribution than the societies they replace, since class upheavals are generally sparked, in part, by concerns about justice, and they modify class relations. Specific aspects of social welfare that might be affected by revolution include how land and income are distributed and health standards.[10] Each is examined below.

Land

In societies in which much of the population is involved in agriculture, land ownership constitutes an important component of social welfare. Landowners control production on their holdings, and they enjoy a social status that farm laborers do not. They can appropriate surplus produced on their properties, the amount of surplus depending, in part, on the size of the holdings and the organization of production.

While information on land ownership is unfortunately incomplete, available data show Cuban land ownership concentration to have been high before the revolution (with a Gini Index value of 0.79) but third lowest (tied with two other countries) in the region (World Bank 1978:2).[11] Moreover, by regional standards *minifundismo* (smallholdings) was not a severe problem in the prerevolutionary period. Only 20 percent of all units were smaller than five hectares (Eckstein 1991:335).

Because land was an important concern of some of the farm population, and because the agrarian labor force was an important political base for the revolutionary movement, Castro promulgated an agrarian reform shortly after taking power. The reform extended property rights to more than 100,000 sharecroppers, tenant farmers, and squatters. Land was redistributed especially in the regions in which pressure on the land had been intense, land security an issue, and peasant support for the revolution considerable. This "land to the tiller" program does not distinguish Cuba's land reform from others in the region, but Cuba is the only Latin American country besides Nicaragua to have also transformed large estates into state farms; this transformation occurred not merely because the government was committed to socialism but also because the farms had been capitalized, making redistribution economically unwise. Prerevolutionary sugar plantations initially were converted into cooperatives, then, like other large holdings, into state farms. Workers on the farms benefited not from acquisition of land rights but, rather, from year-round employment, social benefits, and wage increases.

The 1959 agrarian reform, however, allowed Cuban nationals to retain up to 402 hectares. A second reform, promulgated four years later, reduced the legal maximum (in most instances) to 67 hectares. Since then about 30 percent of the farm population and an even smaller percentage of the farm land remain in private hands, although the government has encouraged the independent farmers to join cooperatives in the 1980s. Cooperatives, it argued, were more consistent with socialist organizing principles, but they also permitted, in principle, economies of scale: they could make use of newly manufactured domestic sugar machinery. Nearly two-thirds of all remaining private farmers received land rights in conjunction with the first agrarian reform.

While land was less concentrated in Cuba than in most countries in the region before the revolution, the two reforms reduced property inequities and changed the bases of property ownership to an extent that no other country in the region has. Among Latin American countries Cuba has the smallest percentage of total and total private land in large estates (see table 5). Also, no other Latin American country has implemented an agrarian reform that has benefited as large a percentage of the farm labor force or distributed as large a percentage of the land area as has Cuba.

Cuba's agrarian reforms result from the leadership's anticapitalist class bias, on the one hand, and its commitment to farm laborers who helped "make" the revolution, on the other hand. The peculiarities of Cuban agriculture, however, above all the centrality of capitalist-intensive sugar to the economy, have shaped postrevolutionary property relations and the organization of production in the countryside as well.

Income Distribution

As societies urbanize and agriculture is capitalized, the size of land-holdings becomes a less important determinant of overall welfare; financial wealth assumes greater importance. The more equitable the distribution of wealth, the more an entire populace can share the benefits

TABLE 5. Regional Rankings, or Measures of Cuban Land and Income Concentration (for Year of Most Recent Information)

	Regional Ranking
Percentage of private farm units in land holdings of:	
Fewer than 5 hectares	6[a]
More than 1,000 hectares	20[b,c]
Percentage of land area in private farms in holdings of:	
Fewer than 5 hectares	—[d]
More than 1,000 hectares	20[b,c]
Percentage economically active males employed in private agriculture who received land title in conjunction with private title	1[e]
Percentage of land area distributed or confirmed with private title	1[e]
Percentage of national income accruing to:	
Bottom 20 percent	1
Top 10 percent	20

Sources: Wilkie 1974:5; Wilkie and Reich 1978:50–53; Aranda 1968:143; World Bank 1978:30; World Bank 1980:156–57; Eckstein 1982a:54–56, 69–70 (and references therein).

[a]The higher the rank (1 = highest), the smaller the percentage of units that are *minifundio*.

[b]The higher the rank (1 = highest), the larger the percentage of farms in holdings of 1,000+ hectares or the larger the percentage of land area in units of 1,000+ hectares.

[c]Ranking (of private sector) inferred; no conclusive information.

[d]Countries not ranked because significance of figures is ambiguous (figures have meaning only in relation to *number* and *percentage* of farm units smaller than five hectares).

[e]Rankings are based on cumulative Latin American figures from Wilkie (1974) plus information on Cuba through the late 1960s and Peru as of 1973; Cuban data refer to the farm population receiving *individual* land rights in conjunction with the 1959 agrarian reform (slightly less than two-thirds of private farmers).

of a society's riches. Income is the best available measure of wealth, although it underestimates the economic worth of people with assets (of minimal significance in Cuba since the revolution).

There are, unfortunately, no official income distribution figures and no recent unofficial figures. Available information suggests that Cuba has equalized earnings to an extent that no other country in the region has. In the most recent year with data, the poorest 20 percent of the population earned proportionally more and the wealthiest 10 percent proportionally less in Cuba than anywhere else in Latin America (table 5). Moreover, the change since the revolution has been dramatic: in the latest prerevolutionary year with income data, the poorest one-fifth of the population received about a quarter as much, while the wealthiest 10 percent received more than twice as much of the national income as in 1978 (see table 6).[12] The real average wage of the poorest 40 percent roughly doubled in the first few years of Castro's rule.

After the first few years of the revolution the rate of redistribution slowed down. A wage policy initiated in 1980 probably reversed earlier egalitarian trends, although only within a narrowly defined range.[13] The 1980 wage scale reduced the earnings spread among manual workers, but it raised the earning potential of, and wage spread among, technicians and executives and, to a lesser extent, administration and service personnel (Brundenius 1981:153).

Whatever unequalizing effect the 1980 wage reform had, in the latter 1980s and early 1990s the government countered this tendency by raising rural wages, farm workers traditionally being the poorest paid group. While thus advancing egalitarian socialist principles, the government had economic reasons for the policy change: it sought thereby to attract more labor to agriculture and to stabilize the rural labor force. Labor instability was a problem in the low-paid agricultural sector, and demand for farm

TABLE 6. Cuban National Income Held by Economically Active Population, Estimated Shares, by Percentile Group

| | Percentile groups | | | | | | |
	Poorest 0–20	21–40	41–60	61–80	81–100	91–100	Richest 96–100
1953	2.1	4.4	11.1	24.5	57.9	38.8	26.5
1962	6.2	11.0	16.3	25.1	41.4	23.0	12.7
1973*	7.8	12.5	19.2	26.0	34.5	19.4	9.8
1978	7.8	12.4	19.7	26.7	33.4	18.1	9.5

Source: Brundenius 1984:113, 114, 116.

*Excludes private sector; 7–8 percent of the labor force remains in the private sector since the nationalization of small businesses in 1968.

labor increased with the launching of the Food Program in 1990, in conjunction with the special period in peacetime. As of 1990, the government offered agriculturalists nonwage benefits that it did not offer to other workers: the only new housing and social service facilities planned for the "special period" are in the countryside.

Indeed, under Castro nonwage policies have eroded much of the historical significance of income. Basic goods are sold, through a ration system, at subsidized prices. Rationing had diminished in importance in the 1970s and 1980s, but it was reinvigorated in 1990, when scarcities caused by the changes in Eastern Europe otherwise would have resulted in high inflation. Most of the labor force, moreover, enjoys benefits that their counterparts in other Latin American countries do not. Cuba, for example, is one of the few nations in the region to offer free and near universal health care, a well-developed education system, retirement pensions, and (until 1991) unemployment insurance, plus free or low-rent housing (never exceeding 10 percent of family income). Scarcities crimp the life-styles of top income earners, all the more so since the government restricted sales of nonessentials in the special period, beginning in 1990. Because many goods and services are free or inexpensive and the income spread is small, low-income groups live better and more like upper-income groups in Cuba than do their equivalents in other Latin American countries. But upper-income groups live less well than their equivalents elsewhere in the region.

Thus, structural reforms have ushered in a significantly more equitable distribution of income, wealth, and consumption in Cuba than in any capitalist country in the region. Low-income groups gained most and upper-income groups least, however, when the new regime first consolidated power. New bases of inequality surfaced in the 1970s and 1980s, but within a narrowly confined range, and the trend may be changing with special-period policies in the 1990s.

Health Standards

Well-being depends not only on material comforts but also on good health. Good health requires a well-balanced and adequate diet and access to a medical delivery system that provides quality care. The quality, of course, is difficult to assess at the macro level, and available data unfortunately only permit cross-national comparisons of health welfare on a per capita basis, not among distinct socioeconomic groups. We will therefore have to assume, when we do not have convincing information to the contrary, that the higher the per capita figures on measures of health welfare, the more all groups benefit. The "in-depth" discussion of Cuba, however, illustrates that health patterns may change over time among groups in ways not reflected in per capita statistics.

The Medical Delivery System

To assess the scope of the delivery system the per capita supply of physicians and nurses is examined. In principle, doctors provide better-quality care than nurses and paraprofessionals because of their more extensive training, but the latter can provide an array of services for which doctors are unnecessary. In resource-poor countries with low health standards there may be a positive trade-off between large staffs of less expensive paraprofessionals and a small cadre of costly physicians. Therefore, we will examine the supply of both.

Cuba's health care delivery system expanded after the revolution. It was also restructured in ways that distinguish it from those in other Latin American countries. According to available information, Cuba ranked among the Latin American countries with the largest number of doctors and nurses per capita before the revolution. Its ranking on both medical facility indicators rose, however, under Castro (see table 7). Immediately after the revolution its population/physician ratio actually had deteriorated, with the exodus of about half the country's stock of doctors (Navarro 1972:413). Beginning in the 1970s, though, the per capita supply of doctors improved and surpassed the prerevolutionary level. The government sponsored a concerted campaign to attract students to medicine. With all graduates guaranteed jobs and with nearly all doctors employed by the government, the expansion of the medical profession is a direct reflection of the state's commitment to health care.

Not only has the government trained a new cadre of doctors, it also has modified its medical care priorities and restructured the delivery system. The system remains doctor based, but health units make extensive use of nurses, pharmaceutics, technicians, and medical and dental assistants. The shift in medical concern is reflected in the much greater improvement in the country's stock of nurses and paraprofessionals than in its stock of doctors.

The reorganization of medical care has included a centralization of administration and a decentralization of the actual delivery of services. A well-organized system of health centers provides ambulatory care in the cities and the countryside. In addition, citizens have been mobilized throughout the country over the years for street cleaning, immunizations, blood donations, and disease control campaigns, in most cases by the block organizations of the mass-based Committees for the Defense of the Revolution.

In 1984 the government went so far as to initiate a program designed to provide a doctor on each city block and a more abundant supply of doctors in isolated mountainous areas. The so-called family doctor program involves professionals trained in social and comprehensive general medicine. They are to focus on both cure and prevention. Most family doctors and nurses live and work on the city block or in the rural community they serve, in order to comprehend better the psychological and biological problems of their patients and to provide immediate and continuous care (Feinsilver 1989:9).

TABLE 7. Availability of Medical Services, 1958–1989

	Number	Latin American Ranking
Population per physician[a]		
1958	1,081	—
1960	1,038[d]	3
1965	1,252	—
1970	1,390	4
1974	1,122	4
1980	638	3
1984	524[c]	2
1989	303	—
Population per nursing population[b]		
1958	1,353[d]	—
1960	1,199[d]	5
1965	810	—
1970	724	2
1974	480	3
1980	358	2
1984	377	1[e]
1989	163	—

Sources: World Bank, *World Development Report* 1978:108–9; 1979:168–69; 1983:194–95; 1990:232–33; World Bank, *World Tables* 1976:518–21; Brundenius 1984:39, 101; Feinsilver 1989:8; Comité Estatal de Estadísticas 1990:7, 9.

[a]Data for eighteen countries for 1974 and for twenty countries for 1960, 1970, and 1980. The two countries lacking 1976 information were assumed to have the same ranking as in the closest year with information.

[b]Data for sixteen countries for 1960, for twenty countries for 1970, for fifteen countries for 1974, and for eighteen countries for 1980. All countries with figures missing for a given year are assumed to have the same ranking as in the closest year with information available.

[c]Approximate

[d]Estimate

[e]No data for Uruguay, Venezuela, and Peru

Cuba is the only Latin American country with an extensive, institutionalized system of universal, free, rural and urban health care. In the capitalist countries in the region public and private medical facilities are more doctor oriented, more concentrated in the principal cities, and less accessible to the masses; they are available primarily to the small percentage of the labor force that either can afford private care or are employed in bureaucratic and industrial jobs that offer health plans partially subsidized by business and the government. There is every reason to believe that the medical needs of low-income groups, above all in rural areas, are better met in Cuba than in any other Latin American country. Cuba is the only Latin American country to make access to health care a basic social right.

Cuba's health care delivery system accordingly differs from those of other countries in the region, in both scope and access. The revolution made the changes possible. The changes reflect the government's class and political biases, on the one hand, and the reduced power of doctors and other private medical interests to influence state policy, on the other hand. Castro's commitment to health care is reflected in his claims to turn Cuba into a world medical power. In this vein doctors and nurses, plus nurse auxiliaries, are being trained for service overseas as well as at home (see Feinsilver 1989).

Nutrition

Health welfare depends, however, not only on the size and scope of the medical delivery system but also on nutrition. Two measures of diet are examined: per capita caloric intake and per capita protein intake. The latter is a better indicator of nutrition, but it accounts for only one source of nutrients. Because poverty is widespread in the Third World, and because poor people often consume insufficient calories, total caloric consumption is considered as well.

Available information on per capita protein and caloric consumption suggests that Cuban nutritional standards deteriorated during the 1960s then improved. Average caloric consumption took about two decades to surpass prerevolutionary levels (see table 8).

Data on food distributed through official channels indicate that per capita consumption of many food items deteriorated in the latter 1960s (see Eckstein 1980:96; and table 8), when the government emphasized investment over consumption and it subordinated production for local

TABLE 8. Nutrition, Life Expectancy and Infant Mortality, 1945–1985

	Total	Latin American Ranking
Daily per capita caloric supply[b]		
1951–57	2,740	—
1961–65	2,430	6
1970	2,688	4
1975	2,726	4
1980	2,762	4
1983–85	3,094	3
Daily per capita protein supply (total grams per day)[b]		
1961	62.8	7
1965	62.5	8
1970	63.1	9
1975	64.4	9
1980	65.7	10
1983–85	76.2	5
Life expectancy		
1950–55	59	3
1960	64	3
1965	67	2
1970	70	1
1975	71	1
1980	74	1
1985	77	1
1989	74	2[c]
Infant mortality (deaths per 1,000 live births of infants aged less than one year)[d]		
1945–49	39	1
1955–59	32	1
1960	35	1
1965	38	1
1970	36	3
1975	27	2
1980	20	1
1985	16	1
1989	11	1[c]

Sources: World Bank, *World Development Report* 1978:108–9; 1979:168–69; 1983:194–95; 1990:232–33; World Bank, *World Tables* 1976:518–21; Brundenius 1984:39, 101; Feinsilver 1989:8; Comité Estatal de Estadísticas 1990:7, 9.

[a]Data for eighteen countries for 1974 and for twenty countries for 1960, 1970, and 1980. The two countries lacking 1976 information were assumed to have the same ranking as in the closest year with information.

[b]Data for sixteen countries for 1960, for twenty countries for 1970, for fifteen countries for 1974, and for eighteen countries for 1980. All countries with figures missing for a given year are assumed to have the same ranking as in the closest year with information available.

[c]Approximate

[d]Estimate

[e]No data for Uruguay, Venezuela, and Peru

consumption to production for export, to generate needed export earnings. Since 1970 the food supply improved with reemphasis on production for domestic consumption and government tolerance of private farm production and, in the first half of the 1980s, private farmer markets (Eckstein 1990:74).

The caloric intake of Cubans has compared much more favorably with that of their Latin American neighbors than their protein intake, at least until the 1980s. The country's regional ranking on the former health welfare measure improved under Castro, while its regional ranking on the latter deteriorated until the 1980s.

Yet protein and caloric intake undoubtedly improved since the revolution among low-income groups, even when per capita intake did not, and improved more among low-income groups in Cuba than in other Latin American countries. Employment, wage, and housing policies, plus the two agrarian reforms, have enhanced the purchasing power of rural and urban poor, while rationing has guaranteed all an affordable basic diet. During the 1970s and 1980s, as more goods were sold off the ration system, dietary standards undoubtedly varied more with income. With the reintroduction of full-scale rationing, with the special period in peacetime, consumption is likely to become more egalitarian again. Scarcities, however, can be expected to cause most people's food intake to deteriorate.

In sum, the revolution has done more to modify dietary patterns among socioeconomic groups than to raise per capita food consumption. Access to foods is more egalitarian in Cuba than in other Latin American countries, but dietary patterns among socioeconomic groups have varied over the years with rationing policy.

Health Well-Being: Infant Mortality and Life Expectancy
Medical delivery system and dietary success at addressing people's health needs should influence infant mortality and life expectancy rates. The number of deaths of infants less than one year old per thousand live births and the number of years people, on average, are likely to live are indicative of how effective medical and societal conditions are in meeting people's health needs.

Cuba has the lowest infant mortality rate and second highest life expectancy rate in Latin America. Its impressive health record, even by First World standards, reflects the allocative possibilities and priorities of a socialist government but also Castro's personal commitment to health welfare and the prerevolutionary social base upon which he had to build. The island already had the lowest infant death rate and the third highest life expectancy rate in Latin America under Batista (see table 8).

Cuba's infant mortality rate is lower and its life expectancy rate is higher than those of other countries with larger national and per capita national products. Resource allocations, not resources per se, prove to have a major bearing on the life chances of the young and old. Allocations vary with the values of the governing class and the organization of production. When the state owns "the means of production" it has more discretionary power than when the economy remains predominantly in private hands.

Cuba's infant mortality rate does not appear to have dropped below the level under Batista until the 1970s. Possibly health care deteriorated under Castro until a new generation of medical cadre was trained to replace the physicians who emigrated, until the health care delivery system was fully reorganized, and until nutritional standards improved. It also may be that the increase in infant mortality registered during Castro's first decade of rule reflects improved data collection, not a worsening in health care: in 1969, for example, 98 percent of all deaths were reported, whereas in 1956 it is thought that only 53 percent were (Navarro 1972:424, 430).

The ambiguity of the data notwithstanding, by the 1970s Cuba could guarantee newborns a better chance of survival than before the revolution and a better chance of survival than in any other Latin American country. If the chances were already high before the revolution, the improvements since then are nonetheless noteworthy.

Conclusion

This article has examined the economic and social impact of the Cuban revolution over a three-decade period, from the 1960s through the 1980s. The analysis compared pre- and postrevolutionary trends in Cuba. It also compared developments in Cuba with developments during the same period in other Latin American countries.

According to available data, Cuba expanded its productive base over the three decades. Its national product grew, in general and on a per capita basis, and so did its industrial capacity. Moreover, Cuba reduced its dependence on a single and highly priced volatile commodity for trade, and it reduced the importance of exports in the national economy;

these were major concerns of Castro when coming to power because many of the problems of the "old order" were attributed to the economy's dependence on sugar. Economic prosperity had hinged on world market sugar prices, which fluctuated markedly over the years.

The economic improvements occurred, however, at certain fiscal costs. The government accumulated a large foreign debt in the process, not only to the Soviet Union but also to Western governments and banks. Owing largely to Washington's efforts to undermine the revolution, Cuba has had greater difficulty than other Latin American countries finding overseas markets for its goods and services, compounding its debt problem. Foreign loans typically must be repaid in foreign currency.

While Cuba has not been the economic basket case portrayed by Washington, its main accomplishments have been social. Wealth, as reflected both in the distribution of income and land, is much more equitably distributed in post- than in prerevolutionary Cuba. Moreover, its health profile looks more like a First than a Third World country's. Its infant mortality rate is barely higher, and its life expectancy rate is barely lower than that of the United States. The revolution made these social improvements possible. The health welfare gains are not, however, an inevitable consequence of a socialist transformation. Castro has been politically committed to using the powers of the state to improve the health well-being of the populace.

Since most countries have improved their economic performances and the levels of well-being of their peoples over the past three decades, the real test of Cuba's revolution is whether it ushered in more change than nonrevolutionary forces in other countries. Table 9 summarizes whether Cuba's Latin American rank improved, fell, or remained unchanged since the prerevolutionary period on the specific indicators of economic and social development examined.

From a regional perspective, Cuba's economic performance through the mid-1980s has been mixed. Relative to other Latin American countries its industrial performance has been most impressive, even though other countries have more effectively expanded their industrial exports. Other countries have been better at reducing their dependence on a single commodity for trade, at the same time that Cuba has, relative to other nations in the region, reduced the importance of exports to the national economy (a development strategy that increasingly, however, has been called into question, as foreign debts have compelled countries to reemphasize exports). Political discrimination against Cuba and lack of access to multinational corporation marketing networks have marginalized Cuba's ability to compete in the world market in products other than sugar. Some Cuban products undoubtedly cannot compete in price and quality, but Cuba, with its educated labor force, could undoubtedly do as well as other Latin American countries in the *maquiladora* sector. Also, Cuba has made great strides in biotechnology, which it could market more successfully abroad.

In the social domain the revolution has been more impressive from a regional vantage point. On all measures Cuba's regional ranking has improved (except infant mortality, Cuba having had the lowest rate already under Batista).

The data therefore indicate that the gains of socialism are social more than economic. The economic potential of socialism, however, has never been fully tested in Cuba, even after thirty years of Castro's rule. The United States has used its hegemonic influence to constrict Cuba's transformational capacity. It has done so by containing trade, investment, loan, and aid options, on which all Third World countries remain highly dependent. Soviet aid and trade have been insufficient to offset the constrictive impact of U.S. foreign policy. With rising Soviet domestic problems and the collapse of the other East European Communist states, whatever possibilities socialism might have ushered in are circumscribed as never before.

TABLE 9. **Summary of Changes in Regional Rankings during Years for Which Data Are Available**

Gross domestic product	Improved
Gross domestic product per capita	Deteriorated
Value of manufacturing output	Improved
Manufacturing as percentage of national product	Improved[a]
Metal and machine industry as percentage of total manufacturing output	Improved[b]
Monoproduct export dependence	Deteriorated
Exports as percentage of national product	Improved
Manufacturing exports as percentage of total exports	Deteriorated
Size of total Western debt	Improved[b]
Western debt as percentage of Western exports	Deteriorated[b]
Western debt service as percentage of Western exports	Deteriorated[b]
Population per physician	Improved[b]
Population per nurse	Improved[b]
Per capita caloric supply	Improved[b]
Per capita protein supply	Improved[b]
Infant mortality rate	Unchanged
Life expectancy rate	Improved

Note: For specific years, see tables 1–8.
[a]Data overestimates postrevolutionary improvements
[b]Information only for postrevolutionary period

The social developments under Castro help explain why Castro weathered the domino collapse of world communism and why domestic dissension has been less than in China and the Soviet Union while still under Communist rule. They do not alone, of course, explain why no "popular" movement for change has emerged in Cuba. Castro still has charismatic appeal, and Castro has stepped up his public appearances to strengthen political loyalty during the period when communism has been so delegitimated internationally. Also, political reforms to streamline bureaucracy probably allowed the national leadership to weed out politicos in favor of major structural change; the establishment of a new political organ in Havana, people's councils, helps the state have a better handle on problems at the grass roots level; and the public trials of high-ranking government, military, and party officials in 1989 probably served the symbolic function of taming regime defiance for a while. The official slogan in 1990, moreover, was "Socialism or Death." Regime preservation became a test of nationalism.

Unfortunately for Castro and Cubans, social as well as economic prospects for the foreseeable future are not promising. As Cuba's economic relations with former COMECON countries have deteriorated, Castro has called a halt to the expansion of social services: to "save the revolution." Through the media, the education system, and mass organizations Castro and the party have instilled in most of the population Socialist social and political values. But no one likes deprivation. If Cubans, under the "new world order," experience en masse a persistent dramatic deterioration in their level of well-being, ever more of them are likely to seek to leave, to "exit," or press for major change at home. There are limits to the sacrifices they can be expected to tolerate to save a revolution that international, if not national, circumstances are making increasingly meaningless.

Should illegal immigration from Cuba to the United States increase, Cuba's problems will become those of the United States as well. Cuba is a short boat ride from Florida. It is therefore in Washington's interests to "normalize" relations with its Caribbean neighbor. Washington has already won the victory against communism, and differences between the two countries are shrinking. While remaining politically hardlined, Cuba has become ever more capitalist in praxis. The Cuban government encourages tourism, foreign investment, and material incentives previously condemned on moral grounds. A "normalization" of relations would strengthen these tendencies and, undoubtedly with time, contribute to domestic pressure for political change as well.

NOTES

An earlier version of this article was awarded the Lourdes Casal Prize in 1983. Claes Brundenius provided helpful comments on the earlier version.

1. The other countries with which Cuba is compared and ranked in the tables are Argentina, Bolivia, Brazil, Chile, Colombia, Costa Rica, the Dominican Republic, Ecuador, El Salvador, Guatemala, Haiti, Honduras, Mexico, Nicaragua, Panama, Paraguay, Peru, Uruguay, and Venezuela. For a discussion of different estimates of the Cuban prerevolutionary national product, see Brundenius (1981:6–27 and references therein).

2. Although data from all Latin American countries should be assumed to be mere approximations, the Cuban time-series figures must be viewed especially cautiously. Few statistics are available for the first three years of Castro's rule; the government methodology employed before the revolution differs from that used afterward; and the revolutionary leadership has changed its methodology several times, in ways not publicly known. On deficiencies in the adequacy, consistency, and reliability of Cuban statistics, see Mesa-Lago (1969; 1979; 1981) and Brundenius (1984:19–40).

3. Following the Marxist principle of estimating only "productive activity" (i.e., the direct production of goods and services), the Castro government omits health, education, and defense activity from its so-called gross material product (GMP) and gross social product (GSP) output calculations. Since GMP, unlike GSP, omits double counting, it is a preferable national product estimate. The work of Brundenius, as summarized here in table 1, attempts to estimate Cuban output in GDP terms.

4. See the debate between Brundenius and Zimbalist on the one side and Perez-Lopez and Mesa-Lago on the other (*Comparative Economic Studies* Spring, Fall, and Winter 1985). The data cited in table 3 on the value of Cuban industrial output represents the more positive assessment of the island economic performance.

5. Washington has, to date, refused to renegotiate relations with Havana, even after relations with Moscow improved under Gorbachev.

6. Total industrial production figures include industrial sugar production. Since the gross value of industrial sugar production, in relation to the value of total industrial output, dropped from 16 to 10 percent betwen 1962 and 1976, Cuban industry has become increasingly based on nonsugar activity. On industrial output, see Brundenius (1979:6–7), Zimbalist and Brundenius (1989:21–34, 73–101), and United Nations (1981:76).

7. Blasier 1979:230, 239; U.S. Congress 1982:10. Aid to the sugar industry is probably included in the industrial figure.

8. Castro's international *political* influence, however, has been exceptional for a country of its size. See Dominguez 1978.

9. It should be kept in mind that the Western debt data refer exclusively to state-guaranteed loans and to loans with maturity periods of more than one year. Since Cuba is the only Latin American country in which all loans are government guaranteed, its regional debt ranking might be better were all foreign loans included in each country calculation. Its ranking might also be better were short as well as medium and long-term loans included in the data for the other countries on the continent.

10. For other analyses of social welfare, or quality of life and basic needs, see Morris 1979 and Brundenius 1981. They concur that the level of well-being, in most respects, is high in Cuba. Brundenius, however, notes that, while education, health, and, to a lesser extent, food consumption have improved under Castro, the consumption of clothing and housing has thus far barely surpassed prerevolutionary levels.

11. Information is available for seventeen countries for years between 1930 and 1961.

12. Moreover, since the rich had assets in 1953 that they lost in the revolution, the equalizing effect of the class transformation is even greater than available information suggests.

13. The scale includes only the basic wage. Earnings for exceptionally productive and skilled workers can be supplemented, especially since 1973, with fringe benefits and bonuses. The wage reform, and increased availability of consumer goods, proved insufficient to stem an exodus of some 125,000 Cubans from the port of Mariel in 1980.

REFERENCES

Aranda, Sergio. 1968. *La revolucion agraria en Cuba.* Mexico, D. F.: Siglo XXI.

Blasier, Cole. 1979. "COMECON in Cuban Development." In *Cuba in the World,* ed. Cole Blasier and Carmelo Mesa-Lago, 225–56. Pittsburgh: University of Pittsburgh Press.

Brundenius, Claes. 1979. "Measuring Economic Growth and Income Distribution in Revolutionary Cuba." Research Policy Studies, Lund University Discussion Paper 130. Lund, Sweden: Research Policy Institute.

———. 1981. *Economic Growth, Basic Needs, and Income Distribution in Revolutionary Cuba.* Lund, Sweden: Research Policy Institute, University of Lund.

———. 1984. *Revolutionary Cuba: The Challenge of Economic Growth with Equity.* Boulder: Westview Press.

Comité Estatal de Estadísticas. 1990. *Cuba en Cifras 1958–89.* Havana: Comité Estatal de Estadísticas.

Dominguez, Jorge. 1978. "Cuban Foreign Policy." *Foreign Affairs* 57, no. 1 (Fall): 83–108.

Eckstein, Susan. 1980. "Income Distribution and Consumption in Post-Revolutionary Cuba: An Addendum to Brundenius." *Cuban Studies* 10 (January): 91–98.

———. 1982. "The Impact of Revolution on Social Welfare in Latin America." *Theory and Society* 1143–94.

———. 1990. "The Rectification of Errors or the Errors of the Rectification Process in Cuba?" *Cuban Studies* 20:67–86.

———. 1991. "How Consequential Are Revolutions?" In *Comparative Political Dynamics*, ed. Dankwart Rustow and Kenneth Erickson, 309–51. New York: Harper and Collins.

Espindola, Roberto. 1983. "Cuba Plays the Field." *South*, June 70–71.

Feinsilver, Julie. 1989. "Cuba as a 'World Medical Power': The Politics of Symbolism." *Latin American Research Review* 23, no. 2: 1–34.

Gunn, Gillian. 1990. "Will Castro Fall?" *Foreign Policy* 79 (Summer): 132–50.

LeoGrande, William. 1979. "Cuban Dependency: A Comparison of Pre-Revolutionary and Post-Revolutionary Cuban International Economic Relations." *Cuban Studies* 9 (July): 1–28.

Mesa-Lago, Carmelo. 1969. "Availability and Reliability of Statistics in Socialist Cuba." *Latin American Research Review* 4, nos. 1–2 (Spring/Summer): 53–91 and 47–81.

———. 1979. "Cuban Statistics Revisited." *Cuban Studies/Estudio's Cubanos* 9, no. 2 (July): 59–62.

———. 1981. *The Economy of Socialist Cuba: A Two-Decade Appraisal.* Albuquerque: University of New Mexico Press.

———. 1990. "On Rectifying Errors of a Courteous Dissenter." *Cuban Studies* 20:87–110.

Morris, Morris. 1979. *Measuring the Conditions of the World's Poor: The Physical Quality of Life Index.* New York: Overseas Development Council.

Navarro, Vicente. 1972. "Health, Health Services, and Health Planning in Cuba." *International Journal of Health Services* 2:424, 430.

United Nations. Economic Commission on Latin America. 1981. *Statistical Yearbook for Latin America 1979.* New York: United Nations.

———. 1983. *Balance preliminar de la economía latinoamericana en 1983.* United Nations: Comisión Economica para America Latina.

U.S. Congress. Joint Economic Committee. 1982. *Cuba Faces the Economic Realities of the 1980s.* 97th Cong. 2d sess., March 22. Washington, D.C.: U.S. Government Printing Office.

Wilkie, James. 1974. *Measuring Land Reform: Supplement to Statistical Abstract of Latin America.* Los Angeles: University of California, Latin American Center.

———. 1980. *Statistical Abstract of Latin America 20.* Los Angeles: University of California, Latin American Center.

Wilkie, James, and Enrique Ochoa. 1989. *Statistical Abstract of Latin America 27.* Los Angeles: University of California, Latin American Center.

World Bank. 1976. *World Tables.* Baltimore: Johns Hopkins University Press.

———. 1976–83. *World Atlas.* Washington, D.C.: World Bank.

————. 1978. *Land Reform in Latin America: Bolivia, Chile, Mexico, Peru, and Venezuela.* Staff Working Paper no. 275. Washington, D.C.: World Bank.

————. 1978–90. *World Development Reports.* New York: Oxford University Press.

————. 1980. *World Tables.* Baltimore: Johns Hopkins University Press.

Zimbalist, Andrew, and Claes Brundenius. 1989. *The Cuban Economy.* Baltimore: Johns Hopkins University Press.

Zorn, Jean, and Harold Mayerson. 1983. "Cuba's Joint Venture Law: New Rules for Foreign Investment." *Columbia Journal of Transnational Law* 21, no. 2: 273–303.

Contributors

Ilya Adler teaches communications at the University of Illinois in Chicago. He wrote his thesis on the relation between the government and the press in Mexico and has published a number of articles on this subject.

Marjorie J. Becker is assistant professor of history at the University of Southern California. Her doctoral dissertation is "Lázaro Cárdenas and the Mexican Counter Revolution: The Struggle over Culture in Michoacán, 1834–1940" (Yale University, 1988). She has written numerous articles on everyday resistance, peasant culture, and the social construction of the state. She is currently completing a book entitled *Humility, Glory, and Other Lessons: The Construction of Hegemony in Post-Revolutionary Mexico.*

William W. Culver is professor of political science at the State University of New York at Plattsburgh and director of SUNY Latin America and Southern Cone programs. He has published numerous articles on politics and the history of copper mining. He is currently completing, with Cornel J. Reinhart, a book manuscript entitled *Chili Bars: The Regulation of Capitalism and Free Trade in the Nineteenth Century Revisited.*

Susan Eckstein is professor of sociology at Boston University. She is the author of *The Poverty of Revolution: The State and Urban Poor in Mexico* (2d. ed., 1989); *The Impact of Revolution: A Comparative Analysis of Mexico and Bolivia* (1976); and numerous articles on Latin America in professional journals. She is also the editor of *Power and Popular Protest: Latin American Social Movements* (1989). Currently, she is writing a book on the impact of the Cuban revolution.

Michael W. Foley is associate professor of politics at the Catholic University of America in Washington, D.C. He has written on peasant mobilization and agricultural policy in Mexico and is currently studying peasant response to neoliberal reform in Mexico, Chile, and Costa Rica.

Randal Johnson is professor of Brazilian literature and culture at the University of Florida. He is the author of *Literatura e cinema:* Macunaíma *do modernismo na literatura ao Cinema Novo* (1982); *Cinema Novo x 5: Masters of Contemporary Brazilian Cinema* (1984); and *The Film Industry in Brazil: Culture and the State* (1987); and editor of *Brazilian Cinema* (1982, 1988; with Roberto Stam); *Tropical Paths: Essays on Modern Brazilian Narrative* (1992); and Pierre Bordieu's *The Field of Cultural Production: Essays on Art and Literature* (1992). His current research concerns structures of authority in Brazilian literature of the 1930s and 1940s.

A. Douglas Kincaid is associate director of the Latin American and Caribbean Center and assistant professor of sociology at Florida International University. Recipient of a Ph.D. degree in sociology from the Johns Hopkins University, he has recently published (with M. Rosenberg and K. Logan) *Americas: An Anthology* (1992) and (with A. Portes) "Comparative National Development: Theory and Facts for the 1990s," a special issue of *Sociological Forum* (1989). His current research focuses on civil-military relations and problems of democratization in Central America.

Daniel H. Levine is professor of political science at the University of Michigan. He has published widely on religion, cultural change, and politics in Latin America. His most recent book is *Popular Voices in Latin American Catholicism*.

Claudio Lomnitz Adler teaches in the anthropology department of New York University. He is author of *Evolución de una sociedad rural* and of various articles on Mexican culture, politics, and anthropology.

Larissa Adler Lomnitz, anthropologist and researcher at the Universidad Nacional Autónoma de México, is the author of numerous books and articles. Her works have focused on the reproduction of social classes in Latin America, concentrating especially on the informal sector, the middle class, and Mexico's bourgeoisie. Her books include *Networks and Marginality* and *A Mexican Elite Family*.

José Murilo de Carvalho received his Ph.D. degree in political science from Stanford University. He is associate professor of Brazilian politics at the *Instituto Universitário de Pesquisas do Rio de Janeiro* (IUPERJ) in Rio de Janeiro. He is the author of five books, including *Teatro de sombras: A Política imperial* (1988; translated into French, 1990) and *A Formação das almas: O Imaginário da república no Brazil* (1990).

Cornel J. Reinhart received his Ph.D. in American history from the University of Oklahoma in 1972. His research interests are in the areas of comparative social and economic history. He is presently assistant professor of history at St. Lawrence University in Canton, New York. He is currently completing, with William W. Culver, a book manuscript entitled *Community to State: Social Welfare Policy in New York, 1824–1900*.

Linda J. Seligmann, anthropologist and associate director of the Latin American and Iberian Studies Program at the University of Wisconsin–Madison, is currently a fellow in Yale University's Program in Agrarian Studies. She has written on issues of gender, class, and ethnicity in the Andean region and is currently writing a book on peasant relations to law.

Carol A. Smith is professor of anthropology at the University of California, Davis. She has published widely on cultural and economic change and politics in Guatemala and Central America. Her most recent book is *Guatemalan Indians and the State, 1540–1988*.

Index

Popular, 7, 10, 12, 171–72; identity, 12, 171–72; subject, 172. *See also* Popular needs; Popular spirituality

Popular needs, 194–97; and churches, 195–96; image of clergy, 196; powerlessness, 195

Popular religious groups, 172. *See also* Bible; CEBs; Popular needs

Popular spirituality, 206; authentic love, 203; bible reading, 198–99, 202–3; christology, 200–201; death, 212; hell, 212; holy water, 210–11; prayer, 206–8; saints, 208–10. *See also* Bible; CEBs; Prayer

Porfiriato, 370, 372

Pornochanchadas, 343, 345

Portes, Alejandro, 9

Poverty: gender differences, 187; needs, 187–88; popular definitions, 187

Practical ethos: Anglo-America and Latin America compared, 4

Prayer, 206, 207, 208; and authenticity, 208. *See also* Popular spirituality

PRI (Partido Revolucionario Institucional), 12, 235, 245, 357, 358, 361, 362, 366, 368, 370, 372, 379, 380, 383, 384, 387, 391, 393, 394; presidential succession, 361; *sexenio,* 363, 391. *See also Mexicanidad;* Mexican political culture; PRI campaign

PRI campaign: ambiguity in, 390–91; candidate image and socialization, 375–77; closures, 364; *destape,* 360, 362; electoral fraud, 372; fetishization of candidate, 376–77; logos, 366–67; negotiation and interpretation in, 373; media role, 384, 388–90; organization of public acts, 377, 380–82; precampaign, 363; president's men and system men, 359–60; propaganda, 378; rituals, 373; special guests, 387–88; stages, 362–68; trips, 364. *See also*

Mexicanidad; Mexican political culture; Salinas de Gortari

Proletarian novel, 14, 321

Proletarianization: and community solidarity, 139–40; El Salvador, 89; Guatemala and El Salvador compared, 89. *See also* Peasant rebellion; Peasants

Protestants, 18, 224

Puritans, 17, 199

Quebradanegra 200, 207

Quechua, 267

Quiche, 95, 105

Quijano, Aníbal, 278

Religion, 14; and authoritarian rule, 177; conventional assumptions, 17; and crisis, 17; crisis-solace models, 17; politicization, 171; redefinitions, 18. *See also* Bible; CEBs; Popular religious groups; Popular spirituality

Resistance, 14–20, 25; expanded concepts, 15; repertoires, 16. *See also* Associations; Capitalism; Sociability

Rigaud, Jacques, 348

Río Bravo, 202

Rokkan, Stein, 60, 62

Romanist tradition, 410

Romero, Archbishop Oscar, 177, 211

Rosaldo, Michelle, 286

Sacatepéquez, 105

Saints, 208–10; as role models, 209; changing image, 208–9. *See also* Popular spirituality

Salamanca, University of, 408

Salinas de Gortari, Carlos, 357, 365, 367, 368, 373, 375, 377, 389–90. *See also* PRI campaign

Salsa, 3

Samaniego, Carlos, 139

Samba, 3, 14, 321

Sandinistas, 19